Psychological Knowledge in Court

Psychological Knowledge in Court
PTSD, Pain, and TBI

Gerald Young   Andrew W. Kane
Keith Nicholson

Editors

With 12 Figures

Gerald Young
Department of Psychology
Glendon College
York University
Toronto, ON M4N 3M6
Canada

Andrew W. Kane
Andrew W. Kane & Associates, S.C.
Milwaukee, WI 53211-3439
USA

Keith Nicholson
Comprehensive Pain Program
Toronto Western Hospital
Toronto, ON M5T 2S8
Canada

Library of Congress Control Number: 2005926340

ISBN-10: 0-387-25609-1   e-ISBN 0-387-25610-5
ISBN-13: 978-0387-25609-2

Printed on acid-free paper.

Printed in the United States of America.   (SPI/MVY)

9 8 7 6 5 4 3 2 1

springer.com

Acknowledgments

The writing of this book has been a genuine collective endeavor and we owe much thanks to all who have helped. First, we have received much encouragement from our families and colleagues. Individuals who have helped directly include Natalie Kardasopoulos, who typed many of the references and did much detective work. At the publishers, Sharon Panulla has shown remarkable patience and expertise in shepherding us through all phases of the book. Anna Tobias and Louise Farkas had the thankless job in the final stages of helping to produce the volume. Gerald Young received several internal research grants from Glendon College, York University, to help in preparing the book.

Contents

Section 6   Conclusions

Index

About the Editors

Gerald Young, Ph.D., C. Psych., is an Associate Professor in the Department of Psychology at Glendon College, York University, Toronto, Canada. He teaches Rehabilitation Psychology to senior undergraduates. In addition, he is a licensed psychologist in Ontario and Quebec, practicing in rehabilitation, in particular. He is the author or co-author of four books and multiple chapters and articles. He is a member of Canadian registers in clinical practice and disability assessment. He has undertaken over 1,000 assessments related to rehabilitation and disability claims for psychological injury, including after referral for medicolegal purposes from attorneys, insurance companies, and assessment companies. He is a member of the college policy and planning committee, having served in this function at the university level, as well. For the field of psychological injury and law, he is organizing (a) the first professional association, (b) the first academic journal, (c) the first graduate-level textbook related to the field, and (d) the first book series. Springer is considering supporting these publishing initiatives.

Andrew W. Kane, Ph.D., **ABAP,** is a licensed psychologist in private practice in Milwaukee, Wisconsin. He is a diplomate of the American Board of Assessment Psychologists, is listed in the National Register of Health Service Providers in Psychology, and is a recipient of the Certificate of Professional Qualification in Psychology of the Association of State and Provincial Psychology Boards. Dr. Kane has served as an expert in more than 2,800 civil cases involving a variety of issues. He is a Professor at the Wisconsin School of Professional Psychology, an Adjunct Clinical Professor in the Department of Psychology at the University of Wisconsin-Milwaukee, and an Associate Clinical Professor in the Department of Psychiatry and Behavioral Medicine at the Medical College of Wisconsin. He is the author or co-author of eight books and some four dozen professional papers and chapters. He was a member of the Expert Panel on Psychiatric and Psychological Evidence of the American Bar Association's Commission on Mental and Physical Disability Law. He is a former president of the Wisconsin Psychological Association and of its Division of Forensic and Correctional Psychologists. Dr. Kane also served as a member of the board of the Wisconsin Psychological Association's forensic division. He served for ten years as a member of the Ethics Committee of the Wisconsin Psychological Association. Dr. Kane founded the Wisconsin Coalition on Sexual Misconduct by Psychotherapists and Counselors, a national model program.

Keith Nicholson, Ph.D., C. Psych, has had extensive clinical experience working with many different clinical populations. He obtained his Ph.D. in Clinical Neuropsychology from the University of Victoria and has worked at the Toronto Western Hospital, now part of the University Health Network in Toronto, in addition to working at several community clinics and maintaining a private practice. Dr. Nicholson is now affiliated with the Comprehensive Pain Program at the Toronto Western Hospital. He has a particular interest in the psychology of chronic pain and clinical neuropsychology and has many publications in these or other areas of interest.

Contributors

Paul A. Arbisi, Ph.D., LP., Staff Psychologist, Minneapolis VA Medical Center and University of Minnesota, Minneapolis, MN 55417 USA

Gordon J.G. Asmundson, Ph.D., University of Regina, Regina, Saskatchewan, Canada S4S 0A2

Jeffrey T. Barth, Ph.D., University of Virginia School of Medicine, Charlottesville, VA 22908-0203 USA

Heather G. Belanger, James A. Haley Veterans Hospital, Tampa, FL 33612 USA

Erin D. Bigler, Ph.D., Brigham Young University, Provo, UT 84602 USA

Edward B. Blanchard, Ph.D., The University at Albany-SUNY, Albany, NY 12222-1000 USA

Richard A. Bryant, Ph.D., University of New South Wales, Sydney, Australia NSW 2052

C. Richard Chapman, Ph.D., University of Utah School of Medicine, Salt Lake City, UT 84108 USA

Mark Creamer, Ph.D., University of Melbourne, West Heidelberg, Victoria, Australia 3081

Glenn Curtiss, Ph.D., James A. Haley Veterans Hospital, Tampa, FL 33612 USA

Patricia Espe-Pfeifer, Ph.D., University of Virginia School of Medicine, Charlottesville, VA 22908-0136 USA

Brian M. Freidenberg, Ph.D., CSW, MA, Institute of Gerontology/School of Social Welfare, Albany, NY 12222 USA

Robert J. Gatchel, Ph.D., University of Texas Southwestern Medical Center at Dallas, Dallas, TX 75390-9044 USA

Edward J. Hickling, Ph.D., Russell Sage College, Troy, NY 12180-1538 USA

Andrew W. Kane, Ph.D., Andrew W. Kane & Associates, S.C., Milwaukee, WI 53211-3439 USA

Joel Katz, Ph.D., C. Psych., York University, Toronto, ON, Canada M3J 1P3

Terence M. Keane, Ph.D., VA Boston Healthcare System, Boston, MA 02130-4893 USA

Nancy Kishino, OTR, CVE, West Coast Spine Restoration Center, Riverside, CA 92507 USA

Loretta S. Malta, Program for Anxiety and Traumatic Stress Studies, Weill Medical College of Cornell, New York, NY 10021 USA

Michael F. Martelli, Ph.D., Concussion Care Centre of Virginia, Pinnacle Rehabilitation and Tree of Life, Glen Allen, VA 23060 USA

Catherine A. Mateer, Ph.D., University of Victoria, Victoria, B.C., Canada V8W 3P5

Ronald Melzack, PhD., McGill University, Montreal, QUE, Canada H3A1B1

Keith Nicholson, Ph.D., Toronto Western Hospital, Toronto, ON, Canada M5T 2S8

Meaghan L. O'Donnell, Ph.D., University of Melbourne, Heidelberg, Victoria, Australia 3081

Richard Ohrbach, DDS, Ph.D., University of Buffalo, Buffalo, NY 14214 USA

John D. Otis, Ph.D., VA Boston Healthcare System, Boston, MA 02130-4893 USA

Emily J. Ozer, Ph.D., University of California-Berkeley, Berkeley, CA 94720-7360 USA

Brigitte N. Patry, M.A., University of Victoria, Victoria, B.C., Canada V8W3P5

Donna B. Pincus, Ph.D., Boston University, Boston, MA 02215 USA

Tamar Pincus, MSc, Ph.D., Mphil, University of London, Egham, Surrey, United Kingdom TW20 0EX

Melissa A. Polusny, Ph.D., L.P., Minneapolis VA Medical Center and University of Minnesota, Minneapolis, MN 55417 USA

Ronald Ruff, Ph.D., University of California-San Francisco, San Francisco, CA 94143-0858 USA

Ulrich Schnyder, M.D., University Hospital, CH-8091 Zurich, Switzerland

Arik Shalev, M.D., Hadassah University Hospital, Kiriat Hadassah, Jerusalem, Israel 91120

Jeffrey J. Sherman, Ph.D., University of Washington School of Dentistry, Seattle, WA 98195 USA

Steven Taylor, Ph.D., R. Psych., University of British Columbia, Vancouver, BC, Canada V6T 2A1

Rodney D. Vanderploeg, Ph.D., James A. Haley Veterans Hospital, Tampa, FL 33612 USA

Daniel S. Weiss, Ph.D., University of California-San Francisco, San Francisco, CA 94143-0984 USA

Rachel Yehuda, Ph.D., Mount Sinai School of Medicine, New York, NY 10029 USA

Gerald Young, Ph.D., C. Psych., Glendon College, York University, Toronto, ON, Canada M4N 3M6

Section 1

Introduction

1

Introduction to Psychological Knowledge in Court: PTSD, Pain, and TBI

GERALD YOUNG, ANDREW W. KANE, AND KEITH NICHOLSON

Psychologists are asked by the courts to provide evidence on a host of issues. The core of many of them concerns causality, causation, and similar concepts. In the area of psychological injury, which concerns the physical and psychological effects of motor vehicle accidents, sexual assaults, and other trauma or injury, psychologists evaluate individuals about their alleged symptoms, disorders, disabilities, and related issues. In order to accomplish this task, they need to be aware of the recent literature on evidence law as it pertains to psychology and the recent literature with respect to areas of psychology subject to tort action, such as Posttraumatic Stress Disorder (PTSD)/distress, chronic pain, and traumatic brain injury (TBI). These three sequelae, either individually or together, are common following traumatic or other events that may be subject to tort actions.

This book falls within the purview of forensic psychology, defined as "the application of the science and profession of psychology to questions and issues relating to law and the legal system" (American Board of Forensic Psychology, in Archer, 2003, p. 317), concentrating especially on psychological injury. We expect that the book will appeal to a broad audience because it covers three areas of psychological practice that are well researched, yet in need of a state-of-the-art review of the literature that can serve psychological, legal, and other interested professionals. Allied mental health professionals who would find the book relevant include psychiatrists, psychiatric nurses, social workers, rehabilitation specialists, and counsellors. Attorneys and judges who deal with psychological injury cases constitute another group that would profit from reading the book.

1. Core Questions, Controversies, and Answers

1.1. Core Questions

There is a very large and growing research literature in the fields of PTSD/distress, chronic pain, and TBI. Therefore, we have assembled leading

3

researchers to provide state-of-the-art reviews in the three domains and have asked them to consider their work in terms of possible applications to the evaluation of causality in forensic assessments. The various chapters consider the following: (1) key concepts, definitions, and models in the three areas, (2) the physiological underpinnings and chronicity of the psychological difficulties that may arise in an individual, (3) how best to assess pertinent difficult-ties in the three areas, (4) their comorbidity and its compounding effects (e.g., with respect to PTSD being experienced concurrently with pain), (5) the multiple factors that may act to maintain them (e.g., the influence of personality, cognitions, and stress on their expression), (6) to what extent these multiple factors relate to the event in question and postevent factors relative to pre-event and unrelated factors, (7) the evaluation of possible confounding factors, such as symptom magnification and malingering, (8) the factors that help predict outcome, (9) methodological issues that need to be considered, and (10) unresolved issues and controversies.

The chapters explore the similarities and differences across several types of event, such as motor vehicle accidents and rapes, in terms of their effect on the development of PTSD, chronic pain, and TBI, in particular. In addition, we provide a detailed presentation of evidence law and what psychologists need to know for court purposes. Our conclusions emphasize that psychologists undertaking forensic, clinical, rehabilitation, or related work need to be aware of the constantly evolving legal and psychological fields pertaining to evidence law, psychological assessments, the areas of PTSD/distress, chronic pain, and TBI, and causality.

Our goal is to provide psychologists with a current account of relevant theory, concepts, research investigations, and practical implications in these three areas. We expect that legal professionals will find the book essential for understanding better the work of psychologists and the psychological difficulties that accident, assault, and other psychological injury victims may face.

A companion book on psychological evidence for court explores in greater depth the concept of causality, the practical aspects of court work, malingering, and evidence law [see *Causality: Psychological Evidence in Court*, by Young, Kane, & Nicholson (2006)].

The present book consists of this introduction by the coeditors, followed by a chapter on psycholegal matters by Andrew Kane. This is followed by several chapters in each of the areas of PTSD/distress, chronic pain, and TBI. Finally, we conclude the book with a chapter that provides a summary and commentary on each of the sections and offers some integrating suggestions.

1.2. Controversies

Some of the open questions covered in the book explore whether the typical diagnoses and formulations of cause made after traumatic events by psychologists and other mental health professionals are valid. Therefore, in terms of the three major sections of the book, questions such as the following have been raised.

1. With respect to the presentation of PTSD, there is ongoing debate about the relative role of traumatic stressors, pre-existing factors such as prior trauma, psychopathology or biological vulnerabilities, concurrent stressors, the role of comorbid conditions such as depression, and several other issues. Do the three major clusters of symptoms in PTSD provide full coverage of its presentation? What are the best predictors of PTSD after exposure to trauma?

   There is considerable variability in estimates of prevalence of PTSD after trauma. The presentation of trauma victims varies according to the nature of the trauma (e.g., motor vehicle accident compared to sexual assault). Further, individuals vary in their pre-existing vulnerabilities, interpretation of the same traumatic event, and eventual outcome despite similar objective parameters of trauma experienced.

   How much do psychological factors and what kind of psychological factors play a role in individual differences in the interpretation of trauma, its course, and its outcome? In any individual case, to what degree can presentation be explained by the gamut of factors unrelated to the trauma itself? Can we adequately detect malingering? What assessment procedures should be used to increase reliability and validity of the data gathered? Can physiological measures be used to confirm diagnostic validity? Has the research examined functional outcome at a level sufficient for court purposes? Does the population level research cover all relevant aspects needed for court purposes, or will there be cases where the assessor will have difficulty bridging the gap from research to evaluation of the individual?

2. The biopsychosocial model considers pain experience the result of multiple factors, with biomedical and psychosocial factors intimately intertwined. However, it is often unclear what the relative role of each factor may be or how they interact. How can the subjective experience of pain be measured in an objective manner? How is the experience of pain related to pain behavior, illness behavior, purported suffering, and claimed disability? What are the relative roles of the patient's style of thinking, beliefs, coping mechanisms, emotions, attitude, behaviors, or other factors in the course or expression of her or his pain? Is there a pain-prone personality? Is Chronic Pain Disorder a valid psychiatric disorder that should continue to be included in the major diagnostic manuals used by psychologists and other mental health professionals? There is often poor explication or understanding of what may be the psychological factors associated with the onset, maintenance, and exacerbation or severity of chronic pain. There is concern that such diagnosis could encourage a false dichotomy between psychological and biomedical factors in chronic pain, reflecting the more general problem of mind–body dualism. Do we know enough to be able to certify with adequate certainty our professional opinions presented in court? Can we meet all *Daubert* challenges to the reliability and validity of our evidence?

3. Given that sequelae associated with mild TBI typically resolve within days to months after injury, are persistent postconcussive effects associated with brain injury or other causes such as pre-existing psychological vulnerabilities or ability structure, psychopathology, concomitant pain (especially headaches), sleep disturbance, event-related stressors, or other confounds? How is mild TBI best defined, and what may be the underlying pathophysiology of persistent mild TBI-related sequelae? What are the neuropsychological sequelae of this or of more significant (i.e., moderate to severe) TBI? Do the same confounding factors apply equally to more significant cases? Have we developed adequate means of assessing TBI? Are we developing adequate models of the causality of mild TBI? Do the data support the models? Can these results be applied to individual cases? Can neuropsychologists specify the long-term behavioral, cognitive, affective, and functional outcomes of TBI with the precision needed by the courts and determine to what degree an index event is responsible, if at all?

1.3.   Core Answers

The editors of this book take the position that research in the three areas under review supports a conclusion that there are often legitimate psychological difficulties that individuals may experience after traumatic events or other injuries that may be subject to medicolegal proceedings and that only comprehensive psychological assessments can adequately analyze for the presence of such psychological sequelae in affected individuals. Comprehensive psychological assessments include patient interviews, behavioral observation, administration of psychological instruments, and review of collateral information, at a minimum.

In their evaluations, assessors may need to consult *The Diagnostic and Statistical Manual of Mental Disorders* [DSM IV, 1994; text revision, DSM IV-TR, 2000 (American Psychiatric Association 1994, 2000)]. The DSM is the primary diagnostic manual of mental disorder in use in North America. It is the standard manual used for court purposes and is considered superior to other classificatory systems of mental disorders, such as the ICD-9/ICD-10 [*International Classification of Diseases* (World Health Organization, 1992)] (Ackerman & Kane, 1998). On the positive side, the process followed in the construction of each of the DSM's multiple versions reflects advances in knowledge based on research. On the negative side, DSM categories are ultimately decided by consensus arrived at by committees and reflect ongoing limitations in understanding of the phenomena in question.

In terms of the three major areas of this book, the practical questions regarding the current diagnostic criteria in use, whether the particular diagnostic categories involved take one form or another, must be distinguished from wider research questions. Fundamental research must continue to investigate the nature and course of stress after a traumatic event, the nature and course of pain experience after physical injury, and the nature and course of neuropsychological effects after a traumatic brain injury. At the same time on the pratical side, careful psychological evaluation can ascertain the need for psychological treatment, the negative affect on functional activity of psychological difficulties being experienced, and the causation of psychological disability. Only by having state-of-the-art knowledge of research addressing these questions in the three psychological areas under review can psychologists expect to meet their professional and ethical obligations and be prepared to defend their evidence when it is presented in court.

2.   Chapter Summaries

2.1.   Introduction

After the introductory chapter by Young, Kane, and Nicholson, in Chapter 2 Kane provides a review of the nature and purpose of expert testimony and the rules and regulations governing evidence law. He describes the three U.S. Supreme Court decisions on evidence law referred to as the *Daubert* trilogy [*Daubert* (*Daubert v. Merrell Dow Pharmaceuticals, Inc.*, 1993), *Joiner* (*General Electric Company v. Joiner*, 1997), *Kumho* (*Kumho Tire Co. v. Carmichael*, 1999)] and the Federal Rules of Evidence (2004) governing evidence presented in federal courts, in particular. Kane concludes that psychologists need to keep abreast of the population-level scientific research (i.e., at the nomothetic level), in order to increase the acceptability of their individual assessments (i.e., at the idiographic level).

2.2.   Posttraumatic Stress Disorder

In Chapter 3, Young and Yehuda describe the DSM IV approach to PTSD and its eliciting stressors, prevalence, predictors, comorbid diagnoses, physiological underpinnings, and related topics. Individual variability characterizes the course of PTSD and reflects a broad multicausal system. Young and Yehuda conclude that research needs to continue to address issues that are central to litigation, improving the quantity and quality of information available to the court regarding the causes of PTSD in individuals who have had traumatic experiences. They emphasize that assessments need to consider pretrauma, trauma, and posttrauma factors.

In Chapter 4, O'Donnell, Creamer, Bryant, Schnyder, and Shalev examine factors that need to be considered in studying the relationship between injury and subsequent PTSD. The authors discuss prevalence rates, Acute Stress Disorder and its relationship to onset of PTSD, the high comorbidity of PTSD with other psychiatric disorders, assessment issues including differential diagnosis with conditions such as TBI or medication side effects, the effect of prior trauma and the contribution of secondary stressors to presentation, the fluctuating course of PTSD, and factors such as selection biases and litigation status on research findings.

In Chapter 5, Weiss and Ozer examine the literature concerning the prediction of PTSD. They note that only a small proportion of individuals who are exposed to potential PTSD-related events proceed to develop the disorder. They review two meta-analyses of the literature, by Brewin et al. (2000) and by Ozer et al. (2003). In both meta-analyses, the most significant predictors concerned proximal and subjective links such as peritraumatic dissociation and subsequent social support, compared to more distal links or general psychological vulnerabilities such as history of prior trauma or education level.

The chapter by Polusny and Arbisi, the sixth chapter, concludes the first part of the PTSD section. Unlike the other chapters in this section, it examines the psychological effects of sexual assault, which is different in certain ways from other types of trauma. They further explore the assessment of PTSD, psychological distress, and related disability. Polusny and Arbisi also discuss biases in assessment and confounding factors, including the role of secondary gain, symptom magnification, or malingering. Polusny and Arbisi advocate for a comprehensive, multimethod assessment.

2.3.   Chronic Pain

In Chapter 7, Melzack and Katz present a brief history of the study of pain, including the 1965 formulation of Melzack and Wall on gate control theory, where central nervous system processes in the spinal cord and brain were considered to modulate perception of pain arising from peripheral pathology. Melzack and Katz stress the importance of the brain in understanding many puzzling chronic pain phenomena, including phantom limb pain. They discuss how the "neuromatrix," a widely distributed neural network in the brain that represents the anatomical substrate of the "body-self," may be involved in chronic pain. The DSM criteria for Pain Disorder are critically reviewed, and it is questioned whether such a diagnosis belongs in a manual of mental disorders.

In Chapter 8, Gatchel and Kishino provide further review of the historical development of thinking about chronic pain, emphasizing the current predominant biopsychosocial model, and discussing a number of important distinctions, such as the difference between illness and disease. They critique the concept of a "pain-prone personality." They present a three-stage model in the development of chronic pain, make recommendations for the assessment–treatment process, and address implications for understanding the causality of pain.

In Chapter 9, Pincus presents an enmeshment model in which cognition is considered to play a central role in the development of chronic pain. Cognitions, including beliefs, attributions, and information processing biases, have been investigated extensively in populations seeking help for pain.

Pincus' model integrates three normally separate internal schemata or cognitive representations, related to self, pain, and illness. When they become enmeshed, heightened distress results, as schemata of disability, helplessness, and threat are enmeshed with those of self and pain.

In Chapter 10, Young and Chapman examine the relationship between chronic pain and affect as a unified, nonlinear dynamical system. Concepts such as dynamical attractors, the "butterfly" effect, and Complex Adaptive Systems (Kauffman, 1993), which may help explain sudden changes of state as well as resistance to change in pain systems, are discussed. The authors apply a five-step model of change (Young, 1997) to the development of chronic pain and consider the five-step change model for therapy in its terms. Young and Chapman conclude that the DSM should consider a unified category of chronic pain, perhaps calling it "Chronic Pain Complications Disorder."

Chapter 11, written by Sherman and Ohrbach, emphasizes that pain experience needs to be measured at the level of subjective impression, thoughts, and emotions, and not only at the level of anatomy, biology, or physiology, consistent with the biopsychosocial model. Chronic pain perception needs to be measured with instruments that possess adequate reliability and validity. In terms of pain appraisal, higher-order processes including personality, cognition, mood, and psychiatric condition can influence pain perception. Maladaptive appraisal, coping style, and cognition can be at the heart of pain problems.

2.4.   The Co-occurrence of PTSD and Chronic Pain

The three chapters in this section address the relationship between chronic pain experience and Posttraumatic Stress Disorder and related distress after injury. This is a new area of research spurred on by the work of Blanchard and Hickling (1997), in particular, and explored in more depth by the authors of the chapters in this section. This represents the first time that a group of leading workers in the area have been brought together to address this question in one forum.

In Chapter 12, Freidenberg et al. examine the relationship between whiplash pain and PTSD in MVA (motor vehicle accident) survivors. In follow-up research to Blanchard and Hickling's (1997) suggestion that the pain that whiplash victims experience might impede recovery of psychological symptoms, a relationship was found between initial diagnosis of whiplash and PTSD status at 6 months. The authors call for more research on the mutual maintenance of PTSD and pain, although the causal relationship between the two remains unclear.

In Chapter 13, Asmundson and Taylor provide an update on their work in the area of anxiety sensitivity in relation to comorbid PTSD and chronic pain. Research from the authors' labs indicates that high levels of anxiety sensitivity are associated with measures of both pain experience and of

PTSD. They provide a case study to illustrate the difficulty in treating comorbid PTSD and chronic pain. Asmundson and Taylor conclude that difficulty in establishing the exact nature of the PTSD–pain linkage and difficulty in treating clients having the conditions comorbidly complicate determining causality in any one individual case.

Chapter 14, by Otis et al. reviews the theories and studies across the life span pertaining to the mutual maintenance of concurrent PTSD and chronic pain, including discussion of the Triple Vulnerability Model (Otis et al., 2003). That model is comprised of (1) a common biological vulnerability, (2) a common early developing psychological vulnerability acquired through experience, resulting in a sense of lessened control of salient events, and (3) a more specific psychological vulnerability in which one learns to focus anxiety on specific situations.

2.5. Traumatic Brain Injury

Barth, Ruff, and Espe-Pfeifer introduce the section on traumatic brain injury in Chapter 15. They review the basic definitions pertaining to mild traumatic brain injury (mTBI). There is no one universally accepted definition of mTBI, despite a 2003 Centre for Disease Control report and a 2004 World Health Organization report on the matter. Postconcussional Disorder or Postconcussive Syndrome are considered controversial, because of a lack of objective data, a lack of generally accepted outcome measures, and variability among individuals in physiological and psychological symptoms.

In Chapter 16, Vanderploeg, et al. contrast the biomedical and psychological mechanisms that could be involved in presentation following mTBI. They review several imaging techniques that may prove useful in identifying underlying physiological processes. They discuss the results of several meta-analyses of neuropsychological outcomes following mTBI. They suggest that there is typically good resolution in outcome in mTBI, although some individuals continue with difficulties. In their own research, the authors found mild difficulties in veterans' 8-year postinjury performance on attention and working memory. Chronic and litigating patients showed worse performance.

Bigler reviews several issues about mTBI in Chapter 17, including the definition of grades in mTBI, its pathophysiological effects, its psychological effects, and the degree to which neuroimaging data in individual cases can support conclusions on causality. Shortly after injury, traditional MRI (magnetic resonance imaging) measures may show degenerative changes even in mTBI. Frontotemporolimbic regions are at risk. Moreover, more refined imaging techniques reveal subtle metabolic changes even where MRI scans are normal. It is noted that there is no precise neuropsychological signature or set of test results associated with mTBI.

In Chapter 18, Nicholson and Martelli review the confounding effects of pain, sleep disturbance, psychoemotional distress and psychiatric disorder, and motivational factors, including malingering, on neuropsychological test performance. For example, headache is considered the primary problem in the Postconcussive Syndrome. The authors conclude that such factors could have seriously confounded not only studies of the Postconcussive Syndrome but also more significant TBI.

Patry and Mateer, in Chapter 19, provide a detailed discussion on the assessment of moderate to severe TBI with particular focus on the neuropsychological domains of attention, memory, language, executive function, visuospatial skills, motor function, and anosmia. They note the wide variability in results of different studies using different techniques. Any assessment instrument used must demonstrate appropriate psychometric properties, such as having adequate reliability and validity. These concepts, important for all the chapters in the book, are explained well in their chapter.

2.6.   Conclusions

In Chapter 20, we review each section of the book, offering comments. Psychology and law exist in a reciprocal relationship. Psychologists must undertake comprehensive assessments while being aware of psychological and legal pitfalls, and keeping up to date with the psychological literature and with the rules and regulations governing their practice.

To conclude our introduction, psychologists are often called upon to determine the degree to which a defined stressor or injury contributes causally to a client's ongoing psychological condition. For example, psychologists assess whether a motor vehicle accident and its effects materially contribute to a survivor's subsequent psychological condition relative to preaccident psychological vulnerabilities, or what effect concurrent stressors may have in conjunction with premorbid factors and accident-related injuries.

This book will help psychologists undertake causal analyses of individual cases by providing a state-of-the-art review of this growing field of research, examining the areas of Posttraumatic Stress Disorder/distress, chronic pain, and traumatic brain injury in a manner applicable to such questions. The information presented in this volume should also assist attorneys or others involved in medicolegal proceedings to better understand the many issues involved.

Finally, we note that although research is advancing knowledge in the fields presented, it needs more critical theoretical underpinnings as well as better interdisciplinary collaboration among psychologists, medical professionals, and the legal community. Both the legal and psychological fields evolve constantly. Law and psychology relate to each other in a reciprocal manner. Psychologists need to know what the legal community expects of us and how judges and attorneys understand our science and the evidence that we offer the court. At the same time, the legal community needs to understand our scientific process and the knowledge that we derive from it.

The law should understand the multifactorial causal models that we adopt, the comprehensive assessments of individual that we undertake to ascertain causality, and the scientific approach that we use in evaluating causality, both in terms of consulting state-of-the-art research on populations and evaluating alternative hypotheses about individuals.

References

Ackerman, M. J. & Kane, A. W. (1998). *Psychological Experts in Personal Injury Actions*, 3rd ed. New York: Aspen Law and Business.

American Psychiatric Association. (1994). *Diagnostic and Statistical Manual of Mental Disorders*, 4th ed. Washington, DC: American Psychiatric Association.

American Psychiatric Association. (2000). *Diagnostic and Statistical Manual of Mental Disorders: Text Revision*, 4th ed. Washington, DC: American Psychiatric Association.

Archer, R. P. (2003). Editor's introduction to a special issue on the topic of forensic assessment. *Assessment, 10*, 317.

Blanchard, E. B. & Hickling, E. J. (1997). *After the Crash: Assessment and Treatment of Motor Vehicle Accident Survivors.* Washington, DC: American Psychological Association.

Brewin, C. R., Andrews, B., & Valentine, J. D. (2000). Meta-analysis of risk factors for posttraumatic stress disorder in trauma-exposed adults. *Journal of Consulting and Clinical Psychology, 68*, 748–766.

Daubert v. Merrell Dow Pharmaceuticals, Inc. (1993). 113 S. Ct. 2786.

Federal Rules of Evidence (2004). Available from http://judiciary.house.gov/med/pdfs/printers/108th/evid2004.pdf (accessed March 14, 2005).

General Electric Company v. Joiner. (1993). 118 S. Ct. 512.

Kauffman, S. A. (1993). *The Origins of Order*. New York: Oxford University Press.

Kumho Tire Co. v. Carmichael. (1999). (119 S. Ct. 1167, March 23, 1999).

Melzack, R. & Wall, P. D. (1965). Pain mechanisms: A new theory. *Science, 150*, 971–979.

National Center for Injury Prevention and Control. (2003). *Report to Congress on Mild Traumatic Brain Injury in the United States: Steps to Prevent a Serious Public Health Problem*. Atlanta, GA: Centers for Disease Control and Prevention.

Otis, J. D., Keane, T. M., & Kerns, R. D. (2003). An examination of the relationship between chronic pain and Posttraumatic Stress Disorder. *Journal of Rehabilitation Research and Development, 40*, 397–406.

Ozer, E. J., Best, S. R., Lipsey, T. L., & Weiss, D. S. (2003). Predictors of Posttraumatic Stress Disorder and symptoms in adults: A meta-analysis. *Psychological Bulletin, 129*, 52–73.

World Health Organization. (1992). *International Classification of Diseases. Mental and Behavioral Disorders (Including Disorders of Psychological Development), Clinical Descriptions and Diagnostic Guidelines*, 10th rev. ed. Geneva: WHO.

Young, G. (1997). *Adult Development, Therapy, and Culture: A Postmodern Synthesis*. New York: Plenum.

Young, G., Kane, A., & Nicholson, K. (eds.) (2006). *Causality: Psychological Evidence in Court*. New York: Springer-Verlag.

2

Psychology, Causality, and Court

ANDREW W. KANE

Causality is a key issue in psychological injury lawsuits involving claims of psychological or emotional injuries. It is likely that the finder of fact (judge or jury) will require input from a psychologist in order to assess the impact of a claimed Posttraumatic Stress Disorder, traumatic brain injury, chronic pain, or another psychophysiological disorder. In order for the assessment to accurately and adequately address the needs of the fact finder, the psychologist must use methods that are valid and reliable and must present the information in a manner consistent with the requirements of the court process. Specifically, psychologists must acquire knowledge regarding the rules of evidence and rules of civil procedure that govern the admissibility of evidence, and they must understand how courts have addressed science and scientific issues in the present and the recent past.

1. Daubert, Joiner, Kumho, Frye, and Mohan

In 1993, in *Daubert v. Merrell Dow Pharmaceuticals, Inc.* (509 U.S. 579, 113 S. Ct. 2786, 125 L.Ed. 2d 469), the U.S. Supreme Court held that the general acceptance test (*Frye v. United States*, 1923, 54 App. D.C. 46, 293 F. 1013, 34 ALR 145) was superceded by the Federal Rules of Evidence (FRE) (2004) and that general acceptance was not a necessary prerequisite for admissibility of expert testimony under Federal Rule of Evidence 702. The Supreme Court held that "all relevant evidence is admissible." As indicated in *Daubert*,

If scientific, technical, or other specialized knowledge will assist the trier of fact to understand the evidence or to determine a fact in issue, a witness qualified as an expert by knowledge, skill, experience, training, or education may testify thereto in the form of an opinion or otherwise. . . .

The inquiry envisioned by Rule 702 is, we emphasize, a flexible one. Its overarching subject is the scientific validity—and thus the evidentiary relevance and reliability—of the principles that underlie a proposed submission. The focus, of course, must be solely on principles and methodology, not on the conclusions that they generate. (pp. 482–484)

Whereas the Supreme Court identified many criteria, the four official "*Daubert* criteria," according to the Court in *Kumho Tire Co. v. Carmichael* (1999), are as follows: (1) "whether it can be and has been tested . . . [and] can be falsified"; (2) whether the "theory or technique has been subjected to peer review and publication"; (3) that consideration be given to the "known or potential rate of error"; and (4) that there is "general acceptance" of the particular technique within the scientific community (p. 137).

Other factors identified by the Supreme Court as relevant to gatekeeping by federal trial courts include the following: (1) that the expert's testimony "pertain to scientific knowledge," (2) that the "evidence or testimony assist the trier of fact to understand the evidence or to determine a fact in issue" (relevance), (3) "whether that reasoning or methodology properly can be applied to the facts in issue," (4) "the existence and maintenance of standards controlling the technique's operation" (the Court used the example of standards for spectrographic analysis) (*Daubert*, 1993, pp. 593–594), and/or (5) that there be "evidentiary reliability" (*Daubert,* 1993, p. 590). In footnote 9, the Supreme Court indicated that although scientists "distinguish between 'validity' . . . and 'reliability' . . . our reference here is to evidentiary reliability—that is, trustworthiness." It should be noted that some legal scholars list the *Daubert* factors slightly differently (e.g., separating testability requirement into "whether it is testable" and "whether it has been," and adding "whether there are standards controlling the technique's operation" as an additional Daubert factor (Imwinkelried, 2000, p. 21). The Supreme Court explicitly indicated that this list is flexible and these and/or other criteria are to be used by the trial courts to address the scientific validity of the evidence or testimony.

According to the Supreme Court ruling in *Barefoot v. Estelle* (1983), if the psychological expert is testifying on the basis of his or her clinical experience, rather than the state of the art of the science of psychology, a different standard is applicable. Although this type of testimony is admissible, the fact finder may give it greater or lesser weight after cross-examination and, if presented, after contrary evidence by the other party. When clinical evidence is based even in part on research (e.g., on a psychological test or diagnostic syndrome), courts have been more willing to subject the testimony to a rigorous degree of scrutiny (Shuman, 2002a).

The Supreme Court remanded *Daubert* to the Ninth Circuit Court of Appeals [*Daubert V. Merrell Dow Pharmaceuticals, Inc.* (1995)], which indicated, in a ruling often referred to as "*Daubert II*," that federal courts must "analyze not what the experts say, but what basis they have for saying it. . . . We read the Supreme Court as instructing us to determine whether the analysis undergirding experts' testimony falls within the range of accepted standards governing how scientists conduct their research and reach their conclusions. . . ." Further, the Court differentiated research conducted independent of a specific case, or whether "they have developed their opinions expressly for purposes of testifying. . . ." The former "provides important, objective proof that the research comports with the dictates of good science..., [and were] derived by the scientific method...." If the proferred testimony is not based on independent research, the party proffering it must present other objective, verifiable evidence that the testimony is based on "scientifically valid principles." One means of demonstrating that the testimony is so based is by showing that it has been subjected to peer review and publication, indicating "that it has been taken seriously by other scientists."

1.1.   Joiner

The U.S. Supreme Court reaffirmed its conclusions in *Daubert* and specified that the standard for reviewing the admission or exclusion of scientific evidence by federal district courts was "abuse of discretion" (*General Electric Company, Inc. v. Joiner,* 1997); that is, the trial court has great discretion, in its role as the gatekeeper, to admit or reject proferred evidence. Appellate courts are to offer deference to the trial court's decision unless the trial court abused its discretion.

1.2.   Kumho

In *Kumho,* the U.S. Supreme Court ruled that an individual may be considered an expert if he or she has any type of specialized knowledge or experience that may contribute to the fact finder's understanding of a case. The knowledge or experience may be technical or "other specialized" knowledge, not only scientific knowledge. Further, the specific factors that the district court may consider are flexible; the court can apply one or many in the process of determining reliability. "The objective... is to make certain that an expert, whether basing testimony upon professional studies or personal experience, employs in the courtroom the same level of intellectual rigor that characterizes the practice of an expert in the relevant field" (*Kumho Tire Co. v. Carmichael,* 1999, p. 152).

1.3.   Trial Judges Need Not Question Expert Testimony

It should be noted that trial judges are not obligated to question expert testimony; rather, it is up to the attorneys to identify admissibility issues and either bring motions before the court, address the issues during testimony before the jury, or choose to disregard them (Shuman & Sales, 2001).

1.4.   Bases for Expert Opinions

According to Federal Rule of Evidence 703, or its state equivalent, expert testimony may be based on facts or information learned by direct observation or by studying various facts or information learned during a trial, as well as facts or information obtained through reading or through discussions with others. It is further required that the facts or data be of the kind upon which other experts in the same field would rely and that relying on that information is reasonable. Information learned at a trial includes information from other witnesses. It is also possible for an attorney to pose a hypothetical question that includes relevant facts from the instant case and to ask the expert to give his or her opinion on the basis of the statements in the hypothetical question (Kirkpatrick & Mueller, 2003).

1.5. Opinion on the Ultimate Issue

Federal Rule of Evidence 704, or its state equivalent, permits experts in civil cases to state opinions regarding the ultimate issue (e.g., whether the alleged trauma caused the psychological damage identified). The expert must be prepared to provide the reasoning that led to reaching that conclusion, and the information must be deemed helpful to the fact finder if it is to be admitted (Shuman, 1994a, 2003 supplement).

1.6. Error Rates

The critical issue is the mandate to avoid false positives and false negatives to the degree possible. Testimony by the expert must address the likelihood that a given result might be a false conclusion, imparting blame or causality when it is not deserved, or indicating a lack of blame or causality when it is in fact present. Other definitions of "error rate" also exist, further ensuring confusion (Kraus & Sales, 2003; Youngstrom & Busch, 2000). In science, absolute truth does not exist. An hypothesis can be demonstrated to be false, but can never be considered absolutely true. The goal of research is to test hypotheses to identify those that are likely to be true based on current knowledge.

Further confusing matters, *Daubert* gives no guidance to judges in trial courts regarding what error rate should be considered unacceptable. One judge might use 10%, another 20%, and a third another amount. One judge might allow a larger error rate if the scientific evidence underlying the expert's opinion has been tested and was published in a peer-reviewed journal, whereas another might demand a low error rate unless the scientific evidence has been generally accepted within the scientific community, regardless of testability or publication issues.

1.7. State Courts

Although the requirements of *Daubert, Joiner*, and *Kumho* are mandatory in federal courts, they are not mandatory in state courts unless a given state has specifically adopted these requirements, either via a decision by its highest court or by action of its legislature (Youngstrom & Busch, 2000). However, the evidence law of most states mirrors the Federal Rules (Saks, 2000; Shuman, 2002a).

1.8.   Practical Effect of Daubert and Its Progeny

According to Shuman and Sales (2001), *Daubert* is perhaps most important because it reminds mental health professionals of their ethical obligation to be aware of the latest research in the areas about which they testify and to offer information to the court that is valid and reliable and has been derived with appropriate methodology. Experts must also be prepared to present evidence that their methodology in a given case is also valid and reliable. In effect, "preparation for a *Daubert* challenge is preparation for cross-examination" (p. 76).

1.9.   Mohan

In *R. v. Mohan*, (1994), the Supreme Court of Canada ruled that

[a]dmission of expert evidence depends on the application of the following criteria: (a) relevance; (b) necessity in assisting the trier of fact; (c) the absence of any exclusionary rule; and (d) a properly qualified expert.

Relevance is a threshold requirement to be decided by the judge as a question of law. . . . Expert evidence should not be admitted where there is a danger that it will be misused or will distort the fact-finding process, or will confuse the jury. . . . [E]xpert evidence which advances a novel scientific theory or technique is subjected to special scrutiny to determine whether it meets a basic threshold of reliability and whether it is essential in the sense that the trier of fact will be unable to come to a satisfactory conclusion without the assistance of the expert. The closer the evidence approaches an opinion on an ultimate issue, the stricter the application of this principle. . . .

An expert's function is precisely this: to provide the judge and jury with a ready-made inference which the judge and jury, due to the technical nature of the facts, are unable to formulate. . . . As in the case of relevance. . . , the need for the evidence is assessed in light of its potential to distort the fact-finding process. . . .

Compliance with criteria (a), (b) and (d) will not ensure the admissibility of expert evidence if it falls afoul of an exclusionary rule of evidence separate and apart from the opinion rule itself. . . .

[T]he evidence must be given by a witness who is shown to have acquired special or peculiar knowledge through study or experience in respect of the matters on which he or she undertakes to testify. . . .

In summary, *Mohan*, like *Daubert, Joiner,* and *Kumho*, requires that the trial judge act as a gatekeeper for expert evidence. Both Supreme Court decisions require relevance and that the expert testimony assist the trier of fact to understand the issues and evidence in order to determine a fact in issue. Both require that the expert testimony pertain to special knowledge that the expert acquired through education or experience (i.e., that the expert be qualified to testify in a particular area of inquiry). Although *Mohan* specifies that there must not be any exclusionary rule that would preclude the expert testimony, this is certainly implied by *Daubert, Joiner*, and *Kumho* and is included in other parts of the Federal Rules of Evidence. The final three *Daubert* criteria are not specifically addressed by *Mohan*; that is, whether there has been peer review and publication, that consideration be given to the known or potential error rate, and/or that there is general acceptance of a particular technique within the scientific community. In most respects, however, *Mohan, Daubert, Joiner*, and *Kumho* are comparable decisions.

2.   Learned Treatises

Federal Rule of Evidence 803(18), or its state equivalent, defines "learned treatises" as "statements contained in published treatises, periodicals, or pamphlets" in a relevant area that are "established as a reliable authority by the testimony or admission of the witness or by other expert testimony or by judicial notice." Such treatises are generally considered trustworthy because they have been published for inspection by other professionals, with the expectation that they will be criticized for any inaccuracies (Kilpatrick & Mueller, 2003). *Daubert* placed special value on peer-reviewed treatises, but treatises that have not gone through that formal review process might be of equal or greater value in a particular case. As indicated in *Daubert*, "[p]ublication... does not necessarily correlate with reliability..., and in some instances well-grounded but innovative theories will not have been published." (p. 483) Experts must be *very* familiar with the professional literature related to issues in a given case, as dictated by codes of ethics, forensic guidelines, and the reasonable expectation of the courts that someone retained as an expert *is* an expert on the subject at bar. It should also be noted that it is the professional literature that provides the nomothetic (population) data (see section 19) with which the expert can compare the idiographic (case-specific) data that results from the assessment of the plaintiff.

According to Kassirer and Cecil (2002), "just because a study has been published in a prestigious peer-reviewed journal is no assurance that its results or conclusions are correct" (p. 1383). Further, they indicate, there remain many areas of practice in which objective data are difficult to find, with most of the literature consisting of case studies.

That publication in a peer-reviewed publication as a relative guarantee of reliability (validity, trustworthiness) should be questioned was supported by a study by Garcia-Berthou and Alcaraz (2004). Reviewing two prestigious journals, they found that 11.6% of the computations in *Nature* were incorrect, as were 11.7% of the computations in the *British Medical Journal*. Further, 38% of *Nature* articles and 25% of *British Medical Journal* articles contained at least one computational error.

3.   Licensing/Certification Across Jurisdictions

A variety of circumstances might lead to a psychologist or other expert to travel to a "foreign jurisdiction" (i.e., one in which the expert is not licensed or certified). Among the reasons could be hospitalization or incarceration of the plaintiff, or a plaintiff who is afraid of flying. In-person interviews of collaterals might also be given more credibility by the fact finder.

Many jurisdictions permit psychologists and other professionals to practice temporarily in their jurisdictions—but many do not, with penalties for unlicensed practice ranging from civil forfeitures of $100 to $50,000 and/or felony charges in five jurisdictions. An expert who does not meet licensing/certification requirements might not be permitted to testify. A recent study of requirements in all states and provinces by Kane (2005) can be found in the companion volume to this text or in the work of Ackerman and Kane (2005). (See also McLearen et al., 2004; Simon & Shuman, 1999; Tucillo et al., 2002). Experts are strongly urged to contact the relevant licensing/certifying board prior to accepting a request to provide an evaluation and testimony in a case in a jurisdiction in which he or she is not licensed. Contact information for all U.S. and Canadian psychology boards is available at www.asppb.org.

4. Tort Law

The purpose of tort law is to distribute the costs of events in which harm was done to an aggrieved individual or entity, on the basis of social policies. For the individual who was harmed, "the commonly understood goal of tort compensation is to restore the injured to their pre-accident condition, to make them whole" (Shuman, 1994b). To address this goal, the plaintiff must demonstrate that the defendant owed a duty to the plaintiff, was derelict in that duty, directly caused harm to the plaintiff, and that the harm was significant and the plaintiff should be compensated for the harm done (damages). Tort law intends to reduce harm by deterring unreasonable conduct and to compensate injured individuals with money that may be used for treatment or other means of compensation. To achieve that goal, "a plaintiff must establish both liability (i.e., that the defendant's conduct was intentionally or negligently unreasonable and should be deterred) and damages (i.e., that the plaintiff has suffered injury and should be compensated" (Shuman & Daley, 1996, pp. 294–295). Both liability and a showing that the defendant's intentional or negligent conduct is below the societal standard for reasonable care must be shown, as well as a direct, causal relationship between the defendant's behavior and the injury—that is, *but for* the defendant's behavior, the injury would not have occurred. The typical standard for negligence is the "reasonable person test" (i.e., whether a reasonable person would have behaved as did the defendant) (McLearen et al., 2004; Shuman & Daley, 1996). Because it is difficult for laymen to evaluate psychological or emotional harm, the assistance of an expert, often a psychologist, is necessary to establish the nature and degree of harm and to assess the degree of disability associated with it (McLearnen et al., 2004).

4.1.   Thin Skulls, Eggshell Personalities, and Crumbling Skulls

The law of torts indicates that the tortfeasor is liable whether the stressor caused the injury or aggravated a pre-existing condition. In many cases, there will be some combination of the two: a direct psychological/emotional injury and a degree to which pre-existing problems are exacerbated by the traumatic event. This has led to use of terms like "thin skulled man" or "eggshell personality" or variations on those terms to describe an individual with a pre-existing disorder or condition that makes the harm by the defendant more significant than it would otherwise be. The psychologist's task is to identify the nature and extent of the pre-existing condition, the additional damage done by the alleged trauma under consideration, and the prognosis.

The Supreme Court of Canada discussed a variation, the "crumbling skull," in *Athey v. Leonati* (1996) (3 S.C.R.458) The case involved an individual who was in two motor vehicle accidents in 1991, one in February and one in April. The Supreme Court indicated that the "crumbling skull" rule establishes that

the pre-existing condition was inherent in the plaintiff's "original position." The defendant need not put the plaintiff in a position *better* than his or her original position. The defendant is liable for the injuries caused, even if they are extreme, but need not compensate the plaintiff for any debilitating effects of the pre-existing condition *that the plaintiff would have experienced anyway....*[emphasis added]

4.2.   Identifying Deficits

For each area of apparent deficit, the evaluator should be able to specify the anticipated influence of the deficit on the person's ability to function: both what the person would be expected to be able to do and what the person would not be expected to be able to do. For example, if memory problems are claimed, the individual should have difficulty learning new information. By addressing each area of anticipated deficit based on the claimed disability or disabilities, the expert can identify the degree to which the person's presentation is consistent with expectations based on the expert's experience and the research literature. Each discrepancy needs to be investigated and resolved (Faust & Heard, 2003b).

5.   Base Rates

The expert also needs to consider base rates. "[B]ase rate refers to... the established probability of events in a population prior to the introduction of any novel procedure..." (Urbina, 2004, p. 262). One area involves the nature of the trauma. If the plaintiff were hit with an object moving at one-half mile per hour, for example, the likelihood of a traumatic brain injury would be very small (Faust, 2003).

Lees-Haley and Brown (1993) identified base rates for a number of complaints common among psychological injury claimants. They found that 93% of claimants reported anxiety or nervousness—but so did 54% of the control group. Three other common complaints among psychological injury claimants are headaches (88% vs. 62% for controls), concentration problems (78% vs. 26% for controls), and memory problems (53% vs. 20% for controls). In each example, the probative value of the expert's testimony is very limited unless base rates have been considered, and a good case can be made for excluding the expert's testimony if they have not (Fleishman et al., 1999). Similarly, the base rate for an anxiety disorder is over 16% for adults 18–54 years of age during 1 year, with the base rate for a Posttraumatic Stress Disorder (PTDS) being 3.6%. The lifetime prevalence of exposure to significant trauma in the United States is between 40% and 70%, and the lifetime prevalence of PTSD is between 8% and 14% (Frueh et al., 2004). The presence of a mood or anxiety disorder, by itself, is not proof that an individual suffered from the trauma claimed in a case.

6. Diagnosis

Diagnoses serve a useful purpose in clinical work, permitting professionals to communicate with one another and to bill health insurance. Diagnoses are not, however, distinct entities that can be objectively identified; rather, they are explanatory fictions or constructs established by the vote of a group of psychiatrists, making the diagnoses to some degree value judgments (Ackerman & Kane, 1998; Shuman, 2002a; State Justice Institute, 1999). They have significant reliability; that is, for most diagnoses, two psychologists or psychiatrists can come to the same or a very similar conclusion regarding a diagnosis. In the United States and Canada, the relevant diagnostic criteria are those of the *Diagnostic and Statistical Manual of Mental Disorders*, 4th ed. (DSM-IV) (American Psychiatric Association, 1994). The diagnostic criteria in the 2000 "Text Revision" of DSM-IV are the same as those in the 1994 DSM.

The strength of the DSM is its standardization and relative comprehensiveness. The authors of DSM-IV addressed its weakness as a legal resource, indicating that "[i]t is to be understood that inclusion here. . . of a diagnostic category. . . does not imply that the condition meets legal or other nonmedical criteria for what constitutes mental disease, mental disorder, or mental disability. . . ." [DSM-IV, 1994, p. xxvii]

The most common diagnosis in psychological injury is Posttraumatic Stress Disorder (PTSD). However, numerous other diagnoses might be relevant in addition to or instead of PTSD.

It should be noted that the DSM diagnostic criteria for PTSD differ significantly from those of the *International Classification of Diseases and Related Problems, Classification of Mental and Behavioral Disorders,* 10th ed. (ICD-10) (WHO, 1992). The ICD-10 criteria are more similar to those of DSM-III-R than to DSM-IV. Peters et al. (1999) found a 12-month prevalence for PTSD of 3% when using DSM-IV criteria, but 6.9% when using ICD-10 criteria in a sample of 1364 individuals. Under ICD-10 criteria, events that do not pose a threat to life or limb qualify for the diagnosis [e.g., a burglary, sexual misconduct by professionals (clergy, physicians, mental health professionals, etc.) or sexual harassment].

Posttraumatic Stress Disorder and Acute Stress Disorder are the only two DSM-IV diagnoses that require that a traumatic event initiate the disorder. Specifically, it is required that "the person experienced, witnessed, or was confronted with an event or events that involved actual or threatened death or serious injury, or a threat to the physical integrity of self or others" (Criterion A). Further, it is required that "the person's response involved intense fear, helplessness, or horror," or, for children, that "this may be expressed instead by disorganized or agitated behavior." There is then a requirement that the individual *re-experiences* (Criterion B) the trauma in one or more of five listed ways, persistently *avoids* "stimuli associated with the trauma and [experiences] *numbing* of general responsiveness" (Criterion C) in three or more of seven listed ways, exhibits "persistent symptoms of increased *arousal* (Criterion D) in two or more of five listed ways, that the symptoms have lasted more than 1 month, and that the symptoms cause "clinically significant distress or impairment in social, occupational, or other important areas of functioning." It is recognized that onset might be delayed 6 or more months after the stressor, in which case one specifies "with delayed onset" (DSM-IV, pp. 427–429, emphasis added).

Posttraumatic Stress Disorder involves both psychological and physiological reactivity to an exceptionally stressful situation (Scrignar, 1996; Wilson, 2004). Components include memory, sensory and/or perceptual experiences, physical symptoms of hyperarousal, disturbance of the sleep cycle, emotional reactivity, and impaired information processing. Further, it must be noted that PTSD is not a singular phenomenon. With the wide variety of ways an individual might react to a severe stressor, there are a number of different presentations that could fall under the PTSD heading. A given individual could also exhibit different aspects of the disorder at one point in time from those exhibited at another point in time. Finally, whereas some people who go through a traumatic experience recover within weeks, others evidence significant symptoms for months, and some for years (Scrignar, 1996; Wilson, 2004).

The goal for the psychological expert is to identify a given individual's areas of dysfunction, determine whether and to what degree those dysfunctions relate to the traumatic event, and couch the description in terms that are relevant to the court process. The expert needs to "present the logic that links these observations to the specific abilities and capacities with which the law is concerned" (Grisso, 2003, pp. 12–13).

In many cases in which an individual shows evidence of symptoms of PTSD, the diagnosis cannot be made because the stressor that caused those symptoms does not meet the requirements of Criterion A [i.e., an event that threatened the individual with death or serious injury, or a threat to his or her physical integrity (or that of others), leading to extreme fear, horror, or helplessness]. When this is the case, the expert might need to refer to a "posttraumatic syndrome" rather than PTSD (Moreau & Zisook, 2002).

Far more important than the specific diagnosis is that the individual's specific symptoms are identified and that all potentially applicable diagnoses are considered, ruling each one in or out on the basis of the person's symptom picture (Ackerman & Kane, 1998; Brown & Eder, 1999). Although the expert does not need to specify why each diagnosis was included or excluded, it is very important to be able to specify that all potentially relevant diagnoses were considered and why the final diagnosis or diagnoses were chosen (Macartney-Filgate & Snow, 2004). Among the diagnoses whose criteria overlap with PTSD are Panic Disorder, Social Phobia (Social Anxiety Disorder), Specific Phobia, Generalized Anxiety Disorder, Major Depressive Episode, Somatoform Disorder, Substance-Related Disorders, some Organic Mental Disorders, and some Adjustment Disorders (Ackerman & Kane, 1998).

The evaluator must also consider other possibilities. There could be malingering or, at least, symptom exaggeration. The evaluator must avoid the logical error of "post hoc, ergo propter hoc" ("after this, therefore because of this"). The facts that an individual experienced a trauma and that he or she was diagnosed with PTSD does not mean that the trauma was the primary or even secondary cause of the PTSD. Rather, the PTSD could have been caused by another event, or a series of events that included the identified traumatic event. Similarly, a *correlation* between an event and a psychological disorder never, alone, indicates *causation*. Height and weight, for example, are correlated, but neither causes the other (Ackerman & Kane, 1998). Every reasonably possible cause of a given injury or condition must be considered, as must other factors that might play a significant role such as pre-existing disorders or problems. Without considering all of these factors, an expert cannot legitimately draw conclusions to a reasonable degree of psychological/medical/scientific certainty (Fleishman et al., 1999). In addition, the Fourth Circuit Court of Appeals indicated, in *Cooper v. Smith & Nephew* (2001), that testimony from an expert who has not conducted a thorough differential diagnostic process could be excluded in federal court. Many state courts would draw the same conclusion.

7. "Reasonable Certainty"

Whereas scientific research generally accepts conclusions only if the probability of getting the result by chance is 5% or less (i.e., a 95% level of certainty), in law the relevant criterion is "more likely than not," and the degree of psychological (or medical, etc.) certainty necessary for "reasonable certainty" is the same (Bradford, 2001). If the expert cannot state that conclusions are made to a reasonable degree of psychological (or medical) certainty, a court may conclude that the required degree of certainty is absent and exclude the testimony (Shuman, 1994a, 2002 supplement)—or, at the least, give less weight to the evidence (Shuman, 1994a, 2003 supplement).

8.   Goals of an Assessment

The primary goal for an evaluator is to be impartial, regardless of who retained him or her, acknowledging the strengths and weaknesses of the data while advocating for the conclusions he or she has drawn from the data, not for a given side in a case. Among the means of maintaining impartiality are to (1) set and maintain professional boundaries regarding the attorney who retained the evaluator, (2) avoid becoming invested in a particular outcome of a case—the evaluator is to advocate for his data and conclusions, not to try to "win" and (3) communicate the results of the evaluation clearly and in simple language, avoiding superlatives (e.g., "absolutely" or "completely"), in both the report and testimony [Greenberg, 2003; Heilbrun et al., 2002; Macartney-Filgate & Snow, 2004; see also the Specialty Guidelines for Forensic Psychologists, Guidelines VII.B., C., and D. (Committee on Ethical Guidelines for Forensic Psychologists, 1991)]. According to Murphy (2000), the American Bar Association has indicated that expert witnesses must be independent, rather than loyal to or an advocate for his or her client, the attorney.

In essence, an expert must analyze, explain, and offer an accurate opinion of the relevant issue before the court, not strive to advocate and persuade the fact-finder of a certain point of view. The expert's main duty to provide truthful and accurate information comes from the court and the ethical guidelines of his professional organization, if any.

The case-related goal of the assessment is to identify whether, and if so to what degree, the traumatic event caused the plaintiff to suffer a psychological injury. The options include the following: (1) The traumatic event was the sole cause of the individual's assessed psychopathology—a rare event. (2) The traumatic event was the major cause of the individual's assessed psychopathology. *But for* the traumatic event, the individual would not have the degree of psychopathology assessed. (3) The traumatic event was a significant contributing factor ("material contribution" or "substantial contribution") to the degree of assessed psychopathology, but not the major factor; that is, the assessed disorder was identifiably worse because the traumatic event occurred. (4) The traumatic event had little affect on the assessed psychopathology of the individual, but could have exacerbated an existing psychopathology to some degree. (5) No significant relationship was identified between the traumatic event and any psychopathology that was found by the assessment. (Ackerman & Kane, 1998; Melton et al., 1997; see also Young, this volume).

The means of identifying which of the above five conclusions is most applicable is scientific reasoning. Hypotheses having been formulated, each is subjected to analysis leading (in most instances) to either confirmation or falsification by the idiographic data of the case. The interpretation of the data should be parsimonious: The best conclusion is generally the one that accounts for the most data with the simplest, most direct explanation. (Greenberg, et al., 2003; Heilbrun, 2001). Because the evaluator does not know until near the end of the evaluation what data will ultimately be relevant, everything that *might* be relevant should be noted, because relevance is the legal standard for discovery. Information that appears relevant but proves to be either irrelevant or immaterial will be in the evaluator's notes, but is left out of the report (Greenberg, 2003).

If a relationship is found between the traumatic event and the individual's psychological condition, recommendations should be made for treatment and a prognosis stated regarding the likelihood of a return to his or her prior level of functioning. Prognosis is, in effect, "future damages" (Greenberg, 2003, p. 245). The evaluator is to make a statement regarding the likelihood the plaintiff can be treated, the likelihood (if there are data to so indicate) that the plaintiff will recover, and an estimate of the period of time required for optimal or maximal recovery to occur if the individual actively participates in treatment. A cost estimate, based on community rates, is usually of value as well.

9.   Conducting the Evaluation

There is no gold standard for the conduct of an evaluation. Each evaluator must design an evaluation that properly and adequately addresses the legal questions at issue in each individual case. A number of authors have suggested models that might be used for an evaluation (see, e.g., Greenberg, 2003; Grisso, 2003; Heilbrun, 2001; Wilson & Moran, 2004).

It is essential that multiple methods and sources be utilized in the assessment, to try to ensure that all important factors are considered and that the data from each factor can be compared with those from the other factors, looking for convergent validity. The issue is not, *per se*, how damaged the individual might now be, but, rather, how different the individual is from the way he or she was prior to the traumatic incident. Significant inconsistencies must also be addressed (Ackerman & Kane, 1998; Greenberg, et al. 2003; Heilbrun, 2001; Heilbrun et al., 2002; McLearen et al., 2004; Walker & Shapiro, 2003; Weiner, 2002). In most cases, this will involve three areas of investigation: review of records, psychological testing, and clinical interviews.

9.1.   Review of Records

The forensic expert needs to review the Complaint (i.e., the allegations) and all records that will potentially shed light upon the functional and mental status of the individual, both pretrauma and posttrauma. The pretrauma information identifies a baseline—what the individual was like prior to the traumatic event. The posttrauma data indicate the changes the individual went through as a result of the trauma or other events in his or her life. In general, the records reviewed should go back at least 5 years, and a minimum of 3 years, prior to the allegedly traumatic event, to try to ensure that nothing important is missed and to form a substantial baseline of pretrauma functioning. The records reviewed should include all medical (including psychotherapy), arrest and conviction, school, employment, military, personnel, and any other records that might shed light on the individual's functional abilities prior to and following the traumatic event. Information regarding changes in the individual's lifestyle since the trauma might be available via checkbook registers and credit card statements (Greenberg, 2003). Physical activities and hobbies engaged in prior to and after the traumatic event should be listed. Medication records should identify any direct or side effects that might affect the clinical picture. Although these data do not stand alone as evidence of changes caused by the traumatic event, without a strong database it will be difficult to clearly identify the pretraumatic status and posttraumatic changes for the individual. Without a strong database, it will also be difficult, if not impossible, for an expert to testify to a "reasonable degree of psychological (or medical or social work, etc.) certainty," and the record review should be considered to be below the standard of practice (Ackerman & Kane, 1998; Grisso, 2003; Heilbrun, 2001).

9.2.   Questionnaires

Self-report questionnaires can provide important information for the evaluation and understanding of an individual's beliefs, attitudes, and behavior (Heilbrun, 2001). There are a number of instruments commercially available or easily constructed that are not necessarily meant to be formal evaluation instruments. Most are face-valid; that is, it is not difficult to tell what the assessor is looking for by simply looking at the items included in the instrument. Most also have no, or minimal, validity scales and could be falsified by an individual who is so inclined. The forensic expert may also design questionnaires to gather relevant information without tying up the limited time of the assessor, who would otherwise have to gather the information through interviews. These instruments should generally be considered to be "information gathering instruments" or "interview extensions," rather than tests. Although most are not standardized, if they are a standard part of an evaluator's assessments they will generally be accepted in courts. Types of information gathered include personal history, work history, medical history, trauma history (accidents or other traumas that preceded the currently alleged trauma), pain history, and so forth. Norris and Hamblen (2004, pp. 66–98) described a number of instruments, with varying degrees of standardization, which address PTSD symptoms. All of them address the key question: *How has the individual changed as a result of the trauma/incident/accident?* What objective evidence is there that the claimed changes are real and are interfering with the individual's ability to function in some way?

9.3.   Informed Consent

Prior to beginning the assessment, the psychologist obtains the informed consent of the individual being assessed. This includes telling the person the nature and purpose of the evaluation (including who retained the psychologist), the fact that the evaluation is not confidential (although the number of people with access to the information might be small), and who might have access to the results of the evaluation (Specialty Guidelines for Forensic Psychologists, Guideline IV.E. [Committee on Ethical Guidlines for Forensic Psychologists (1991)]. If there is any reason to question the individual's understanding of the explanation given, the person should be asked to paraphrase the information. If the individual does not understand and therefore cannot give informed consent, this should be discussed with the retaining attorney, who (if not the attorney for the individual) should contact the individual's attorney prior to proceeding with the evaluation, unless the evaluation is court ordered or otherwise not voluntary. In that case, a simple explanation should be given, but assent rather than informed consent may be sufficient. The psychologist's report should indicate the questionable understanding and discuss the apparent reason(s) for it and any impact that it is likely to have on the results of the evaluation (Heilbrun, 2001).

9.4.   Psychological Testing

Although a "test" is technically a highly structured instrument with responses that are evaluated for quality or correctness, in general the use of the terms "test," "inventory," "scale," and "instrument" is interchangeable (American Educational Research Association, 1999). Experts can use psychological tests and other sources of information to reliably describe individuals' emotional, motivational, intellectual, neuropsychological, and social characteristics, as well as their daily behavior. In addition, there is empirical research that connects these types of information with past, present, and future behavior and outcomes. Further, there are theories of both normal and abnormal behavior that use constructs and assumptions to connect behavior with its causes. Such a theory is a "convenient fiction that is useful for generating hypotheses about how various events, behaviors, and human characteristics interrelate" (Grisso, 2003, p. 31).

10.   Clinical Versus Actuarial Assessment

Although there has been debate among psychologists for decades regarding the relative merits of actuarial [statistical, e.g., the Minnesota Multiphasic Personality Inventory, Second Edition (MMPI-2)] versus clinical (e.g., interviews, some projective techniques) assessment, both methods have a substantial amount to offer in an evaluation. Research suggests that the actuarial method is better about half the time, and there is no significant difference the other half of the time, indicating that the actuarial method does not always lead to better information (Heilbrun, 2001). When there is an actuarial instrument available and appropriate to the nature of the assessment, it should generally be used, along with appropriate means of clinical assessment.

11.   Correct Administration Is Essential

To be valid and reliable, a psychological instrument must be correctly administered. Each instrument has been standardized with a specific population under specific testing conditions. The further one deviates from the standardized conditions, the less likely one is to have test results that are valid. Among the considerations indicated by Ackerman and Kane (1998) are the following:

1. Tests and other assessment instruments, and interviews, should be administered in a relatively quiet area that is free of distractions. If conditions deviate significantly from this requirement, it might not be possible to conduct a valid assessment. Any environmental factors believed to have affected the results should be noted in the report (see also Heilbrun, 2001).
2. The individual being assessed should be alone with the examiner, because assessment instruments are standardized under this condition and there is no research literature indicating whether, and to what degree, the results from a nonstandardized administration might change the results of a particular instrument. This is also true with regard to audio or video recording. There is no research indicating that the assessment is as valid when a third party is present or the assessment is recorded as when it is not. (See also Constantinou & McCaffrey, 2003; Constantinou et al., 2002; Kehrer et al., 2000; Lezak et al., 2004). Further, the U.S. Supreme Court, in *Estelle v. Smith* (1981) indicated that the physical presence of an attorney during an evaluation "could contribute little and might seriously disrupt the examination." Ethical standards also suggest that there might be serious problems with validity if there is a third party present or if other nonstandard conditions are present. [See Ethical Standards 9.02, 9.06, and 9.11 of the *Ethical Principles of Psychologists and Code of Conduct* (2002); Standards 1.4, 5.4, and 12.19 of the *Standards for Educational and*

Psychological Testing (1999).] Further, Dean (2002, p. 141) indicated that "a medical examination itself is not part of the adversarial proceedings," so federal courts do not permit the presence of attorneys at evaluations without a compelling reason.

3. The psychologist should personally administer all tests and other formal instruments, if possible, to ensure that standard testing conditions were in place and to record extratest behavior (e.g., reactions, expressions, side comments) as well. If absolutely necessary, testing may be done by the psychologist's well-trained staff, under the psychologist's direct supervision.

4. *No standardized test should ever be taken home by or left with the individual being assessed.* If the administration is not directly observed, the psychologist cannot guarantee that the test or other instrument was in fact answered by the individual being assessed, or that the individual was sober while taking the test, or that other people did not influence the individual's responses to the test (Ethics Committee, American Psychological Association, 1993).

5. Tests and other assessment instruments must be appropriate for the individual being assessed. If reading level is a concern, it must be assessed prior to test administration.

6. If the psychologist makes any substantial changes from the standardized conditions for test administration, it is the responsibility of the psychologist to demonstrate that the test remains valid and reliable despite the changes. If the psychologist cannot do so, he or she cannot testify to a reasonable degree of psychological certainty that the results are valid.

12.   Response Style

The individual's response style, or "test-taking attitude," must be assessed. Specifically, the psychologist must identify whether the individual is responding honestly, is malingering, is defensive, is responding in a relevant manner, is cooperative, and is not impaired by communication problems related to age, thought or speech disorganization, deficits of intellect, and/or problems with memory (Heilbrun, 2001; Heilbrun et al., 2003; Rogers, 1997; Rogers & Bender, 2003). The most widely used instrument for addressing an individual's response style is the MMPI-2 (Boccaccini & Brodsky, 1999; Greenberg et al., 2003; Lees-Haley, 1992; Otto, 2002; Posthuma et al., 2002; Shuman, 1994a, 2002 supplement) The MMPI-2 is particularly well suited for addressing whether an individual is malingering or otherwise not answering questions in an open, forthright manner (Rogers, 2003). Further, the MMPI-2 should have no difficulty meeting the requirements of the Federal Rules of Evidence (or their state equivalents), including the requirements for relevance, reliability, falsifiability, peer review and publication, and general acceptance with the scientific community (Otto, 2002).

A related question is that of *motivation*. Does it appear that the individual did his or her best in responding to the tests and other instruments? Does it appear that the individual wants to get better, or is there evidence that he or she is comfortable in the "sick role?" Some of these data will come from the above instruments and some from the clinical and collateral interviews.

13.   Specific Tests

Although the popularity of a test or other instrument does not guarantee either validity or reliability, in most cases the most frequently used instruments will be both valid and reliable, as well as satisfying the criterion for "general acceptance" by psychologists. The most widely used test in both forensic and clinical evaluations is the MMPI-2 (Boccaccini & Brodsky, 1999; Camara et al., 2000; Watkins et al., Hallmark, 1995), in part because of its success at identifying the individual's response style. Although it is certainly not guaranteed, the individual who responds consistently, nondefensively, and so forth on the MMPI-2 is relatively likely to respond similarly throughout the evaluation (Ackerman & Kane, 1998; Boccaccini & Brodsky, 1999; Graham, 1993; Pope et al., 2000).

The second most widely used test in forensic evaluations is the Wechsler Adult Intelligence Scale, the current edition of which is the third (WAIS-III) (Boccaccini & Brodsky, 1999; Camara et al., 2000; Watkins et al., 1995). Third is the Millon Clinical Multiaxial Inventory, Second or Third Edition (MCMI-II or III) (Boccaccini & Brodsky, 1999; Camara et al., 2000; Watkins et al., 1995). This last finding is a matter of concern because there was no normal comparison group in the standardization sample, which was comprised solely of psychiatric patients. As a result, it is well documented that the MCMI–II and MCMI–III exaggerate an individual's psychopathology (Ackerman & Kane, 2005; Craig, 1999; Faust & Heard, 2003a; Groth-Marnat, 2003; Hess, 1998; Hynan, 2004; Rogers et al., 1999; Rogers, Salekin & Sewell, 2000; Schutte, 2000). Although the MCMI's emphasizing of psychopathology helps clinicians identify personality disorders that might require treatment, the overpathologizing is a serious confounding factor in forensic evaluations.

Other tests used by at least 25% of psychologists in at least one survey include the Rorschach Inkblot Technique (or Method), the Beck Depression Inventory, the Thematic Apperception Test, and the Symptom Check List-90 (Boccaccini & Brodsky, 1999; Camara et al., 2000; Watkins et al., 1995). The most widely used tests by neuropsychologists, according to Lees-Haley et al. (1995) are, in order, the Wechsler Adult Intelligence Scale, the current edition being the third (WAIS-III), the Minnesota Multiphasic Personality Inventory, Second Edition (MMPI-2), and the Wechsler Memory Scale, the current edition of which is the third (WMS-III).

14.   PTSD Instruments

If the plaintiff is indicating symptoms consistent with a PTSD, the areas of symptoms to address are those involving three components: reexperiencing, avoidance, and hyperarousal. (Briere, 2004, p. 102). Although few instruments address all three of these areas, two that do are the Trauma Symptom Inventory (TSI) and the Detailed Assessment of Posttraumatic Stress (DAPS). The former addresses 10 types of posttraumatic response, as well as having three validity scales (Briere, 2004; Briere et al., 1995; Demare' & Briere, 1996; Edens et al., 1998). An alternative for the expert who wishes to use an instrument with documented psychometric properties is the DAPS, which directly correlates with the criteria of PTSD in DSM-IV-TR (Briere, 2004; Greenberg et al., 2003; McLearen et al., 2004). The DAPS also includes two validity scales and assesses comorbid conditions often found with PTSD: dissociation, substance abuse, and suicidality (Briere, 2004, see also Chapters 6–8; see also the chapter by Polosny in this volume.)

15.   Malingering and Exaggerated Responding

There are a number of instruments designed to identify whether the individual is malingering. In a psychological injury case, at least one such instrument should be utilized. The validity scales of the MMPI-2 are the most frequently used scales for this purpose (Fishbain et al., 2003; Kane, 1999; Pope et al., 2000; Rogers, 1997). The individual who is forthright and consistent on the MMPI-2's validity scales is relatively likely to be forthright and consistent throughout the evaluation. Conversely, the individual who significantly exaggerates is extremely defensive, is inconsistent, or otherwise obfuscates raises a question about the veracity of the balance of the evaluation. Significantly elevated validity scales might be indications of malingering, a "cry for help," or of severe psychopathology. Individuals who have been stigmatized or rejected because of posttraumatic changes might respond in a manner that draws attention to their felt pain and injury, so that their problems do not get overlooked (Briere, 2004).

The MMPI-2 has a number of validity scales and one additional factor, the number of items to which no response was given or for which both "true" and "false" were marked, the "Cannot Say" or "?" Scale. Samuel et al. (1995) indicated that significantly more blanks are left by people involved in psychological injury litigation than among people who are not so involved. They also indicate that the closer the evaluation is to the date of the injury, the more likely it is that the individual will leave more than 30 items blank, producing a profile that is likely to be invalid, or, at the least, questionable.

Next, the consistency of responding is addressed with two scales, the Variable Response Inconsistency Scale (VRIN) and the True Response

Inconsistency Scale (TRIN). Either random responding or a fixed response set could lead to an invalidating score (above a T score of 79) on either or both of these scales.

The L Scale addresses the degree to which the individual tries to appear "perfect" or especially "virtuous." T Scores of 70–79 suggest blatant exaggeration of positive qualities (Pope et al., 2000). MMPI-2 profiles are generally invalidated by T scores of 80 or more on the L Scale (Butcher et al., 2001).

The F (Infrequency) Scale includes items that were endorsed by 10% or fewer of the normative population. T scores of 80–89 suggest questionable validity, whereas T scores of 90 or greater indicate that the test is likely to be invalid (Butcher et al., 2001). An invalid score could be the result of malingering, exaggeration of problems (including a cry for help), extreme defensiveness, random responding, and/or significant psychopathology (Groth-Marnat, 2003). Research indicates that there is a positive correlation between high F Scale scores and histories of trauma, depression, dissociation, PTSD, and traumatic environments in the family of origin, making the F Scale much less useful in assessing malingering among trauma victims (Elhai et al., 2004).

The F_B (F Back) Scale primarily addresses items in the second half of the test. The same cutoff scores should be used as for the F Scale (Butcher et al., 2001).

The K Scale addresses a more subtle and sophisticated defensiveness than does the L Scale. A high score does not imply psychopathology. T Scores from 65 to 74 suggest substantial defensiveness, whereas T scores of 75 or higher suggest "faking good." High K Scale T scores make it much less likely that psychopathology will be indicated on the clinical scales (Butcher et al., 2001). Individuals with advanced education and/or high socioeconomic status are relatively likely to get high K Scale scores regardless of whether they are intentionally being defensive (Pope et al., 2000).

The S (Superlative Self-Presentation) Scale is similar to the K Scale, but includes items from throughout the test, rather than only the first 370. Individuals with high scores might be claiming one or more positive qualities (e.g., a belief in human goodness, a feeling of serenity, feeling content with life, denial of negative feelings, and/or denial of moral flaws). T scores of 69 or less suggest a valid test protocol, scores of 70–74 indicate moderate defensiveness, and scores of 75 or higher indicate that the protocol might be invalid because of "faking good." If the T score is 65 or higher, the five subscales of the S Scale may be interpreted (Butcher et al., 2001; Pope et al., 2000).

The F_P (Infrequency-Psychopathology) Scale consists of items that were answered in the scored direction by no more than 20% of either the normative sample or a sample of psychiatric inpatients. When the F Scale is elevated and random responding has been ruled out, a T score of 100 or higher on F_P suggests significantly excessive reporting of psychopathology (i.e., "faking bad"). In contrast, if F_P is below 70, it is relatively likely that severe psychopathology reported is real. T Scores between 70 and 99 suggest either exaggeration of symptoms or a "cry for help" (Butcher et al., 2001; Nichols, 2001). The F_p Scale is the most specific and most sensitive measure of over-reporting on the MMPI-2 (Nichols, 2001; Pope et al., 2000). Briere (2004) and Elhai et al. (2004) indicated that F_p appears to be more sensitive than the F Scale in determining whether a PTSD protocol is valid.

The F–K (F minus K) Index, also known as the Dissimulation Index, suggests "faking bad" if the *raw* score for the F Scale is 15 or more points greater than the *raw* score for the K Scale (Butcher et al., 2001). Scores of 25 or more strongly suggest exaggeration of psychopathology (Nichols, 2001; Rogers et al., 1994). If F–K is equal to or less than –8, it is very unlikely that the person was feigning (Rogers et al., 1994). The F–K Index has been found to be especially good at identifying "motivated faking" (Briere, 2004).

Other commonly used instruments that have been demonstrated to be both valid and reliable measures of malingering include the Structured Interview of Reported Symptoms (SIRS), the Personality Assessment Inventory (PAI), the Test of Memory Malingering (TOMM), and the Validity Indicator Profile (VIP) (Ackerman & Kane, 1998; Briere, 2004; Rogers, 1997; Rogers & Bender, 2003). Neuropsychologists assessing malingering are also likely to use the MMPI-2, with one of the others above as an alternative or addition, or they might use a forced-choice test [e.g., the Portland Digit Recognition Test (PDRT)] (Lally, 2003). With these and/or other instruments designed to detect malingering, it is usually possible to at least raise a significant question about malingering and often to make a statement with a substantial degree of certainty.

To further assess malingering, Wilson and Moran (2004, p. 628) have developed a list of "critical cues to malingering," including lack of cooperation with psychological and medical assessment procedures and requests, evasiveness and vagueness, incorrect details or implausible information, evidencing behavior inconsistent with PTSD, blaming all problems on the traumatic symptoms, falsifying or altering documentation, overemphasis on "flashbacks," inconsistent, defensive, or malingering patterns in test responses, a history of antisocial personality or behavior, or previous legal claims for injuries.

Because an accusation of malingering is very serious, multiple methods should be used to assess it, coming to a positive conclusion only if malingering is strongly indicated, and contrary results, if any, can be explained as well (Rogers & Bender, 2003). Discordant results are hypotheses to be addressed, not results that are contradictory (Greenberg, 2003).

16.   Other Factors

Any test or other standardized instrument utilized should have an identified level of *sensitivity* and *specificity*. The former refers to the ability of the instrument to correctly detect pathology that is present (correct positives). The latter refers to the ability to identify when the pathology is *not* present (correct negatives). The goal is to minimize both false positives and false negatives (Gouvier et al., 2003).

Part of the evaluation of malingering or secondary gain is the assessment of secondary *cost*. The sick role involves a variety of limitations on behavior, travel, and general functioning. If the potential gain from a lawsuit is relatively small (e.g., a few thousand dollars), there is little reason to suspect that the individual is consciously (malingering) or unconsciously (secondary gain) demonstrating the degree of dysfunction associated with the injury (Miller, 2003).

17. Interviews

A personal interview of the plaintiff is extremely important in any evaluation. Without it, there is a marked limitation to the conclusions that can be drawn about the individual and the impact of the traumatic event on that individual, even if the expert has access to psychological testing of and other information regarding the plaintiff and his or her description of the traumatic event (Greenberg, 2003; Heilbrun, 2001). The *Specialty Guidelines for Forensic Psychologists* (Committee on Ethical Guidelines for Forensic Psychologists, 1991) indicated that forensic psychologists must attempt to have an "examination of the individual adequate to the scope of the statements, opinions, or conclusions to be issued. . . . When it is not possible or feasible to do so, they make clear the impact of such limitations on the reliability and validity of their professional products, evidence, or testimony." Without an interview, the expert lacks a key source of data concerning the connection between historical, test, and other information and the legal question at issue. Even if there is an interview, the clinician might not have an adequate basis for an opinion if the interview had been too short, if essential areas were not covered, if there was not sufficient privacy during the interview, and so forth. Courts generally admit testimony under these conditions (Shuman, 1994a, 2002 supplement). However,

standard psychiatric and psychological diagnostic techniques include an examination of the patient. . . . Thus, an in-court opinion not based on a personal examination of the patient, when it is possible to do so, violates accepted practice. This failure should bear on the weight given the resulting opinions

as well. (Shuman, 1994a, 2003 supplement, p. 9–7)

In the United States, Rule 35(a) of the Federal Rules of Civil Procedure permits a party to the litigation to have an evaluation of the plaintiff by an independent expert in nearly every case "when the mental or physical condition. . . of a party. . . is in controversy. . . ." The party requesting the examination must make the report of the examination available to the opposing party if so requested. If the report is not given to the requesting party, the expert's testimony may be excluded. If the attorney requesting the examination does not like the contents or conclusions of the verbal report by the expert, however, he or she will most likely not request a written report, thereby eliminating the unfavorable testimony by the expert (Greenberg, 2003). States generally have similar provisions in their statutes.

Whereas some psychologists prefer a structured interview, others prefer to use formal and informal instruments such as those listed above to address most, if not all, of the areas that must be considered and to spend several hours interviewing the individual regarding his or her experience and the responses to the tests and questionnaires (Greenberg et al., 2003).

The goal is to not only formally evaluate the individual but also to understand *what the trauma means to the individual*, as no two people have exactly the same response to a given event (Ackerman & Kane, 1998; Wilson & Moran, 2004). It is *essential* that the evaluator understand the meaning of the stressor for the individual being evaluated—this is in many ways the primary purpose of the interview.

Another aspect of identifying the meaning of the trauma for the individual is the assessment of whether the person has an unconscious psychological need to identify a physical or other traumatic cause for his or her symptoms. The individual who does is *not* malingering; his or her pain and suffering are real.

Because there is evidence that social support following traumatic events is associated with an improved prognosis, it is important to assess the individual's perceived and actual levels of social support (Briere, 2004). The individual whose family and friends accept the fact that emotional injuries are as real as physical injuries is relatively likely to simply discuss his or her symptoms in a straightforward manner. Lacking the social support of family and friends, however, an individual might feel a need to "prove" that the disability is real, including asserting that his or her injury is organic (e.g., a mild traumatic brain injury or a soft tissue injury). These individuals are generally not primarily seeking financial gain; they are trying to have their suffering acknowledged by family and friends and, in the legal context, by having the jury independently confirm that the individual has really been hurt *and* that it is not his or her fault (Miller, 2003). Some individuals have such goals as trying to prevent the defendant from hurting someone else, punishing the defendant, or other "social justice" goals (Ackerman & Kane, 1998).

18.   Number and Length of Assessment Sessions

A complete evaluation requires at least two meetings with the plaintiff, and often more (Ackerman & Kane, 1998; Wilson & Moran, 2004). It is simply not possible to do a complete evaluation in a single session; the story of the traumatic experience requires ample time if it is to be fully told

(Wilson & Moran, 2004). Although the needed tasks might be accomplished in one 8-hour day, there will be a real question about whether fatigue is an increasing factor as the day wears on, making conclusions potentially less valid. It is also very difficult to get a complete picture of an individual in a single day. Further, scheduling a second session a week or so later permits the tests and other instruments from the first day to be scored and interpreted, and some, if not all, collateral calls to be made, so that the value of the clinical interview (at session two) is greater. If the plaintiff or his or her attorney refuses to permit sufficient time for a complete evaluation, it might be necessary to request that the court order that the plaintiff be available for sufficient time to permit a complete evaluation to occur.

19.   Review of Research

There is a large body of research addressing aspects of causality and the assessment of psychological status, disability, and related factors. The research addresses samples of people with various characteristics (e.g., age, education, gender, trauma history, education) who have been assessed using specified instruments under various conditions. This is referred to as *nomothetic* data. Nomothetic data are group or population based and are especially useful for establishing the validity and reliability of instruments (tests, information forms, etc.) used for forensic assessments and for prediction related to the course of psychological disorders and impairments. Nomothetic data also tell us what is statistically "normal" and what is significantly different from normal. In addition, base rates are established by nomothetic data. Hypotheses can be generated on the basis of research regarding the typical behavior (including test results) of individuals who have experienced one or more specific types of traumatic event and/or the absence of behavior or other characteristics *not* typical of individuals who have experienced a traumatic event (Heilbrun, 2001). Experts must be able to identify relevant professional articles or other learned treatises that support their methodology, if asked, and it might be appropriate for the expert to include that information in his or her report. (Baer & Neal, 2000).

Idiographic data are those pertaining to the individual who is being assessed. Through psychological testing, use of information-gathering forms and interviews, and review of documents related to the case, the psychologist identifies relevant characteristics of the individual, the nature of the alleged traumatic incident and its meaning for the individual, and the impact of the alleged traumatic incident on the individual (Ackerman & Kane, 1998; Wilson & Moran, 2004). In the course of doing so, the psychologist develops a number of hypotheses, each of which can be tested against further data that become available from some source. The greater the consistency among sources (e.g., tests, life history information, interviews of the individual, and collaterals), the greater the likelihood that a given piece of data is accurate.

Through the analysis of idiographic data, the psychologist identifies possible causal links between changes in the condition of the individual and the alleged traumatic incident (Greenberg et al., 2003; Heilbrun, 2001).

The primary difficulty that could arise is if the individual (ideographic) data does not match the parameters of the group (nomothetic) data, so that hypotheses about the individual cannot adequately be tested or, therefore, firm conclusions drawn. If all research in a particular area of inquiry has been conducted on men, for example, it might not be possible to accurately generalize to women. If the normative group consists solely of psychiatric patients, it might not be possible to accurately generalize to individuals who are not psychiatric patients (see the discussion of the MCMI, p. 30). Further, some information is available based on controlled experiments, whereas other information is based on naturalistic groups. For example, it would be unethical to do controlled research that involved causing severe pain to the experimental group in order to ascertain how people respond to a variety of pain experiences. Instead, we have to do research with people who have already been injured and who already feel severe pain to try to understand their pain experience. It is the task of the expert to accurately identify the ways the individual is similar to and different from both the controlled and naturalistic research populations and to carefully draw conclusions from that data (Haney & Smith, 2003). The expert must also be at all times cognizant of the fact that "trial courts are usually concerned with specific effects on specific individuals. While science attempts to discover the universals hiding among the particulars, trial courts attempt to discover the particulars hiding among the universals" (Faigman, 1999, p. 340).

20.   Every Evaluation Has Some Limits

Every evaluation leaves some questions unanswered or marginally answered. Exhausting every possible avenue of inquiry and administration of every psychological test or other instrument that might have utility would take so much time and be so expensive that it could not be justified. In addition, limits imposed by the parties or the court (e.g., number of hours permitted for the assessment) could also hinder the ability of an evaluator to provide a strong statement regarding some of his or her conclusions. There might also be inconsistencies among the results of different parts of the evaluation, including two tests, or a test and an interview, and so forth. Further, information considered important or essential might not be available (e.g., school records, medical records, or other objective information). It is incumbent on the evaluator to try to identify any significant limits of the evaluation and to indicate them in his or her report, together with a statement regarding the impact of those limits on the validity of his or her conclusions. The expert also has an obligation to indicate any significant findings that are not consistent with his or her conclusions (Heilbrun, 2001). Because every evaluation has some limits, experts are expected to testify not to absolute certainty but, instead, to "a reasonable degree" of certainty.

21.   Ecological Validity

"Ecological validity" refers to the degree to which an instrument or procedure yields information applicable not only to the standardization sample or theoretical model but also to an individual's real-world functioning. A given injury might cause one individual to spend much of each day in bed, whereas another person with a seemingly identical injury is much more active, goes to work, and so forth. Further, a "normal" psychological or neuropsychological test result does not mean that the individual does not have a real problem and a real inability to function in certain areas (Miller, 2003).

The ecological validity of the individual's complaints might also be addressed by interviewing people familiar with the plaintiff's daily functioning. Both the plaintiff and the collaterals might be asked questions regarding exactly what the individual is able or unable to do. Does the individual actually do things that he or she has told the evaluator cannot be done (Faust & Heard, 2003a)?

Information from collaterals also increases the face validity of the evaluation and can help identify whether an apparent or claimed deficit is a problem in the individual's daily life (Heilbrun, 2001; Heilbrun et al., 2002). There is research suggesting that telephone collateral interviews regarding the plaintiff may also be equivalent to face-to-face interviews (Heilbrun, 2001). The possibility of biased responding by a collateral can be addressed by gathering information from multiple sources, developing conclusions based on trends in the data collected rather than any single response. The evaluator should limit inquiries to what the collateral source saw and heard, not any conclusions drawn by the collateral source (Greenberg, 2003; Heilbrun, 2001). To identify collaterals who might be interviewed, the evaluator might request that the plaintiff provide the names and telephone numbers of individuals who have knowledge about his or her functioning (Greenberg, 2003).

If the plaintiff is part of a couple, there is often value in having the partner come to the first evaluation session but sit in a different room and fill out questionnaires that address his or her perceptions of the plaintiff and the plaintiff's functional abilities. Among the information requested would be, for example, "things my husband/wife/spouse used to do alone, but which I now have to help with or do for him or her." The partner could describe an average day for the plaintiff and could describe the plaintiff before and after the traumatic event. This information needs to be gathered at the first evaluation session because the couple is likely to discuss the nature of the testing and interviewing of the plaintiff after the first session and the partner's responses might be different after hearing what the plaintiff had said.

22.   Incremental Validity

Each source of data in a forensic evaluation adds some amount of *information*, but not necessarily *new* or *useful* information. The goal is to investigate all of the relevant and important issues and to stop there (Faust, 2003; Hunsley, 2003; Hunsley & Meyer, 2003). Because the evaluator cannot be certain what a given test, interview, or review of records will produce, he or she should generally stop when a substantial amount of data has been collected and there is a clear direction to the data. According to Garb (2003), personality inventories, interviews, and brief self-rating instruments generally add incremental validity in both diagnosis and the assessment of psychpathology and personality. Projective tests might provide a rich source of hypotheses that can be addressed in the evaluation (Ackerman & Kane, 1998).

23.   Controversy Regarding the Comprehensive System for the Rorschach

Although the Rorschach Inkblot Method (or Test) is the most widely used projective test, questions have been raised regarding the validity of many scales of the most widely used scoring and interpretive system, the Comprehensive System by John Exner. Since 1999, many articles by prominent authors such as Gregory Meyer, Irving Weiner, James Wood, and Howard Garb have been published that either defend the Comprehensive System or point out its alleged problems. A psychologist who uses the Rorschach as part of an evaluation must be aware of the controversy and, if he or she uses the Comprehensive System to score and interpret the test, to defend the use of any of the questioned scales.

The present author believes that the Rorschach has much to offer in forensic evaluations, particularly through the generation of hypotheses about an individual that might have been missed without this test. As is true of all tests, the Rorschach should not be used in isolation; it should be part of a complete evaluation involving other tests, interviews, and review of records.

24.   Sources of Bias

There are many types of bias that could interfere with the validity of an evaluation:

1. *Observer effects* refer to the fact that the thoughts, feelings, experiences, and expectations of scientists, like any people, could influence their perceptions and conclusions. The expert must be aware of his or her biases and try to ensure that they do not interfere with the validity of the evaluation (Risinger et al., 2002).

2. *Anchoring bias* refers to research indicating that information received early in the evaluation process is remembered better and used more than information received later in the process. The evaluator needs to ensure that this tendency is monitored so that it does not interfere with the validity of the evaluation (Bowman, 2003; Risinger et al., 2002).

3. *Confirmation bias* refers to evaluators giving more weight to information that is consistent with their own beliefs. This might cause the evaluator to pay more attention to information confirming his or her bias and disregarding contrary information (Bowman, 2003; Risinger et al., 2002).

4. *Overconfidence bias* results when the evaluator feels certain of his or her conclusions and therefore assumes they are valid. However, confidence in and validity of conclusions are not correlated. The evaluator must keep an open mind while examining all of the relevant data (Bowman, 2003).

5. *Attribution bias* involves "discounting contextual factors accounting for behavior and imputing it instead to a permanent characteristic of an individual" (Sageman, 2003, p. 325). For example, an individual might act aggressively when attacked, but at no other time, but the evaluator might assume that it is a personality characteristic.

6. *Hindsight bias* occurs when people who are aware of how an incident turns out believe that that outcome was more likely than objective prediction would indicate. Because both experts and fact finders know how an incident turned out, they might attribute more foreseeability than appropriate (Shuman, 1995; Wayte et al., 2002).

Awareness is the primary means of addressing these forms of bias. The expert must guard against the validity of the evaluation being compromised by any form of bias and must always endeavor to remain impartial.

25. Treating Versus Independent Expert

Whereas a treating psychologist, psychiatrist, or other mental health professional has a great deal of information about an individual who has been traumatized, it is not possible for the treating professional to be an independent expert, and it is very likely an ethical violation for the treater to attempt to maintain these conflicting roles. Further, if the "treating expert" recommended psychotherapy, it might appear to be feathering his or her own nest. Because malingering must be considered by the expert in a case, the therapeutic relationship could be irreparably damaged if the treater were to find evidence of malingering. There are, thus, many incompatibilities between the treating and expert witness roles (Ackerman & Kane, 2005; Greenberg, & Shuman, 1997; Heilbrun, 2001; Shuman, 1994a, 2002 supplement; Simon & Wettstein, 1997; Strassburger et al., 1997). This does not preclude the therapist from being interviewed by the independent evaluator or from testifying as a fact witness. In both cases, the therapist should be circumspect regarding information released and should get the written consent of the patient, if possible, prior to releasing or discussing information that is potentially harmful or embarrassing (Greenberg & Shuman, 1997).

26. Expert Consultant Versus Expert Witness

An expert may be retained to advise an attorney rather than to testify. As a paid consultant to the attorney, the expert is bound by the attorney's work product privilege. The retaining attorney does not have to tell the opposing attorney that the expert has been retained.

27. For Whom Does the Expert Advocate?

Whether retained by either side or appointed by the court, experts are bound by the ethics codes of their professions and the statutes and administrative codes governing their licenses. The expert is to advocate for his or her data and conclusions, not for either side, regardless of who is paying the fees. This will not produce agreement among experts, because each comes to any given case with beliefs based on both theory and experience and might draw conclusions far different from those of a different expert (Heilbrun, 2001). The Specialty Guidelines for Forensic Psychologists (1991, p. 665) indicate that the psychologist's "essential role [is] as expert to the court. . . ."

28. Expert Ethics

The American Psychological Association adopted a revised Ethical Principles of Psychologists and Code of Conduct (EPPCC) in 2002, which became effective on June 1, 2003. Many of the changes are in response to the requirements of *Daubert* and its progeny.

Psychologists' work is to be based on "established scientific and professional knowledge" (EPPCC, Std. 2.04). Their opinions are to be based "on information and techniques sufficient to substantiate their findings" [EPPCC, Std. 9.01(a)]. In all cases except those in which only a records review is deemed sufficient for a given purpose, "psychologists provide opinions of the psychological characteristics of individuals only after they have conducted an examination of the individuals adequate to support their statements or conclusions" [EPPCC, Std. 9.01(b)]. If a personal examination is not possible, psychologists must indicate the "probable impact of their limited information on the reliability and validity of their opinions, and appropriate limit the nature and extent of their conclusions or recommendations" [EPPCC, Std. 9.01(b)]. Similarly, assessment instruments and methods are to be used only for populations upon which they have been standardized and for which validity and reliability have been established. If the psychologist utilizes instruments and methods that do not meet this requirement, the psychologist is required to indicate how that might impact the validity and reliability of his or her findings and interpretations [EPPCC, Std. 9.02(b)].

Psychologists also indicate any significant limitations on their interpretations as a result of the characteristics of the person being evaluated (e.g., language or cultural differences) (EPPCC, Std. 9.06). The *Canadian Code of Ethics for Psychologists* covers essentially the same points as well, although in less detail (Canadian Psychological Association 2000). Because certain behavior might be considered normal in one culture but aberrant in another, cultural factors must be carefully considered by the evaluator (Briere, 2004).

An area of contention for many years is the conflicting responsibilities of psychologists and attorneys regarding raw test data. The psychologist has an ethical and legal duty to maintain the integrity of the testing materials, whereas an attorney wants to obtain all information upon which a psychologist bases his or her opinion. This battle may be eased somewhat by an attempt to differentiate *test data* from *test materials*. Thus, *test data* refer to raw and scaled scores, client/patient responses to test questions or stimuli, and psychologists' notes and recordings concerning client/patient statements and behavior during an examination. Those portions of test materials that include client/patient responses are included in the definition of *test data* [EPPCC, 9.04(a)].

If the psychologist has a signed release, he or she can provide test data to the client/patient or other persons who are identified in the release. However,

Psychologists may refrain from releasing test data to protect a client/patient or others from substantial harm or misuse or misrepresentation of the data or the test, recognizing that in many instances release of confidential information under these circumstances is regulated by law. [EPPCC, 9.04(a)]

This section is generally taken to indicate that the raw (test) data must be released to someone who is able to interpret it (i.e., another licensed or certified psychologist) to prevent the harm that might occur if the data are misinterpreted or misrepresented.

This Ethical Standard must be considered along with Ethical Standard 9.11, Maintaining Test Security:

The term *test materials* refers to manuals, instruments, protocols, and test questions or stimuli, which do not include *test data* as defined in Standard 9.04, Release of Test Data. Psychologists make reasonable efforts to maintain the integrity and security of test materials and other assessment techniques consistent with law and contractual obligations, and in a manner that permits adherence to this Ethics Code. [EPPCC, Std. 9.11]

Thus, *test data* refer to a specific client/patient and to the responses of that particular individual, whereas *test materials* refer to the instrument or test to which the client/patient was responding. Test material, therefore, contains nothing that is unique to a given individual. Taken together, these two Ethical Standards indicate the following:

1. Psychologists may provide test data, as defined, to attorneys, provided that the client/patient has given informed consent, in writing, to that release.
2. However, the psychologist may withhold test data from the client/patient, from the attorney, and/or from others if the psychologist believes that release of the test data might cause substantial harm to the client/patient or others or if the psychologist believes that the test data that are released might be misused or misrepresented.
3. Statutory law takes precedence over ethical standards. If a state law prohibits release under the circumstances in a given case, the psychologist would not release the test data. The same would be true if release of the test data was believed by the psychologist to violate the U.S. Health Insurance Portability and Accountability Act (HIPAA). However, "HIPAA does not require release of [records] in situations in which information is compiled in reasonable anticipation of, or for use in, civil, criminal, or administrative actions or proceedings" (Fisher, 2003, p. 195).
4. If the client/patient has not provided a written, informed consent for release, the psychologist is not permitted to release the test data without specific statutory authority or a court order. A subpoena from an attorney is not a sufficient basis for the release of test data. Further, because attorneys are not trained to understand or evaluate most of the raw obtained data from an evaluation, in most cases raw data may be released only to a psychologist retained by that attorney. A psychologist who releases test data with neither a signed, informed consent from the client/patient nor a court order is likely to be in violation of Standard 9.04.
5. "Test materials" are defined as the test instruments themselves. If the client/patient responds by writing on the test materials or if the psychologist writes the individual's responses on the test materials, the test materials *become* test data because of the presence of those client/patient responses. If, however, the responses are recorded on a separate document or paper, it is only the responses, not the test questions or stimuli, that can be released.
6. If the psychologist has been retained by an attorney, appointed by a court, or otherwise retained by an organization rather than by the individual who is being evaluated, the test data do not have to be released to that individual because he or she is not the client.
7. Whenever possible, psychologists have a responsibility to avoid releasing test materials, because of the need to maintain the integrity and security of those test materials, the contractual agreements between the psychologist and the test publisher, and the need to minimize entry of the test materials into the public domain.
8. Ethical Standard 9.04 specifies that "test data" include "psychologists' notes and recordings concerning client/patient statements and behavior *during an examination*." [emphasis added] "The term 'notes' in this standard is limited to the assessment or test and does not include

psychotherapy notes documenting or analyzing the contents of conversation during a private counseling session."

29.   Specialty Guidelines for Forensic Psychologists

There are also Specialty Guidelines for Forensic Psychologists (Committee on Ethical Guidelines for Forensic Psychologists, 1991). The Specialty Guidelines are aspirational, not binding, but many courts and licensing boards have considered them when addressing the conduct of forensic psychologists.

Specialty Guideline VI.A. indicates that "[b]ecause of their special status as persons qualified as experts to the court, forensic psychologists have an obligation to maintain current knowledge of scientific, professional and legal developments within their area of claimed competence".... Specialty Guideline VI.B. indicates that "[f]orensic psychologists have an obligation to document and be prepared to make available... all data that form the basis for their evidence or services...." Specialty Guideline VI.H. indicates that "[f]orensic psychologists avoid giving written or oral evidence about the psychological characteristics of particular individuals when they have not had an opportunity to conduct an examination of the individual adequate to the scope of the statements, opinions, or conclusions to be issued...." Specialty Guideline VII.F indicates that "[f]orensic psychologists are aware that their essential role as expert to the court is to assist the trier of fact to understand the evidence or to determine a fact in issue."

30.   Potential Liability of the Psychologist

In *Deatherage v. Washington Examining Board of Psychology* (1997), the Washington Supreme Court ruled that a psychologist did not have immunity from discipline by the state's psychology licensing board for failing to qualify statements made in child custody evaluations, mischaracterizing information, failing to verify information, and misinterpreting test data (Cohen, 2004; Ewing, 2004). Further, although witness and/or quasi-judicial immunity prevents civil lawsuits against experts by nearly anyone, a few courts have permitted litigants to sue their own experts for malpractice, alleging that the expert was negligent and/or practiced below the minimum standard for his or her profession (Cohen, 2004; Ewing, 2004). In any forensic evaluation, the expert must do a competent job of gathering and processing information.

31.   Conclusions

1. Psychologists are well equipped by training, experience, codes of ethics, and specialty guidelines to follow the requirements of *Daubert, Mohan,* and their progeny.

2. The expert must adhere to the best practices of his or her profession, because this will help ensure that the expert's testimony will be admitted into evidence.

3. The expert must be aware of the latest scientific evidence (learned treatises) concerning causality and the assessment of individuals who have allegedly sustained a traumatic injury.

4. Multiple methods must be used to assess an individual, including, when appropriate, psychological testing, interviews, and review of all relevant medical, work, arrest/conviction, school, military, and other records.

5. Most, if not all, of the methodology of an assessment should utilize instruments and methods widely accepted in the professional community, with well-established reliability and validity. These instruments must also be used according to the standardization and validation procedures of the instrument's originators, as well as other uses validated by the research literature.

6. The expert should be prepared to defend the appropriateness of procedures utilized in an assessment.

7. Experts may utilize information-gathering forms that are, in effect, "written interviews" rather than tests and that are not necessarily standardized instruments.

8. Experts providing psychological services outside of the jurisdiction in which he or she is licensed/certified must verify that he or she will not be violating the statutes or administrative code of the "foreign" jurisdiction by providing those services.

9. The expert must be familiar with the relevant case law in any jurisdiction in which he or she practices.

10. In arriving at conclusions, experts must weigh all the evidence gathered in their assessments, consider all reasonably possible causal factors, and rule in or rule out all potentially relevant explanations for the findings.

32.   The Rest of the Book

This chapter has been an introduction to the ethics and the legal and practical information and procedures that a psychologist needs to know prior to being involved as a consultant or testifying expert assessing causality in a psychological injury lawsuit. The balance of this book is devoted to the psychological knowledge that is also essential to have if one is to be part of the legal process.

For those who wish a substantially greater background in the legal and psychological processes and procedures involved, the companion book to this volume, *Causality: Psychological Evidence in Court*, is highly recommended.

References

Ackerman, M. J. & Kane, A. W. (1998). *Psychological Experts in Personal Injury Actions*, 3rd ed. New York: Aspen Law and Business.

Ackerman, M. J. & Kane, A. W. (2005). Psychological Experts in Divorce Actions, 4th ed. New York: Aspen Law and Business.

American Educational Research Association. (1999). *Standards for Educational and Psychological Testing*. Washington, DC: American Educational Research Association.

American Psychiatric Association. (1994). Diagnostic and Statistical Manual of Mental Disorders, 4th ed. Washington, DC: American Psychiatric Association.

American Psychological Association. (2002). Ethical principles of psychologists and code of conduct. *American Psychologist, 57*, 1060–1073.

Athey v. Leonati. (1996). 3 S.C.R. 458.

Baer, L. G. & Neal, J. K. (2000). Admissibility of medical causation expert opinions in federal courts, part I: The current state of the law. *The Trial Lawyer, 23*, 323–334.

Barefoot v. Estelle. (1983). 463 US 880.

Boccaccini. M. T. & Brodsky, S. L. (1999). Diagnostic test usage by forensic psychologists in emotional injury cases. *Professional Psychology: Research and Practice, 30*, 253–259.

Bowman, M. L. (2003). Problems inherent to the diagnosis of Posttraumatic Stress Disorder. In I. Z. Schulze & D.O. Brady (Eds.). *Psychological Injuries at Trial*. Chicago, IL: American Bar Association, pp. 820–849.

Bradford, G. E. (2001). Dissecting Missouri's requirement of "reasonable medical certainty." *Journal of the Missouri Bar, 57*, 3 (January 1, 2004), Available from www.mobar.org (accessed August 12, 2004).

Briere, J. (2004). *Psychological Assessment of Adult Posttraumatic States, 2nd ed.* Washington, *DC:* American Psychological Association.

Briere, J., Elliott, D. M., Harris, K., & Cotman, A. (1995). Trauma Symptom Inventory: Psychometrics and association with childhood and adult victimization in clinical samples. *Journal of Interpersonal Violence, 10,* 387–401.

Brown, J. J. & Eder, E. (1999). The standards of admissibility of scientific and technical evidence. In J. J. Brown (Ed.). *Scientific Evidence and Experts Handbook*. New York: Aspen Law & Business, pp. 1–42.

Butcher, J. N., Graham, J. R., Ben-Porath, Y. S., Tellegen, A., Dahlstrom, W. G., & Kaemmer, B. (2001). *MMPI-2 Manual for Administration, Scoring, and Interpretation*, rev. ed. Minneapolis, MN: University of Minnesota Press.

Camara, W. J., Nathan, J. S. & Puente, A. E. (2000). Psychological test usage: Implications in professional psychology. *Professional Psychology: Research & Practice, 31,* 141–154.

Canadian Psychological Association. (2000). *Canadian Code of Ethics for Psychologists*, 3rd ed. Ottawa; Canadian Psychological Association. Available from www.cpa.ca/ethics.html (accessed February 2, 2005).

Cohen, F. L. (2004). The expert medical witness in legal perspective. *The Journal of Legal Medicine, 25,* 185–209.

Committee on Ethical Guidelines for Forensic Psychologists. (1991). Specialty guidelines for forensic psychologists. *Law and Human Behavior, 15*, 655–665.

Constantinou, M. & McCaffrey, R. J. (2003). The effects of 3rd party observation: When the observer is a video camera. *Archives of Clinical Neuropsychology, 18*, 788–789.

Constantinou, M., Ashendorf, L. & McCaffrey, R. J. (2002). When the 3rd party observer of a neuropsychological evaluation is an audio-recorder. *The Clinical Neuropsychologist, 16*, 407–412

Cooper v. Smith & Nephew. (2001). 259 F.3d 194.

Craig, R. J. (1999). Testimony based on the Millon Clinical Multiaxial Inventory: Review, commentary, and guidelines, *Journal of Personality Assessment, 73*, 290–304.

Daubert v. Merrell Dow Pharmaceuticals, Inc. (1993). 509 U.S. 579, 113 S. Ct. 2786, 125 L.Ed. 2d 469.

Daubert v. Merrell Dow Pharmaceuticals, Inc. (1995). 43 F.3d 1311 (9th Cir).

Dean, B. P. (2004). Discovery in scientific evidence cases. In J.J. Brown, *Scientific Evidence and Experts Handbook*. New York: Aspen Law & Business, 2004 cumulative supplement (pp. 137–229).

Deatherage v. Washington Examining Board of Psychology. (1997). 134 Wn.2d 131, 948 P.2d 828 (Washington Sup. Ct, 1997).

Demaré, D. & Briere, J. (1996). Validation of the Trauma Symptom Inventory with abused and nonabused university students. Paper presented at the 104th Annual Convention of the American Psychological Association, Toronto, Canada.

Edens, J. F., Otto, R. K., & Dwyer, T. J. (1998). Susceptibility of the Trauma Symptom Inventory to malingering. *Journal of Personality Assessment, 71*, 379–392.

Elhai, J. D., Naifeh, J. A., Zucker, I. S., Gold, S. N., Deitsch, S. E., & Frueh, B. C. (2004). Discriminating malingered from genuine civilian Posttraumatic Stress Disorder: A validation of three MMPI-2 infrequency scales (F, Fp, and Fptsd). *Assessment, 11*, 139–144.

Estelle v. Smith. (1981). 451 U.S. 454, 14.

Ethics Committee, American Psychological Association. (1994). "Take home" tests. *American Psychologist, 49*, 665–666.

Ewing, C. P. (2004). Expert testimony: Law and practice. In A. M. Goldstein (Ed.). *Handbook of Psychology*, vol. 11, pp. 55–66. Hoboken, NJ: Wiley

Faigman, D. L. (1999). The gatekeepers: Scientific expert testimony in the trial process. *The Trial Lawyer, 23*, 335–346.

Faust, D. (2003). Holistic thinking is not the whole story: Alternative or adjunct approaches for increasing the accuracy of legal evaluations. *Assessment, 10*, 428–41.

Faust D. & Heard, K. V. (2003a). Biased experts: Some practical suggestions for identifying and demonstrating unfair practices. In I. Z. Schulze & D. O. Brady (Eds.). *Psychological Injuries at Trial*. Chicago, IL: American Bar Association, pp. 1706–1739.

Faust, D. & Heard, K. V. (2003b). Objectifying subjective injury claims. In I. Z. Schulze & D. O. Brady (Eds.). *Psychological Injuries at Trial*. Chicago, IL: American Bar Association, pp. 1686–1705.

Federal Rules of Evidence. (2004). Available from http://judiciary.house.gov/media/pdfs/printers/108th/evid2004.pdf (accessed February 20, 2005).

Fishbain, D. A., Cutler, R., Rosomoff, H. L., & Rosomoff, R. S. (2003). Chronic pain disability exaggeration/malingering and submaximal effort research. In I. Z. Schultz & D. O. Brady (Eds.). *Psychological Injuries at Trial.* Chicago, IL: American Bar Association.

Fisher, C. (2003). *Decoding the Ethics Code: A Practical Guide for Psychologists.* Thousand Oaks, CA: Sage.

Fleishman, W., Jackson, J. R., & Rothschild, M. (1999). Defensive litigation strategy in scientific evidence cases. In J.J. Brown (Ed.). *Scientific Evidence and Experts Handbook*. New York: Aspen Law and Business, pp. 305–385.

Frueh, B. C., Elhai, J. D., & Kaloupek, D. G. (2004). Unresolved issues in the assessment of trauma exposure and posttraumatic reactions. In G. M. Rosen (Ed.). *Posttraumatic Stress Disorder: Issues and Controversies*. West Sussex, UK: England: Wiley.

Frye v. United States (1923). 54 App. D.C. 46, 293 F. 1013, 34 ALR 145.

Garb, H. N. (2003). Incremental validity and the assessment of psychopathology in adults. *Psychological Assessment, 15*, 508–20.

Garcia-Berthou, E. & Alcaraz, C. (2004). Incongruence between test statistics and p values in medical papers. *BMC Medical Research Methodology, 4*. Available from www.biomedcentral.com/1471–2288/4/13 (accessed August 12, 2004).

General Electric Company v. Joiner. (1997). 118 S.Ct. 512, 522 U.S. 136.

Graham, J. R. (1993). *MMPI-2 Assessing Personality and Psychopathology,* 2nd ed. New York: Oxford University Press.

Greenberg, S. (2003) Personal injury examinations in torts for emotional distress. In A. M. Goldstein (Ed.). *Handbook of Psychology, Vol. 11, Forensic Psychology.* Hoboken, NJ: Wiley, pp. 233–258.

Greenberg, S. & Shuman, D.W. (1997). Irreconcilable conflict between therapeutic and forensic roles. *Professional Psychology: Research and Practice, 28*, 50–57.

Greenberg, S. A., Otto, R. K., & Long, A. C. (2003). The utility of psychological testing in assessing emotional damages in personal injury litigation. *Assessment, 10*, 411–419.

Grisso, T. (2003). *Evaluating Competencies*, 2nd ed. New York: Kluwer/Plenum.

Groth-Marnat, G. (2003). *Handbook of Psychological Assessment.* Hoboken, NJ: Wiley.

Gouvier, W. D., Hayes, J. S., & Smiroldo, B. B. (2003). The significance of base rates, test sensitivity, test specificity, and subjects' knowledge of symptoms in assessing TBI sequelae and malingering. In I.Z. Schulze & D.O. Brady (Eds.). *Psychological Injuries at Trial.* Chicago, IL: American Bar Association, pp. 641–671.

Haney, C. & Smith, A. (2003). Science, law, and psychological injury: The Daubert standards and beyond. In I. Z. Schulze & D. O. Brady (Eds.). *Psychological Injuries at Trial.* Chicago, IL: American Bar Association, pp. 184–201.

Heilbrun, K. (2001). *Principles of Forensic Mental Health Assessment.* New York: Kluwer/Plenum.

Heilbrun, K., Marczyk, G.R., & DeMatteo, D. (2002) *Forensic Mental Health Assessment: A Casebook.* Oxford: Oxford University Press.

Heilbrun, K., Warren, J., & Picarello, K. (2003). Third party information in forensic assessment. In Goldstein, A.M., (Ed.). *Handbook of Psychology, Vol. 11, Forensic Psychology.* Hoboken, NJ: Wiley, pp. 69–86.

Hess, A. (1998). Millon Clinical Multiaxial Inventory-III. In J. C. Impara and B. S. Plake (Eds.). *The Thirteenth Mental Measurements Yearbook.* Lincoln, NE: University of Nebraska–Lincoln, pp. 665–667.

Hunsley, J. (2003). Introduction to the special section on incremental validity and utility in clinical assessment. *Psychological Assessment, 15*, 443–45.

Hunsley, J. & Meyer, G. J. (2003). The incremental validity of psychological testing and assessment: Conceptual, methodological, and statistical issues. *Psychological Assessment, 15*, 446–455.

Hynan, D. J. (2004). Unsupported general differences on some personality disorder scales of the Millon Clinical Multiaxial Inventory-III. *Professional Psychology: Research and Practice, 35*, 105–110.

Imwinkelried, E. J. (2000). Evaluating the reliability of nonscientific expert testimony: A partial answer to the questions left unresolved by *Kumho Tire Co. v. Carmichael. Maine Law Review, 52*, 20–41.

Kane, A. W. (1999). Essentials of malingering assessment. In M.J. Ackerman (Ed.). *Essentials of Forensic Psychological Assessment.* New York: Wiley, pp. 78–99.

Kane, A. W. (2006). Causality in court: Psychological considerations. In G. Young, A. W. Kane, & K. Nicholson, (Eds). *Causality: Psychological Evidence in Court*. New York: Springer-Verlag.

Kassirer, J. P. & Cecil, J. S. (2002). Inconsistency in evidentiary standards for medical testimony. *Journal of the American Medical Association, 288*, 1382–1387.

Kehrer, C. A., Sanchez, P. N., Habif, U., Rosenbaum, J. G., & Townes, B. D. (2000). Effects of a significant-other observer on neuropsychological test performance. *The Clinical Neuropsychologist, 14*, 67–71.

Kirkpatrick, L. C. & Mueller, C. B. (2003). *Evidence: Practice Under the Rules.* New York: Aspen Law and Business.

Kraus, D. A. & Sales, B. D. (2003). Forensic psychology, public policy, and the law. In A.M. Goldstein, (Ed.). *Handbook of Psychology, Vol. 11, Forensic Psychology*. Hoboken, NJ: Wiley, pp. 543–560.

Kumho Tire Co. v. Carmichael. (1999). 119 S.Ct. 1167, 526 U.S. 137.

Lally, S. J. (2003). What tests are acceptable for use in forensic evaluations? A survey of experts. *Professional Psychology: Research and Practice, 34*, 491–498.

Lees-Haley, P. (1992). Psychodiagnostic test usage by forensic psychologists. *American Journal of Forensic Psychology, 10*, 25–30.

Lees-Haley, P. & Brown, R. S. (1993). Neuropsychological complaint base rates of 170 personal injury claimants. *Archives of Clinical Neuropsychology, 8*, 203–209.

Lees-Haley, P., Smith, H. H., Williams, C. W., & Dunn, J. T. (1995). Forensic neuropsychological test usage: An empirical survey. *Archives of Clinical Neuropsychology, 11*, 45–51.

Lezak, M. D., Howieson, D. B., & Loring, D. W. (2004). *Neuropsychological Assessment*, 4th ed. Oxford: Oxford University Press.

Macartney-Filgate, M. S. & Snow, G. W. (2004). The practitioner as expert witness. In D.R. Evans (Ed.). *The Law, Standards, and Ethics in the Practice of Psychology*, 2nd ed. Toronto: Edmond Montgomery Publications, pp. 287–309.

McLearen, A. M., Pietz, C. A., & Denney, R. L. (2004). Evaluation of psychological damages. In W. T. O'Donohue & E.R. Levensky (Eds.). *Handbook of Forensic Psychology*. Amsterdam: Elsevier, pp. 267–299.

Melton, G. B., Petrila, J.. Poythress, N. G., & Slobogin, C. (1997). *Psychological Evaluations for the Courts*, 2nd ed. New York: Guilford Press.

Miller, W. (2003). Evidentiary issues in the psychological injury case. In I.Z. Schulze & D.O. Brady (Eds.). *Psychological Injuries at Trial*. Chicago, IL: American Bar Association, pp. 202–235.

Moreau, C. & Zisook, S. (2002). Rationale for a posttraumatic stress spectrum disorder. *Psychiatric Clinics of North America, 25*, 775–790.

Murphy, J. P. (2000). Expert witnesses at trial: Where are the ethics? *Georgetown Journal of Legal Ethics, 14*. Available from www.law-forensics.com/ethic_and_experts.htm (accessed April 4, 2003).

Nichols, D. S. (2001). *Essentials of MMPI-2 Assessment.* New York: Wiley.

Norris, F. N. & Hamblen, J. L. (2004). Standardized self-report measures of civilian trauma and PTSD. In J.P. Wilson & T.M. Keane (Eds.). *Assessing Psychological Trauma and PTSD*, 2nd ed. New York: Guilford Press, pp. 63–102.

Otto, R. K. (2002). Use of the MMPI-2 in forensic settings. *Journal of Forensic Psychology Practice, 2*, 71–91.

Peters, L., Slade, T., & Andrews, G. (1999). A comparison of ICD-10 and DSM-IV criteria for posttraumatic stress disorder. *Journal of Traumatic Stress, 12,* 335–343.

Pope, K. S., Butcher, J. N., & Seelen, J. (2000). *The MMPI, MMPI-2 & MMPI-A in Court*, 2nd ed. Washington, DC: American Psychological Association.

Posthuma, A., Podrouzek, W., & Crisp, D. (2002). The implications of Daubert on neuropsychological evidence in the assessment of remote mild traumatic brain injury. *American Journal of Forensic Psychology, 20,* 21–37.

R. v. Mohan, (1994) 2 S.C.R.9.

Risinger, D. M., Saks, M. J., Thompson, W.C., & Rosenthal, R. (2002). The *Daubert/Kumho* implications of observer effects in forensic science: Hidden problems of expectation and suggestion. *California Law Review, 90,* 1–56.

Rogers, R. (1997). Structured interviews and dissimulation. In R. Rogers (Ed.). *Clinical Assessment of Malingering and Deception*, 2nd ed., New York: Guilford Press, pp. 301–327.

Rogers, R. (2003). Forensic use and abuse of psychological tests: Multiscale inventories. *Journal of Psychiatric Practice, 9,* 316–320.

Rogers, R. & Bender, S. D. (2003). Evaluation of malingering and deception. In A.M. Goldstein (Ed.). *Handbook of Psychology, Vol. 11, Forensic Psychology*. Hoboken, NJ: Wiley, pp. 109–129.

Rogers, R., Sewell, K. W., & Salekin, R. T. (1994). A meta-analysis of malingering on the MMPI-2. *Assessment, 1,* 227–237.

Rogers, R., Salekin, R. T., & Sewell, K.W. (1999). Validation of the Millon Clinical Multiaxial Inventory for axis II disorders: Does it meet the *Daubert* standard? *Law and Human Behavior, 23,* 425–443.

Rogers, R., Salekin, R. T., & Sewell, K. W. (2000). The MCMI-III and the *Daubert* standard: Separating rhetoric from reality. *Law and Human Behavior, 24,* 501–506.

Sageman, M. (2003). Three types of skills for effective forensic psychological assessments. *Assessment, 10,* 321–328.

Saks, M. J. (2000). The aftermath of *Daubert*: An evolving jurisprudence of expert evidence. *Jurimetrics, 40,* 229–41.

Samuel, S. E., DeGirolamo, J., Michals, T. J., & O'Brien, J. (1995). Preliminary findings on the MMPI "Cannot Say" responses with personal injury litigants. *American Journal of Forensic Psychiatry, 16,* 59–72.

Schutte, J. W. (2000). Using the MCMI-III in Forensic Evaluations, *American Journal of Forensic Psychology, 19,* 5–20.

Scrignar, C. B. (1996). *Post-traumatic Stress Disorder: Diagnosis, Treatment, and Legal Issues*, 3rd ed. New Orleans, LA: Bruno Press.

Shuman, D. W. (1994a). *Psychiatric and Psychological Evidence*, 2nd ed. Deerfield, IL: Clark, Boardman, Callaghan (supplemented 2002, 2003, 2004).

Shuman, D. W. (1994b). The psychology of compensation in tort law. *Kansas Law Review, 43.* Available from www.lexis.com (accessed April 6, 2003).

Shuman, D. W. (1995). Persistent reexperiences in psychiatry and law. In R. I. Simon (Ed.). *Posttraumatic Stress Disorder in Litigation*. Washington, DC: American Psychiatric Press.

Shuman, D. W. (2002a). Retrospective assessment of mental states and the law. In R.I. Simon & D.W. Shuman (Eds.). *Retrospective Assessment of Mental States in Litigation*. Washington, DC: American Psychiatric Publishing, pp. 21–45.

Shuman, D. W. & Daley, C. E. (1996). Compensation for mental and emotional distress. In D. B. Sales & D. W. Shuman, (Eds.). *Law, Mental Health, and Mental Disorder*. Pacific Grove, CA: Brooks/Cole.

Shuman, D. W. & Sales, B. D. (2001). Daubert's wager. *Journal of Forensic Psychology Practice, 1*, 69–77.

Simon, R. I. & Shuman, D. W. (1999). Conducting forensic examinations on the road: Are you practicing your profession without a license? *Journal of the American Academy of Psychiatry and Law, 27*, 75–82.

Simon, R. I. & Wettstein, R. M. (1997). Toward the development of guidelines for the conduct of forensic psychiatric examinations. *Journal of the American Academy of Psychiatry and Law, 25,* 17–30.

State Justice Institute. (1999). The Bench: Companion to a judge's deskbook on the basic philosophies and methods of science. Available from www.unr.edu/bench/ (accessed November 6, 2003).

Strassburger, L., Gutheil, T., & Brodsky, A. (1997). On wearing two hats: Role conflict in service as both psychotherapist and expert witness. *American Journal of Psychiatry, 154*, 448–450.

Tucillo, J. A., DeFilippis, N. A., Denney, R. L., & Dsurney, J. (2002). Licensure requirements for interjurisdictional forensic evaluations. *Professional Psychology: Research and Practice, 33*, 377–383.

Urbina, A. (2004). *Essentials of Psychological Testing.* Hoboken, NJ: Wiley.

Walker, L. E. A. & Shapiro, D. L. (2003). *Introduction to Forensic Psychology.* New York: Kluwer/Plenum.

Watkins, C. E., Campbell, V. L., Nieberding, R., & Hallmark, R. (1995). Contemporary practice of psychological assessment by clinical psychologists. *Professional Psychology: Research and Practice, 26,* 54–60.

Wayte, T., Samra, J., Robbennolt, J.K., Heuer, L., & Koch, W.J. (2002). Psychological issues in civil law. In J. R. P. Ogloff, (Ed.). *Taking Psychology and Law into the Twenty-First Century.* New York: Kluwer/Plenum, pp. 323–369.

Weiner, I. B. (2002). Psychodiagnostic testing in forensic psychology: A commentary. *Journal of Forensic Psychology Practice, 2*, 113–119.

Wilson, J. P. (2004). PTSD and complex PTSD. In J.P. Wilson & T.M. Keane (Eds.). *Assessing Psychological Trauma and PTSD*, 2nd ed. New York: Guilford Press, pp. 7–44.

Wilson, J. P. & Moran, T. A. (2004). In J. P. Wilson, J. P. & T.M. Keane (Eds.). *Assessing Psychological Trauma and PTSD*, 2nd ed. New York: Guilford Press, pp. 603–636.

World Health Organization. (1992). *International Classification of Diseases and Related Problems, 10th Revision. Clinical Description and Diagnostic Guidelines, Classification of Mental and Behavioral Disorders.* Geneva: World Health Organization.

Youngstrom, E. A. & Busch, C. P. (2000). Expert testimony in psychology: Ramifications of Supreme Court decision in *Kumho Tire Co., Ltd. v. Carmichael, Ethics & Behavior, 10*, 185–193.

Section 2

PTSD/Distress

3

Understanding PTSD: Implications for Court

GERALD YOUNG AND RACHEL YEHUDA

Posttraumatic Stress Disorder (PTSD) is a disorder that has captivated the attention of the legal profession in the area of psychological injury, in some part perhaps by providing for plaintiffs a more tangible way of expressing "pain and suffering" inflicted by injury. This view assumes that the research regarding etiology, phenomenology, prevalence, course, comorbidity, and biologic underpinnings has fully resolved all outstanding issues. Yet, the nature and description of PTSD is still in the process of being more carefully studied. In this review, we highlight some of the current issues that researchers are studying and suggest which ones necessitate caution in the legal arena.

1. PTSD as a Multicausal System

The Diagnostic and Statistical Manual of Mental Disorders (DSM-IV and DSM-IV-TR) (American Psychiatric Association, 1994, 2000) specifies the diagnostic criteria for PTSD. The diagnosis has undergone several revisions over the years, mostly in relation to defining trauma exposure rather than describing phenomenology of this disorder. When first introduced in the DSM-III in 1980, individual differences in PTSD were minimized (American Psychiatric Association, 1980; Miller, 2003) because the underlying assumption behind the diagnosis was that traumatic stress constituted the most important, if not sole, etiologic agent or cause of PTSD (Yehuda & McFarlane, 1995). The traumatic events considered necessary to elicit PTSD were defined as "outside the range of usual human experience" (American Psychiatric Association, 1980, p. 238) and, therefore, would evoke "significant symptoms of distress" in most victims of the events. Implicitly, PTSD was conceived as a normal response to extraordinary traumatic events (Yehuda & McFarlane, 1995).

Yehuda et al. (2005) pointed out that the current fourth version of the DSM represents a paradigm shift with regard to the issue of the "Criterion A" stressor, because it placed emphasis on the variability in individuals' responses to traumatic events, instead of treating PTSD as a very likely response to extreme traumatic stressors. Epidemiologic studies (Kessler et al., 1995) have supported this paradigm shift, for they show that exposure to potentially life-threatening or horrifying events is not that unusual in the population. Furthermore, most individuals exposed to traumatic events recover (i.e., either do not develop PTSD symptoms or develop them only transiently). That only a minority of individuals develop chronic PTSD in response to trauma exposure was not a known fact when PTSD was initially included in the DSM. However, these observations resulted in shifting the focus of our understanding of the etiology of PTSD from the nature of the traumatic stressors to the nature of the individual experiencing the trauma.

Accordingly, research related to risk for PTSD has burgeoned in the last decade, and pretrauma, peritraumatic, and posttraumatic factors have emerged as important in influencing the response to trauma. Two major subtypes of variable that have been discussed concern those related to event characteristics and those related to individual differences.

In terms of pretrauma factors, a wide range has been identified, from contextual factors to familial and genetic ones. For example, individuals at greater risk for developing PTSD after trauma may have had a family history of psychopathology, prior development of PTSD, lower IQ, poor social support, and/or certain pre-existing personality traits, such as proneness to experiencing negative emotions (Brewin, 2003; Yehuda, 1999).

Furthermore, peritraumatic factors, such as the nature of the individual's immediate responses to trauma, may be strong predictors of those who will not recover. In particular, the presence of peritraumatic panic and of peritraumatic dissociation have been shown to differentiate those who will develop PTSD from those who will not (see Nixon & Bryant, 2003; Ozer et al., 2003).

For posttrauma factors, researchers have highlighted the importance of evaluating the psychosocial stressors and other burdens in the aftermath of trauma: whether there has been property damage, medical injury, or loss; what is the degree of social support, the availability of adequate therapy matched to the individual, and contextual factors such as job loss.

Schnurr et al. (2004) have attempted to describe the interplay between pretraumatic, peritraumatic, and posttraumatic factors. They primarily demonstrated that failure to remit from military-related PTSD in veterans was related to factors during and after trauma, but not before. Premilitary variables included experiences of abuse and prior trauma. Postmilitary factors included social support. Research such as this will help elucidate models of the development of chronic PTSD that account for pretrauma, trauma, and posttrauma factors in interactive manners, where different combinations relate to different points in time in posttrauma course and outcome.

However, given the multiplicity of factors involved, assessors will be left with the difficult task of applying population-level models to individual cases. The field has still not evolved to the point where it can apply the study of risk factors to individual cases of PTSD in a systematic manner; that is, it is hard to attribute the "PTSD" of any single person to the presence of any single risk factor.

In assessments for court, there is often an expectation that pretraumatic, posttraumatic, and peritraumatic factors can easily be disentangled from one another. However, even if the critical risk factors contributing to an individual's PTSD can be identified, it is not necessarily easy to determine the relative impact of each of these factors on the severity of posttraumatic symptoms. For example, lack of social support following trauma exposure is presumably a posttraumatic factor that inhibits recovery. However, those who lack such supports may lack this because of pretraumatic risk factors (e.g., psychopathology or avoidant personality styles). Thus, although it is possible to measure social support posttrauma, this measure could be constituted by various earlier risk factors.

2.   Criteria of PTSD

According to the DSM-IV, there are three major clusters of symptoms, and the symptoms must be present for at least 1 month (Criterion E). The three clusters involve persistent re-experiencing, persistent avoidance/numbing, and a persistent increase in arousal (Criteria B, C, and D, respectively). In addition, the disturbance must cause "clinically significant distress or impairment" in important areas of function (Criterion F). The traumatic event needs to have involved a response of "intense fear, helplessness, or horror" to "actual or threatened death or serious injury, or a threat to the physical integrity of self or others" (Criteria A2 and A1, respectively), (American Psychiatric Association, 1994, p. 467). The criteria for children vary at three points; that is, children may be more disorganized and/or agitated, may replay the trauma in their play behavior, and may have nonspecific frightening dreams. After 3 months duration, PTSD is considered chronic, not acute. Its onset may be delayed by at least 6 months and is sometimes delayed much longer.

Like many DSM-IV diagnoses, the three primary symptom clusters in PTSD are structured polythetically, where individuals need to present only with a partial set of the full list for a cluster to meet threshold requirements for diagnosis. In the case of persistent re-experiencing, only one of five ways of expressing the category must be evident on presentation, although more than one may be present. This allows for substantial individual variability in symptom expression. In the next category, persistent avoidance, the minimum of symptoms needed is three, but the list from which they can be drawn is longer, involving seven symptoms. Finally, for persistent increased arousal, two or more of five symptoms constitute the criterion.

Courtois (2004) proposed the creation of the diagnostic category Complex PTSD (CPTSD). Similarly, Wilson (2004) emphasized that PTSD involves complex, long-term, stress-related responses. He suggested that one category encompassing a range of intensity types of PTSD may not be sufficient. Moreover, he developed a model of PTSD involving dimensions of self and social support in addition to the three primary clusters. In this regard, Asmundson et al. (2000) reported a confirmatory factor analysis involving four factors that best fit the data; with respect to symptoms related to the combined avoidance/numbing cluster, they appeared as separate factors, in contrast to what is suggested in the DSM criteria.

It is probably most useful to understand this literature that struggles with the incompleteness of the current PTSD definition as an attempt to delineate a wider spectrum of responses to trauma rather than an attempt to invalidate the diagnosis of PTSD. The literature just cited are all attempts to underscore that, in many cases, a person with PTSD can have an extremely severe condition complicated by other symptoms or circumstances as also evidenced in the literature on comorbidity in PTSD (see Section 3 below). The intention of broadening the diagnosis is to include symptoms and constructs from "comorbid" psychiatric diagnoses and to allow these to be viewed within the framework of traumatic stress responses. In the absence of such attempts, the diagnosis of PTSD might be dwarfed by the presence of comorbidity in a manner that would marginalize its symptoms occurring as a result of trauma exposure.

When response to trauma develops into a chronic, complicated condition, the courts need to know that the symptom complex may be more resistant to treatment. Chapter 13 by Asmundson and Taylor in the present volume cogently explores this point.

In addition, we caution that comorbid diagnoses should not be construed as reasons to minimize the central role that PTSD may have in an individual's complex response to trauma. Rather, just the opposite obtains: The presence of comorbid conditions are amplifiers of the traumatic stress response. Moreover, this exacerbation takes place even if comorbid conditions have predated trauma exposure.

At the same time, when individuals present with complex responses to trauma such as these, the courts need to know that assessors should adopt a multicausal perspective, examining pretrauma, trauma, and posttrauma factors, consistent with the multicausal model presented above and in Yehuda et al. (2005).

Just as there were no data about the prevalence of trauma exposure when PTSD was initially formulated, the PTSD diagnosis was initially conceptualized in the absence of any prospective, longitudinal data about the natural course of symptoms. Rather, ideas about phenomenology and course were based on the clinical presentation of chronically symptomatic and often disabled patients. No attempt was made to differentiate the symptoms of trauma survivors who appeared less disabled and showed greater overall functioning (Yehuda & McFarlane, 1995; Yehuda et al., 2005). It is now clear that trauma survivors who do not meet full diagnostic criteria for PTSD and who appear to be functioning well (e.g., do not report high levels of subjective distress and largely maintain pre-exposure levels of occupational and relationship functioning) may still endorse experiencing intrusive symptoms, such as distress at reminders of the traumatic event, and active avoidance symptoms, such as forgetting aspects of the traumatic event and avoiding reminders of the event. Can these symptoms be considered pathological if they are not associated with clinically significant subjective distress and increased utilization of health care systems? In assessing whether long-term responses are pathological, do we need to address more specific criteria reflecting the affect of trauma exposure on absenteeism from work, reduced productivity, loss of employment, and functional impairment?

Without a re-examination of these issues, it becomes difficult to consider the different individual trajectories from the acute response to pathology. Had PTSD been defined by marker symptoms that characterize it relative to the symptoms found in individuals exposed to trauma who do not develop PTSD, including those symptoms relative to functional impairment, we would now be in a better position to identify symptoms differentiating individuals who fail to recover and those with resilience. In particular, which symptoms from the clusters of reliving, avoidance/numbing, and hyperarousal and which functional outcome measures will be shown by future research to best predict substantial long-term functional impairment, or disability, and which will best predict resilience, improvement with appropriate treatment, and a full return to work or other pretrauma functional activity?

We conclude that PTSD represents a useful construct as it is presently constituted and that it can be reliably evaluated. Nevertheless, research of its criteria, their organization, its relationship to comorbid disorders, its long-term functional effects, and other issues related to its description and diagnosis should continue in order to offer clinicians and courts an increased understanding of its presentation. We explore some of these issues in greater detail below.

3.   Trauma and Stress: Relationship to PTSD

According to Briere (2004), PTSD is not the only clinically significant response to trauma that can be manifested. Victims can develop a wide range of anxiety or depressive disorders following trauma even if they do not meet the criteria for PTSD. In addition, victims may experience Acute Stress Disorder in the first month posttrauma before PTSD can be diagnosed. Other diagnoses that may be relevant include Brief Psychotic Disorder with Marked Stressors, Dissociative Disorders, Adjustment Disorder, posttraumatic grief, assault syndromes, Conversion Disorder, Somatization Disorder, and cultural-specific disorders. Thus, the absence of PTSD is not evidence of a lack of trauma exposure.

Several disorders often co-occur with PTSD, such as substance abuse, chronic pain, and depression. For example, in chapter 14, Otis, Pincus, and Keane explore the comorbidity of PTSD and chronic pain. Similarly, O'Donnell et al. (2004) concluded that PTSD and depression at 1 year after trauma may be integrated. This underscores our position that the response to trauma exposure can include a broad trauma response, only part of which is encompassed by the PTSD diagnosis.

The critical question that often arises is whether the presence of PTSD affirms the presence of a traumatic stressor. What becomes difficult here is that so many disparate types of event can precipitate PTSD. These include disasters, mass violence against noncombatants, transportation accidents, motor vehicle accidents (MVAs), emergency worker exposure to trauma, war, rape and sexual assault, intimate partner violence, stalking, torture, life-threatening illness, child abuse, and other traumas. Note that in chapter 6, Polusny and Arbisi examine the psychological consequences of sexual assault in adults.

McNally (2003) pointed out that for almost all of its categories, the DSM-IV does not require a specific etiological event. However, PTSD can be differentiated from other psychiatric disorders in that Criterion A defines PTSD in terms of an external traumatic stressor. Moreover, the event is defined partly by the trauma victim's emotional response, not simply by the magnitude of the event.

Also, a witness or recipient of information about a traumatic event can be diagnosed with PTSD even if the victim is not a family member. The definition allows a broad range of events to qualify. Even sexual harassment of an apparently relatively minor nature may qualify as sufficient to elicit PTSD. In this regard, McNally referred to conceptual bracket creep.

However, the presence of an identifiable PTSD syndrome is not meant to make statements about the objective characteristics of an event, but, rather, represents an amalgamation of the stressor characteristics and subjective responses to them. Thus, a woman responding with extreme distress and subsequent intrusive, avoidance, and hyperarousal symptoms to sexual harassment is likely to have perceived a level of implicit threat or may have experienced a sense of vulnerability in the face of that threat, which may have precipitated PTSD. This PTSD, in turn, is a legitimate entity formed in response to the stressor in this particular individual and is no less valid than a PTSD that might have occurred in response to a more serious physical assault or rape; that is, the symptoms are manifestations of how events are interpreted.

However, the event itself must provide some objective reality in terms of its potential to elicit fear, helplessness, or horror. What is likely in the case of persons who develop PTSD to events that do not, prima facie, seem particular traumatic is that they might have pretraumatic vulnerability factors, including genetic ones; that is, such persons might be analogous to "eggshell plaintiffs"; however, if the PTSD can be related to the traumatic event, this indicates that the harassment or other trauma had contributed to "cracking their fragile skull." (See chapter 2 by Kane in the present volume, and the section by Young in Young, Kane, and Nicholson (2006)).

At the other extreme, if victims cannot recall well the events that had transpired because of a dissociative response, they may not qualify for a diagnosis of PTSD no matter how bad symptoms are experienced because they may be unaware of whether they experienced intense fear, helplessness, or horror. However, this also does not mean that they are not responding to traumatic stress. In court, the fact of dissociation can be used to attempt to invalidate testimony of a survivor as being unreliable. However, from a diagnostic perspective, presentation of dissociation may imply traumatic induction.

Although there is pressure in court to focus on the intensity of a traumatic stressor and not the intensity of the response, the assessor needs to consider that the severity of the reaction to trauma does not follow a dose–response relationship with the purported objective criteria of the stressor. In reality, traumatic stressors are defined especially by the individual's interpretation of the event and not simply the objective parameters of the event. When it comes to traumatic reactions, the intensity of the event is most legitimately defined in the eyes of the person experiencing the event.

4.   Prevalence, Prognosis, and Predictors

In the following, we provide a sample of recent research on aspects of PTSD related to course and outcome in the minority of individuals who develop it. In this regard, the court must understand that diagnoses made on an individual basis do not involve probabilities or base rates in the population, but the presence or absence of symptoms in an individual being assessed.

4.1.   Prevalence in MVAs

O'Donnell et al. (2004) examined prevalence rates of various psychiatric diagnoses following consecutive admissions to a trauma service, with 75% of victims involved in MVAs and with 64% of the admissions having a moderate to severe physical injury. Over 20% of the study participants were diagnosed with at least one psychiatric condition at 12 months, including 10% with PTSD. This study illustrates that PTSD develops in only a minority of individuals exposed to a traumatic stressor. Chapter 4 by O'Donnell and colleagues presents their research in greater detail.

4.2.   Prognosis

Schnurr et al. (2000) found that 32% of World War II veterans who had been exposed to mustard gas experiments 50 years previously still met the criteria for PTSD. In addition, 10% met the criteria for subsyndromal PTSD. In Blanchard et al. (2003), 30% of patients in MVAs failed to remit after undergoing a course of cognitive behavioral therapy, which is generally considered an appropriate evidence-based treatment for PTSD. Chapter 12 by Freidenberg, Hickling, Blanchard, and Malta summarizes this research. Although not all of the research in the field finds the same degree of long-term difficulty in the course of PTSD, these studies illustrate that in cases of psychological injury, a certain proportion of the minority of victims who develop PTSD have it prolonged or do not recover at all.

4.3.   Predictors

Ozer et al. (2003) performed a meta-analysis of prior research on predictors of PTSD, statistically analyzing trends over studies. Across studies, compared to pretrauma and other variables, peritraumatic dissociation emerged among the best predictors of PTSD. All seven predictors distilled from the literature were found to significantly predict PTSD status. Chapter 5 by Weiss and Ozer summarizes their research. Bowman and Yehuda (2004) indicated that risk factors include a history of trauma, personality traits, coping styles, psychiatric history, personality disorders, low intelligence, pre-event beliefs and attributions, and biological and genetic factors. Overall, as we have indicated previously, predictor variables of PTSD relate to a full range of prettrauma, peritraumatic, and posttrauma factors in a multicausal perspective.

Nevertheless, in court it is often asked whether PTSD in an individual results from trauma exposure. The limited prevalence of PTSD and the idea of pretraumatic risk factors together give some experts the opportunity to present the argument that the response of the person experiencing a trauma is not caused by the trauma, but, rather, reflects a constitutional risk factor.

Miller (2003), in his review of the literature, supported a model indicating that negative emotionality (NEM), in particular, plays a "strong predisposing" role in predicting PTSD status. Miller also found that other personality dimensions play varying roles in the development of PTSD, especially positive emotionality (often called extraversion) and constraint/inhibition. In support of Miller's model that NEM is prominent as a contributing variable in the presentation of PTSD, Cox et al. (2004) found that the psychological trait of neuroticism is associated with PTSD. Moreover, van den Hout and Engelhard (2004) found that negative appraisal of symptoms predicts PTSD symptoms independently of neuroticism.

Nevertheless, despite positive findings on the relationship between personality variables and PTSD, there are no prospective studies that compare persons with these personality traits to demonstrate that those who subsequently become exposed to trauma would show different reactions from persons without such traits. Without such studies, this type of research cannot demonstrate causation. More important, although we do not deny the influence of personality in response to trauma, we adhere to a multicausal perspective, because that perspective is, by far, the one best supported by the research literature.

5.   Individual Differences

Although several risk factors for PTSD have been elucidated in the population-level research, there is still no way of being able to use risk factors in the prediction of which particular individuals will recover from an initial diagnosis of PTSD. The diagnosis itself does not give the factors and context needed by the assessor to help determine the prognosis and course. Therefore, by itself, the diagnosis of PTSD is limited in allowing us to make decisions about issues crucial to the court, related to long-term trajectory and outcome. Prognosis is never simply a function of the initial diagnosis of PTSD. Rather, a prognosis is formulated after a comprehensive assessment by interview, psychological testing, and other means that examine attenuators or amplifiers of the disorder over time and an individual's risks, vulnerabilities, response to therapy, and protective and other factors.

The assessor might arrive at reasoned conclusions regarding the course of the disorder for a particular PTSD victim because valid assessments take all of the relevant information available in the literature and data gathered on the individual and proceed from there in a careful, scientific manner. As mentioned earlier, diagnoses are not about base rates in the population, but about individuals being assessed. The same proviso applies to prognoses. Assessors should focus on the specific issues that contributed to the PTSD diagnosis and understanding of the course and outcome of the particular person being assessed.

6. Psychobiological Underpinnings

In this section, in particular, we review the research by Yehuda on the underlying physiology that is elicited in PTSD.

6.1. Brain

Posttraumatic Stress Disorder is accompanied by neurobiologic changes. Nutt and Malizia (2004) reviewed neuroimaging studies implicating three areas of the brain in PTSD: the hippocampus (involved in memory), the amygdala (involved in emotions), and the medial frontal cortex (involved in executive functions). The authors posited that the cardinal symptoms of PTSD, such as flashbacks and excessive startle, may be related to a lowered dampening or inhibitory control of the amygdala by higher brain regions such as in the hippocampus and the frontal cortex.

6.2. Physiology

Yehuda (2004) explored the role of neuroendocrine changes in PTSD such as lowered cortisol and alterations in the HPA (hypothalamic–pituitary–adrenocortical) axis. PTSD may cause long-lasting physiological changes as much as more overtly organic injuries such as pain as a result of physical injury or traumatic brain injury. Moreover, Yehuda and Bierer (2005, p. 72), maintained that the findings in the literature suggest that the psychobiological response in PTSD is not a simple reflection of a normal response to stress, but, rather, a "pathologic" one. In particular, neurobiological results with trauma survivors indicate that the development of PTSD may be facilitated "by a failure to contain the normal stress response at the time of the trauma." (p. 73). This leads to a cascade of biological consequences that eventually facilitate the expression of PTSD symptoms that may include enhancement of recall, distress at reminders of the trauma, avoidance of reminders, and hyperarousal. Relative to individuals who do not develop PTSD after trauma, PTSD patients have attenuated cortisol levels. Normally, cortisol response to stress is elevated, which at first is adaptive. However, when the stress response continues because of actual or perceived danger, or overly catastrophic thinking, and the body remains in a hyperalert state, the individual is placed at risk for deleterious consequences.

As described by one of us (Yehuda, 2004; Yehuda & Bierer, 2005), cortisol inhibits its own release through negative feedback at various levels of the neuroendocrine system, especially the pituitary gland and the hypothalamus. Therefore, lower levels of cortisol in PTSD patients may disrupt or delay the process of recovering physiologically from stress, by failing to inhibit the activation of the HPA axis. As a further consequence, CRF (corticotrophin-releasing factor) production is stimulated, in concert with other neuropeptides, resulting in increased ACTH (adrenocorticotrophin hormone). In turn, this may further stimulate the sympathetic nervous system, in general, creating additional vicious cycles. Moreover, because glucocorticoids act to inhibit the release of norepinephrine from sympathetic system nerve terminals, individuals manifesting relatively low levels of circulating cortisol may experience longer norepinephrine availability at synapses both peripherally and centrally. This prepares for further adverse neurohormonal consequences in the cascade effects that may accompany PTSD.

A complicating factor in this cascade effect of trauma on physiological functioning relates to pretrauma variables. For example, not only can the adaptive negative feedback on cortisol at the beginning of the stress cycle be inhibited by posttraumatic stress, but also there can also be pre-existing enhanced negative feedback inhibition contributing to dysregulated ACTH and cortisol suppression, exacerbating the risk represented by the PTSD reaction itself to trauma.

The confluence of these neurohormonal changes precipitated or exacerbated by trauma is consistent with the behavioral changes considered as typically elicited by the trauma. For example, adrenergic activity combined with low cortisol levels has been reported to facilitate learning in animals. Therefore, initial trauma sequelae may set the stage for learned fears, avoidance, altered beliefs, and so on, which, in turn, may become further accentuated by ongoing physiological cascades, leading to the development of full-blown PTSD by 1 month posttrauma. Further cascades are potentiated after a trauma, in that biological sensitization to subsequent traumatic events takes place. PTSD is associated with other biological effects, which, together, constitute a biological risk for PTSD.

6.3. Implications

The physiological research on PTSD needs to be seen in the context of a multicausal perspective. A constellation of multiple variables contributes to an interactive synergy with biological risk factors. As we have seen, these multiple variables in the determination of PTSD status include (1) psychological risk/vulnerability factors, resilience/coping skills, and degree of responsiveness to any therapy undertaken, in conjunction with (2) the specifics of trauma, and the appraisals, interpretations, or meaning given to such events, and (3) posttrauma factors. Once initiated, the course of PTSD is governed by a system with multiple or multivariate influences and multiple or individual outcomes, even if there is a core stress response fairly constant across individuals that may be initiated in the immediate aftermath of trauma.

Nevertheless, it is important that the court understand that although research is increasingly identifying how individuals may react physiologically to trauma, the knowledge being acquired cannot be used to specify concomitant physiological reactivity in individual cases for court purposes. There is too much individual variation in PTSD expression, there is no specific biological marker of PTSD, and it would be difficult to obtain the appropriate biological samples needed to establish the long-term cascade that we have described in any one individual case.

7. PTSD as Negative Emotionality

7.1. Pretrauma Emotionality

Koch et al. (2005) emphasized pre-existing factors, such as personality styles, as prominent in understanding psychological symptoms in response to trauma exposure. These investigators posited that PTSD is an extreme state of NEM (a personality characteristic, often called neuroticism), composed of pre-existing levels of a superordinate NEM, exacerbation of the NEM by the stress of an index event, and "unique dysfunctional characteristics" related to PTSD. They supported this view by noting that NEM, in particular, plays a "strong predisposing" role in predicting PTSD status [citing the research by Miller (2003) reviewed earlier].

There are problems with determining emotionality after trauma, because trauma survivors often are quite emotional after the trauma. Thus, the argument that trauma survivors are emotional after the event because they were emotional before the event involves arguments that add nothing to predictability. Long-term prospective research needs to be undertaken that will lead to a better understanding of the difference between pretrauma emotionality and personality and posttrauma emotionality and alterations in pre-existing long-term personality variables related to emotionality.

Ironically, the position articulated by Koch et al. represents a throwback to the times before PTSD was established, in which trauma survivors who could not recover from symptoms were often diagnosed with an anxiety or depressive neurosis (Yehuda & McFarlane, 1995). Such a diagnosis often left the patient feeling misunderstood (sometimes to the extent of avoiding treatment) or stigmatized because the emphasis in therapy was not on the fact that trauma had occurred and changed one's life, but, rather, that the survivor's constitutional weakness was to blame for the failure to "get over" what had happened. As early as 1944, Lindemann (1944) had shown that an argument such as this is false, but the fact that it keeps reappearing illustrates that some researchers draw conclusions that are not supported by the available evidence. As the pendulum swings back from viewing PTSD as completely determined by traumatic exposure, care must be taken that the gains that have been made in highlighting the contribution of trauma exposure to symptom presentation in PTSD not be lost.

The challenge in assessment of PTSD is to understand individual variation in responding to trauma, including the influence of pretraumatic contributions, without minimizing the importance of trauma exposure as a possible major force in eliciting symptom presentation. Koch et al.'s (2005) suggestion that forensic assessors need to differentiate or find marker symptoms of PTSD that are different from those of high levels of NEM, low levels of positive emotionality, or other facets of dysfunctional personality functioning is difficult to accomplish. Without having evaluated a particular trauma survivor prior to a traumatic experience, this becomes a difficult proposition. Moreover, even if one had access to a pretrauma interview in which emotionality or other characteristics were clearly delineated prior to a traumatic event, it is not clear that a finding of negative emotionality prior to trauma would in any way invalidate a diagnosis of PTSD based on posttraumatic presentation. Furthermore emotionality, *per se*, is not a symptom of PTSD. A more emotional person may be more likely to have intrusive thoughts or hyperarousal following trauma exposure, but whether or not those symptoms are present, "PTSD" is no less valid than someone else's who may have been less emotional prior to trauma exposure. This being said, the weight of the evidence continues to support a multicausal perspective on the development of PTSD.

7.2. Pretrauma Mental State

Koch et al. (2005) questioned whether forensic assessors can reliably estimate pretrauma status based on retrospective recall of the trauma survivor and collateral information in documentation. However, inconsistencies presented by patients might be attributed to areas of confusion that need to be resolved. Furthermore, there are some measures developed for the assessment of PTSD that contain validity scales, addressing positive bias or underreporting and negative bias or overreporting [e.g., Detailed Assessment of Posttraumatic Stress (DAPS), (Briere, 2001); see also Chapter 2 by Kane and Chapter 6 by

Polusny and Arbisi in this volume for discussion of additional instruments relevant to the assessment of PTSD]. These instruments may provide data available for examination by the expert to assist with making a clinical diagnosis and to inform the court about the relationship between trauma exposure and symptoms, based on further analysis of the full range of pretrauma, peritrauma, and posttrauma evidence available.

8.   Conclusion

In the development of PTSD after trauma, individual variability or unique, individual pathways mark the course of the disorder. Moreover, multicausal mechanisms contribute to its outcome. Comprehensive assessments that consider the scientific literature and that analyze the scientifically gathered data are the best ways to ensure that evidence offered to the court meets standards for the validity and reliability of evidence. There are gaps in our knowledge of PTSD, especially in terms of long-term functional and psychological outcome. Nevertheless, bridges can be made from the literature to the individual, as long as the multicausal nature of PTSD is recognized.

References

American Psychiatric Association. (1980). *Diagnostic and Statistical Manual of Mental Disorders*, 3rd ed. Washington, DC: American Psychiatric Association.

American Psychiatric Association. (1994). *Diagnostic and Statistical Manual of Mental Disorders*, 4th ed. Washington, DC: American Psychiatric Association.

American Psychiatric Association. (2000). *Diagnostic and Statistical Manual of Mental Disorders: Text Revision*, 4th ed. Washington, DC: American Psychiatric Association.

Asmundson, G. J., G., Frombach, I., McQuaid, J., Pedrelli, P., Lenox, R., & Stein, M. B. (2000). Dimensionality of Posttraumatic Stress symptoms: A confirmatory factor analysis of DSM-IV symptom clusters and other symptom models. *Behaviour Research and Therapy, 38*, 203–214.

Blanchard, E. B., Hickling, E. J., Devineni, T., Veazey, C. H., Galovski, T. E., Mundy, E., Malta, L. S., & Buckley, T. C. (2003). A controlled evaluation of cognitive behavioral therapy for posttraumatic stress in motor vehicle accident survivors. *Behavior Research and Therapy, 41,* 79–96.

Bowman, M. L. & Yehuda, R. (2004). Risk factors and the adversity-stress model. In G. M. Rosen (Ed.), *Posttraumatic Stress Disorder: Issues and Controversies*. Chichester, UK: Wiley, pp. 15–38.

Brewin, C.R. (2003). *Post-traumatic Stress Disorder: Malady or Myth?* New Haven, CT: Yale University Press.

Briere, J. (2001). *Detailed Assessment of Posttraumatic Stress: Professional Manual*. Odessa, FL: Psychological Assessment Resources.

Briere, J. (2004). *Psychological Assessment of Adult Posttraumatic States: Phenomenology, Diagnosis, and Measurement*, 2nd ed. Washington, DC: American Psychological Association.

Courtois, C. (2004). Complex trauma, complex reactions: Assessment and treatment. *Psychotherapy: Theory, Research, Practice, Training, 41*, 412–425.

Cox, B. J., MacPherson, P. S. R., Enns, M. W., & McWilliams, L. A. (2004). Neuroticism and self-criticism associated with Posttraumatic Stress Disorder. *Behaviour Research and Therapy, 42*, 105–114.

Kessler, R. C., Sonnega, A., Hughes, E., Bromet, M.H., & Nelson, C.B. (1995). Posttraumatic stress disorder in the National Comorbidity Survey. *Archives of General Psychiatry, 52*, 1046–1060.

Koch, W.J., O'Neill, M., & Douglas, K.S. (2005). Empirical limits for the forensic assessment of PTSD litigants. *Law and Human Behavior, 29*, 121–149.

Lindemann, E. (1944). Symptomology and management of acute grief. *American Journal of Psychiatry, 101*, 141–148.

McNally, R.J. (2003). *Remembering Trauma*. Cambridge, MA: Harvard University Press.

Miller, M.W. (2003). Personality and the etiology and expression of PTSD: A three-factor perspective. *Clinical Psychology: Science and Practice, 10*, 373–393.

Nixon, R. D. V., & Bryant, R. A. (2003). Peritraumatic and persistent panic attacks in acute stress disorder. *Behaviour Research and Therapy, 41*, 1237–1242.

Nutt, D. J. & Malizia, A. L. (2004). Structural and functional brain changes in Posttraumatic Stress Disorder. *Journal of Clinical Psychiatry, 65*, 11–17.

O' Donnell, M. L., Creamer, M., & Pattison, P. (2004). Posttraumatic Stress Disorder and depression following trauma: Understanding comorbidity. *American Journal of Psychiatry, 161*, 1390–1396.

O'Donnell, M. L., Creamer, M., Pattison, P., & Atkin, C. (2004). Psychiatric morbidity following injury. *American Journal of Psychiatry, 161*, 507–514.

Ozer, E. J., Best, S. R., Lipsey, T. L., & Weiss, D. S. (2003). Predictors of Posttraumatic Stress Disorder and symptoms in adults: A meta-analysis. *Psychological Bulletin, 129*, 52–73.

Schnurr, P. P., Lunney, C.A., & Sengupta, A. (2004). Risk factors for the development versus the maintenance of Posttraumatic Stress Disorder. *Journal of Traumatic Stress, 17*, 85–95.

Schnurr, P. P., Ford, J., D., Friedman, M., J., Green, B. L., Dain, B. J., & Sengupta, J. (2000). A descriptive analysis of PTSD chronicity in Vietnam veterans. *Journal of Traumatic Stress, 16*, 545–553.

van den Hout, M. A. & Engelhard, I. M. (2004). Pretrauma neuroticism, negative appraisals of intrusions, and severity of PTSD symptoms. *Journal of Psychopathology and Behavioral Assessment, 26*, 181–183.

Wilson, J. P. (2004). PTSD and complex PTSD: Symptoms, syndromes, and diagnosis. In J. P. Wilson & T. M. Keane (Eds.), *Assessing Psychological Trauma and PTSD*. (2nd ed.). New York: Guilford Press, pp. 7–44.

Yehuda, R. (1999). *Risk Factors for Posttraumatic Stress Disorder*. Washington, DC: American Psychiatric Press.

Yehuda, R. (2004). Risk and resilience in Posttraumatic Stress Disorder. *Journal of Clinical Psychiatry, 65*, 29–36.

Yehuda, R. & Bierer, L. M. (2005). Re-evaluating the link between disasters and psychopathology. In J. J. Lopez-Ibor, G. Christodoulou, M. Maj, N. Sartorius, & A. Okasha (Eds.), *Disasters and Mental Health*. New York: Wiley, pp. 65–80.

Yehuda, R. & McFarlane, A.C. (1995). Conflict between current knowledge about Posttraumatic Stress Disorder and its original conceptual basis. *American Journal of Psychiatry, 152*, 1705–1713.

Yehuda, R., Bryant, R., Marmar, C., & Zohar, J. (2005). Pathological responses to terrorism. Prepared for the ACNP Terrorism Task Force. Chair: Steven E. Hyman.

Young, G., Kane, A.W., & Nicholson, K. (Eds.). (2006). *Causality: Psychological Evidence in Court*. New York: Springer-Verlag.

4

Posttraumatic Disorders Following Injury: Assessment and Other Methodological Considerations

MEAGHAN L. O'DONNELL, MARK CREAMER, RICHARD A. BRYANT, ULRICH SCHNYDER, AND ARIK SHALEV

Physical injury in civilian populations is a frequent event. In 2000, 11% of the U.S. population (approximately 30 million people) were treated in emergency departments following nonfatal injuries (National Centre for Injury Prevention and Control—Electronic Database, 2000). Not only does injury occur frequently, but it often occurs at a severity to be classified as a traumatic event. Breslau et al. (1991) found that a lifetime prevalence of serious injury or serious motor vehicle crash was 41.9%, rating second in frequency of traumatic events.

The conditional risk for developing Posttraumatic Stress Disorder (PTSD) following serious accidents and injury is relatively low (Kessler et al., 1995); that is, the risk of developing PTSD in all those who are exposed to traumatic injury is low relative to other traumatic events such as interpersonal violence (Breslau et al., 1998). Nevertheless, serious injury is a leading cause of PTSD because of the frequency with which injury occurs. For example, Breslau et al. (1998) found that serious injury accounted for nearly one-quarter of the PTSD cases in their community sample. This was also the case in both the National Comorbidity Survey (Kessler et al., 1995) and the equivalent Australian study (Creamer et al., 2001). Taken together, although the conditional risk of developing PTSD following serious injury is low, the substantial frequency with which injury occurs makes injury one of the most frequent causes of PTSD.

This chapter aims to orient both practitioner and researcher to the current status of research regarding PTSD following injury. However, when evaluating this literature and when conducting assessments with injury survivors, researchers and practitioners alike must be cognizant of a number of key issues that may impact on the diagnosis of PTSD. These factors include the following: differentiating among the physical, psychological, and environmental origin of symptoms; head injury and how it complicates assessment;

the impact of secondary stressors; the influence of medications on symptom presentation; and the role of litigation. Appropriate attention to these factors will help to optimize the reliability and consistency of mental health assessments following injury.

1.   Prevalence of Psychopathology Following Injury

1.1.   PTSD

The reported prevalence of PTSD following injury is highly variable, which may be, in part, a function of the inherent difficulty of conducting psychological research in injury populations (O'Donnell et al., 2003). A number of studies have found a prevalence rate of PTSD within the first 6 months posttrauma of around 20% (Ehlers et al., 1998; Zatzick et al., 2004). These results are similar despite the fact that some of the populations included individuals with traumatic brain injury (Bryant & Harvey, 1998). Rates of over 30% within the first 6 months posttrauma have also been identified (Holbrook et al., 2001), as have rates of over 39% (Michaels et al., 1999). Finally, in a methodologically conservative study, O'Donnell et al. (2004b) found a PTSD rate of 9% at 3 months postinjury.

Posttraumatic Stress Disorder prevalence rates at 12 months postinjury range between 2% and 36%. Schnyder et al. (2001a) found a rate of only 2% in consecutively admitted Intensive Care Unit (ICU) patients 12 months following severe injury. Moderate levels have been found in the range of 10–20% (e.g., Ehlers et al., 1998; O'Donnell et al., 2004b). A number of studies have found a 12-month PTSD rate in the 30–36% range (Zatzick et al., 2002b). There is some evidence to suggest that burn patients, as a subset of injury survivors, may be at higher risk for PTSD with 12-month prevalence rates as high as 45% (Perry et al., 1992; Van Loey & Van Son, 2003). However, it is important to note that the majority of these studies have small sample sizes.

Although rates of PTSD vary across studies and across time periods, longitudinal studies generally point to decreased prevalence over time. For example, Murray et al. (2002) found a PTSD rate of 32% 1 month postinjury that declined to 19% at 6 months postinjury. Moreover, despite the decreased prevalence of PTSD over time, prospective longitudinal studies with survivors of traffic accidents have shown that of those with a diagnosis of PTSD at 12 months, up to 57% will retain this diagnosis over 3 years postinjury (Koren et al., 2001; Mayou et al., 2002).

1.2.   Acute Stress Disorder

Acute stress disorder (ASD), describes pathological stress reactions within the first 4 weeks following trauma. ASD prevalence rates of 14% have been reported for motor vehicle accident (MVA) survivors with mild traumatic brain injury (MTBI) (Bryant & Harvey, 1998), 16% of non-MTBI MVA survivors (Harvey & Bryant, 1999b), and 12% of industrial accident and burns survivors (Harvey & Bryant, 1999a). Similarly, a rate of 16–21% of ASD was found among admissions to emergency departments and trauma services (Mellman et al., 2001; Zatzick et al., 2004).

In contrast, other studies have reported much lower rates of ASD such as 1% (O'Donnell et al., 2004b) and 6% (Fuglsang et al., 2002). Variance in ASD prevalence rates may reflect the difficulty with the ASD diagnostic criteria and may be a function of how researchers have defined peritraumatic dissociation. Furthermore, studies that have utilized structured clinical interviews relative to self-report scales generally have found lower ASD prevalence rates.

1.3.   ASD as a Predictor of PTSD

Although its diagnosis has been the subject of controversy and debate (Bryant & Harvey, 1997; Marshall et al., 1999), ASD's utility in predicting PTSD has been a focus in recent research. Among prospective studies, there are findings that reveal ASD as a strong predictor of PTSD (Harvey & Bryant, 1999c). There is a growing body of literature, however, that suggests that the ability of an ASD diagnosis to reliably identify all those who will go on to develop PTSD is somewhat limited (McNally et al., 2003). Although it appears that most of those who meet criteria for a diagnosis of ASD will go on to develop PTSD, a large proportion of those who develop PTSD do not meet criteria for an ASD diagnosis within 1 month of the trauma. McNally et al. (2004) cited two reasons for this. First, the timing of ASD assessments within studies varies substantially. An early diagnosis (i.e., within 2 days) increases the likelihood of transient or rapidly changing stress reactions becoming incorrectly classified as ASD, which, in turn, decreases its predictive ability. Murray et al's. (2002) study of MVA survivors demonstrated that the timing of an ASD diagnosis had a significant effect on its predictive ability; that is, those who met ASD criteria at 4 weeks were more likely to develop later PTSD than those who met criteria at 1 week. Second, because an ASD diagnosis requires the presence of three dissociative symptoms, this might exclude survivors who go on to develop PTSD without an initial dissociative response. Creamer et al. (2004) found that although dissociative symptoms had a high sensitivity, they had a low specificity; that is, the majority of those who developed PTSD did not have dissociative symptoms within the first month posttrauma.

Although the predictive value of an ASD diagnosis is unresolved, there are features of PTSD symptomatology that are strongly predictive. Studies of injury survivors suggest that the presence of severe acute re-experiencing phenomena increases the likelihood of early and later-onset PTSD (Koren et al., 1999). Moreover, as re-experiencing symptoms do not appear to predict psychopathology in general, their significance as a marker of PTSD is enhanced (Schnyder et al., 2001b). Avoidance is less common in the early aftermath of injury and its predictive utility is relatively low in injury survivors (Creamer et al., 2004). Over time, however, avoidance symptoms become more important in predicting PTSD (Schnyder et al., 2001b). Finally, there is growing evidence to suggest that high levels of acute arousal symptoms are a strong predictor of later PTSD (Creamer et al., 2004; Schell et al., 2004).

1.4. Comorbidity and Other Psychopathology

Posttraumatic Stress Disorder rarely occurs in isolation. Large epidemiological studies using community samples show that between 80% and 85% of individuals with a diagnosis of PTSD also meet criteria for at least one other psychiatric condition (Creamer et al., 2001). Generalized Anxiety Disorder (GAD), substance abuse, phobias and Major Depressive Disorder often co-occur with PTSD (Brown et al., 2000). Few studies using injury populations have examined the issue of comorbidity, although the studies that do examine this issue report similar findings. For example, in a series of two studies following up treatment-seeking survivors of MVA at 1 and 2 years postinjury, Blanchard et al. (2004) found comorbid major depression in approximately half of those diagnosed with PTSD. A sizable number of those diagnosed with PTSD also had other comorbid anxiety disorders. The most common anxiety disorders to occur comorbidly with PTSD are generalized Anxiety Disorder and agoraphobia (Maes et al., 2000).

In their longitudinal study of consecutively admitted injury survivors, O'Donnell et al. (2004a) found that only 30% of individuals with PTSD had it as their only diagnosis, with over half of those with PTSD having comorbid depression (59%). These authors found that when PTSD co-occurred with depression, the two disorders shared the same predictors as when PTSD occurred alone. They concluded that depression occurring in the context of PTSD was part of a broader construct of general traumatic stress. However, when depression occurred in the absence of PTSD, it represented a distinctly different construct.

Alongside comorbid depression and other anxiety disorders, PTSD has also been shown to co-occur with substance use disorders (O'Donnell et al., 2004b). Substance abuse/dependence is a particular problem in injury populations. There is a large body of literature that indicates that current or lifetime histories of alcohol or other drug use/dependence is particularly prevalent in this group. For example, Rivara et al. (1993) found that 35.8% of injury admissions were intoxicated at the time of the injury and that 75% of this intoxicated group had evidence of chronic alcoholism. Zatzick et al. (2004) found that 25% of admissions to a trauma service had problem drinking at 12 months postinjury and 8% had comorbid alcohol problems and PTSD. Not surprisingly, survivors who suffer from other psychiatric conditions in addition to PTSD are likely to report more clinical distress and present with greater symptom severity and functional and role impairment (Blanchard & Penk, 1998; Maes et al., 2000; Shalev et al., 1998).

2.   Assessment Issues

It is important to recognize that assessing the psychological consequences associated with physical injury is inherently difficult. Issues such as the overlap between symptoms of different origin (e.g., organic, environmental, psychological) have implications for understanding the literature, conducting forensic assessment, and research design. By highlighting these issues, this chapter aims to provide a guide to those who have an interest in comprehending the relationship between physical injury and PTSD.

2.1.   Physical Injury

In assessing PTSD following injury, it is important to attempt to elucidate the nature of symptoms and not to automatically assume that a given symptom is part of a psychiatric condition. For example, hyperarousal symptoms such as sleep disturbance, concentration difficulties, and irritability are core features of PTSD. However, in injury survivors, these may be secondary to pain, the injury itself (especially traumatic brain injury), or, in the case of the hospitalized patient, the hospital environment. Similarly, in assessing behavioral avoidance, one should consider that behaviors resembling avoidance might be a function of physical limitations rather than psychopathology. For example, failing to drive following a motor vehicle crash could be associated with having poor movement in an ankle rather than an attempt to prevent exposure to distressing reminders of the trauma.

Re-experiencing distressing memories of the traumatic event often is seen as the hallmark of PTSD. It is important when assessing PTSD that one differentiates between intrusive memories of the traumatic event and voluntary ruminations about the incident and its potential sequelae. Injury survivors are often preoccupied with the injury-causing event and the impact it has had on their lives. This intentional thinking is usually elaborated within a broader autobiographical contextual framework. It is, therefore, different from the intrusive re-experiencing central to PTSD, which tends to be unmodified and unelaborated.

In order to consider these issues when assessing PTSD, it is essential that a clinical interview be conducted. Structured clinical interviews such as the Clinician Administered PTSD Scale for DSM-IV (CAPS), (Blake et al., 1998), the Structured Clinical Interview for DSM-IV (SCID-IV), (Spitzer et al., 1995), and the Structured Interview for PTSD (Davidson et al., 1997) offer valid and reliable tools for assessing PTSD. The CAPS offers both dimensional and categorical scores and, importantly, indices of clinical distress and impairment in social and occupational functioning (Criterion F, DSM-IV) (American Psychiatric Association, 1994). When conducting the clinical interview, attempts should be made to establish that symptoms such as altered sleep patterns, decreased interest, and poor concentration are not simply a function of the physical recovery process or the environment. In general, symptoms that can be better accounted for by an alternative explanation should not be reported as a psychological symptom.

2.2. Traumatic Brain Injury

Traumatic brain injury (TBI) is a particular form of injury that presents marked difficulty when assessing psychological responses to injury. The symptoms associated with TBI are shared with a number of psychiatric disorders, but, in particular, PTSD and ASD. For example, dissociative symptoms such as derealization, reduced awareness of one's surroundings, and depersonalization overlap with postconcussive symptoms resulting from TBI. Of importance is the difficulty in distinguishing between psychogenic amnesia (amnesia with a psychological origin) characteristic of ASD/PTSD and organic amnesia, which occurs frequently following TBI. In addition to dissociative symptoms, a number of hyperarousal symptoms can also be a part of the postconcussive syndrome following TBI including irritability, sleep disturbance, concentration deficits, and agitation. There are no simple answers to these issues. Many researchers have excluded amnesia from ASD/PTSD criteria when assessing PTSD following TBI (e.g., Harvey & Bryant, 2000; O'Donnell et al., 2004b) in an attempt to address the overlap between psychogenic and organic amnesia. Others have attempted to differentiate between dissociativelike neurological symptoms and those with a psychogenic origin (e.g., Sivec & Lynn, 1995). However, it remains remarkably difficult (Bryant, 2001).

Another issue of contention is that of the appropriateness of Criterion A2 in the diagnosis of ASD/PTSD for injury survivors following TBI. As part of the entry criteria, Criterion A2 requires that the individual's response involve "intense fear, helplessness, or horror." However, if amnesia precludes the recall of any subjective experience associated with the traumatic event, the question is raised as to whether the individual can be diagnosed with PTSD without satisfying this criterion. From a theoretical perspective, a fear response at the time of the trauma is critical in the development of a traumatic memory network, which, when reactivated, causes intrusive memories of the event to invade consciousness (e.g., Foa et al., 1989). Amnesia for the event should, therefore, prevent the occurrence of intrusive memories and the development of PTSD. However, there is growing evidence that although individuals who are amnesic to the event have lower frequency of intrusive memories, they do show high levels of emotional and physiological reactivity in response to trauma reminders (Bryant et al., 2000). It may be that trauma re-experiencing can be mediated by fear conditioning or by nonconscious mental representations of the trauma in the absence of visual and verbal memory (Bryant et al., 2000). Alternatively, amnesic patients may reconstruct memories of the event through secondary sources such as photographs or elaborations from tiny fragments of existing memory (Harvey & Bryant, 2001). Although these manifestations of PTSD may appear atypical, there is increasing evidence to suggest that they need to be recognized as valid indications of PTSD following TBI.

2.3.   Subsequent and Prior Traumatization

Traumatic events can be divided into primary or secondary stressors (Shalev, 2002). Primary stressors relate to the impact phase of the event, whereas secondary stressors refer to the aftermath of the event (i.e., its consequences). Secondary stressors significantly and independently contribute to psychopathology following trauma (Brewin et al., 2000) and, therefore, secondary as well as primary traumatization should be considered when assessing PTSD following injury. Examples of subsequent traumatization that have been investigated in the literature include trauma experienced secondary to medical factors, including uncontrollable pain (Schreiber & Galai Gat, 1993) or pain related to treatment (as in burns victims) (Yu & Dimsdale, 1999), ongoing medical problems (Ehlers et al., 1998), or physical disability (Michaels et al., 2000). As mental health research develops within injury populations, the relationships among primary stressor, secondary stressor, and psychopathology need to be explored further.

There is a growing body of literature indicating that injury populations are highly likely to having experienced prior traumatic events. Zatzick et al. (2002b) found that hospitalized injury survivors were 4.5 times more likely to experience four or more prior traumatic life events relative to the general population. Exploring this further, Zatzick et al. (2004) found that over 40% of admissions had experienced a prior assault and more than 35% had experienced a prior life-threatening accident, providing evidence of chronic recidivistic injury in this population. As recurrent traumatic life events are an established risk factor for the high levels of immediate distress following injury (Zatzick et al., 2004) and the development of PTSD (Brewin et al., 2000; Ozer et al., 2003), a thorough assessment of an individual's prior trauma history is important.

2.4.   Measurement of Outcome

In addition to the development of psychopathology in the aftermath of traumatic injury, it is important to consider a broad array of other possible outcomes. Specifically, the impact of psychopathology on the many domains of an individual's life should be considered. A number of studies have shown that symptoms of PTSD independently contributed to lowered quality of life and impaired occupational function at 1–2 years postinjury (e.g., Holbrook, Anderson, Sieber, Browner, & Hoyt, 1998; Michaels et al., 1998; Zatzick, Jurkovich, Gentilello, Wisner, & Rivara, 2002a). More research, however, is required to develop our understanding of the complex relationship among psychopathology, disability, quality of life, and other major parameters relevant to this population.

2.5.   Current Medications

When assessing injured individuals following injury, it is important to consider current medications and how these may affect the presentation. Of particular note is the presence of narcotic analgesia that may be taken for many months following the injury. The side effects of narcotic analgesia could include sweating, confusion, mood changes, restlessness, sedation, drowsiness, depersonalization, derealization, and nausea. These symptoms overlap with a range of dissociative and anxiety reactions and, therefore, must be considered when assessing individuals. To date, very few research studies have considered how medications may impact on an individual's presentation. Two studies, however, have examined narcotic analgesia administration in the acute setting and found that there was no significant difference in reported dissociative symptoms between those taking or not taking narcotics (O'Donnell et al., 2004b) or in the relationship between dissociation and the amount of narcotics received in the 2 weeks prior to the assessment (Difede et al., 2002). Although these studies go some way to suggest that narcotics may not affect dissociative symptom reporting in the acute setting, these findings must be replicated both in acute and chronic settings. Furthermore, the effects of narcotics on other psychological symptom reporting (like intrusions or concentration deficits) need to be addressed. Finally, the impact of other medications on symptom reporting warrants further investigation (e.g., glucocorticoids on reporting of lowered mood or emotional numbing).

2.6.   Symptom Fluctuation

Clinicians and researchers conducting posttraumatic stress assessments should be aware that symptoms of PTSD tend to fluctuate across time. O'Donnell et al. (2004b) found that although the 3- and 12-month prevalence rate for PTSD was relatively similar (9% and 10%, respectively), individuals who met 12-month PTSD criteria were not necessarily those who had met 3-month PTSD. Specifically, 46% of those with a PTSD diagnosis at 3 months did not have a PTSD diagnosis at 12 months, whereas 31% of those with PTSD at 12 months had no PTSD at 3 months. One explanation for the changing PTSD over time is that of delayed onset PTSD (PTSD that develops at least 6 months following a traumatic event). The injury literature reports relatively small numbers of delayed onset PTSD, around 5–6% of the total population (Bryant & Harvey, 2002; Ehlers et al., 1998). However, this constitutes a reasonably high proportion of those who actually develop PTSD (18%, by Bryant & Harvey (2002); 33% by Ehlers et al. (1998); 31%, by O'Donnell et al., 2004a).

One possible explanation for delayed onset PTSD is that those individuals had high levels of early symptoms but did not report a sufficient number or severity to meet diagnostic criteria (Bryant & Harvey, 2002). Delayed onset PTSD could also be associated with ongoing stressors that occur during the posttrauma period (Green et al., 1990). This is particularly relevant to injury survivors who, as discussed earlier, are subjected to high levels of secondary stressors postinjury, including pain, physical disabilities, and financial difficulties.

Further evidence for symptom fluctuation is that individuals with a PTSD diagnosis at 6 months who no longer meet criteria at 12 months are likely to experience some ongoing symptomatology. Ehlers et al. (1998) and Mertin and Mohr (2001), for example, have shown that individuals who no longer qualify for full PTSD frequently report occurrence of some PTSD symptoms and that these symptoms are often associated with considerable psychiatric and social morbidity.

It is important to note that in the absence of any early PTSD symptoms, it is unlikely that the disorder will develop subsequently (Shalev, 2002). This is supported by the findings by Orcutt et al. (2004), who assessed the trajectory of PTSD symptoms across time in Gulf veterans. They found over a 6-year period following the war that the course of PTSD symptoms was best described as having two distinct trajectories: those who begin with low levels of symptomatology that increase little (if at all) over time and those who begin with high levels of symptomatology that significantly increase over time. The course of symptoms, the fluctuation of symptomatology, and the factors that influence these fluctuations are, therefore, important considerations when assessing individuals across time.

2.7.   Selection Bias

One factor to consider when understanding the prevalence estimates of psychopathology following injury is that of selection bias. Prevalence estimates are extremely sensitive to sampling. Very few studies pertaining to injury survivors utilize consecutive admissions or truly randomized sampling techniques. Furthermore, even those studies that have seemingly unbiased sampling techniques might be indirectly biased by emergency room and hospital policies that determine the mix of patients. In addition to this, hospital catchment areas may influence prevalence rates. Given the different conditional risk of various traumas (Breslau et al., 1998), trauma centers that have high levels of injury caused by interpersonal violence would probably have higher rates of PTSD than those in which motor vehicle crashes are the major mechanism of injury. Finally, most of the studies examining psychopathology following injury utilize samples of less than 200. The literature is now at a point where large, multisited, international studies are required to address some of these more complex questions.

2.8.   Litigation

An increasing number of studies have identified that PTSD symptom severity in injury populations is often higher in those who are undergoing litigation procedures (e.g., Mayou et al., 2002). This is consistent with reports from the combat veteran psychiatric literature that individuals may overreport psychiatric symptoms in order to obtain disability-related compensation (For review, see Frueh et al., 2000). Studies of civilian populations have similarly established close relationships between symptom severity and litigation status (Bryant & Harvey, 1995).

Conversely, a number of studies with injury populations have found that PTSD symptom severity was not a function of compensation settlement. Blanchard et al's. (1998) Albany MVA prospective study, for example, compared PTSD symptoms over 12 months in those who settled litigation claims versus those who did not. No differences in PTSD symptomatology was observed across these groups. More recently, Bryant and Harvey (2003) found that following a MVA, litigation had no effect on return to work status and that similar proportions of those who had settled or not settled their compensation were receiving psychological therapy. In addition, the presence of litigation did not affect individuals' responses to psychological therapy (Bryant & Harvey, 1995).

It has been hypothesized that litigation stress may contribute to the elevation of PTSD severity symptoms rather than intentional malingering processes (Koch et al., 1999). Although the finding that symptoms do not decline postsettlement may not support this view, litigation could be yet another secondary stressor that adds to the ongoing traumatization of injury survivors. It could also be the case that individuals who are more severely injured or who have comorbid psychiatric problems such as depression are more likely to initiate litigation processes. Although this was not the case in the Bryant and Harvey (2003) study, these findings need to be replicated before this rationale can be discounted.

Understanding the effects of litigation on PTSD following injury is in its infancy. Studies to date have been from different jurisdictions with very distinct compensation systems, making interpretation of results difficult. Furthermore, they have tended to use simple measures of measuring litigation (such as yes/no, settled/not settled) and tended to rely on self-report measures. Future research should use other measures in addition to self-report instruments. These include psychophysiological recordings, functional indicators, and behavioral assessments, which are likely to enhance our comprehension of the relationship between PTSD and litigation. Specifically, the research needs to better index the nature of litigation and to assess the mediating roles of pain, disability, and quality of life on PTSD and litigation. Additionally, understanding not only the legal jurisdiction but also the cultural milieu of populations that seek compensation (e.g., veterans, MVA populations) would assist in determining those contexts in which litigation occurs. There may be specific factors, for example, surrounding veterans, that directly impact on symptoms reported and the subsequent nature of compensatory claims—factors that may not be present in other traumatized populations (Blanchard et al., 1998).

3. Implications for the Clinician and Forensic Practitioner

This chapter aimed to present a brief overview of the literature pertaining to Posttraumatic Stress Disorder within injury populations. Although the evidence base relating to the psychological consequences of physical injury has expanded markedly in recent years, this review has emphasized that conducting psychiatric research within injury populations is fraught with difficulty. Consistent and empirically defensible methodologies within future research are crucial in order to enhance our understanding and management of mental health problems in injury survivors.

The clinician or forensic assessor should, therefore, exercise prudence when making claims based on the literature. Quoting studies without reference to their limitations will only serve to increase skepticism in the courtroom environment. However, awareness of the issues addressed in this chapter allows the literature to be interpreted from a critical perspective, one that can also be used to identify strengths within studies.

The assessment recommendations highlighted in this chapter have direct implications for practitioners and forensic assessors. By being cognizant of issues such as attempting to differentiate the physical, psychological, and environmental origin of symptoms or the influence medications might have on the reporting of symptoms, the clinician too is taking steps toward more accurate assessments of injury survivors. The informed clinician and forensic assessor who uses structured clinical interviews as well as other psychological tests with sound psychometric properties, who considers the impact of the environment, pain, the injury itself, medication, and secondary stressors, and who examines other outcomes such as psychiatric comorbidity, quality of life, and disability offers his/her client a competent and comprehensive psychological assessment.

References

American Psychiatric Association. (1994). *Diagnostic and Statistical Manual of Mental Disorders, 4th ed.* Washington DC: American Psychiatric Association.

Blake, D. D., Weathers, F. W., Nagy, L. M., Kaloupek, D. G., Charney, D. S., & Keane, T. M. (1998). *Clinician-Administered PTSD Scale for DSM-IV.* Boston: National Center For Posttraumatic Stress Disorder.

Blanchard, E. B., Hickling, E. J., Freidenberg, B. M., Malta, L. S., Kuhn, E., & Sykes, M. A. (2004). Two studies of psychiatric morbidity among motor vehicle accident survivors 1 year after the crash. *Behaviour Research and Therapy, 42(5)*, 569–583.

Blanchard, E. B., Hickling, E. J., Taylor, A. E., Buckley, T. C., Loos, W. R., & Walsh, J. (1998). Effects of litigation settlements on posttraumatic stress symptoms in motor vehicle accident victims. *Journal of Traumatic Stress, 11(2)*, 337–354.

Blanchard, E. B. & Penk, W. E. (1998). Posttraumatic Stress Disorder and comorbid major depression: Is the correlation an illusion? *Journal of Anxiety Disorders, 12(1)*, 21–37.

Breslau, N., Davis, G., Andreski, P., & Peterson, E. (1991). Traumatic events and Posttraumatic Stress Disorder in an urban population of young adults. *Archives of General Psychiatry, 48*, 216–222.

Breslau, N., Kessler, R. C., Chilcoat, H. D., Schultz, L. R., Davis, G. C., & Andreski, P. (1998). Trauma and Posttraumatic Stress Disorder in the community. *Archives of General Psychiatry, 55*, 626–632.

Brewin, C. R., Andrews, B., & Valentine, J. D. (2000). Meta-analysis of risk factors for Posttraumatic Stress Disorder in trauma-exposed adults. *Journal of Consulting and Clinical Psychology, 68(5)*, 748–766.

Brown, E. S., Fulton, M. K., Wilkeson, A., & Petty, F. (2000). The psychiatric sequelae of civilian trauma. *Comprehensive Psychiatry, 41(1)*, 19–23.

Bryant, R. A. (2001). Posttraumatic Stress Disorder and mild brain injury: controversies, causes and consequences. *Journal of Clinical & Experimental Neuropsychology, 23(6)*, 718–728.

Bryant, R. A. & Harvey, A. G. (1995). Avoidant coping style and Posttraumatic stress following motor vehicle accidents. *Behaviour Research and Therapy, 33(6)*, 631–635.

Bryant, R. A. & Harvey, A. G. (1997). Acute Stress Disorder—A critical review of diagnostic issues. *Clinical Psychology Review, 17(7)*, 757–773.

Bryant, R. A. & Harvey, A. G. (1998). Relationship between Acute Stress Disorder and Posttraumatic Stress Disorder following mild traumatic brain injury. *American Journal of Psychiatry, 155(5)*, 625–629.

Bryant, R. A. & Harvey, A. G. (2002). Delayed-onset Posttraumatic Stress Disorder: A prospective evaluation. *Australian & New Zealand Journal of Psychiatry, 36(2)*, 205–209.

Bryant, R. A. & Harvey, A. G. (2003). The influence of litigation on maintenance of Posttraumatic Stress Disorder. *Journal of Nervous & Mental Disease, 191(3)*, 191–193.

Bryant, R. A., Marosszeky, J. E., Crooks, J., & Gurka, J. A. (2000). Posttraumatic Stress Disorder after severe traumatic brain injury. *American Journal of Psychiatry, 157(4)*, 629–631.

Creamer, M., Burgess, P., & McFarlane, A. C. (2001). Posttraumatic Stress Disorder: Findings from the Australian National Survey of Mental Health and Well-being. *Psychological Medicine, 31(7)*, 1237–1247.

Creamer, M., O'Donnell, M. L., & Pattison, P. (2004). The relationship between Acute Stress Disorder and Posttraumatic Stress Disorder in severely injured trauma survivors. *Behaviour Research and Therapy, 42(3)*, 315–328.

Davidson, J., Malik, M., & Travers, J. (1997). Structured interview for PTSD (SIP): Psychometric validation for DSM-IV criteria. *Depression and Anxiety, 5*, 127–129.

Difede, J., Ptacek, J. T., Roberts, J., Barocas, D., Rives, W., Apfeldorf, W., et al. (2002). Acute Stress Disorder after burn injury: A predictor of Posttraumatic Stress Disorder? *Psychosomatic Medicine, 64(5)*, 826–834.

Ehlers, A., Mayou, R. A., & Bryant, B. (1998). Psychological predictors of chronic Posttraumatic Stress Disorder after motor vehicle accidents. *Journal of Abnormal Psychology, 107(3)*, 508–519.

Foa, E. B., Steketee, G., & Rothbaum, B. O. (1989). Behavioral/cognitive conceptualizations of Posttraumatic Stress Disorder. *Behavior Therapy, 20(2)*, 155–176.

Frueh, B. C., Hammer, M. B., Cahill, S. P., Gold, P. B., & Hamlin, K. (2000). Apparent symptom overreporting in combat veterans evaluated for PTSD. *Clinical Psychological Review, 20*, 853–885.

Fuglsang, A. K., Moergeli, H., Hepp-Beg, S., & Schnyder, U. (2002). Who develops Acute Stress Disorder after accidental injuries? *Psychotherapy and Psychosomatics, 71*, 214–222.

Green, B. L., Lindy, J. D., Grace, M. C., Gleser, G. C., Leonard, A. C., Korol, M., et al. (1990). Buffalo Creek survivors in the second decade: Stability of stress symptoms. *American Journal of Orthopsychiatry, 60(1)*, 43–54.

Harvey, A. G. & Bryant, R. A. (1999a). Acute Stress Disorder across trauma populations. *Journal of Nervous and Mental Disease, 187(7)*, 443–446.

Harvey, A. G. & Bryant, R. A. (1999b). Predictors of acute stress following motor vehicle accidents. *Journal of Traumatic Stress, 12(3)*, 519–525.

Harvey, A. G. & Bryant, R. A. (1999c). The relationship between acute stress disorder and Posttraumatic Stress Disorder: A 2-year prospective evaluation. *Journal of Consulting & Clinical Psychology, 67(6)*, 985–988.

Harvey, A. G. & Bryant, R. A. (2000). Two-year prospective evaluation of the relationship between acute Stress Disorder and posttraumatic Stress Disorder following mild traumatic brain injury. *American Journal of Psychiatry, 157(4)*, 626–628.

Harvey, A. G. & Bryant, R. A. (2001). Reconstructing trauma memories: A prospective study of "amnesic" trauma survivors. *Journal of Traumatic Stress, 14(2)*, 277–282.

Holbrook, T. L., Anderson, J. P., Sieber, W. J., Browner, D., & Hoyt, D. B. (1998). Outcome after major trauma: Discharge and 6-month follow-up results from the trauma recovery project. *Journal of Trauma-Injury Infection and Critical Care, 45(2)*, 315–323.

Holbrook, T. L., Hoyt, D. B., Stein, M. B., & Sieber, W. J. (2001). Perceived threat to life predicts Posttraumatic Stress Disorder after major trauma: Risk factors and functional outcome. *Journal of Trauma-Injury Infection & Critical Care, 51(2)*, 287–293.

Kessler, R. C., Sonnega, A., Hughes, M., & Nelson, C. B. (1995). Posttraumatic Stress Disorder in the national comorbidity survey. *Archives of General Psychiatry, 52*, 1048–1060.

Koch, W. J., Shercliffe, M. A., Fedoroff, I. C., Iverson, G. L., & Taylor, S. (1999). Malingering and litigation stress in motor vehicle accident victims. In E. J. Hickling & E. B. Blanchard (Eds.). *Road Traffic Accidents and Psychological Trauma*. Oxford: Elsevier Science.

Koren, D., Arnon, I., & Klein, E. (1999). Acute stress response and posttraumatic Stress Disorder in traffic accident victims: A one-year prospective, follow-up study. *American Journal of Psychiatry, 156(3)*, 367–373.

Koren, D., Arnon, I., & Klein, E. (2001). Long term course of chronic posttraumatic Stress Disorder in traffic accident victims: A three-year prospective follow-up study. *Behaviour Research & Therapy, 39(12)*, 1449–1458.

Maes, M., Mylle, J., Delmeire, L., & Altamura, C. (2000). Psychiatric morbidity and comorbidity following accidental man-made traumatic events: Incidence and risk factors. *European Archives of Psychiatry and Clinical Neuroscience, 250(3)*, 156–162.

Marshall, R. D., Spitzer, R., & Liebowitz, M. R. (1999). Review and critique of the new DSM-IV diagnosis of acute Stress Disorder. *American Journal of Psychiatry, 156(11)*, 1677–1685.

Mayou, R. A., Ehlers, A., & Bryant, B. (2002). Posttraumatic Stress Disorder after motor vehicle accidents: 3-Year follow-up of a prospective longitudinal study. *Behaviour Research & Therapy, 40(6)*, 665–675.

McNally, R.J., Bryant, R.A., & Ehlers, A. (2003). Does early psychological intervention promote recovery from posttraumatic stress? *Psychological Science,* 45–79.

Mellman, T. A., David, D., Bustamante, V., Fins, A. I., & Esposito, K. (2001). Predictors of Posttraumatic Stress Disorder following severe injury. *Depression & Anxiety, 14(4)*, 226–231.

Mertin, P., & Mohr, P.B. (2001). A follow-up study of Posttraumatic Stress Disorder, anxiety, and depression in Australian victims of domestic violence. *Violence & Victims, 16(6)*, 645–654.

Michaels, A. J., Michaels, C. E., Moon, C. H., Smith, J. S., Zimmerman, M. A., Taheri, P. A., et al. (1999). Posttraumatic Stress Disorder after injury: Impact on general health outcome and early risk assessment. *Journal of Trauma-Injury Infection and Critical Care, 47(3)*, 460–466.

Michaels, A. J., Michaels, C. E., Moon, C. H., Zimmerman, M. A., Peterson, C., & Rodriguez, J. L. (1998). Psychosocial factors limit outcomes after trauma. *Journal of Trauma-Injury Infection and Critical Care, 44(4)*, 644–648.

Michaels, A. J., Michaels, C. E., Smith, J. S., Moon, C. H., Peterson, C., & Long, W. B. (2000). Outcome from injury: General health, work status, and satisfaction 12 months after trauma. *Journal of Trauma-Injury Infection and Critical Care, 48(5)*, 841–848; discussion 848–850.

Murray, J., Ehlers, A., & Mayou, R. A. (2002). Dissociation and Posttraumatic Stress Disorder: two prospective studies of road traffic accident survivors. *British Journal of Psychiatry, 180*, 363–368.

National Centre for Injury Prevention and Control—Electronic Database. (2000). *Non-Fatal Injury Report*, 2000.

O'Donnell, M. L., Creamer, M., & Pattison, P. (2004a). PTSD and depression following trauma: Understanding comorbidity. *American Journal Psychiatry, 161*, 1–7.

O'Donnell, M. L., Creamer, M., Pattison, P., & Atkin, C. (2004b). Psychiatric morbidity following injury. *American Journal of Psychiatry, 161*, 507–514.

O'Donnell, M. L., Creamer, M., Bryant, R. A., Schnyder, U., & Shalev, A. (2003). Posttraumatic disorders following injury: An empirical and methodological review. *Clinical Psychology Review, 23(4)*, 587–603.

Orcutt, H.K., Erickson, D.J., & Wolfe, J. (2004). The course of PTSD symptoms among Gulf War veterans: A growth mixture modeling approach. *Journal of Traumatic Stress, 17(3)*, 195–202.

Ozer, E. J., Best, S. R., Lipsey, T. L., & Weiss, D. S. (2003). Predictors of Posttraumatic Stress Disorder and symptoms in adults: A meta-analysis. *Psychological Bulletin, 129(1)*, 52–73.

Perry, S. W., Difede, J., Musngi, G., Frances, A. J., et al. (1992). Predictors of Posttraumatic Stress Disorder after burn injury. *American Journal of Psychiatry, 149(7)*, 931–935.

Rivara, F. P., Jurkovich, G. J., Gurney, J. G., Seguin, D., Fligner, C. L., Ries, R., et al. (1993). The magnitude of acute and chronic alcohol-abuse in trauma patients. *Archives of Surgery, 128(8)*, 907–913.

Schell, T. L., Marshall, G. N., & Jaycox, L. H. (2004). All symptoms are not created equal: The prominent role of hyperarousal in the natural course of posttraumatic psychological distress. *Journal of Abnormal Psychology, 113(2)*, 189–197.

Schnyder, U., Moergeli, H., Klaghofer, R., & Buddeberg, C. (2001a). Incidence and prediction of Posttraumatic Stress Disorder symptoms in severely injured accident victims. *American Journal of Psychiatry, 158(4)*, 594–599.

Schnyder, U., Moergeli, H., Trentz, O., Klaghofer, R., & Buddeberg, C. (2001b). Prediction of psychiatric morbidity in severely injured accident victims at one-year follow-up. *American Journal of Respiratory & Critical Care Medicine, 164(4)*, 653–656.

Schreiber, S. & Galai Gat, T. (1993). Uncontrolled pain following physical injury as the core-trauma in the Posttraumatic Stress Disorder. *Pain, 54(1)*, 107–110.

Shalev, A. Y. (2002). Acute stress reactions in adults. *Biological Psychiatry, 51(7)*, 532–543.

Shalev, A. Y., Freedman, A., Peri, T., Brandes, D., Sahara, T., Orr, S., et al. (1998). Prospective study of Posttraumatic Stress Disorder and depression following trauma. *American Journal of Psychiatry, 155(5)*, 630–637.

Sivec, H. J., & Lynn, S. J. (1995). Dissociative and neuropsychological symptoms: The question of differential diagnosis. *Clinical Psychology Review, 15*, 297–316.

Spitzer, R. L., Williams, J. B., Gibbon, M., & First, M. B. (1995). *Structured Clinical Interview for DSM-IV–Patient Version (SCID-P, Version 2.0)*. Washington DC: American Psychiatric Press.

Van Loey, N. E. & Van Son, M. J. (2003). Psychopathology and psychological problems in patients with burn scars: Epidemiology and management. *American Journal of Clinical Dermatology, 4(4)*, 245–272.

Yu, B. H. & Dimsdale, J. E. (1999). Posttraumatic Stress Disorder in patients with burn injuries. *Journal of Burn Care & Rehabilitation, 20(5)*, 426–433.

Zatzick, D. F., Jurkovich, G. J., Gentilello, L., Wisner, D., & Rivara, F. P. (2002a). Posttraumatic stress, problem drinking, and functional outcomes after injury. *Archives of Surgery, 137(2)*, 200–205.

Zatzick, D. F., Jurkovich, G., Russo, J., Roy-Byrne, P., Katon, W., Wagner, A., et al. (2004). Posttraumatic distress, alcohol disorders, and recurrent trauma across level 1 trauma centers. *Journal of Trauma-Injury Infection & Critical Care, 57(2)*, 360–366.

Zatzick, D. F., Kang, S. M., Muller, H. G., Russo, J. E., Rivara, F. P., Katon, W., et al. (2002b). Predicting Posttraumatic distress in hospitalized trauma survivors with acute injuries. *American Journal of Psychiatry, 159(6)*, 941–946.

5

Predicting Who Will Develop Posttraumatic Stress Disorder

Daniel S. Weiss and Emily J. Ozer

1. Statement of the Problem

Posttraumatic Stress Disorder (PTSD) (American Psychiatric Association, 1994) is unusual among psychiatric disorders in that it requires specification of an external event (as does Acute Stress Disorder and Adjustment Disorder) and a specified reaction to witnessing or being exposed to that event. The symptomatic sequelae were well characterized and specified (e.g., Keiser, 1968) long before the DSM-III (American Psychiatric Association, 1980) included PTSD as a diagnostic entity. These sequelae have important neurobiological underpinnings (LeDoux, 2000; Yehuda, 1998) and the nature of the symptoms when present in individuals differentiate PTSD from the adjustment disorders.

A central question in understanding the impact of exposure to a traumatic event is being able to predict who will develop PTSD after exposure and who will not. Epidemiological data (Kessler et al., 1995; Resnick et al., 1993; Schlenger et al., 1992; Weiss et al., 1992) clearly document that the prevalence of exposure to traumatic life events greatly exceeds the prevalence of PTSD, although the ratio differs across groups with differing rates of exposure. For example, Kessler et al.'s National Comorbidity Study (1995), using a nationally representative sample, estimated that, although during their lifetime one of two people would be exposed to an event that would meet the requirements for a diagnosis of PTSD, the lifetime prevalence of the disorder is only 5% in men and 10% in women. Consequently, researchers have sought to identify the risk factors for the development of PTSD and to understand how they explain the phenomenon.

We will present the results of the two most comprehensive summaries to date that together suggest that psychological factors are more important than demographic or intellectual variables in predicting who develops PTSD. We also observe that there is great complexity in almost every aspect of predicting PTSD: subjective appraisal of the event, the pattern of symptoms, the longitudinal course, and the measurement of these features. We propose that this complexity is at least partially a result of four attributes: (1) the biological and psychological characteristics of the individual, (2) the individual's history, (3) the social context of the individual, and (4) how the individual interprets and understands the meaning of having been victimized. Among the factors contributing to these individual differences are sense of agency, self-efficacy, and coping skills (e.g., Benight & Bandura, 2004). We make the case that because there are substantial individual differences in how potentially traumatic experiences are understood, even the strongest predictors will remain probabilistic. Research approaches that incorporate idiographic data into quantitative analyses might enhance our prediction of the development of PTSD as well as our understanding.

2.   Early Efforts and Limitations

Early in the study of PTSD, research that included an association between variables, or correlates, were the main source of data available. Until recently, reviews of sets of studies were unavailable. Initially, these summaries were qualitative (Emery et al., 1991; Fontana & Rosenheck, 1994; Green, 1994). The main deficiencies of a subjective box score approach (e.g., Meehl, 1992, 2002) include lack of comprehensiveness of the studies reviewed and absence of a method for synthesizing findings and drawing conclusions. The generic solution to these problems is a meta-analysis (e.g., Rosenthal, 1984; Smith & Glass, 1977; Smith, et al., 1980), a now popular and well-known approach that actually dates back to the 1930s (Lush, 1931). Recently, two meta-analyses of the risk factors (Brewin et al., 2000) or predictors (Ozer et al., 2003) of PTSD have been added to the literature. They have an important bearing on our knowledge about the development of PTSD, as well as to our understanding of the impact of exposure to traumatic life events. After presenting the results of these summaries, we will discuss the limitations of this knowledge base and broader issues regarding challenges and opportunities in the prediction of who develops PTSD.

3.   Meta-analysis of Brewin et al. (2000)

There were 14 variables examined in Brewin et al.'s meta-analysis (2000; see Table 1, p. 751): (1) gender, (2) age, (3) socioeconomic status, (4) education, (5) intelligence, (6) race, (7) psychiatric history, (8) childhood abuse, (9) other previous trauma, (10) other adverse childhood, (11) family history of psychiatric disorder, (12) trauma severity, (13) social support, and (14) life stress. In order to simplify interpretation, we (Ozer et al., 2003, p. 14) grouped this set of 14 variables into 4 categories: (1) demographics, (2) historical or static person characteristics, (3) trauma severity, and (4) social support and intercurrent life stress in the interval between traumatic exposure and assessment of PTSD symptoms and/or diagnosis.

Brewin et al. (2000) reported results of 77 studies, the yield from the literature identified by their search and subsequent pruning. The results of their analyses were complex. Each of the 14 variables generated a weighted-average effect size[1] (ES) that was statistically significant. Thus, having PTSD symptoms was associated with every variable examined, a result that provides little differentiation of the state of the literature. The magnitude of the associations, however, varied considerably; some predictors were stronger than others. Race was the weakest predictor with an average ES (in the same metric as a correlation coefficient) of 0.05, a particularly weak relationship.[2] Social support was the strongest predictor, with an average ES of 0.40. The remaining ESs were in the span of 0.10 to 0.19, but did not produce an obvious pattern. For all the predictors examined, there was considerable heterogeneity in the magnitude of the individual coefficients from each of the studies that contributed to the average ES. For example, 1 study of the 49 that contributed to the average ES for trauma severity had an ES of +0.76. Conversely, there was also a study that reported a relationship of −0.14. As a result, the inference that the average ES is typical of the ES for all studies for that predictor is unwarranted.

Across the set of 14 predictors, there were no regularities of ES based on the characteristics of the sample. For example, comparing studies using social support to predict PTSD resulted in different ESs, depending on whether the sample comprised civilians or members of the military. This difference was statistically significant. The same comparison (civilian vs. military), however, did not yield a significant difference in average ES for studies using life stress as the predictor.

Whether PTSD was indexed by a score (Lauterbach et al., 1997), set of scores (Weiss, 2004a), or a diagnosis with a validated structured interview (Weathers et al., 2001; Weiss, 2004b) produced a variable result across predictors as well. Again, an analysis of the difference between two of the predictors, trauma severity and social support, showed that the method of measurement used to establish that symptoms of PTSD were present made a difference. The size of the effect within the set of studies examining trauma severity showed that the method of measurement did make a difference, whereas in the set of studies examining social support, it did not.

Given these results, it is understandable why Brewin et al. (2000) were unable to offer a straightforward theoretical or conceptual statement that encompassed the full set of comprehensive findings examined in their meta-analysis.

---

[1] Detailed discussion about the methodology of meta-analysis, including explanations of the methods of literature searching, selection, coding, assigned effects, weighting for sample size, and related topics can be found in the works of Rosenthal (1991) and Cooper and Hedges (1994).
[2] Statistical significance is a joint function of effect size and sample size; consequently, even very small effects will achieve statistical significance with sufficiently large samples.

An understanding that explained why, for example, family psychiatric history produced an average ES of 0.13 but lower intelligence yielded an average ES of 0.18 and also accounted for the heterogeneity within and across studies was elusive. Concluding that any particular conceptualization is untenable may nevertheless, be the most useful contribution that can be made, especially when a field is in its early stages of scientific development, as is the current one, a point clearly articulated by Meehl (1973). Brewin et al. presented such a conclusion. They stated that "a general vulnerability model for all cases of PTSD" was not supported by their review, but that "it may be more productive to investigate more proximal links in the causal chain, such as the association between pretrauma risk factors and immediate trauma responses" (Brewin et al., 2000, p. 756).

4.   Meta-analysis of Ozer et al. (2003)

Prior to becoming aware of the meta-analysis of Brewin et al., as well as their key conclusion, we (Ozer et al., 2003) had initiated a meta-analysis that included person characteristics that we considered to be germane to the development of PTSD. We also included phenomena that were part of, or immediately followed, the traumatic event. There were seven of these that we examined (see Ozer et al., 2003, Table 8, p. 66) (1) prior trauma, (2) prior adjustment, (3) family history of psychopathology, (4) perceived life threat, (5) perceived support, (6) peritraumatic emotions, and (7) peritraumatic dissociation. The term "peritraumatic" refers to the time during and immediately after exposure to the traumatic event.

Our meta-analysis pruned a set of 2,647 studies down to 476, and then further to a final set of 68. The analysis of this set of studies yielded some general conclusions as well as some important specific findings. First, the average ES for all predictors was significantly different from zero. This means that the set of variables that were not covered by Brewin et al. (2000) were also important predictors of PTSD, despite the set of 68 studies having different types of event, different measurement methods, and, perhaps most important, differing amounts of time between exposure and assessment of symptoms.

Second, the strength of the predictors, as indexed by the average ES, was similar to those in Brewin et al. (2000), with a high of 0.35 for peritraumatic dissociation and a low of 0.21 for prior trauma, prior adjustment, and family history of psychopathology. These results, when taken with the complete set from Brewin et al. (2000) underscored their key conclusion for understanding who develops and/or has a more severe course of PTSD: Distal predictors such as prior adjustment or education are less strong predictors than proximal variables such as perceived support, life threat, peritraumatic emotionality, and peritraumatic dissociation, all phenomena that are subjectively appraised and not easily subject to outside evaluation.

Third, even within the same category of predictor (e.g., prior trauma, peritraumatic dissociation), there was substantial heterogeneity in the strength of the ESs. This heterogeneity, however, was somewhat less for predictors that were more proximal to the event. We sought to understand whether features of the research studies moderated the relationship between the predictor and PTSD. Thus, we systematically examined four potential moderators: (1) the type of sample studied; (2) the time elapsed between exposure and assessment; (3) the type of trauma experienced; and (4) the method used to assess PTSD. Our most consistent finding was that stronger predictive relationships generally emerged from research in which the traumatic event was interpersonal violence that did not occur in the context of military service. The other broad categories of trauma included accidents, disaster, or combat/military service. No other consistent patterns were found for these moderation analyses. This set of results was not sufficiently consistent to allow us to offer the field an empirically supported conceptualization that brought order to the varied ESs. We could not demonstrate, for example, that predictors showed consistently stronger effects when less time had elapsed since being exposed to the traumatic event or when a structured interview method was used to assess PTSD.

5.   Complexities in Predicting PTSD

The findings of both major meta-analytic reviews of predictors of PTSD suggest that the field has identified multiple person-level factors that are associated with a higher likelihood of PTSD but has yet to provide evidence for any straightforward causal models. Clearly, the explanation of phenomena in human behavior is inherently challenging. That this is so follows from the initial observation that formed the basis for the study of predictors: a considerably lower lifetime prevalence of PTSD than the lifetime prevalence of events that could qualify for the diagnosis.

5.1.   Appraisal of the Event

Although the challenge of predicting human behavior is relevant to research on all types of psychopathology, PTSD has unique features that we propose provide additional challenges to the study of causality in this area. First, unlike any other serious psychiatric disorder (we exclude here the adjustment disorders), the diagnosis of PTSD requires exposure to a specifiable traumatic event, independent of the typical pattern of signs and symptoms. Elsewhere (Weiss et al., submitted) we have argued that the definition of an event as traumatic is considerably more complex than might appear at first glance. We suggested that the notion that an event is traumatic because of its objective characteristics is more illusory than real. The DSM-IV (American Psychiatric Association, 1994), in defining trauma, specifies that "[t]he person has been exposed to a traumatic event in which both of the following were present: (a) (A1) the person experienced, witnessed, or was confronted with an event or events that involved actual or threatened death or serious injury, or a threat to the physical integrity of self and others; and (b) A2, 'the person's response involved intense fear, helplessness, or horror' (p. 427).

These changed criteria made the primary definitory feature for an event to be considered traumatic not an objective assessment of severity, however crudely measured, but, rather, the response to the event. Consider this illustration. A large sample of police officers was asked to report on their frequency of exposure to critical incidents (Weiss et al., submitted). They also estimated the difficulty entailed in coping with the event. The results suggested that determining whether a particular event is considered traumatic is not clear-cut, nor is assessing the degree of severity straightforward. The findings indicated that the nature and characteristics of an event are often not independent of the context or particular group encountering that event. Thus, even though witnessing an event that led to someone's death is clearly within the purview of the A1 criterion for PTSD, the further requirement of a certain response (intense fear, helplessness, or horror) to qualify the event as traumatic for the purpose of making a diagnosis of PTSD appears to mix stressor with stress response. The prevailing view that the severity (see below) of the stressor is sufficient to provoke the criterion A2 responses may be somewhat flawed because the response may well depend on the amount of previous exposure. The amount of previous exposure, in turn, may be determined by one's occupation, one's gender, one's socioeconomic status, and one's previous reactions to events (Brunet et al., 2001), which is similar, but not identical, to the meta-analysis variable of previous trauma.

The typical use of the term "severity," when applied to types of critical incidents, is understood to imply a normative expectation in the same way that the language in the DSM implies a normative expectation; that one event is judged to be more severe than another if, all other things being equal, the average reaction to the first event is greater than to the second. It is expectable that certain events (e.g., torture, sexual assault with deadly force) will always be located at the far tail of the severity distribution. What complicates judging if other kinds of critical incident are more severe than others is that the normative expectation for exposure may be considerably different for different groups.

The expectations of police officers demonstrate this phenomenon in that their coping ratings for a number of events are low. In those data, for example, encountering a body that was recently dead yielded a rating of less than moderately difficult and was among the lowest rated incidents. Although data have not been gathered for an unselected sample, it is unlikely that such an event would be seen as less than moderately difficult; indeed, it would likely be described as a traumatic event with which it would be quite difficult to cope. Analogously, having to drill open a skull would undoubtedly be rated as less severe by a sample of forensic pathologists or a sample of neurosurgeons than by a sample of construction workers or dancers. Thus, without some empirical anchors, such as rating of coping difficulty, the departures from the implicit normative response for any particular category of individuals (e.g., Navy Seals, symphony violinists) are simply not able to be determined. Nonetheless, the notion abandoned by the DSM-III-R that an event's rarity is related to its potential to lead to PTSD symptoms is supported by a negative relationship of –0.61 in these data between frequency of exposure and difficulty coping.

5.2.   Relationship Between Event and Symptoms

Exposure to an event is a necessary but not sufficient condition in the diagnostic algorithm for PTSD, but there is a considerably more intimate connection between the event and the symptomatology of PTSD that follows exposure. Intrusive images and thoughts are about the traumatic event (or derivatives), not just any stimulus. Avoidance does not initially include a wide variety of stimuli, but, instead, is more narrowly focused on reminders, activities, or stimuli that are connected to the event in the individual's understanding of the experience. Although initially circumscribed, avoidance can become more generalized. We argue that this might be the result of changes over time in what it means to have been traumatized.[3] Hyperarousal symptoms appear less related to the specific content of the event, but that remains an open question. Thus, it is both the nature and the meaning of the traumatic event that give rise to the content of the mental activities of intrusion and avoidance.

5.3.   Course of PTSD

Because PTSD is a chronic waxing and waning disorder (Bromet et al., 1998; Dirkzwager et al., 2001; Johnson et al., 2004; Yule et al., 2000; Zeiss & Dickman, 1989; Zlotnick et al., 2004), there appears to be considerable variability in symptom patterns (Solomon, 1989) over time. If having a diagnosis of PTSD is a requirement for a legal proceeding of some sort, a person exposed at an earlier point in time might not, at the time of the proceeding, meet the formal criteria for a diagnosis of PTSD. This can create an easily

---

[3]   One explanation of the spread of stimuli and circumstances that are avoided is that the meaning of the event (e.g., a motor vehicle accident) to the victim confers the property of danger to neutral circumstances that were not previously perceived as dangerous. Crossing bridges or traveling through tunnels becomes an ordeal to be feared or avoided not because the traumatic event involved either of these venues, but because one of the meanings of having been exposed to a traumatic event is the new conviction that the world is more dangerous than previously understood. This view appears more plausible than the traditional view that the spread is merely stimulus generalization (indeed, the phenomenon of stimulus generalization itself requires explanation).

misunderstood circumstance that mistakes fluctuating symptomatology for improvement or recovery.

Another difficulty exists with the practice of using diagnostic status as the only evidence that disabling symptomatology exists as a result of exposure to a traumatic event, such as being electrocuted at a work site. There is evidence that following exposure to a traumatic event, some victims will never evidence a symptom pattern that meets the full criteria for PTSD, but whose symptom status and subsequent disability or impairment in functioning is virtually indistinguishable from those who do (Carlier & Gersons, 1995; Mylle & Maes, 2004; Weiss et al., 1992). Thus, just as biostatisticians advise against making a continuous variable into a categorical one (e.g., Cohen & Cohen, 1983), clarifying the relationship between continuous measures of symptoms and diagnostic status in PTSD, especially as it applies longitudinally, can be vital in forensic settings. Because structured interviews are typically the method by which diagnostic decisions are made (Weiss, 2004b), when symptom measures are available they can be an important complement to the categorical decisions. A rather dramatic example of a pure categorical position occurred in July 2002, when the World Health Organization changed the fasting plasma glucose criterion for diabetes from 7.8 mmol/L to 7.0 mmol/L. People who were not diabetic on June 30 became diabetic on July 1 with no change whatsoever in their clinical status.

5.4.   Methodological Implications of Complexity

Several methodological points should be made about the meta-analyses and literature on which they were based. First, consistent with standard meta-analytic methods, the meta-analyses combined zero-order effect size that estimated the linear relationship between each predictor and PTSD. Even though some original research studies also provided ES estimates from multivariate analyses that controlled for other variables or represented tests of the interactions between characteristics of the event and characteristics of the individual, estimates representing multivariate relationships cannot be combined across studies unless there is a sufficient number that represent the identical set of variables tested. Because it is unlikely that this will change, one limitation of the meta-analytic findings is its focus on noncontingent linear relationships. If, in the future, the research literature were to permit it, meta-analyses could examine multivariate ESs that might yield better prediction of PTSD.

We propose, however, that the challenges inherent in predicting PTSD are more fundamental than moving from univariate to multivariate ESs. Rather, we argue that the study of the predictors of PTSD must integrate variables measuring subjective meanings and contextual factors. As discussed earlier, humans habitually attribute meaning to their experiences, especially those that are traumatic. If the development of PTSD depends at least partially on the subjective meaning attributed to the event in the short- and long-term aftermaths as well as efforts to cope with the event and subsequent stress-related symptoms, research seeking to predict PTSD must gather data on these dimensions. Because the attribution of meaning is idiographic rather than nomothetic, anticipating an upper limit on the ability to predict who develops PTSD using solely nomothetic research models and methods is appropriate. The use of person-centered analytic approaches (e.g., Bergman & Magnusson, 2001) provide opportunities to identify clusters of variability with respect to characteristics such as subjective and objective aspects of the event, the individual, and symptom course that might provide insight into potentially meaningful patterns of the development of the disorder beyond that which can be predicted by variable-centered quantitative research designs.

6.   Summary

Findings from meta-analyses of predictors of PTSD suggest that using variables that are both more proximal to the event and more subjective than objective, such as peritraumatic dissociative experiences or subsequent social support, enhances prediction. Our examination of the knowledge base of predicting who develops PTSD appears to corroborate the sage observation made by Cluckhorn and Murray (1948) more than half a century ago: "Every man is in certain respects *a.* like all other men, *b.* like some other men, *c.* like no other man" (p. 35). Exposure to an event experienced as traumatic (a combination of *b* and *c*), elicits an initial fight or flight response and a period of oscillating avoidance and re-experiencing (*a*). As a varying amount (*b*) of time passes, the intrusion, avoidance, and hyperarousal phenomena either dissipate or become established symptoms (*b*) partly as a function of a variety of predictors or risk factors (*b*) and partly as a function of idiographic factors (*c*). Whether or not a treatment intervention occurs (e.g., Hembree et al., 2003; Resick, Nishith, Weaver, Astin, & Feuer, 2002; Weiss, in press), many experience symptoms of PTSD for a prolonged period of time (*b*) perhaps with a pattern or waxing and waning symptoms (*b*). The nature of the symptomatic course and the connection to the traumatic event are mostly unique (*c*). This perspective underscores the necessity to acknowledge the role of individualized interpretations and construal of meanings and the logical consequence that there is likely a ceiling on how accurate prediction can be. From a forensic point of view, this current state of affairs is likely unsatisfactory. It underscores the need for a thorough evaluation in every legal case involving PTSD.

References

American Psychiatric Association. (1980). *Diagnostic and Statistical Manual of Mental Disorders*, 3rd ed. Washington, DC: American Psychiatric Association.

American Psychiatric Association. (1994). *Diagnostic and Statistical Manual of Mental Disorders*, 4th ed. Washington, DC: American Psychiatric Association.

Benight, C.C. & Bandura, A. (2004). Social cognitive theory of posttraumatic recovery: The role of perceived self-efficacy. *Behaviour Research & Therapy, 42*, 1129–1148.

Bergman, L. R. & Magnusson, D. (2001). Person-centered research. In T. Cook & C. Ragin (Eds.). *The International Encyclopedia of the Social and Behavioral Sciences: Logic of Inquiry and Research Design.* Oxford: Elsevier, pp. 11,333–11,339.

Brewin, C. R., Andrews, B., & Valentine, J. D. (2000). Meta-analysis of risk factors for Posttraumatic Stress Disorder in trauma-exposed adults. *Journal of Consulting & Clinical Psychology, 68*, 748–766.

Bromet, E., Sonnega, A., & Kessler, R. C. (1998). Risk factors for DSM-III-R Posttraumatic Stress Disorder: Findings from the National Comorbidity Survey. *American Journal of Epidemiology, 147*, 353–361.

Brunet, A., Boyer, R., Weiss, D. S., & Marmar, C. R. (2001). The effects of initial trauma exposure on the symptomatic response to a subsequent trauma. *Canadian Journal of Behavioral Sciences, 33*, 97–102.

Carlier, I. V. & Gersons, B. P. (1995). Partial Posttraumatic Stress Disorder (PTSD): the issue of psychological scars and the occurrence of PTSD symptoms. *Journal of Nervous and Mental Disease, 183*, 107–109.

Cluckhorn, C. & Murray, H. A. (1948). Personality formation: The determinants. In C. Cluckhorn & H. A. Murray (Eds.). *Personality in Nature, Society, and Culture.* New York: Alfred A. Knopf, pp. 35–48.

Cohen, J. & Cohen, P. (1983). *Applied Multiple Regression/Correlation Analysis for the Behavioral Sciences, 2*nd ed. Hillsdale, NJ: Erlbaum.

Cooper, H., & Hedges, L. V. (Eds.). (1994). *The Handbook of Research Synthesis.* New York: Russell Sage Foundation.

Dirkzwager, A. J. E., Bramsen, I., & Van Der Ploeg, H. M. (2001). The longitudinal course of Posttraumatic Stress Disorder symptoms among aging military veterans. *Journal of Nervous & Mental Disease, 189*, 846–853.

Emery, V. O., Emery, P. E., Shama, D. K., Quiana, N. A., & Jassani, A. K. (1991). Predisposing variables in PTSD patients. *Journal of Traumatic Stress, 4*, 325–343.

Fontana, A. & Rosenheck, R. (1994). Posttraumatic Stress Disorder among Vietnam theater veterans. A causal model of etiology in a community sample. *Journal of Nervous and Mental Disease, 182*, 677–684.

Green, B. L. (1994). Psychosocial research in traumatic stress: An update. *Journal of Traumatic Stress, 7*, 341–362.

Hembree, E. A., Rauch, S. A. M., & Foa, E. B. (2003). Beyond the manual: The insider's guide to prolonged exposure therapy for PTSD. *Cognitive & Behavioral Practice, 10*, 22–30.

Johnson, D. R., Fontana, A., Lubin, H., Corn, B., & Rosenheck, R. (2004). Long-term course of treatment-seeking Vietnam veterans with Posttraumatic Stress Disorder: Mortality, clinical condition, and life satisfaction. *Journal of Nervous & Mental Disease, 192*, 35–41.

Keiser, L. (1968). *The Traumatic Neurosis.* Philadelphia: J.B. Lippincott Company.

Kessler, R. C., Sonnega, A., Bromet, E., Hughes, M., & Nelson, C. B. (1995). Posttraumatic Stress Disorder in the National Comorbidity Survey. *Archives of General Psychiatry, 52*, 1048–1060.

Lauterbach, D., Vrana, S., King, D. W., & King, L. A. (1997). Psychometric properties of the Civilian Version of the Mississippi PTSD scale. *Journal of Traumatic Stress, 10*, 499–513.

LeDoux, J. E. (2000). Emotion circuits in the brain. *Annual Review of Neuroscience, 23*, 155–184.

Lush, J. L. (1931). Predicting gains in feeder cattle and pigs. *Journal of Agricultural Research, 42*, 853–881.

Meehl, P. E. (1973). *Psychodiagnosis: Selected Papers.* Minneapolis, MN: University of Minnesota Press.

Meehl, P. E. (1992). Cliometric metatheory: The actuarial approach to empirical, history-based philosophy of science. *Psychological Reports, 71*, 339–467.

Meehl, P. E. (2002). Cliometric metatheory: II. Criteria scientists use in theory appraisal and why it is rational to do so. *Psychological Reports, 91*, 339–404.

Mylle, J. & Maes, M. (2004). Partial Posttraumatic Stress Disorder revisited. *Journal of Affective Disorders, 78*, 37–48.

Ozer, E. J., Best, S. R., Lipsey, T. L., & Weiss, D. S. (2003). Predictors of Posttraumatic Stress Disorder symptoms in adults: A meta-analysis. *Psychological Bulletin, 129*, 52–73.

Resick, P. A., Nishith, P., Weaver, T. L., Astin, M. C., & Feuer, C. A. (2002). A comparison of cognitive-processing therapy with prolonged exposure and a waiting condition for the treatment of chronic Posttraumatic Stress Disorder in female rape victims. *Journal of Consulting & Clinical Psychology, 70*, 867–879.

Resnick, H. S., Kilpatrick, D. G., Dansky, B. S., Saunders, B. E., & Best, C. L. (1993). Prevalence of civilian trauma and Posttraumatic Stress Disorder in a representative national sample of women. *Journal of Consulting and Clinical Psychology, 61*, 984–991.

Rosenthal, R. (1984). *Meta-analytic Procedures for Social Research.* Newbury Park, CA: Sage.

Rosenthal, R. (1991). *Meta-analytic Procedures for Social Research*, rev. ed.: Newbury Park, CA: Sage.

Schlenger, W. E., Kulka, R. A., Fairbank, J. A., Hough, R. L., Jordan, B. K., Marmar, C. R., et al. (1992). The prevalence of Posttraumatic Stress Disorder in the Vietnam generation: A multimethod, multisource assessment of psychiatric disorder. *Journal of Traumatic Stress, 5*, 333–363.

Smith, M. L. & Glass, G. V. (1977). Meta-analysis of psychotherapy outcome studies. *American Psychologist, 32*, 752–760.

Smith, M. L., Glass, G. V., & Miller, T. I. (1980). *The Benefits of Psychotherapy.* Baltimore, MD: Johns Hopkins University Press.

Solomon, Z. (1989). A 3-year prospective study of Posttraumatic Stress Disorder in Israeli combat veterans. *Journal of Traumatic Stress, 2*, 59–73.

Weathers, F. W., Keane, T. M., & Davidson, J. R. (2001). Clinician-administered PTSD scale: A review of the first ten years of research. *Depress Anxiety, 13*, 132–156.

Weiss, D. S. (2004a). Impact of Event Scale-Revised. In J. P. Wilson & T. M. Keane (Eds.). *Assessing Psychological Trauma and PTSD: A Practitioner's Handbook*, 2nd ed., New York: Guilford Press, pp. 168–169.

Weiss, D. S. (2004b). Structured clinical interview techniques for PTSD. In J. P. Wilson & T. M. Keane (Eds.). *Assessing Psychological Trauma and PTSD: A Practitioner's Handbook*, 2nd ed. New York: Guilford Press.

Weiss, D. S. (in press). Psychodynamic group treatment. In L. Schein, G. Burlingame, H. Spitz, & P. Muskin (Eds.). *Group Approaches for the Psychological Effects of Terrorist Disasters.* New York: Guilford Press, pp. 103–121.

Weiss, D. S., Brunet, A., Best, S. R., Metzler, T. J., Liberman, A. M., Fagan, J. A., et al. (submitted). The Critical Incident History Questionnaire: A method for measuring total cumulative exposure to critical incidents in police officers.

Weiss, D. S., Marmar, C. R., Schlenger, W. E., Fairbank, J. A., Jordan, B. K., Hough, R. L., et al. (1992). The prevalence of lifetime and partial Posttraumatic Stress Disorder in Vietnam theatre veterans. *Journal of Traumatic Stress, 5,* 365–376.

Yehuda, R. (1998). Psychoneuroendocrinology of Posttraumatic Stress Disorder. *Psychiatric Clinics of North America, 21,* 359–379.

Yule, W., Bolton, D., Udwin, O., Boyle, S., O'Ryan, D., & Nurrish, J. (2000). The long-term psychological effects of a disaster experienced in adolescence: I: The incidence and course of PTSD. *Journal of Child Psychology & Psychiatry & Allied Disciplines, 41,* 503–511.

Zeiss, R. A. & Dickman, H. R. (1989). PTSD 40 years later: Incidence and person situation correlates in former POWs. *Journal of Clinical Psychology, 45,* 80–87.

Zlotnick, C., Rodriguez, B. F., Weisberg, R. B., Bruce, S. E., Spencer, M. A., Culpepper, L., et al. (2004). Chronicity in Posttraumatic Stress Disorder and predictors of the course of Posttraumatic Stress Disorder among primary care patients. *Journal of Nervous & Mental Disease, 192,* 153–159.

6

Assessment of Psychological Distress and Disability After Sexual Assault in Adults

Melissa A. Polusny and Paul A. Arbisi

1. Introduction

Sexual assault involves any attempted or completed sexual act, ranging from intentional sexual contact against a victim's will or without a victim's consent to forcible sexual intercourse. Bureau of Justice statistics estimated about 250,000 sexual assaults occurred in 2002 alone (US Department of Justice, 2003). Although sexual violence affects both sexes, women are clearly more likely than men to be victims and men perpetrate the majority of sexual violence (DeLahunta & Baram, 1997). According to the National Violence Against Women Survey, 1 in 6 women and 1 in 33 men have experienced attempted or completed sexual assault (Tjaden & Thoennes, 2000). Rates of sexual assault are even higher among some populations, such as women seeking mental health treatment (Goodman et al., 2001) and women serving in the military. For example, nearly a quarter of female veterans report having experienced sexual assault during their military service (Hankin et al., 1999).

The Department of Veterans Affairs (VA) is currently the largest provider of treatment for Posttraumatic Stress Disorder (PTSD) in the United States. PTSD is a chronic disabling condition caused by witnessing or experiencing a life-threatening and horrifying, traumatic event and is the most common psychiatric condition for which veterans seek VA disability benefits (Frueh et al., 2000; Statistics, 1995). As the occurrence of sexual assault while serving in the military has gained recognition, the rate of claims for disability secondary to sexual assault has increased (Murdoch et al., 2003). Thus, a significant number of female veterans apply for and receive benefits or compensation related to sexual assault that occurred while serving in the military. Moreover, claims for federal disability through the Social Security System have also increased steadily in recent years, with mental stresses as one of the most frequently cited reasons for disability claims (Arbisi, 2005).

Given the high rates of sexual violence among clients presenting for mental health treatment and increasing rates of disability claims, there is a strong likelihood that psychologists will see patients who present with problems that may serve as the basis for a claim of disability or compensation. Practicing psychologists must be aware of sexual trauma issues and regularly screen for these events in their patients' histories. Although psychologists providing treatment to sexual assault victims should not serve in the dual roles of treating professional and forensic expert, the treating professional must be familiar with disability issues and be aware that his or her assessment conducted in a treatment setting could later become evidence for a subsequent disability claim in a litigation context. Given this, any assessment of a sexual assault victim presenting for treatment should carefully address issues of causality, impairment, and subsequent disability with the view that whatever conclusion is reached may be challenged, and objective evidence is required in support of such conclusions. As we will discuss in this chapter, a multimethod assessment strategy, including the use of structured and semistructured interviews, objective psychological testing, and focused self-report questionnaires, can greatly assist the psychologist in making judgments regarding the validity of a claim of disability and support an opinion regarding the level of distress that may lead to compromised adaptive functioning and serve as a cause of damage.

2.   General Issues Related to the Assessment of Adult Sexual Assault

2.1.   *Emotional and Psychological Sequelae of Sexual Assault*

Since Burgess and Holmstrom's (1974) pioneering work on rape trauma syndrome, there has been a great deal of empirical research on the immediate and longer-term impact of sexual assault. Sexual assault is a particularly potent predictor of PTSD (Kessler et al., 1995). Lifetime prevalence rates of PTSD for women who have experienced completed rape range from approximately 32% to 80% (Breslau et al., 1991; Resnick et al., 1993), and women appear to experience greater chronicity of PTSD symptoms than do men (e.g., Breslau et al., 1998; Norris et al., 2002).

Although the diagnosis of PTSD has been useful in forensic situations as a scientifically valid description of the impact of sexual assault (Boeschen et al., 1998), the PTSD conceptualization has been criticized for failing to capture the complexity of victims' responses to sexual assault (Koss et al., 2003; McGowan & Helms, 2003). In addition to PTSD, sexual assault might lead to a range of disabling problems, including depression, suicidality, substance abuse, sexual dysfunction, physical health outcomes, and changes in core beliefs about one's self and the world.

Depression is one of the most common reactions to sexual assault and those sexual assault victims suffering from PTSD are more likely to meet criteria for major depression (Brady et al., 2000; Breslau et al., 1997; Koss et al., 2003). Further, sexual assault survivors are at significantly greater odds of having attempted suicide during their lifetime (Ullman, 2004). Even subthreshold PTSD symptoms have been associated with greater impairments and suicidal ideation (Marshall et al., 2001).

2.2.   Substance Abuse and Dependence

Substance abuse or dependence problems are also more likely to occur among sexual assault survivors (e.g., Lang et al., 2003). In a 2-year longitudinal analysis of the relationship between violent assault and substance use in a national sample of women, Kilpatrick et al. (1997) found that after an assault, the odds of both alcohol and other drug use were significantly increased, even among women with no previous use or assault history. Sexually assaulted individuals may use alcohol or other drugs to reduce or avoid distressing symptoms associated with the diagnosis of PTSD (Saladin et al., 2003), especially sleep disturbances and nightmares (Nishith et al., 2001).

2.3.   Sexual Dysfunction

Female sexual assault survivors are more than twice as likely as women without a sexual assault history to experience sexual dysfunction (Kilpatrick et al., 1988). In a random community sample of 3,132 adults, Siegel and colleagues (1990) reported that female sexual assault victims were more likely to be fearful of sex (22%), have less sexual interest (33%), and experience less pleasurable sexual relations (27%) than nonvictims. Women whose sexual assault experience involved a completed rape or physical injury during the crime or who subsequently developed depression and PTSD are more likely to develop sexual problems (Letourneau et al., 1996). Sexual dissatisfaction and disruptions in sexual functioning may be longstanding and continue for years following a sexual assault (Becker et al., 1986).

2.4.   Somatic Complaints and Health Care Utilization

In addition to impairments in psychosocial functioning, a number of physical complaints and illnesses have been associated with sexual assault, including chronic pelvic pain, premenstrual syndrome, and gastrointestinal disorders (Clum et al., 2000; Leserman, et al., 1996). Between 4% and 30% of rape victims contract sexually transmitted diseases as a result of being sexually assaulted (Resnick et al., 1997). Although somatic complaints generally diminish over the year following assault, sexually victimized women's medical health care utilization remains elevated compared with utilization of nonvictimized women (Kimerling & Calhoun, 1994).

2.5.   Sexual Revictimization

A significant proportion of women seen by psychologists following rape or attempted rape will have a history of previous sexual victimization during childhood or adolescence (Messman-Moore & Long, 2002; Polusny & Follette, 1995; Roy-Byrne et al., 2004). In a sample of 1,887 female Navy recruits, women who had experienced childhood sexual abuse reported rape nearly five times more frequently than women with no childhood sexual abuse history (Merrill et al., 1999). There is also growing evidence that the severity of problems associated with adult sexual assault become greater among women who have had multiple victimization experiences. Revictimized women report more PTSD symptoms and greater substance abuse and dependence, experience greater problems in areas such as intimacy and trust, and are more likely to have attempted suicide than either women who had never been sexually victimized or women who experienced adult sexual assault only (Cloitre et al., 1997; Follette et al., 1996; Gold et al., 1994; Nishith et al., 2000; Thompson et al., 2003).

2.6.   Recovery from Sexual Assault

Clearly, sexual assault can lead to significant and lasting psychosocial impairments. However, the ideas that severe and lasting psychological effects are the natural consequence of exposure to potentially traumatic events and that resiliency is a relatively rare phenomenon seem to be fairly widely held beliefs among professionals in both the psychological (Bonanno, 2004; Galea et al., 2002; McNally, 2003a) and legal (Gaughwin, 2001) communities. Early conceptualizations of PTSD defined traumatic stressors as events "outside the range of human experiences" and that those would be "markedly distressing to almost anyone." The disorder was described as a normative response to exposure to a traumatic event (Yehuda & McFarlane, 1995). However, the resiliency of trauma survivors to psychological disruptions appears to have been underestimated (Bonanno, 2004). Although the majority of the U.S. population has been exposed to at least one traumatic stressor during the course of their lives, only a small percentage of trauma survivors develop PTSD (Ozer et al., 2003).

Prospective studies have documented high levels of distress among victims in the initial weeks following sexual assault. Rothbaum et al. (1992) found that 94% of one sample of rape victims met symptomatic criteria for PTSD in the first week following assault. The rate of PTSD dropped to 47% at 3 months postassault. Although early studies indicated that little additional improvement in symptoms occurs after 3 months postrape (Atkeson et al., 1982; Kilpatrick, et al., 1981), recent data suggests that about half of trauma survivors in general who are still symptomatic at 3 months will recover over the next few years (Ehlers et al., 1998). However, these recent findings are based on the study of a general trauma population, and sexual-assault-related

PTSD appears to be more resistant to recovery than PTSD stemming from other traumatic stressors (Gilboa-Schechtman & Foa, 2001).

3.   Dilemmas in Forensic Evaluations Following Adult Sexual Assault

The psychologist who is evaluating an individual who has suffered sexual assault and is claiming disability is frequently challenged by a number of dilemmas that can complicate the evaluation process. For example, the forensic psychologist is focused on a number of assessment goals that differentiate the forensic evaluations from the goals of assessment within a treatment context (Arbisi, 2005). Therefore, forensic psychological evaluations that involve claims of disability or psychological damage after a sexual assault should not be conducted by the professional who is providing treatment because the goal of a forensic evaluation may be at odds with the goal of an evaluation conducted within the context of the provision of treatment. Indeed, forensic evaluations are necessarily time-limited and require that the examiner elicit information that can be used in establishing a direct link between the alleged traumatic event and the development of symptoms and functional impairment. The forensic examiner does not have the opportunity to develop the type of alliance that is commonly developed between a therapist and client before sensitive material is elicited. Thus, despite the best efforts of the forensic examiner, the individual being evaluated may view the evaluation as intrusive or adversarial.

3.1.   Subjectivity and Bias

The forensic psychologist is asked to establish whether a diagnosis or diagnoses are present, address the degree to which the condition(s) are currently present, and estimate the impact of those conditions on the examinee's current level of disability, or ability to carry out his or her daily activities. Disputes may arise in litigation over the existence of a specific psychiatric diagnosis or whether, if present, the psychiatric condition led to the alleged disability. Clinical judgments may also be unintentionally or intentionally biased by financial factors inherent in the forensic evaluation process in which the examiner's fee is paid by one side in the dispute. Evidence pointing to this potential bias comes from research in the area of sexual harassment litigation, which has documented discrepancies between diagnoses obtained by plaintiff and defense expert examiners in cases of sexual harassment. Long (1994) found that PTSD was diagnosed in 17 out of 47 cases by the plaintiff examiner and in only 2 cases (both PTSD cases were attributed to previous victimization) by the defense examiners. Alternatively, personality disorder diagnoses were given in only 5 out of 47 cases by the plaintiff examiner and in 33 out of the same 47 (75%) cases by the defense examiner.

In order to avoid subjective and/or biased evaluation of an individual's claimed distress and impairment, it is recommended that standardized assessment procedures be used to arrive at diagnoses, including structured or semi-structured interviews and validated self-report instruments. Results from psychological testing can provide an objective measure of the individual's current level of distress and functioning compared to normative data.

3.2.   Secondary Gain in the Litigation Context

The issue of secondary gain is almost always an issue in forensic evaluations, and the psychologist may be asked to address the extent to which secondary gain is influencing the examinee's presentation of symptoms and report of impairment. Unfortunately, the validity of both clinical interviews and self-report questionnaires can be compromised by intentional defensiveness and symptom magnification. A number of researchers have documented the relative ease of feigning or exaggerating the presence of symptoms associated with PTSD because the diagnosis of PTSD is almost completely related to the patient's self-report and PTSD symptoms can be easily learned from a variety of sources (Bury & Bagby, 2002; Resnick, 1997).

Whenever secondary gain is an issue, as is the case within the context of litigation, the presence of symptom exaggeration or malingering should be considered and objectively evaluated. Thus, the use of objective psychological tests, such as the revised Minnesota Multiphasic Personality Inventory (MMPI-2) with well-established validity scales, is an essential complement to clinical interview and other self-report data collected in forensic evaluations (Arbisi, 2005). Data from the MMPI-2 validity scales provide objective information on the individual's approach to the assessment process, including the extent to which the self-report is distorted or malingered.

3.3.   Dilemmas in Inferring Causality

In a forensic evaluation of a sexually assaulted individual, it is critical to establish whether the presence of a psychiatric condition is causally linked to an alleged sexual assault claimed in litigation. Psychologists conducting such evaluations are asked to determine the likelihood that a particular sexual assault directly led to a claimed psychiatric condition and disability. If the sexual assault in question did not directly lead to distress and impairment, then the psychologist may be asked to define the likelihood that the recent sexual assault aggravated a pre-existing psychiatric condition that contributes to a greater degree of impairment or disability. The psychologist considering issues of causality in a sexual assault disability evaluation may be challenged by a number of issues.

As mentioned earlier, sexual assault may produce a variety of psychosocial impairments. One common error in the evaluation of a sexually assaulted individual is to focus narrowly on the presence or absence of PTSD. Failure to examine other possible traumatic responses that may result from sexual assault could lead to the erroneous conclusion that a particular sexual assault has not caused injury to an individual if the diagnosis of PTSD is not present. It is recommended that a comprehensive evaluation using a structured or semistructured interview gather information about a range of pre-existing and current psychological disorders. The use of objective psychological testing that assesses a broad range of psychopathology may be particularly helpful.

Another dilemma that could arise when making causal inferences relates to the magnitude of the alleged sexual victimization experience on the examiner's evaluation of subsequent symptomatology. A number of studies across populations have documented a trauma dose–response relationship. For example, Follette et al. (1996) reported evidence for the cumulative impact of interpersonal victimization experiences. Women reporting greater sexual and physical abuse experiences showed increasing levels of posttrauma symptoms. Combat veterans who were POWs or wounded in action are more likely to have a PTSD diagnosis than those veterans never captured, tortured, or wounded (Kulka et al., 1990; Sutker et al., 1993). Greater proximity to the site of a terrorist attack has been shown to predict PTSD severity (Galea et al., 2002). However, not all studies have shown correlations between the severity of trauma exposure and the severity of posttrauma symptoms (McNally, 2003a). Consequently, the examiner must be careful not to assume that severe symptoms necessarily result from severe assault. A graphic description by an individual of his or her survival of a horrific sexual assault is not, itself, sufficient to determine that psychological impairment has necessarily resulted.

The halo effect may operate when an examiner's evaluation of an individual's symptomatology is influenced by the nature of the traumatic event reported by the individual (Nisbett & Wilson, 1977). Listening to details of a brutal sexual assault may elicit greater sympathy on the part of the psychologist that could subsequently bias impressions about an individual's level of distress, functioning, or impairment. According to the halo effect, severe traumatic events that clearly meet Criterion A for PTSD may result in greater severity ratings of other symptoms that may not actually be present. Examiners must be alert to how listening to details of sexual assault could impact their own emotional responses in the interview that could potentially bias subsequent evaluation of impairment and disability. Objective assessment of symptoms and distress using standard, reliable diagnostic interviews and psychological testing serves as a check on the subjectivity of the examiner and prevents overreliance on data from unstructured clinical interviews.

On the other hand, the examiner may be challenged with evaluating an individual claiming severe symptoms in response to a relatively low-magnitude stressor (e.g., an unwanted sexual advance). In legal terms, this concept has been referred to as the "eggshell plaintiff." The eggshell plaintiff rule was intended to protect the rights of individuals whose pre-existing risk factors make them particularly vulnerable to injury following even minor traumatic events (Levy & Rosenberg, 2003). Although epidemiological studies indicate that it is rare for individuals to suffer severe, disabling symptoms following low-magnitude stressors, some individuals may have pre-existing risk factors that could increase their vulnerability to developing PTSD following trauma exposure. For example, individuals with previous trauma histories are more likely than those not previously trauma exposed to develop PTSD following subsequent victimization (Nishith et al., 2000). Examiners are advised to take a cautious and common-sense approach to questioning claims of excessive vulnerability and severe consequences in response to seemingly trivial events (Tennant, 2001). Additionally, examiners should observe evidence regarding population base rates for injury and disability following trauma exposure. Objective evidence should be gathered to support the argument that the examinee was vulnerable to becoming distressed following the alleged event (Tennant, 2001). For example, medical records may document a history of impairment following similar low-intensity stressors when litigation was not involved.

When making inferences about causality, it is important that the assessment consider alternative explanations for the association of sexual assault and psychological distress. Because errors in causal inferences are especially likely to occur when alternative explanations are not assessed and the relationship between two variables is consistent with the examiner's a priori causal hypothesis, the psychologist is advised to conduct a comprehensive examination that explores alternative explanations. Postassault psychosocial stressors, such as medical illness, unemployment, family conflict, and the stress associated with criminal investigation and litigation may contribute to the link between sexual assault and subsequent distress and disability. Consideration of alternative explanations for claimed disability is especially important when an individual claims injury and disability to have resulted from exposure to a minor stressor. In addition to evaluating the individual for vulnerability factors that would indicate an "eggshell plaintiff," the examiner should also consider whether the alleged stressor is indeed the causal agent responsible for producing injury and disability, whether other more severe traumatic stressors may better account for the claimed stressors, or whether the individual is malingering symptoms to obtain benefits.

The task of attributing distress and disability with certainty to only one event becomes challenging when the individual has a history of exposure to multiple traumatic events that could potentially lead to the development of a psychiatric condition. The research literature clearly suggests that this set of antecedents is more likely to be present in individuals who were sexually victimized. Through careful evaluation of temporal sequencing of events and responses, the relative contribution of the sexual assault in question along with other traumatic stressors in determining causality must be carefully teased apart. In addition, obtaining a detailed description of the nature of the victim's intrusive symptoms (e.g., Are flashbacks and intrusive images specific to the recent rape experience?) could also help strengthen the causal inferences that can be made about the impact of a particular sexual assault experience. This process of attributing causality becomes even more complex when considering that individuals with previous trauma histories and PTSD are more likely to develop PTSD, or existing symptoms might be exacerbated by a subsequent stressor. Assessing the sequence of events might help to determine the impact of a particular event, or stressor, the impact of subsequent events, and the extent to which sexual assault exacerbated pre-existing conditions.

3.4.   Dilemmas Related to Memory and Sexual Assault

A rather heated and somewhat divisive debate regarding the veracity of memories for sexual trauma has been played out over the years in the trauma literature. Given the focus of this chapter on psychological assessment following adult sexual assault, we will not review the important issues regarding children's memory for sexual abuse as well as adults reporting recovery of memories of having been allegedly sexually abused during childhood. Here, we address the dilemma of the veracity of memory for adult sexual assault and the implications of this question for the assessment of distress and disability.

It is believed that, in order for a sexual assault experience to result in subsequent symptoms, it must first be encoded in memory (McNally, 2003b). In some sexual assaults, the victim may be unconscious during the rape because of drug intoxication or physical injury and thus is incapable of encoding the sexual assault experience. However, even if a sexual assault victim is unconscious during the traumatic event, PTSD symptoms could develop (Simon, 2003). Bryant et al. (2000) found that 26 out of 96 accident survivors who suffered a severe brain injury developed PTSD. Although most patients with PTSD did not report intrusive memories of the accident, the majority experienced emotional reactivity to stimuli associated with the traumatic accident.

When PTSD symptoms are assessed for the individual who does not have conscious recollection of the actual sexual assault, the symptoms should be evaluated with regard to events surrounding the aftermath of the traumatic event (e.g., recovering consciousness in the emergency room, learning from someone else that one has been sexually assaulted) rather than the sexual assault itself. To meet criteria for PTSD, re-experiencing symptom content should reflect the stressful events surrounding recovery or being informed of the rape. Reports of experiencing vivid intrusive recollections of a traumatic event that occurred when the individual was allegedly unconscious should be carefully questioned.

The extent to which a sexual assault experience is encoded in memory is influenced by the process of selective encoding as well as peritraumatic cognitive processing that occur during and immediately following the event.

There is substantial evidence that central features of a sexual assault experience are most likely to be encoded in memory (McNally, 2003b). This phenomenon is known as the Easterbrook principle (Easterbrook, 1959, cited in McNally), which holds that the central features of an experience receive priority coding, often at the expense of peripheral features. If aspects of a sexual assault fail to be encoded and thus are unable to be retrieved, it will most likely be peripheral details (e.g., description of a rapist's clothing), not the central essence of the experience (e.g., presence of weapon, occurrence of forcible intercourse).

Peritraumatic cognitive processing during and immediately following sexual assault may lead to disorganized memories of the assault and also increase vulnerability for the development of PTSD. Halligan et al. (2003) found that cognitive processing, memory disorganization, and appraisals significantly predicted PTSD 6 months posttrauma even after accounting for assault severity. Poorer recall of specific memories of the traumatic event 1 week following a motor vehicle accident (MVA) predicted trauma survivors PTSD severity 6 months later (Harvey et al., 1998).

4. Guidelines for Assessment of Sexual-Assault-Related Distress and Disability

Over the past 20 years, there have been significant scientific advances in the development and standardization of procedures for the assessment of traumatic stress responses (see Carlson, 1997; Keane et al., 2000, 2003; Resnick, 2003; Simon, 2003). In this section, we describe a comprehensive multimethod assessment strategy recommended for the psychological evaluation of the adult who claims to have suffered injury and disability as a result of being sexually assaulted. A comprehensive evaluation requires that the psychologist gather detailed and objective evidence regarding the individual's psychosocial history, the alleged sexual assault experience, and the individual's history of psychological distress, impairment, treatment, and claimed disability.

4.1. Assessment of Psychosocial History

A comprehensive assessment strategy gathers information about the individual's developmental and social history prior to and following the sexual assault. Structured or semistructured clinical interviews should include assessment of the individual's strengths, weaknesses, support systems, as well as beliefs and coping abilities that could reasonably predict resiliency in the aftermath of trauma exposure. In conducting an assessment of the individual's coping abilities, maladaptive coping methods used to control or dampen symptomatology (e.g., substance use) should be evaluated. The individual's prior life stressors, psychiatric history, medical history, litigation history, and criminal record should also be assessed. These domains may point to alternative explanations that may better account for the individual's claim of distress and disability. Evaluating the individual's family background for a history of psychopathology and family dysfunction is important given the potential contribution of these factors for increasing risk for individual psychopathology following trauma exposure (Foy, 1992). In addition, current stressors that have intervened in the individual's life since the sexual assault may be a source of increased vulnerability to distress and disability, and should also be evaluated.

It is crucial to evaluate the individual's history of prior trauma exposure, which may better account for current symptomatology or may increase vulnerability to the development of distress following subsequent sexual assault (Resnick et al., 1991). Other potentially traumatic events include war-zone stressors, previous sexual assault in childhood, adolescence, or adulthood, criminal victimization through robbery or mugging, witnessing or experiencing physical violence, motor vehicle accidents, technological or natural disasters, sudden death of a loved one, and surviving a life-threatening illness. A number of psychometrically sound self-report instruments designed to assess PTSD symptomatology include questions that systematically assess lifetime exposure to a broad range of potentially traumatic events in a fairly economical manner. The Post-traumatic Stress Diagnostic Scale (PDS) (Foa et al., 1997) contains a 12-item checklist of potentially traumatic events that the individual might have experienced. The Traumatic Life Events Questionnaire (TLEQ) (Kubany et al., 2000) assesses 21 potentially traumatic events in behaviorally specific terms. Both the PDS and TLEQ assess the presence of physical injury and emotional responses to distressing event such as fear, helplessness, and horror. The Life Events Stressor Checklist (Wolfe & Kimerling, 1997) similarly assesses high-magnitude events as well as broader developmental experiences (e.g., permanent separation from a child) that may be gender-specific and linked to psychosocial disruptions.

4.2. Assessment of the Sexual Assault Experience

It is advised that the psychologist gather a detailed history of the sexual victimization, using behaviorally specific questions that elicit information about the presence of threat and injury as well as elements that define different types of assault (Resnick et al., 1993; Weaver, 1998). The examiner should avoid using jargon such as "abuse" or "rape" that may be misunderstood by the individual and may rely on individual interpretations and cultural stereotypes. Specific information about the duration and intensity of the assault, chronology of events, and consequences of the assault such as changes in living patterns and treatment received should also be gathered.

In order to determine whether the individual's alleged sexual assault experience meets both Criteria A-1 and A-2 for a diagnosis of PTSD, it is essential to thoroughly evaluate the individual's emotional, cognitive, and behavioral responses during the traumatic event. The individual's subjective appraisal of the stressor event and his or her self-reported emotional response to the alleged stressor may be distorted in litigation situations (Tennant, 2001). For example, the individual may unintentionally or intentionally overestimate the magnitude of distress experienced during the event under litigation and minimize or underestimate the impact of other prior or subsequent stressors.

Collateral information about the sexual assault experience, such as witness statements, police reports, emergency room treatment notes, or other medical records may be useful in evaluating the subjective appraisal offered by the individual. Although most sexual assault victims do not report their victimization experiences to authorities, victim reports to police are more likely when the incident involved a weapon or a stranger or the victim perceived the event as "rape" (Fisher et al., 2003). Although police reports may or may not be available as collateral evidence, many sexual assault survivors disclose their assault to a friend, family member, or intimate partner and collateral information and statements about the sexual assault can be gathered from these sources. Moreover, treatment notes from emergency room care and therapy could provide collateral sources of evidence regarding the nature of the sexual assault.

4.3.   Assessment of Psychological Distress and Psychopathology

Psychological evaluation of the individual claiming injury and disability following a sexual assault must be solidly based on the official diagnostic criteria outlined in the most current version of the *Diagnostic and Statistical Manual* (DSM-IV) as well as the growing body of empirical literature related to sexual assault (DSM-IV, American Psychiatric Association, 2000). At a minimum, the psychologist should assess for the presence of PTSD and other anxiety disorders, affective disorders, substance use disorders, and psychotic symptoms, as those conditions are most likely to occur following trauma. In conducting a valid assessment of current and past psychiatric conditions, it is critical that the evaluation closely consider the presence and severity of each diagnostic criterion required to arrive at a formal diagnosis.

Training in and use of structured or semistructured diagnostic interviews helps ensure that psychiatric conditions are evaluated in detail using a standard, less subjective method. There are a number of important issues relevant to the forensic context that clinicians should consider when selecting instruments most appropriate to their purpose. In forensic evaluations, it is critical that clinicians choose measures with the strongest psychometric properties (e.g., reliability, validity, and diagnostic utility) and that allow for collection of the most detail (Carlson, 1997). Structured interviews that assess the severity of each symptom offer more flexibility in differentiating individuals with severe or mild psychopathology as well as those with subthreshold, but clinically significant symptoms (Weathers et al., 1999). Although all psychological measures are imperfect, efficient instruments are those that possess both good sensitivity (the probability that those with the disorder will be identified) and specificity (the probability that those without the disorder will score below the cutoff for the test) and are preferred. In addition, psychological examiners should consider the impact of selecting various scoring algorithms for converting continuous scores into dichotomous diagnoses on the probabilities of obtaining false positives and false negatives (Weathers et al., 1999).

4.3.1.   Structured Interviews

The psychometric properties of various structured and semistructured diagnostic interviews used to assess trauma-related sequelae have been reviewed elsewhere (Keane et al., 2000, 2003). It is beyond the scope of this chapter to comprehensively review all assessment instruments available; however, we will highlight some of the more widely used instruments. The Structured Clinical Interview for DSM (SCID) (Spitzer et al., 1990) is the most widely used structured clinical interview and provides a comprehensive examination of both Axis I and Axis II diagnoses. The SCID has demonstrated good reliability and validity. However, one limitation of the SCID is that symptoms are rated dichotomously (symptoms meet full criteria/threshold or symptoms are absent or present at the subthreshold level and do not meet full criteria) and do not account for the dimensional nature of symptomatology. Resnick et al. (1991) have recommended a modified administration of the SCID that allows the interviewer to better determine the etiology of lifetime symptoms. After identifying a multiple-trauma event history, additional probe questions could be included that determine whether each symptom occurred before or after each victimization experience. Moreover, evaluating the content of trauma-specific PTSD symptoms (e.g., nightmares, flashbacks) may help establish whether current symptoms relate to a specific victimization experience or, more generally, to multiple victimization experiences.

   The Clinician Administered PTSD Scale (CAPS) (Blake et al., 1995) is one of the most frequently used measures of PTSD. The CAPS is a semistructured interview that assesses the frequency and severity of each of the 17 PTSD symptoms as well as measuring associated features and social and occupational functioning. Both lifetime and current versions of the CAPS are available. The CAPS provides behaviorally anchored probe questions and prompts that aid the clinician in using his or her clinical training, judgment, and expertise to make scaled ratings of the individual's symptomatology. If needed, the clinician generates follow-up questions for further clarification. The CAPS yields both dichotomous scores for determining the presence of the disorder and continuous scores for quantifying the severity of symptoms. The CAPS has demonstrated excellent psychometric properties with veteran populations (Keane et al., 2000). Test–retest reliability, internal consistency (alpha = 0.95), sensitivity (the proportion of true cases correctly identified by a test; 0.84), specificity (the proportion of noncases correctly identified by a test; 0.95), and agreement with the SCID (kappa = 0.72 to 0.87) support the selection of this instrument for the diagnosis of PTSD (Weathers et al., 2001). The CAPS has been referred to as the "gold standard" measure of PTSD in combat veteran populations; however, the psychometric properties of the CAPS in nonveteran populations are not well known (Blanchard et al., 1996; Foa & Tolin, 2000).

The PTSD Symptom Scale-Interview (PSS-I) (Foa et al., 1993) is a semi-structured interview that assesses the current severity of each of the 17 symptoms of PTSD as defined by DSM-IV. The individual's responses are rated on a four-point scale (0–3), and symptoms are considered present if they are rated as 1 (once per week or less/a little) or greater. The PSS-I was developed and validated with female victims of sexual assault and nonsexual assault and has demonstrated excellent psychometric properties. The PSS-I has been shown to be internally consistent (alpha = 0.65 to 0.71) and has demonstrated high test-retest reliability (0.66 to 0.77) over a 1-month period and good concurrent validity as measured by significant correlations with other measures of PTSD symptoms. Foa and Tolin (2000) compared the psychometric properties of the CAPS and the PSS-I in civilian trauma survivors. Those researchers found that the PSS-I compares favorably to the CAPS, with both showing strong reliability. Although the PSS-I subscale scores correlate highly with the corresponding CAPS subscale scores, the PSS-I yields slightly higher sensitivity and may be more useful for detecting true cases of PTSD. The CAPS demonstrates slightly higher specificity and could perform better than the PSS-I at ruling out false positives.

4.3.2. Psychological Testing

Broad-band measures of psychopathology, such as the MMPI-2, can provide the examiner with important objective information related to the examinee's openness of self-report, level of experienced distress, and an objective indication of presence or absence of symptoms (Arbisi, 2000). As mentioned earlier, within the context of a forensic evaluation of emotional consequence after sexual assault including PTSD, several factors can serve to confound assessment. These factors include the wide range and varied presentation of the emotional consequences of sexual assault and the presence of unintentional symptom magnification or minimization in distressed individuals. For example, an assault victim may present to the clinic with somatic complaints and pain, but fail to attribute the onset of these problems and symptoms directly to the sexual assault. Further, it is common for victims of childhood sexual abuse who meet criteria for PTSD to produce elevations on MMPI-2 scales traditionally associated with exaggeration (Elhai et al., 2001). This "symptom magnification," as determined by the MMPI-2 F scale, does not necessarily reflect symptom overreporting in this population and appears associated with genuine distress (Flitter et al., 2003). Determining to what extent the clinical presentation is consistent with a diagnosis such as PTSD or is consistent in general with the emotional aftermath of a sexual assault and whether the report of symptoms is significantly distorted by exaggeration is greatly facilitated by the use of a broad-band measure of psychopathology such as the MMPI-2. The MMPI-2 provides an objective estimate of response distortion as well as objective measurement of broad dimensions of psychopathology including somatic preoccupation, depression, substance abuse/dependence, and anxiety (Arbisi, 2005).

The base rate for symptom exaggeration or malingering is higher in forensic settings than in general clinical practice and is estimated to be between 14% and 30% by surveyed forensic experts (Lees-Haley, 1992, 1997; Rogers, 1997; Rogers et al., 1994). Further, some have argued that PTSD is a particularly easy condition to feign for a number of reasons. For example, there is a broad range of symptoms associated with PTSD that are frequently reported to be highly distressing. Indeed, individuals who wish to feign PTSD can draw upon personal experience of their own nonpathological reaction to a traumatic event to provide credible appearing symptoms (Bury & Bagby, 2002; Resnick, 1997). Consequently, given the expected base rate of malingering of PTSD and the ease with which symptoms are feigned, it is critical that the examiner utilize a valid and reliable measure of symptom magnification and malingering when assessing PTSD in order to identify those individuals who are likely to be feigning the disorder. The consequence of the failure to detect feigned PTSD within the context of sexual assault is perhaps more dire than with other traumas that elicit PTSD because individuals who need to report sexual assaults frequently have difficulty disclosing this information and are reluctant to do so for fear that their complaints will not be validated. Consequently, great care must be used in assessing for symptom exaggeration or minimization to avoid false positives or false negatives (i.e., accusing someone of malingering who is in fact reporting genuine symptoms of PTSD stemming from a sexual trauma).

The MMPI-2 contains several validity scales that have demonstrated the ability to accurately distinguish between patients with genuine psychopathology and those malingering various psychiatric conditions, including PTSD (Elhai et al., 2001; Rogers et al., 2003). Indeed, the MMPI-2 F(p) scale has been shown to be the most effective MMPI-2 validity scale in the detection of malingering of psychopathology in general and "civilian" PTSD in particular compared with other routinely scored MMPI-2 validity scales (Elhai et al., 2001, 2004; Rogers et al., 2003). In contrast to the MMPI-2 F and F_B scales, the F(p) scale was designed to detect exaggeration and malingering by identifying items that were not only infrequently endorsed by the normative group but were also endorsed by fewer than 20% of psychiatric inpatients (Arbisi & Ben-Porath, 1995). By examining elevations on the MMPI-2 F(p) scale, the examiner can determine to what degree the individual resembles severely disturbed psychiatric patients in their response to the instrument. As the elevation on the F(p) scale deviates from the mean, confidence in the accuracy of the individuals self-report erodes to the point (a T score of 100) where there is no useful information being conveyed regarding the individuals' current emotional or psychological state. In particular, the F(p) scale can provide information to the evaluator that is useful in distinguishing between the person who is feigning PTSD and the highly distressed individual who has genuine PTSD.

The vast majority of the empirical literature regarding the MMPI-2 and PTSD comes from studies of combat-related trauma and were conducted with veterans (Frueh et al., 1996a, 1996b). In contrast, there are relatively few MMPI-2 studies of women who have experienced sexual assault in adulthood. The existing studies of sexual victimization involving the MMPI-2 primarily involve individuals who experienced childhood sexual abuse and domestic violence (Elhai et al., 2001; Follette et al., 1997; Morrell & Rubin, 2001). Questions have been raised regarding the advisability of generalizing MMPI-based assessment strategies developed in combat veterans with PTSD to civilians who have developed PTSD as a result of sexual assault (Gaston et al., 1996). Specifically, the PK scale (Keane et al., 1984) developed by contrasting hospitalized Vietnam combat veterans with PTSD with Vietnam combat veterans without PTSD does not appear to be particularly effective in identifying PTSD resulting from noncombat trauma (Gaston et al., 1996; Scheibe et al., 2001). Indeed, this scale primarily assesses nonspecific distress and is frequently elevated in groups of psychiatric patients without PTSD (Graham, 2000). Thus, the PK scale is less a measure of PTSD than a measure of general distress and should not be used as an independent index of the presence of PTSD in victims of sexual assault.

The report of a broad range of symptoms, including somatic and affective symptoms, the intensity of expressed distress, and the frequent comorbidity of PTSD with major depression and substance abuse, make the psychometric assessment of PTSD a challenging endeavor particularly when using a broad-band instrument such as the MMPI-2. As discussed earlier, the emotional and psychological aftermath of sexual assault can include depression, somatic preoccupation, and substance abuse. The MMPI-2 contains scales that objectively assess the presence of these problems and can provide the examiner with a broad picture of the examinee's presentation after the alleged assault. Indeed, the MMPI-2 (elevations on scales F, 2, and 8) was able to discriminate between patients with PTSD after a sexual assault and patients without PTSD (Kirz et al., 2001). The examiner can thereby determine if the report of symptoms and emotional distress as reflected by the MMPI-2 profile is broadly consistent with the emotional and psychological sequalae of sexual assault by examining the specific MMPI-2 scales that are elevated as well as the pattern of MMPI-2 scale elevations.

Recently, a new set of scales for the MMPI-2, the Restructured Clinical (RC) scales, was introduced with the goal of improving the discriminant validity of MMPI-2. This improvement in discriminant validity was accomplished through the removal of shared variance associated with general distress or demoralization from each scale and the identification of the core component of each clinical scale in order to enhance the restructured scale's uniqueness (Tellegen et al., 2003). In several independent samples, including 1,200 psychiatric outpatients and 2,424 psychiatric inpatients where relevant extra test clinical criteria were available, the RC scales have demonstrated comparable convergent validity and improved discriminant validity relative to the MMPI-2 clinical scales (Sellbom & Ben-Porath, in press Tellegen et al., 2003;). Consequently, the use of the RC scales along with the MMPI-2 clinical and content scales can assist the evaluator in disentangling the impact of general distress and demoralization and improve the identification of specific symptoms commonly associated with PTSD after sexual assault.

4.3.3.   Focused Self-Report Questionnaires

As part of a multimethod assessment strategy, an individual's performance on self-report questionnaires can be objectively compared with the clinician's ratings of PTSD and other psychopathology gained through clinical interview. In addition, an individual's score on a particular measure can be compared against relevant norms established for that instrument to provide an objective index of the intensity of current distress. However, recent experimental data showing that trauma simulators could not be reliability differentiated from trauma patients on self-report data suggest that it is important to recognize that many self-report rating instruments may be vulnerable to symptom magnification and manipulation (McGuire, 2002). Therefore, the interpretation of self-report data must be considered with caution in forensic settings and carefully examined in relation to other clinical data, including clinical interviews and objective psychological testing.

With this caveat, a number of standardized self-report instruments have been developed for measuring PTSD symptoms (Keane et al., 2003) and other comorbid symptoms such as depression (Nezu et al., 2000), anxiety (Antony et al., 2001), and substance use (Miller et al., 1995). It is beyond the scope of this chapter to comprehensively review all focused self-report questionnaires available. [See Keane et al. (2003) for a review.] Instead, we highlight some of the more widely used instruments here.

One of the first self-report scales developed to assess posttrauma distress was the Impact of Events Scale (IES) (Horowitz et al., 1979). This measure has been widely used as a measure of subjective distress associated with exposure to traumatic events. The IES yields two reliable subscale scores (Reexperiencing/Intrusion and Avoidance/Numbing). This measure does not correspond to the 17 symptoms outlined in the DSM-IV criteria for PTSD. Although a revised version that includes hyperarousal symptoms has demonstrated high internal consistency, adequate test–retest reliability and factor structure have not been supported (Creamer et al., 2003; Weiss & Marmar, 1997). The IES may be a reasonable choice for evaluating "current subjective distress" (Joseph, 2000), but it appears that students are able to easily simulate responses on the IES that are similar to responses provided by genuinely injured patients (Lees-Haley, 1990). The utility of the IES was also recently questioned by Lees-Haley and colleagues (2001) after nearly three-fourths of undergraduate students scored in the medium to highly distressed range on the IES in response to ratings of an event that clearly did not meet traumatic stressor criteria according to DSM-IV criteria for PTSD. Given these concerns, the IES is not recommended for forensic evaluations.

Developed by researchers at the National Center for PTSD in Boston, Massachusetts, the PTSD Checklist-Civilian Version (PCL-C) (Weathers et al., 1994) is a 17-item self-report rating scale designed to assess the presence and severity of distress corresponding with DSM-IV criteria for re-experiencing, avoidance, and hyperarousal symptoms of PTSD. The PCL-C has demonstrated high internal consistency (alpha = 0.94 for the total score) (Ruggiero et al., 2003) and strong test–retest reliability (0.88) during a 1-week period. The PCL-C has been shown to correlate highly with the CAPS among victims of MVAs and sexual assault (Blanchard et al., 1996). Correlations between the PCL-C and other measures of PTSD were higher than those obtained between the PCL-C and more global measures of distress, suggesting some evidence for discriminant validity (Ruggiero et al., 2003).

As noted earlier, the PDS (Foa et al., 1997) was designed to assess PTSD diagnosis and symptom severity corresponding to DSM-IV criteria and has been validated using a diverse sample of men and women who have experienced a range of traumatic stressors. After screening for exposure to a range of potentially traumatic events, individuals are instructed to indicate which event has been the most distressing in the past month and this event is further evaluated to determine whether Criterion A is met. In the next subsection, individuals provide ratings of the frequency of 17 items that directly correspond with DSM-IV criteria for PTSD. The last section includes items that assess impairment in different areas of life functioning. The PDS can be scored to determine whether the individual meets DSM-IV criteria for the diagnosis of PTSD and also yields a symptom-severity score. The mean symptom-severity score for individuals who met SCID criteria for PTSD was 33.59 (SD = 9.96), compared to those with no PTSD diagnosis (12.54) (SD = 10.54). The PDS has demonstrated high internal consistency (alpha = 0.92) and strong test–retest reliability (kappa = 0.74) with 87% agreement between diagnoses obtained at two time periods. Convergent validity of the PDS is demonstrated by good agreement (82%) between the PDS and SCID diagnosis. However, scores on the PDS correlated with measures of PTSD, depression, and anxiety, raising the question of whether the PDS is a general measure of psychological distress versus a specific measure of PTSD. Foa and colleagues suggest that this finding may be the result of symptoms of PTSD overlapping with symptoms of depression and general anxiety. Correlational patterns between corresponding subscales of the PDS and another measure of posttrauma symptoms lend support to the construct validity of the PDS.

The Distressing Life Events Questionnaire (DEQ) (Kubany et al., 2000) was designed to assess symptoms of PTSD and associated problems and includes 17 items corresponding to each of the symptoms included in the DSM-IV diagnosis of PTSD. The psychometric properties of the DEQ have been evaluated using samples of combat veterans, treatment-seeking women survivors of childhood sexual abuse, rape, and partner abuse, and women with histories of prostitution, substance abuse, and sexual abuse. The instrument has demonstrated high internal consistency (alpha = 0.93) and test–retest reliability of 0.95 for the total DEQ symptom score. In samples of women as well as combat veterans, evidence for convergent validity comes from high correlations between the DEQ and other measures of PTSD (e.g., CAPS and Modified PTSD Symptom Scale). Finally, the DEQ was not correlated with scores on a measure of social desirability, providing evidence for the instrument's discriminant validity.

4.4. Assessment of Functional Impairment and Damages

A significant challenge in the evaluation of PTSD resulting from sexual victimization is to establish the level of impairment experienced by the traumatized individual. As mentioned earlier, the establishment of causality is particularly challenging under these circumstances. One of the challenges is the issue of "false imputation" (Resnick, 1997) (i.e., where individuals erroneously specify an event that directly causes the development of a set of symptoms that produces the current level of subjective distress or genuine disability). Indeed, the claim that a sexual trauma directly and substantially resulted in functional impairment and distress is frequently the disputed issue that led to the forensic assessment in the first place. A rather interesting observation that illustrates the challenge in conducting assessment of PTSD after sexual assault and establishing disability comes from studies of former POWs. As a group, former POWs who met criteria for PTSD produced normal limits MMPI-2 (Engdahl et al., 1996). Although the POWs continued to experience symptoms of PTSD over 40 years after the traumatic event, as a group they generally were not functionally disabled (Goldstein et al., 1987). On the other hand, PTSD symptoms that do not meet full criteria for the disorder can be debilitating (Amaya-Jackson et al., 1999). Marshall and colleagues (2001) found that levels of impairment increased with increasing psychiatric comorbidity in a cohort of adults with subthreshold PTSD. Further, the level of impairment increased with increasing numbers of PTSD symptoms that fell to a subthreshold level. Consequently, whether an individual meets diagnostic criteria for PTSD does not necessarily indicate functional impairment/disability (see Engdahl et al., 1996). Functional disability must be evaluated separately and tied directly to the psychiatric symptoms produced in response to sexual victimization.

In reaching a decision regarding the degree of impairment and disability resulting from PTSD after sexual trauma, the evaluator will need to rely upon multiple sources of information, including the patient's self-report and observations made during the course of the evaluation. The evaluator will need to answer questions such as the following: Are behavioral observations during the evaluation consistent or discrepant with self-report? Do specific symptoms of PTSD or another condition directly resulting from the sexual assault compromise or prevent the individual from performing all or some of the principle duties of their primary occupation? With accommodations, could the individual perform these duties? For example, if an individual employed as a health care professional was sexually assaulted by a patient at work on a late shift, then similar duties and schedule of work hours could serve as triggers for PTSD symptoms and these triggers may likely generalize away from the workplace to other settings. Under these circumstances, could the individual be provided with an alternate work shift, and, with support, function adequately in the workplace? The examiner must also bear in mind that a preexisting psychiatric condition could be exacerbated by a sexual assault, and must therefore attempt to quantify the effect of the sexual victimization by establishing a decrement in functioning since the trauma.

Given that conclusions about permanent impairment can only be made reliably after the examinee has received a sufficient trial of an appropriate treatment, the psychologist may be asked to evaluate the adequacy of the treatment provided to the examinee for the condition. A number of empirically supported pharmacological treatments (Friedman et al., 2000) and cognitive–behavioral interventions (Rothbaum et al., 2000) exist for treating specific psychological problems associated with sexual assault.

5.   Conclusions

Within the context of *Daubert v. Merrell Dow Pharmaceuticals* (1993), in order to be judged admissible, expert testimony related to PTSD and other psychological impairments following sexual victimization must be informed by the scientific literature and accurately reflect that literature. Based on a review of the literature, it becomes evident that PTSD following sexual victimization appears to present clinically in a somewhat distinct fashion when compared with PTSD stemming from military combat (Deering et al., 1996). Victims of sexual trauma generally present with depression, suicidal ideation, somatic complaints, sexual dysfunction, and alcohol or other drug abuse issues, and frequently do not initially identify the sexual assault as a precipitating event (Naugle et al., 2003). Additionally, victims of adult sexual trauma are also often victims of childhood sexual abuse. These characteristics differentiate the clinical presentation of individuals who have survived sexual victimization from survivors of other forms of trauma and may not be completely captured under the DSM-IV PTSD rubric. At this point, the differences in clinical presentation between individuals who develop PTSD as a result of sexual trauma and those who develop PTSD as a result of other types of trauma are confounded by the fact that sexually victimized populations studied thus far have been exclusively women, while much of the descriptive data regarding PTSD has been derived from male combat veterans (Cusack et al., 2002; Orsillo et al., 2002).

Given the characteristic clinical presentation of sexually victimized women, the literature suggests that most individuals recover from acute symptoms within 3 months of the traumatic event (Rothbaum et al., 1992). Of those who had been symptomatic 1 year after the sexual assault, 50% recovered over the next several years. Consequently, for the forensic examiner, the natural course of PTSD symptoms after sexual victimization is an important factor to consider when evaluating individual victims. The greater the length of time between the assault and the evaluation, particularly if this period was associated with the provision of empirically-supported treatment for psychological problems associated with sexual trauma, the less the likelihood that the individual will continue to experience debilitating psychological symptoms.

In conducting an evaluation for PTSD and subsequent disability after a sexual assault, it is essential that the examiner establish the presence and/or absence of symptoms, demonstrate that these symptoms are causally related to the sexual trauma, and establish that the symptoms result in significant impairment through the use of objective procedures and techniques that meet *Daubert* standards. A multimethod assessment approach that integrates the following is recommended: (1) structured or semistructured interviews [e.g., SCID, CAPS (Rogers, 2001; Weathers et al., 2001)]; (2) a broad-band measure of psychopathology that contains validity indices for assessing the presence or absence of self-report distortion and objectively measures symptoms [e.g., MMPI-2 (Boccaccini & Brodsky, 1999; Elhai et al., 2004; Franklin et al., 2002; Rogers et al., 2003)]; and (3) focused self-report questionnaires [e.g., PDS (Flitter et al., 2003; Foa et al., 1997)].

That being said, many of the studies of the objective assessment of PTSD, particularly with regard to the MMPI-2, have been conducted with male combat veterans. To our knowledge, there is a single MMPI-2 study that examines sexual assault in adulthood and no studies of adult victim of sexual assault who are claiming disability and seeking compensation. Consequently, there is a sore need for such studies to support the use of psychometric and objective measures of PTSD in populations who experienced sexual victimization as adults.

Once a diagnosis is established, the degree of impairment must be tied to the presence of symptoms resulting from the trauma. In the case of a pre-existing condition, any impairment associated with that condition must be shown to have been exacerbated by the traumatic event. It is important to recognize that simply because the diagnostic criteria for PTSD are met, significant functional or vocational impairment may not follow (Engdahl et al.,

1996). Consequently, a thorough review of social and occupational functioning must be undertaken in order to determine whether the presence of PTSD or other psychological symptoms effectively compromises the ability of the individual to engage in activities of daily living or principal occupational duties.

References

Amaya-Jackson, L., Davidson, J. R. T., Hughes, D. C., Swartz, M., Reynolds, V., George, L. K., & Blazer, D. G. (1999). Functional impairment and utilization of services associated with Posttraumatic stress in the community. *Journal of Traumatic Stress, 12*, 709–724.

American Psychiatric Association. (2000). Diagnositic and Statistical Manual of Mental Disorders (4th ed.) Washington, D.C. Author.

Antony, M. M., Orsillo, S. M., & Roemer, L. (2001). *Practitioner's Guide to Empirically Based Measures of Anxiety.* New York: Kluwer.

Arbisi, P. A. (2005). Use of the MMPI-2 in personal injury and disability evaluations. In J. N. Butcher (Ed.), *Practitioners Handbook for the MMPI-2.* Washington, DC: American Psychological Association, pp. 407–442.

Arbisi, P. A. & Ben-Porath, Y. S. (1995). An MMPI-2 infrequent response scale for use with psychopathological populations: The Infrequency-Psychopathology Scale (F(p)). *Psychological Assessment, 7*, 424–431.

Atkeson, B., Calhoun, K. S., Resick, P. A., & Ellis, E. (1982). Victims of rape: Repeated assessment of depressive symptoms. *Journal of Consulting and Clinical Psychology, 50*, 96–102.

Becker, J. V., Skinner, L. J., Abel, G. G., & Cichon, J. (1986). Level of Postassault sexual functioning in rape and incest victims. *Archives of Sexual Behavior, 15*, 37–49.

Blake, D. D., Weathers, F. W., Nagy, L. M., Kaloupek, D. G., Charney, D. S., & Keane, T. M. (1995). Clinician-administered PTSD Scale for DSM-IV. *Journal of Traumatic Stress, 8*, 75–90.

Blanchard, E. B., Jones-Alexander, J., Buckley, T. C., & Forneris, C. A. (1996). Psychometric properties of the PTSD Checklist (PCL). *Behaviour Research & Therapy, 34*, 669–673.

Boccaccini, M. T. & Brodsky, S. L. (1999). Diagnostic test usage by forensic psychologists in emotional injury cases. *Professional Psychology: Research and Practice, 30*, 253–259.

Boeschen, L. E., Sales, B. D., & Koss, M. P. (1998). Rape trauma experts in the courtroom. *Psychology, Public Policy, & Law, 4*, 414–432.

Bonanno, G. A. (2004). Loss, trauma, and human resilience: Have we underestimated the human capacity to thrive after extremely aversive events? *American Psychologist, 59*, 20–28.

Brady, K. T., Killeen, T. K., Brewerton, T., & Lucerini, S. (2000). Comorbidity of psychiatric disorders and Posttraumatic Stress Disorder. *Journal of Clinical Psychiatry, 61*, 22–32.

Breslau, N., Davis, G. C., Andreski, P., & Peterson, E. (1991). Traumatic events and Posttraumatic Stress Disorder in an urban population of young adults. *Archives of General Psychiatry, 48*, 216–222.

Breslau, N., Davis, G. C., Peterson, E. L., & Schultz, L. (1997). Psychiatric sequelae of Posttraumatic Stress Disorder in women. *Archives of General Psychiatry, 54*, 81–87.

Breslau, N., Kessler, R. C., Chilcoat, H. D., Schultz, L. R., Davis, G. C., & Andreski, P. (1998). Trauma and Posttraumatic Stress Disorder in the community. *Archives of General Psychiatry, 55,* 626–632.

Bryant, R. A., Marosszeky, J. E., Crooks, J., & Gurka, J. A. (2000). Posttraumatic Stress Disorder after severe traumatic brain injury. *American Journal of Psychiatry, 157,* 629–631.

Burgess, A. W. & Holmstrom, L. L. (1974). Rape trauma syndrome. *American Journal of Psychiatry, 131,* 981–986.

Bury, A. S. & Bagby, R. M. (2002). The detection of feigned uncoached and coached Posttraumatic Stress Disorder with the MMPI-2 in a sample of workplace accident victims. *Psychological Assessment, 14,* 472–483.

Carlson, E. B. (1997). *Trauma Assessment: A Clinician's Guide.* New York: Guilford Press.

Cloitre, M., Scarvalone, P., & Difede, J. (1997). Posttraumatic Stress Disorder, self- and interpersonal dysfunction among sexually retraumatized women. *Journal of Traumatic Stress, 10,* 437–452.

Clum, G. A., Calhoun, K. S., & Kimerling, R. (2000). Associations among symptoms of depression and Posttraumatic Stress Disorder and self-reported health in sexually assaulted women. *Journal of Nervous & Mental Disease, 188,* 671–678.

Creamer, M., Bell, R., & Failla, S. (2003). Psychometric properties of the Impact of Event Scale-Revised. *Behaviour Research and Therapy, 41,* 1489–1496.

Cusack, K., Falsetti, S., & De Arellano, M. (2002). Gender considerations in the psychometric assessment of PTSD. In R. Kimerling, P. Ouimette & J. Wolfe (Eds.). *Gender and PTSD.* New York: Guilford Press, pp. 150–176.

Daubert v. Merrell Dow Pharmaceuticals. (1993). 727 F. Supp. 570 (S.D. Cal. 1989), aff'd, 951 F.2d 1128 (9th Cir. 1990), vacated, 113 S. Ct. 2786.

Deering, C. G., Glover, S. G., Ready, D., Eddleman, H. C., & Alarcon, R. D. (1996). Unique patterns of comorbidity in Posttraumatic Stress Disorder from different sources of trauma. *Comprehensive Psychiatry, 37,* 336–346.

DeLahunta, E. A. & Baram, D. A. (1997). Sexual assault. *Clinical Obstetrics and Gynecology, 40,* 648–660.

Easterbrook, J. A. (1959). The effect of emotion on cue utilization and the organization of behavior. *Psychological Review, 66,* 183–201.

Ehlers, A., Mayou, R. A., & Bryant, B. (1998). Psychological predictors of chronic Posttraumatic Stress Disorder after motor vehicle accidents. *Journal of Abnormal Psychology, 107,* 508–519.

Elhai, J. D., Flitter, J. M. Koltz, Gold, S. N., & Sellers, A. H. (2001). Identifying subtypes of women survivors of childhood sexual abuse: An MMPI-2 cluster analysis. *Journal of Traumatic Stress, 14,* 157–175.

Elhai, J. D., Gold, S. N., Sellers, A. H., & Dorfman, W. I. (2001). The detection of malingered Posttraumatic Stress Disorder with MMPI-2 fake bad indices. *Assessment, 8,* 221–236.

Elhai, J. D., Naifeh, J. A., Zucker, I. S., Gold, S. N., Deitsch, S. E., & Frueh, B. C. (2004). Discriminating malingered from genuine civilian Posttraumatic Stress Disorder: A validation of three MMPI-2 infrequency scales (F, Fp, and Fptsd). *Assessment, 11,* 139–144.

Engdahl, B. E., Eberly, R. E., & Blake, J. D. (1996). Assessment of Posttraumatic Stress Disorder in World War II veterans. *Psychological Assessment, 8,* 445–449.

Fisher, B. S., Daigle, L. E., Cullen, F. T., & Turner, M. G. (2003). Reporting sexual victimization to the police and others. *Criminal Justice and Behavior, 30,* 6–38.

Flitter, J. M. Klotz, Elhai, J. D., & Gold, S. N. (2003). MMPI-2 F scale elevations in adult victims of child sexual abuse. *Journal of Traumatic Stress, 16,* 269–274.

Foa, E. B., Cashman, L., Jaycox, L., & Perry, K. (1997). The validation of a self-report measure of Posttraumatic Stress Disorder: The Posttraumatic Diagnostic Scale. *Psychological Assessment, 9,* 445–451.

Foa, E.B., Riggs, D.S., Daneu, C.V., & Rothbaum, B.O. (1993). Reliability and validity of a brief instrument for assessing Posttraumatic Stress Disorder. *Journal of Traumatic Stress, 6,* 459–473.

Foa, E. B. & Tolin, D. F. (2000). Comparison of the PTSD Symptom Scale-Interview Version and the Clinician-Administered PTSD Scale. *Journal of Traumatic Stress, 13,* 181–191.

Follette, V. M., Polusny, M. M., Bechtle, A. E., & Naugle, A. E. (1996). Cumulative trauma effects: The impact of child sexual abuse, adult sexual abuse, and spouse abuse. *Journal of Traumatic Stress, 9,* 15–25.

Follette, W. C., Naugle, A. E., & Follette, V. M. (1997). MMPI-2 profiles of adult women with child sexual abuse histories: Cluster-analytic findings. *Journal of Consulting and Clinical Psychology, 65,* 858–866.

Foy, D. W. (1992). Introduction and description of the disorder. In D. W. Foy (Ed.), *Treating PTSD: Cognitive–Behavioral Strategies.* New York: Guilford Press, pp. 1–12.

Franklin, C. L., Repasky, S. A., Thompson, K. E., Shelton, S. A., & Uddo, M. (2002). Differentiating overreporting and extreme distress: MMPI-2 use with compensation-seeking veterans with PTSD. *Journal of Personality Assessment, 79,* 274–285.

Friedman, M. J., Davidson, J. R. T., Mellman, T. A., & Southwick, S. M. (2000). Pharmacology. In E. B. Foa, T. M. Keane, & M. J. Friedman (Eds.). *Effective Treatments for PTSD.* New York: Guilford Press, pp. 84–105.

Frueh, B. C., Hamner, M. B., Cahill, S. P., Gold, P. B., & Hamlin, K. L. (2000). Apparent symptom overreporting in combat veterans evaluated for PTSD. *Clinical Psychology Review, 20,* 853–885.

Frueh, B. C., Smith, D. W., & Barker, S. E. (1996a). Compensation seeking status and psychometric assessment of combat veterans seeking treatment for PTSD. *Journal of Traumatic Stress, 9,* 427–439.

Frueh, B. C., Smith, D. W., & Libet, J. M. (1996b). Racial differences on psychological measures in combat veterans seeking treatment for PTSD. *Journal of Personality Assessment, 66,* 41–53.

Galea, S., Ahern, J., Resnick, H., Kilpatrick, D., Bucuvalas, M., Gold, J., & Vlahov, D. (2002). Psychological sequelae of the September 11 terrorist attacks in New York City. *New England Journal of Medicine, 346,* 982–987.

Gaston, L., Brunet, A., Koszycki, D., & Bradwejn, J. (1996). MMPI profiles of acute and chronic PTSD in civilian samples. *Journal of Traumatic Stress, 9,* 817–832.

Gaughwin, P. C. (2001). Trauma evidence and litigation. *Australian & New Zealand Journal of Psychiatry, 35,* 857.

Gilboa-Schechtman, E. & Foa, E. B. (2001). Patterns of recovery from trauma: The use of intraindividual analysis. *Journal of Abnormal Psychology, 110,* 392–400.

Gold, S. R., Milan, L. D., Mayall, A., & Johnson, A. E. (1994). A cross-validation study of the Trauma Symptom Checklist: The role of mediating variables. *Journal of Interpersonal Violence, 9,* 12–26.

Goldstein, G., van Kammen, W., Shelly, C., & Miller, D. J. (1987). Survivors of imprisonment in the Pacific theater during World War II. *American Journal of Psychiatry, 144,* 1210–1213.

Goodman, L. A., Salyers, M. P., Mueser, K. T., Rosenberg. S. D., Swartz, M., Essock, S. M., Osher, F. C., Butterfield, M. I., & Swanson, J. (2001). Recent victimization in women and men with severe mental illness: Prevalence and correlates. *Journal of Traumatic Stress, 14,* 615–632.

Graham, J. R. (2000). *MMPI-2: Assessing Personality and Psychopathology,* (3rd ed.). New York: Oxford University Press.

Halligan, S. L., Michael, T, Clark, D. M., & Ehlers, A. (2003). Posttraumatic Stress Disorder following assault: The role of cognitive processing, trauma memory, and appraisals. *Journal of Consulting and Clinical Psychology, 71,* 419–431.

Hankin, C. S., Spiro, A., Miller, D. R., & Kazis, L. (1999). Mental disorders and mental health treatment among U.S. Department of Veterans Affairs outpatients: The veterans health study. *American Journal of Psychiatry, 156,* 1924–1930.

Harvey, A. G., Bryant, R. A., & Dang, S. T. (1998). Autobiographical memory in acute Stress Disorder. *Journal of Consulting and Clinical Psychology, 66,* 500–506.

Horowitz, M. J., Wilner, N., & Alvarez, W. (1979). Impact of Event Scale: A measure of subjective stress. *Psychosomatic Medicine, 41,* 209–218.

Joseph, S. (2000). Psychometric evaluation of Horowitz's Impact of Event Scale: A review. *Journal of Traumatic Stress, 13,* 101–113.

Keane, T. M., Buckley, T. C., & Miller, M. W. (2003). Forensic psychological assessment in PTSD. In R. I. Simon (Ed.), *Posttraumatic Stress Disorder in Litigation: Guidelines for Forensic Assessment* (2nd ed.). Washington, DC: American Psychiatric Publishing, Inc., pp. 119–140.

Keane, T. M., Mallyo, P. F., & Fairbank, J. A. (1984). Empirical development of an MMPI subscale for the assessment of Posttraumatic Stress Disorder. *Journal of Consulting and Clinical Psychology, 52,* 888–891.

Keane, T. M., Weathers, F. W., & Foa, E. B. (2000). Diagnosis and assessment. In E. B. Foa, T. M. Keane, M.J. Friedman. (Eds.), *Effective treatments for PTSD: Practice Guidelines from the International Society for Traumatic Stress Studies.* New York: Guilford Press, pp. 18–36.

Kessler, R. C., Sonnega, A., Bromet, E., Hughes, M., & Nelson, C. B. (1995). Posttraumatic Stress Disorder in the National Comorbidity Survey. *Archives of General Psychiatry, 52,* 1048–1060.

Kilpatrick, D. G., Acierno, R., Resnick, H. S., Saunders, B. E., & Best, C. L. (1997). A 2-year longitudinal analysis of the relationships between violent assault and substance use in women. *Journal of Consulting and Clinical Psychology, 65,* 834–847.

Kilpatrick, D. G., Best, C. L., Saunders, B. E., & Veronen, L. J. (1988). Rape in marriage and in dating relationships: How bad is it for mental health? *Annals of the New York Academy of Sciences, 528,* 335–344.

Kilpatrick, D. G., Resick P. A., & Veronen, L. J. (1981). Effects of a rape experience: A longitudinal study. *Journal of Social Issues, 37,* 105–121.

Kimerling, R. & Calhoun, K. S. (1994). Somatic symptoms, social support, and treatment seeking among sexual assault victims. *Journal of Consulting and Clinical Psychology, 62,* 333–340.

Kirz, J. L., Drescher, K. D., Klein, J. L., Gusman, F. D., & Schwartz, M. F. (2001). MMPI-2 assessment of differential Posttraumatic Stress Disorder patterns in combat veterans and sexual assault victims. *Journal of Interpersonal Violence, 16,* 619–639.

Koss, M. P., Bailey, J. A., Yuam, N. P., Herrera, V. M., & Lichter, E. L. (2003). Depression and PTSD in survivors of male violence: Research and training initiatives to facilitate recovery. *Psychology of Women Quarterly, 27,* 130–142.

Kubany, E. S., Leisen, M. B., Kaplan, A. S., & Kelly, M. P. (2000). Validation of a brief measure of Posttraumatic Stress Disorder: The Distressing Event Questionnaire (DEQ). *Psychological Assessment, 12,* 197–209.

Kubany, E. S., Leisen, M. B., Kaplan, A. S., Watson, S. B., Haynes, S. N., Owens, J. A., & Burns, K. (2000). Development and preliminary validation of a brief broad-spectrum measure of trauma exposure: The Traumatic Life Events Questionnaire. *Psychological Assessment, 12,* 210–224.

Kulka, R. A., Schlenger, W. E., Fairbank, J. A., Hough, R. L., Jordan, B. K., Marmar, C. R., & Weiss, D. S. (1990). *Trauma and the Vietnam War Generation: Report on Findings from the National Vietnam Veterans Readjustment Study.* New York: Brunner/Mazel.

Lang, A. J., Rodgers, C. S., Laffaye, C., Satz, L. E., Dresselhaus, T. R., & Stein, M. B. (2003). Sexual trauma, Posttraumatic Stress Disorder, and health behavior. *Behavioral Medicine, 28,* 150–158.

Lees-Haley, P. R. (1990). Malingering mental disorder on the Impact of Event Scale (IES): Toxic exposure and cancerphobia. *Journal of Traumatic Stress, 3,* 315–321.

Lees-Haley, P. R. (1992). Efficacy of MMPI-2 validity scale and MCMI-II modifier scales for detecting spurious PTSD claims: F, F-K, Fake Bad Scale, Ego Strength, Subtle-Obvious subscales, DIS, and DEB. *Journal of Clinical Psychology, 48,* 681–689.

Lees-Haley, P. R. (1997). MMPI-2 base rates for 492 personal injury plaintiffs: Implications and challenges for forensic assessment. *Journal of Clinical Psychology, 53,* 745–755.

Lees-Haley, P. R., Price, J. R., Williams, C. W., & Betz, B. P. (2001). Use of the Impact of Events Scale in the assessment of emotional distress and PTSD may produce misleading results. *Journal of Forensic Neuropsychology, 2,* 45–52.

Leserman, J., Drossman, D. A., Li, Z., Toomey, T. C., Nachman, G., & Glogau L. (1996). Sexual and physical abuse history in gastroenterology practice: How types of abuse impact health status. *Psychosomatic Medicine, 58,* 4–15.

Letourneau, E. J., Resnick, H. S., Kilpatrick, D. G., Saunders, B. E., & Best, C. L. (1996). Comorbidity of sexual problems and Posttraumatic Stress Disorder in female crime victims. *Behavior Therapy, 27,* 321–336.

Levy, M. I. & Rosenberg, S. E. (2003). The "eggshell plaintiff" revisited: Causation of mental damages in civil litigation. *Mental & Physical Disability Law Reporter, 27,* 204–206.

Long, B. L. (1994). Psychiatric diagnoses in sexual harassment cases. *Bulletin of the American Academy of Psychiatry & the Law, 22,* 195–203.

Marshall, R. D., Olfson, M., Hellman, F., Blanco, C., Guardino, M., & Struening, E. L. (2001). Comorbidity, impairment, and suicidality in subthreshold PTSD. *American Journal of Psychiatry, 158,* 1467–1473.

McGowan, M. G. & Helms, J. L. (2003). The utility of the expert witness in a rape case: Reconsidering rape trauma syndrome. *Journal of Forensic Psychology Practice, 3,* 51–60.

McGuire, B. E. (2002). Malingered Posttraumatic stress symptoms on the Impact of Event Scale. *Legal and Criminological Psychology, 7,* 165–171.

McNally, R. J. (2003a). Progress and controversy in the study of Posttraumatic Stress Disorder. *Annual Review of Psychology, 54,* 229–252.

McNally, R. J. (2003b). Psychological mechanisms in acute response to trauma. *Biological Psychiatry, 53,* 779–788.

Merrill, L. L., Newell, C. E., Thomsen, C. J., Gold, S. R., Milner, J. S., Koss, M. P., & Rosswork, S. G. (1999). Childhood abuse and sexual revictimization in a female Navy recruit sample. *Journal of Traumatic Stress, 12,* 211–225.

Messman-Moore, T. L. & Long, P. J. (2003). The role of childhood sexual abuse sequelae in the sexual revictimization of women: An empirical review and theoretical reformulation. *Clinical Psychology Review, 23,* 537–571.

Miller, W. R., Westerberg, V. S., & Waldron, H. B. (1995). Evaluating alcohol problems in adults and adolescents. In R. K. Hester & W. R. Miller (Eds.), *Handbook of Alcoholism Treatment Approaches: Effective Alternatives.* Boston, MA: Allyn and Bacon, pp. 61–88.

Morrell, J. S., & Rubin, J. L. (2001). The Minnesota Multiphasic Personality Inventory-2, Posttraumatic Stress Disorder, and women domestic violence survivors. *Professional Psychology: Research and Practice, 32,* 151–156.

Murdoch, M., Nelson, D., & Fortier, L. (2003). Time, gender, and regional trends in the application for service-related Posttraumatic Stress Disorder disability benefits, 1980–1998. *Military Medicine, 168,* 662–670.

National Center for Veteran Analysis and Statistics (1995). *National Survey of Veterans (NSV9503).* Washington DC: U.S. Government Printing Office.

Naugle, A. E., Bell, K. M., & Polusny, M. A. (2003). Clinical considerations for treating sexually revictimized women. *National Center for PTSD Clinical Quarterly, 12,* 12–16.

Nezu, A. M., Ronan, G. F., Meadows, E. A., & McClure, K. S. (2000). *Practitioner's Guide to Empirically Based Measures of Depression.* New York: Kluwer.

Nisbett, R. E. & Wilson, T. D. (1977). The halo effect: Evidence for unconscious alteration of judgments. *Journal of Personality & Social Psychology, 35,* 250–256.

Nishith, P., Mechanic, M. B., & Resick, P. A. (2000). Prior interpersonal trauma: The contribution to current PTSD symptoms in female rape victims. *Journal of Abnormal Psychology, 109,* 20–25.

Nishith, P., Resick, P. A., & Mueser, K. T. (2001). Sleep difficulties and alcohol use motives in female rape victims with Posttraumatic Stress Disorder. *Journal of Traumatic Stress, 14,* 469–479.

Norris, F. H., Foster, J. D., & Weisshaar, D. L. (2002). The epidemiology of sex differences in PTSD across developmental, societal, and research contexts. In R. Kimerling, P. Ouimette, & J. Wolfe (Eds.). *Gender and PTSD.* New York: Guilford Press, pp. 3–42.

Orsillo, S. M., Raja, S., & Hammond, C. (2002). Gender issues in PTSD with comorbid mental health disorders. In R. Kimerling, P. Ouimette, & J. Wolfe (Eds.). *Gender and PTSD.* New York: Guilford Press, pp. 207–231.

Ozer, E. J., Best, S. R., Lipsey, T. L., & Weiss, D. S. (2003). Predictors of Posttraumatic Stress Disorder and symptoms in adults: A meta-analysis. *Psychological Bulletin, 129,* 52–71.

Polusny, M. A. & Follette, V. M. (1995). Long-term correlates of child sexual abuse: Theory and review of the empirical literature. *Applied & Preventative Psychology, 4,* 143–166.

Resnick, H. S., Acierno, R., & Kilpatrick, D. G. (1997). Health impact of interpersonal violence 2: Medical and mental health outcomes. *Behavioral Medicine, 23,* 65–78.

Resnick, H. S., Kilpatrick, D. G., & Lipovsky, J. A. (1991). Assessment of rape-related Posttraumatic Stress Disorder: Stressor and symptom dimensions. *Psychological Assessment, 3,* 561–572.

Resnick, H. S., Kilpatrick, D. G., Dansky, B. S., Saunders, B. E., & Best, C. L. (1993). Prevalence of civilian trauma and Posttraumatic Stress Disorder in a representative national sample of women. *Journal of Consulting and Clinical Psychology, 61,* 984–991.

Resnick, P. J. (1997). Malingering of Posttraumatic disorders. In R. Rogers (Ed.). *Clinical Assessment of Malingering and Deception,* 2nd ed. New York: Guilford Press, pp. 130–152.

Resnick, P. J. (2003). Guidelines for evaluation of malingering patients in PTSD. In R. I. Simon (Ed.). *Posttraumatic Stress Disorder in Litigation: Guidelines for Forensic Assessment,* 2nd ed. pp. 187–205. Washington, D.C.: American Psychiatric Publishing Inc.

Rogers, R. (1997). Introduction. In R. Rogers (Ed.) *Clinical Assessment of Malingering and Deception,* 2nd ed. New York: Guilford Press, pp. 1–22.

Rogers, R. (2001). *Handbook of Diagnostic and Structured Interviewing.* New York: Guilford Press.

Rogers, R., Sewell, K. W., & Goldstein, A. (1994). Explanatory models of malingering: A prototypical analysis. *Law and Human Behavior, 8,* 543–552.

Rogers, R., Sewell, K. W., Martin, M. A., & Vitacco, M. J. (2003). Detection of feigned mental disorders: A Meta-analysis of the MMPI-2 and malingering. *Assessment, 10,* 160–177.

Rothbaum, B. O., Foa, E. B., Riggs, D. S., Murdock, T., & Walsh, W. (1992). A prospective examination of symptoms of Posttraumatic Stress Disorder in rape victims. *Journal of Traumatic Stress, 5,* 455–475.

Rothbaum, B. O., Meadows, E. A., Resick, P., & Foy, D. W. (2000). In E. B. Foa, T. M. Keane, & M. J. Friedman (Eds.). *Effective Treatments for PTSD.* New York: Guilford Press, pp. 60–83.

Roy-Byrne, P. P., Russo, J., Michelson, E., Zatzick, D., Pitman, R. K., & Berliner, L. (2004). Risk factors and outcome in ambulatory assault victims presenting to the acute emergency department setting: Implications for secondary prevention studies in PTSD. *Depression & Anxiety, 19,* 77–84.

Ruggiero, K. J., Del Ben, K., Scotti, J. R., & Rabalais, A. E. (2003). Psychometric properties of the PTSD Checklist-Civilian Version. *Journal of Traumatic Stress, 16,* 495–502.

Saladin, M. E., Drobes, D. J., Coffey, S. F., Dansky, B. S., Brady, K. T., & Kilpatrick, D. G. (2003). PTSD symptom severity as a predictor of cue-elicited drug craving in victims of violent crime. *Addictive Behaviors, 28,* 1611–1629.

Scheibe, S., Bagby, R. M., Miller, L. S., & Dorian, B. J. (2001). Assessing Posttraumatic Stress Disorder with the MMPI-2 in a sample of workplace accident victims. *Psychological Assessment, 13,* 369–374.

Siegel, J. M., Golding, J. M., Stein, J. A., Burnam, M. A., et al. (1990). Reactions to sexual assault: A community study. *Journal of Interpersonal Violence, 5,* 229–246.

Simon, R. I. (Ed). (2003). *Posttraumatic Stress Disorder in Litigation: Guidelines for Forensic Assessment,* 2nd ed. Washington, DC: American Psychiatric Publishing, Inc.

Spitzer, R. L., Williams, J. B. W., Gibbon, M., & First, M. A. (1990). *Structured Clinical Interview for DSM-III-R.* Washington, DC: American Psychiatric Press.

Sutker, P. B., Allain, A. N., & Winstead, D. K. (1993). Psychopathology and psychiatric diagnoses of World War II Pacific theater prisoner of war survivors and combat veterans. *American Journal of Psychiatry, 150,* 240–245.

Tellegen, A., Ben-Porath, Y. S., McNulty, J. L., Arbisi, P. A., Graham, J. R., & Kaemmer, B. (2003). *The MMPI-2 Restructured Clinical (RC) Scales: Development, Validation, and Interpretation.* Minneapolis, MN: University of Minnesota Press.

Tennant, C. (2001). Assessing stressful life events in relation to liability and compensation. *Australian & New Zealand Journal of Psychiatry, 35,* 81–85.

Thompson, K. M., Crosby, R. D., Wonderlich, S. A., Mitchell, J. E., Redlin, J., Demuth, G., Smyth, J., & Haseltine, B. (2003). Psychopathology and sexual trauma in childhood and adulthood. *Journal of Traumatic Stress, 16,* 35–38.

Tjaden, P. & Thoennes, N. (2000). Prevalence and consequences of male-to-female and female-to-male intimate partner violence as measured by the National Violence Against Women Survey. *Violence Against Women, 6,* 142–161.

Ullman, S E. (2004). Sexual assault victimization and suicidal behavior in women: A review of the literature. *Aggression & Violent Behavior, 9,* 331–351.

U.S. Department of Justice. (2003). *Criminal Victimization 2002.* Washington, DC: U.S. Government Printing Office. Available from http://www.ojp.usdoj.gov/bjs/abstract/cv02.htm.

Weathers, F. W., Keane, T. M., & Davidson, J. R. T. (2001). Clinician-Administered PTSD Scale: A review of the first ten years of research. *Depression & Anxiety, 13,* 132–156.

Weathers, F. W., Litz, B. T., Huska, J. A., & Keane, T. M. (1994). *The PTSD Checklist-Civilian Version (PCL-C).* Boston, MA: National Center for PTSD.

Weathers, F. W., Ruscio, A. M., & Keane, T. M. (1999). Psychometric properties of nine scoring rules for the Clinician-Administered Posttraumatic Stress Disorder Scale. *Psychological Assessment, 11,* 124–133.

Weaver, T. L. (1998). Method variance and sensitivity of screening for traumatic stressors. *Journal of Traumatic Stress, 11,* 181–185.

Weiss, D. S. & Marmar, C. R. (1997). The Impact of Event Scale—Revised. In J. P. Wilson, & T. M. Keane (Eds.). *Assessing Psychological Trauma and PTSD.* New York: Guilford Press, pp. 399–411.

Wolfe, J. & Kimerling, R. (1997). Gender issues in the assessment of Posttraumatic Stress Disorder. In J. P. Wilson & T. M. Keane (Eds.). *Assessing Psychological Trauma and PTSD.* New York: Guilford Press, pp. 192–238.

Yehuda, R. & McFarlane, A. C. (1995). Conflict between current knowledge about Posttraumatic Stress Disorder and its original conceptual basis. *American Journal of Psychiatry, 152,* 1705–1713.

Section 3

Chronic Pain

7

Pain in the 21ˢᵗ Century: The Neuromatrix and Beyond

RONALD MELZACK AND JOEL KATZ

1. Introduction

Theories of pain, like all scientific theories, evolve as result of the accumulation of new facts as well as leaps of the imagination (Kuhn, 1970). The gate control theory's most revolutionary contribution to understanding pain was its emphasis on central neural mechanisms (Melzack & Wall, 1965). The theory forced the medical and biological sciences to accept the brain as an active system that filters, selects, and modulates inputs. The dorsal horns, too, are not merely passive transmission stations but sites at which dynamic activities—inhibition, excitation, and modulation—occur. The great challenge ahead of us is to understand how the brain functions.

2. A Brief History of Pain in the 20th Century

The theory of pain we inherited in the 20th century was proposed by Descartes three centuries earlier (see Melzack & Wall, 1996). The impact of Descartes' specificity theory was enormous. It influenced experiments on the anatomy and physiology of pain up to the first half of the 20th century (reviewed in Melzack & Wall, 1996). This body of research is marked by a search for specific pain fibers and pathways and a pain center in the brain. The result was a concept of pain as a specific, straight-through sensory projection system. This rigid anatomy of pain in the 1950s led to attempts to treat severe chronic pain by a variety of neurosurgical lesions. Descartes' specificity theory, then, determined the "facts" as they were known up to the middle of the 20th century, and even determined therapy.

Specificity theory proposed that injury activates specific pain receptors and fibers that, in turn, project pain impulses through a spinal pain pathway to a pain center in the brain. The psychological experience of pain, therefore, was virtually equated with peripheral injury. In the 1950s, there was no room for psychological contributions to pain, such as attention, past experience, anxiety, depression, and the meaning of the situation. Instead, pain experience was held to be proportional to peripheral injury or pathology. Patients who suffered back pain without presenting signs of organic disease were often labeled as psychologically disturbed and sent to psychiatrists. The concept, in short, was simple and, not surprisingly, often failed to help patients who suffered severe chronic pain. To thoughtful clinical observers, specificity theory was clearly wrong.

There were several attempts to find a new theory. The major opponent to specificity was labeled "pattern theory," but there were several different pattern theories and they were generally vague and inadequate (see Melzack & Wall, 1996). However, seen in retrospect, pattern theories gradually evolved (Fig. 7.1) and set the stage for the gate control theory. Goldscheider (1894) proposed that central summation in the dorsal horns is one of the critical determinants of pain. Livingston's (1943) theory postulated a reverberatory circuit in the dorsal horns to explain summation, referred pain, and pain that persisted long after healing was completed. Noordenbos' (1959) theory proposed that large-diameter fibers inhibited small-diameter fibers, and he even suggested that the substantia gelatinosa in the dorsal horns plays a major role in the summation and other dynamic processes described by Livingston. However, in none of these theories was there an explicit role for the brain other than as a passive receiver of messages. Nevertheless, the successive theoretical concepts moved the field in the right direction: into the spinal cord and away from the periphery as the exclusive answer to pain. At least, the field of pain was making its way up toward the brain.

3.   The Gate Control Theory of Pain

In 1965, Melzack and Wall proposed the gate control theory of pain. The final model, depicted in Figure 7.1D in the context of earlier theories of pain, is the first theory of pain that incorporated the central control processes of the brain.

The gate control theory of pain (Melzack & Wall, 1965) proposed that the transmission of nerve impulses from afferent fibers to spinal cord transmission (T) cells is modulated by a gating mechanism in the spinal dorsal horn. This gating mechanism is influenced by the relative amount of activity in large- and small-diameter fibers, so that large fibers tend to inhibit transmission (close the gate) and small fibers tend to facilitate transmission (open the gate). In addition, the spinal gating mechanism is influenced by nerve impulses that descend from the brain. When the output of the spinal T-cells exceeds a critical level, it activates the Action System—those neural areas that underlie the complex, sequential patterns of behavior and experience the characteristic of pain.

The theory's emphasis on the modulation of inputs in the spinal dorsal horns and the dynamic role of the brain in pain processes had a clinical as well as a scientific impact. Psychological factors, which were previously

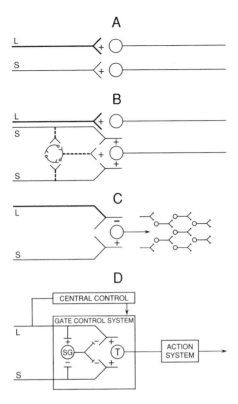

FIGURE 7.1. Schematic representation of conceptual models of pain mechanisms. **(A)** Specificity theory. Large (L) and small (S) fibers are assumed to transmit touch and pain impulses, respectively, in separate, specific, straight-through pathways to touch and pain centers in the brain. **(B)** Goldscheider's (1894) summation theory, showing convergence of small fibers onto a dorsal horn cell. The central network projecting to the central cell represents Livingston's (1943) conceptual model of reverberatory circuits underlying pathological pain states. Touch is assumed to be carried by large fibers. **(C)** Sensory interaction theory, in which large (L) fibers inhibit (−) and small (S) fibers excite (+) central transmission neurons. The output projects to spinal cord neurons, which are conceived by Noordenbos (1959) to comprise a multisynaptic afferent system. **(D)** Gate control theory. The large (L) and small (S) fibers project to the substantia gelatinosa (SG) and first central transmission (T) cells. The central control trigger is represented by a line running from the large fiber system to central control mechanisms, which, in turn, project back to the gate control system. The T-cells project to the entry cells of the action system. +, excitation; −, inhibition. [From Melzack (1991), with permission.]

dismissed as "reactions to pain," were now seen to be an integral part of pain processing and new avenues for pain control by psychological therapies were opened. Similarly, cutting nerves and pathways was gradually replaced by a host of methods to modulate the input. Physical therapists and other health care professionals who use a multitude of modulation techniques were brought into the picture, and transcutaneous electrical nerve stimulation (TENS) became an important modality for the treatment of chronic and acute pain. The current status of pain research and therapy indicates that, despite the addition of a massive amount of detail, the conceptual components of the theory remain basically intact up to the present.

4.   Beyond the Gate

We believe the great challenge ahead of us is to understand brain function. Melzack and Casey (1968) made a start by proposing that specialized systems in the brain are involved in the sensory–discriminative, motivational–affective, and cognitive–evaluative dimensions of subjective pain experience (Fig. 7.2). These names for the dimensions of subjective experience seemed strange when they are coined, but they are now used so frequently and seem so "logical" that they have become part of our language. So too, the McGill Pain Questionnaire, which taps into subjective experience—one of the functions of the brain—is widely used to measure pain (Melzack, 1975, 1987).

In 1978, Melzack and Loeser described severe pains in the phantom body of paraplegics with verified total sections of the spinal cord and proposed a central "pattern generating mechanism" above the level of the section (Melzack & Loeser, 1978). This concept, generally ignored for more than a decade, is now beginning to be accepted. It represents a revolutionary

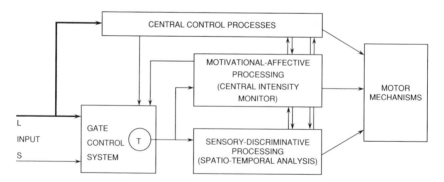

FIGURE 7.2. Conceptual model of the sensory, motivational, and central control determinants of pain. The output of the T-cells of the gate control system projects to the sensory–discriminative system and the motivational–affective system. The central control trigger is represented by a line running from the large fiber system to central control processes; these, in turn, project back to the gate control system and to the sensory–discriminative and motivational–affective systems. All three systems interact with one another and project to the motor system. [From Melzack and Casey (1968), with permission.]

advance: It did not merely extend the gate; it said that pain could be generated by brain mechanisms in paraplegics in the absence of a spinal gate because the brain is completely disconnected from the cord. Psychophysical specificity, in such a concept, makes no sense; instead, we must explore how patterns of nerve impulses generated in the brain can give rise to somesthetic experience.

5.   Phantom Limbs and the Concept of a Neuromatrix

It is evident that the gate control theory has taken us a long way. Yet, as historians of science have pointed out, good theories are instrumental in producing facts that eventually require a new theory to incorporate them. This is what has happened. It is possible to make adjustments to the gate theory so that, for example, it includes long-lasting activity of the sort Wall has described (see Melzack & Wall, 1996). However, there is a set of observations on pain in paraplegics that just does not fit the theory. This does not negate the gate theory, of course. Peripheral and spinal processes are obviously an important part of pain and we need to know more about the mechanisms of peripheral inflammation, spinal modulation, midbrain descending control, and so forth. However, the data on painful phantoms below the level of total spinal section (Melzack, 1989, 1990) indicate that we need to go above the spinal cord and into the brain. Note that we mean more than the spinal projection areas in the thalamus and cortex. These areas are important, of course, but they are only part of the neural processes that underlie perception. The cortex, Gybels and Tasker (1999) made amply clear, is not the pain center and neither is the thalamus. The areas of the brain involved in pain experience and behavior must include somatosensory projections as well as the limbic system. Furthermore, cognitive processes are known to involve widespread areas of the brain. Despite this increased knowledge, we do not have yet an adequate theory of how the brain works.

Melzack's (1989) analysis of phantom limb phenomena, particularly the astonishing reports of a phantom body and severe phantom limb pain in people with a total thoracic spinal cord section (Melzack & Loeser, 1978), has led to four conclusions that point to a new conceptual model of the nervous system. First, because the phantom limb (or other body part) feels so real, it is reasonable to conclude that the body we normally feel is subserved by the same neural processes in the brain as the phantom; these brain processes are normally activated and modulated by inputs from the body, but they can act in the absence of any inputs. Second, all of the qualities we normally feel from the body, including pain, are also felt in the absence of inputs from the body; from this, we can conclude that the origins of the patterns that underlie the qualities of experience lie in neural networks in the brain; stimuli can trigger the patterns but do not produce them. Third, the body is perceived as a unity and is identified as the "body-self," distinct from other people and the surrounding world. The experience of a unity of such diverse feelings, including the self as the point of orientation in the surrounding environment, is produced by central neural processes and cannot derive from the peripheral nervous system or spinal cord. Fourth, the brain processes that underlie the body-self are "built in" by genetic specification, although this built-in substrate must, of course, be modified by experience. These conclusions provide the basis of the new conceptual model (Melzack, 1989, 1990; 2001, Fig. 4)

5.1.   Outline of the Theory

The anatomical substrate of the body-self, Melzack proposed, is a large, widespread network of neurons that consists of loops between the thalamus and cortex as well as between the cortex and limbic system. He has labeled the entire network, whose spatial distribution and synaptic links are initially determined genetically and are later sculpted by sensory inputs, as a *neuromatrix*. The loops diverge to permit parallel processing in different components of the neuromatrix and converge repeatedly to permit interactions between the output products of processing. The repeated *cyclical processing and synthesis* of nerve impulses through the neuromatrix imparts a characteristic pattern: the *neurosignature*. The neurosignature of the neuromatrix is imparted on all nerve impulse patterns that flow through it; the neurosignature is produced by the patterns of synaptic connections in the entire neuromatrix. All inputs from the body undergo cyclical processing and synthesis so that characteristic patterns are impressed on them in the neuromatrix. Portions of the neuromatrix are specialized to process information related to major sensory events (such as injury, temperature change, and stimulation of erogenous tissue) and can be labeled as neuromodules that impress subsignatures on the larger neurosignature.

   The neurosignature, which is a continuous output from the body-self neuromatrix, is projected to areas in the brain—the *sentient neural hub*—in which the stream of nerve impulses (the neurosignature modulated by ongoing inputs) is converted into a continually changing stream of awareness. Furthermore, the neurosignature patterns may also activate a neuromatrix to produce movement; that is, the signature patterns bifurcate so that a pattern proceeds to the sentient neural hub (where the pattern is transformed into the experience of movement) and a similar pattern proceeds through a neuromatrix that eventually activates spinal cord neurons to produce muscle patterns for complex actions. Figure 7.3 summarizes the factors that contribute to the output pattern from the neuromatrix that produce the sensory, affective, and cognitive dimensions of pain experience and the resultant behavior.

5.2.   The Body-Self Neuromatrix

The body is felt as a unity, with different qualities at different times. Melzack proposed that the brain mechanism that underlies the experience also comprises a unified system that acts as a whole and produces a neurosignature

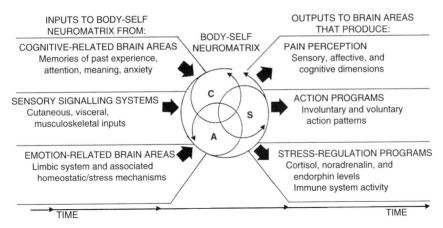

FIGURE 7.3. Factors that contribute to the patterns of activity generated by the body-self neuromatrix, which is comprised of sensory, affective, and cognitive neuromodules. The output patterns from the neuromatrix produce the multiple dimensions of pain experience as well as concurrent homeostatic and behavioral responses. [From Melzack (2001), with permission.]

pattern of a whole body. The conceptualization of this unified brain mechanism lies at the heart of the new theory, and the word "neuromatrix" best characterizes it. The neuromatrix (not the stimulus, peripheral nerves, or "brain center") is the origin of the neurosignature; the neurosignature originates and takes form in the neuromatrix. Although the neurosignature may be triggered or modulated by input, the input is only a "trigger" and does not produce the neurosignature itself. The neuromatrix "casts" its distinctive signature on all inputs (nerve impulse patterns) that flow through it. Finally, the array of neurons in a neuromatrix is genetically programmed to perform the specific function of producing the signature pattern. The final integrated neurosignature pattern for the body-self ultimately produces awareness and action.

The neuromatrix, distributed throughout many areas of the brain, comprises a widespread network of neurons that generates patterns, processes information that flows through it, and ultimately produces the pattern that is felt as a whole body. The stream of neurosignature output with constantly varying patterns riding on the main signature pattern produces the feelings of the whole body with constantly changing qualities.

5.3.   Conceptual Reasons for a Neuromatrix

It is difficult to comprehend how individual bits of information from skin, joints, or muscles can all come together to produce the experience of a coherent, articulated body. At any instant in time, millions of nerve impulses arrive at the brain from all of the body's sensory systems, including the proprioceptive and vestibular systems. How can all this be integrated in a constantly changing unity of experience? Where does it all come together?

Melzack conceptualized a genetically built-in neuromatrix for the whole body, producing a characteristic neurosignature for the body that carries with it patterns for the myriad qualities we feel. The neuromatrix, as Melzack conceived of it, produces a continuous message that represents the whole body in which details are differentiated within the whole as inputs come into it. We start from the top, with the experience of a unity of the body, and look for differentiation of detail within the whole. The neuromatrix, then, is a template of the whole, which provides the characteristic neural pattern for the whole body (the body's neurosignature) as well as subsets of signature patterns (from neuromodules) that relate to events at (or in) different parts of the body.

These views are in sharp contrast to the classical specificity theory in which the qualities of experience are presumed to be inherent in peripheral nerve fibers. Pain is not injury; the *quality of pain experiences* must not be confused with the physical event of breaking skin or bone. Warmth and cold are not "out there" and temperature changes occur "out there," but the *qualities of experience* must be generated by structures in the brain. There are no external equivalents to stinging, smarting, tickling, itch; the *qualities* are produced by built-in neuromodules whose neurosignatures innately produce the qualities.

We do not learn to feel qualities of experience: Our brains are built to produce them. The inadequacy of the traditional peripheralist view becomes especially evident when we consider paraplegics with high-level complete spinal breaks. In spite of the absence of inputs from the body, virtually every quality of sensation and affect is experienced. It is known that the absence of input produces hyperactivity and abnormal firing patterns in spinal cells above the level of the break (Melzack & Loeser, 1978). However, how, from this jumble of activity, do we get the meaningful experience of movement, the coordination of limbs with other limbs, cramping pain in specific (nonexistent) muscle groups, and so on? This must occur in the brain, in which neurosignatures are produced by neuromatrixes that are triggered by the output of hyperactive cells.

When all sensory systems are intact, inputs modulate the continuous neuromatrix output to produce the wide variety of experiences we feel. We may feel position, warmth, and several kinds of pain and pressure all at once. It is a single unitary feeling, just as an orchestra produces a single unitary sound at any moment even though the sound comprises violins, cellos, horns, and so forth. Similarly, at a particular moment in time, we feel complex qualities from all of the body. In addition, our experience of the body includes visual images, affect, "knowledge" of the self (vs. not-self) as well as the meaning of body parts in terms of social norms and values. It is hard to conceive of all of these bits and pieces coming together to produce a unitary body-self, but we can visualize a neuromatrix that impresses a characteristic signature on all the inputs that converge on it and thereby produces the never-ending stream of feeling from the body. The experience of the body-self involves multiple dimensions—sensory, affective, evaluative, postural, and many others. The sensory dimensions are subserved, in part at least, by portions of the neuromatrix that lie in the sensory projection areas of the brain; the affective dimensions, Melzack assumed, are subserved by areas in the brainstem and limbic system. Each major psychological dimension (or quality) of experience, Melzack proposed, is subserved by a particular portion of the neuromatrix that contributes a distinct portion of the total neurosignature. To use a musical analogy once again, it is like the strings, tympani, woodwinds, and brasses of a symphony orchestra that each comprise a part of the whole; each makes its unique contribution, yet is an integral part of a single symphony that varies continually from beginning to end.

The neuromatrix resembles Hebb's "cell assembly" by being a widespread network of cells that subserves a particular psychological function. However, Hebb (1949) conceived of the cell assembly as a network developed by gradual sensory learning, whereas Melzack proposed that the structure of the neuromatrix is predominantly determined by genetic factors, although its eventual synaptic architecture is influenced by sensory inputs. This emphasis on the genetic contribution to the brain does not diminish the importance of sensory inputs. The neuromatrix is a psychologically meaningful unit, developed by both heredity and learning, that represents an entire unified entity.

5.4.   Action Patterns: The Action Neuromatrix

The output of the body neuromatrix, Melzack proposed, is directed at two systems: (1) the neuromatrix that produces awareness of the output and (2) a neuromatrix involved in overt action patterns. In this discussion, it is important to keep in mind that just as there is a steady stream of awareness, there is also a steady output of behavior (including movements during sleep). It is important to recognize that behavior occurs only after the input has been at least partially synthesized and recognized. For example, when we respond to the experience of pain or itch, it is evident that the experience has been synthesized by the body-self neuromatrix (or relevant neuromodules) sufficiently for the neuromatrix to have imparted the neurosignature patterns that underlie the quality of experience, affect, and meaning. Apart from a few reflexes (such as withdrawal of a limb, eye-blink, and so on), behavior occurs only after inputs have been analyzed and synthesized sufficiently to produce meaningful experience. When we reach for an apple, the visual input has clearly been synthesized by a neuromatrix so that it has three-dimensional shape, color, and meaning as an edible, desirable object, all of which are produced by the brain and are not in the object "out there." When we respond to pain (by withdrawal or even by telephoning for an ambulance), we respond to an experience that has sensory qualities, affect, and meaning as a dangerous (or potentially dangerous) event to the body.

Melzack proposed that after inputs from the body undergo transformation in the body neuromatrix, the appropriate action patterns are activated concurrently (or nearly so) with the neuromatrix for experience. Thus, in the action neuromatrix, cyclical processing and synthesis produces activation of several possible patterns and their successive elimination until one particular pattern emerges as the most appropriate for the circumstances at the moment. In this way, input and output are synthesized simultaneously, in parallel, not in series. This permits a smooth, continuous stream of action patterns.

The command, which originates in the brain, to perform a pattern such as running activates the neuromodule, which then produces firing in sequences of neurons that send precise messages through ventral horn neuron pools to appropriate sets of muscles. At the same time, the output patterns from the body neuromatrix that engage the neuromodules for particular actions are also projected to the sentient neural hub and produce experience. In this way, the brain commands can produce the experience of movement of phantom limbs even though there are no limbs to move and no proprioceptive feedback. Indeed, reports by paraplegics of terrible fatigue as a result of persistent bicycling movements (Conomy, 1973) and the painful fatigue in a tightly clenched phantom fist in arm amputees (Katz, 2000) indicate that feelings of effort and fatigue are produced by the signature of a neuromodule rather than particular input patterns from muscles and joints.

The phenomenon of phantom limbs has allowed us to examine some fundamental assumptions in psychology. One assumption is that sensations are produced only by stimuli and that perceptions in the absence of stimuli are psychologically abnormal. Yet, phantom limbs, as well as phantom seeing (Schultz & Melzack, 1991), indicate that this notion is wrong. The brain does more than detect and analyze inputs; it generates perceptual experience even when no external inputs occur.

Another entrenched assumption is that perception of one's body results from sensory inputs that leave a memory in the brain; the total of these signals becomes the body image. However, the existence of phantoms in people born without a limb or who have lost a limb at an early age suggests that the neural networks for perceiving the body and its parts are built into the brain (Melzack, 1989, 1990, 1995; Melzack et al., 1997). The absence of inputs does not stop the networks from generating messages about missing body parts; they continue to produce such messages throughout life. In short, phantom limbs are a mystery only if we assume the body sends sensory messages to a passively receiving brain. Phantoms become comprehensible once we recognize that the brain generates the experience of the body. Sensory inputs merely modulate that experience; they do not directly cause it.

6.   Pain and Neuroplasticity

There was no place in the specificity concept of the nervous system for "plasticity," in which neuronal and synaptic functions are capable of being molded or shaped so that they influence subsequent perceptual experiences. Plasticity related to pain represents persistent functional changes, or "somatic memories" (Katz & Melzack, 1990; Salomons et al., 2004), produced in the nervous system by injuries or other pathological events. The recognition that such changes can occur is essential to understanding chronic pain syndromes, such as low back pain and phantom limb pain, that persist and often destroy the lives of the people who suffer them.

7.   Denervation Hypersensitivity and Neuronal Hyperactivity

Sensory disturbances associated with nerve injury have been closely linked to alterations in Central Nervous System (CNS) function. Markus et al., (1984) have demonstrated that the development of hypersensitivity in a rat's hind paw following sciatic nerve section occurs concurrently with the expansion of the saphenous nerve's somatotopic projection in the spinal cord. Nerve injury can also lead to the development of increased neuronal activity at various levels of the somatosensory system (see review by Coderre et al., 1993). In addition to spontaneous activity generated from the neuroma, peripheral neurectomy also leads to increased spontaneous activity in the dorsal root ganglion and spinal cord. Furthermore, after dorsal rhizotomy, there are increases in spontaneous neural activity in the dorsal horn, the spinal trigeminal nucleus, and the thalamus.

Clinical neurosurgery studies reveal a similar relationship between denervation and CNS hyperactivity. Neurons in the somatosensory thalamus of patients with neuropathic pain display high spontaneous firing rates, abnormal bursting activity, and evoked responses to stimulation of body areas that normally do not activate these neurons (Lenz et al., 1987, 1989). The site of abnormality in thalamic function appears to be somatotopically related to the painful region. In patients with complete spinal cord transection and dysesthesias referred below the level of the break, neuronal hyperactivity was observed in thalamic regions that had lost their normal sensory input, but not in regions with apparently normal afferent input (Lenz et al., 1987). Furthermore, in patients with neuropathic pain, electrical stimulation of subthalamic, thalamic, and capsular regions may evoke pain (Tasker, 1989) and, in some instances, even reproduce the patient's pain (Davis et al., 1995; Lenz et al., 1994; Nathan, 1985). Direct electrical stimulation of spontaneously hyperactive cells evokes pain in some but not all pain patients, raising the possibility that in certain patients, the observed changes in neuronal activity may contribute to the perception of pain (Lenz et al., 1987). Studies of patients undergoing electrical brain stimulation during brain surgery reveal that pain is rarely elicited by test stimuli unless the patient suffers from a chronic pain problem. However, brain stimulation can elicit pain responses in patients with chronic pain that does not involve extensive nerve injury or deafferentation. Lenz et al. (1994, p. 121) described the case of a woman with unstable angina who, during electrical stimulation of the thalamus, reported "heart pain like what I took nitroglycerin for" except that "it starts and stops suddenly." The possibility that the patient's angina was the result of myocardial strain, not the activation of a somatosensory pain memory, was ruled out by demonstrating that EKG, blood pressure, and cardiac enzymes remained unchanged over the course of stimulation.

It is possible that receptive field expansions and spontaneous activity generated in the CNS following peripheral nerve injury are, in part, mediated by alterations in normal inhibitory processes in the dorsal horn. Within 4 days of a peripheral nerve section, there is a reduction in the dorsal root potential and, therefore, in the presynaptic inhibition it represents (Wall & Devor, 1981). Nerve section also induces a reduction in the inhibitory effect of A-fiber stimulation on the activity in dorsal horn neurons (Woolf & Wall, 1982). Furthermore, nerve injury affects descending inhibitory controls from brainstem nuclei. In the intact nervous system, stimulation of the locus coeruleus (Segal & Sandberg, 1977) or the nucleus raphe magnus (Oliveras et al., 1979) produces an inhibition of dorsal horn neurons. Following dorsal rhizotomy, however, stimulation of these areas produces excitation, rather than inhibition, in half of the cells studied (Hodge et al., 1983).

Recent advances in our understanding of the mechanisms that underlie pathological pain have important implications for the treatment of both acute and chronic pain. Because it has been established that intense noxious stimulation produces a sensitization of CNS neurons, it is possible to direct treatments not only at the site of peripheral tissue damage but also at the site of central changes (see the review by Coderre & Katz, 1997). Furthermore, it might be possible in some instances to prevent the development of central sensitization, which contributes to pathological pain states. The evidence that acute postoperative pain intensity and/or the amount of pain medication patients require after surgery are reduced by preoperative administration of variety of agents via the epidural (Katz et al., 1992, 1994, 2003) or systemic route (Katz et al., 1996, 2004; Snijdelaar et al., 2004) suggests that the surgically induced afferent injury barrage arriving within the CNS, and the central sensitization it induces, can be prevented or at least obtunded significantly (see review by Katz, 2003). The reduction in acute pain intensity associated with preoperative epidural anesthesia may even translate into reduced pain experience (Gottschalk et al., 1998) and pain disability (Katz & Cohen, 2004) weeks after patients have left the hospital and returned home.

The fact that amputees are more likely to develop phantom limb pain if there is pain in the limb prior to amputation (Katz & Melzack, 1990) raises the possibility that the development of longer-term neuropathic pain also can be prevented by reducing the potential for central sensitization at the time of amputation (see Katz & Melzack, 2003). Whether chronic postoperative problems such as painful scars, postthoracotomy chest wall pain, and phantom limb and stump pain can be reduced by blocking perioperative nociceptive inputs awaits additional well-controlled clinical trials (see Katz, 1997).

Furthermore, research is required to determine whether multiple-treatment approaches (involving local and epidural anesthesia as well as pretreatment with opiates and anti-inflammatory drugs) that produce an effective blockade of afferent input, may also prevent or relieve other forms of severe chronic pain such as postherpetic neuralgia (Manabe et al., 2004) and reflex sympathetic dystrophy. It is hoped that a combination of new pharmacological developments, careful clinical trials, and an increased understanding of the contribution and mechanisms of noxious stimulus-induced neuroplasticity will lead to improved clinical treatment and prevention of pathological pain.

8.   Pain and Psychopathology

Pains that do not conform to present-day anatomical and neurophysiological knowledge are often attributed to psychological dysfunction.

'There are many pains whose cause is not known. If a diligent search has been made in the periphery and no cause is found, we have seen that clinicians act as though there was only one alternative. They blame faulty thinking, which for many classically-thinking doctors is the same thing as saying that there is no cause and even no disease. They ignore a century's work on disorders of the spinal cord and brainstem and target the mind … These are the doctors who repeat again and again to a Second World War amputee in pain that there is nothing wrong with him and that it is all in his head' (Wall, 1999, p. 107).

This view of the role of psychological generation in pain persists to this day notwithstanding evidence to the contrary. Psychopathology has been proposed to underlie phantom limb pain (Katz, 2000), dyspareunia (Meana & Binik, 1994), orofacial pain (Gagliese & Katz, 2000), and a host of others, including pelvic pain, abdominal pain, chest pain, and headache (Stoudemire & Sandhu, 1987). However, the complexity of the pain transmission circuitry described in the previous sections means that many pains that defy our current understanding will ultimately be explained without having to resort to a psychopathological etiology. Pain that is "nonanatomical" in distribution, spread of pain to noninjured territory, pain that is said to be out of proportion to the degree of injury, and pain in the absence of injury have all, at one time or another, been used as evidence to support the idea that psychological disturbance underlies the pain. Yet, each of these features of supposed psychopathology can now be explained by neurophysiological mechanisms that involve an interplay between peripheral and central neural activity (Gagliese & Katz, 2000; Melzack & Wall, 1996).

Recent data linking the immune system and the CNS have provided an explanation for another heretofore medically unexplained pain problem. Mirror-image pain or *allochira* has puzzled clinicians and basic scientists ever since it was first documented in the late 1800s (Basbaum, 2004). Injury to one side of the body is experienced as pain at the site of injury as well as at the contralateral, mirror-image point (Livingston, 1998; Maleki et al., 2000). Recent animal studies show induction of a sciatic inflammatory neuritis by perisciatic microinjection of immune system activators results in both an ipsilateral hyperalgesia and hyperalgesia at the mirror-image point on the opposite side in the territory of the contralateral healthy sciatic nerve (Chacur et al., 2001). Moreover, both the ipsilateral and contralateral hyperalgesia are prevented or reversed by intrathecal injection of a variety of proinflammatory cytokine antagonists (Milligan et al., 2003).

Mirror-image pain is likely not a unitary phenomenon and other nonimmune mechanisms may also be involved (Koltzenburg et al., 1999). For example, recent human (Oaklander et al., 1998) and animal evidence (Oaklander & Brown, 2004) point to a potential combination of central and peripheral contributions to mirror-image pain because nerve injury to one side of the body has been shown to result in a 50% reduction in the innervation of the territory of the same nerve on the opposite side of the body in uninjured skin (Oaklander & Brown, 2004). Interestingly, although documented contralateral neurite loss can occur in the absence of contralateral pain or hyperalgesia, pain intensity at the site of the injury correlates significantly with the extent of contralateral neurite loss (Oaklander et al., 1998). This raises the intriguing possibility that the intensity of pain at the site of an injury may be facilitated by contralateral neurite loss induced by the ipsilateral injury (Oaklander & Brown, 2004)—a situation that most clinicians would never have imagined possible.

9.   Implications for Diagnosis: DSM-IV Pain Disorder and Beyond

Taken together, these novel mechanisms that explain some of the most puzzling pain symptoms must keep us mindful that emotional distress and psychological disturbance in our patients are not at the root of the pain. Attributing pain to a psychological disturbance is damaging to the patient and provider alike; it poisons the patient–provider relationship by introducing an element of mutual distrust and implicit (and, at times, explicit) blame. It is devastating to the patient who feels at fault, disbelieved, and alone.

The current DSM-IV classification of Pain Disorder (American Psychiatric Association, 1994) contributes to the existing confusion about the role of psychological factors in the etiology of pain. The dualism inherent in specificity theory is reflected in the diagnosis of Pain Disorder, which attributes pain to psychological or physical factors (Table 7.1).

The diagnosis of Pain Disorder is coded as Pain Disorder Associated with Psychological Factors or Pain Disorder Associated with Both Psychological Factors and a General Medical Condition. A third DSM-IV disorder, Pain Disorder Associated with a General Medical Condition, is described but "it is not considered to be a mental disorder" for "[i]f psychological factors are

Table 7.1. Diagnostic Criteria for DSM-IV Pain Disorder

A. Pain in one or more anatomical sites is the predominant focus of the clinical presentation and is of sufficient severity to warrant clinical attention.
B. The pain causes clinically significant distress or impairment in social, occupational, or other important areas of functioning.
C. Psychological factors are judged to have an important role in the onset, severity, exacerbation, or maintenance of the pain.
D. The symptom or deficit is not intentionally produced or feigned (as in Factitious Disorder or Malingering).
E. The pain is not better accounted for by a Mood, Anxiety, or Psychotic Disorder and does not meet criteria for Dyspareunia.

Code as follows:

Pain Disorder Associated with Psychological Factors: Psychological factors are judged to have the major role in the onset, severity, exacerbation, or maintenance of the pain. (If a general medical condition is present, it does not have a major role in the onset, severity, exacerbation, or maintenance of the pain.) This type of Pain Disorder is not diagnosed if criteria are also met for Somatization Disorder.

Pain Disorder Associated with Both Psychological Factors and a General Medical Condition: Both psychological factors and a general medical condition are judged to have important roles in the onset, severity, exacerbation, or maintenance of the pain. The associated general medical condition or anatomical site of the pain is coded on Axis III.

Note: The following is not considered to be a mental disorder and is included here to facilitate differential diagnosis.

Pain Disorder Associated with a General Medical Condition: A general medical condition has a major role in the onset, severity, exacerbation, or maintenance of the pain. (If psychological factors are present, they are not judged to have a major role in the onset, severity, exacerbation, or maintenance of the pain.) The diagnostic code for the pain is selected based on the associated general medical condition if one has been established or on the anatomical location of the pain if the underlying general medical condition is not yet clearly established.

Specify if:
Acute: duration of less than 6 months
Chronic: duration of 6 months or longer

present, they are not judged to have a major role in the onset, severity, exacerbation or maintenance of the pain" (American Psychiatric Association, 1994, p. 462). Here, we are presented with the possibility, borne of dualistic thinking, of having pain without psychological factors, which is considered to be a sign of mental health—or at least the absence of a mental disorder. It has been proposed that the lack of a definition of "psychological factors" or a description of when they are of sufficient importance to play a role in the pain experience in the presence of a general medical condition makes this a diagnosis of exclusion (Sullivan, 2000).

The argument has been made for a "dualism of etiology" recognizing multiple causes of pain" and a "monistic view of the pain experience" (Merskey, 2004), but this distinction maintains a separation between mind and body by suggesting that pain can be caused by one factor in the absence of the others.

The idea of "psychogenic pain" (i.e., pain without physical contribution) remains as untenable as that of "pain associated with medical factors" (without psychological involvement) (Sullivan, 2000). The DSM-IV requirement (Criterion E) that the pain is "not better accounted for" by other mental disorders, especially mood and anxiety disorders, achieves the intent of making this a rare diagnosis. However, it seems incompatible with Criteria A and B specifying pain of sufficient severity to produce clinically significant distress or impairment in important areas of functioning.

The idea that emotional and psychological processes can cause pain traditionally has been tied to the notion of psychopathology. The argument we are making is not that psychological and emotional factors cannot trigger an experience of pain, but that psychopathology *per se* is not at the root of unexplained pain. There is ample evidence that pain may be triggered by emotional and psychological processes in psychologically healthy individuals (Katz, 2000). Although the DSM-IV classification represents an improvement over previous editions, the main issue is whether Pain Disorder really belongs in a manual of mental disorders (Sullivan, 2000). Logic dictates that the concept of pain due to psychopathology can never be disproved and so it appears that the classification of Pain Disorder has been retained.

10.   Conclusion: The Multiple Determinants of Pain

The neuromatrix theory of pain proposes that the neurosignature for pain experience is determined by the synaptic architecture of the neuromatrix, which is produced by genetic and sensory influences. The neurosignature pattern is also modulated by sensory inputs and by cognitive events, such as psychological stress (Melzack, 1999). Furthermore, stressors, physical as well as psychological, act on stress-regulation systems, which may produce lesions of muscle, bone, and nerve tissue, thereby contributing to the neurosignature patterns that give rise to chronic pain. In short, the neuromatrix, as a result of homeostasis-regulation patterns that have failed, may produce the destructive conditions that give rise to many of the chronic pains that so far have been resistant to treatments developed primarily to manage pains that are triggered by sensory inputs. The stress-regulation system, with its complex, delicately balanced interactions, is an integral part of the multiple contributions that give rise to chronic pain.

The neuromatrix theory guides us away from the Cartesian concept of pain as a sensation produced by injury or other tissue pathology and toward the concept of pain as a multidimensional experience produced by multiple influences. These influences range from the existing synaptic architecture of the neuromatrix to influences from within the body and from other areas in the brain. Genetic influences on synaptic architecture could determine—or predispose toward—the development of chronic pain syndromes.

Multiple inputs act on the neuromatrix programs and contribute to the *output* neurosignature. They include (1) sensory inputs (cutaneous, visceral, and other somatic receptors), (2) visual and other sensory inputs that influence the cognitive interpretation of the situation, (3) phasic and tonic cognitive and emotional inputs from other areas of the brain, (4) intrinsic neural inhibitory modulation inherent in all brain function, and (5) the activity of the body's stress-regulation systems, including cytokines as well as the endocrine, autonomic, immune, and opioid systems. We have traveled a long way from the psychophysical concept that seeks a simple one-to-one relationship between injury and pain. We now have a theoretical framework in which a genetically determined template for the body-self is modulated by the powerful stress system and the cognitive functions of the brain, in addition to the traditional sensory inputs.

References

American Psychiatric Association. (1994). *Diagnostic and Statistical Manual of Mental Disorders*, 4th ed. Washington, DC: American Psychiatric Association.

Basbaum, A. I. (2004). A new way to lose your nerve. *Science of Aging Knowledge Environment, 2004(15)*, pe15.

Chacur, M., Milligan, E. D., Gazda, L. S., Armstrong, C., Wang, H., Tracey, K. J., Maier, S.F. & Watkins, L.R. (2001). A new model of sciatic inflammatory neuritis (SIN): Induction of unilateral and bilateral mechanical allodynia following acute unilateral peri-sciatic immune activation in rats. *Pain, 94*(3), 231–244.

Coderre, T. J. & Katz, J. (1997). Peripheral and central hyperexcitability: Differential signs and symptoms in persistent pain. *Behavioral and Brain Sciences, 20*, 404–419.

Coderre, T. J., Katz, J., Vaccarino, A. L., & Melzack, R. (1993). Contribution of central neuroplasticity to pathological pain: Review of clinical and experimental evidence. *Pain, 52*, 259–285.

Conomy, J. P. (1973). Disorders of body image after spinal cord injury. *Neurology, 23(8)*, 842–850.

Davis, K. D., Tasker, R. R., Kiss, Z. H., Hutchison, W. D., & Dostrovsky, J. O. (1995). Visceral pain evoked by thalamic microstimulation in humans. *Neuroreport, 6(2)*, 369–374.

Gagliese, L. & Katz, J. (2000). Medically unexplained pain is not caused by psychopathology. *Pain Research and Management, 5*, 251–257.

Goldscheider, A. (1894). *Uber den Schmerzes in Physiologischer and Klinicher Hinsicht*. Berlin: Hirchwald.

Gottschalk, A., Smith, D. S., Jobes, D. R., Kennedy, S. K., Lally, S. E., Noble, V. E., Grugan, K.F., Seifert, H.A., Cheung, A., Malkowicz, S.B., Gutsche, B.B. & Wein, A.J. (1998). Preemptive epidural analgesia and recovery from radical prostatectomy: A randomized controlled trial. *JAMA, 279(14)*, 1076–1082.

Gybels, J. M. & Tasker, R. R. (1999). Central neurosurgery. In P. D. Wall & R. Melzack (Eds.). *Textbook of Pain*. Edinburgh: Churchill Livingstone, pp. 1307–1339.

Hebb, D. O. (1949). *The Organization of Behavior*. New York: Wiley.

Hodge, C. J., Jr., Apkarian, A. V., Owen, M. P., & Hanson, B. S. (1983). Changes in the effects of stimulation of locus coeruleus and nucleus raphe magnus following dorsal rhizotomy. *Brain Res, 288(1–2)*, 325–329.

Katz, J. (1997). Prevention of phantom limb pain by regional anaesthesia. *Lancet, 349*, 519–520.

Katz, J. (2000). Individual differences in the consciousness of phantom limbs. In R. G. Kunzendorf & B. Wallace (Eds.). *Individual Differences in Conscious Experience: First-Person Constraints on Theories of Consciousness, Self-consciousness, and Subconsciousness*. Amsterdam: John Benjamins, pp. 45–97.

Katz, J. (2003). Timing of treatment and pre-emptive analgesia. In D. J. Rowbotham & P. E. Macintyre (Eds.). *Acute Pain*. London: Arnold, pp. 113–163.

Katz, J. & Cohen, L. (2004). Preventive analgesia is associated with reduced pain disability three weeks but not six months after abdominal gynecological surgery by laparotomy. *Anesthesiology, 101*, 169–174.

Katz, J. & Melzack, R. (1990). Pain "memories" in phantom limbs: Review and clinical observations. *Pain, 43*, 319–336.

Katz, J. & Melzack, R. (2003). Phantom limb pain. In J. Grafman & I. H. Robertson (Eds.). *Handbook of Neuropsychology*, 2nd ed. Oxford: Elsevier, Vol. 9, pp. 205–230.

Katz, J., Cohen, L., Schmid, R., Chan, V. W. S., & Wowk, A. (2003). Postoperative morphine use and hyperalgesia are reduced by preoperative but not intraoperative epidural analgesia: Implications for preemptive analgesia and the prevention of central sensitization. *Anesthesiology, 98*, 1449–1460.

Katz, J., Clairoux, M., Kavanagh, B. P., Roger, S., Nierenberg, H., Redahan, C., & Sandler, A.N. (1994). Pre-emptive lumbar epidural anaesthesia reduces postoperative pain and patient-controlled morphine consumption after lower abdominal surgery. *Pain, 59*, 395–403.

Katz, J., Clairoux, M., Redahan, C., Kavanagh, B. P., Carroll, S., Nierenberg, H., Jackson, M., Beattie, J., Taddio, A. & Sandler, A.N. (1996). High dose alfentanil pre-empts pain after abdominal hysterectomy. *Pain, 68(1)*, 109–118.

Katz, J., Schmid, R., Snijdelaar, D. G., Coderre, T. J., McCartney, C. J., & Wowk, A. (2004). Pre-emptive analgesia using intravenous fentanyl plus low-dose ketamine for radical prostatectomy under general anesthesia does not produce short-term or long-term reductions in pain or analgesic use. *Pain, 110(3)*, 707–718.

Katz, J., Kavanagh, B. P., Sandler, A. N., Nierenberg, H., Boylan, J. F., Friedlander, M., & Shaw, B.F. (1992). Preemptive analgesia: Clinical evidence of neuroplasticity contributing to post-operative pain. *Anesthesiology, 77*, 439–446.

Koltzenburg, M., Wall, P. D., & McMahon, S. B. (1999). Does the right side know what the left is doing? *Trends in Neuroscience, 22(3)*, 122–127.

Kuhn, T. S. (1970). *The Structure of Scientific Revolutions*, 2nd ed. Chicago, IL: University of Chicago Press.

Lenz, F. A., Gracely, R. H., Hope, E. J., Baker, F. H., Rowland, L. H., Dougherty, P. M., & Richardson, R.T. (1994). The sensation of angina can be evoked by stimulation of the human thalamus. *Pain, 59(1)*, 119–125.

Lenz, F. A., Kwan, H. C., Dostrovsky, J. O., & Tasker, R. R. (1989). Characteristics of the bursting pattern of action potential that occurs in the thalamus of patients with central pain. *Brain Research, 496*, 357–360.

Lenz, F. A., Tasker, R. R., Dostrovsky, J. O., Kwan, H. C., Gorecki, J., Hirayama, T., & Murphy, J.T. (1987). Abnormal single-unit activity recorded in the somatosensory thalamus of a quadriplegic patient with central pain. *Pain, 31*, 225–236.

Livingston, W. K. (1943). *Pain Mechanisms*. New York: Macmillan.

Livingston, W. K. (1998). *Pain and Suffering*. Seattle, WA: IASP Press.

Maleki, J., LeBel, A. A., Bennett, G. J., & Schwartzman, R. J. (2000). Patterns of spread in complex regional pain syndrome, type I (reflex sympathetic dystrophy). *Pain, 88(3)*, 259–266.

Manabe, H., Dan, K., Hirata, K., Hori, K., Shono, S., Tateshi, S., Ishino, H. & Higa, K. (2004). Optimum pain relief with continuous epidural infusion of local anesthetics shortens the duration of zoster-associated pain. *Clinical Journal of Pain, 20*, 302–308.

Markus, H., Pomeranz, B., & Krushelnyky, D. (1984). Spread of saphenous somatotopic projection map in spinal cord and hypersensitivity of the foot after chronic sciatic denervation in adult rat. *Brain Research, 296*, 27–39.

Meana, M. & Binik, Y. M. (1994). Painful coitus: A review of female dyspareunia. *Journal of Nervous and Mental Disorders, 182(5)*, 264–272.

Melzack, R. (1975). The McGill Pain Questionnaire: Major properties and scoring methods. *Pain, 1*, 277–299.

Melzack, R. (1987). The short-form McGill Pain Questionnaire. *Pain, 30*, 191–197.

Melzack, R. (1989). Phantom limbs, the self, and the brain (The D. O. Hebb memorial lecture). *Canadian Psychology, 30*, 1–16.

Melzack, R. (1990). Phantom limbs and the concept of neuromatrix. *Trends in Neuroscience, 13*, 88–92.

Melzack, R. (1991). The gate control theory 25 years later: New perspectives on phantom limb pain. In M. R. Bond, J. E. Charlton, & C. J. Woolf (Eds.). *Pain Research and Therapy: Proceedings of the VIth World Congress on Pain*. Amsterdam: Elsevier, pp. 9–21.

Melzack, R. (1995). Phantom limb pain and the brain. In B. Bromm & J. E. Desmedt (Eds.). *Pain and the Brain*. New York: Raven Press, pp. 73–82.

Melzack, R. (1999). From the gate to the neuromatrix. *Pain, Suppl 6*, S121–S126.

Melzack, R. (2001). Pain and the neuromatrix in the brain. *Journal of Dental Education, 65*, 1378–1382.

Melzack, R. & Casey, K. L. (1968). Sensory, motivational, and central control determinants of pain. In D. Kenshalo (Ed.). *The Skin Senses*. Springfield, IL: Charles C Thomas, pp. 423–443.

Melzack, R. & Loeser, J. D. (1978). Phantom body pain in paraplegics: Evidence for a central "pattern generating mechanism" for pain. *Pain, 4(3)*, 195–210.

Melzack, R. & Wall, P. D. (1965). Pain mechanisms: A new theory. *Science, 150(699)*, 971–979.

Melzack, R. & Wall, P. D. (1996). *The Challenge of Pain*, 2nd ed. New York: Basic Books.

Melzack, R., Israel, R., Lacroix, R., & Schultz, G. (1997). Phantom limbs in people with congenital limb deficiency or amputation in early childhood. *Brain, 120*, 1603–1620.

Merskey, H. (2004). Pain disorder, hysteria or somatization? *Pain Research and Management, 9(2)*, 67–71.

Milligan, E. D., Twining, C., Chacur, M., Biedenkapp, J., O'Connor, K., Poole, S., Tracey, K., Martin, D., Maier, S.F. & Watkins, L.R. (2003). Spinal glia and proinflammatory cytokines mediate mirror-image neuropathic pain in rats. *Journal of Neuroscience, 23(3)*, 1026–1040.

Nathan, P. W. (1985). Pain and nociception in the clinical context. *Philosophical Transactions of the Royal Society of London, 308*, 219–226.

Noordenbos, W. (1959). *Pain*. Amsterdam: Elsevier.

Oaklander, A. L. & Brown, J. M. (2004). Unilateral nerve injury produces bilateral loss of distal innervation. *Annals of Neurology, 55(5)*, 639–644.

Oaklander, A. L., Romans, K., Horasek, S., Stocks, A., Hauer, P., & Meyer, R. A. (1998). Unilateral postherpetic neuralgia is associated with bilateral sensory neuron damage. *Annals of Neurology, 44(5)*, 789–795.

Oliveras, J. L., Guilbaud, G., & Besson, J. M. (1979). A map of serotoninergic structures involved in stimulation producing analgesia in unrestrained freely moving cats. *Brain Research, 164*, 317–322.

Salomons, T., Osterman, J. E., Gagliese, L., & Katz, J. (2004). Pain flashbacks in Posttraumatic Stress Disorder. *Clinical Journal of Pain, 20*, 83–87.

Schultz, G. & Melzack, R. (1991). The Charles Bonnet syndrome: "Phantom visual images." *Perception, 20*, 809–825.

Segal, M. & Sandberg, D. (1977). Analgesia produced by electrical stimulation of catecholamine nuclei in the rat brain. *Brain Research, 123(2)*, 369–372.

Snijdelaar, D. G., Cornelisse, H. B., Schmid, R. L., & Katz, J. (2004). A randomised, controlled study of peri-operative low dose s(+)-ketamine in combination with postoperative patient-controlled s(+)-ketamine and morphine after radical prostatectomy. *Anaesthesia, 59(3)*, 222–228.

Stoudemire, A. & Sandhu, J. (1987). Psychogenic/idiopathic pain syndromes. *General Hospital Psychiatry, 9(2)*, 79–86.

Sullivan, M. (2000). DSM-IV Pain Disorder: A case against the diagnosis. *International Review of Psychiatry, 12*, 91–98.

Tasker, R. R. (1989). Stereotactic surgery. In P. D. Wall & R. Melzack (Eds.). *The Textbook of Pain*. Edinburgh: Churchill Livingstone, pp. 840–855.

Wall, P. D. (1999). *Pain: The Science of Suffering*. London: Weidenfeld & Nicolson.

Wall, P. D. & Devor, M. (1981). The effect of peripheral nerve injury on dorsal root potentials and on transmission of afferent signals into the spinal cord. *Brain Research, 209(1)*, 95–111.

Woolf, C. J. & Wall, P. D. (1982). Chronic peripheral nerve section diminishes the primary afferent A-fibre mediated inhibition of rat dorsal horn neurones. *Brain Research, 242(1)*, 77–85.

8

Influence of Personality Characteristics of Pain Patients: Implications for Causality in Pain

ROBERT J. GATCHEL AND NANCY KISHINO

Today, pain is still a very pervasive medical problem and is associated with the following statistics: It accounts for over 80% of all physician visits; it affects over 50 million Americans; each year, an estimated 176,850 patients seek treatment in pain centers in the United States alone; and there is a cost of over $70 billion annually in health care and lost productivity (such cost includes lost earnings, decreased productivity, and increased health care utilization expenses and disability benefits). Moreover, based on interviews with over 197,000 individuals assessed in the National Health Interview Survey conducted in 1998, Pleis and Coles (1998) estimated that in the 3-month period prior to the survey, 28% of the adult population in the United States had experienced pain in the lower back, 16% had migraine or severe headaches, 15% had experienced pain in the neck region, and 4% had pain in the face or jaw area. In addition, overall, 32% of the sample reported limitations that affected their ability to walk a quarter of a mile, stand for 2 hours, reach over their heads, use their fingers to grasp small objects, or lift or carry 10-pound items. It should also be noted that in addition to these enormous socioeconomic costs to society, there is a great deal of emotional suffering experienced by patients with pain.

1. Historical Overview of Pain Conceptualizations

As previously reviewed (Gatchel, 1999), the history of attempts at understanding the etiology and treatment of pain parallels the historical changes that have occurred in medicine in general. Starting during the Renaissance period, with the great revolution in scientific knowledge in the areas of anatomy, biology, physiology and physics, a *biomedical reductionism* perspective developed. This approach argued that concepts such as the mind or soul were not needed to explain physical functioning or behavior. It also stimulated a great new revolution in knowledge, with sciences such as anatomy, biology, and physiology evolving simultaneously, all of which would be based on the

149

principles of scientific investigation. Such a "mechanistic" approach to the study of human anatomy and physiology began to foster a "dualistic" viewpoint that the body and mind function separately and independently. The 17th-century French philosopher René Descartes (1596–1650) postulated that the mind or soul was a completely separate entity parallel to and incapable of affecting physical matter or somatic processes in any significant or direct way. Such a dualistic viewpoint gained additional acceptance during the 19th century, with the discovery that micro-organisms caused certain diseases. This novel and revolutionary biomedical reductionism philosophy of medicine then became viewed as the only acceptable basis for explaining diseases through understanding mechanical laws and physiological processes and principles.

Although the above reductionistic approach to medicine played a valuable role in bringing medicine "out of the Dark Ages" and prompting significant discoveries and maturation of the field as a science, it subsequently had a stifling effect on the field during the 19th and 20th centuries, when clinical research began to appear that emphasized the importance of taking into account the mind (or psychological factors) for a more thorough understanding of a physical disorder. Fortunately, however, this strict mechanistic, biomedical reductionist approach to medicine began to subside somewhat because of the advent of important work implicating the role of psychosocial factors in medical disorders. Indeed, Bonica (1953) had pointed out the various shortcomings of earlier purely mechanistic models of pain.

During the past three decades, there have been major advances in the understanding of the close interaction of physiological and psychosocial processes in pain perception. The first major theory of pain, which emphasized the close interaction between psychosocial and physiological processes affecting pain, was that of Melzack and Wall (1965). They introduced the *gate control theory of pain*, which accounted for many diverse factors involved in pain perception. Its primary contribution to the scientific community was the introduction of the importance of the central nervous system *and* psychosocial variables in the pain perception process. It highlighted the potentially significant role of psychosocial factors in the perception of pain (Melzack, 1993). Subsequently, Melzack (1999) extended the gate control theory of pain and integrated it with models of stress [which Selye (1956) first introduced]. His *neuromatrix theory* assumes that pain is a multidimensional experience and is produced by specific patterns of nerve impulses generated by a widely distributed neural network or "neuromatrix." Nerve impulse patterns can be triggered either by peripheral sensory input or centrally without peripheral stimulation. The final neuromatrix is determined and modified by multiple factors: genetics, sensory experiences, and learning influences. This neuromatrix theory can be viewed as a *diathesis stress model*, in which predispositional factors interact with an acute stressor such as pain. Once pain is established, it becomes a stressor in its own right. This neuromatrix theory of pain integrates a great deal of physiological and psychological evidence.

Although the various components of the theory, as well as the theory itself, still require a great deal of systematic investigation, it offers another promising way of conceptualizing pain. It should stimulate a great deal of clinical research in the future.

2.   The Biopsychosocial Perspective of Pain

Both the gate control model and the neuromatrix theory have attempted to integrate a great deal of psychological and physiological scientific data. Although both require additional investigation, they highlight the most promising approach to understanding pain: the *biopsychosocial approach*. Indeed, the biopsychosocial model of pain is now accepted as the most heuristic approach to the understanding and treatment of pain disorders. It views physical disorders such as pain as a result of a complex and dynamic interaction among physiologic, psychologic, and social factors, which perpetuates and could worsen the clinical presentation. Each individual experiences pain uniquely. The range of psychological, social, and economic factors can interact with physical pathology to modulate a patient's report of symptoms and subsequent disability. In fact, Loeser (1982) originally formulated a model outlining four dimensions associated with the concept of pain: nociception, pain, suffering, and pain behavior. *Nociception* refers to the actual physical units (chemical, mechanical, or thermal) that might impact on specialized nerve fibers and signal the central nervous system that an aversive event has occurred. *Pain* is the sensation arising as the result of perceived nociception. However, this definition is overly simplistic and less than certain because, sometimes, pain is perceived in the absence of nociception (e.g., phantom limb pain) or, conversely, when nociception occurs without being perceived (e.g., an individual being severely wounded without becoming immediately aware of the pain).

Nociception and pain act as signals to the central nervous system. In contrast, *suffering* and *pain behavior* are reactions to these signals that can be affected by past experiences as well as anticipation of future events. Specifically, according to Loeser (1982), *suffering* refers to the emotional responses that are triggered by nociception or some other aversive event associated with it, such as fear, threat, or loss. Because of a specific painful episode, the individual might lose his or her job and, as a consequence, develop anxiety and depression. *Pain behavior* refers to those things that individuals do when they are suffering or are in pain. For example, they might avoid exercise or any activity for fear of reinjury. Thus, there might be a complex interaction of a range of biopsychosocial factors.

The development of this biopsychosocial approach has grown rapidly during the past decade, and a great deal of scientific knowledge has been produced in this short period of time concerning the best care of individuals with complex pain problems as well as pain prevention and coping techniques.

As Turk and Monarch (2002) have discussed in their comprehensive review of the biopsychosocial perspective on chronic pain, individuals differ significantly in how frequently they report physical symptoms, in their tendency to visit physicians when experiencing identical symptoms, and their responses to the same treatments. Quite frequently, the nature of a patient's response to treatment has little to do with his or her objective physical condition. For example, White and colleagues (1961) noted earlier that less than one third of all individuals with clinically significant symptoms consult a physician. On the other hand, from 30% to 50% of patients who seek treatment in primary care do not have specific diagnosable disorders (Dworkin & Massoth, 1994).

3.   Disease Versus Illness

Turk and Monarch (2002) go on to make the distinction between disease and illness in better understanding chronic pain. The term *disease* is generally used to define "an objective biological event" that involves the disruption of specific body structures or organ systems caused by either anatomical, pathological, or physiological changes. *Illness*, in contrast, is generally defined as a "subjective experience or self-attribution" that a disease is present. An illness will yield physical discomfort, behavioral limitations, and psychosocial distress. Thus, illness references how a sick individual and members of his or her family live with, and respond to, symptoms and disability. This distinction between disease and illness is analogous to the distinction made between pain and nociception. As noted earlier, nociception involves the stimulation of nerves that convey information about tissue damage to the brain. Pain, on the other hand, is a more subjective perception that is the result of the transduction, transmission, and modulation of sensory input. This input may be filtered through an individual's genetic composition, prior learning history, current physiological status, and sociocultural influences. Pain, therefore, cannot be comprehensively assessed without a full understanding of the person who is exposed to the nociception. The biopsychosocial model focuses on illness, which is the result of the complex interaction of biological, psychological, and social factors. With this perspective, a diversity in pain or illness expression (including its severity, duration, and psychosocial consequences) can be expected. The interrelationships among biological changes, psychological status, and the social and cultural context need to be taken into account in fully understanding the pain patient's perception and response to illness. A model or treatment approach that focuses on only one of these core sets of factors will be incomplete. Indeed, the treatment efficacy of a biopsychosocial approach to pain has consistently demonstrated the heuristic value of this model (Turk & Monarch, 2002).

One important postulate of the above disease versus illness distinction is that pain, as an illness, cannot usually be "cured" but only *managed*. This is also true for other chronic medical conditions such as hypertension, diabetes, and asthma. Moreover, currently, a major trend in the pain management literature is a movement away from the "homogeneity of pain patients myth" and toward attempts to match treatment to specific assessment outcomes of patients (e.g., Turk & Gatchel, 1999; Turk & Monarch, 2002; Turk & Okifuji, 2001). Because groups of patients may differ in psychosocial and behavioral characteristics, even when the medical diagnosis is identical, such patient differences and treatment matching is important to consider. Traditionally, patients with the same medical diagnosis or set of symptoms were "lumped" together (e.g., chronic back pain, fibromyalgia, neuropathic pain) and then treated in the same way, as though "one size fits all." However, it has been shown that there are differential responses of pain patients with the same diagnosis to the same treatment. Consequently, it is important that treatment should be individually tailored for each patient based on the careful biopsychosocial assessment of that particular patient. It is often the case that two chronic low back pain patients, for example, will require slightly different treatment programs because of differences in their physical, psychosocial, or socioeconomic presentations. Turk and Okifuji (2001) have provided a comprehensive review of the importance of this treatment-matching process and literature to support the greater clinical efficacy of such a matching approach strategy. Indeed, taking the approach of delineating homogeneous *subgroups* among patients with pain will provide an extremely important basis for the development of more specific, optimal treatment regimens for these different subgroups of patients.

4. Personality and Pain

The search for specific personality or psychosocial factors predisposing individuals to develop pain problems has always been a major focus in the field of psychosomatic medicine and mental health research. Indeed, there is a close comorbidity of mental health and physical health problems that needs to be more carefully understood in order to develop the most effective intervention strategies. Recently, the most promising work that has been conducted has, again, embraced a biopsychosocial approach to intervention, in which the mental health needs of patients require careful evaluation and treatment, along with the intertwined physical components of the pain problem. For example, well-documented clinical evaluations have concluded that patients with chronic pain often manifest concurrent psychiatric illness, most commonly depression, anxiety disorders, and substance abuse disorders (Dersh et al., 2002). Also, there are close associations among chronic pain, depression, and suicide. Patients with chronic pain are at increased risk for depression (Rush et al., 2000), suicide (Fishbain, 1999; Parker, 1998), identified by the Surgeon General as one of the top public health concerns in the United States, and sleep disorders (Hanscom & Jex, 2001). As pain becomes more chronic, emotional factors play an increasingly dominant role in the maintenance of dysfunction and suffering (Dersh et al., 2002). Indeed, Dersh and colleagues (2002) have reviewed research demonstrating a greater prevalence of psychiatric disorders in patients with chronic pain relative to those with acute pain.

4.1. Conceptual Model of the Transition from Acute to Chronic Pain Disability

Gatchel (1991, 1996) developed a three-stage conceptual model to further understand the transition from acute to chronic pain disability and accompanying psychosocial distress. In Stage 1 of this model, referred to as the *acute phase*, normal emotional reactions (such as fear, anxiety, and worry) develop subsequent to the patient's perception of pain. As noted earlier, this is a natural emotional reaction that often serves a protective function by prompting the individual to heed the pain signal and, if necessary, seek out medical attention for it. However, if the perception of pain exists beyond a 2–4-month period (which is usually considered a normal healing time for most pain syndromes), the pain begins to develop into a more chronic condition, leading into Stage 2 of the model. During this second stage, physiological, behavioral, and personality problems are often exacerbated. Learned helplessness, anger, distress, and somatization are typical symptoms of patients in this stage. Often, the extent of these symptoms usually depends on the individual's pre-existing personality/psychosocial structure, in addition to socioeconomic and environmental conditions. The model proposes a *diathesis–stress* perspective, in which the stress of coping with pain can lead to exacerbation of the individual's underlying psychological characteristics. Finally, the progression to complex interactions of physical, psychological, and social processes characterize Stage 3, which represents the *chronic phase* of the model. As the result of the chronic nature of the pain experience and the stress that it creates, the patient's life begins to revolve around the pain and the behaviors that maintain it. The patient begins to adopt a "sick role," in which any excuse from social and occupational responsibilities becomes routine. As a consequence, the patient now becomes accustomed to the avoidance of responsibility, and other reinforcers serve to maintain such maladaptive behavior.

Superimposed on these three stages is what is referred to as the "physical deconditioning syndrome," originally emphasized by Mayer and Gatchel (1988). This refers to a significant decrease in physical capacity (such as strength, mobility, and endurance) resulting from disuse and the resultant atrophy of the injured area. There is usually a two-way pathway between the physical deconditioning and the three stages described earlier. For example, physical deconditioning can "feed back" and negatively affect the emotional well-being and self-esteem of individuals. This can lead to further negative psychosocial sequelae. Conversely, negative emotional reactions such as depression can "feed back" to physical functioning (e.g., by decreasing the motivation to get involved in work or recreational activities and thereby contributing further to physical deconditioning).

4.2.   The "Pain-Prone Personality"

Currently, the notion that there is a unique "pain-prone personality" characteristic is quite outdated. Early works attempted to differentiate "functional" from "organic pain." The term psychogenic was used to suggest that the pain was the result of psychological causes only and that it was not "real" pain because no specific organic basis for it could be found. Unfortunately, this significantly hindered the development of effective psychiatric and pain management strategies. Today, fortunately, the *Diagnostic and Statistical Manual*, 4th ed. (DSM-IV) of the American Psychiatric Association (1994) does not list "psychogenic pain" as a diagnostic entity. The assessment or diagnosis of organically caused pain does not rule out the important role that psychosocial factors play for any particular patient. Again, the biopsychosocial model now views physical disorders, such as pain, as the result of a complex and dynamic interaction among physiologic, psychologic, and social factors, which perpetuates and may worsen clinical presentation. Therefore, the proper question to pose is not whether personality characteristics cause pain, but what are their relative contributions to the pain perception process?

In terms of personality disorders in general, research has consistently found that such disorders are more common in the chronic pain population (Dersh et al., 2002). However, little consistency has been found concerning specific types of personality disorder among chronic pain patients. For example, Gatchel and colleagues found that prevalences of personality disorders were much higher in a sample of chronic low back pain patients (60%) relative to samples of acute low back pain patients (Kinney et al., 1993), and acute carpal tunnel syndrome patients (Mathis et al., 1994). These results further support Gatchel's above-reviewed model of the progression from acute to chronic pain. Gatchel et al. (1995) also found that the presence of *any* diagnosed personality disorder, along with several other psychosocial variables, was predictive of which acute low back pain patients had not returned to work 6 months later. These authors note that no specific type of personality order was found to predict chronicity, leading them to suggest that an Axis II diagnosis of any type may reflect a general deficit in coping skills that is linked to chronic disability. Indeed, according to DSM-IV,

Personality traits are enduring patterns of perceiving, relating to, and thinking about the environment and oneself that are exhibited in a wide range of social and personal contexts. Only when personality traits are inflexible and maladaptive and cause significant functional impairment or subjective distress do they constitute personality disorders. The essential feature of a personality disorder is an enduring pattern of inner experience and behavior that deviates markedly from the expectations of the individual's culture and is manifested in at least two of the following areas: cognition, affectivity, interpersonal functioning, or impulse control (American Psychiatric Association, 1994 p. 633).

Moreover, personality disorders are thought to develop during childhood or adolescence and must be evident by late adolescent or early adulthood. As long-term patterns, these disorders, by definition, precede the development of pain episodes. As such, in the context of pain, personality disorders are best conceptualized as marginally adaptive coping styles that can often decompensate under distress of injury, pain, and disability, in an exacerbation of the expression of a personality disorder.

5.   The Assessment–Treatment Process

Gatchel and Weisberg (2000) comprehensively reviewed the various personality issues that need to be considered in the assessment and treatment process of patients with pain. As they highlighted, a *"stepwise approach"* to assessment needs to be used in which one proceeds from global indices of personality characteristics to more detailed evaluations of specific diagnoses. For example, as Gatchel (2000) has noted, most clinicians are currently under various time constraints, as well as billing constraints imposed by third-party payers, when considering the best method of evaluating possible personality/psychosocial pathology in their patients with pain. Thus, commonly, a frequently asked question is: "If I were to choose the most time- and cost–efficient assessment method, which one should I select?" Unfortunately, one must not make the assumption that there is a single instrument that can serve as the best assessment. For many patients, several assessments will be needed. Rather than asking which instrument should be used, a better question is: "What sequence of testing should I consider to obtain the best understanding of potential personality problems that might be encountered with patients experiencing pain?" As such, psychosocial/personality assessment should be viewed as a "stepwise" process, proceeding from global indices of emotional distress and disturbance to more detailed evaluations of specific diagnoses of Axis I Clinical and Axis II Personality Disorders.

   An initial screening process to identify the obvious psychological distress, which can be done efficiently, might consist of the administration of the Beck Depression Inventory (BDI-II), the Symptom Checklist-90-Revised (SCL-90-R), and the SF-36. Pronounced scale elevations on these instruments would alert clinical staff to the degree of emotional distress and dysfunction in a pain patient and would indicate the need for a more thorough evaluation. This would include the administration of the MMPI-2, as well as the Structured Clinical Interview for DSM Diagnosis (SCID). Note that if no pronounced elevations were displayed on the BDI-II, SCL-90-R, and the SF-36, the MMPI-2 would still be administered. If there were no meaningful profile elevations on the MMPI-2, then one could proceed directly to a clinical interview. If the elevations on the MMPI-2 were exhibited, the SCID would be administered. Administration of it would support an official DSM-IV-based diagnosis of an Axis I and/or Axis II disorder. The next step would be the administration of a psychosocial clinical interview, which is, indeed, a powerful assessment tool of the clinician. In addition to the traditional areas explored in a clinical history, there are other areas that should be examined, especially with chronic pain patients. The clinician will be sensitized to which needs attention as a result of the structured psychosocial–personality test results. Some issues that are important to cover in a clinical interview consist of potential barriers to recovery that could affect response to treatment:

• Patient and family history of mental health, such as depression and substance abuse
• History of head injury, convulsions, or impairment of function
• Any stressful changes in lifestyle or marital status before or since the injury that precipitated the pain
• Work history, including explanation of job losses, changes, and dissatisfaction
• Financial history, contrasting current income with past, and comparing these with current cost-of-living requirements
• Any litigation pending for the patient's current medical and pain problem
• Any potential drug/medication abuse patterns

In addition to the above, the determination of a patient's motivation for change is another important and unstated purpose of the interview process. Many patients with pain, especially if the pain is chronic, restrict their lives by avoiding any risk of experiencing pain, through immobilization and use of analgesics. Patients who are not candidates for surgical intervention (for any reason) and who refuse to work toward active rehabilitation clearly have suspect motivation for change. There are now methods for enhancing patient motivation in pain treatment programs.

The above clinical interview allows the clinician to contrast a patient's current psychosocial functioning with past functioning and to compare the testing data with the interview data. The clinician can then estimate the potential for getting the patient to change behavior and work toward rehabilitation. Finally, with this clinical assessment material in hand, if it is decided that the patient is a suitable candidate to enter a comprehensive pain management program, an additional set of assessment instruments should be administered: the Multidimensional Pain Inventory (MPI) and the Millon Behavioral Health Inventory (MBHI). These instruments are beneficial for treatment personnel who can use the results to identify the best approach for pain management and to anticipate potential problems in the pain management program. As an extension to the MBHI, Millon and colleagues have recently developed the Millon Behavioral Medicine Diagnostic (MBMD). This was done because several important psychosocial characteristics were not evaluated by the MBHI (Bockian et al., 2000).

6.   Implications for Effective Pain Management

A number of important personality, emotional, and psychopathology issues have been discussed that can directly or indirectly affect a patient's report of pain and overall response to a pain management program. Thus, again, a biopsychosocial treatment approach emphasizes that a full range of psychosocial factors have to be addressed, in addition to any biological basis of symptoms. Interdisciplinary treatment focuses on providing patients with methods to better manage their pain and the biopsychosocial concomitants of it by providing an array of beneficial therapeutic modalities, ranging from physical therapy for reconditioning purposes, to psychopharmacological therapy to deal with emotional distress, to cognitive–behavioral therapy to deal with affective, behavioral, and cognitive facets of the pain experience. Such a comprehensive treatment approach will result in significant changes in developing more appropriate beliefs about pain, better coping styles, positive behavioral changes, as well as decreases in reported pain severity. It is important to increase the function and perceptions of control over pain because that will result in decreases in emotional distress and perceived pain–severity ratings. Once again, in order to accomplish these treatment goals, it will be important to individually tailor treatment programs that are matched to a particular patient's biopsychosocial characteristics. Fortunately, we now have a broad range of pain management techniques in our treatment armamentarium to help tailor the specific treatment needs for each patient we see, after careful pretreatment assessment.

7.   Implications for Causality

Finally, in addition to the important issue of considering the relative role that personality factors play in pain, health care professionals need to be aware of the number of other important issues pertaining to pain patients. One important such issue is that of discordance among medical/administrative diagnostic concepts. Waddell (1987) was the first to note that although correlations are found among pain, disability, and impairment, there is not perfect overlapping among these categories. Although they are all logically and clinically related to one another, there is usually not a 1:1:1 relationship among them. *Impairment* is a medical term used to refer to an alteration of a patient's usual health status (i.e., some anatomical or pathological abnormality) that is evaluated by medical means. The evaluation of impairment is solely a medical responsibility in which there is an attempt to evaluate structural limitations objectively and it also has become a term used in psychological research. However, unfortunately, no technology currently exists that would allow impairment evaluation to be totally accurate or objective. At the present time, such evaluation relies upon methods that are not highly reliable and are often subject to patient and examiner bias. *"Disability"* is an administrative term that refers to the diminished capacity or inability to perform certain activities of everyday living. Disability evaluations, too, are not totally reliable and are subject to various examiner and patient response biases. The assessment of disability is usually based on subjective report measures. Finally, '*pain*' is a psychophysiological concept based primarily on experiential or subjective evaluation. Likewise, it is often difficult to quantify in an objective or reliable manner. Overall, the wide individual differences and the discordance among these three concepts from one patient to the next make this imperfect correlation even more complex. Therefore, assessment/treatment personnel need to be aware of the varying relationships among these concepts. Attempts to develop an algorithm or model to help guide and direct the therapeutic process on the basis of measurement of these various components have not been successful (Gatchel, 1996). Another important issue yet to be effectively addressed is what role personality plays in affecting the degree of discordance displayed by individuals.

Needless to say, it is important to address all three concepts in specific situations whenever possible, with the expectation that there may be complex interactions among them that may differ from one patient to the next, as well as from one time to the next. One patient may verbally report a significant amount of pain, but yet may show very little impairment that can be objectively evaluated, with disability perhaps lying somewhere in between the two in terms of severity. Another patient may report little pain, but may display great disability and some impairment. Moreover, an important issue that has not received much empirical attention to date is the role that personality plays in this relationship process.

8.   Summary and Conclusions

In summary, as noted earlier, the most proper question to ask when considering the potential influence of personality characteristics of pain patients on causality in pain is not whether personality characteristics cause pain but, rather, what are their relative contributions to the pain perception process. For an even more comprehensive review of the complexity of this biopsychosocial causality perspective, the reader is referred to a recent chapter by Wright and McGeary (2005). Finally, there are a number of "assumption traps" or fallacies that pain management professionals and forensic psychologists will need to avoid when considering the relationship between personality influences on pain experience as well as judgments of causality. These are delineated as follows:

- There is no specific "pain-prone personality."
- One cannot automatically assume, on an a priori basis, that one assessment method of personality will necessarily be more valid or reliable than another. One must rely on empirical data to determine what method is psychometrically best for what individuals in certain situations.

- Relatedly, the common denominator of all assessment methods is the qualities of validity, reliability (reproducibility), and predictive value. However, there often remain frequent misunderstandings over the appropriate use of assessments based on the generalizability of the scientific reports of validity to the circumstances in which the health care professional is using the assessment method. Such ambiguities can be minimized by examining the match between the clinical context in which a test is evaluated and the patient to whom it is applied in the clinical setting. Basically, it is answering the question of test validity by addressing the "valid for what?" issue. Assessment methods might be valid for measuring specific biologic/physiologic states but have no validity in predicting, for example, impairment, disability or activities of daily living.
- Likewise, in evaluating pain, one cannot assume that one assessment measure will necessarily be more valid or reliable than another. Generally, the more objectively quantified the measure is, the more likely it can be empirically established as a valid and reliable referent or marker.
- A physical measure will not always be more objective than self-report psychosocial measures. No matter what the level of accuracy or sophistication of a mechanical device used in collecting physiologic measures, it is always the case that human interpretation often must be used in the understanding of the resulting findings.
- A patient's performance during an assessment protocol will not always be the same from one time to another. It can be greatly influenced by a number of factors, such as fear of pain or injury, motivation, secondary gain, instructional set, and so forth (Gatchel, 2001).
- Neither personality assessment nor pain assessment is an exact science. As a result, causality can rarely be unequivocally proven. One should be content with making a probability statement concerning possible relationships between personality and pain, rather than cause–effect statements concerning such an association.

Acknowledgment

The writing of this chapter was supported in part by grants from the National Institute of Health (3R01-MH046452; 2R01-DE010713; 2K02-MH01107; IK05-MH071892).

References

American Psychiatric Association. (1994). *Diagnostic and Statistical Manual of Mental Disorders*, 4th ed. Washington, DC: American Psychiatric Association.

Bockian, N., Meager, S., & Millon, T. (2000). Assessing personality with the Millon Behavioral Health Inventory, the Millon Behavioral Medicine Diagnostic, and the Millon Clinical Multiaxial Inventory. In R. J. Gatchel & J. N. Weisberg (Eds.). *Personality Characteristics of Patients with Pain*. Washington, DC: American Psychological Association Press.

Bonica, J. J. (1953). *The Management of Pain*. Philadelphia: Lea & Febiger.

Dersh, J., Polatin, P., & Gatchel, R. (2002). Chronic pain and psychopathology: Research findings and theoretical considerations. *Psychosomatic Medicine, 64*, 773–786.

Dworkin, S. F., & Massoth, D. L. (1994). Temporomandibular disorders and chronic pain: Disease or illness? *Journal of Prosthetic Dentistry, 72(1)*, 29–38.

Fishbain, D. (1999). The association of chronic pain and suicide. *Seminars in Clinical Neuropsychiatry, 4*, 221–227.

Gatchel, R. J. (1991). Psychosocial assessment and disability management in the rehabilitation of painful spinal disorders. In T. Mayer, V. Mooney, & R. Gatchel (Eds.). *Contemporary Conservative Care for Painful Spinal Disorders*. Philadelphia: Lea & Febiger.

Gatchel, R. J. (1996). Psychological disorders and chronic pain: Cause and effect relationships. In R. J. Gatchel & D. C. Turk (Eds.). *Psychological Approaches to Pain Management: A Practitioner's Handbook*. New York: Guilford Press, pp. 33–52.

Gatchel, R. J. (1999). Perspectives on pain: A historical overview. In R. J. Gatchel & D. C. Turk (Eds.). *Psychosocial Factors in Pain: Critical Perspectives*. New York: Guilford Press, pp. 3–17.

Gatchel, R. J. (2000). How practitioners should evaluate personality to help manage chronic pain patients. In R. J. Gatchel & J. N. Weisberg (Eds.). *Personality Characteristics of Patients with Pain*. Washington, DC: American Psychological Association.

Gatchel, R. J. (2001). A biopsychosocial overview of pre-treatment screening of patients with pain. *The Clinical Journal of Pain, 17*, 192–199.

Gatchel, R. J., Polatin, P. B., & Kinney, R. K. (1995). Predicting outcome of chronic back pain using clinical predictors of psychopathology: A prospective analysis. *Health Psychology, 14*(5), 415–420.

Gatchel, R. J. & Weisberg, J. N. (2000). *Personality Characteristics of Patients with Pain*. Washington, DC: American Psychological Association Press.

Hanscom, D. & Jex, R. (2001). Sleep disorders, depression and musculoskeletal pain. *Spineline, Sept./Oct.*pp. 20–31.

Kinney, R. K., Gatchel, R. J., Polatin, P. B., Fogarty, W. J., & Mayer, T. G. (1993). Prevalence of psychopathology in acute and chronic low back pain patients. *Journal of Occupational Rehabilitation, 1993*, 95–103.

Loeser, J. D. (1982). Concepts of pain. In J. Stanton-Hicks & R. Boaz (Eds.). *Chronic Low Back Pain*. New York: Raven Press.

Mathis, L. B., Gatchel, R. J., Polatin, P. B., Boulas, J., & Kinney, R. (1994). Prevalence of psychopathology in carpal tunnel syndrome patients. *Journal of Occupational Rehabilitation, 4*, 199–210.

Mayer, T.G & Gatchel, R.J. (1988). *Functional Restoration for Spinal Disorders : The Sports Medicine Approach.* Philadelphia : Lea & Febiger.

Melzack, R. (1993). Pain: Past, present and future. *Canadian Journal of Experimental Psychology, 47*(4), 615–629.

Melzack, R. (1999). Pain and stress: A new perspective. In R. J. Gatchel & D. C. Turk (Eds.). *Psychosocial Factors in Pain: Critical Perspectives*. New York: Guilford Press.

Melzack, R. & Wall, P. D. (1965). Pain mechanisms: A new theory. *Science, 50*, 971–979.

Parker, D. (1998). See suicide as preventable: A national strategy emerges. *Christian Science Monitor, 3*.

Pleis, J. R. & Coles, R. (1998). Summary Health Statistics for U.S. Adults: *National Health Interview Survey, 202*(10), 209.

Rush, A., Polatin, P., & Gatchel, R. J. (2000). Depression and chronic low back pain: Establishing priorities in treatment. *Spine, 25,* 2566–2571.

Selye, H. *The Stress of Life.* New York: McGraw-Hill. 1956.

Turk, D. C. & Gatchel, R. J. (1999). Psychosocial factors and pain: Revolution and evolution. In R. J. Gatchel & D. C. Turk (Eds.). *Psychosocial Factors in Pain: Critical Perspectives.* New York: Guilford Press.

Turk, D. C. & Monarch, E. S. (2002). Biopsychosocial perspective on chronic pain. In D. C. Turk & R. J. Gatchel (Eds.). *Psychological Approaches to Pain Management: A Practitioner's Handbook,* 2nd ed. New York: Guilford Press.

Turk, D. C. & Okifuji, A. (2001). Matching treatment to assessment of patients with chronic pain. In D. C. Turk & R. Melzack (Eds.). *Handbook of Pain Assessment,* 2nd ed. New York: Guilford Press.

Waddell, G. (1987). A new clinical method for the treatment of low back pain. *Spine, 12,* 632–644.

White, K. L., Williams, F., & Greenberg, B. G. (1961). The etiology of medical care. *New England Journal of Medicine, 265,* 885–886.

Wright, A. R. & McGeary, D. D. (2005). Musculoskeletal injury: A three-stage continuum from cause to disability to decision. In I. Z. Schultz & R. J. Gatchel (Eds.). *At Risk Claims: Predicting and Managing Occupational Disabilities.* New York: Kluwer Academic/Plenum.

9

Effect of Cognition on Pain Experience and Pain Behavior: Diathesis–Stress and the Causal Conundrum

Tamar Pincus

1. Introduction and Definition of Risk

1.1. The Burden of Pain

Pain has been described as "the most widespread and intractable of all health problems" (Wall & Jones, 1991, p. 7). It has been estimated that in industrialized countries, as many as 20% of the population experience acute pain yearly and as many as 30% report suffering from chronic pain (Bonica & Loeser, 2001). This chapter aims to describe the concepts and measurement of cognitive factors that have been considered risk factors in pain populations, outline the shortcomings in current research, and suggest some promising avenues for future research.

1.2. Risk and Vulnerability

The concept of "risk" applies to an increased likelihood of developing a poor outcome if the factor is present (Ingram et al., 1998). It does not necessarily imply a causal path between the presence of the risk factor and the subsequent outcome. In the context of this chapter, the concept of "risk" is considered distinct from causality. The discussion will explain how theories have assumed such a causal path, thereby suggesting that the factors they describe are in fact vulnerability factors. The concept of "vulnerability" (Ingram et al., 1998) is related to relatively stable, endogenous characteristics that are causally linked to pathology. Typically, these are genetic or are acquired early in life. We currently have no definitive knowledge about cognitive factors and pain syndromes, although it often appears otherwise in the literature. However, we do have theories, models, and logical conjectures about the nature of cognitive factors as vulnerability factors. I propose that at present these should be seen as promising suggestions.

1.3. "Good Evidence": Evidence-Based Criteria for Establishing Risk of Poor Outcome

The literature on risk factors (psychological and otherwise) that contribute to pain syndromes is extensive. It consists of useful theories and models, some attempts to systematically assess the evidence, and much conjecture and myth. Correlations have been found between dozens of potential risk factors and outcome factors such as pain, disability, and distress in literally thousands of cross-sectional studies. Although they inform us that sets of factors tend to occur together in certain populations, they tell us little about the causal path between the factors. Even the most sophisticated statistical analysis (e.g., causal path analysis using Structural Equation Modeling) cannot test causality in the absence of research using a time line. Ultimately, the time line must include some measure of risk before acute pain has developed (Pincus & Morley, 2001). Furthermore, such vulnerability could lie dormant, until "switched on" by a stressful event (e.g., Banks & Kerns, 1996). To assess the evidence for causality in cognitive factors in pain populations, we therefore need to examine primarily longitudinal cohort studies and experimental approaches, including controlled trials.

The majority of people with acute pain recover or learn to live with pain without seeking medical care (Papageorgiou & Wells, 1998; Thomas & Roy, 1999). Thus, having pain, even on a regular basis, is not considered in itself a negative outcome. Seeking multiple care, restricting life activities, and being distressed are considered poor long-term outcomes. These are the ones we want to prevent. This chapter, therefore, deals primarily with the transition from acute to chronic pain, as defined by these markers of poor outcome.

2. Cognition and Pain

2.1. The Gate Control Theory of Pain

The publication of Gate Control Theory (Melzack & Wall, 1965) brought about a revolution in the way pain is conceptualized. The "gate" itself is a hypothesized neural mechanism in the spinal cord, which operates to allow through pain information signals. The degree to which it opens and closes depends not only on ascending neural signals about injury and damage but also on descending signals from the central nervous system. These are affected by emotional states such as fear and anxiety and by cognitive processing such as attention, memory, and expectation. Modern models of pain owe their basic premises to the gate control model. Researchers have adopted universally its central theoretical proposition that psychological states, including emotion and cognition, are part and parcel of pain processing. Even the definition of pain has been altered to incorporate these ideas: The International Association for the Study of Pain (IASP) defines pain as "an unpleasant sensory and emotional experience associated with actual or potential tissue damage, or described in terms of such damage" (Merskey & Bogduk, 1994, p. 210).

2.2.   The Interaction Between Cognition and Pain

The study of the effect of cognition on pain processing and pain experience has not always yielded clear-cut findings. Intuitively, it is easier to grasp why the way we think, our beliefs, and attributions can affect our behavior. Pain behavior, including care seeking, medication consumption, avoidance of work, and reduction in daily activities, are clearly affected by the way we think. It is harder to understand how our beliefs can affect the pain experience *per se*. Examples are readily available from the more dramatic events in life: the dancer who continues to dance to the end of the show despite injury, the athlete who wins the race without even noticing the damage until later. We call it "mind over matter," thus demonstrating our reluctance to accept that mind and matter are one, working together.

Perhaps the most obvious example of the interaction between cognitive and physiological processing is the placebo effect. Evidence suggests that this effect might in part at least be the result of an endogenous opiod mediating system (e.g., Gibson et al., 1994). However, there is no explanation for the fact that individuals differ in their responses to placebo and that this response changes over time, in direct relation to their expectations and their past experience (reviewed in Field, 2004). In summary, if we believe that something will help us, at least in the short term, it probably will. This will be reflected not only in our subsequent behavior and self-report, but it can be detected by objective physiological measures. No intervention is free of the placebo effect, therefore every intervention harnesses patients' cognition to some extent.

Apart from the placebo effect, research has generally concentrated on what makes people worse, rather than better. There is some evidence that certain beliefs and attributions are related to poor outcome. For example, the belief that normal daily activities will exacerbate the injury can result in needless and often damaging behavior. The belief that one is helpless in the face of an overwhelming physical threat can result in distress, overmonitoring of physical sensations, fear, and even thoughts of suicide. For decades, researchers and clinicians have been puzzled by the apparent finding that some patients, presenting with the same degree of injury and damage as others, appear to experience more distress and suffering, resulting in higher rates of disability, care seeking, medication consumption, and overall reduction in quality of life. It is now believed that, at least in part, these negative outcomes are the result of individual psychological characteristics, including certain cognitions and a tendency toward negative affect (Pincus & Morley, 2001; Pincus et al., 2002; Sullivan et al., 1998). The last two decades have seen a flurry of studies attempting to identify such factors, conceptualized as "vulnerability" factors.

These factors combined with specific stressors, such as work pressure, bereavement, or illness (conceptualized as "diathesis") are thought to be responsible for negative outcomes (Dworkin & Banks, 1999).

2.3. The Evidence of Cognitive Risk Factors for Poor Outcome

There have been several systematic reviews of psychological factors and their influence on disability and pain in pain patients (Linton & Skevington, 1999), working populations (Bongers et al., 1993; Hoogendoorn et al., 2000), and specifically in musculoskeletal pain populations (Linton, 2000; Pincus et al, 2002; Truchon & Fillion, 2000). Most of them conclude that there is strong evidence for a role played by a variety of psychological factors, including catastrophizing, locus of control, coping strategies, helplessness, somatization, personality traits, fear avoidance, and attention (summarized in Linton et al., 2002). Although most of the reviews systematically searched the literature and describe the findings, only one (Pincus et al., 2002) applied objective criteria to assess the quality of the evidence. The conclusion was that the evidence, contrary to common claims, was limited. There were considerably less studies than believed: This was a result of several publications based on single cohorts. The methodology of many studies fell short of that needed to draw conclusions from the findings. Large loss to follow-up in relatively small samples reduced power; patients were recruited too late along their pain time line; and measurement of psychological factors was poor.

Several famous studies, cited time and again in the literature as strong evidence for psychological risk factors, in fact provided only limited evidence. These included the evidence for coping strategies affecting poor long-term outcome in acute low back pain (Burton et al., 1995), the evidence for personality traits significantly predicting poor outcome (Gatchel et al., 1995), and the evidence for fear avoidance as a predictor of outcome (Klenerman et al., 1995). New evidence has been found for each of these factors: Gatchel and Kishino in Chapter 8 describe the evidence for personality traits; the evidence for catastrophizing and fear avoidance is described in this chapter.

Nonetheless, the claim that there is an abundance of strong evidence for cognitive risk factors in pain populations is based on a misconception or myth, and it misinforms clinicians and researchers. It also limits the willingness of funding bodies to provide support for further large-scale prospective cohorts.

In fact, there is only limited evidence for the role of most risk factors studied so far (excluding bed rest as a risk factor for developing long-term back problems). However, the evidence is promising, and some of it is based on novel studies utilizing a high standard of methodological rigor. The following is a description and a critique of the evidence and its implications for assessment and intervention.

3.   Self-reported Cognitive Factors and Pain

3.1.   *Cognition and Pain*

Cognition is an umbrella term that is thought to include perceiving, recognizing, conceiving, judging, sensing, reasoning, and imagining (Weisenberg, 1984). It is the mental act by which knowledge is acquired (Collins English Dictionary, 1993). It relates to the way people view themselves and the world. The general hypothesis in research on the effect of cognitions on pain outcomes is that some individuals have had, or have acquired, a style of interacting with the world that interferes with adjustment. Some of the cognitive factors that have been studied include coping style (including catastrophizing), self-efficacy, locus of control, and fear avoidance. Each of these is described and discussed in this section. A different approach to cognition and pain has utilized experimental paradigms to study processing of stimuli. This will be described in a following section.

It has long been recognized that cognitive factors are related to distressed, depressive thoughts, and even disability and work loss, even when pain has been controlled for (Main & Waddell, 1991). However, the study of such factors has been plagued by problems. Some of these are methodological in nature and were covered earlier. Others are the result of a lack of clarity about the psychological concepts themselves. Another problem is that the factors studied are clearly strongly interrelated; for example, strong correlations have been found between external locus of control and catastrophizing (Harkapaa et al., 1996). Extracting the unique contribution of cognitive factors can, therefore, be a problem.

3.2.   *Coping*

Coping is "a complex set of behaviours and is determined by a number of factors including perceived available resources (personal and situational), expectation of outcome and ascribed characteristics of the event to be coped with" (Horn & Monafo, 1997, p. 77). The patterns of behaviors utilized to cope with a perceived threat are defined as "coping strategies" (Cohen, 1987). Certain styles of coping with pain have been categorized by different researchers into those they considered "healthy" and those they considered "unhealthy." Such categorization also includes defining strategies aimed at reducing psychological distress, such as praying and hoping, as "emotion based," in contrast to strategies aimed at seeking to change the situation, such as care seeking, which are described as "problem based" (Schussler, 1992). A related dichotomy has been presented by Brown and Nicassio (1987), who described "active" versus "passive" strategies, based on factor analysis of the Vanderbilt Pain Management Inventory (VPMI).

Passive coping items measured in chronic pain patients with rheumatoid arthritis were found to relate to pain, depression, helplessness, and lower self-efficacy 6 month later, whereas active coping was related to lower ratings of depression. Although the negative effects of passive coping strategies have been replicated in groups with long-term rheumatoid arthritis (Brown et al., 1989) and in healthy populations (Mercado et al., 2000), the causal path between the two factors is not clear. A negative mood may increase the tendency towards passivity, which, in turn, results in increased disability and subsequent distress.

Despite attempts to categorize coping styles as positive and negative in terms of outcomes, findings in fact suggest two tendencies:

1. People change their styles over time and in response to changing environments (Newman et al., 1990).
2. Certain styles that have been described as maladaptive can at times help patients in terms of recovery. An example of this is denial, which was considered an avoidant strategy of coping, but which has in fact been demonstrated to facilitate reduction in anxiety and improve recovery postsurgery (Suls & Fletcher, 1985).

Several problems are associated with measuring coping. The use of self-report is primary among these and applies to all of the factors described in this section. Self-report relies not only on willingness to accurately report cognitive events, but it assumes that people are able to accurately describe such processes. Another problem that has been associated with measuring coping is that many of the measurements confuse cognitions and behaviors; praying might be a strategy of coping with pain, or a cultural habit.

3.3.   Locus of Control

The concept of locus of control relates to the attribution people make about who has control over their lives. Rotter (1966) suggested that some people have a high internal locus of control: they believe that what happens to them is a result of their own actions or lack of action. In contrast to this, the belief that ones own actions matter little and that one's condition depends on fate, chance, or luck is considered an external locus of control. To this category was added the belief that what happens depends on other people—family, friends, or professionals such as doctors. This belief has been described as a belief in "powerful others." The most common measurement of locus of control is the Multidimensional Health Locus of Control Scale (MHLC) Wallston et al., 1978). In fact, the concept of locus of control as measured by the MHLC has been found to be a poor predictor of health outcome in a number of studies (reviewed in Stainton, 1991). However, it is closely related to the concept of self-efficacy, which might be an important factor to recovery or poor outcome.

3.4. Self-efficacy

Self-efficacy has been defined as "the product of a complex process of self-persuasion that relies on the cognitive processing of diverse sources of efficacy information conveyed enactively, vicariously, socially, and physiologically" (Bandura, 1989, p. 423). In simple words, it is related to our confidence and belief in our ability to control/change our circumstances. Thus, self-efficacy could be linked both to distress and to pain behavior in pain patients. The evidence, especially for groups with rheumatoid arthritis, is promising. In cross-sectional studies, self-efficacy beliefs have been related to pain behaviors (Jensen et al., 1991), but prospective studies have shown contradictory findings. In groups with rheumatoid arthritis, measures of self-efficacy early on in the diagnosis have been shown to predict later functional disability (Brekke et al., 2001; Schiaffino et al., 1991; Shifren et al., 1999). In the short term, levels of self-efficacy have been shown to relate to daily ratings of pain, mood, and coping (Lefebvre et al., 1999). However, these studies have not been analyzed systematically applying criteria for adequate methodology. In contrast, self-efficacy failed to predict health status at 12 months in a large sample of people with acute musculoskeletal pain (Estlander et al., 1998). However, recruitment took place relatively late in the time line (Pincus et al., 2002). More research is necessary to discover the interaction among patient self-efficacy, interventions, clinicians' beliefs (including about their self-efficacy!), and outcome.

3.5. Catastrophizing

Catastrophizing is described as an exaggerated orientation toward pain stimuli and pain experience (Sullivan et al., 1995). It is closely related to depression and perceived disability (Sullivan et al., 1998; Tan et al., 2001). Typically, it has been measured using the Coping Strategy Questionnaire (Rosensteil & Keefe, 1983) or the Pain Catastrophizing Scale (Sullivan et al., 1995). Items include cognitions such as "It's terrible and I feel it's never going to get any better." Most of the research concluding that catastrophizing is a reliable predictor of outcome in pain patients is based on cross-sectional studies. However, the few prospective cohorts that have included an explicit measure of catastrophizing at baseline (e.g., Burton et al., 1995) have shown some evidence to support this conclusion. A novel study of the effect that catastrophizing could have on patients was carried out by Lefebvre and Keefe (2002), who asked patients with rheumatoid arthritis to keep a pain diary for 30 days. They then tested recall of these pain ratings and related the accuracy of pain recall to catastrophizing. They concluded that patients who scored high on catastrophizing were more accurate, even after controlling for actual levels of pain.

The overlap between catastrophizing and other cognitive constructs further complicates the picture: In a study of women with rheumatoid arthritis, predictors of catastrophizing in later stages of the disease were found to be dispositional pessimism, passive coping, venting as a pain coping behavior, and arthritis helplessness (Sinclair, 2001). One of the main criticisms of the concept of catastrophizing is the overlap with depression/distress. Two of the main theoretical constructs that are thought to make up catastrophizing (Sullivan et al., 1995) are rumination and helplessness, which are also hypothesized to be major aspects of depression.

Catastrophizing has been considered to be a major contributing factor for the development of fear avoidance, discussed later in this chapter (Vlaeyen & Linton, 2000). A recent cross-sectional study investigated the hypothesis that a stable personality trait, specifically neuroticism (defined as a traitlike tendency to experience a broad range of negative feelings such as distress, worry, and anxiety), impacts on catastrophizing, which, in turn, affects fear of movement, leading to hypervigilance and, ultimately, to increased pain (Goubert et al., 2004). Despite the fact that catastrophizing and fear of movement could be interchanged in their presumed order, without compromising the goodness of fit, and the limitations because of the retrospective design, the study provides some evidence to suggest that both of these factors impact on pain.

3.6.   Summary

There is contradictory evidence about the role that different styles of thought play in predicting behavior and health in the long term. Although there are plenty of studies looking at cognition and pain, many of them are limited because of methodological issues. In addition, the research often overlooks the role that pain and disability play in creating and reinforcing certain cognitions (i.e., reversed causality). Another major limitation is the overlap of certain cognitive concepts with emotional states. This is evident in the nature of the content of certain factors (e.g., catastrophizing), whereas other constructs are presented in the literature alternatively as cognitive or emotional ones, depending on the researcher's theoretical approach (e.g., fear avoidance/fear of pain).

4.   The Role of Emotions

4.1.   Emotions, Cognition, and Pain

The interaction between emotion and cognition has long been a subject of study and debate in psychology, behavioral medicine, psychiatry, and even philosophy. It is generally agreed now that the two interact in a circular manner and occur in parallel (reviewed in Williams et al., 1997). Neither is considered to be completely volitional, and both can occur at preconscious levels. Both impact on behavior. The implication of this is that in pain populations, the study of cognitions and their impact on outcome also needs to address their interaction with emotions.

4.2. Depression

The majority of research in pain populations has focused on depression and anxiety. Patients have been classified as "depressed" if they have scored above a given cut point on self-report scales. The debate about the inadequacies of these measurements has been outlined elsewhere (Clyde & Williams 2002; Pincus & Williams, 1999). In addition to other problems involved in the psychometric assessment of depression, the majority of the measurements are contaminated by somatic items asking about symptoms (e.g., fatigue, loss of appetite, loss of weight) that could reflect pain rather than depression, possibly inflating scores. Many measurements were developed in psychiatric populations, intentionally excluding groups with physiological problems. The focus of distress and low mood in pain populations has been shown to revolve around loss, but it lacks the classic self-blame and generalized pessimism associated with clinical depression (Pincus & Morley, 2001; Pincus et al., 1995). Almost all of the measurements focus on negative to neutral emotions, but fail to account for neutral to positive feelings, despite the fact that a positive affect has been found to be an important predictor of outcome in other physical conditions (Huppert & Whittington, 2003). Finally, anxiety and depression have been shown time and time again to occur together in pain patients, so the diagnostic split reflected in separate measurements lacks validity. Both anxiety and depression are multidimensional constructs with complex interrelationships, and both interact with pain behavior and pain experience (Campbell et al., 2003).

4.3. Fear and Anxiety

Research on cognition and emotions in pain populations has provided useful evidence, of which the quality is directly related to the level of focus. In other words, attempts to measure global states of anxiety (i.e., steady traits, without specifying the nature of the perceived threat) have not shown significant effects (Haldorsen et al., 1998), partly because of the methodological shortcomings of the design and analysis. However, investigations into health-related anxiety and, specifically, pain-related fear (e.g., Vlaeyen & Linton, 2000) have provided promising evidence for the role that these concepts might play in affecting people's behavior and experience of pain.

4.4. Health-Related Anxiety and Anxiety Sensitivity

Anxiety sensitivity, in contrast to the fear of danger or the fear of being harmed, is about "fear of fear," the propensity to experience fear in response to one's bodily arousal sensations; typically, the concept is measured using the Anxiety Sensitivity Index (ASI), (Reiss et al., 1986), of which one subscale measures physical concerns.

Research on anxiety sensitivity and its impact on the experience of pain is surprisingly scarce. However, the idea that fearfulness will impact on pain has been investigated. In an experiment using pain induction, Keogh and Cochrane (2002) found that high-anxiety-sensitivity participants exhibited a greater interpretative bias and reported more negative pain experiences than those low in anxiety sensitivity. In a prospective study of chronic pain patients, Hadjistavropoulos et al. (2004) compared the impact of four different measurements of trait and state fear/anxiety on functioning 3 months later. The regression analysis suggested that after controlling for pain intensity at baseline, both health anxiety and anxiety sensitivity predicted unique variance in negative affect at 3 months, whereas health anxiety alone predicted disability.

4.5. Fear of Pain

The role of pain-specific fear is a perfect example of the enmeshment between cognition and emotion. Although fear itself is an emotion, instruments measure the thoughts and beliefs associated with it. Research on pain-related fear has been extremely successful in clarifying some of the difficulties that patients face. When withdrawal and emotions associated with pain (fear and distress) continue in the absence of a new injury, because of catastrophic misinterpretation of benign or ambiguous physical sensations, the process becomes maladaptive. It leads to a cascade of negative events, including hypervigilance, muscular reactivity, avoidance, guarding behavior, and reduction in mobility and daily activities, which, in turn, lead to increased disability and distress (Vlaeyen & Linton, 2002). There are several theoretical models, of which the best known is probably that by Vlaeyen et al. (1995). The model describes two possible responses to the experience of pain: confrontation resulting in recovery, or catastrophizing (influenced in turn by negative affectivity), which results in pain-related fear. In this context, catastrophizing is described as an exaggerated negative orientation toward noxious stimuli, which has shown to increase distress (Sullivan et al., 1995).

Although this model has proved popular and offers a focused approach to intervention (e.g., Boersma et al., 2004), it raises a few problems from the point of view of causal attributions. There is no reason why catastrophizing should be necessary or, indeed, sufficient for the emergence of fear avoidance. Fear avoidance can be acquired through classical or operant conditioning mechanisms in which it reflects a reality: In the short term, movement might well lead to increased and even severe pain. In addition, the causal path might be reversed: A strong response of fear, based on exposure to high levels of pain, could result in catastrophizing. In a recent study, Sieben et al. (2002) used a sophisticated design to seek relationships across time among fear of movement, catastrophizing, and pain severity. Their results indicate that peaks on all three measures occur together, thus providing little evidence for a causal path among the variables.

Crombez et al. (1998), who maintain that one of the most important mechanisms to predict poor outcome is through attention and hypervigilance (without necessarily catastrophizing), have proposed a related, but slightly different causal path. The presence of pain interrupts and disrupts other tasks and processes (reviewed in Eccelston & Crombez, 1999). Using self-report measures, correlations have been found among attention to pain, avoiding straining activities (Crombez et al., 1998), and the presence of high fear of pain (Peters et al., 2000; Peters et al., 2002). In an experimental study, disruption on a task, taken as an index of attentional interference due to bodily hypervigilance, has been shown to be related to high pain intensity, negative affect, and high somatic awareness (Eccleston & Crombez, 1999). There is also supportive evidence from psychophysiological approaches using elevated electromyogram levels as indicators of symptom-specific muscular reactivity in patients high in fear of pain (Flor et al., 1992). The most consistent findings are for a relationship between fear of pain and reduced physical performance. In weight-lifting and trunk extension–flexion tasks, Crombez et al. (1999) were able to demonstrate that fear of pain was a significant predictor of patients' behavior, even after partialing out their reported pain intensity. However, these studies took place in laboratory conditions and do not involve a long enough time line to provide evidence for a causal link between fear avoidance in early stages of pain and the development of long-term disability.

Does fear of pain increase disability? There is some evidence suggesting that fear of movement impacts on pain behavior and distress. Several prospective studies focusing on short-term outcome in patients with acute pain have used valid measurement of fear avoidance at baseline. For example, Fritz and George (2002) found that scores on the Fear-Avoidance Beliefs Questionnaire (FAB), (Waddell et al., 1993) were the strongest predictor of return to work after 4 weeks in 78 injured workers.

4.6.   Other Emotional States and Pain

Finally, a better understanding of the set of emotions so far neglected by research—anger, frustration, and irritation,—might prove extremely important in changing health-related behavior in pain patients. To date, there is no sound theoretical framework for understanding frustration in psychology, let alone frustration related to physical illness and disability. A recent review (Greenwood et al., 2003) concluded that there is fairly consistent support for the impact of high anger on pain experience and some evidence for the role of people's anger management style in the outcome of pain interventions.

5. New Models and Conceptual Approaches

One way of conceptualizing the host of interrelated psychological factors is in three "constellations": those associated with self (including self-concept, self-efficacy, and self-loss), those associated with threat (including fear of pain and health anxiety), and the interaction between the two (which involves the concept of control). Several new models have tried to account for poor outcome in individuals with chronic pain using similar ideas.

5.1. Studies of Information Processing in Pain Patients

The definition of cognition (see Section 2) includes the term "process": the mental act carried out by the individual in an attempt to perceive, comprehend, and acquire knowledge about the world. Studies of these processes include the investigation of attention and recall in pain patients and are typically experimental in their design. The techniques used have been adapted from research in psychopathology and especially in groups with clinical depression and anxiety. An important feature of this approach is that it enables testing of processes that are outside of awareness and, therefore, does not rely on introspection, as is the case with self-report measurement. Some of the studies rely on pain language, which is interpreted to represent activation of a pain schema (e.g., Pincus et al., 1993). Other experimental approaches rely on reaction time to complete tasks under different conditions, including induction of pain (e.g., Peters et al., 2002). Typically, a group of chronic pain patients is compared to control groups. A review of the evidence on attention, interpretation, and recall bias in chronic pain patients (Pincus & Morley 2001) concluded that there was robust evidence for a recall bias toward pain-related stimuli in such groups, especially when the information referred to the self. Weaker evidence suggested that pain patients were more likely to interpret ambiguous information as pain related. The authors attempted to synthesize this evidence into a model, from which explicit predictions could be extracted.

5.2. The Enmeshment Model of Pain

The *enmeshment* model (Pincus & Morley, 2001) owes much of its principles to the more generic model of vulnerability–diathesis–stress. It builds on the idea of the interaction between features of information/situation and internal structures. The focus of the model is the idea that three separate internal representations (schemata), which normally operate independently of each other, become enmeshed. These schemata are of the self, of pain, and of illness. The model suggests that enmeshment of pain schema and self-schema alone does not necessarily lead to distress or poor outcome, as in the case of pain associated with sport training. However, when illness schemata, incorporating features about disability, helplessness, and threat, are enmeshed with self and pain schemata, the result is heightened distress and possibly poor prognosis. This enmeshment is maintained by processing biases, such as selective recall of illness-related stimuli (Pincus et al., 1995), and interpretation of ambiguous stimuli as pain-related (Pincus et al., 1994, 1996). The model is yet to be tested in prospective designs, and the predictive power of information processing biases is currently unknown. However, the advantage of the model is in the methodology it advocates. This highly controlled approach, combined with a sound theoretical model, is promising.

6.   Summary

Should we assess cognitions? The evidence for a causal link between cognitive factors and outcome in patients with painful physical conditions is not as strong as it is at times presented in the literature. However, the evidence is promising enough to suggest that research continue. It is reasonable to assume that the role of beliefs and attributions impacts on patients' well-being and behavior no less than physiological measures or even pain itself. When we have a much better understanding of *which* cognitions have *what* effect, under *what circumstances*, and at *what point in time*, we should be able to significantly reduce suffering, decrease health costs, and improve the quality of our lives.

Which cognitions should be assessed? Although the jury is out on the causal role of cognitive factors, some appear to derive from more coherent conceptual model than others. This, in turn, means that interventions attempting to change cognitions can become more focused and that the assessment of success in such interventions is more transparent. Among these are fear avoidance/fear of pain and negative affect/distress. Other factors where research is needed include coping strategies and especially catastrophizing.

How should cognitions be assessed? The issue of valid, reliable, and sensitive measurement of psychological factors is a vast Pandora's box. It is easy, however, to indicate how they should not be assessed: We should cease pulling questionnaires off the shelf indiscriminately, regardless of the population in which they were developed. Single items should not be considered adequate measurement, especially if removed from in-depth instruments without further validation. We should attempt triangulation whenever possible, by testing the relationship between different measurements and behavior and by including more objective measures, such as experimental tests when there is a good theoretical rationale for their inclusion. Another conundrum (which will not be discussed here) is who should carry out this assessment and what skills/training are needed to carry it out efficiently.

Although it would be nice to have an optimal time to assess cognition in patients with pain, so that interventions can be carried out at early stages and risk resulting from cognitive maladaptive factors is reduced, this reductionist approach will only yield limited success. Cognitions must be regarded as part of human experience at all rehabilitation and developmental stages, through pain and healing and through health and illness. Cognitions change, are impacted by external events, and impact behavior in a parallel fashion. More research is needed on health outcome, cognitions, and their interactions with the person and her or his context throughout the lifespan (e.g., on the relationship between the meta-cognitions of different cultural groups and how they affect their well-being and health).

References

Bandura, A. (1989). Perceived self-efficacy in the exercise of personal agency. *The Psychologist, 10*, 411–424.

Banks, S. M. & Kerns, R. D. (1996). Explaining high rates of depression in chronic pain: A diathesis–stress framework. *Psychological Bulletin, 199*, 95–110.

Boersma, K., Linton, S., Overmeer, T., Jansson, M., Vlaeyen, J., & de Jong, J. (2004). Lowering fear-avoidance and enhancing function through exposure in vivo: A multiple baseline study across six patients with back pain. *Pain, 108*, 8–16.

Bongers, P. M., de Winter, C. R., Kompier, M. A. J., & Hildebrandt, V. H. (1993). Psychosocial factors at work and musculoskeletal disease. *Scandinavian Journal of Work, Environment and Health, 19*, 297–312.

Bonica, J. J. & Loeser, J. D. (2001). History of pain concepts and therapies. In J. D. Loeser (Ed.). *Bonica's Management of Pain*, 3rd ed. Philadelphia: Lippincott Williams & Wilkins.

Brekke, M., Hjortdahl, P., & Kvien, T. K. (2001). Self-efficacy and health status in rheumatoid arthritis: A two-year longitudinal observatorial study. *Rheumatology, 40*, 387–392.

Brown, G. K. & Niccasio, P. M. (1987). Development of a questionnaire for the assessment of active and passive coping strategies in chronic pain patients. *Pain, 31*, 53–64.

Brown, G. K., Nicassio P. M., & Wallston, K. A. (1989). Pain coping strategies and depression in rheumatoid arthritis. *Journal of Consulting and Clinical Psychology, 57*, 652–657.

Burton, A. K., Tillotson K., Main, C., & Hollis, M. (1995). Psychosocial predictors of outcome in acute and sub-acute low back trouble. *Spine, 20*, 722–728.

Campbell, L. C., Clauw, D. J., & Keefe, F. J. (2003). Persistent pain and depression: A biopsychosocial perspective. *Biological Psychiatry, 54*, 399–409.

Clyde, Z. & Williams, A. C. de C. (2002). Depression and mood. In S. J. Linton (Ed.). *New Avenues for the Prevention of Chronic Musculoskeletal Pain and Disability*. London: Elsevier, pp. 105–122.

Cohen, F. (1987). Measurement of coping. In S. V. Kaol & C. L. Cooper (Eds.). *Stress and Health: Issues in Health Methodology*. New York: Wiley.

Collins English Dictionary (1993). London: William Collins & Sons & Co. Ltd.

Crombez, G., Eccleston, C., Baeyens, F., & Eelen, P. (1998). When somatic information threatens, pain catastrophizing enhances attentional interference. *Pain, 75*, 187–198.

Crombez, G., Vlaeyen, J. W. S., Heuts, P. H. T. G., & Lysens, R. (1999). Pain-related fear is more disabling than pain itself: Evidence on the role of pain-related fear in chronic back pain disability. *Pain, 80*, 329–339.

Dworkin, R. H. & Banks, S. M. (1999). A vulnerability–diathesis–stress model of chronic pain: Herpers zoster and the development of postherpic neuraligia.

In R. J. Gatchel & D. C. Turk (Eds.). *Psychosocial Factors in Pain: Critical Perspectives*. New York: Guildford Press, pp. 247–269.

Eccleston, C. & Crombez, G. (1999). Pain demands attention: A cognitive-affective model of the interruptive function of pain. *Psychological Bulletin, 125*, 356–366.

Estlander, A. M., Tkala, E. P., & Viikari-Juntura, E. (1998). Do psychological factors predict changes in musculoskeletal pain? A prospective, two year follow-up study of the working population. *Journal of Occupational and Environment Medicine, 40*, 445–453.

Field, H. L. (2004). Placebo analgesia. In H. R. H. Dworkin & W. S. Breitbart (Eds.). *Psychosocial Aspects of Pain: A Handbook for Health Care Providers. Progress in Pain Research and Management* Vol. 27. Seattle WA: IASP Press.

Flor, H., Birbaumer, N., Schugens, M. M., & Lutzenberger, W. (1992). Symptom-specific psychophysiological responses in chronic pain patients. *Psychophysiology, 29*, 452–460.

Fritz, J. M. & George, S. Z. (2002). Identifying psychosocial variables in patients with acute work-related low back pain: The importance of fear avoidance beliefs. *Physical Therapy, 82*, 973–983.

Gatchel, R. J., Polantin, P. B., & Mayer, T. G. (1995). The dominant role of psychosocial risk factors in the development of chronic low back pain disability. *Spine, 20*, 2702–2709.

Gibson, S. J., Katz, B., Corran T. M., Farrell M. J., & Helme R. D. (1994). Pain in older persons. *Disability and Rehabilitation, 16*, 127–139.

Goubert, L., Crombez, G., & Van Damme, S. (2004). The role of neuroticism, pain catastrophizing and pain-related fear in vigilance to pain: A structural equations approach. *Pain, 107*, 234–241.

Greenwood, K. A., Thurston, R., Rumble, M., Waters, S. J., & Keefe, F. J. (2003). Anger and persistent pain: current status and future directions. *Pain, 103*, 1–5.

Hadjistavropoulos, H. D., Asmundson, G. J. G., & Kowalyk, K. (2004). Measures of various anxiety constructs: Is there a difference in their ability to predict long-term functioning among pain patients? *European Journal of Pain, 8*, 1–11.

Haldorsen, E. M. H., Indahl, A., & Ursin, H. (1998). Patients with low back pain not returning to work: A 12-month follow-up study. *Spine, 23*, 1202–1208.

Harkapaa, K., Jarvikoski, A., & Vakkari, T. (1996). Locus of control beliefs in back pain patients. *British Journal of Health Psychology, 1*, 51–63.

Hoogendoorn, W. E., van Poppel, M. N., Bongers, P. M., Koes, B. W., & Bouter, L. M. (2000). Systematic review of psychosocial factors at work and private life as risk factors for back pain. *Spine, 25*, 2114–2125.

Horn, S. & Monafo, M. (1997). *Pain: Theory, Research and Intervention*. Philadelphia: Open University Press.

Huppert, F. A. & Whittington, J. E. (2003). Evidence for the independence of positive and negative well-being: Implications for quality of life assessment. *British Journal of Health Psychology, 8*, 107–122.

Ingram, R. E., Miranda, J., & Segal, Z. V. (1998). *Cognitive Vulnerability to Depression*. New York: Guilford Press.

Jensen, M. P., Turner, J. A., & Romano, J. M. (1991). Self efficacy and outcome expectations: Relationship to chronic pain coping strategies and adjustment. *Pain, 44*, 263–269.

Keogh, E. & Cochrane, M. (2002). Anxiety sensitivity, cognitive biases and pain. *Journal of Pain, 3*, 320–329.

Klenerman, L., Slade, P. D., Stanley, M., Tennie, B., Reilly, J. P., Atchison, L. E., Troop, J. D., & Rose, M. J. (1995). The prediction of chronicity in patients with an acute attack of low back pain in a general practice setting. *Spine, 20*, 478–484.

Lefebvre, J. C. & Keefe, F. J. (2002). Memory for pain: The relationship of pain catastrophizing to the recall of daily rheumatoid arthritis pain. *Clinical Journal of Pain, 18*, 56–63.

Lefebvre, J. C., Keefe, F. J., Affleck, G., Raezer, L. B., Starr, K., Caldwell, D. S., & Tennen, H. (1999). The relationship of arthritis self efficacy to daily pain, daily mood and daily coping in rheumatoid arthritis patients. *Pain, 80*, 425–435.

Linton, S. J. (2000). A Review of psychological risk factors in back and neck pain. *Spine, 25*, 1148–1156.

Linton, S. J. & Skevington, S. M. (1999). Psychological factors and the epidemiology of pain. In I. Crombie, P. R. Croft, S. J. Linton, L. LeResche, & Von Kroff (Eds.). *The Epidemiology of Pain.* Seattle, WA: IASP Press, pp. 25–42.

Linton, S. J., Vlaeyen, J., & Ostelo, R. (2002). The back pain beliefs of health care providers: Are we fear-avoidant? *Journal of Occupational Rehabilitation, 12*, 223–232.

Main, C. J. & Waddell, G. (1991). A comparison of cognitive measures in low back pain: Statistical structure and clinical validity at initial assessment. *Pain, 46*, 287–98.

McCracken, L. M., Gross, R. T., Sorg, P. J., & Edmands, T. A. (1993). Prediction of pain in patients with chronic low back pain: Effects of inaccurate prediction and pain-related anxiety. *Behaviour Research and Therapy, 31*, 647–652.

Mercado, A. C., Carroll, L. J., Cassidy, J. D., & Cote, P. (2000). Coping with neck and low back pain in the general population. *Health Psychology, 19*, 333–338.

Merskey, H. & Bogduk, N. (1994). *Classification of Chronic Pain: Descriptions of Chronic Pain Syndromes and Definitions of Pain Terms*, 2nd ed. Seattle, WA: IASP Press.

Newman, S., Fitzpatrick, R., Lamb, R., & Shipley, M. (1990). An analysis of coping strategies in rheumatoid arthritis. In L. R. Schmidt, P. Schwenkmesger, J. Weinman, & S. Maes (Eds.). *Theoretical and Applied Aspects of Health Psychology.* Amsterdam: Harwood Academic.

Papageorgiou, C. & Wells, A. (1998). Effects of attention training on hypochondriasis: A brief case series. *Psychological Medicine, 28*, 193–200.

Peters, M. L., Vlaeyen, J. W., & Kunnen, A. M. (2002). Is pain related fear a predictor of somatosensory hypervigilance in chronic low back pain patients. *Behaviour Research and Therapy, 40*, 85–103.

Peters, M. L., Vlaeyen, J. W., & Van Drunen, C. (2000). Do fibromyalgia patients display hypervigilance for innoxious somatosensory stimuli? Application of a body scanning reaction time paradigm. *Pain, 86*, 283–292.

Pincus, T. & Morley, S. (2001). Cognitive processing bias in chronic pain: A review and integration. *Psychological Bulletin, 127*, 599–617.

Pincus, T. & Williams, A. (1999). Models and measurements of depression in chronic pain. *Journal of Psychosomatic Research, 47*, 211–219.

Pincus, T., Burton, K., Vogel, S., & Field, A. (2002). A systematic review of psychological risk factors for chronicity/disability in prospective cohorts of low back pain. *Spine, 27*, 109–120.

Pincus, T., Pearce, S., McClelland, A., Farley, S., & Vogel, S. (1994). Interpretation bias in response to ambiguous cues in pain patients. *Journal of Psychosomatic Research, 38*, 347–353.

Pincus T., Pearce, S., McClelland, A., & Isenberg, D. (1995). Endorsement and memory bias for pain stimuli in pain patients. *British Journal of Clinical Psychology, 34*, 267–277.

Pincus T., Pearce, S., & Perrot, E. (1996). The interpretation of ambiguous homophones in chronic pain patients, *British Journal of Medical Psychology, 69*, 259–266.

Pincus, T., Pearce, S., McClelland, A., & Turner-Stokes, L. (1993). Self referential selective memory in pain patients, *British Journal of Clinical Psychology, 32*, 365–374.

Reiss, S., Peterson, R. A., Gursky, D. M., & McNally, R. J. (1986). Anxiety sensitivity, anxiety frequency and the predictions of fearfulness. *Behaviour Research and Therapy, 24*, 1–8.

Rosenstiel, A. K. & Keefe, F. J. (1983). The use of coping strategies in chronic low back pain patients: Relationship to patient characteristics and current adjustment. *Pain, 17*, 33–44.

Rotter, J. B. (1966). Generalized expectancies for internal versus external control of reinforcement. *Psychological Monographs, 80*, 1–28.

Schiaffino, K. M., Revenson, T. A., & Gibovsky, A. (1991). Assessing the impact of self efficacy beliefs on adaptation to rheumatoid arthritis. *Arthritis Care Research, 4*, 150–157.

Schussler, G. (1992). Coping strategies and individual meaning of illness. *Social Science Medicine, 34*, 427–32.

Shifren, K., Park, D. C., Bennett, J. M., & Morrell, R. W. (1999). Do cognitive processes predict mental health in individuals with rheumatoid arthritis? *Journal of Behavioral Medicine, 22*, 529–547.

Sieben, J. M., Vlaeyen, J. W. S., Tuerlinckx, S., & Portegijs, P. J. M. (2002). Pain-related fear in acute low back pain: The first two weeks of a new episode. *European Journal of Pain, 6*, 229–237.

Sinclair, V. G. (2001). Predictors of pain catastrophizing in women with rheumatoid arthritis. *Archives of Psychiatric Nursing, 15*, 279–288.

Stainton, R. S. (1991). *Explaining Health and Illness: An Exploration of Diversity*. Hemel Hempstead, UK: Harvester Wheatsheaf.

Sullivan, M. J. L., Bishop, S., & Pivik, J. (1995). The pain catastrophizing scale: Development and validation. *Psychological Assessment, 7*, 524–532.

Sullivan, J. L., Stanish, W., Waite, H., Sullivan, M., & Tripp, D. A. (1998). Catastrophizing, pain, and disability in patients with soft tissue injuries. *Pain, 77*, 253–260.

Suls, J. & Fletcher, B. (1985). The relative efficacy of avoidant and non-avoidant coping strategies: A meta-analysis. *Health Psychology, 4*, 249–288.

Tan, G., Jensen, M. P., Robinson-Whelen, S., Thornby, J. I., & Monga, T. N. (2001). Coping with chronic pain: A comparison of two measures. *Pain, 90*, 127–133.

Thomas, M. R. & Roy, R. (1999). *The Changing Nature of Pain Complaints over the Lifespan*. The Plenum Series in Adult Development and Aging. New York: Plenum.

Truchon, M. & Fillion L. (2000). Biopsychosocial determinants of chronic disability and low back pain: A review. *Journal of Occupational Rehabilitation, 10*, 117–142.

Vlaeyen, J. W. & Linton, S. J. (2000). Fear-avoidance and its consequences in chronic musculoskeletal pain: A state of the art. *Pain, 85*, 317–332.

Vlaeyen, J. W. & Linton, S. J. (2002). Pain-related fear and its consequences in chronic musculoskeletal pain. In S. J. Linton (Ed.). *New Avenues for the Prevention of Chronic Musculoskeletal Pain and Disability*. London: Elsevier, pp. 83–103.

Vlaeyen, J. W., Kole-Snijders, A. M., Boeren, R. G., & van Eek, H. (1995). Fear of movement (re) injury in chronic low back pain and its relationship to behavioral performance. *Pain, 62*, 363–372.

Waddell, G., Newton, M., Henderson, I., Somerville, D., & Main, C. (1993). A fear-avoidance beliefs questionnaire (FABQ) and the role of fear-avoidance beliefs in chronic low back pain and disability. *Pain, 93*, 157–168.

Wall, P. D. & Jones, M. (1991). *Defeating Pain: The War Against a Silent Epidemic*. New York: Plenum.

Wallston, K. A., Wallston, B. S., & De Vellis, R. (1978). Development of multidimensional health locus of control (MHLC) scales. *Health Education Monographs, 6*, 160–170.

Williams, J. M. G., Watts, F. N., MacLeod, C., & Mathews, A. (1997). *Cognitive Psychology and Emotional Disorders, 2nd ed.* New York: Wiley.

Weisenberg, M. (1984). Cognitive aspects of pain. In P. D. Wall & R. Melzack (Eds.). *Textbook of Pain*, 3rd ed. Edinburgh: Churchill Livingston, pp. 315–336.

10

Chronic Pain and Affect as a Nonlinear Dynamical System

GERALD YOUNG AND C. RICHARD CHAPMAN

The relationship between pain and emotions has generated substantial research (Robinson & Riley, 1999). Pain co-occurs with negative affective states, such as depression, anxiety, anger, physical disease and PTSD (Kruegger et al., 2004; Von Korff et al., 2005). However, research indicates that individual patients experience chronic pain in different ways and that it is important to tailor treatment to the individual (Gatchel, 2005; Turk et al., 2004). For example, the classic work by Turk and and Rudy (1988) described subgroups of pain patients as dysfunctional, interpersonally distressed, and adaptive pain copers, with hybrid styles possible.

Pain typically begins with nociception, but a patient might experience pain in the absence of nociceptive input, as in the case of phantom limb pain (see Chapter 7 by Melzack and Katz). Moreover, when nociception is present, there is often a poor correspondence between the severity of a wound or pathological condition and the intensity of pain reported subjectively. A linear description of the relationship between tissue damage and pain does not summarize well how pain occurs in response to injury.

1. Stage Models of Chronic Pain and of Therapy

1.1. Gatchel's Three-Step Stage Model of Chronic Pain

Gatchel (1991, 1996, 2005) postulated that acute pain develops into chronic pain after passing through a transition stage. At each stage of the model, the development of chronic pain is linked with emotional factors. In the first phase of acute pain, affective distress reactions normally develop, such as worry, anxiety, and fear, along with physical deconditioning. By about 3 months, the patient develops depression, demoralization, learned helplessness, anger, frustration, distrust, and various psychological disorders, worsened by legal and related stresses. Pre-existing vulnerabilities such as personality, psychosocial, and social and economic issues often affect the degree of the exacerbation, and predisposing characteristics are exacerbated, in turn.

Somatization and symptom magnification might develop, although physical processes play a role. In Stage 3, the pain becomes chronic. The patient might adopt a pain-focused lifestyle and sick role, avoiding responsibility.

Gatchel has presented an important model of the development of chronic pain. However, he described the middle stage of transition as a gradual transition. Alternatively, we propose a five-stage model in the development of chronic pain, which includes three transitional steps compared to the one in Gatchel's model. (See Figure 10.1 and Section 4. Also see Young and Chapman (2006) for a further elaboration).

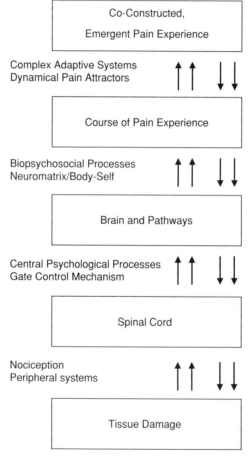

FIGURE 10.1. A nonlinear dynamical systems model of pain. The lower level indicates the early reactions of the body to tissue damage. There are transduction, transmission, and modulation processes at work; peripheral nerves fire after tissue damage. Already at this level, Melzack has shown that descending pathways from the brain might influence pain-related processes (nociception) [e.g., through hypothalamus-mediated opioid mechanisms (see Chapter 7 by Melzack and Katz)]. Gating mecha-

1.2.   A Five-Step Model of Change in Therapy

Gatchel (2005) also described Prochaska et al.'s change model in the context of chronic pain (see Figure 10.1). In this change model, updated in the works by Prochaska et al. (1994) and Maddox (1995), patients pass through five stages, and the model also allows for relapse. Patients in pain may begin in the phase of precontemplation—not being ready for change.

---

nisms in the spinal cord constitute the next level in nociceptive processing. Nociceptors transmit information to the dorsal horns, which can act to open or close the gate, depending on the types of fiber sending messages and whether activation or inhibition processes are involved. Opening the gate (e.g., through small-fiber stimulation) facilitates the transmission of tissue injury signals to the brain. Melzack has shown that central control mechanisms in the brain involving psychological processes might contribute to opening or closing the gate. As influences on pain experience, psychological or central control processes concern affect (e.g., depression, anxiety, fear, anger), stress [e.g., chronic activation of the hypothalamic–pituitary–adrenocortical (HPA) axis, which releases excessive, deletrious cortisol], motivation (e.g., social withdrawal, crying out for help, keeping financial compensation in mind), and cognitive factors (e.g., catastrophizing, pessimism).

In the next level of nociceptive processing, multiple, parallel, distributed neural networks in different regions of the brain are activated, concerning the multiple central factors involved. There is not a pain center in the brain or one nociceptive pathway. Nevertheless, there are certain regions more involved (e.g., the hypothalamus, limbic system, and portions of the cortex). Melzack and Katz refer to the neuromatrix in this regard, which generates a continuously-forming unitary body-self experience as its primary output, a backdrop onto which pain experience is integrated. This view of pain is consistent with the biopsychosocial model, in which sensory, biological, psychological, and social factors interact in generating pain experience.

The nonlinear dynamical systems view contributes to our understanding of pain by adding that pain experience is constantly reconstructed, or reconfigured, from the matrix of components comprising the pain-related system. Components of the pain system include not only sensory information (e.g., currently and on its course since the tissue damage) but also cognitions, emotions, stress, and motivation. There is also context, treatment, disability, litigation status, and so on. An individual's pain experience constantly emerges anew or is constantly reassembled according to the pattern of elements comprising the system at any one time. These factors could include pre-existing ones such as prior depression and ongoing ones such as increased pain-related transmission after a physical activity and the anticipated stress of losing one's employment because of the injury. In terms of nonlinear dynamical systems modeling, in chronic pain, patterns of system activation that have emerged after the injury are sensitized. The patient lapses into illness lifestyles. These patterns can be called dynamical attractors, or areas in the system's state space to which the system might gravitate more readily. In terms of complexity theory, chronic pain patients appear to follow a course toward an order that is entrenched, less flexible, and maladaptive from the psychological point of view. They gravitate from a region in their state space lying between order and disorder, as they descend into a state resistant to therapy.

In the last phase, they enter the stage of problem resolution, confidence, and control. In between lie four stages, three being transitional. The patient passes from contemplating change, involving weighing pros and cons, to the transition stages of preparing/deciding/determining, and undertaking concrete activities that will lead to change, in the action stage. In the last transition step, the maintenance phase, gains are consolidated and preventative steps are instituted.

Gatchel's (2005) three-step stage model of chronic pain describes a degenerative process, whereas Prochaska and DiClemente's five-step therapeutic model describes a constructive one. However, change processes may follow the same dynamic whether regressive or progressive, and the transitions in the negative direction may be multiple and follow several steps rather than just one. In this regard, as mentioned in Section 1.1, and in Section 4 we propose that chronic pain follows a five-step change model.

2.   Nonlinear Dynamical Systems Models

Chapman and colleagues (Chapman, 2004; Chapman et al., 1999) have suggested a nonlinear dynamical systems approach to chronic pain. They describe chronic pain as an emergent, constructed conscious experience.

2.1.   Systems

A system is comprised of a set of interconnected variables that interact and change over time (Boom, 2004). In a dynamical system, the system's present state among its variables is influenced by the system's prior state. If the dynamical system is deterministic, its present state is completely dependent on the prior state. If it is linear, a combination of linear equations can specify all dependence. In a nonlinear dynamical system, linear equations cannot account adequately for its dependence.

Freeman (1995a) contended that human brains function like complex nonlinear dynamical systems that continuously adapt to the bodies they inhabit, the external environment, and other brains. Simpler levels of a system are nested within more complex levels. Self-organization is a primary characteristic of systems, facilitating adaptation and spontaneous emergence of coherent patterns and order from the nonlinear interactions of component system parts. The whole is characterized by a property not predictable from the sum of the parts. In self-organization, a complex global pattern emerges with new properties not involved in the local interactions of the system elements from which it arises. For example, water is an emergent liquid form of the system created by mixing hydrogen and oxygen gases at room temperature. Subjective awareness, including somatic awareness, appears to be an emergent property of brain activity. Such processes can be multidirectional, involving feedback cycles, and they are responsive to changes in other, related systems.

Self-organization produces states of the system, and often the system has a limited number of possible states. Therefore, the system might jump abruptly from one state to another, especially at bifurcation points or in response to some perturbation or trigger. The trigger might be small in relation to a large or disproportionate change that it initiates.

Chronic, disabling pain that develops through the prolongation of acute pain appears to be an entrenched state of accommodation to a complex array of physiological, psychological, and social components. The person in pain, as a system, is adapting to the entire array of elements involved in the system, including those related to prior system states. However, once chronic pain sets in, the relevant system patterns seem to hold the person in a state of illness and disability that is not adaptive. Attempts to change the chronic pain at a simple mechanism level, such as through surgery, typically fail because the system as a whole eventually returns to the entrenched state of disability, dysphoria, and hopelessness. Affective status plays an important role in sustaining chronic pain and disability, but the literature to date has produced piecemeal knowledge that addresses mechanisms without regard to integrated systems.

In the following, we undertake further elaboration of nonlinear dynamical systems theory in terms of the concepts of attractors and complexity (see Figure 10.1).

2.2.   Attractor Modeling

When system dynamics repeatedly end at the same place in its trajectories, attractors characterize the system. Imagine a child's marble rolling in a bowl and going up and down the sides until it stops moving. The trajectory of the marble on the sides of the bowl could serve as a metaphor for the repeated differing trajectories of a system's path as it moves in its basin and eventually settles into an attractor state—in this case of zero velocity, at equilibrium.

Attractors govern a system when it almost always gravitates over time to certain fixed values or to an oscillation among several values, irrespective of the initial value and later perturbations in the system (Boom, 2004; Freeman, 1995a, 1995b; Gleick, 1987; Guastello, 1995; Schore, 2000). Attractors are represented by mathematical equations that describe certain classes of motion of objects in space. Mathematically, an attractor exists within a system space where every point stays nearby and approaches the attractor, except under certain conditions.

As infants develop their leg movement capacities, the data suggest that they function from an initial attractor state of repetitions of springlike, alternating flexions and extensions (Thelen & Smith, 1994). However, the system is soft-assembled, or prone to instability as other elements in the motor system are acquired in development. The system's soft assembly is adaptive, as it allows system exploration of more complex attractors corresponding to walking. This example suggests that rigid stability in attractor system assembly is not adaptive in the long term. Attractors are always stable, at least in the short term; they reach equilibrium. However, even as they do so, they may cycle between different poles.

There are several kinds of attractors. For example, cyclical attractors gravitate periodically between two different poles in its state space. Chaotic attractors are characterized by unpredictable behavior, so that the system may reach a threshold of change and gravitate to new system configurations. There is sensitivity to initial conditions, the so-called "butterfly effect," but once nonlinear transformation in a far-from-equilibrium system takes place because of the sensitivity, the attractor functions stably. Nevertheless, evolving system dynamics may be preparatory to discontinuous change.

2.3.   Complexity Modeling

Complex systems lie at the interface of cyclic and chaotic attractors (Kauffman, 1993; Lansing, 2003). As systems gravitate to increasing complexity through adaptive spontaneous emergence and other complexity processes, this leads to the emergence of integrated structures called Complex Adaptive Systems. Systems with multiple elements adapt to the patterns created by the elements. Lansing (2003) gave the example of the terraced water irrigation systems created by Balinese villages, a complex system that emerges spontaneously because it facilitates adaptation, taking place without a prefigured master plan. The actions of local actors balancing constraints in context lead to the emergence of global control of terrace ecology.

Systems may stand at the cusp of change, poised at the transition between stability and instability, or order and disorder (Kauffman, 1993). In fact, systems may seek out this dynamic region, because being in it facilitates movement toward increasing complexity, which normally maximizes adaptation. In other words, systems may live on "the edge of chaos" (or at the edge of order-disorder), because systems living on cusps of possible change increase the probability of increasing their complexity, which is normally beneficial.

To conclude, systems tend to gravitate to regions in their state space that facilitate movement toward increasing order and complexity. However, in some circumstances, movement toward instability and disorder can occur. Chronic pain is difficult to model according to systems theory, because the chronic pain system appears to stabilize around the attractor of pain and its consequences; yet, in contrast, the system appears unstable, or in a runaway dynamic toward increasing disability. Furthermore, we need to consider individual differences, for some pain patients are responsive to therapy and improve. Next, we examine chronic pain further from the perspective of attractors and complexity theory.

3.   Nonlinear Dynamical Systems Modeling of Chronic Pain

3.1.   Illness and Health Attractors

According to Francis (1995), a cyclical attractor can represent acute illness, with health and illness behavior as the two poles involved. Additionally, Francis speculated that chaotic attractors potentially can characterize improvement in chronic illness. He contended that especially with appropriate therapy, chronically ill individuals may follow trajectories into unpredictable behavior or challenges to growth beyond the threshold of change, allowing the possibility of healthier ways of living to emerge.

Francis applied the concept of attractors to the constructive evolution from an illness lifestyle to a more adaptive one, at a higher level of integration because of therapy. In the following, we see that attractors can also be used to represent systems tending toward instability rather than stability.

Gottman (1991) has described negative family dynamics in terms of attractors. His research can be applied to help understand chronic pain. In terms of his approach, chronic pain appears to be the product of a system governed by attractors with runaway processes. In the context of chronic pain, this means negative emotions, persistent and pervasive pain experience, instability in mood, less predictability, and increased dysfunctionality, disability, and poor adaptive flexibility. When an individual's pain experience appears to be governed by dynamical attractors such as these, we suggest that they may be labeled "dynamical pain experience attractors" or "dynamical pain attractors." At the same time, we caution that chronic pain patients are not all the same, that one model cannot fit all, for they manifest individual differences.

3.2.   Complexity in Chronic Pain

From the perspective of complexity theory, therapy in the pain patient is a process that inhibits the pathway to disorder and facilitates reorganization or movement toward the cusp of change, balancing between order and disorder. This is the healthy dynamic region, because it can lead to more ordered, complex states, where attractors related to or representing a return to flexibility, readiness for or openness to constructive change, optimal adaptation, rehabilitation, restoration of function, and healing govern the patient. When effective, therapy essentially functions as a guide to reorganization, and the movement is toward higher-order, more complex, adaptive states. However, many chronic pain patients enter therapy with entrenched pain, and therapy is ineffective in altering their system dynamics.

4.   A Five-Step Stage Model of Chronic Pain

As we have seen earlier, Gatchel (2005) has formulated a stage model of the development of chronic pain, which is interlinked with emotional factors. Young (1997) has developed a general five-step model of change, showing that it is compatible with the five steps in the change model proposed by Prochaska et al. (1994). The five steps in Young's model are called coordination, hierarchization, systematization, multiplication, and integration. Within this model, as systems evolve, at first they start to coordinate new acquisitions, then the coupled acquisitions develop a dominant–subordinate relationship with one as primary, and then the two acquisitions coalesce into a single new structure. In the fourth step, the new structure propagates throughout the system in which it is embedded, and, finally, the full system is characterized by the new structure and is ready for renewed coordination.

The five-step change model developed by Young (1997) accounts for the development of chronic pain in the following way (see Table 10.1). In the coordination phase, the negative effects of an individual's acute pain are coordinated with her or his ongoing lifestyle. In the hierarchization stage, chronic pain becomes predominant in the coordination. In the third phase, a debilitating chronic pain lifestyle emerges. Next, the chronic pain gradually propagates throughout all aspects of the individual's life. Fifth, the individual transforms fully into a chronic pain patient, where her or his pain is deeply entrenched, resistant to treatment, and impregnated in personal identity.

In a further proposal, we suggest that transition processes described in nonlinear dynamical systems theory may facilitate passage through the five-step model of chronic pain because the steps may reflect chaotic and complex

TABLE 10.1. Parallel Five Step Models of Stages of Change in Therapy and in Chronic Pain, with Proposed Nonlinear Dynamical System Transitions

Stages of Change in Therapy	Stages of Change in Chronic Pain	Nonlinear Dynamical System Transitions
Contemplation	Coordination	
		Cyclical attractor
Preparation	Hierarchization	
		Chaotic attractor
Action	Systematization	
		Inhabiting cusp between order and disorder
Maintenance	Multiplication	
		Complex adaptive system processes
Resolution	Integration	

Note: The stage model of therapy is presented the works of Prochaska et al. (1994) and Maddox (1995). The stage model of pain is based on an elaboration of Gatchel (2005) and Young (1997). The transition sequence in nonlinear dynamical systems theory is explained in the text.

processes at work. For full details of the model, summarized in Table 10.1, see Young and Chapman (2006). Briefly, the model shows how a transition from cyclical to chaotic attractors and then to the state of gravitating to the cusp of change and other complexity theory processes may facilitate passage through the steps in chronic pain. There are many possible dynamic schemes, and the four-step one suggested may self-organize under appropriate conditions.

Finally, it is important to note that for any stage model, individual differences are not excluded. There may be different patterns; for example, at any one stage, individuals may express the stage differently. Moreover, not all pain patients will pass through these stages; in fact, some may respond well to therapy, whereas others may get on as best as they can with their life despite their pain experience, and so on.

5.   Is There a Chronic Pain Disorder?

In Chapter 7, Melzack and Katz underscore that pain patients diagnosed with chronic Pain Disorder due to psychological factors may be unjustly given a psychiatric diagnosis because in cases of pain, there are always physiological concomitants. They disagree that pain can be constituted by primarily psychological factors (presumably excluding cases of malingering and the like in this contention). Moreover, they suggest that when clinicians use the label chronic Pain Disorder, they may be understood as saying that the pain is fully psychological in origin; that is, pain is not a genuine signal of tissue injury. Therefore, Melzack and Katz question the value of the diagnosis of chronic Pain Disorder in the DSM (*Diagnostic and Statistical Manual of Mental Disorders*) (DSM-IV and DSM-IV-TR) (American Psychiatric Association, 1994, 2000).

However, if the working committee of the DSM-V keeps the diagnosis of Chronic Pain Disorder, either as a unified entity, or as several different types, it may want to consider using a category such as "Chronic Pain Complications Disorder." A diagnosis such as this would allow specification of the psychological distress and functional effects of the patient's pain experience without leaving a negative connotation, and still allow the assessor in other cases to list litigation and malingering factors where warranted. It would be explained in the text that valid cases of chronic pain always express an interaction of physiological, psychological, and social factors.

6.   Conclusions

In the companion volume to this book, Young and Chapman (2006) explore in detail the relationship between pain and affect, showing how the development of chronic pain appears to have been organized within a nonlinear dynamical system. In this chapter, we provide a summary.

We conclude that it is useful to construe chronic pain as a nonlinear dynamical pain experience system that is "stuck" in certain states. Pain reflects the ongoing emergence of subjective awareness emanating from the confluence of components involved in tissue damage and its consequences over time at the physiological, psychological, and social levels, and the influence of past states, but it is always constructed *de novo* from moment to moment. The neuronal networking that is part of the pain system undergoes continuous and active reconstruction. Affect and the physiological disruption accompanying pain are interdependent, part of the larger system, and are not separate in a mind–body dualism. The nonlinear dynamical systems model provides a framework conducive to understanding individual differences in pain experience. For example, to use the language of nonlinear dynamical systems theory, for any one individual, a newly learned psychotherapeutic procedure may initiate a process of attractor network reassembly, with less pain experience.

The regressive process apparent at the psychological level in the development of chronic pain does not fit a pattern of increasing adaptive complexity. In particular, at the psychological level, there appears to be increasing maladaptive behavior. However, in terms of the quality of the system being formed in chronic pain, in terms of its networked elements, integration of different levels, inclusion of significant others into the system dynamic, and so on, the increasing domination of pain in the individual's life suggests an increasingly ordered and complex system, *qua system*, which stands in contrast to the increasing disorder at the psychological level. Therefore, whether there is progressive change in therapy or regressive change in the development of chronic pain, the pain patient may undergo the same qualitative shifts through the five stages described, with nonlinear dynamic transition systems underlying self-organizational mechanisms of change.

The proposed five-step change model in the development of chronic pain, given its underlying activation through different nonlinear dynamic system modalities, supports the inclusion of the complexity theory approach to nonlinear dynamical systems into a theory of stages in pain development along with the more commonly used attractor/chaos theory. The two approaches have proved complementary in our efforts to clarify an understanding of pain, and in addition, the proposed model does suggest different roles for these approaches in the transition from acute to chronic pain.

The danger in using terminology derived from nonlinear dynamical systems theory is that the terms can become reified when, in fact, they are merely constructs and cannot replace the hard empirical data that they are meant to represent. At the same time, nonlinear dynamical systems modeling provides a powerful theoretical structure and language for characterizing chronic pain.

Finally, nonlinear dynamical systems models seek predictability in finding overarching patterns, but acknowledge difficulties in making particular predictions about any one data trajectory. Granted, the nonlinear dynamical systems approach emphasizes the unique nature of the individual case. Nevertheless, from an empirical point of view, in individual cases involving psychological injury, the nonlinear dynamical systems approach and the data that it might generate would need to be applied prudently to the evaluation of causality. In this sense, it resembles any other approach to the question of addressing psychological injury in court.

6.1. Comorbid PTSD and Pain as a Superordinate System

The nonlinear dynamical systems approach to chronic pain experience presented in this chapter speaks to the relatively new area of research on the interaction of Posttraumatic Stress Disorder and chronic pain (addressed in several chapters in this Volume), which describes their mutual maintenance and exacerbation. Chapters 13 and 14 by Asmundson and Taylor and by Otis, Pincus, and Keane, for example, have shown that pain and PTSD share common vulnerabilities and partially share triggers. We propose that their co-occurrence may reflect their integration, within a single pain–trauma system. To use systems theory language, in cases of comorbid chronic pain and PTSD, dynamical attractors in neuronal firings and related components may become tightly integrated across two subsystems, forming an integrated attractor of subordinate systems.

References

American Psychiatric Association. (1994). *Diagnostic and Statistical Manual of Mental Disorders*, 4th ed. Washington, DC: American Psychiatric Association.

American Psychiatric Association. (2000). *Diagnostic and Statistical Manual of Mental Disorders: Text Revision*, 4th ed. Washington, DC: American Psychiatric Association.

Boom, J. (2004). Individualism and collectivism: A dynamic systems interpretation of Piaget's interactionism. In J. I. M. Carpendale & U. Müller (Eds.). *Social Interaction and the Development of Knowledge*. Mahwah, NJ: Erlbaum, pp. 67–85.

Chapman, C. R. (2004). Pain perception, affective mechanisms, and conscious experience. In T. Hadjistavropoulos & K. D. Craig (Eds.). *Pain: Psychological Perspectives*. Mahwah, NJ: Erlbaum, pp. 59–85.

Chapman, C. R., Nakamura, Y., & Flores, L. Y. (1999). Chronic pain and consciousness: A constructivist perspective. In R. J. Gatchel & D. C. Turk (Eds.). *Psychosocial Factors in Pain: Critical Perspectives*. New York: Guilford Press, pp. 35–55.

Francis, S. E. (1995). Chaotic phenomena in psychophysiological self-regulation. In R. Robertson & A. Combs (Eds.). *Chaos Theory in Psychology and the Life Sciences*. Mahwah, NJ: Erlbaum, pp. 253–265.

Freeman, W. J. (1995a). *Societies of Brain: A Study in the Neuroscience of Love and Hate*. Hillsdale, NJ: Erlbaum.

Freeman, W. J. (1995b). The kiss of chaos and the sleeping beauty of psychology. In F. D. Abraham & A. R. Gilgen (Eds.). *Chaos Theory in Psychology*. Westport, CT: Greenwood, pp. 19–29.

Gatchel, R. J. (1991). Early development of physical and mental deconditioning in painful spinal disorders. In T. G. Mayer, V. Mooney, & R. J. Gatchel (Eds.). *Contemporary Conservative Care for Painful Spinal Disorders*. Philadelphia: Lea & Febiger, pp. 278–289.

Gatchel, R. J. (1996). Psychological disorders and chronic pain: Cause and effect relationships. In R. J. Gatchel & D. C. Turk (Eds.). *Psychological Approaches to Pain Management: A Practitioner's Handbook*. New York: Guilford Press, pp. 33–52.

Gatchel, R. J. (2005). *Clinical Essentials of Pain Management*. Washington, DC: American Psychological Association.

Gleick, J. (1987). *Chaos*. New York: Viking Penguin.

Gottman, J. M. (1991). Chaos and regulated change in families: A metaphor for the study of transitions. In P. A. Cowen & M. Hetherington (Eds.). *Family Transitions*. Hillsdale, NJ: Erlbaum, pp. 247–272.

Guastello, S. J. (1995). *Chaos, Catastrophe, and Human Affairs: Application of Nonlinear Dynamics to Work, Organizations, and Social Evolution*. Mahwah, NJ: Erlbaum.

Kauffman, S. A. (1993). *The Origins of Order*. New York: Oxford University Press.

Krueger, R. F., Tackett, J. L., & Markon, K. E. (2004). Structural models of comorbidity among common mental disorders: Connections to chronic pain. *Advances in Psychosomatic Medicine, 25*, 63–77.

Lansing, J. S. (2003). Complex adaptive systems. *Annual Review of Anthropology, 32*, 183–204.

Maddox, J. E. (1995). Yes, people can change, but can psychotherapists? *Contemporary Psychology, 40*, 1047–1048.

Prochaska, J. O., Norcross, J. C., & DiClemente, C. C. (1994). *Changing for Good: The Revolutionary Program That Explains the Six Stages of Change and Teaches You How to Free Yourself from Bad Habits*. New York: Morrow.

Robinson, M. E. & Riley, J. L., III. (1999). The role of emotion in pain. In R. J. Gatchel & D. C. Turk (Eds.). *Psychosocial Factors in Pain*. New York: Guilford Press, pp. 74–88.

Schore, A. N. (2000). The self-organization of the right brain and the neurobiology of emotional development. In M. D. Lewis & I. Granic (Eds.). *Emotion, Development, and Self-Organization: Dynamic Systems Approaches to Emotional Development*. Cambridge: Cambridge University Press, pp. 155–185.

Thelen, E. & Smith, L. B. (1994). *A Dynamical Systems Approach to the Development of Cognition and Action*. Cambridge, MA: MIT Press.

Turk, D. C. & Rudy, T. E. (1988). Toward an empirically-derived taxonomy of chronic pain patients: Integration of psychological assessment data. *Journal of Consulting and Clinical Psychology, 56*, 233–238.

Turk, D. C., Monarch, E. S., & Williams, A. D. (2004). Assessment of chronic pain sufferers. In T. Hadjistravropoulos & K. D. Craig (Eds.). *Pain: Psychological Perspectives*. Mahwah, NJ: Erlbaum, pp. 209–243.

Von Korff, M., Crane, P., Lane, M., Miglioretti, D. L., Simon, G., Saunders, K., Stang, P., Brandenburg, N., & Kessler, R. (2005). Chronic spinal pain and physical-mental comorbidity in the United States: Results from the national comorbidity survey replication. *Pain, 113*, 331–339.

Young, G. (1997). *Adult Development, Therapy, and Culture: A Postmodern Synthesis*. New York: Plenum.

Young, G. & Chapman, C. R. (2006). Pain, affect, nonlinear dynamical systems, and chronic pain: Bringing order to disorder. In G. Young, A. Kane, & K. Nicholson (Eds.). *Causality: Psychological Evidence in Court*. New York: Springer-Verlag.

11

Objective and Subjective Measurement of Pain: Current Approaches for Forensic Applications

JEFFREY J. SHERMAN AND RICHARD OHRBACH

Pain, as with all conditions described in this volume, is a multidimensional experience (Melzack & Wall, 1965). The experience is described along two main axes: the sensory–discriminative dimension, comprising spatial, temporal, and intensity properties, and the affective–motivational dimension, related to the unpleasantness, behavioral, emotional, and social properties of the experience (Fernandez & Turk, 1992). Pain is defined as an unpleasant sensory and emotional experience associated with actual or potential tissue damage, or it is described in terms of such damage. Each individual learns the meaning of the word through experiences related to injury in early life (Merskey & Bogduk, 1994). This definition, now adopted by the International Association for the Study of Pain (IASP), recognizes that the experience of pain is measured as much by subjective thoughts, emotions, and behaviors as by objective measurement of anatomical, biological, or physiological pathology. As such, the experience of pain can never fully be confirmed or disconfirmed with absolute certainty by an external observer. However, the sequelae of pain, the resulting disability associated with pain, and the moderating perceptual, experiential, cognitive, and social factors can be assessed comprehensively, reliably, and validly to provide the professional with considerable information about the individual's experience of pain.

This chapter will present a pragmatic framework for a comprehensive understanding of chronic pain. Three central questions should guide assessment of people with chronic pain: (1) What is the extent of the individual's disease or injury? (2) What is the magnitude of the illness?—that is, to what extent is the individual suffering, disabled, or unable to engage in activities? (3) Does the individual's behavior seem appropriate to the injury, evident pathology, or laboratory findings?—that is, are symptoms amplified or minimized for psychological or social reasons? We believe that in order to answer these questions, all of the perceptual and experiential dimensions of pain must be considered. The biopsychosocial model of chronic pain provides a multifactorial, heuristic model that depicts the various dimensions of pain experience. After presenting and describing the model, we review some of the most widely used and studied measures of pain that capture each dimension. Specific tools for measuring aspects of pain will be described with regard to the reliability and validity of each measure. We also focus on measures with predictive validity for chronicity and disability, believing that this aspect of validity is important to the readers of this volume. Finally, we consider future directions of research into functional brain mapping, as it might relate to objective measurement of brain areas underlying the experience of pain.

1.   Using a Theoretical Model to Guide Measurement

In the clinical assessment of chronic pain associated with a prior injury, one must first consider the severity of the initial injury and pain experienced immediately thereafter. Individuals who report high levels of subjective pain intensity during an acute injury phase consistently report greater levels of subsequent disability (Dworkin, 1997), but initial levels of injury and acute pain do not perfectly predict ongoing pain and disability (Turk and Melzack, 2001). A purely biomedical approach that excludes assessment of psychological and environmental factors is insufficient.

The traditional biomedical model that views physical illness as resulting from aberrations in biochemistry, physiology, or anatomy is inadequate in the valid assessment of chronic pain. In contrast, the biopsychosocial model views health and illness as reflecting the reciprocal influences among biological, psychological, and social/environmental factors and lends itself to assessment of all relevant dimensions of health and illness.

1.1.   Biopsychosocial Perspective

The biopsychosocial model provides an integrated framework for understanding chronic pain and guides selection of measures. The model (see Fig.11.1) presumes physical pathology or at least physical changes in muscles, joints, and nerves sufficient to generate nociceptive signals, but it also presumes that psychological and social processes interact with pathology to result in overt expressions of pain such as functional impairment, disability, and distress. Reciprocal relationships among pain perception, mood, cognition, appraisals, and behaviors ultimately influence the experience of pain. Initial signals of pathology occur at the nociceptive level, where stimulation at the periphery above a certain threshold creates an electrical impulse carried along nerve fibers that selectively respond to injurious stimuli (e.g., A-delta and C-nerve fibers). These signals travel along peripheral pain fibers to the dorsal horn in the spinal cord. The experience of pain occurs when peripheral nociceptive information undergoes central nervous system processes that involve perception and appraisal. The result of the appraisal is a behavior, or response, that is expressed in the context of the individual's social role and environment.

Each of these domains can result in an exaggerated or minimized response. Dworkin et al. (1992) have suggested this model as a useful tool in describing the multiple processes that occur simultaneously in individual's pain. We now describe the measurement process within each level.

2.   Deciding What to Measure

2.1.   Nociception

Our model assumes, at the biologic level, that pain report is associated with information, or signals, being transmitted in the nervous system that have the potential for being perceived and appraised as noxious, aversive, or painful. Although this assumption might not be true in certain cases (e.g., malingering), we, nevertheless, make the assumption that there are signals generated in the body that give rise to pain experiences, until we find clinical evidence to the contrary. In terms of peripheral activity, psychologists have become considerably more adept at detecting pathophysiology that can lead to nociception. Hendler et al. (1996) reviewed data from 120 patients referred to a multidisciplinary pain clinic with diagnoses such as "psychogenic pain," "chronic pain," or "lumbar strain." After complete diagnostic studies including magnetic resonance imaging, computed tomography, and nerve blocks, a putative organic origin for the pain was found in 98% of the patients.

Chronic pain patients differ in their level of sensitization to nociceptive input. Increased sensitization might be induced at peripheral sites via peripheral mediators or nociceptor changes (Mendell, 1966; Mense, 1993) or at the central nervous system level (e.g., central sensitization) (Melzack et al., 2001). Although it appears that sensitization to thermal and mechanical nociceptive stimuli can adequately discriminate chronic pain patients from healthy controls and that some chronic pain patients are less able to activate endogenous pain regulatory mechanisms when compared to those with no pain (Kleinbohl et al., 1999; Maixner et al., 1997, 1998), sensitivity and specificity of such measures are not sufficient for forensic applications.

2.1.1.   Interobserver Reliability and Validity of Clinical Signs

In most settings in which human pain data are gathered, it is not possible to obtain information at the level of basic nociceptive processes (such as neurotransmitter concentrations or specific neural pathways being discharged). In clinical settings, there is typically measurement of pain-related clinical signs through physical examination and, to a lesser extent, through laboratory tests (Polatin & Meyer, 2001; Waddell & Turk, 2001). The resultant findings, commonly labeled "signs," are often thought of as objective measures of the physical components of pain because they do not appear to require a subjectively derived self-report. Examples of common clinical measures include assessment of range of motion for musculoskeletal pains, use of radiographic and other imaging methods to detect abnormal structural changes, and laboratory tests for indications of painful systemic diseases, such as rheumatoid arthritis or ischemic cardiac pain. Although many of these measures are truly free of the client's subjective report, they are not necessarily reliable or valid measures of pain symptoms, pain behaviors, functioning, suffering, or outcome.

For example, Waddell signs (Waddell et al., 1980), a group of appropriate and inappropriate responses to physical examination once considered to be an objective indicator of exaggeration or "functional overlay" (i.e., behaviorally or psychologically driven "nonorganic signs") are now understood to not discriminate between organic and nonorganic pain and have low test–retest reliability (Fishbain et al., 2003). Waddell and Turk (2001) note that although Waddell signs are seen in the medicolegal context, they are also commonly observed in the clinic setting in patients with no legal proceedings or compensation claims. They suggest that these signs should not be viewed simplistically as faking, but, rather, as part of the complex emotional and behavioral patterns of chronic pain.

One might expect reliability and validity to be better for "objective signs" than for "subjective self-report," but this often is not the case. We (Dworkin & Sherman, 2001) have previously reviewed the literature demonstrating that reliability for interpretations based on various imaging techniques is notoriously low, as is reliability for clinical measures such as spine motion, muscle strength, and spinal alignment. Further, the validity of "objective signs" is sometimes questionable as well. Muscle strength, range of motion, and radiographic indicators correlate poorly with actual behaviors and are only weak predictors of long-term disability (Frymoyer et al., 1978; Ohrbach & Dworkin, 1998). We suggest that subjective pain reports may be gathered with more reliability and validity than clinical observations. Dworkin and Sherman (2001) discussed several methods for maximizing examiner agreement and increasing interexaminer reliability. These include the following: having a clear definition, in operational terms, of the behavior to be assessed; having written specifications for examiners; and repeatedly calibrating examiners with each other and, if possible, with a gold standard.

An ongoing challenge of pain assessment is that measurements at the physical level, typically clinical signs in the case of pain patients, are often inconsistent with, or inadequate to explain, subjective reports of persistent pain and suffering accompanied by frequently dysfunctional chronic pain behaviors (Sternbach, 1990). Thus, assessment of higher-order functioning is necessary in order to understand an individual's report of pain.

2.2. Pain Perception

The first opportunity to measure the subjective experience of pain is at the sensory–discriminative level, whereby one determines presence–absence, intensity, temporal characteristics, and reported locations of pain as well as the affect associated with the pain (Jensen & Karoly, 2001). Temporal characteristics include episode frequency and duration. Pain intensity can be defined as a quantitative estimate of how much a person hurts, and pain affect can be defined as the emotional arousal and valence attached to the pain experience. Pain location refers to the areas reported on the body affected by pain. The quality of pain perception is based on descriptors of the sensation such as burning, throbbing, and dull or sharp (sensory qualities). We briefly review measures of each of these dimensions of pain perception below.

2.2.1.   Notable Instruments for the Measurement of Chronic Pain Perception

The most common measures of pain perception for intensity include visual analog scales (VAS), verbal rating scales (VRS), and numerical rating scales (NRS) (for a review, see Jensen & Karoly, 2001; Melzack & Katz, 2001). VRSs typically consist of a series of verbal pain descriptors ordered from least to most intense (e.g., no pain, mild, moderate, severe). The individual chooses the word that best describes his or her pain intensity. NRSs consist of a series of numbers with end points representing extremes of pain (e.g., no pain, worst possible pain). The individual chooses the number that best corresponds to his or her pain intensity. VASs usually consist of 100-mm horizontal or vertical lines with two end points representing extremes (e.g., "no pain" and "worst possible pain"). The individual places a mark somewhere on the line that most closely corresponds to his or her level of pain intensity, and the mark is measured in millimeters from the "no pain" end. Common time frames for assessment include "the present" or "now," as well as average, worst, and least pain intensities over some time interval such as 1 month or 6 months.

The VRS, NRS, and VAS are all simple to administer and have demonstrated reliability and validity (Melzack & Katz, 2001). The type of population and pain conditions to be assessed should guide instrument selection. In a study of postoperative pain, Jensen and colleagues (1996) showed that an 11-point box scale NRS showed higher validity than a linear VAS. Two others studies showed preferences for the NRS over the VAS in two chronic pain populations (Jensen et al., 1986; Strong et al., 1991). On the other hand, the VAS scale has been shown to be sensitive to clinical change, is reproducible, and is nearly universally understood (Collins et al., 1997).

A visual representation of pain can be derived from a pain drawing that consists of outline drawings of the human body, front and back, on which the client indicates where he or she feels pain by shading the appropriate sections on the figure. Numerous scoring systems exist for the pain drawing (Margolis et al., 1988) and some (Ransford et al., 1976) suggest that the pain drawing can be used as a measure of emotional distress. However, Parker et al. (1995) showed that although patients with pain drawings containing excessive shading are often psychologically distressed, 50% of the psychologically distressed pain patients in their sample produced normal pain drawings. When used as a measure of pain location, the pain drawing shows high test–retest reliability even with a 3-month interval between testings (Margolis et al., 1988) and good predictive validity in patients with recent-onset low back pain and disability (Ohland et al., 1996).

The McGill Pain Questionnaire (MPQ) (Melzack, 1975), used primarily to assess the qualitative aspects of pain experience, is composed of 19 categories of adjectives that describe the qualities of pain and 1 category containing a 5-point verbal descriptor scale for pain intensity. Individuals are asked to endorse those words that describe their feelings and sensations at that moment. The rank values of the words chosen are summed to obtain a total pain rating index (PRI-T) and separate scores for the sensory (PRI-S), affective (PRI-A), evaluative (PRI-E), and miscellaneous (PRI-M) subscales. There are alternate procedures for scoring the MPQ, and a short form is available. The evidence for the validity, reliability, sensitivity, and discriminative abilities of the MPQ and its alternate forms is reviewed by Melzack and Katz (2001). It is sufficient to say that the factor structure has considerable support, the measure is sensitive to clinical interventions, it is likely the most widely used pain inventory in the world, it is translated into at least 20 languages, and it has been used in several hundred studies of acute, chronic and laboratory pain (Melzack & Katz, 2001). Further, there is evidence for its ability to discriminate between patients who have detectable physical causes (e.g., evident organic pathology) and those who have no detectable physical cause (Perry et al., 1988, 1991). The choice to omit rather than include administration of the MPQ would have to be more strongly defended in a forensic setting.

2.3. Pain Appraisal

Underlying physiologic processes that create large individual differences in pain thresholds and tolerance levels can influence pain perception. However, "higher-order" processes that characterize the cognitive and emotional appraisal of pain and other events and what people think and feel also can influence pain perception and subsequent functioning in response to pain. Psychiatric conditions such as depression and anxiety can magnify pain perception and perpetuate the disability associated with pain (Sullivan, 2001). We will not review measures of psychiatric disorders and personality in depth, as they are covered elsewhere in this text and other texts (Sullivan, 2001). Measures such as the Minnesota Multiphasic Personality Inventory-2 (MMPI-2) (Hathaway et al., 1989), the Symptom Checklist-90 Revised (SCL-90R) (Derogatis, 1983), and the Millon

Behavioral Health Inventory (MBHI) (Millon et al., 1983) have a long history of demonstrated utility and validity in the assessment of psychiatric status and personality characteristics. Those characteristics influence the appraisal of pain in much the same way that they influence the appraisal of all other stressful events and personal experiences.

Other psychological factors such as low self-efficacy, low expectations about one's capacity to execute behavior required for a successful outcome, catastrophizing (Sullivan et al., 1998), and an exaggerated negative orientation toward pain are predictive of greater disability because of pain and are only recently receiving attention in the assessment of pain.

Maladaptive beliefs (Table 11.1) about the diagnosis and treatment of pain can result in an individual's overuse of healthcare in an unending search for the answer to the source of pain and an unwillingness to engage in the self-management activities necessary to reduce pain and avoid disability. Rigid convictions that the source of the pain is physical and as yet undiagnosed, that one is helpless to reduce the pain with self-management strategies such as relaxation and gradual increases in activity, or that one lacks the coping abilities and resources to manage, can contribute to the pain and disability experience. DeGood and Tait (2001) suggested that beliefs about the nature of pain and about coping should not be viewed as artifacts of injury, but, rather, that maladaptive appraisal, coping styles, and cognitions can lie at the heart of the pain problem.

When pain perception is intensified beyond adaptive levels, it is often assessed as inappropriate augmentation of physical sensations (Barsky, 1979) or as somatization (Simon & Von Korff, 1991). In the case of somatization, intensified pain perception may reflect a more generalized tendency to report multiple physical symptoms (e.g., numbness, tingling, shortness of breath, pounding heart), perhaps modifying the diagnostic saliency of the observed pain report (Dworkin et al., 1990).

TABLE 11.1 Distorted Beliefs About Chronic Pain

Type of Belief	Examples
Explanatory model	Somatic/physical/injury explanation for pain onset versus interaction of multiple factors.
	Pain as a symptom of a disease process.
Beliefs about self	Individual is unable to self-manage symptoms.
	Low self-efficacy.
	Life should be free of pain and suffering.
	Pain is unfair/someone is to blame.
Beliefs about treatment	Health care practitioner is responsible for curing the pain.
	Patient is passive recipient of cure.
Beliefs about outcome	Prognosis is hopeless.
	Complete cure versus partial relief.
	Return to prior full and pain-free functioning versus functional adjustments.

2.3.1.   Notable Instruments for the Assessment of Pain Appraisal

There are numerous measures of pain-related beliefs, attitudes, appraisals, and coping responses, many thoroughly reviewed in other texts (DeGood & Tait, 2001). However, because of their relevance to an assessment of causality, we briefly review three that are widely used, extensively studied, and predictive of chronicity and disability.

The Survey of Pain Attitudes (SOPA) (Jensen et al., 1987) is perhaps the most widely used attitudinal pain measure (DeGood & Tait, 2001). It has six scales measuring beliefs about pain-related control, disability, medical cures, solicitude, medications, and emotions. In addition to possessing high validity and reliability (Jensen et al., 1996), the measure is predictive of treatment outcome (Jensen et al., 1996). Its utility is also apparent in its ability to measure self-efficacy and conviction that health care should provide a cure for chronic pain. One limitation of the SOPA is its current lack of normative standards by which to compare individual responses. The Coping Strategies Questionnaire (CSQ) (Rosenstiel & Keefe, 1983) assesses seven coping strategies, including diverting attention from the pain, reinterpreting pain, coping self-statements, ignoring pain, praying/hoping, catastrophizing, and increasing activity. Additionally, there are two self-efficacy items reflecting "perceived control over pain" and "ability to decrease pain." Subscales can be considered alone or composite scales can be derived by combining items and subscales. Subscales and composite measures from the CSQ are predictive of distress and disability (Beckham et al., 1991; Dozois et al., 1996). As an appraisal or coping response, catastrophizing, in particular, has been shown to be an important predictor of psychological distress, adjustment to pain, and disability (Burton et al., 1995; Lester et al., 1996). The Pain Catastrophizing Scale (Sullivan et al., 1995), a 13-item scale that examines 3 components of catastrophizing (rumination, magnification, helplessness), has been shown to predict pain, disability, and employment status among patients with intractable musculoskeletal pain (Sullivan et al., 1998).

2.4.   Pain Behaviors

The nociceptive, perceptual, and appraisal processes underlying pain experience depicted in Figure 11.1 and discussed so far reflect intrapersonal events occurring within the individual. However, those with pain display a broad range of interpersonal reactions that are indicative of pain, distress, and suffering. People with pain might cry, moan, complain, or exhibit pain-related body postures or facial expressions. These behaviors elicit responses from others and those responses can serve to reinforce and thus increase the frequency of those behaviors or punish and thus diminish the frequency of those behaviors. Pain behaviors are exhibited in a social context, can simultaneously influence the environment and be influenced by the environment, and are often measured together, leading us to consider the two dimensions together in this text.

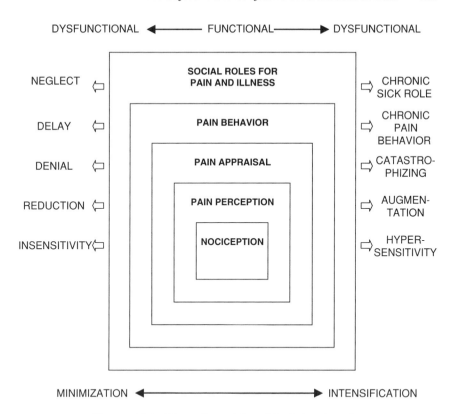

FIGURE 11.1. Biopsychosocial model of chronic pain.

Overt pain behaviors can be self-reports or observations by a significant other or health care provider making the assessment (Table 11.2). Largely due to the efforts of Fordyce (1976) and Keefe and Gil (1986), measures of pain behavior have emerged as potent indicators of current pain status and as measures of change in response to treatment. Measuring pain in terms of observable behavior (e.g., facial expressions, body positioning, activity level) offers the possibility of assessing the person without recourse to subjective self-report. Measuring pain behaviors is particularly important in the assessment of chronic pain patients because many of these patients exhibit a pattern of behavior characterized by a sedentary and restricted lifestyle, dependence on pain medication, and reliance on family members. In addition to their association with pain, pain behaviors are important in their own right, in that they are observable, elicit responses from others, and are subject to the same principles of learning and reinforcement as all other behaviors. Various positive and negative reinforcements (e.g., attention, avoidance of undesirable activities, financial compensation) may maintain pain behaviors.

TABLE 11.2. Observable Pain Behaviors

Pain Behavior	Observation
Facial expressions	Grimacing, frowning, clenching teeth
Body postures	Holding or supporting affected body part or area, slouching, awkward or unusual body position, sitting with a rigid posture
Movement	Limping or distorted gait, frequent shifting of posture or position, moving in a guarded or protective fashion, stooping while walking
Motor activity	Extremely slow movements, hand-wringing
Paralingual vocalizations	Moaning, sighing, crying
Assistive devices	Using a cane, cervical collar, relying on others for help in performing tasks or carrying objects

The dilemma faced by the evaluator making the assessment of causality is that the intensity of pain perception or physical signs in those with chronic pain is often unrelated to self-report of physical disability (Patrick & D'Eon, 1996). This is further complicated by the understandable expectation held by a lay person, such as a jury member, that extent of disability should be proportionately related to severity of pain. When the two are not related, one might argue that the person's report of pain is exaggerated or invalid; however, the two constructs might be entirely distinct and independently provide valid information about the individual with chronic pain. Adaptive or maladaptive behavioral mechanisms are pervasive and can be thought of as one group of variables that explain much of the discrepancy between reported pain and disability.

2.4.1.   Notable Instruments for the Measurement of Pain Behaviors

As with all observational methods, observer training is important in developing and maintaining the psychometric properties of a pain observational method (Keefe et al., 2001). Keefe and colleagues (2001) have developed a model behavioral observation system for the assessment of pain behaviors in patients with osteoarthritis and describe the rationale behind observer training, sampling of behaviors, and applications of behavioral observation. In the absence of formal training, we would recommend that the evaluator use both informal behavioral observations during the interview and formal self-reports of pain behaviors.

Instruments to assess self-reported functioning and limitations in behaviors are economical and efficient and can assess a wide range of behaviors and levels of functioning. Commonly used functional assessment scales include the Roland-Morris Disability Scale (RMDS) (Roland & Morris, 1983) and the Oswestry Disability Questionnaire (ODQ) (Fairbank et al., 1980). Both have demonstrated reliability, validity, and clinical utility, have been widely used with pain patients, and are translated widely into 12 and 9 languages, respectively (for a review of both of these measures, see Roland & Fairbank, 2000).

The RMDS is a widely used 24-item self-report inventory designed to assess disability associated with low back pain. The RMDS is short, simple to complete, and readily understood by patients. It demonstrates excellent internal consistency and high correlations when compared to other measures of physical functioning (Turner et al., 2003). The ODQ is a 10-item self-report instrument with each item consisting of a set of 6 statements describing level of functioning or disability. All statements indicate a level of severity of disability or impairment of functioning in a set of life activities, including personal care, lifting, walking, sitting, standing, sleeping, sexual activity, and social life. Although Stratford et al. (1994) found fewer incomplete or ambiguous responses to the RMDS than to the Oswestry questionnaire, Turner et al. (2003) found that 15% of 309 respondents omitted at least 1 response from the RMDS.

2.5.   Social Roles for the Pain Patient

Fordyce (1976) suggested that responses by family members and others to the behavior of those with pain could maintain pain behaviors, worsen disability, and increase functional impairment. Chronic pain behaviors are embedded in social roles for pain patients (see Fig. 11.1) that might sanction withdrawal from personal and work responsibilities and an increase in treatment-seeking behaviors. The notion of a sick role implies measuring the reciprocating impact of pain on both the person and the environment. Comprehensive assessment of chronic pain cannot occur in the absence of measurement of pain behaviors and the social roles those behaviors respond to and elicit.

2.5.1.   Notable Instruments for the Measurement of Social Role of the Pain Patient

The Multidimensional Pain Inventory (MPI) is a 60-item self-report instrument designed to assess cognitive, behavioral, and affective responses to pain (Kerns et al., 1985). The MPI consists of 12 empirically derived scales grouped into 3 sections. Section I includes five scales that describe pain severity and cognitive and affective responses to pain. Section II assesses perception of how significant others respond to pain complaints. Section III consists of various types of common activity altered by pain. The MPI has good internal consistency for all scales (0.70–0.90) and satisfactory test–retest stability (Rudy et al., 1989; Turk & Rudy, 1988). The validity of the MPI has been demonstrated across a number of samples of chronic pain syndromes, including patients with fibromyalgia, temporomandibular disorder, back pain, and headache (Jacob & Kerns, 2001). The MPI also provides three empirically derived primary profiles, namely (1) Dysfunctional individuals, who report high levels of pain, distress, and disability and feel pessimistic and helpless about their pain conditions, (2) Interpersonally Distressed individuals, who also report high levels of pain, distress, and disability, but additionally report low levels of perceived social support, solicitous responses, or high levels of negative responses from their significant others, and (3) Copers who, compared to other chronic pain patients, report relatively low levels of pain, disability, and distress, minimal functional limitations, and high levels of life control.

The Graded Chronic Pain Scale (GCPS) (Von Korff et al., 1992) includes a measure of pain intensity and the extent to which pain is psychosocially disabling. The average of three pain intensity items is used to measure characteristic pain intensity (Dworkin et al., 1990). Disability days and ratings of interference with social, occupational, and recreational activities result in a disability score and a grade of severity of chronic pain status. Graded chronic pain categories correspond to the following: grade 0, pain free; grade I, low-intensity pain and low interference; grade II, high-intensity pain, low interference; grade III, moderate interference; grade IV, high interference. Grades I and II correspond to a pain patient who is functioning adaptively to his pain, whereas grades III and IV correspond to dysfunctional adaptation. Comparing the GCPS to the MPI, we (Dworkin et al., 2002) have shown that GCPS classifications are closely related to MPI classifications, with GCPS Grades I and II highly related to Adaptive Copers and GCPS Grades III and IV highly related to the Dysfunctional and Interpersonally Distressed profiles. The GCPS is short, and in settings where gaining information rapidly is imperative, it may compare favorably to longer measures such as the MPI.

3.   Objective Versus Subjective Assessment of Pain and Detection of Malingering

The objective assessment of pain involves an ongoing pursuit to develop measures that cannot be biased by an individual. To that end, pain is assessed by observable performance measures such as strength, lifting capacity, and range of motion as well as physiological measures at the periphery such as electromyography, nerve blocks, computed tomography, and magnetic resonance imaging. We have shown how such "objective" measures are subject to their own degree of questionable validity and reliability. We have also shown that measures of functional performance are also influenced by patient presentation, beliefs, and appraisals. Because pain is a subjective experience influenced by motivational, cognitive, and affective factors, assessment of pain cannot be independent of assessment relevant characteristics of the individual. Furthermore, given the considerable interindividual variability in nociceptive, perceptual, and appraisal processes, it is doubtful that brain imaging can provide a reliable way of distinguishing "real" from "imagined" or malingered pain (Jones, 2001). We will probably never be able to evaluate pain without some reliance on subjective reports (Turk, 2001), and this reliance introduces the possibility of difficulty in detecting malingering of symptoms in the forensic setting.

Malingering has been discussed in earlier chapters (see Kane, chapter 2), and in the detection of malingering of psychiatric and cognitive problems, it has received considerable research attention. There is far less research regarding chronic pain malingering; however, the available research has received considerable scrutiny in a careful review. Fishbain and colleagues (1999) determined the prevalence of malingering in the chronic pain setting and whether evidence exists that malingering can be reliably detected within that setting. After reviewing 12 studies on the topic, they concluded that malingering could be present in 1.25–10.4% of cases in the chronic pain setting. However, they noted that the evidence is extremely weak and that there are no well-designed experimental studies in the area. Further, there is very little evidence that we can detect malingering in the chronic pain setting in a reliable manner using traditional psychometric devices (Butcher et al., 2003; Khostanteen et al., 2000).

Clearly, this is an area requiring considerable continued research, but until better pain malingering instruments are developed, the evaluator should focus on a thorough assessment of all dimensions of pain and, as is the case in any complete assessment, consider the domains that could result in malingering. For example, in addition to financial gain, are there other sources of secondary gain such as solicitous responses from significant others that may be perpetuating the sick role? Has the client's report of other symptoms been incompatible with other objective findings? Has the client been known to malinger in the past? Does the client's work, social, and educational history suggest that he or she conforms to authority and is guided by our societal views of moral behavior? Are findings consistent over time and over repeated examinations? We believe that whether we can trust an individual in his or her pain report is related to how well we can trust the individual with reference to all other reports of physical and psychological symptoms.

4.   Conclusions

An exciting direction for pain research that has opened up in the last decade involves use of positron emission tomography scan, functional magnetic resonance imaging, and other imaging techniques to view pain information as it is being dynamically processed by the brain (Derbyshire, 1999). Brain areas implicated in pain processing include the prefrontal cortex, cingulate cortex, somatosensory cortex, amygdala, insula, basal ganglia, thalamus, and the brainstem (Jones, 2001). However, the same brain areas active under pain conditions are active under heightened emotional conditions corresponding to the higher-order perceptual and appraisal processes described in this chapter. Such studies suggest to some that, in the future, we might have a truly objective measure of pain. However, do these studies suggest that functional brain imaging will allow us to measure "true pain"—so much so that an evaluator will be able to tell a patient reporting pain, "no, you do not have pain

TABLE 11.3. Key Pain Domains and Recommended Instruments

Domain	Instruments	Strengths	Limitations
Nociception	Radiologic findings, MRI, nerve blocks, computed tomography, EMG	No patient reporting bias.	Interpretation of findings might be unreliable without calibration of radiologists. Costly; and correlation between objective findings and disability might be low.
Perception	NRS, VRS, VAS, Pain drawing, MPQ	All measures have high validity and reliability. Compliance rate for VRS and NRS is higher than VAS. MPQ is widely used and provides insight into quantitative and qualitative aspects of pain.	High failure rates and difficulty in interpretation by some populations for VAS. Language barrier for VRS. Rating scales for pain drawing have poor validity.
Pain appraisal	SOPA, CSQ	Internal consistency, predictive validity, and factor structure are all adequate. SOPA provides insight into patients functional and dysfunctional beliefs and CSQ provides insight into functional and dysfunctional attempts at coping with pain.	SOPA and CSQ lack normative standards against which to compare individual response profiles.
Pain behaviors	Observations of pain behaviors, RMDS, ODQ	Observations of pain behaviors provide detailed descriptions of behaviors that might be contributing to disability and help in detection of exaggeration or malingering. Both are widely used and have high reliability and validity. Both are short self-reports of disability behaviors.	Reliable observation of pain behavior requires training. RMDS and ODQ are limited to back pain.
Social roles	MPI, GCPS	Both measures are widely used and have excellent reliability and validity. Both measures provide measures of psychosocial functioning. MPI provides patient profiles and comparison norms for pain population.	MPI is longer than GCPS MPI can result in high proportion of invalid profiles.

even though you think you do"? We regard this example as nonsensical. Although biomedical factors appear to instigate the initial report of pain in most cases, psychosocial and behavioral factors may serve to exacerbate and maintain pain and disability (Turk & Melzack, 2001). The ultimate information source of one's pain is the individual. Although there is no single agreed upon method for evaluating patients with pain, there is agreement that chronic pain assessment should include both physical and psychosocial domains to assess the person with pain. We have proposed a theory-based orientation for selection of psychometrically valid instruments and summarize the theory and corresponding instruments in Table 11.3. When measuring pain and the individual with pain, it is important to remember that pain is culturally specific and unique to that individual. Hence, the instruments chosen should be relevant for the age, culture, and cognitive abilities of the individual. We advise that the evaluator choose and use these instruments to complement rather than supplant clinical impressions formed through comprehensive interview.

References

Barsky, A. J. (1979). Patients who amplify bodily sensations. *Annals of Internal Medicine, 91*, 63–70.

Beckham, J. C., Keefe, F. J., Caldwell, D. S., & Roodman, A. A. (1991). Pain coping strategies in rheumatoid arthritis: Relationship to pain, disability, depression and daily hassles. *Behavior Therapy, 22*, 113–124.

Burton, A. K., Tillotson, K. M., Main, C. J., & Hollis, S. (1995). Psychosocial predictors of outcome in acute and subchronic low back trouble. *Spine, 20*, 722–728.

Butcher, J. N., Arbisi, P. A., Atlis, M. M., & McNulty, J. L. (2003). The construct validity of the Lees-Haley Fake Bad Scale (FBS): Does this scale measure malingering and feigned emotional distress? *Archives of Clinical Neuropsychology, 18*, 473–485.

Collins, S. L., Moore, R. A., & McQuay, H. J. (1997). The visual analogue pain intensity scale: What is moderate pain in millimeters? *Pain, 72*, 95–97.

DeGood, D. E. & Tait, R. C. (2001). Assessment of pain beliefs and coping. In D. C. Turk & R. Melzack (Eds.). *Handbook of Pain Assessment*, 2nd ed. New York: Guilford Press, pp. 320–345.

Derbyshire, S. W. (1999). Meta-analysis of thirty-four independent samples studied using PET reveals a significantly attenuated central response to noxious stimulation in clinical pain patients. *Current Pain and Headache Reports, 3*, 266–280.

Derogatis, L. (1983). *The SCL90-R Manual II: Administration, Scoring and Procedures*. Towson, MD: Clinical Psychometric Research.

Dozois, D. J., Dobson, K. S., Wong, M., Hughes, D., & Long, A. (1996). Predictive utility of the CSQ in low back pain: Individual vs. composite measures. *Pain, 66*, 171–180.

Dworkin, R. H. (1997). Which individuals with acute pain are most likely to develop a chronic pain syndrome? *Pain Forum, 6*, 127–136.

Dworkin, S. F. & Sherman, J. J. (2001). Relying on objective and subjective measures of chronic pain: Guideline for use and interpretation. In D. C. Turk & R. Melzack (Eds.). *Handbook of Pain Assessment*, 2nd ed. New York: Guilford Press, pp. 619–638.

Dworkin, S. F., Sherman, J., Mancl, L., Ohrbach, R., LeResche, L., & Truelove, E. (2002). Reliability, validity, and clinical utility of the research diagnostic criteria for Temporomandibular Disorders Axis II Scales: Depression, non-specific physical symptoms, and graded chronic pain. *Journal of Orofacial Pain, 16*, 207–220.

Dworkin, S. F., Von Korff, M., & LeResche, L. (1990). Multiple pains and psychiatric disturbance. An epidemiologic investigation. *Archives of General Psychiatry, 47*, 239–244.

Dworkin, S. F., Von Korff, M., & LeResche, L. (1992). Epidemiologic studies of chronic pain: A dynamic-ecologic perspective. *Annals of Behavioral Medicine, 14*, 3–11.

Fairbank, J. C., Couper, J., Davies, J. B., & O'Brien, J. P. (1980). The Oswestry Low Back Pain Questionnaire. *Physiotherapy, 66*, 271–273.

Fernandez, E. & Turk, D. C. (1992). Sensory and affective components of pain: Separation and synthesis. *Psychology Bulletin, 112*, 205–217.

Fishbain, D. A., Cole, B., Cutler, R. B., Lewis J., Rosomoff, H. L., & Rosomoff, R. S. (2003). A structured evidence-based review on the meaning of nonorganic physical signs: Waddell signs. *Pain Medicine, 4*, 141–181.

Fishbain, D. A., Cutler, R. B., Lewis J., Rosomoff, H. L., & Rosomoff, R. S. (1999). Chronic pain disability exaggeration/malingering and submaximal effort research. *Clinical Journal of Pain, 15*, 244–274.

Fordyce, W. E. (1976). *Behavioral Methods in Chronic Pain and Illness*. St. Louis, MO: C. V. Mosby.

Frymoyer, J. W., Matteri, R. E., Hanley, E. N., Kuhlmann, D., & Howe, J. (1978). Failed lumbar disc surgery requiring second operation. A long term follow-up study. *Spine, 3*, 7–11.

Hathaway, S. R., McKinley, J. C., Butcher, J. N., Dahlstrom, W. G., Graham, J. R., Tellegen, A., & Kaemmer, B. (1989). *Minnesota Multiphasic Personality Inventory 2: Manual for Administration*. Minneapolis, MN: University of Minnesota Press.

Hendler, N., Bergson, C., & Morrison, C. (1996). Overlooked physical diagnoses in chronic pain patients involved in litigation, Part 2. The addition of MRI, nerve blocks, 3-D CT, and qualitative flow meter. *Psychosomatics, 37*, 509–17.

Jacob, M. C. & Kerns R. D. (2001). Assessment of the psychosocial context of the experience of chronic pain. In D. C. Turk & R. Melzack (Eds.). *Handbook of Pain Assessment*, 2nd ed. New York: Guilford Press, pp. 362–384.

Jensen, M. P. & Karoly, P. (2001). Self-report scales and procedures for assessing pain in adults. In D. C. Turk & R. Melzack (Eds.). *Handbook of Pain Assessment*, 2nd ed. New York: Guilford Press, pp. 15–34.

Jensen, M. P., Karoly, P., & Braver S. (1986). The measurement of clinical pain intensity: A comparison of six methods. *Pain, 27*, 117–126.

Jensen, M. P., Karoly, P., & Huger, R. (1987). The development and preliminary validation of an instrument to assess patients' attitudes toward pain. *Journal of Psychosomatic Research, 31*, 393–400.

Jensen, M. P., Turner, L. R., Turner, J. A., & Romano, J. M. (1996). The use of multiple item scales for pain intensity measurement in chronic pain patients. *Pain, 67*, 35–40.

Jones, A. (2001). The future of imaging in assessment of chronic musculoskeletal pain. In D. C. Turk & R. Melzack (Eds.). *Handbook of Pain Assessment*, 2nd ed. New York: Guilford Press, pp. 693–704.

Keefe, F. J. & Gil, K. M. (1986). Behavioral concepts in the analysis of chronic pain. *Journal of Consulting and Clinical Psychology, 54*, 776–783.

Keefe, F. J., Williams, D. A., & Smith, S. J. (2001). Assessment of pain behaviors. In D. C. Turk & R. Melzack (Eds.). *Handbook of Pain Assessment*, 2nd ed. New York: Guilford Press, pp. 170–187.

Kerns, R. D., Turk, D. C., & Rudy, T. E., (1985). The West Haven-Yale Multidimensional Pain Inventory (WHYMPI). *Pain, 23*, 345–356.

Khostanteen, I., Tanks, E. R., Goldsmith, C. H., & Ennis, J. (2000). Fibromyalgia: Can one distinguish it from simulation? An observer-blind controlled study. *Journal of Rheumatology, 27*, 2671–2676.

Kleinbohl, D., Holzl, R., Moltner, A., Rommel, C., Weber, C., & Osswald, P. M. (1999). Psychophysical measures of sensitization to tonic heat discriminate chronic pain patients. *Pain, 81*, 35–43.

Lester, N., Lefebvre, J., & Keefe, F. (1996). Pain in young adults—III: Relationships of three pain coping measures to pain and activity interference. *Clinical Journal of Pain, 12*, 291–300.

Maixner, W., Fillingim, R., Kincaid, S., Sigurdsson, A., & Harris, M. B. (1997). Relationship between pain sensitivity and resting arterial blood pressure in patients with temporomandibular disorders. *Psychosomatic Medicine, 59*, 503–511.

Maixner, W., Fillingim, R., Sigurdsson, A., Kincaid, S., & Silva, S. (1998). Sensitivity of patients with temporomandibular disorders to experimentally evoked pain: Evidence for altered temporal summation of pain. *Pain, 76*, 71–81.

Margolis, R. B., Chibnall, J. T., & Tait, R. C. (1988). Test-retest reliability of the pain drawing instrument. *Pain, 33*, 49–51.

Melzack, R. (1975). The McGill Pain Questionnaire: Major properties and scoring methods. *Pain, 1*, 277–299.

Melzack, R. & Katz, J. (2001). The McGill Pain Questionnaire: Appraisal and current status. In D. C. Turk & R. Melzack (Eds.). *Handbook of Pain Assessment*, 2nd ed. New York: Guilford Press, pp. 35–52.

Melzack, R. & Wall, P. D. (1965). Pain mechanisms: A new theory. *Science, 150*, 971–979.

Melzack, R., Coderre, T. J., Katz, J., & Vaccarino, A. L. (2001). Central neuroplasticity and pathological pain. *Annals of the New York Academy of Science, 933*, 157–174.

Mendell, L. M. (1966). Physiological properties of unmyelinated fiber projection to the spinal cord. *Experimental Neurology, 16*, 316–332.

Mense, S. (1993). Nociception from skeletal muscle in relation to clinical muscle pain. *Pain, 54*, 241–289.

Merskey, H. & Bogduk, N. (Eds.). (1994). *Classification of Chronic Pain*, 2nd ed. Seattle, WA: International Association for the Study of Pain Press.

Millon, T., Green, C., & Meagher, R. (1983). Millon Behavioral Health Inventory Manual, 3rd ed. Minneapolis, MN: National Computer Systems.

Ohland, C., Eek, C., Palmbald, S., Areskoug, B., & Nachemson, A. (1996). Quantified pain drawing in subacute low back pain. Validation in a nonselected outpatient industrial sample. *Spine, 21*, 1021–1031.

Ohrbach, R. & Dworkin, S. F. (1998). Five-year outcomes in TMD: Relationship of changes in pain to changes in physical and psychological variables. *Pain, 74*, 315–326.

Parker, H., Wood, P. L. R., & Main, C. J. (1995). The use of the pain drawing as a screening measure to predict psychological distress in chronic low back pain. *Spine, 20*, 236–243.

Patrick, L. & D'Eon, J. (1996). Social support and functional status in chronic pain patients. *Canadian Journal of Rehabilitation, 9*, 195–201.

Perry, F., Heller, P. H., & Levine, J. D. (1988). Differing correlations between pain measures in syndromes with or without explicable organic pathology. *Pain, 34*, 185–189.

Perry, F., Heller, P. H., & Levine, J. D. (1991). A possible indicator of functional pain: Poor scale correlation. *Pain 46*, 191–193.

Polatin, P. B. & Meyer, T. G. (2001). Quantification of function in chronic low back pain. In D. C. Turk & R. Melzack (Eds.). *Handbook of Pain Assessment*, 2nd ed. New York: Guilford Press, pp. 191–203.

Ransford, A. O., Cairns, D., & Mooney, V. (1976). The pain drawing as an aid to the psychologic evaluation of patients with low back pain. *Spine, 1*, 127–134.

Roland, M. & Fairbank, J. (2000). The Roland–Morris Disability Questionnaire and the Oswestry Disability Questionnaire. *Spine, 26*, 847.

Roland, M. & Morris, R., (1983). A study of the natural history of back pain. Part I: Development of a reliable and sensitive measure of disability in low-back pain. *Spine, 8*, 41–144.

Rosenstiel, A. K. & Keefe, F. J. (1983). The use of coping strategies in chronic low back pain patients: Relationship to patient characteristics and current adjustment. *Pain, 17*, 33–44.

Rudy, T. E., Turk, D. C., Zaki, H. S., & Curtin, H. D. (1989). An empirical taxometric alternative to traditional classification of temporomandibular disorders. *Pain, 36*, 311–320.

Simon, G. E. & Von Korff, M. (1991). Somatization and psychiatric disorders in the NIMH Epidemiologic Catchment Area Study. *American Journal of Psychiatry, 148*, 1494–1500.

Sternbach, G. (1990). The world in cervical spine precautions. *Journal of Emergency Medicine, 8*, 207–208.

Stratford, P. W., Binkley, J., Solomon, P., Gill, C., & Finch, E. (1994). Assessing change over time in patients with low back pain. *Physical Therapy, 74*, 528–533.

Strong, J., Ashton, R., & Chant, D. (1991). Pain intensity measurement in chronic low back pain. *Clinical Journal of Pain, 7*, 209–218.

Sullivan, M. D. (2001). Assessment of psychiatric disorders. In D. C. Turk & R. Melzack (Eds.). *Handbook of Pain Assessment*, 2nd ed. New York: Guilford Press, pp. 275–291.

Sullivan, M. J. L., Bishop, S. R., & Pivik, J. (1995). The pain catastrophizing scale: Development and validation. *Psychological Assessment, 7*, 524–532.

Sullivan, M. J. L., Stanish, W., Waite, H., Sullivan, M., & Tripp, D. A. (1998). Catastrophizing, pain and disability in patients with soft tissue injuries. *Pain, 77*, 253–260.

Turk, D. C. (2001). Trends and future directions in human pain assessment. In D. C. Turk & R. Melzack (Eds.). *Handbook of Pain Assessment*, 2nd ed. New York: Guilford Press, pp. 707–715.

Turk, D. C. & Melzack, R. (2001). The measurement of pain and the assessment of people experiencing pain. In D. C. Turk & R. Melzack (Eds.). *Handbook of Pain Assessment*, 2nd ed. New York: Guilford Press, pp. 3–14.

Turk, D. C. & Rudy, T. E. (1988). Toward an empirically derived taxonomy of chronic pain patients: Integration of psychological assessment data. *Journal of Consulting and Clinical Psychology, 56*, 233–238.

Turk, D. C., & Rudy, T. E. (1990). The robustness of an empirically derived taxonomy of chronic pain patients. *Pain, 43*, 27–35.

Turner, J. A., Fulton-Kehoe, D., Franklin, G., Wickizer, T., & Wu, R. (2003). Comparison of the Roland–Morris Disability Questionnaire and Generic Health Status Measures: A population-based study of Workers' Compensation back injury claimants. *Spine, 28*, 1061–1067.

Von Korff, M., Ormel, J., Keefe, F. J., & Dworkin, S. F. (1992). Grading the severity of chronic pain. *Pain, 50*, 133–149.

Waddell, G., & Turk, D. C. (2001). Clinical assessment of low back pain. In D. C. Turk & R. Melzack (Eds.). *Handbook of Pain Assessment*, 2nd ed. New York: Guilford Press, pp. 431–453.

Waddell, G., McCulloch, J. A., Kummel, E., & Venner, R. M. (1980). Nonorganic physical signs in low-back pain. *Spine, 5*, 117–125.

Section 4

PTSD and Pain

12

Posttraumatic Stress Disorder and Whiplash After Motor Vehicle Accidents

BRIAN M. FREIDENBERG, EDWARD J. HICKLING,
EDWARD B. BLANCHARD, AND LORETTA S. MALTA

Motor vehicle accidents (MVAs) that involve personal injuries are extremely common in the United States (nearly 3 million people annually) (National Highway Traffic Safety Administration, 2003). The development of Posttraumatic Stress Disorder (PTSD) is a frequent potential consequence of MVAs (Blanchard & Hickling, 1997).

1. Definition of Whiplash Injuries

Whiplash injuries have been defined as bony or soft tissue injuries of the neck and upper back, caused by flexion and extension of the neck (Spitzer et al., 1995). The injuries are a common result of MVAs (Mayou & Bryant, 1996) as indicated by the 1 million annual occurrences of MVA-related whiplash injuries in the United States alone (Silverman & Devineni, 1999). The injuries typically involve rear, side, or front impact collisions in which accelerative–decelerative forces impact the head and neck, causing them to be thrown back and forth (Silverman & Devineni, 1999). The primary symptom in all cases is neck pain, which is often described as either a dull ache or a series of sharp pains. The pain usually intensifies during movement of the neck. Furthermore, whiplash is frequently associated with stiffness in the neck, as well as restricted movement of the neck (Barnsley et al., 1998). Whiplash also has been found to have a profound impact on physical, social, and vocational functioning (e.g., Barnsley et al., 1994; Smed, 1997; Teasell & Shapiro, 1999).

2. The Relationship Between Whiplash Recovery and PTSD Recovery

It has been found that whiplash injuries can take a long time to remit (i.e., several months or even years) (Mayou & Bryant, 1996). Given this chronicity in addition to the injury's intrusive nature, it has been suggested that whiplash injuries may impede recovery of psychological symptoms (Blanchard & Hickling, 1997). However, there has been little research to help shed light on the issue.

3.   Assessment of Whiplash

Physicians often find whiplash injuries difficult to assess (Mayou, 1999). The diagnosis of whiplash tends to be less definitive than the diagnoses of other physical conditions (e.g., broken arm, dislocated shoulder). To our knowledge, there are no physiologically based tests [e.g., magnetic resonance imaging (MRI)] that can confirm the diagnosis of whiplash injury. As a result, the assessor must rely upon patient self-report of the injury, including the continued complaints of pain, restricted range of motion, and that certain movements cause pain. In our work at the Center for Stress and Anxiety Disorders, we have relied exclusively upon patient self-report and have consulted medical reports when available.

4.   Psychological Distress as a Consequence of Whiplash Injury

It has been documented that psychosocial problems often occur in reaction to persistent whiplash-associated pain (Teasell & Shapiro, 1999). Also, research has shown that psychological distress tends to develop following whiplash injuries (Barnsley et al., 1994; Smed, 1997).

Mayou and colleagues (Mayou & Bryant, 1996, 2002) have been the primary contributors to the literature on psychiatric consequences of whiplash injuries following MVAs. In their first report, Mayou and Bryant (1996) described the 12-month outcome for 74 patients who had whiplash injury from their prospective follow-up study of MVA survivors who visited the emergency department (Mayou et al., 1993). Sixty-one patients were reassessed at 3 months and 57 of them (77.0%) at 1 year. Whereas 84% complained explicitly of neck pain at the initial evaluation (a mean of 25 days post-MVA), this was reduced to 51% at 3 months and 37% at 1 year. The decreasing frequency implies gradual relief from the pain and discomfort. According to these researchers, there were no special psychiatric outcomes for these whiplash patients, with 18% qualifying as a "case" at 3 months and 12% at 1 year based on the Present State Examination (Wing et al., 1974). Moreover, psychosocial outcomes were predicted by variables other than the injury status. Wing et al. (1974, p. 621) concluded "that the continuing report of neck symptoms at 3 months and 1 year is largely unrelated to any of the psychological and social variables assessed at, or soon after, injury or to compensation."

The second report from these investigators is from the 3-year follow-up data on the prospective study (by Ehlers et al., 1998) of a very large cohort of MVA survivors attending the emergency room in Oxford, UK. Of the 1148 patients who were initially assessed, 278 (24.2%) had whiplash injuries. The whiplash subsample was reassessed by questionnaire [N=208 (74.8%) at 3 months, 187 (67.3%) at 1 year, and 124 (44.6%) at 3 years]. The percent of whiplash patients claiming moderate to very severe pain over time was 37% at 3 months, 27% at 1 year, and 30% at 3 years. These values showed little change over time. They exceed those for patients with other soft tissue injuries and are on a par with those who had bony injuries. The fraction with any noticeable psychological difficulty was fairly consistent, being at 37% at 3 months, 35% at 1 year, and 35% at 3 years; again, the results were comparable to those with bony injury. The only significant multivariate predictor of pain level at 1 year was whether the patient had filed a legal suit for compensation within 3 months of the accident. The authors concluded that "there is no special psychiatry of whiplash" (Ehlers et al., 1998, p. 447). In summary, Mayou and Bryant (1996, 2002) noted that the minority of whiplash patients had long-standing physical, and, to some extent, social and psychological problems.

To understand more on psychiatric consequences of whiplash injuries, data from one of our Center for Stress and Anxiety Disorder cohorts (Blanchard & Hickling, 1997), which we will call cohort 1, will now be presented to examine how the role of physical healing specific to whiplash injury may play a role in the maintenance of, or recovery from, psychological symptoms, particularly PTSD, stemming from an MVA. Specifically, we were interested in testing the following questions: (1) Is the presence of whiplash at initial assessment associated with differences in PTSD symptom levels at any point in time? (2) Is the continuing presence of whiplash later associated with differences in PTSD symptom levels at any point in time? (3) Does pretreatment presence of whiplash interact with treatment condition, affecting posttreatment CAPS (Clinician-Administered PTSD Scale) scores? (4) Does psychological treatment have an affect on pain ratings of those individuals who had whiplash?

4.1. Cohort 1

4.1.1. Method: Participants

Our original sample was composed of 158 MVA survivors who sought medical attention within 48 hours of their accident. The sample was not a consecutive series. For this report, we analyzed data for 87 participants who initially met diagnostic criteria for either full or subsyndromal PTSD (see diagnostic criteria below) and for whom data were available at all 3 assessment points, ranging from 1 to 12 months. Of the 87 participants, 24 were male and 63 were female. The mean age of the sample was 35.5 years. There were 81 Caucasian Americans and 6 non-Caucasian Americans.

4.1.2. Method: Procedure

The sample was recruited via referral from medical professionals, local media coverage, and advertising. There was an initial assessment 1–4 months after the MVA (Time 1; T1), a 6-month follow-up (Time 2; T2), and a 1-year follow-up (Time 3; T3). Participants were paid for their time after assessments were completed ($50 at Time 1, $50 at Time 2, $75 at Time 3). The length of interviews ranged from 2 to 6 hours. The Clinician Administered Post-Traumatic Stress Disorder Scale (CAPS; Blake et al., 1990a, 1990b, 1998) was used to assess for PTSD. The CAPS is a commonly accepted valid and reliable measure for assessing PTSD (Weathers et al., 1992; Weathers & Litz, 1994; Weathers et al., 2001). The CAPS is a clinician-administered, structured interview. For each of the 17 symptoms of PTSD, the CAPS can be used to assess both frequency of occurrence and severity of the symptoms. To diagnose PTSD, several different scoring rules can be adopted. For further information on the various scoring rules for different assessment tasks, one should refer to Weathers et al. (1999).

4.1.3. Diagnoses

In order for a diagnosis of whiplash to be made, participants must have met the following criteria: (1) during the MVA, their head whipped back and forth and (2) they complained of neck pain, tenderness, or stiffness. Whiplash was considered to be in remission once participants rated the problem as absent.

Full and subsyndromal PTSD diagnoses were made using the Diagnostic and Statistical Manual of Mental Disorders, Fourth Edition (DSM-IV) (American Psychiatric Association, 1994) and CAPS interview. Subsyndromal PTSD was diagnosed if participants met the symptomatic criteria for Criterion B (the re-experiencing cluster) and either Criterion C (avoidance and numbing cluster) or Criterion D (hyperarousal cluster). A similar subsyndromal category for PTSD has been used in previous research (Blanchard & Hickling, 1997; Feinstein & Dolan, 1991; Green et al., 1993).

4.1.4. Analyses

Only the analyses involving the sample size with full data ($N=87$) are presented. Analyses were also performed (but are not presented) on those participants who met full criteria for PTSD; those diagnosed with subsyndromal PTSD were excluded. However, there was not enough power to detect meaningful differences when the smaller sample size ($N=45$) was divided into even smaller comparison groups for the analyses.

4.1.5. Results: Descriptive

At the initial assessment (T1), 69 participants were positive for whiplash injuries and 18 participants were negative.

4.1.6. Results and Conclusions: Question 1—Is the Presence of Whiplash at T1 Associated with Differences in PTSD Symptom Levels at a Later Point? Answer: Yes

We examined clinical diagnostic status at T2 and T3 (as indicated by the CAPS interviews) as a function of whether or not participants had whiplash injury at T1 (see Table 12.1). A chi-square analysis indicated a significant group difference in PTSD diagnosis at T2, $\chi^2(1, N=87) = 6.21, p<.025$ (specifically that more PTSD remitted in those without whiplash compared to those with whiplash), but no significant difference at T3, $\chi^2(1, N=87) = 2.71, p=ns$. Thus, the presence of whiplash at the initial assessment appears to have had an impact on PTSD 6 months later.

4.1.7. Results and Conclusions: Question 2—Is the Continuing Presence of Whiplash at T2 Associated with Differences in PTSD Symptom Levels at Any Time Point? Answer: Yes

We examined clinical diagnostic status at T2 and T3 as a function of whether participants continued to have whiplash, no longer had whiplash, or never had whiplash at T2 (see Table 12.2). A chi-square analysis indicated a significant group differences in PTSD diagnosis at T2, $\chi^2(2, N=87) = 7.03, p<.05$ [in particular, a significant difference between those who still had whiplash and those who never had whiplash, $\chi^2(1, N=61) = 7.03, p<.01$], but no significant difference at T3, $\chi^2(2, N=87) = 3.46, p=ns$ (Table 2). Thus, at the 6-month follow-up assessment, those participants whose whiplash injuries

TABLE 12.1. CAPS-Derived Clinical Status at 6- and 12-Month Follow-Ups as a Function of Whiplash Injury Status During the Initial Assessment (T1)

	Clinical Status at 6 Months		Clinical Status at 12 Months	
Injury Status at T1	PTSD Remitted	PTSD Not Remitted	PTSD Remitted	PTSD Not Remitted
Whiplash	35	34	39	30
No whiplash	15	3	14	4
	$\chi^2(1, N = 87) = 6.21, p<.025$		$\chi^2(1, N = 87) = 2.71, p=ns$	

TABLE 12.2. CAPS-Derived Clinical Status at 6- and 12-Month Follow-Ups as a Function of Whiplash Injury Status During the 6-Month Follow-Up (T2)

	Clinical Status at 6 Months		Clinical Status at 12 Months	
Injury Status at T2	PTSD Remitted	PTSD Not Remitted	PTSD Remitted	PTSD Not Remitted
Still [a] whiplash	20	23	26	17
Whiplash remitted	15	11	13	13
Never [a] had whiplash	15	3	14	4
	$\chi^2(2, N=87) = 7.03, p<.05$		$\chi^2(2, N=87) = 3.46, p=ns$	

Note: Groups that share the superscript a are significantly different.

had not remitted were significantly more likely to still have PTSD at that point in time than those who never had whiplash injuries.

4.1.8. Results and Conclusions: Question 3—Is the Continuing Presence of Whiplash at T3 Associated with Differences in PTSD Symptom Levels at Any Time Point? Answer: No

We examined clinical diagnostic status at T3 as a function of whether participants continued to have whiplash, no longer had whiplash, or never had whiplash at T3 (see Table 12.3). A chi-square analysis indicated no significant between group differences in PTSD diagnosis at T3, $\chi^2(2, N=87) = 3.28$, p=ns. Thus, whiplash status at the 12-month follow-up had no impact on PTSD status at that point in time.

4.1.9. Conclusions: Final Remark

Thus, it seems that there is a concurrent relation between physical healing (remission of pain and stiffness of whiplash) and psychological healing (improved psychological status) with respect to PTSD given the answers to the above questions.

5.   The Role of Whiplash Injury in the Psychological Treatment of PTSD

Next, it is important to identify whether whiplash injuries impede psychological treatment that targets PTSD secondary to MVAs. To our knowledge, the impact of whiplash on treatment outcome has yet to be examined. To learn more about this, data from another cohort of MVA survivors (Cohort 2) (Blanchard et al., 2003) are briefly summarized in this section.

5.1.   Cohort 2

5.1.1.   Method: Participants

In the study, we analyzed data for 78 MVA survivors who sought medical attention within 48 hours of their accident. The sample was not a consecutive series. All participants met diagnostic criteria for either full or subsyn-

TABLE 12.3. CAPS-Derived Clinical Status at 12-Month Follow-Up as a Function of Whiplash Injury Status During the 12-Month Follow-Up (T3)

Injury Status at T3	Clinical Status at 12 Months	
	PTSD Remitted	PTSD Not Remitted
Still whiplash	23	15
Whiplash remitted	16	15
Never had whiplash	14	4

dromal PTSD at an initial assessment 6–24 months post-MVA. Of the 78 participants, 21 were male and 57 were female. The mean age of the sample was 40.9 years. There were 72 Caucasian Americans and 6 non-Caucasian Americans.

5.1.2. Method: Procedure

The sample was recruited via referral from medical professionals, local media coverage, and advertising. Assessments took place both before and after one of three conditions to which participants were randomly assigned. Participants were assigned to enter one of the three conditions at the conclusion of the precondition interview. The three conditions were cognitive–behavior therapy (CBT; 27 participants), supportive psychotherapy (SUPP; 27 participants), and a waiting list control condition (WL; 24 participants). If assigned to one of the two psychotherapy conditions, participants were treated by one of three experienced clinical psychologists from the community for 10 one-hour sessions using a manualized treatment (for specific details of the treatment conditions, please refer to Blanchard et al., 2003). The length of the initial interviews ranged from 2 to 6 hours, and the length of postcondition interviews averaged 1 hour. These interviews were conducted by advanced clinical psychology doctoral students and were not part of therapy. The CAPS was used to assess for PTSD.

5.1.3. Diagnoses

Diagnoses were derived using the same methods used in Cohort 1.

5.1.4. Results and Conclusions

Posttreatment changes in CAPS scores were not affected by pretreatment whiplash status, regardless of treatment condition completed. Furthermore, we examined pretreatment and posttreatment mean self-reported whiplash pain rating scores (rated on a 10-point subjective intensity scale) as a function of assigned condition. Results revealed that psychological treatment did not have an affect on pain ratings by those participants who had whiplash.

Overall Conclusions

Although the presence of whiplash might be relevant in the recovery of PTSD, the importance of this relationship is still not well understood. In the above research, we have assumed a causal direction—that after accidents physical injury in the accidents and its healing influences individuals' psychological state. It is equally possible that the survivor's psychological state influences his/her perception of (1) degree of healing and (2) present physical state.

This topic area is in need of more extensive collaborative research among orthopedists, physical therapists, and mental health professionals. As if to answer our 1997 call for more research on this topic, Sharp and Harvey (2001) published a theoretical paper in which they speculate about the possible mutual maintenance between PTSD and chronic pain (Blanchard & Hickling, 2004; Otis et al., 2003). They noted the scattered reports of high levels of comorbidity between PTSD and chronic pain and went on to speculate on possible mechanisms by which these two problems reinforce one another. Chief among these are (1) that the pain serves as a reminder of the trauma, (2) that chronic levels of anxiety and arousal (from PTSD) make the sufferer more sensitive to painful stimuli, and (3) that both problems lead to efforts at avoidance of situations that remind sufferers of the source of the pain and situations that involve actual pain from any source. We certainly agree with this formulation. Given that our data did not permit a fine-grained analysis that would allow one to draw strong causal inferences, future research examining each of the above-mentioned mechanisms is warranted.

Acknowledgment

This research was supported by a grant from NIMH (MH-48476).

References

American Psychiatric Association. (1994). *Diagnostic and Statistical manual of Mental Disorders*, 4th ed. Washington, DC: American Psychiatric Association.

Barnsley, L., Lord, S., & Bogduk, N. (1994). Whiplash injury. *Pain, 58*, 283–307.

Barnsley, L., Lord, S. M., & Bogduk, N. (1998). The pathophysiology of whiplash. In G. A. Malanga (Ed.). *Spine: State of the Art Reviews, 12*. Philadelphia, PA: Hanley & Belfus.

Blake, D., Weathers, F., Nagy, L., Kaloupek, D., Klauminzer, G., Charney, D., & Keane, T. (1990a). *Clinician-Administered PTSD Scale (CAPS)*. Boston, MA: National Center for Post-Traumatic Stress Disorder, Behavioral Science Division.

Blake, D., Weathers, F., Nagy, L., Kaloupek, D., Klauminzer, G., Charney, D., & Keane, T. (1990b). *Clinician-Administered PTSD Scale (CAPS), Form 2-One-Week Symptom Status Version*. Boston, MA: National Center for Post-Traumatic Stress Disorder, Behavioral Science Division.

Blake, D., Weathers, F., Nagy, L., Kaloupek, D., Klauminzer, G., Charney, D., & Keane, T. (1998). *Clinician-Administered PTSD Scale (CAPS)*. Boston, MA: National Center for Post-Traumatic Stress Disorder, Behavioral Science Division.

Blanchard, E. B. & Hickling, E. J. (1997). *After the Crash: Assessment and Treatment of Motor Vehicle Accident Survivors,* 1st ed. Washington, DC: American Psychological Association.

Blanchard, E. B. & Hickling, E. J. (2004). *After the Crash: Assessment and Treatment of Motor Vehicle Accident Survivors,* 2nd ed. Washington, DC: American Psychological Association.

Blanchard, E. B., Hickling, E. J., Devineni, T., Veazey, C. H., Galovski, T. E., Mundy, E., Malta, L. S., & Buckley, T. C. (2003). A controlled evaluation of cognitive behavioral therapy for posttraumatic stress in motor vehicle accident survivors. *Behaviour Research and Therapy, 41*, 79–96.

Ehlers, A., Mayou, R. A., & Bryant, B. (1998). Psychological predictors of chronic Posttraumatic Stress Disorder after motor vehicle accidents. *Journal of Abnormal Psychology, 107*, 508–519.

Feinstein, A. & Dolan, R. (1991). Predictors of Posttraumatic Stress Disorder following physical trauma: An examination of the stressor criterion. *Psychological Medicine, 21*, 85–91.

Green, M. M., McFarlane, A. C., Hunter, C. E., & Griggs W. M. (1993). Undiagnosed Posttraumatic Stress Disorder following motor vehicle accidents. *The Medical Journal of Australia, 159*, 529–534.

Mayou, R. (1999). Medical, social, and legal consequences. In E. J. Hickling, & E. B. Blanchard (Eds.). *The International Handbook of Road Traffic Accidents & Psychological Trauma: Current Understanding Treatment and Law*. New York: Elsevier, pp. 43–56.

Mayou, R. & Bryant, B. (1996). Outcome of 'whiplash' neck injury. *Injury, 27*, 617–623.

Mayou, R. & Bryant, B. (2002). Psychiatry of whiplash neck injury. *British Journal of Psychiatry, 180*, 441–448.

Mayou, R., Bryant, B., & Duthie, R. (1993). Psychiatric consequences of road traffic accidents. *British Medical Journal, 307*, 647–651.

National Highway Traffic Safety Administration, U.S. Department of Transportation. (2003). Traffic safety facts 2002: A public information fact sheet on motor vehicle and traffic safety.

Otis, J. D., Keane, T. M., & Kerns, R. D. (2003). An examination of the relationship between chronic pain and Posttraumatic Stress Disorder. *Journal of Rehabilitation Research and Development, 40*(5), 397–405.

Sharp, T. J. & Harvey, A. G. (2001). Chronic pain and Posttraumatic Stress Disorder: Mutual maintenance? *Clinical Psychology Review, 21*, 857–877.

Silverman, D. & Devineni, T. (1999). Injuries to the brain. In E. J. Hickling, & E. B. Blanchard (Eds.). *The International Handbook of Road Traffic Accidents & Psychological Trauma: Current Understanding Treatment and Law*. New York: Elsevier, pp. 67–87.

Smed, A. (1997). Cognitive function and distress after common whiplash injury. *Acta Neurologica Scandinavica, 95*, 73–80.

Spitzer, W. O., Skovron, M. L., Salmi, L. R., Cassidy, J. D., Durancean, J., Suissa, S., & Zeiss, E. (1995). Quebec Task Force on whiplash-associated disorders. *Spine, 20*, 1S–73S.

Teasell, R. W. & Shapiro, A. P. (1999). Whiplash injuries. In A. R. Block, E. F. Kremer, & E. Fernandez (Eds.). *Handbook of Pain Syndromes: Biopsychosocial Perspectives*. Mahwah, NJ: Erlbaum, pp. 235–257.

Weathers, F. W. & Litz, B. T. (1994). Psychometric properties of the Clinician-Administered PTSD Scale, CAPS-I. *PTSD Research Quarterly, 5*, 2–6.

Weathers, F. W., Blake, D. D., Krinsley, K. E., Haddad, W., Huska, J. A., & Keane, T. M. (1992). The Clinician-Administered PTSD Scale: Reliability and construct validity. Paper presented at the 26th annual meeting of the Association for the Advancement of Behavior Therapy, Boston, MA.

Weathers, F. W., Keane, T. M., & Davidson, J. R. T. (2001). Clinician-Administered PTSD Scale: A review of the first ten years of research. *Depression and Anxiety, 13*, 132–156.

Weathers, F. W., Ruscio, A. M., & Keane, T. M. (1999). Psychometric properties of nine scoring rules for the Clinician-Administered PTSD Scale (CAPS). *Psychological Assessment, 11*, 124–133.

Wing, J. K., Cooper, J. E., & Sartorious, N (1974). *Measurement and Classification of Psychiatric Symptoms*. Cambridge: Cambridge University Press.

13

PTSD and Chronic Pain: Cognitive–Behavioral Perspectives and Practical Implications

Gordon J. G. Asmundson and Steven Taylor

GH, a 40-year-old software engineer, was referred to the second author by his primary care physician for treatment of Posttraumatic Stress Disorder (PTSD) that developed subsequent to a road traffic collision 9 months earlier. A vehicle struck GH at moderate speed while he was cycling to work during rush-hour traffic and, as a result, he was flipped over the handlebars and thrown against a building wall. He hit his head, cracking the helmet he was wearing, and sustained multiple soft tissue injuries to his neck, upper back, and shoulders that were considered mild in nature. GH was deemed to be not at fault for the accident, and his insurance company replaced his bicycle and helmet and covered his hospital expenses and wage loss. He took 6 weeks off work and resumed full-time employment after receiving a transfer 6 months after the accident. During his intake interview, GH reported having difficulty performing his job and being easily irritated by colleagues. On examination, he was found to meet diagnostic criteria for PTSD, with scores on various assessment instruments indicating his symptoms to be severe. He was also moderately depressed and was experiencing daily pain in his neck and back, which, although fluctuating in severity from mild to moderate, had persisted over the past 9 months.

There is a growing body of research that indicates clearly that Posttraumatic Stress Disorder (PTSD) and chronic pain frequently co-occur. People with both PTSD and chronic pain tend to have greater distress and impairment compared to those with only one of these conditions and, as might be expected, assessment and treatment are more complicated. The co-occurrence of these conditions is, unfortunately, often overlooked in clinical practice and, as a result, treatment outcomes are often less encouraging than hoped. The present chapter has several goals. First, we briefly review the core characteristics of PTSD and chronic pain, and present data regarding the extent of their co-occurrence. Second, we summarize cognitive–behavioral models that have been offered to explain the co-occurrence of these conditions and briefly review the supporting evidence. Third, we explore specific areas of overlap between PTSD symptom clusters and the cognitive, emotional, behavioral, and physiological aspects of chronic pain. Fourth, elaborating on the case of GH introduced earlier, we describe practical implications stemming from key aspects of the cognitive–behavioral models that might improve outcomes for people with co-occurring PTSD and chronic pain. We close that chapter by noting several issues that warrant future research attention.

1. Characteristics of PTSD

Posttraumatic Stress Disorder has been described in detail elsewhere in this volume. Notwithstanding, it is important for our purposes to review its core characteristics. PTSD typically develops following exposure to a situation or event that is, or is perceived to be, threatening to the safety or physical integrity of one's self or others. Upward of 90% of the general population report having experienced an event of this type at some time during their life (Breslau, 2002) and, fortunately, not all go on the develop PTSD. Posttraumatic Stress Disorder is experienced by somewhere between 7% and 12% of the general population (Seedat & Stein, 2001). Prevalence estimates are typically much higher in populations that might be considered at risk (e.g., disadvantaged urban dwellers, deployed military personnel, emergency response personnel, motor vehicle accident survivors) (American Psychiatric Association, 2000). So, despite not affecting everyone who experiences a traumatic event, PTSD is associated with significant morbidity.

The current *Diagnostic and Statistical Manual of Mental Disorders* (4th ed., text revision; DSM-IV-TR) (American Psychiatric Association, 2000) groups symptoms into three clusters, including re-experiencing of the event (e.g., recurrent and intrusive thoughts, distressing dreams), avoidance and emotional numbing (e.g., avoidance of reminders of the traumatic event, restricted range of affect), and hyperarousal (e.g., exaggerated startle response). Recent evidence indicates that avoidance and numbing represent distinct symptom clusters that differentially influence prognosis and treatment outcome (Asmundson et al., 2004).

Current diagnostic criteria require that individuals be exposed to a traumatic event with actual or perceived threat, experience intense fear or helplessness, and have at least one re-experiencing symptom, at least three avoidance and numbing symptoms, and at least two hyperarousal symptoms in order to be diagnosed with PTSD. They also must have experienced these symptoms for more than 1 month in the context of significant distress or impairment in their social and occupational activities.

In recent years, it has become increasingly evident that people with PTSD present with a number of co-occurring physical and mental health problems. Increased reporting of physical health problems as well as depressed mood and alcohol use and abuse are common in those with PTSD (Resnick et al., 1997; Sareen et al., 2005; Schnurr & Jankowski, 1999). Pain and chronic pain problems are reported with striking frequency in people with a primary diagnosis of PTSD (Asmundson et al., 2002). Indeed, 20–30% of those with PTSD seeking outpatient treatment from community and mental health clinics report chronic pain (Amir et al., 1997; Hubbard et al., 1995). Co-occurrence estimates have, in most cases, been even higher in military veterans as well as volunteer firefighters who have PTSD, ranging anywhere from 20% to 80% (for recent reviews, see Asmundson et al., 2002; Otis et al., 2003; Sharp & Harvey, 2001). Although most studies in this area have used samples consisting primarily (if not exclusively) of males, recent findings from a sample of female veterans using the VA Health Care System confirm that these finding generalize across gender (Asmundson et al., 2004).

2.   Characteristics of Chronic Pain

Although once conceptualized strictly as a sensory experience resulting from stimulation of specific noxious receptors, such as might be the case when physical injury occurs, contemporary models of pain recognize that it is a complex perceptual experience that is determined by sensory as well as psychological (i.e., thinking, emotions, behaviors) and social influences (Asmundson & Wright, 2004). Pain serves an adaptive function: It alerts us that potential or actual tissue damage might be pending and it motivates us to take action to limit damage and recover from it (Wall, 1978). Pain typically abates with physical recovery; however, in some cases it becomes chronic (i.e., persists for 3 months or more) (International Association for the Study of Pain, 1986), losing its adaptive qualities, and, instead, causes considerable emotional distress and impairment of social and occupational abilities.[1]

Many people with chronic pain make frequent physician visits, sometimes undergo inappropriate medical evaluations, and miss work and other important activities because of their symptoms and associated suffering (Nachemson, 1992; Spengler et al., 1986; also see Gureje et al., 1998). As a result, chronic pain has become the second most common chronic health condition in Canada and accounts for approximately $18 billion dollars annually in lost productivity and health care costs (Statistics Canada, 1999). Estimates from the United States indicate that approximately 7% of the general population has experienced chronic pain in the past 12 months

---

[1]   The DSM-IV-TR includes the diagnosis of Pain Disorder in its somatoform disorder section; however, many researchers and clinicians who work with chronic pain patients find the DSM-IV criteria for Pain Disorder to be problematic and of limited usefulness in guiding assessment and diagnosis. Problems and limitations are succinctly outlined by Fishbain (1995) and Sharp (2004). We find it more useful to distinguish between acute and chronic pain experiences and, in case of the latter, to individual differences in pain severity, emotional distress, and functional limitations in social and occupational milieus.

(McWilliams et al., 2003) at a cost of about $100 billion annually (Weisberg & Vaillancourt, 1999).

Recent models have recognized the role that fear and avoidance behavior play in perpetuating the physical deconditioning and pain in a significant subset of people with chronic pain, despite standard (e.g., medical, physical therapy) interventions (Asmundson et al., 2004; Norton & Asmundson, 2003; Vlaeyen & Linton, 2000). Similarly, investigators have consistently observed that rates of some anxiety disorders, particularly PTSD, are elevated in people with chronic pain and pain-related conditions like fibromyalgia (Sherman et al., 2000). McWilliams et al. (2003), using data gathered from a large sample representative of the general U.S. civilian population, reported that people with chronic pain are almost four times more likely to experience PTSD than those without chronic pain. Recent reviews (Asmundson et al., 2002; Otis et al., 2003) indicate that between 10% and 50% of patients receiving rehabilitation services for chronic musculoskeletal pain and related conditions also have PTSD. Likewise, up to 45% of patients with pain subsequent to burn-related injury exhibit significant posttraumatic stress symptoms (Saxe et al., 2001; for review also see Yu & Dimsdale, 1999). Consistent with postulates of the fear-avoidance models of chronic pain alluded to above, we have shown that PTSD is much more prevalent in chronic pain patients characterized by high levels of fear and functional disability when compared to those with interpersonal issues and those who are functioning well (70% vs 21% vs 35%, respectively; Asmundson, et al., 2000a).

3.   Explanatory Models

The preceding paragraphs indicate that chronic pain is frequently experienced by people seeking treatment for PTSD and, conversely, that PTSD is common in people with chronic pain. The consistency of findings suggests that PTSD and chronic pain are related in some way. To date, there have been several models posited to explain the relationship between PTSD and chronic pain. These models, described below, all draw on tenants of empirically supported cognitive–behavioral models of PTSD (e.g., Ehlers & Clark, 2000; Foa & Rothbaum, 1998) and chronic pain (e.g., Norton & Asmundson, 2003; Vlaeyen & Linton, 2000) in efforts to provide a basis from which to extend understanding and thereby improve treatment of those people who experience both together.

3.1.   Mutual Maintenance Model

The mutual maintenance model (Sharp & Harvey, 2001) holds that certain components of PTSD (e.g., physiological arousal, emotional numbing, behavioral avoidance) maintain or exacerbate symptoms of pain and, similarly, that certain components of chronic pain (e.g., physiological arousal, catastrophizing, behavioral avoidance) maintain or exacerbate symptoms of PTSD. The model predicts, for example, that pain sensations experienced by a person in chronic pain will be a persistent and arousal-provoking reminder of the trauma that precipitated the pain. The physiological arousal in response to recollection of the trauma will, in turn, promote avoidance of pain-related activities and (over time) physical deconditioning, which makes the experience of pain more likely. The person thereby becomes trapped in a vicious cycle whereby the symptoms of PTSD and chronic pain interact to produce self-perpetuating distress and functional disability.

3.2. Shared Vulnerability Model

Of the several postulates of the mutual maintenance model, one provided direct impetus for our shared vulnerability model (Asmundson et al., 2002a). Specifically, Sharp and Harvey (2001, p. 870) suggested that "the tendency toward anxiety sensitivity in chronic pain and PTSD may fuel a vulnerability to the misinterpretation… and catastrophization… of physical sensations associated with pain and the bodily sensations accompanying arousal [from PTSD]" and thereby act to maintain the symptoms of both conditions. We extended this postulate in order to clarify the role of anxiety sensitivity as both a maintaining factor and as a vulnerability factor.

Our shared vulnerability model holds that there are individual difference factors that predispose people to develop both PTSD and chronic pain; that is, these factors increase the risk of developing these conditions. Of several potential individual difference factors (e.g., trait negative affectivity, harm avoidance, intolerance of uncertainty), anxiety sensitivity appears most promising. Anxiety sensitivity is defined as the fear of anxiety-related bodily sensations based on the belief that they may have harmful cognitive, somatic, or social consequences (Reiss & McNally, 1985). To illustrate, a person with high anxiety sensitivity may believe that stabbing head pain signifies the onset of brain cancer or impending stroke, whereas a person with low anxiety sensitivity would regard this sensation merely as unpleasant. Importantly, anxiety sensitivity is believed to amplify the intensity of fear and anxiety responses (Taylor, 1999), such as those associated with exposure to trauma and the experience of persistent pain (Taylor, 2004).

Anxiety sensitivity, as measured by the Anxiety Sensitivity Index (ASI) (Peterson & Reiss, 1992), has been shown to be elevated in patients with PTSD (Taylor et al., 1992, 2001, 2003) as well as in patients with chronic pain who present with significant functional limitations (see review by Asmundson et al., 2000b). The degree of anxiety sensitivity is positively correlated with the severity of PTSD symptoms; that is, the higher the anxiety sensitivity, the more severe the PTSD symptoms (Fedoroff et al., 2000). Accumulating evidence from samples of musculoskeletal (Asmundson & Norton, 1995; Asmundson & Taylor, 1996; Greenberg & Burns, 2003) and heterogeneous (Zvolensky et al., 2001) pain patients supports the hypothesis that high levels of anxiety sensitivity increase the risk of pain-related avoidance and disability following physical injury (for review, also see Keogh & Asmundson, 2004).

It has yet to be established that elevated anxiety sensitivity precedes the development of PTSD and chronic pain. Longitudinal studies are needed to do so. It remains a possibility that anxiety sensitivity becomes elevated as a consequence of PTSD and chronic pain and thereafter serves to maintain symptoms. However, the aforementioned collection of findings, combined with emerging evidence that anxiety sensitivity may be genetically determined (Jang et al., 1999; Stein et al., 1999), suggest that people with high levels of anxiety sensitivity are prone to respond to traumatic stressors involving painful physical injury with more intense emotional reactions. This, we believe, makes them vulnerable to developing one or both of these conditions.

3.3.   Triple Vulnerability Model

Otis et al. (2003) have argued that a model previously proposed to account for the development of PTSD—the triple vulnerability model (Keane & Barlow, 2002)—can also be applied to explain the development of chronic pain. The triple vulnerability model holds that PTSD will develop in cases where there is (1) a general biological vulnerability for alarm reactions (i.e., physiological reactivity) to stressors, (2) a general psychological vulnerability for feeling that things are beyond one's control, and (3) a specific psychological vulnerability for developing a focus on anxiety. In other words, PTSD is probable in people who are predisposed to react to traumatic stressors with alarm and feelings that the situation and their emotional response to it are beyond their control. Similarly, the model holds that chronic pain is most likely to develop in people who believe that the pain they are experiencing and their emotional responses (e.g., anxiety, worry, fear, agitation) to it are uncontrollable. The empirical literature stemming from the identification of pain subtypes (e.g., Asmundson et al., 1997; Kerns et al., 1985; Turk & Rudy, 1988) supports this supposition.

The postulates of the triple vulnerability model are consistent with the diathesis–stress model of chronic pain and disability following traumatic injury recently proposed by Turk (2002). Building on evidence that physical pathology is not a good predictor of functional ability (Burton et al., 1995), Turk (2002) suggested that it is the interaction of predispositional characteristics (the diathesis) and an instigating event (the stressor) that explain individual differences in pain chronicity and degree of functional disability. He posited that pain and disability are more likely to persist following a pain-precipitating event (e.g., road traffic collision, work-related injury) in people who a prone to respond to their symptoms with fear, interpret their symptoms catastrophically, and avoid activities they believe will increase pain, as a means of limiting chances of further pain. Anxiety sensitivity and related constructs (e.g., negative affectivity, catastrophic thinking; for review see Keogh & Asmundson, 2004) are identified as predisposing factors that when coupled with a stressful event as well as other cognitive factors, such as anticipatory anxiety and low self-efficacy (i.e., feelings of lack of control), promote persistent pain and disability.

From these models it follows, then, that co-occurring PTSD and chronic pain are most likely to develop in cases where vulnerable people—those predisposed to be physiologically labile, to feel a sense of lack of control, and to focus on their anxiety and respond to it with fear—are exposed to an event that is both traumatic and painful. Otis et al. (2003) further suggested that both reminders of the trauma and sensations of pain can serve as triggers for alarm reactions. The triple vulnerability and diathesis–stress models, despite some content differences, are in many ways consistent with our concept of shared vulnerability described earlier.

4. A Closer Look at Symptom Overlap

The models that we have just described, which incorporate the shared vulnerability construct, explain the etiology of co-occurring PTSD and chronic pain. However, it is the mutual maintenance model that explains how the symptoms perpetuate and exacerbate each other. We have described above how anxiety sensitivity may contribute to the maintenance and exacerbation of both conditions. Sharp and Harvey (2001) have also suggested how the overlap of particular symptoms might serve this function. Indeed, biases in attention toward threatening environmental stimuli, hypervigilance, startle, emotional numbing, avoidance, and dysregulations in stress response and pain modulation have been observed in both conditions (Asmundson et al., 2002; Sharp & Harvey, 2001).

There is also emerging evidence to suggest that specific PTSD symptom clusters are more closely associated with certain aspects of the pain experience. Several investigators (Asmundson et al., 2004; Beckham et al., 1997), for example, have demonstrated that from among the major clusters of PTSD symptoms that re-experiencing symptoms are uniquely associated with pain severity and limitations in functional ability. It is plausible that pain serves as a somatic reminder of the traumatic experience—a somatic flashback of sorts—and thereby impacts on re-experiencing. It has recently been demonstrated that pain experiences that closely resemble the quality and location of pain experienced at the time of trauma can be triggered by reminders of the trauma (Salomons et al., 2004). To illustrate, one patient developed PTSD following a surgical situation during which she was unable to respond but remained aware under anesthesia and experienced pain during intubation and incision. Seeing a nurse in a blue surgical scrub suit later triggered feelings of painful pressure against her sternum. These finding support the postulate, as suggested by Otis et al. (2003), that reminders of trauma and of pain can serve as triggers for alarm that perpetuate re-experiencing.

Using factor analysis, we have observed that the structure of PTSD symptom clusters, with one potentially important exception, is very similar when compared between veteran peacekeepers with and without chronic pain (Asmundson et al., 2003). In addition to finding relative stability of re-experiencing, avoidance, and numbing between groups, we found that hypervigilance (i.e., being highly alert for danger, watchful, or on guard) was a particularly salient symptom of hyperarousal in those with chronic pain compared to those without. Cattell (1978) has argued that distinct factors identified through factor analysis correspond to discrete mechanisms (or operational processes). The between-groups consistency on re-experiencing, avoidance, and numbing symptom clusters suggests that the associated operational processes are not significantly altered by the co-occurrence of pain (and pain behavior) but, in cases of co-occurrence, may serve a maintaining or exacerbating role. The mechanisms by which hypervigilance impacts on co-occurring PTSD and chronic pain remains to be determined. It is possible that hypervigilance increases the likelihood of detecting subtle somatic changes or environmental stimuli that might serve as posttrauma triggers for alarm and thereby functions to maintain co-occurring PTSD and pain symptoms. It is equally plausible that hypervigilance is closely associated with shared vulnerability factors—that is, the predisposition to attend to certain events or the preparedness to respond to certain kinds of stimuli from the external or internal environment (see Mackworth, 1950) may put one at risk for both PTSD and chronic pain.

5. Practical Implications

The available evidence suggests that the concepts of shared vulnerability and mutual maintenance are both relevant to understanding the co-occurrence of PTSD and chronic pain. Both are also important in guiding practice. Armed with knowledge of the emerging cognitive–behavioral theories regarding the relationship between PTSD and chronic pain, practitioners will have a strong foundation on which to base assessment, case conceptualization, and treatment planning for these potentially complicated cases. Likewise, other professionals, including psychiatrists and occupational therapists as well as members of the legal profession, will have a more thorough understanding of the multitude of factors that can impact on co-occurrence of these conditions and what should be considered in reviewing a case file.

The risks of not understanding the nature of the relationship between co-occurring PTSD and pain are several. In settings in which patients present with PTSD as the primary concern, pain symptoms may go undetected unless specifically mentioned by the patient. Conversely, patients who present with a primary concern of pain may not be assessed for PTSD. The most likely outcome of overlooking co-occurring symptoms is that planned treatment will be less effective than anticipated. Indeed, it is difficult to plan the most appropriate treatment without having a thorough understanding of all factors—predisposing (or vulnerability), precipitating (or triggering and exacerbating), perpetuating (or maintenance), and protective—that influence symptom presentation and course. It is also possible that failure to make progress may result in some patients deciding to drop out of treatment prior to its completion.

5.1. Assessment

Based solely on the prevalence of co-occurrence of PTSD and chronic pain, we recommend that, regardless of the patient's primary presenting concern, brief screening for comorbidity should be a standard part of assessment. This need not be a complex or time-consuming exercise. To illustrate, asking patients with PTSD a few direct questions about their current experiences with pain, its severity, and its location is often sufficient for identifying problem areas that might require more thorough assessment. This can be supplemented with questions about pain triggers and pain-related interference with daily living, if time permits. Likewise, simple queries about history of exposure to traumatic events and current re-experiencing symptoms (e.g., recurring nightmares related to an event, intrusive recollections of an event) can serve as an efficient method for identifying whether a patient with chronic pain requires a comprehensive PTSD assessment.[2]

GH was referred for treatment of PTSD that developed subsequent to his road traffic accident. His chronic pain symptoms were known at the time of assessment. Notwithstanding, he was asked questions about his current pain experiences in order to characterize their nature and quality. It was determined that he experienced neck and back pain of fluctuating severity that occurred on a daily basis. This pain was aggravated by working at the computer, while driving, on occasions when he attempted to resume physical activity, and when stressed. GH also reported having experienced migraines shortly after the accident and that these had become less frequent as of late. He found the pain to be frustrating because of its impact on his ability to do things.

When it appears that patients have both PTSD and chronic pain, a comprehensive assessment of both should be conducted. Experienced practitioners might elect to conduct their assessment using an unstructured clinical interview; however, for purposes of facilitating systematic evaluation of treatment outcomes, we recommend the use of standardized assessment tools. PTSD can be assessed using structured clinical interviews, including the PTSD module of the Structured Clinical Interview for DSM-IV (SCID-IV) (First et al., 1996) and the Clinician Administered PTSD Scale (CAPS)

---

[2] Methods for assessing malingering and symptom exaggeration are beyond this scope of this chapter. This issue is discussed elsewhere (Halligan et al., 2003; Pope et al., 2000; Simon, 2003).

(Blake et al., 1995), as well as one or more of numerous self-report instruments that have been created to measure a variety of posttrauma phenomena. Key dimensions of pain that warrant consideration in comprehensive assessment include pain severity, pain location, attitudes and beliefs about pain and its effects, ways of coping with pain, pain-specific emotional distress (i.e., fear, anxiety, mood changes), and functional abilities and limitations (Asmundson, 2002; Tait, 1999). We recommend that clinical interview be supplemented with a package of questionnaires comprising three core measures—the McGill Pain Questionnaire–short form (Melzack, 1987), Multidimensional Pain Inventory (Kerns et al., 1985), and Pain Anxiety Symptoms Scale (McCracken et al., 1992)—and other measures (e.g., of pain coping or pain catastrophizing) on an as-needed basis. Self-report measures of PTSD and pain are described in detail in other chapters of this volume. Finally, given its prominence in the aforementioned explanatory models of co-occurring PTSD and chronic pain, we recommend that anxiety sensitivity be assessed. This is most easily and efficiently accomplished using the 16-item ASI (Peterson & Reiss, 1992).

GH was assessed using a structured interview and a companion package of self-report instruments similar to that described in this subsection. The trauma-related self-report instruments confirmed that his PSTD symptoms were severe in nature and further revealed that he was feeling trauma-related guilt and anger, had strong negative beliefs about himself and the world, and strong beliefs that he was to blame for his trauma. The pain-related instruments confirmed that his pain was currently mild to moderate in severity, that he felt he had little control over his pain, and that the pain was causing limitations in home and social functioning. The ASI revealed an exceptionally elevated score (i.e., 2.5 standard deviations above the mean for healthy people and 1 standard deviation above the mean for patients with PTSD). This indicated that GH holds strong beliefs that his anxiety-related sensations signal extreme personal danger and that he is prone to significant emotional reactions to fear and anxiety.

Other issues that warrant attention in comprehensive assessment include other presenting problems—general mood, general levels of anxiety, other current Axis I disorders, past history of psychiatric disorder or substance abuse—as well as treatment history and current medication. Because some symptoms associated with concussion and Postconcussion Syndrome (e.g., concentration difficulties, irritability, depressed mood) overlap considerably with both PTSD and chronic pain, they also warrant careful consideration in cases where the traumatic event involved potential brain injury. Traumatic brain injury and its association with PTSD is discussed in detail elsewhere (Bryant, 2001).

During the intake interview, GH reported that a neuropsychologist said he had "mild, sustained, brain damage." The need for conducting a neuropsychological screening assessment was carefully considered. Because his irritability, concen-

tration difficulties, and depressed mood were mild in nature and possibly a product of PTSD, chronic pain, or both, it was decided that delaying assessment and treatment of GH's clearly identifiable presenting conditions in order to obtain additional neuropsychological screening was not warranted.

5.2.   Treatment

Very few studies have reported on the outcomes of treating patients with co-occurring PTSD and chronic pain. There is evidence from uncontrolled studies suggesting that targeting the PTSD alone using cognitive–behavioral interventions may be effective in alleviating PTSD symptoms but not functional limitations in work-related activities (Hickling & Blanchard, 1997; Muse, 1993). More recent findings have shown that PTSD intervention, although not effective in reducing pain-severity reports, positively influences pain-related functional limitations (Shipherd et al., 2003). Other research, however, has found that pain symptoms can interfere with the PTSD treatment by affecting the patient's ability to engage in and benefit from the intervention (Taylor et al., 2001).

Modified cognitive–behavioral interventions may also be of benefit when PTSD and pain co-occur. This might include, for example, the incorporation of passive relaxation techniques (exercises that avoid "tense–release" instructions in order to circumvent pain flare-ups), brief relaxation exercises between exposure therapy trials, cognitive restructuring of catastrophic pain-related beliefs, reducing the length of exposure therapy within a session, and the incorporation of interoceptive exposure exercises designed to reduce anxiety sensitivity (Asmundson & Hadjistavropoulos, in press; Wald et al., 2004).

In the case of GH, his treatment was part of a series of investigations into the merits of combining exposure therapies with pain management procedures (Wald & Taylor, in press-a, in press-b). He was treated using in vivo and imaginal exposure as the primary PTSD interventions because these are among the most powerful empirically supported treatments for PTSD (Taylor, 2004). Additional interventions included interoceptive exposure, which is a method for reducing anxiety sensitivity. This included exercises designed to deliberately induce feared but harmless anxiety-related bodily sensations (e.g., deliberately hyperventilating for short periods of time to learn that the associated sensations, such as dizziness and palpitations, have no harmful consequences). Emerging evidence suggests that interoceptive exposure might play a useful role in reducing PTSD, at least when chronic pain is not present (Wald & Taylor, 2005). It is not yet known whether interoceptive exposure is effective for co-occurring PTSD and pain. GH was also treated with cognitive–behavioral pain management interventions (e.g., relaxation training, cognitive restructuring to reduce catastrophic beliefs about pain, such as the belief that "hurt equals harm"). GH's treatment consisted of 12 weekly 60-minute sessions.

Treatment was associated with a reduction in PTSD symptoms from pre-treatment to posttreatment, but no change in chronic pain. The gains were short-lived, and GH had a relapse of PTSD symptoms at 10-week follow-up (Wald & Taylor, in press-b). Given that GH's chronic pain did not change during treatment and that previous studies suggest that PTSD and pain may mutually maintain (exacerbate) one another (Asmundson et al., 2002; Sharp & Harvey, 2001), the findings are consistent with the concept of mutual maintenance; if treatment reduces PTSD but leaves pain unchanged, then pain might fuel the recrudescence of PTSD. The findings suggest that even mild or moderately severe pain can be clinically important when treating PTSD.

Further advances in treatments for pain and PTSD could better serve patients such as GH. Recent advances in pain pharmacotherapy, such as second-generation anticonvulsants (e.g., gabapentin, topirimate), will likely lead to more effective treatment options (Finnerup et al., 2002) and potentially reduce the risk of developing chronic pain (Schwartzman et al., 2001). Pilot data from a small, randomized trial indicate that propranolol, a beta-blocker with analgesic effects, reduces the symptoms of PTSD (Pitman et al., 2002). This suggests that it may be effective when PTSD and chronic pain co-occur. Given that recent expert consensus guidelines recommend combined cognitive–behavioral intervention and pharmacotherapy for comorbid PTSD and chronic pain (Foa et al., 1999), further exploration of the various combinations and their effects of the symptoms of both conditions is clearly warranted.

Notwithstanding the importance of the recent treatment advances mentioned earlier, treatment decisions at present need to be made on a case-by-case basis. Controlled trials are needed to determine how cognitive–behavioral interventions can be optimally tailored for these individuals. Also, the merits of various types of medication, alone and in combination with cognitive–behavioral intervention, have yet to be determined.

6.   Conclusions and Future Directions

Comorbid PTSD and chronic pain is a common, costly, disabling, and often chronic clinical condition. In recent years, there have been several important conceptual developments that have shed light on how and why these disorders often co-occur and how they can interact with one another. The models address different aspects of the PTSD–pain relationship, and so can be considered to be broadly compatible with one another. Although the empirical evaluation of these models is still at the early stages, there is encouraging preliminary support for each of them.

The models have influenced assessment procedures for PTSD and pain. For example, anxiety sensitivity is now often assessed because of the possibility that it may represent a shared vulnerability for PTSD and chronic pain.

The models have also suggested strategies for treating PTSD. The case of GH illustrates this "conceptually driven" approach to treatment. Although GH's treatment was ultimately unsuccessful, the conceptually driven approach provides some suggestions for improving outcome with other interventions (e.g., by giving more attention to the treatment of pain).

The conceptually driven approach to treatment can be contrasted with what is sometimes called the "product development" approach, whereby investigators (often funded by the pharmaceutical industry) seek to develop the range of indications for a given treatment; that is, they take a treatment that is effective for a given disorder (e.g., a drug that is effective for epilepsy) and see whether it is effective for other clinical conditions (e.g., pain or PTSD). The use of gabapentin and topiramate are two examples of this approach.

The product development and conceptually driven approaches represent two different strategies for improving treatment outcome for comorbid PTSD and chronic pain. Future research drawing on both approaches may eventually lead to highly effective treatments for this complex and challenging clinical condition. Research that furthers our understanding of the mechanisms of shared vulnerability may also lead to improvements in treatment efficacy and potentially guide the development of effective preventive interventions. At present, it remains a pressing challenge for investigators to establish the precise nature of the PTSD–pain linkage and to find effective, empirically justified treatments for their comorbid presentation. In the absence of this crucial information, the causality picture will remain complicated.

References

American Psychiatric Association. (2000). *Diagnostic and Statistical Manual of Mental Disorders—Text Revision*, 4th ed. Washington, DC: American Psychiatric Association.

Amir, M., Kaplan, Z., Neumann, L., Sharabani, R., Shani, N., & Buskila, D. (1997). Posttraumatic stress disorder, tenderness and fibromyalgia. *Journal of Psychosomatic Research, 42*, 607–613.

Asmundson, G. J. G. (2002). Pain assessment: State-of-the-art applications from the cognitive–behavioural perspective. *Behaviour Research and Therapy, 40*, 547–550.

Asmundson, G. J. G. & Hadjistavropoulos, H. D. (in press). Addressing shared vulnerability for comorbid PTSD and chronic pain: A cognitive–behavioral perspective. *Cognitive and Behavioral Practice*.

Asmundson, G. J. G. & Norton, G. R. (1995). Anxiety sensitivity in patients with physically unexplained chronic back pain: A preliminary report. *Behaviour Research and Therapy, 33*, 771–777.

Asmundson, G. J. G. & Taylor, S. (1996). Role of anxiety sensitivity in pain-related fear and avoidance. *Journal of Behavioral Medicine, 19*, 573–582.

Asmundson, G. J. G. & Wright, K. D. (2004). The biopsychosocial model of pain. In T. Hadjistavropoulos & K. D. Craig (Eds.). *Pain: Psychological Perspectives*. Mahwah, NJ: Erlbaum, pp. 35–57.

Asmundson, G. J. G., Bonin, M., Frombach, I. K., & Norton, G. R. (2000a). Evidence of a disposition toward fearfulness and vulnerability to posttraumatic stress in dysfunctional pain patients. *Behaviour Research and Therapy, 38*, 801–812.

Asmundson, G. J. G., Coons, M. J., Taylor, S., & Katz, J. (2002). PTSD and the experience of pain: Research and clinical implications of shared vulnerability and mutual maintenance models. *Canadian Journal of Psychiatry, 47*, 930–937.

Asmundson, G. J. G., Norton, G. R., & Allerdings, M. D. (1997). Fear and avoidance in dysfunctional chronic back pain patients. *Pain, 69*, 231–236.

Asmundson, G. J. G., Stapleton, J. A., & Taylor, S. (2004). Avoidance and numbing are distinct PTSD symptom clusters. *Journal of Traumatic Stress, 17*, 467–475.

Asmundson, G. J. G., Wright, K. D., & Hadjistavropoulos, H. D. (2000b). Anxiety sensitivity and disabling chronic health conditions: State of the art and future directions. *Scandinavian Journal of Behaviour Therapy, 29*, 100–117.

Asmundson, G. J. G., Wright, K. D., McCreary, D. R., & Pedlar, D. (2003). Posttraumatic Stress Disorder symptoms in United Nations peacekeepers: An examination of facture structure in peacekeepers with and without chronic pain. *Cognitive Behaviour Therapy, 32*, 26–37.

Asmundson, G. J. G., Wright, K. D., & Stein, M. B. (2004). Pain and PTSD symptoms in female veterans. *European Journal of Pain, 8*, 345–350.

Beckham, J. C., Crawford, A. L., & Feldman, M. E. (1997). Chronic posttraumatic stress disorder and chronic pain in Vietnam combat veterans. *Journal of Psychosomatic Research, 43*, 379–389.

Blake, D. D., Weathers, F. W., Nagy, L. M., Kaloupek, D. G., Gusman, F. D., Charney, D. S., & Keane, T. M. (1995). The development of a clinician-administered PTSD scale. *Journal of Traumatic Stress, 8*, 75–90.

Breslau, N. (2002). Epidemiologic studies of trauma, Posttraumatic Stress Disorders, and other psychiatric disorders. *Canadian J of Psychiatry, 97*, 923–929.

Bryant, R. A. (2001). Posttraumatic stress disorder and traumatic brain injury: Can they co-exist? *Clinical Psychology Review, 21*, 931–948.

Burton, A. K., Tillotson, K. M., Main, C. J., & Hollis, S. (1995). Psychosocial predictors of outcome in acute and subchronic low back trouble. *Spine, 20*, 722–728.

Cattell, R.B. (1978). The Scientific Use of Factor Analysis in Behavioral Life Sciences. New York: Graywind.

Ehlers, A. & Clark, D. M.. (2000). A cognitive model of posttraumatic stress disorder. *Behaviour Research and Therapy, 38*, 319–345.

Fedoroff, I. C., Taylor, S., Asmundson, G. J. G., & Koch, W. J. (2000). Cognitive factors in traumatic stress reactions: Predicting PTSD symptoms from anxiety sensitivity and beliefs about harmful events. *Behavioural and Cognitive Psychotherapy, 28*, 5–15.

Finnerup, N. B., Gottrup, H., & Jensen, T. S. (2002). Anticonvulsants in central pain. *Expert Opinion on Pharmacotherapy, 3*, 1411–1420.

First, M. B., Spitzer, R. L., Gibbon, M., & Williams, J. B. W. (1996). *Structured Clinical Interview for DSM-IV — Patient Edition (SCID-I/P)*. New York: New York State Psychiatric Institute.

Fishbain, D. (1995). DSM-IV: Implications and issues for the pain clinician. *American Pain Society Bulletin, March–April*, 6–18.

Foa, E. B. & Rothbaum, B. O. (1998). *Treating the Trauma of Rape*. New York: Guilford Press.

Foa, E. B., Davidson, J. R. T., & Frances, A. (1999). Treatment of PTSD: The NIH expert consensus guideline series. *Journal of Clinical Psychiatry, 60(Suppl. 16)*, 4–76.

Greenberg, J. & Burns, J. W. (2003). Pain anxiety among chronic pain patients: Specific phobia or manifestation of anxiety sensitivity? *Behaviour Research and Therapy, 41*, 223–240.

Gureje, O., Von Korff, M., Simon, G. E., & Gater, R. (1998). Persistent pain and well being: A World Health Organization study in primary care. *Journal of the American Medical Association, 280*, 147–151.

Halligan, P. W., Bass, C., & Oakley, D. A. (2003). *Malingering and Illness Deception*. New York: Oxford University Press.

Hickling, E. J. & Blanchard, E. B. (1997). The private practice psychologist and manual-based treatments: A case study in the treatment of Posttraumatic Stress Disorder secondary to motor vehicle accidents. *Behaviour Research and Therapy, 35*, 191–203.

Hubbard, J., Realmuto, G. M., Northwood, A. K., & Masten, A. S. (1995). Comorbidity of psychiatric diagnoses with Posttraumatic Stress Disorder in survivors of childhood trauma. *Journal of the American Academy of Child and Adolescent Psychiatry, 34*, 1167–1173.

International Association for the Study of Pain. (1986). Classification of chronic pain. *Pain (Suppl. 3)*, 1–226.

Jang, K. L., Stein, M. B., Taylor, S., & Livesley, W. J. (1999). Gender differences in the etiology of anxiety sensitivity: A twin study. *Journal of Gender Specific Medicine, 2*, 39–44.

Keane, T. M. & Barlow, D. H. (2002). Posttraumatic Stress Disorder. In D. H. Barlow (Ed.). *Anxiety and Its Disorders*. New York: Guilford Press, pp. 418–453.

Keogh E. & Asmundson, G. J. G. (2004). Negative affectivity, catastrophizing, and anxiety sensitivity. In G. J. G. Asmundson, J. W. S. Vlaeyen, & G. Crombez (Eds.). *Understanding and Treating Fear of Pain*. New York: Oxford University Press, pp. 91–115.

Kerns, R. D., Turk, D. C., & Rudy, T. E. (1985). The West Haven–Yale Multidimensional Pain Inventory (WHYMPI). *Pain, 23*, 345–356.

Mackworth, N. H. (1950). *Researches in the Measurement of Human Performance*. Medical Research Council Special Report Series. Ottawa: Medical Research Council, p. 268.

McCracken, L. M., Zayfert, C., & Gross, R. T. (1992). The Pain Anxiety Symptoms Scale: Development and validation of a scale to measure fear of pain. *Pain, 50*, 67–73.

McWilliams, L. A., Cox, B. J., & Enns, M. W. (2003). Mood and anxiety disorders associated with chronic pain: An examination in a nationally representative sample. *Pain, 106*, 127–133.

Melzack, R. (1987). The short-form McGill Pain Questionnaire. *Pain, 30*, 191–197.

Muse, M. (1986). Stress-related, posttraumatic chronic pain syndrome: Behavioral treatment approach. *Pain, 25*, 389–394.

Nachemson, A. L. (1992). Newest knowledge of low back pain. *Clinical Orthopedics, 279*, 8–20.

Norton, P. J. & Asmundson, G. J. G. (2003). Amending the fear-avoidance models of chronic pain: What is the role of physiological arousal? *Behavior Therapy, 34*, 17–30.

Otis, J. D., Keane, T. M., & Kerns, R. D. (2003). An examination of the relationship between chronic pain and Posttraumatic Stress Disorder. *Journal of Rehabilitation Research and Development, 40*, 397–406.

Peterson, R. A. & Reiss, S. (1992). *Anxiety Sensitivity Index Manual*, 2nd ed. Worthington, OH: International Diagnostic Systems.

Pitman, R. K., Sanders, K. M., Zusman, R. M., Healy, A. R., Cheema, F., Lasko, N. B., Cahill, L., & Orr, S. P. (2002). Pilot study of secondary prevention of Posttraumatic Stress Disorder with propranolol. *Biological Psychiatry, 51,* 189–192.

Pope, K. S., Butcher, J. N., & Seelen, J. (2000). *The MMPI, MMPI-2, and MMPI-A in Court,* 2nd ed. Washington, DC: American Psychological Association.

Reiss S. & McNally, R. J. (1985). The expectancy model of fear. In S. Reiss & R. R. Bootzin (Eds.). *Theoretical Issues in Behaviour Therapy.* New York: Academic.

Resnick, H. S., Acierno, R., & Kilpatrick, D. G. (1997). Health impact of interpersonal violence 2: Medical and mental health outcomes. *Behavioral Medicine, 23,* 65–78.

Salomons, T. V., Osterman, J. E., Gagliese, L., & Katz, J. (2004). Pain flashbacks in Posttraumatic Stress Disorder. *Clinical Journal of Pain, 20,* 83–87.

Sareen, J., Cox, B. J., Clara, I., & Asmundson, G. J. G. (2005). The relationship between anxiety disorders and physical disorders in the US National Comorbidity Survey. *Depression and Anxiety, 21,* 193–202.

Saxe, G., Stoddard, F., Courtney, D., Cunningham, K., Chawla, N., Sheridan, R., King, D., & King, L. (2001). Relationship between acute morphine and the course of PTSD in children with burns. *Journal of the American Academy of Child and Adolescent Psychiatry, 40,* 915–921.

Schnurr, P. P. & Jankowski, M. K. (1999). Physical health and Posttraumatic Stress Disorder: Review and synthesis. *Seminars in Clinical Neuropsychiatry, 4,* 295–304.

Schwartzman, R. J., Grothusen, J., Kiefer, T. R., & Rohr, P. (2001). Neuropathic central pain: Epidemiology, etiology, and treatment options. *Archives of Neurology, 58,* 1547–1550.

Seedat, S. & Stein, M. B. (2001). Posttraumatic Stress Disorder: A review of recent findings. *Current Psychiatry Reports, 3,* 288–294.

Sharp, T. J. (2004). The prevalence of Posttraumatic Stress Disorder in chronic pain patients. *Current Pain and Headache Reports, 8,* 111–115.

Sharp, T. J. & Harvey, A. G. (2001). Chronic pain and Posttraumatic Stress Disorder: Mutual maintenance? *Clinical Psychology Review, 21,* 857–877.

Sherman, J. J., Turk, D. C., & Okifuji, A. (2000). Prevalence and impact of Posttraumatic Stress Disorder-like symptoms on patients with fibromyalgia syndrome. *Clinical Journal of Pain, 16,* 127–134.

Shipherd, J. C., Beck, J. G., Hamblen, J. L., Lackner, J. M., & Freeman, J. B. (2003). A preliminary examination of treatment of Posttraumatic Stress Disorder in chronic pain patients: A case study. *Journal of Traumatic Stress, 16,* 451–457.

Simon, R. I. (2003). *Posttraumatic Stress Disorder in Litigation: Guidelines for Forensic Assessment,* 2nd ed. Washington, DC: American Psychiatric Publishing.

Spengler, D. M., Bigos, S. J., & Martin, N. A. (1986). Back injuries in industry: A retrospective study: Overview and cost analysis. *Spine, 11,* 241–245.

Stein, M. B., Jang, K. L., & Livesley, W. J. (1999). Heritability of anxiety sensitivity: A twin study. *American Journal of Psychiatry, 156,* 246–251.

Statistics Canada. (1999). *Statistical Report on the Health of Canadians.* Ottawa: Statistics Canada.

Tait, R. C. (1999). Evaluation of treatment effectiveness in patients with intractable pain: Measures and methods. In R. J. Gatchel & D. C. Turk (Eds.). *Psychological Factors in Pain: Clinical Perspectives.* New York: Guilford Press, pp. 457–480.

Taylor, S. (1999). *Anxiety Sensitivity: Theory, Research, and Treatment of the Fear of Anxiety.* Mahwah, NJ: Erlbaum.

Taylor, S. (2004). *Advances in the Treatment of Posttraumatic Stress Disorder: Cognitive–Behavioral Approaches.* New York: Springer-Verlag.

Taylor, S., Fedoroff, I. C., Koch, W. J., Thordarson, D. S., Fecteau, G., & Nicki, R. (2001). Posttraumatic Stress Disorder arising after road traffic collisions: Patterns of response to cognitive–behavior therapy. *Journal of Consulting and Clinical Psychology, 69,* 541–551.

Taylor, S., Koch, W. J., & McNally, R. J. (1992). How does anxiety sensitivity vary across the anxiety disorders? *Journal of Anxiety Disorders, 6,* 249–259.

Taylor, S., Thordarson, D. S., Maxfield, L., Fedoroff, I. C., Lovell, K., & Ogrodniciuk, J. (2003). Comparative efficacy, speed, and adverse effects of three PTSD treatments: Exposure therapy, EMDR, and relaxation training. *Journal of Consulting and Clinical Psychology, 71,* 330–338.

Turk, D. C. (2002). A diathesis-stress model of chronic pain and disability following traumatic injury. *Pain Research and Management, 7,* 9–19.

Turk, D. C. & Rudy, T. E. (1988). Toward an empirically derived taxonomy of chronic pain patients: Integration of psychological assessment. *Journal of Consulting and Clinical Psychology, 56,* 233–238.

Vlaeyen, J. W. S. & Linton, S. J. (2000). Fear-avoidance and its consequences in chronic musculoskeletal pain: A state of the art. *Pain, 85,* 317–332.

Wald, J., & Taylor, S. (2005). Interoceptive exposure therapy combined with trauma-related exposure therapy for Posttraumatic Stress Disorder: A case report. *Cognitive Behaviour Therapy, 34,* 34–40.

Wald, J. & Taylor, S. (in press-a). Trauma to the psyche and soma: A case of Posttraumatic Stress Disorder arising from a road traffic accident. *Cognitive and Behavioral Practice.*

Wald, J. & Taylor, S. (in press-b). Cognitive behavioral case conference: Synthesis and outcome. *Cognitive and Behavioral Practice.*

Wald, J., Taylor, S., & Fedoroff, I. C. (2004). The challenge of treating PTSD in the context of chronic pain. In S. Taylor (Ed.). *Advances in the Treatment of Posttraumatic Stress Disorder: Cognitive–Behavioral Perspectives.* New York: Springer-Verlag, pp. 197–222.

Wall, P. W. (1978). On the relation of injury to pain. *Pain, 6,* 253–264.

Weisberg, J. N. & Vaillancourt, P. D. (1999). Personality factors and disorders in chronic pain. *Seminars in Clinical Neuropsychiatry, 4,* 156–166.

Yu, B-H. & Dimsdale, J. E. (1999). Posttraumatic Stress Disorder in patients with burn injuries. *Journal of Burn Care and Rehabilitation, 20,* 426–433.

Zvolensky, M. J., Goodie, J. L., McNeil, D. W., Sperry, J. A., & Sorrell, J. T. (2001). Anxiety sensitivity in the prediction of pain-related fear and anxiety in a heterogeneous chronic pain population. *Behaviour Research and Therapy, 39,* 683–696.

14

Comorbid Chronic Pain and Posttraumatic Stress Disorder Across the Lifespan: A Review of Theoretical Models

John D. Otis, Donna B. Pincus, and Terence M. Keane

Chronic pain is often associated with functional, psychological, and social problems that can have a significant negative impact on a person's quality of life. Substantial literature currently exists documenting the relationship between chronic pain and commonly co-occurring disorders such as substance abuse (Brown et al., 1996), depression (Banks & Kerns, 1996), and anxiety disorders (Asmundson et al., 1996). Importantly, interest in the relationship between chronic pain and these disorders has expanded the field of pain research, has improved our understanding of how these conditions may interact with one another, and has contributed to improvements in pain management.

Pain is often related to naturally occurring degenerative changes in the body that develop gradually over time; however, some pain conditions may develop secondary to injury related to traumatic life events such as motor vehicle accidents, occupational injuries, or military combat. This has led to a growing interest in the relationship between pain and Posttraumatic Stress Disorder (PTSD), as clinical practice and research indicate that the two disorders frequently co-occur and may interact in such a way as to negatively impact the course and outcome of treatment of either disorder. Several theoretical models and potential mechanisms have been proposed to explain the relationship between chronic pain and PTSD. Despite this recent interest in studying pain and PTSD, no empirical studies have been conducted to test theoretical models explaining the comorbidity of these two disorders, and no well-controlled studies have investigated the efficacy of tailoring treatments for individuals with these disorders. Such studies have the potential to advance theory development and improve treatment efficacy.

The primary aim of this chapter is to provide a critical review and synthesis of the existing literature investigating the relationship between chronic pain and PTSD. The chapter begins with a presentation of the diagnostic criteria,

242

prevalence, and theoretical models of chronic pain and PTSD. Research is then presented describing the co-occurrence of the two disorders, and several theoretical models are highlighted that may serve to explain the similar mechanisms by which these two disorders may be maintained. This chapter then addresses how comorbid chronic pain and PTSD may present differently in youth, with consideration of how theoretical models of the comorbidity of pain and PTSD may be modified to incorporate developmental factors. Furthermore, the chapter helps to explicate how the experience of comorbid chronic pain and PTSD can vary from childhood to adulthood. Finally, the chapter closes with a section on implications for treatment as well as a call for continued research to further refine the models reviewed.

1.   Chronic Pain

Although pain is typically a transient experience, for some people pain persists past the point where it is considered adaptive and results in emotional distress, impaired occupational and social functioning, and increased use of health care system resources (Benedetto et al., 1998). For example, individuals with chronic pain often report that pain interferes with their ability to engage in occupational, social, or recreational activities. Their inability to engage in these reinforcing activities may contribute to increased isolation, negative mood (e.g., feelings of worthlessness and depression), and physical deconditioning, which, in turn, can contribute to their experience of pain. Over time, these types of deleterious cognitive and behavioral patterns can become more resistant to change.

Pain is currently defined as an unpleasant sensory and emotional experience associated with actual or potential tissue damage or is described in terms of such damage. Pain that persists for an extended period of time (i.e., months or years), that accompanies a disease process, or that is associated with a bodily injury that has not resolved over time may be referred to as "chronic" pain (IASP Task Force on Taxonomy, 1994). Pain is one of the most common complaints made to primary care providers (Gureje et al., 1998) and has significant implications for health care costs. For example, a recent study estimated that the total health care expenditures for back pain alone reached over $90.7 billion in 1998 (Xuemei et al., 2004).

Biopsychosocial models suggest that pain is not just a biological process involving the transmission of sensory information about tissue damage to the brain, but is the product of the interactions among biological, psychological, and social factors. All of these factors have an impact on a person's experience of pain, including pain intensity, duration, and its consequences. Models have been proposed to incorporate the many factors that might contribute to the development of chronic pain. For example, Kerns et al. (2002a) proposed a cognitive–behavioral, transactional model of chronic pain, emphasizing the importance of social support and the family in the development and maintenance of chronic pain. Research supports the hypothesis that positive attention from a spouse in response to a patient's expression of pain is associated with higher levels of pain (Kerns et al., 1990), higher frequency of observed pain behaviors (e.g., grimacing, bracing, and distorted ambulation) (Romano et al., 1992), and reports of greater disability and interference (Turk et al., 1992). In addition, there is evidence that a high frequency of negative responding to pain is reliably associated with severity of affective distress (Kerns et al., 1990).

Vlaeyen and Linton (2000) proposed a cognitive–behavioral, fear-avoidance model of chronic pain to explain the role of fear and avoidance behaviors in the development and maintenance of chronic pain and related functional limitations. According to this model, there are two opposing responses an individual may have when experiencing pain. One response is that an individual may consider pain to be nonthreatening and consequently engage in adaptive behaviors that promote the restoration of function. In contrast, pain may be interpreted as overly threatening, a process called "catastrophizing." Vlaeyen and Linton (2000) proposed that catastrophizing contributes to a fear of pain and may lead to avoidance of activities that could elicit pain, guarding behaviors, and hypervigilance to bodily sensations. Consistent with principles of operant reinforcement, as activities are avoided and feelings of fear subside, avoidance behaviors are positively reinforced. As an individual becomes more depressed and inactive, the cycle of pain is fueled even further, and fear and avoidance is further increased. Thus, avoidance has the potential to increase disability and negative mood and ultimately contribute to the experience of pain. Research supports a relationship between fear-avoidance and chronic pain (Asmundson & Taylor, 1996; Crombez et al., 1999).

2.   Posttraumatic Stress Disorder

Posttraumatic Stress Disorder can occur following exposure to an event that is, or is perceived to be, threatening to the well-being of oneself or another person. The distinctive profile of symptoms in PTSD include (1) exposure to a traumatic event that involved the threat of death or serious injury (Criterion A), (2) re-experiencing the event in the form of intrusive thoughts, nightmares, flashbacks to the traumatic event, and psychophysiological reactivity to cues of the traumatic event (Criterion B), (3) avoidance of thoughts, people, and places that resemble the traumatic event, emotional numbing, and an absence of emotional attachments (Criterion C), and (4) symptoms of hyperarousal, including heightened startle sensitivity, sleep problems, attentional difficulties, hypervigilance, and the presence of irritability and anger (Criterion D) (American Psychiatric Association, *Diagnostic and statistical manual of mental disorders* 1994). High levels of anxiety, depression, panic, and substance abuse are frequently observed in individuals with PTSD (Keane & Wolf, 1990).

It has been estimated that the prevalence of PTSD in the United States is 6% in males and 12% in females (Kessler et al., 1995). However, exposure to traumatic events has been estimated to be as high as 70% of the adult population (Norris, 1992). These numbers suggest that PTSD is among the most frequent of psychological disorders, ranking behind substance abuse and depression. In the most comprehensive study of the effects of war on its combatants, the National Vietnam Veterans Readjustment Study (Kulka et al., 1990) found a lifetime rate of PTSD of 30% and a current rate of 15%.

Although many people may be exposed to the same potentially traumatic event, not everyone will develop PTSD. The literature suggests that although the experience of a traumatic event certainly contributes to the development of PTSD, other factors also play an important role (Keane & Barlow, 2002; McNally, 2003). Psychosocial factors such as personal hardiness, structural and functional social support, and stressful life events have all been identified as having direct effects on the development of PTSD, and it is believed that these effects may differ for men and women (King et al., 1998). Research also suggests that peritraumatic psychological processes such as dissociation are strong predictors of PTSD (Ozer et al., 2003). Although there is some preliminary evidence to suggest that there may be a genetic or hereditary component to the development of PTSD (Davidson et al., 1991), most studies conducted in this area have had methodological limitations, and continued research with improved experimental design is needed before firm conclusions can be drawn. Thus, it appears that psychosocial factors and personal vulnerabilities may play a significant role in influencing the impact a traumatic event has on a person's life.

A number of theories have been proposed for the development of PTSD (Brewin & Holmes, 2003). Behavioral conceptualizations of PTSD are based on the two-factor learning theory (Mowrer, 1960). The theory proposes that fear is first learned via classical conditioning in which neutral stimuli present in the traumatic situation acquire fear-eliciting properties through their association with elements of the traumatic situation that arouse fear. The second stage is marked by avoidance behavior that minimizes the contact time with the conditioned cues, thus impairing the extinction of the learned fear. Keane et al. (1985) extended this model to humans and proposed that an extreme stressor, such as a traumatic event, acts as an unconditioned stimulus that can create learned associations with internal and external cues (e.g., sights, sounds, or smells) that are present at the time of the stressor. After these conditioned associations are established, previously neutral cues can then elicit strong autonomic and physiological responses that are similar to those experienced at the time of the stressor. These responses may be so aversive that the individual begins to avoid the triggering cues as a way to decrease his or her own fearful reactions (Keane et al., 2000).

Cognitive and information-processing theories of PTSD have been developed from Lang's (1979) bio-informational theory of emotion. According to Lang

(1979), "fear networks" store representations in memory of anxiety-provoking events and contain information about a feared stimulus or situation, the person's cognitive, psychophysiological, and behavioral response to the stimuli or situation, and information about the meaning of the feared stimuli. Anxiety disorders develop when the fear network contains faulty connections and information that does not truly represent the state of the world. Foa and Kozak (1986) have proposed that when compared to other anxiety disorders, the size of the fear network in PTSD is larger, the network is more easily activated, and the affective and physiological response elements of the network are more intense.

In addition to these early theoretical approaches, a number of more recent theories regarding the etiology of PTSD have been proposed. Several of these recent theories are described in detail by Brewin and Holmes (2003). Among those reviewed are Foa and Rothbaum's (1998) emotional processing theory, Brewin et al. (1996) dual representation theory, and Ehlers and Clark's (2000) cognitive theory. It should be noted that there is a high degree of overlap between these recent models of PTSD, with all models incorporating a wide range of findings on the importance of factors affecting encoding, alterations in memory functioning, appraisals, coping strategies and cognitive styles, and the importance of prior beliefs and trauma exposure. They differ significantly, however, in their accounts of how trauma impacts on memory, the processes whereby changes are brought about in memory, and how these changes are related to recovery (Brewin & Holmes, 2003).

3.   Comorbid Pain and PTSD

Several studies have assessed the co-occurrence of PTSD and chronic pain symptoms. For example, using DSM-III-based diagnostic criteria, one study found that 10% of patients referred to a chronic pain clinic met criteria for PTSD (Benedikt & Kolb, 1986), whereas another study reported that 9.5% met criteria for "posttraumatic pain syndrome" (Muse, 1986). A review of the more recent literature suggests that between 20% and 34% of patients referred for the treatment of chronic pain have significant PTSD symptomatology or are diagnosed with PTSD (Asmundson et al., 1998; Geisser et al., 1996). Asmundson et al. (1998) performed a study to assess the extent to which work-related injuries were associated with PTSD. Assessments were conducted on 139 injured workers with chronic pain who were referred to a rehabilitation program. The results indicated that 34.7% of the sample reported PTSD symptoms. Research indicates that rates of PTSD in patients for which pain is secondary to motor vehicle accidents (MVAs) range from 30% to 50% (Chibnall & Duckro, 1994; Hickling & Blanchard, 1992; Hickling et al., 1992; Taylor & Koch, 1995). Studies suggest that from 24% to 47% of fibromyalgia patients attribute the onset of their symptoms to a physical injury associated with an MVA (Sherman et al., 2000; Turk et al., 1996).

Geisser et al. (1996) examined the self-report of pain, affective distress, and disability in pain patients with and without PTSD symptoms. Their results indicated that patients with accident-related pain and high PTSD symptoms reported higher levels of pain and affective distress relative to patients with accident-related pain and without PTSD, or nonaccident-related pain.

Studies examining the prevalence of chronic pain in individuals with a primary diagnosis of PTSD have reported even higher coprevalence rates. Amir et al. (1997) examined a sample of 29 PTSD patients and found the prevalence of fibromyalgia syndrome to be 21%. McFarlane et al. (1994) reported that in a sample of PTSD patients reporting physical symptoms, pain was the most common physical complaint (45% reported back pain and 34% reported headaches). White and Faustman (1989) performed a review of discharge summaries of 543 veterans treated for PTSD to assess the frequency and nature of medical problems. Their results indicated that 60% had an identified medical problem, and one in four showed some type of musculoskeletal or pain problem. Beckham et al. (1997) investigated chronic pain patterns in Vietnam veterans with PTSD. A sample of 129 combat veterans with PSTD completed self-report questionnaires assessing PTSD symptoms and current pain status. Eighty percent of the sample reported the presence of a chronic pain condition. In addition, increased levels of PTSD re-experiencing symptoms were associated with increased pain and disability.

There could be several reasons for the high degree of variability in the prevalence rates reported in these studies of comorbid pain and PTSD. An inspection of these studies indicates that there were differences in the populations sampled (e.g., pain clinics vs. PTSD clinics). In addition, some of the studies cited based their coprevalence rates on diagnostic criteria from the DSM-III, whereas other studies based their prevalence rates on more recent diagnostic criteria. Further, assessment instruments utilized in the above studies varied widely; for example, some studies relied on the retrospective review of medical records to diagnose PTSD or chronic pain, whereas other studies utilized more sophisticated diagnostic and assessment instruments such as the CAPS (for PTSD) (Blake et al., 1990) or the WHYMPI (for pain) (Kerns et al., 1985). Thus, given the limitations of previous research, it is difficult to determine exact figures regarding the prevalence of comorbid pain and PTSD. Future studies should include state-of-the-art diagnostic measures to gain an accurate picture of the coprevalence of these conditions.

The co-occurrence of chronic pain and PTSD may have implications in terms of an individual's experience of each condition. Research indicates that patients with chronic pain related to trauma or PTSD experience more intense pain and affective distress (Geisser et al., 1996; Toomey et al., 1994), higher levels of life interference (Turk & Okifuji, 1996), and greater disability (Sherman et al., 2000) than pain patients without trauma or PTSD. For example, Chibnall and Duckro (1994) examined a sample of chronic post-traumatic headache patients and found that patients with PTSD and pain had higher levels of depression and suppressed anger than pain patients without PTSD. Tushima and Stoddard (1990) found that patients with post-traumatic headache reported more frequent pain and had a poorer prognosis than did nontraumatic headache patients. Sherman et al. (2000) found that in a sample of 93 treatment-seeking fibromyalgia patients, those who experienced PTSD-related symptoms reported significantly greater levels of pain, life interference, emotional distress, and inactivity than did patients who did not report PTSD-like symptoms. Over 85% of the sample with significant PTSD-like symptoms demonstrated significant disability compared to 50% of the patients without significant PTSD-like symptoms. Sherman and colleagues suggested that clinicians should address these PTSD symptoms in pain treatment, as failure to attend to them could limit successful outcomes. Thus, taken together, these studies suggest that the presence of both PTSD and chronic pain can increase patients' overall symptom severity.

4.   Possible Explanations of the Relationship Between Chronic Pain and PTSD: Examination of Theoretical Models

The high rate of comorbidity and symptom overlap between chronic pain and PTSD suggests that the two disorders might be related in some way. Clearly, this review of studies establishing the co-occurrence between pain and PTSD does not provide an explanation of the mechanisms by which they are linked. Although theoretical models have been proposed to account for the co-occurrence of pain and PTSD, these theoretical models have yet to be tested. However, there are numerous factors presented in these models that might be implicated in the etiology and maintenance of both conditions. In several recent articles (Asmundson et al., 2002; Otis et al., 2003; Sharp & Harvey, 2001), theories hypothesizing the relationship between chronic pain and PTSD were reviewed and several potential mechanisms of action were described. For clarity, each model will be reviewed in turn.

4.1.   Mutual Maintenance Model

According to Sharp and Harvey's (2001) Mutual Maintenance Model of chronic pain and PTSD, seven specific factors are identified by which mutual maintenance of chronic pain and PTSD could occur. Although many of the factors described by Sharp and Harvey have not been empirically investigated, they are useful in that they may serve to stimulate more critical examinations of the comorbidity of chronic pain and PTSD and provide several possible directions for future research. These factors include (1) attentional biases (which may cause patients to attend to threatening or painful stimuli), (2) anxiety sensitivity (which may contribute to a vulnerability to catastrophize about pain or trauma), (3) pain as a reminder of trauma (triggering an arousal response, avoidance of the cause of pain, and any memories of the trauma), (4) avoidance (may be adopted as a means to minimize pain and disturbing thoughts of the trauma), (5) fatigue and lethargy (associated with depression), (6) general anxiety, and (7) cognitive demands (caused by symptoms of pain and PTSD, may limit the use of adaptive coping strategies). Several other models have been developed by other researchers that have also included one or more of these factors to help explain the relationship between chronic pain and PTSD. Descriptions of these models, including existing empirical research on the factors maintaining pain and PTSD, will be presented below.

4.2.   Shared Vulnerability Model

Anxiety sensitivity is the fear of arousal-related sensations, arising from beliefs that these sensations have harmful consequences. Evidence suggests that anxiety sensitivity contributes to or amplifies the intensity of emotional reactions, particularly those with an anxiety component such as panic (Taylor, 2003). For example, persons with high anxiety sensitivity may become anxious when confronted with a feared situation as a result of their experience and as a result of their fearful interpretation of the physiological sensations of anxiety (e.g., racing heart, perspiration, shortness of breath). Asmundson et al. (2002) proposed a shared vulnerability model of chronic pain and PTSD in which anxiety sensitivity is a predisposing factor contributing to the development of both conditions. According to this model, a person with high levels of anxiety sensitivity is likely to become fearful in response to physical sensations such as heart pounding and breathlessness, thinking that these symptoms may signal impending doom. When people with high anxiety sensitivity encounter either a traumatic stressor or pain (or both), they are believed to respond with more fear than those with low anxiety sensitivity. Thus, the tendency to respond with fear to physical symptoms of anxiety is seen as a shared vulnerability contributing to the development of either disorder. In the case of PTSD, the degree of alarm caused by the stressor is combined with the alarm of physiological sensations to further exacerbate the emotional reaction, thereby increasing the risk of developing PTSD. In the case of chronic pain, anxiety sensitivity heightens fear and avoidance of activities that could induce pain, which further increases the chances that pain will be maintained over time.

Clinical pain research supports a relationship between anxiety sensitivity and pain. For example, Asmundson and Norton (1995) found that patients with higher anxiety sensitivity were more likely to experience greater anxiety and fear of pain, more negative affect, and greater avoidance of activities. Asmundson and Taylor (1996) found that anxiety sensitivity directly increased fear of pain; however, anxiety sensitivity indirectly influenced avoidance and escape behaviors through fear of pain. More recently, Zvolensky et al. (2000) evaluated anxiety sensitivity, depression, and pain severity as potential predictors of pain-related fear in a heterogeneous chronic pain population. Their findings indicated that anxiety sensitivity, as measured by the Anxiety Sensitivity Index (ASI; Reiss et al., 1986) was a better predictor of fear of pain and anxiety about pain than other relevant variables. Finally, Greenberg and Burns (2003) examined pain-related anxiety in a group of chronic musculoskeletal pain patients who underwent an experimentally induced pain induction procedure (i.e., cold pressor) and had to complete mental arithmetic tasks. Their results indicated that almost all of the effects of pain anxiety on task responses were accounted for by anxiety sensitivity. Taken together, results of all of these studies support the hypothesis that anxiety sensitivity may represent a vulnerability factor in the development and maintenance of pain-related anxiety and avoidance behaviors.

Although the majority of studies on anxiety sensitivity indicate that it may play a role in the development of anxiety disorders such as panic (Barlow, 2002), there are also several studies that support the model of anxiety sensitivity as a vulnerability factor in PTSD. In a study that examined the presence of anxiety sensitivity in 313 individuals with anxiety disorders, Taylor et al. (1992) found that patients with PTSD were the second highest on the ASI measure, with patients diagnosed with panic being the highest. Lang et al. (2002) found that anxiety sensitivity was a significant predictor of PTSD symptoms in women. In another study, anxiety sensitivity was related to severity of PTSD symptoms, and a reduction in anxiety sensitivity after participation in a cognitive–behavioral therapy (CBT) treatment program was related to a reduction in PTSD symptoms (Fedorff et al., 2000). Thus, although preliminary research is supportive, additional research on the interaction of anxiety sensitivity and PTSD would help to clarify the role of anxiety sensitivity as a potential vulnerability factor contributing to the development of PTSD.

4.3.   Fear-Avoidance Model

Building upon Vlaeyen and Linton's (2000) cognitive–behavioral fear-avoidance model of chronic pain, Norton and Asmundson (2003) recently proposed a fear-avoidance model of chronic pain that places a larger emphasis on the contributions of physiological activity and arousal (e.g., increased blood flow, heart rate, or muscle tension) in the perpetuation of fear and avoidance related to pain. There are two primary amendments to the model: (1) Physiological sensations could increase avoidance by aggravating damaged or weakened tissues and increasing pain and (2) physiological sensations of arousal could be misinterpreted as being pain related. These misinterpretations may be influenced by an individual's tendency to respond with fear to sensations that are anxiety provoking (e.g., individuals with high anxiety sensitivity). For example, an individual with a tendency to be hypervigilant to pain-related bodily sensations may interpret the physiological sensations as evidence of impending harm or pain, which would reinforce fears and beliefs that activities will be painful, and thus reinforce avoidance.

Avoidance also plays a significant role in models of chronic pain and PTSD. In chronic pain, avoidance can contribute to decreased feelings of self-efficacy related to pain, negative expectations and beliefs about an individual's ability to cope with pain, and increased disability (Waddell et al., 1993). The avoidance of reinforcing activities and social situations can contribute to affective distress, which can further exacerbate the experience of pain (Romano & Turner, 1985). Similarly, for a person with PTSD, fear of re-experiencing disturbing thoughts of events and avoidance of reminders associated with the trauma are core components of this disorder. This fear and avoidance can serve to prevent effective processing of the traumatic event and may lead to the maintenance of intrusive symptoms of re-exeriencing the trauma and increased arousal (Keane et al., 2000).

Catastrophizing is another factor that has been implicated in Vlaeyen and Linton's (2000) fear-avoidance model, and catastrophizing may also play a significant role in the development and maintenance of both chronic pain and PTSD. For example, pain research indicates that patients who use passive and maladaptive coping strategies such as catastrophizing are more likely to report greater pain and disability than patients who use active and adaptive coping strategies such as exercise, ignoring pain, and positive self-coping statements (Boothby et al., 1999; Jensen et al., 1999; Severeijns et al., 2001). In a recent study by Jensen et al. (2001), it was found that decreases in catastrophizing and the belief that one is disabled and increases in perceived control over pain were associated with decreases in pain, disability, and depression in a sample of 141 patients receiving multidisciplinary treatment for chronic pain. Likewise, for individuals with PTSD, catastrophizing thoughts regarding what might occur in feared situations may cause increased avoidance, unrealistic expectations, and increased distress regarding resumption of everyday activities (Asmundson et al., 2002).

4.4. Triple Vulnerability Model

Otis et al. (2003) applied the Triple Vulnerability Model (Barlow, 2000, 2002) to explain the development of chronic pain and PTSD. According to the Triple Vulnerability Model of anxiety (Barlow, 2000, 2002), an integrated set of triple vulnerabilities need to be present for developing an anxiety disorder: a generalized biological vulnerability, a generalized psychological vulnerability based on early experiences of lack of control over salient events, and a more specific psychological vulnerability in which one learns to focus anxiety on specific situations. Whereas the Triple Vulnerability Model applies to the development of anxiety in general, Keane and Barlow (2002) proposed a model of the development of PTSD specifically. According to their model, a true or false alarm develops during exposure to situations that symbolize or resemble an aspect of a traumatic event. However, the experience of alarm or other intense emotions is not sufficient in and of itself for the development of PTSD. In order to develop PTSD, one must develop anxiety or the sense that these events, including one's own emotional reactions to them, are preceding in an unpredictable and uncontrollable manner. Thus, when negative affect and a sense of uncontrollability develop, PTSD may emerge. Although this model implies that a psychological and biological vulnerability to develop the disorder exists, it has been found that anxiety is always moderated to some extent by variables such as the presence of adequate coping skills and social support (Keane & Barlow, 2002).

Although designed to describe the development of PTSD, this model could also relate to the development of chronic pain. For example, pain may have a biological basis and persons may have a genetic predisposition to develop certain pain conditions, as has been suggested in the case of headache (Larsson et al., 1995; Russell, 2004). Also, pain can be the result of a physical injury or the gradual deterioration of tissue over time. However, it has been consistently demonstrated that the presence and extent of physical pathology by itself is often not sufficient to account for the report of pain. For example, there is a low correlation between abnormal magnetic resonance imaging (MRI) and pain report, and many individuals with abnormal MRIs do not report impairment (Wood et al., 1995). Thus, just as a biological vulnerability is one risk factor in the development of anxiety, yet is not sufficient to cause an anxiety disorder; pain, too, may have a biological basis, but the presence of tissue damage or pathology alone is not sufficient to cause a chronic pain condition. Similar to the Triple Vulnerability Model developed for anxiety, a generalized psychological vulnerability may also be present prior to the development of a chronic pain condition. Numerous studies indicate that many chronic pain patients do experience perceptions of low social support, poorly developed coping skills, and failed past attempts to cope with stressful life events (e.g., job stressors, marital stressors), as well as perceptions of lack of control over life events (DeGood & Tait, 2001). More specifically, it is possible that for some people to develop a chronic pain condition, they must also develop a belief that the pain is preceding in an unpredictable and uncontrollable manner. When combined with a previous experience of coping poorly with a painful condition, this could contribute to decreased self-efficacy and low expectations of adaptively coping with future experiences of pain, which may constitute a specific psychological vulnerability to developing chronic pain. There are numerous studies that indicate that many chronic pain sufferers do, in fact, typically perceive a lack of personal control over their pain (Turk & Rudy, 1988). The relationship between perceived controllability and pain has been demonstrated in a variety of chronic pain syndromes, including migraine headache patients (Mizener et al., 1988), and low back pain patients and rheumatoid arthritis patients (Flor & Turk, 1988). When persons perceive their pain to be uncontrollable, feelings of low self-efficacy may develop, along with negative affect. Thus, a fear may develop of entering situations or performing activities in which pain could occur, leading to avoidance of situations in daily life. This avoidance will further fuel negative affect, feelings of uncontrollability, and

low self-efficacy, resulting in increased disability. Similar to the PTSD literature, it has been found that pain is always moderated to some extent by variables such as the presence of adequate coping skills and social support
(Kerns et al., 2002a, 2002b). Thus, whether the "alarm" is a trauma reminder
or pain reminder, the development of a sense of uncontrollability could precede the development of both disorders.

5.   Comorbidity of Chronic Pain and PTSD: Developmental Considerations

Although the models and empirical research presented earlier are almost
entirely based on work with adults, it is important to consider that comorbid
pain and PTSD could occur throughout one's life span. Although thorough
reviews of the literature on pain and PTSD in children could certainly stand
alone as separate chapters, some of the developmental issues to consider are
presented briefly here in order to provide a broader scope regarding issues of
comorbidity and how they may relate to youth. In the following section,
developmental issues affecting PTSD and chronic pain in children are discussed, followed by a section highlighting potential ways that the theoretical
models of the maintenance of the two disorders may be tailored to incorporate developmental factors.

6.   PTSD in Children and Adolescents

Each year in the United States, more than 5 million children are exposed to
some form of extreme traumatic stressor, such as natural disasters, physical
abuse, sexual assault, MVAs, life-threatening illnesses, painful medical procedures, witnessing of community or domestic violence, sudden death of a parent or loved one, or traumatic injuries or illnesses (Pfefferbaum, 1997). More
than 30% of those children exposed to an extreme traumatic stressor develop
PTSD, and as a result they experience symptoms that may affect them physically, emotionally, cognitively, behaviorally, and socially (Perry, 1999).
Similar to adults, children can develop PTSD in response to a range of traumatic stressors; however, children may express distress as a result of a trauma
quite differently from adults, with the child's initial reaction to trauma
including the possibility of disorganized or agitated behavior, such as crying,
clinging, or hyperkinesis (Perrin et al., 2000). Furthermore, although children
may re-experience a traumatic event just as adults do, young children may not
be able to verbalize their thoughts or have the cognitive capacity to recall
important aspects of the trauma. Nightmares involving the theme of the
trauma are common in children of all ages, and young children often display
signs of re-experiencing through vivid re-enactment of the trauma in the
form of drawings, stories, and play (Scheeringa et al., 1995). Thus, although

children experience both Criterion A (the traumatic event) as well as Criterion B (re-experiencing), these symptoms may be observed differently in children than in adults. Children also experience Criterion C (persistent avoidance and numbing of general responsiveness), and avoidance of both external and internal trauma reminders are common in traumatized children and adolescents. Just as adults may avoid traumatic reminders, and this avoidance can be reinforced by significant others such as a spouse, children also may avoid traumatic reminders, and parents' reactions to the trauma can significantly influence children's reaction. For example, some parents may inadvertently (or even purposefully) reinforce children's avoidance of reminders of the trauma (e.g., allow the child to sleep with them rather than alone, allow the child to avoid school), whereas other parents will not permit such avoidance. Thus, as sequelae to trauma, children may lose interest in participating in significant activities that are part of normal development; this avoidance can further perpetuate the child's vulnerability to feelings of depression or anxiety. Furthermore, older children and adolescents may develop a view of life as being quite fragile after a traumatic event, leading to expectations of negative events happening to them in the future and leading to further avoidance of normal daily activities. Finally, similar to adults, children may also experience persistent symptoms of increased arousal (Criterion D). For example, somatic complaints such as headaches or stomachaches are commonly reported by children who have been traumatized, in addition to intense fears. Irritability and outbursts of anger are also common. As could be expected, children who have been traumatized often find it difficult to concentrate in school and may evidence inattentiveness or hyperactivity (Lyons & Adams, 1999). In addition, children may also report hypervigilance, overprotectiveness of caregivers, separation anxiety, and prolonged upset in response to loud noises and/or arguing (Steward & O'Connor, 1994). Given the differences between the presentation of PTSD in adults and children, assessment and treatment strategies must be developmentally tailored to address the many factors that may be specific to the age of the patient.

7.   Chronic Pain in Children and Adolescents

Brief episodes of acute pain related to routine injuries and illnesses in childhood are common, with 15% of healthy school-aged children reporting brief episodes of pain (Chambliss et al., 2002). Children's typical responses to acute pain are usually short-lived, and normal activity is often quickly resumed, as is typically observed with adults. However, chronic pain in children, often associated with an underlying disease, a traumatic injury, or an ongoing trauma causing sustained injury, can result in unnecessary suffering of the child and family, disruption of the family routine, and restriction of the child's daily activities, thereby increasing the risk of long-term disability (Caffo & Belaise, 2003). In fact, chronic pain in childhood can often result in somatic and psychiatric dysfunction, with studies showing that children experiencing chronic pain are more likely than other children to complain of anxiety, to demonstrate hypochondriacal beliefs, to engage less frequently in social activities, and to experience higher levels of generalized anxiety (Campo et al., 2001). Chronic pain conditions in childhood may arise because of known injury (such as rheumatologic disease, sickle cell disease, or human immunodeficiency virus infection), or to traumatic injury (because of burns, physical abuse, or MVAs), whereas some chronic pain conditions in childhood may have less clear etiologies (e.g., chronic headache) (Chambliss et al., 2002). As a result of increased research over the past 20 years on chronic pain in children, we now understand that child pain, like adult pain, is not simply directly related to the extent of physical injury or level of tissue damage, but is influenced by many psychological factors that can modify the neural signals for pain and increase or decrease a child's distress. It has been suggested that children's pain is more "plastic" than that of adults, such that psychosocial factors could exert an even more powerful influence on children's pain perception than on adults' pain perception (McGrath & Hillier, 2002).

The presentation of chronic pain in children may also differ from that of adults, and there are numerous factors that may influence the child's experience of pain, including child factors (such as age, cognitive level, or temperament), cognitive factors (e.g., expectations about treatment efficacy), behavioral factors (e.g., child's distress responses, avoidance of activities), and emotional factors (anticipatory anxiety, depression) (McGrath & Hillier, 2002). Although some of these factors are stable for a child (e.g., temperament), other factors change progressively (e.g., age, cognitive level, physical state, and family learning). Child factors and situational factors (e.g., level of control over situation) may interrelate to shape how children generally interpret the various sensations caused by tissue damage. For example, as children grow, they learn ways to express pain and ways to cope with pain, and their experience is certainly shaped by their family, culture, and interactions with caregivers and peers. This notion is consistent with Melzack and Wall's (1965) definition of pain as a multidimensional and subjective experience, characterized by physiologic, affective, cognitive, behavioral, and cultural dimensions. Thus, even though the tissue damage for several children may be the same, certain factors specific to each child or to each child's environment can intensify pain and distress, trigger pain episodes, and prolong pain-related disability, whereas other factors may buffer the effects of the pain, enable the child to engage in healthy coping, and lessen distress. Thus, a thorough assessment is crucial to determine the extent to which cognitive, behavioral, emotional, or situational factors contribute to or buffer the pain experience for a child, with understanding that these factors are likely to vary between children and may even vary over time for the same child.

Children's ongoing physical growth may also play a role in their ability to recover more quickly than adults from injury. Pain behavior in children has also been found to vary as a function of the child's developmental level. Older children will be able to describe the location, intensity, duration, and sensation of pain, whereas younger children may not be able to distinguish pain from other negative affective states (Tarnowski & Brown, 1999). Pain behavior in children has also been found to differ depending on the presence or absence of a caregiver during a painful medical procedure, with some studies finding that children whose mothers were present were more distressed, but that children prefer parents or caregivers to be present (Gonzalez et al., 1989). Parents' attitudes and expectations, their anxiety levels, and whether they are overly protective and reinforcing of dependence are variables that may affect children's ability to successfully cope. Also, parents may inadvertently cue and reinforce their child's distress, whereas others may promote coping by the child (Blount et al., 1991). Because of the number of parental variables that could influence child coping, there is need to assess characteristics of the parent, child, and parent–child interactions when assessing pain in children. Given the host of factors that may influence a child's experience of pain, it is not surprising that the treatment of pain in childhood requires an integrated approach, informed by the many factors that may influence a child's pain, including the family and cultural factors that might impact the child, and the child's current methods of coping with pain. Cognitive behavioral treatments for chronic pain in children should take these factors into consideration by giving children effective strategies that will lessen their pain and distress and help them return to developmentally appropriate activities.

8.   Comorbid Chronic Pain and PTSD in Children and Adolescents

Given the range of symptoms experienced by youth experiencing PTSD and chronic pain, it is surprising that there has not been more extensive research specifically on children who experience comorbid chronic pain and PTSD. The majority of the research that has been conducted has focused on children who suffer traumatic injury (pain resulting from trauma or abuse). Stoddard and Saxe (2001) stated that traumatic injuries are the single largest cause of morbidity among children in the United States. In fact, 8.7 million children under the age of 15 are seen in emergency departments because of traumatic injuries resulting from automobile accidents, falls, violence, or sports-related injuries (Scheidt et al., 1995). More than 30% of children who experience a painful traumatic injury develop PTSD and experience its associated emotional, behavioral, cognitive, social, and physical symptoms (Perry, 1999). Another study showed 35% of adolescents with cancer also met criteria for PTSD, with 15% of children surviving cancer still having moderate to severe PTSD (Pelcovitz et al., 1998). Overall, it is clear that traumatic injury or illness may be a cause of comorbid pain and PTSD in children.

Very few studies have examined the relationship between pain and the course of PTSD. However, Saxe et al. (2001) examined the relationship between pain and the course of PTSD in 24 children who experienced burns, with the aim of investigating the efficacy of using opiate medications (morphine) as a possible preventive agent in children with burn-related PTSD. Results indicated that the dose of morphine administered to these children was associated with a significant reduction of PTSD symptoms over a 6-month period, after controlling for other factors. The authors suggest that acute trauma leads to enhanced fear conditioning and memory consolidation of the trauma and that morphine may have diminished the hyperadrenergic state in these children by inhibiting the fear conditioning and memory consolidation. However, because of the small sample size of children assessed and lack of an experimental design, the authors suggested that future studies should examine more specifically the relationship among opiate dose, noradrenergic function, and PTSD symptoms using a randomized treatment design.

An emerging research question concerns the degree to which comorbid pain and trauma in children interrelate to produce risk for psychopathology. Pine and Cohen (2002) reviewed evidence that suggested that the degree of psychopathology resulting from pain and PTSD in children may depend on the specific form of trauma. For example, compared with children exposed to accidents or natural disasters, children who experience pain as a result of physical or sexual abuse exhibit higher rates of psychopathology. Other factors that may influence differential symptom trajectories in children exposed to traumatic injury include level of trauma exposure, proximity to the trauma, prior trauma exposure, extent of disruption in social support systems, pretrauma levels of psychopathology, child age, gender, and developmental level, and child/parent coping styles (Caffo & Belaise, 2003). Although there are many psychiatric implications after painful injury due to trauma, a review of the literature indicates that PTSD is the most common psychiatric disorder found in children and adolescents. Other comorbid diagnoses, such as mood disorders, anxiety disorders, and conduct disorders, may also occur.

Although no specific developmental models have been proposed to help explain the possible relationship between childhood chronic pain and PTSD, several developmental factors could be important to consider when developing a model that might explain the mutual maintenance of the two disorders. Similar to an adult model described in a previous section of this chapter (i.e., Mutual Maintenance Model; Sharp & Harvey, 2001), pain may serve as a reminder of the trauma in children, triggering an arousal response, leading to avoidance of the cause of pain and any memories of the trauma. Avoidance may be adapted as a way of minimizing pain and any disturbing thoughts of the trauma. Such avoidance can be particularly disruptive to a child, who may be avoiding daily activities such as school or social activities that are crucial for continuing to meet developmental milestones. Further, a child's avoidance may be reinforced by caregivers, who may have low tolerance for their child's distress or who may have also experienced the trauma themselves. Avoidance can contribute to a child's decreased feelings of self-efficacy related to pain, negative expectations about the ability to cope with pain, increased feelings of distress, and an amplified focus of attention on painful sensations. Cognitive demands caused by symptoms of pain and PTSD could limit the child's use of adaptive coping strategies such as exercise, ignoring pain, and use of positive self-coping statements.

Borrowing from Asmundson et al.'s (2002) proposed shared vulnerability model of chronic pain and PTSD, anxiety sensitivity may also be a predisposing factor contributing to the maintenance of chronic pain and PTSD in children. Children with high levels of anxiety sensitivity may become more fearful in response to physical sensations such as breathlessness or dizziness, thinking that these symptoms could signal doom; thus, these children may avoid activities that trigger physical sensations because of fear of the sensations and of the traumatic cues that they may trigger. These physiological sensations of arousal because of anxiety or PTSD may even be mistaken for being pain related. In fact, in a study of the relationship between anxiety sensitivity and fear of pain in healthy adolescents, anxiety sensitivity was found to account for a unique proportion of the variance in pain anxiety symptoms, even after controlling for other potential predictors of fear of pain (Muris et al., 2001). Although there are studies that have indicated that anxiety sensitivity may play a role in anxiety disorders such as panic in children (Mattis & Pincus, 2003), there are no known studies specifically examining anxiety sensitivity as a potential vulnerability factor for children contributing to the maintenance of chronic pain and PTSD. Thus, the construct of anxiety sensitivity should be explored in future research with this population, and treatments might then be tailored to help children become less fearful of these symptoms through symptom induction techniques such as interoceptive exposure.

The Triple Vulnerability Model, developed by Barlow (2000, 2002) to explain the development of anxiety and panic, may also be relevant to help explain the maintenance and development of psychopathology in children experiencing comorbid chronic pain and PTSD. For example, according to the Triple Vulnerability Model (reviewed earlier), children may have inherited a biological vulnerability to experience psychopathology. Early experiences of lack of control over salient events may be especially relevant for children experiencing trauma and pain (two salient experiences for which the child has little control), contributing to the child's generalized psychological vulnerability. As a result of these early experiences, children may learn to focus their anxiety on specific situations (presumably those that trigger reminders of the pain or trauma). When negative affect and a sense of uncontrollability develop, PTSD and chronic pain conditions may emerge. Development of psychopathology, however, should be moderated to some extent by variables such as the presence of "protective factors," including adequate coping skills, social support, and parenting styles that support the child's continued positive growth and development. Both risk and protective factors should be considered in developing a model of the maintenance of pain and PTSD in children.

Developmental psychopathology literature has examined the concept of child resilience and has been concerned with identifying factors associated with increased risk (vulnerability) or decreased risk (resilience) for developing psychopathology after exposure to extreme stress (Masten & Reed, 2002). Such factors should be considered in the development of a model of chronic pain and PTSD in children, rather than simply applying adult models indiscriminately to children. For example, protective factors, or measurable characteristics of a child or situation that predict positive outcome in the context of high risk or adversity, should be incorporated in a theoretical model attempting to explain why some children do not experience high distress and disability from comorbid chronic pain and PTSD, whereas others do. Some common "protective factors" for children that have been identified from a host of studies include good cognitive and coping abilities, positive self-perceptions, faith and meaning in life, close relationships with care-giving adults, an organized home environment, socioeconomic advantages, and close relationships with prosocial and rule-abiding peers (Masten & Reed, 2002). Thus, treatment might focus on increasing the presence of such protective factors in a child's life to maximize chances that children can "bounce back" from the distress caused by chronic pain and PTSD.

9.   Implications for Assessment and Treatment of Comorbid Pain and PTSD

Given the high rates of comorbidity of chronic pain and PTSD, clinicians conducting diagnostic assessments of patients with either condition should assess for both disorders, regardless of the age of the patient. There are several well-validated self-report questionnaires that can be used to assist in determining a diagnosis and the severity of symptoms. Self-report measures of pain for adults include the 0 to 10 numerical pain rating scale, the McGill Pain Questionnaire (Melzack, 1975), or the West Haven–Yale Multidimensional Pain Inventory (Kerns et al., 1985). Measures of PTSD for adults include the Posttraumatic Stress Disorder Checklist (Weathers et al., 1993) or the Clinician-Administered PTSD Scale (used to establish a diagnosis of PTSD) (Blake et al., 1990). For a comprehensive review of PTSD assessment measures, see Wilson and Keane (2004). Measures of anxiety sensitivity (Reiss et al., 1986), pain-coping style (Riley et al., 1999), beliefs and expectations related to pain (Jensen et al., 1994), cognitive and behavioral avoidance, and self-efficacy could also be included in the assessment to gain a comprehensive understanding of the factors contributing to and maintaining these conditions.

For children, assessing pain and PTSD can be even more challenging, as age can affect the expression of pain and their ability to report pain or trauma. Typically, below the age of 3 years, children express pain through behavioral manifestation, whereas by the age of 4 years, most children can express pain verbally and indicate the severity of pain using pain-rating scales. The assessment of pain should be sensitive to the child's age, the type of pain, the situation in which pain occurs, the child's prior pain experience, behavioral and emotional factors, and the caregiver's responses and attitudes. There are several child self-report measures of pain, including the Faces Scale (Hicks et al., 2001), the Varni–Thompson Pediatric Pain Questionnaire (Frank et al., 2000), and the Children's Comprehensive Pain Questionnaire (McGrath, 1989). In addition, children may be asked to keep a pain diary. For PTSD, in addition to structured clinical interviews, self-report questionnaires such as the PTSD Reaction Index (Belter et al., 1991), the Children's Posttraumatic Stress Disorder Inventory (Saigh, 1989), or the Impact of Events Scale (Horowitz et al., 1979) are also used. Although it is beyond the scope of this chapter to describe each assessment tool in detail, treatment of children with chronic pain and PTSD should begin with a careful assessment, which should continue throughout treatment.

Only a few studies have reported results of treatments designed to address co-occurring chronic pain and PTSD. Preliminary research suggests that treatment of adults with propanolol following an acute psychologically traumatic event may have a preventative effect on subsequent PTSD; however, further research is needed in this area (Pitman et al., 2002). Muse (1986) described the sequential treatment of three individuals with co-occurring chronic pain and PTSD. Each patient was treated for pain using a behavioral approach that included techniques such as relaxation training, exercise, and biofeedback training. Following treatment for pain, patients were enrolled in a program of systematic desensitization for PTSD. Although the author's discussion of the techniques employed when providing pain treatment and of pain treatment outcomes were vague, the results indicated that subsequent behavioral treatment for PTSD was effective for this population. Of note, treatment in these case studies was sequential; patients were treated first for chronic pain and then for PTSD. In a related study, Shipherd et al. (2003) described a series of case studies that utilized a 12-week manualized PTSD treatment for six women diagnosed with chronic pain and PTSD secondary to MVAs. The treatment included techniques such as imaginal exposure, cognitive restructuring, relaxation techniques, and pleasant activity scheduling. At the 1-month follow-up, patients showed improvements of some PTSD symptoms, but no decrease in pain was noted. Hickling et al. (1992) described 12 patients with posttraumatic headache secondary to a MVA who were effectively treated with CBT. It was reported that the eight participants diagnosed with PTSD failed to show positive results with the headache until the PTSD symptoms were addressed, and they required significantly longer treatment than those who did not meet diagnostic criteria for PTSD. As there are no studies that have examined the efficacy of integrated treatments for comorbid pain and PTSD, further investigation of the potential efficacy of an integrated treatment is warranted. As both chronic pain and PTSD respond well to CBT approaches, an integrated CBT protocol may be the most efficient form of treatment.

The theoretical models presented have yet to be fully tested, and further research is needed to determine how clinical treatment protocols should be modified to integrate treatments for both disorders. However, data from existing case studies point toward several techniques that might be useful to utilize when treating a person with comorbid pain and PTSD. The strategies would likely include standard CBT techniques such as cognitive restructuring or coping skills training, education about the function of avoidance, and ways to conduct situational exposures (e.g., doing activities that were previously avoided), as well as interoceptive exposures (e.g., exercises used to bring on physical sensations). Patients could also be taught to reinforce positive self-efficacy beliefs, correct attentional biases, and reduce catastrophizing. Overall, it is important to help patients with pain and PTSD understand the ways these two disorders may be maintained and the importance of decreasing avoidance. As patients begin to increase their participation in daily activities, they may be better able to obtain a more positive quality of life.

10.   Future Directions

The research summarized in this review suggests that chronic pain and PTSD frequently co-occur throughout one's life span, and that similar mechanisms, such as fear and avoidance, anxiety sensitivity, and catastrophizing, as well as general and specific psychological vulnerabilities, may help account for the development and maintenance of both conditions. Although several models have been proposed to explain the relationship between chronic pain and PTSD, continued research in this area is needed to more fully develop and test these models. Several factors have been presented that might be important to include in the conceptualization of a model of pain and PTSD in childhood, so that adult models are not indiscriminately applied to children without considering developmental factors. Regardless of patient age, given the high rate at which chronic pain and PTSD co-occur, it is imperative that researchers develop more integrated assessment and treatment techniques for this population. In pursuit of this goal, a study recently funded by the Department of Veterans Affairs Rehabilitation Research and Development Service is being conducted by Otis and Keane at the VA Boston Healthcare System to examine the efficacy of an integrated cognitive–behavioral treatment program for veterans with comorbid chronic pain and PTSD; the study will also examine potential mechanisms of action that may explain the relationship between chronic pain and PTSD. As such studies are launched and treatment strategies are tested with patients of all ages with comorbid pain and PTSD, we may then begin to refine our existing treatment protocols. This can only be done through systematic and well-controlled research.

Acknowledgment

Preparation of this manuscript was support by a grant from the Veterans Health Administration Rehabilitation, Research and Development Service (Grant No. C3322R).

References

American Psychiatric Association. (1994). *Diagnostic and Statistical Manual of Mental Disorders*, 4th ed. Washington, DC: American Psychiatric Association.

Amir, M., Kaplan, Z., Neumann, L., Sharabani, R., Shani, N., & Buskila, D. (1997). Posttraumatic Stress Disorder, tenderness and fibromyalgia. *Journal of Psychosomatic Research, 42*, 607–613.

Asmundson, G. J. & Norton, G. (1995). Anxiety sensitivity in patients with physically unexplained chronic back pain: A preliminary report. *Behaviour Research and Therapy, 33*, 771–777.

Asmundson, G. J. & Taylor, S. (1996). Role of anxiety sensitivity in pain-related fear and avoidance. *Journal of Behavioral Medicine, 19*, 577–586.

Asmundson, G. J., Coons, M. J., Taylor, S., & Katz, J. (2002). PTSD and the experience of pain: Research and clinical implications of shared vulnerability and mutual maintenance models. *Canadian Journal of Psychiatry, 47*, 930–937.

Asmundson, G. J., Jacobson, S. J., Allerdings, M., & Norton, G. R. (1996). Social phobia in disabled workers with chronic musculoskeletal pain. *Behavior Research and Therapy, 34*, 939–943.

Asmundson, G., J., Norton, G., Allerdings, M., Norton, P., & Larsen, D. (1998). Posttraumatic Stress Disorder and work-related injury. *Journal of Anxiety Disorders, 12*, 57–69.

Banks, S. M. & Kerns, R. D., (1996). Explaining the high rates of depression in chronic pain: A stress diathesis framework. *Psychological Bulletin, 119*, 95–110.

Barlow, D. H. (2000). Unraveling the mysteries of anxiety and its disorders from the perspective of emotion theory. *American Psychologist, 55*, 1247–1263.

Barlow, D. H. (2002). *Anxiety and Its Disorders*, 2nd ed. New York, Guilford Press.

Beckham, J. C., Crawford, A. L., Feldman, M. E., Kirby, A. C., Hertzberg, M. A., Davidson, R. J. T., Moore, S. (1997). Chronic Posttraumatic Stress Disorder and chronic pain in Vietnam combat veterans. *Journal of Psychosomatic Research, 43*, 379–389.

Belter, R. W., Dunn, S. E., & Jeney, P. (1991). The psychological impact of Hurricane Hugo on children: A needs assessment. *Advances in Behavior Research and Therapy, 13*, 155–161.

Benedetto, M. C., Kerns, R. D., & Rosenberg, R. (1998). Health risk behaviors and healthcare utilization among veterans receiving primary medical care. *Journal of Clinical Psychology in Medical Settings, 5*, 441–447.

Benedikt, R. A. & Kolb, L. C. (1986). Preliminary findings on chronic pain and Posttraumatic Stress Disorder. *American Journal of Psychiatry, 143*, 908–910.

Blake, D. D., Weathers, F. W., Nagy, L. M., Kaloupek, D. G., Klauminzer, G., Charney, D. S., & Keane, T. M. (1990). A clinician rating scale for assessing current and lifetime PTSD: The CAPS-1. *The Behavior Therapist, 13*, 187–188.

Blount, R. L., Landolf-Fritsche, B., Powers, S. W., & Sturges, J. W. (1991). Differences between high and low coping children and between parent and staff behaviors during painful medical procedures. *Journal of Pediatric Psychology, 16*, 795–809.

Boothby, J. L., Thorn, B. E., Stroud, M. W., & Jensen, M. P. (1999). Coping with pain. In R. J. Gatchel & D. C. Turk (Eds.). *Psychosocial Factors in Pain*, New York: Guilford Press, pp. 343–359.

Brewin, C. R. & Holmes, E. A. (2003). Psychological theories of Posttraumatic Stress Disorder. *Clinical Psychology Review, 23*, 339–376.

Brewin, C. R., Dalgleish, T., & Joseph, S. (1996). A dual representation theory of Posttraumatic Stress Disorder. *Psychological Review, 103*, 670–686.

Brown, R. L., Patterson, J. J., Rounds, L. A., & Papasouliotis, O. (1996). Substance use among patients with chronic back pain. *Journal of Family Practice, 43*, 152–160.

Caffo, E. & Belaise, C. (2003). Psychological aspects of traumatic injury in children and adolescents. *Child and Adolescent Psychiatric Clinics of North America, 12*, 493–535.

Campo, J. V., DiLorenzo, C., & Chiappetta, L., (2001). Adult outcomes of pediatric recurrent abdominal pain: Do they just grow out of it. *Pediatrics, 108 (1)*, E1–E7.

Chambliss, C. R., Heggen, J., Copelan, D. N., & Pettignano, R., (2002). The assessment and management of chronic pain in children. *Pediatric Drugs, 4(11)*, 737–746.

Chibnall J. T. & Duckro, P. N. (1994). Posttraumatic Stress Disorder and motor vehicle accidents. *Headache, 34*, 357–361.

Crombez, G., Vlaeyen, J. W. S., Heuts, P. H. T. G., & Lysens, R. (1999). Pain-related fear is more disabling than pain itself: Evidence of the role of pain-related fear in chronic back pain disability. *Pain, 80*, 329–339.

Davidson, J., Hughes, D., Blazer, D. G., & George, L. K. (1991). Posttraumatic Stress Disorder in the community: An epidemiological study. *Psychological Medicine, 21(3)*, 713–721.

DeGood, D. E. & Tait, R. C. (2001). Assessment of pain beliefs and pain coping. In D. C. Turk & R. Melzack (Eds.). *Handbook of Pain Assessment*. New York: Guilford Press, pp. 320–345.

Ehlers, A. & Clark, D. M. (2000). A cognitive model of Posttraumatic Stress Disorder. *Behaviour Research and Therapy, 38*, 319–345.

Fedorff, I. C., Taylor, S., Asmundson, G. J. G., & Koch, W. J. (2000). Cognitive factors in traumatic stress reactions: Predicting PTSD symptoms from anxiety sensitivity and beliefs about harmful events. *Behavioral Cognitive Psychotherapy, 28*, 5–15.

Flor, H. & Turk, D. C. (1988). Chronic back pain and rheumatoid arthritis: Predicting pain and disability from cognitive variables, *Journal of Behavioral Medicine, 11*, 251–265.

Foa, E. B. & Kozak, M. J. (1986). Emotional processing of fear: Exposure to corrective information. *Psychological Bulletin, 99*, 20–35.

Foa, E. B. & Rothbaum, B. O. (1998). Treating the trauma of rape: Cognitive behavioral therapy for PTSD. New York: Guilford Press.

Frank, L. S., Greenberg, C. S., & Stevens, B. (2000). Pain assessment in infants and children. *Pediatric Clinics of North America, 47(3)*, 487–512.

Geisser, M. E., Roth, R. S., Bachman, J. E., & Eckert, T. A. (1996). The relationship between symptoms of Posttraumatic Stress Disorder and pain, affective disturbance and disability among patients with accident and non-accident related pain. *Pain, 66*, 207–214.

Gonzalez, J. C., Routh, D. K., Saab, P. G., Armstrong, F. D., Shifman, L. Guerra, E., & Fawcett, N. (1989). Effects of parent presence on children's reactions to injections: Behavioral, physiological, and subjective aspects. *Journal of Pediatric Psychology, 14(3)*, 449–462.

Greenberg, J. & Burns, J. W. (2003). Pain anxiety among chronic pain patients: Specific phobia or manifestation of anxiety sensitivity? *Behaviour Research and Therapy, 41*, 223–240.

Gureje, O., Von Korff, M., Simon, G. E., & Gater, R. (1998). Persistent pain and well-being. A world health organization study in primary care. *Journal of the American Medical Association, 280*, 147–151.

Hickling, E. J. & Blanchard, E. B. (1992). Posttraumatic Stress Disorder and motor vehicle accidents. *Journal of Anxiety Disorders, 6*, 285–291.

Hickling, E. J., Blanchard, E. B., Silverman, D. J., & Schwartz, S. P. (1992). Motor vehicle accidents, headaches, and Posttraumatic Stress Disorder: Assessment findings in a consecutive series. *Headache, 32*, 147–151.

Hicks, C. L., von Baeyer, C. L., Spafford, P., van Korlaar, I., & Goodenough, B. (2001). The faces pain scale-revised: Toward a common metric in pediatric pain measurement. *Pain, 93*, 173–183.

Horowitz, M., Wilner, M., & Alvarez, W. (1979). Impact of Event Scale: A measure of subjective stress. *Psychosomatic Medicine, 41*, 209–218.

IASP Task Force on Taxonomy. (1994). *Classification of Chronic Pain* H. Merskey & N. Bogduk (Eds.). Seattle, WA: IASP Press.

Jensen, M. P., Romano, J. M., Turner, J. A., Good, A. B., & Wald, L. H. (1999). Patient beliefs predict patient functioning: Further support for a cognitive-behavioral model of chronic pain. *Pain, 81*, 95–104.

Jensen, M. P., Turner, J. A., & Romano, J. M. (2001). Changes in beliefs, catastrophizing, and coping are associated with improvement in multidisciplinary pain treatment. *Journal of Consulting and Clinical Psychology, 69*, 655–662.

Jensen, M. P., Turner, J. A., Romano, J. M., & Lawler, B. K. (1994). Relationship of pain-specific beliefs to chronic pain adjustment. *Pain, 57*, 301–309.

Keane, T. M. & Barlow, D. H. (2002). Posttraumatic Stress Disorder. In D. H. Barlow (Ed.). *Anxiety and Its Disorders*. New York: Guilford Press, pp. 418–453.

Keane, T. M. & Wolf, J. (1990). Comorbidity in Posttraumatic Stress Disorder: An analysis of community and clinical studies. *Journal of Applied Social Psychology, 20*, 1776–1788.

Keane, T. M., Zimmering, R. T., & Caddell, J. M. (1985). A behavioral formulation of Posttraumatic Stress Disorder in Vietnam veterans. *The Behavioral Therapist, 8*, 9–12.

Keane, T. M., Zimmering, R. T., & Kaloupek, D. G. (2000). Posttraumatic Stress Disorder. In M. Hernsen & A. S. Bellack (Eds.). *Psychopathology in Adulthood: An Advanced Test*. Needham Heights, MA: Allyn & Bacon, pp. 208–231.

Kerns, R. D., Haythornthwaite, J., Southwick, S., & Giller, E. L. (1990). The role of marital interaction in chronic pain and depressive symptom severity. *Journal of Psychosomatic Research, 34*, 401–408.

Kerns, R. D., Otis, J. D., & Wise, E. (2002a). Treating families of chronic pain patients: Application of a cognitive–behavioral transactional model. In

R. J. Gatchel & D. C. Turk (Eds.). *Psychological Approaches to Pain Management*. New York: Guilford Press, pp. 256–275.

Kerns, R. D., Rosenberg, R., & Otis, J. D. (2002b). Self-appraised problem-solving competence and pain relevant social support as predictors of the experience of chronic pain. *Annals of Behavioral Medicine, 24(2)*, 100–105.

Kerns, R. D., Turk, D. C., & Rudy, T. E. (1985). West Haven–Yale Multidimensional Pain Inventory (WHYMPI). *Pain, 23*, 345–356.

Kessler, R., Sonnega, A., Bromet, E., Hughes, M., & Nelson, C. (1995). Posttraumatic Stress Disorder in the National Comorbidity Survey. *Archives of General Psychiatry, 52*, 1048–1060.

King, D. W., King, L. A., Fairbank, J. A., Keane, T. M., & Adams, G. (1998). Resilience–recovery factors in Posttraumatic Stress Disorder among female and male Vietnam veterans: Hardiness, postwar social support, and additional stressful life events. *Journal of Personality and Social Psychology, 74*, 420–434.

Kulka, R. A., Schlenger, W. E., Fairbank, J. A., Hough, R. L., Jordan, K. B., Marmar, C. R., & Weiss, D. S. (1990). Trauma and the Vietnam War generation: Report of findings for the National Vietnam Veterans Re-adjustment Study. New York: Brunner/Mazel.

Lang, A. J., Kennedy, C. M., & Stein, M. B. (2002). Anxiety sensitivity and PTSD among female victims of intimate partner violence. *Depression and Anxiety, 16*, 77–83.

Lang, P. J. (1979). A bioinformational theory of emotional imagery. *Psychophysiology, 52*, 1048–1060.

Larsson, B., Bille, B., & Pedersen N. L. (1995). Genetic influence in headaches: A Swedish twin study. *Headache, 35(9)*, 513–519.

Lyons, J. A. & Adams, C. (1999). Posttraumatic Stress Disorder. In A. J. Goreczny & M. Hersen (Eds.). *Handbook of Pediatric and Adolescent Health Psychology*. Needham Heights, MA: Allyn & Bacon.

Masten, A. S. & Reed, M. G. J. (2002). Resilience in development. In C. R. Snyder, S. J. Lopez (Eds). *Handbook of Positive Psychology*. New York: Oxford University Press, pp. 74–88.

Mattis, S. G. & Pincus, D. B. (2003). Treatment of SAD and panic disorder in children and adolescents. In P. Barrett & T. Ollendick (Eds). *Handbook of Interventions That Work with Children and Adolescents: Prevention and Treatment*. West Sussex, UK: Wiley.

McFarlane, A. C., Atchison, M., Rafalowicz, E., & Papay, P. (1994). Physical symptoms in Posttraumatic Stress Disorder. *Journal of Psychosomatic Research, 42*, 607–617.

McGrath, P. A. (1989). Evaluating a child's pain. *Journal of Pain Symptom Management, 4(4)*, 198–214.

McGrath, P. A. & Hillier, L. M. (2002). A practical cognitive behavioral approach for treating children's pain. In D. C. Turk & R. J. Gatchel (Eds.). *Psychological Approaches to Pain Management: A Practitioners Handbook*, 2nd ed. New York: The Guilford Press, pp. 534–552.

McNally, R. J. (2003). Psychological mechanisms in acute response to trauma. *Biological Psychiatry, 53(9)*, 779–788.

Melzack, R. (1975). McGill Pain Questionnaire: Major properties and scoring methods. *Pain, 1*, 277–299.

Melzack, R. & Wall, P. D. (1965). Pain mechanisms: A new theory. *Science, 150*, 971–979.

Mizener, D., Thomas, M., & Billings, R. (1988). Cognitive changes of migraineurs receiving biofeedback training. *Headache, 28(5)*, 339–343.

Mowrer, O. H. (1960). *Learning Theory and Behavior*. New York: Wiley.

Muris, P., Vlaeyen, J., & Meesters, C. (2001). The relationship between anxiety sensitivity and fear of pain in healthy adolescents, *Behaviour Research and Therapy, 39*, 1357–1368.

Muse, M. (1986). Stress-related, Posttraumatic chronic pain syndrome: Behavioral treatment approach. *Pain, 25*, 389–394.

Norris, F. H. (1992). Epidemiology of trauma: Frequency and impact of different potentially traumatic events on different demographic groups. *Journal of Consulting and Clinical Psychology, 60*, 409–418.

Norton, P. J. & Asmundson, G. J. G. (2003). Amending the fear-avoidance model of chronic pain: What is the role of physiological arousal? *Behavior Therapy, 34*, 17–30.

Otis, J. D., Keane, T. M., & Kerns, R. D. (2003). An examination of the relationship between chronic pain and Posttraumatic Stress Disorder. *Journal of Rehabilitation, Research and Development, 40(5)*, 397–406.

Ozer, E. J., Best, S. R., Lipsey, T. L., & Weiss, D. S., (2003). Predictors of Posttraumatic Stress Disorder and symptoms in adults: A meta-analysis. *Psychological Bulletin, 129(1)*, 52–73.

Pelcovitz, D. Libov, B. G., Mandel, F., Kaplan, S., Weinblatt, M., & Septimus, A. (1998). Posttraumatic Stress Disorder and family functioning in adolescent cancer. *Journal of Traumatic Stress, 11*, 205–221.

Perrin, S., Smith, P., & Yule, W. (2000). The assessment and treatment of Posttraumatic Stress Disorder in children and adolescents. *Journal of Child Psychology and Psychiatry, 41 (3)*, 277–289.

Perry, B. (1999). Posttraumatic Stress Disorder in children and adolescents. *Current Opinion in Pediatrics, 11*, 310–320.

Pfefferbaum, B. (1997). Posttraumatic Stress Disorder in children: A review of the past 10 years. *Journal of the American Academy of Child and Adolescent Psychiatry, 36*, 1503–1511.

Pine, D. S. & Cohen, J. A. (2002). Trauma in children and children and adolescents: Risk and treatment of psychiatric sequelae. *Biological Psychiatry, 51*, 519–531.

Pitman, R. K., Sanders, K. M., Zusman, R. M., Healey, A. R., Cheema, F., & Lasko, N. B. (2002). Pilot study of secondary prevention of Posttraumatic Stress Disorder with propranolol. *Biological Psychiatry, 51*, 189–192.

Reiss, S., Peterson, R., Gursky, D., & McNally, R. (1986). Anxiety sensitivity, anxiety frequency, and the prediction of fearfulness. *Behavior Research and Therapy, 24*, 1–8.

Riley, J., Robinson, M. E., & Geisser, M. E. (1999). Empirical subgroups of the Coping Strategies Questionnaire Revised: A multisample study. *Clinical Journal of Pain, 15(2)*, 111–116.

Romano, J.M., & Turner, J.A. (1985). Chronic pain and depression: Does the evidence support a relationship? *Psychological Bulletin, 97*, 18–34.

Romano, J. M., Turner, J. A., Friedman, L. S., Bulcroft, R. A., Jensen, M. P., Hops, H., & Wright, S. F. (1992). Sequential analysis of chronic pain behaviors and spouse responses. *Journal of Consulting and Clinical Psychology, 60*, 777–782.

Russell, M. (2004). Epidemiology and genetics of cluster headache. *Lancet, 3(5)*, 279–283.

Saigh, P. A. (1989). The development and validation of the children's Posttraumatic Stress Disorder inventory. *International Journal of Special Education, 4*, 75–84.

Saxe, G., Stoddard, F., Courtney, D., Cunningham, K., Chawla, N., Sheridan, R., King, D., & King, L. (2001). Relationship between acute morphine and course of PTSD in children with burns. *Journal of the American Academy of Child and Adolescent Psychiatry, 40(8)*, 915–921.

Scheeringa, M. S., Zeanah, C. H., Drell, M. J., & Larrieu, J. A. (1995). Two approaches to the diagnosis of Posttraumatic Stress Disorder in infancy and early childhood. *Journal of the American Academy of Child and Adolescent Psychiatry, 34(2)*, 191–200.

Scheidt, P. C., Harel, Y., Trumble, A. C., Jones, D. H. Overpeck, M. D., & Bijur, P. E. (1995). The epidemiology of nonfatal injuries among US children and youth. *American Journal of Public Health, 85*, 932–938.

Severeijns, R., Vlaeyen, J. W., van den Hout, M. A., & Weber, W. E. (2001). Pain catastrophizing predicts pain intensity, disability, and psychological distress independent of level of physical impairment. *Clinical Journal of Pain, 17*, 165–172.

Sharp, T. J. & Harvey, A. G. (2001). Chronic pain and Posttraumatic Stress Disorder: Mutual maintenance? *Clinical Psychology Review, 21*, 857–877.

Sherman, J. J., Turk, D. C., & Okifuji, A. (2000). Prevalence and impact of Posttraumatic Stress Disorder-like symptoms on patients with fibromyalgia syndrome. *The Clinical Journal of Pain, 16*, 127–134.

Shipherd, J. C, Beck, J. G., Hamblen, J. L., Lackner, J. M., & Freeman, J. B. (2003). A preliminary examination of treatment for Posttraumatic Stress Disorder in chronic pain patients: A case study. *Journal of Traumatic Stress, 16*, 451–457.

Steward, M. S., & O'Connor, J. (1994). Pediatric pain, trauma, and memory. *Current Opinion in Pediatrics, 6*, 411–417.

Stoddard, F. J. & Saxe, G. (2001). Ten-year research review of physical injuries. *Journal of the American Academy of Child and Adolescent Psychiatry, 40*, 1128–1145.

Tarnowski, K. J. & Brown, R. T. (1999). Burn injuries. In A. J. Goreczny & M. Hersen (Eds.). *Handbook of Pediatric and Adolescent Health Psychology*. Needham, MA: Allyn & Bacon.

Taylor, S. (2003). Anxiety sensitivity and its implications for understanding and treating PTSD. *Journal of Cognitive Psychotherapy: An International Quarterly, 17(2)*, 179–186.

Taylor, S. & Koch, W. J. (1995). Anxiety disorders due to motor vehicle accidents: Nature and treatment. *Clinical Psychology Review, 15*, 721–738.

Taylor, S., Koch, W. J., & McNally, R. J. (1992). How does anxiety sensitivity vary across the anxiety disorders? *Journal of Anxiety Disorders, 6*, 249–259.

Toomey, T. C., Seville, J. L., Abashian, S. W., Finkel, A. G., & Mann, J. D. (1994). *Circumstances of Chronic Pain Onset: Relationship to Pain Description, Coping and Psychological Distress*. 23rd American Pain Society Annual Scientific Meeting, Vancouver, BC Canada. Abstract A-76.

Turk, D. C. & Okifuji, A. (1996). Perception of traumatic onset, compensation status, and physical findings: Impact on pain severity, emotional distress, and disability in chronic pain patients. *Journal of Behavioral Medicine, 19*, 435–453.

Turk, D. C. & Rudy, T. E. (1988). Toward an empirically derived taxonomy of chronic pain patients: Integration of psychological assessment data. *Journal of Consulting and Clinical Psychology, 56*, 233–238.

Turk, D. C., Kerns, R. D., & Rosenberg, R. (1992). Effects of marital interaction on chronic pain and disability: examining the down side of social support. *Rehabilitation Psychology, 37*, 259–274.

Turk, D. C., Okifuji, A., Starz, T. W., & Sinclaire, J. D. (1996). Effects of type of symptom onset on psychological distress and disability in fibromyalgia syndrome patients. *Pain, 68*, 678–681.

Tushima, W. T. & Stoddard, V. M. (1990). Ethnic group similarities in the biofeedback treatment of pain. *Medical Psychotherapy, 3*, 69–75.

Vlaeyen, J. W. S., & Linton, S. J. (2000). Fear-avoidance and its consequences in musculoskeletal pain: A state of the art. *Pain, 85*, 317–332.

Waddell, G., Newton, M., Henderson, I., Sommerville, D., & Main, C. J. (1993). Fear avoidance beliefs questionnaire (FABQ) and the role of fear-avoidance beliefs in chronic low back pain and disability. *Pain, 52*, 157–168.

Weathers, F. W., Litz, B. T., Herman, D. S., Huska, J. A., & Keane, T. M. (1993). The PTSD Checklist (PCL): Reliability, validity, and diagnostic utility. Paper presented at the annual meeting of the International Society for Traumatic Stress Studies.

White, P. & Faustman, W. (1989). Coexisting physical conditions among inpatients with Posttraumatic Stress Disorder. *Military Medicine, 154*, 66–71.

Wilson, J., P. & Keane, T. M. (2004). *Assessing Psychological Trauma and PTSD*. New York: Guilford Press.

Wood K. B., Garvey, T. A., Gundry, C., & Heithoff, K. B. (1995). Magnetic resonance imaging of the thoracic spine. Evaluation of asymptomatic individuals. *Journal of Bone Joint Surgery, 77(11)*, 1631–1638.

Xuemei, R., Pietrobon, Sun, S., Liu, G., & Hey, L. (2004). Estimates and patterns of direct healthcare expenditures among individuals with back pain in the US. *Spine, 29(1)*, 79–86.

Zvolensky, M. J., Eifert, G. H., Lejuez, C. W., Hopko, D. R., & Forsyth, J. P. (2000). Assessing the perceived predictability of anxiety-related events: A report on the perceived predictability index, *Journal of Behavior Therapy and Experimental Psychiatry, 31*, 201–218.

Section 5

Traumatic Brain Injury

15

Mild Traumatic Brain Injury: Definitions

Jeffrey T. Barth, Ronald Ruff, and Patricia Espe-Pfeifer

1. Forensic Neuropsychology

Forensic neuropsychology is one of the fastest growing subspecializations within clinical neuropsychology (Sweet et al., 2000). Prior to 1980, neuropsychologists had very little impact on court decisions (Taylor, 1999). Twenty years later, most practicing neuropsychologists are involved in forensic evaluations. It is noteworthy that these forensic assessments typically involve mild traumatic brain injuries (mTBIs). This is because most neurological disorders (e.g., multiple sclerosis, Alzheimer's disease, Huntington's disease, Parkinson's disease, cerebrovascular disease) do not result in litigation, except when the treatment is below the standard of care and a medical malpractice claim is filed. Patients with TBIs, however, are far more likely to enter into litigation, because the cause of their neurological illness is neither genetic nor brought on by another disorder. Instead, often the brain traumas are caused by accidents that involve the responsibility of another party (e.g., a driver being rear-ended by another driver, a pedestrian being struck by a motor vehicle while crossing an intersection, a heavy object falling on the head of an individual).

What strengths or advantages does neuropsychology offer to the court? An expert must assist the triers of fact (judges and juries) in understanding the biopsychosocial sequelae of mTBI and the resultant cognitive, emotional, and physical symptoms. Psychometric instruments are typically very sensitive and their use must be balanced by a careful evaluation of the litigant's history, onset of symptoms, symptom course, functional effects, and level of motivation, effort, and potential for secondary gain (e.g., malingering). Neuropsychologists are called upon to provide the court with scientifically valid assessments of neurocognitive and emotional functions and their relationship to cerebral trauma and recovery. As experts, neuropsychologists are ethically obligated to base their opinions on solid scientific methodology, bearing in mind that it is a research-driven discipline. Thus, the benefits that clinical neuropsychology should provide to the triers of fact are empirically derived quantifications of the patient's cognitive and emotional status postinjury.

What are the weaknesses or disadvantages of forensic neuropsychology? From the perspective of neurologists, a subcommittee of the American Academy of Neurology (1996, p. 595) offered the following conclusion:

Neuropsychological information is subject to intensive scrutiny in forensic proceedings and can be successfully challenged if it is over interpreted, obtained during the acute phase of an injury or when the patient is taking medications that might affect performance, ignores the presence of depression or anxiety when the tests were performed, or fails to take premorbid characteristics, developmental irregularities, and substance abuse into account.

These issues must be carefully addressed in a comprehensive forensic neuropsychological report. The higher the standard of science that is relied upon, the more value the neuropsychologist provides to the patient and to the courts. For patients with Postconcussional Disorder (i.e., those mTBI patients who fall in the "Miserable Minority" of patients with slow or poor recovery), the neuropsychologist's expertise is ideally suited for examining the interactions among premorbid, comorbid and postcomorbid symptoms (Ruff, 1999; Ruff & Hibbard, 2003; Ruff et al., 1996a, 1996b).

In the U.S. because board certification in neuropsychology is not mandated by any of the 50 State Boards of Psychology or any neuropsychological organization such as the National Academy of Neuropsychology, International Neuropsychological Association, or Division 40 of the American Psychological Association, being a licensed psychologist and well trained as a neuropsychologist with 2 years of supervised experience is sufficient to qualify as a forensic expert. The expert must remember that the purpose of testifying is to assist the jurors or judge in making important decisions based on scientific evaluations and clinical judgments. The expert's role is not that of an advocate or warrior. Our discipline is not well served by attacks on colleagues. Moreover, being highly competitive and advocating on behalf of the plaintiff or defense is a trap that must be avoided in an independent neuropsychological examination. Forensic neuropsychologists are well advised to be scientists and clinicians who are advocates for truth being accurate in their services to the courts.

2. Epidemiology

Since the mid-1970s and early 1980s, public health and health care communities have become increasingly aware of the negative impact that mTBIs have on society (Barth et al., 1996; National Center for Injury Prevention and Disease Control, 2003). Although the term "mild" is used to describe this category of head injury, the term is misleading because the long-term or permanent physical, cognitive, emotional, social, and vocational impairments and disabilities that can arise from mTBI can be quite significant.

A September 2003 report by the Centers for Disease Control and Prevention (CDC) estimated that as many as 75% of the 1.5 million TBIs that are documented each year are classified as mild in severity. Given that many individuals who sustain an mTBI do not seek treatment and/or receive medical care immediately following injury, these statistics are an underestimation and provide only a glimpse of the true magnitude of this epidemic. A review of the literature suggests that mTBIs account for approximately 50–75% of all patients hospitalized with a brain injury (McAllister, 1994). People between the ages of 15 and 34 comprise the group that is at highest risk for incidence of mTBI in the United States (Parker, 2001). Guerrero et al. (2000) reported that an estimated 15% of persons who sustain an mTBI continue to experience serious, self-reported negative consequences 1 year postinjury. Unemployment rates among previously employed mTBI victims were reported to be 34% at 3 months and 9% at 12 months postinjury in an early study (Rimel et al., 1981).

3.   Causes and Mechanisms of mTBI

Although numerous events can result in a head injury, the leading causes of mTBI are motor vehicle accidents (42%; occupant, motorcyclist, pedestrian, bicyclist), falls (24%), assaults with a firearm (14%), and sports-related concussions (12%) (Parker, 2001). Regardless of the mode of injury, clinical research has shown that there is clear neuropathological evidence to suggest that diffuse physiological and metabolic disruption can occur with mTBI (Barth et al., 2002; Bigler, 1990; Binder & Rattock, 1989; Hovda et al., 1994). Notably, some of the pathophysiologic changes may not occur immediately, but could take hours or days to develop (Barth et al., 2002). The rapid acceleration and subsequent deceleration that occurs during events such as motor vehicle accidents, falls, and sports-related concussions can cause shear–strain effects. Shear–strain effects occur when axonal fibers stretch and break because of rotational and deceleration forces in the head injury (Bigler, 1990). The generalized and widespread cellular damage that occurs secondary to acceleration–deceleration and rotational forces of the brain inside the skull is referred to as diffuse axonal injury. Related histological changes such as extracellular potassium flow in intracellular influx of calcium is also problematic in mTBI, and reversing this process can take days. Mild traumatic brain injury can lead to disruptions in cerebral autoregulation, which is the metabolic system that serves to maintain sufficient cerebral blood flow to facilitate homeostasis between blood supply and cellular glucose metabolism demands. Mild traumatic brain injury may also lead to slowed cerebral blood flow, which, again, may not reach a maximum until several days postinjury.

4.   Lack of Unified Definition for mTBI

Mild traumatic brain injury is one of the most common neurological disorders that clinical neuropsychologists assess. In contrast to moderate or severe brain injuries that are associated with extended periods of unconsciousness (> 30 minutes), greater than 24 hours of posttraumatic amnesia, or penetrating skull injury, mTBI results in less than 20 (or 30) minutes of unconsciousness or a brief alteration in consciousness and no serious extracranial injuries. Although the distinction between mTBI and more severe head trauma appears straightforward, the establishment of definitive, measurable criteria to identify and quantify the occurrence of mTBI has proven challenging. Such challenges have occurred because clinicians and investigators have been using different diagnostic criteria and methodologies to study this condition (Ruff & Jurica, 1999). As a result, the field of neuropsychology has lacked an accepted and unified definition for mTBI. For example, there are multiple overlapping terms and descriptors used in the literature when describing mTBI, such as cerebral concussion, minor head injury, minor brain injury, minor head trauma, minor traumatic brain injury, complicated mild head injury, Postconcussional Disorder, the silent epidemic, and the miserable minority.

Originally, mTBIs were termed "mild head injury." One of the initial research definitions for mild head injury was developed by investigators at the University of Virginia in the early 1980s and included the following: head injury with Glasgow Coma Scale greater than 12, loss of consciousness of less than 20 minutes, and hospitalization less than 48 hours (Barth et al., 1996, 2002). This definition was later expanded to include the absence of neuroimaging data of cerebral lesion(s) (Levin et al., 1987, 1989). Over the past 20 years, minor modifications and variations of this definition have been the mainstay for mild head injury and concussion research within the field of neuropsychology, and incorporating the term mTBI [which was championed by the American Congress of Rehabilitation Medicine (1993)] in place of mild head injury has helped sensitize the health care community and society to the potential seriousness of this trauma.

In the September 2003 CDC report to Congress on mild brain injury in the United States (National Center for Injury Prevention and Disease Control, 2003, p. 16), mTBI was defined as an occurrence of injury to the head resulting from blunt trauma or acceleration or deceleration forces with one or more of the following conditions attributable to the head injury: (1) any period of observed or self-reported transient confusion, disorientation, or impaired consciousness; (2) any period of observed or self-reported dysfunction of memory (amnesia) around the time of the injury; (3) observed signs of other neurological or neuropsychological dysfunction such as seizures acutely following head injury; irritability, lethargy, or vomiting following head injury among infants and very young children, and symptoms among older children and adults such as headache, dizziness, irritability, fatigue, or poor concentration when identified soon after injury; and (4) any period of observed or self-reported loss of consciousness lasting 30 minutes or less. Even though there is no universally accepted definition of mTBI, the World Health Organization Collaborating Center for Neurotrauma Task Force on Mild Traumatic Brain Injury in its review of methodological issues in the study of mTBI recommended common definitional criteria in future research (Carroll et al., 2004). Their recommended definition of mTBI included

an acute brain injury resulting from mechanical energy to the head from external physical forces. Operational criteria for clinical identification include: (i) 1 or more of the following: confusion or disorientation, loss of consciousness for 30 minutes or less, post traumatic amnesia for less than 24 hours,, and/or other transient neurological abnormalities such as focal signs, seizures, and intracranial lesions not requiring surgery; (ii) Glasgow Coma Scale score of 13–15 after 30 minutes post-injury or later upon presentation for healthcare (Carroll et al., 2004, p. 115).

Neuropsychological assessment of cognitive and psychological sequelae as well as interview and observation are the recognized methods used to verify the diagnosis of mTBI.

5.   Lack of Objective Data for Postconcussion Syndrome

The terms "Postconcussional Disorder" (PCD) and "Postconcussive Syndrome" (PCS) refer to the acquired physical, emotional, and cognitive symptoms that persist at least 3 months following a cerebral concussion or mTBI (Ruff, 1999). In the past, organic bases for the persistence of neurocognitive complaints were often dismissed in favor of psychological or motivational explanations (Lucas, 1998). However, prospective studies have shown that prolonged symptomatology is found after cerebral concussion, particularly in light of the structural and metabolic changes that take place within the brain following acceleration–deceleration injuries (Binder & Rattok, 1989). Although it has been estimated that 80–90% of all individuals with a single uncomplicated mTBI will eventually have a successful recovery, approximately 10–20% of patients with mTBIs continue to experience serious, negative symptoms 1 year after their injury (Guerrero et al., 2000; Ruff, 1999). It has been estimated that after 1 month, 88% of patients continued to experience symptoms, including headaches (71%), reduced energy levels (60%), and dizziness (53%); yet by 3 months postinjury, the vast majority of mTBI patients have made full recoveries (Dikmen et al., 1986). However, the nature of PCS remains controversial because of several findings, including the lack of objective data to support the constellation of symptoms and the lack of a generally accepted outcome measures for mTBI. Parker (2001) suggested that controversy arises from the findings that seemingly mild trauma to the head, even in the absence of loss of consciousness, can cause neurocognitive dysfunction and the variability of physiological and psychological symptoms among individuals.

TABLE 15.1. Common Terms and Definitions

Term	Definition
Acceleration–deceleration injury	Brain injury typically noted at the cellular level (diffuse axonal injury), caused by high-speed deceleration.
Anterograde amnesia	An inability to learn new information subsequent to a brain trauma.
Cerebral autoregulation	System that serves to maintain sufficient cerebral flow to balance blood supply and cellular glucose metabolism demands (i.e., facilitate homeostasis).
Cerebral concussion	Mild traumatic brain injury with posttraumatic amnesia and/or a brief or no loss of consciousness; typically no permanent neuropathological deficits or changes.
Complicated mild head injury	Trauma to the head that results in sequelae that meet the criteria for mild head injury but that reveals neuroimaging evidence of a related cerebral lesion; may also refer to mild head injury with persistent postconcussion disorder.
Diffuse axonal injury	Widespread histological brain trauma characterized by stretching and breaking of neuronal fibers, usually secondary to acceleration–deceleration and rotational forces of the brain inside the skull.
Glasgow Coma Scale (GCS)	A brief head injury observational scale that assesses the general level of consciousness and correlates moderately with severity of injury. This measure involves the evaluation of a patient's best oculomotor, verbal, and motor responses, yielding a severity score from 3 to 15 (3–8, severe; 9–12, moderate; 13–15, mild).
Glucose metabolism	The use of glucose (sugars) to create energy for neural activation related to cerebral autoregulation.
Mild traumatic brain injury	Blunt trauma or acceleration–deceleration injury to the brain resulting in a GCS > 12, some brief alteration in consciousness that is less than 20–30 minutes, and a posttraumatic amnesia of less that 24 hours.
Postconcussional Disorder; Postconcussion Syndrome	A constellation of symptoms including one or more of the following: headache, dizziness, nausea, vomiting, memory, learning and problem-solving impairment, attentional difficulties, problems in abstract reasoning, confusion, fatigue, frustration, depression, sleep disturbance, apathy, diplopia, tinnitus, and slowed thinking, which may persist in some mild head injuries for 3 months postinjury or longer. Postconcussional disorder is the term used in the DSM-IV and Postconcussion Syndrome is the terminology listed in the International Classification of Diseases-9-CM.
Posttraumatic amnesia	A disturbance of memory and confusion for events immediately following a brain injury.
Retrograde amnesia	Deficient recall of events preceding the onset of the brain injury.
Second impact syndrome	An often catastrophic neurological trauma resulting from two mild head injuries in close temporal proximity to each other involving disconnection of the cerebral blood flow autoregulation system, vascular engorgement, and intracranial pressure, resulting in significant morbidity and/or mortality.
Shear strain	Stretching and breaking of the axonal fibers because of rotational and deceleration forces in mild head injury. Shearing trauma is usually associated with diffuse axonal injury, but it may also be focal in nature.

6.   Clarification of Some of the Symptoms of PCS and PCD

Postconcussion Syndrome and PCD are defined as a constellation of physical, emotional, and cognitive symptoms, including one or more of the following: headache, dizziness, nausea, vomiting, memory, learning, and problem-solving impairment, attentional difficulties, problems in abstract reasoning, confusion, fatigue, frustration, depression, sleep disturbance, apathy, diplopia, tinnitus, and slowed thinking, which might persist in some mild head injuries for 3 months postinjury or longer. Although the two terms share the same definition, they differ in regard to classification system. Postconcussional Disorder is the term used in the *Diagnostic and Statistical Manual of Mental Disorders* (American Psychiatric Association, 2000) and Postconcussion Syndrome is the terminology listed in the International Classification of Diseases-9-CM (Hart & Hopkins, 2003–2004).

7.   Terminology

The terminology with definitions is provided in Table 15.1.

References

American Academy of Neurology (Therapeutics and Technology Assessment Subcommittee). (1996). Assessment: Neuropsychological testing of adults: Consideration for neurologists. *Neurology, 47*, 592–599.

American Congress of Rehabilitation Medicine. (1993). Definition of mild traumatic brain injury. *Journal of Head Trauma Rehabilitation, 8(3)*, 86–87.

American Psychiatric Association. (2000). *Diagnostic and Statistical Manual of Mental Disorders*, 4th ed. Washington, DC: American Psychiatric Association.

Barth, J. T., Diamond, R., & Errico, A. (1996). Mild head injury and post concussion syndrome: Does anyone really suffer? *Clinical Electroencephalography, 27(4)*, 183–186.

Barth, J. T., Freeman, J. R., & Broshek, D. K. (2002). Mild head injury. In *Encyclopedia of the Human Brain, V.S. Ramachandran, ed*. New York: Elsevier, Vol. 3, pp. 81–91.

Bigler, E. D. (Ed.). (1990). *Traumatic Brain Injury: Mechanisms of Damage, Assessment, Intervention, and Outcome*. Austin, TX: Pro-Ed.

Binder, L. M. & Rattok, J. (1989). Assessment of the postconcussive syndrome after mild head trauma. In M. Lezak (Ed.). *Frontiers of Clinical Neuroscience, Volume 7, Assessment of the Behavioral Consequences of Head Trauma*. New York: Liss, pp. 37–48.

Carroll, L. J., Cassidy, D., Holm, L., Kraus, J., & Coronado, V. G. (2004). Methodological issues and research recommendations for mild traumatic brain injury: The WHO Collaborating Center Task Force on Mild Traumatic Brain Injury. *Journal of Rehabilitation Medicine, 43(Suppl.)*, 113–125.

Dikmen, S., McLean, A., & Temkin, N. (1986). Neuropsychological and psychosocial consequences of minor head injury. *Journal of Neurology, Neurosurgery, and Psychiatry, 49*, 1227–1232.

Guerrero, J., Thurman, D. J., & Sniezek, J. E. (2000). Emergency department visits associated with traumatic brain injury: United States, 1995–1996. *Brain Injury, 14(2)*, 181–186.

Hart, A. C., & Hopkins, C. A. (Eds.). (2003–2004). *International Classification of Diseases*, 9th rev., 6th ed. Salt Lake City; Utah: St. Anthony Publishing/Medicode.

Hovda, D. A., Le, H. M., Lifshitz, J., Berry, J. A., Badie, H., Yoshino, A., & Lee, S. M. (1994). Long terms changes in metabolic rates for glucose following mild, moderate, and severe concussive head injuries in adult rats. *Society of Neurosciences, 20*, 845 (abstract).

Lucas, J. (1998). Traumatic brain injury: In P. Synder and P. Nussbaum (Eds.). *Clinical Neuropsychology*. Washington, DC: American Psychological Association, pp. 243–265.

Levin, H. S., Eisenberg, H. M., & Benton, A. L. (Eds.). (1989). *Mild Head Injury*. New York: Oxford University Press.

Levin, H. S., Mattis, S., Ruff, R. M., Eisenberg, H. M., Marshall, L. F., Tabaddor, K., & High, W. M, Jr. (1987). Neurobehavioral outcome following minor head injury: A three-center study. *Journal of Neurosurgery, 66*, 234–243.

McAllister, T. (1994). Mild traumatic brain injury and the post concussive syndrome. In J. Silver, S. Yudofsky, & R. Hales (Eds.). *The Neuropsychiatry of Traumatic Brain Injury*. Washington, DC: American Psychiatric Press, pp. 357–392.

National Center for Injury Prevention and Disease Control. (2003). *Report to Congress on Mild Traumatic Brain Injury in the United States: Steps to Prevent a Serious Public Health Problem*. Atlanta, GA: Centers for Disease Control and Prevention.

Parker, R. S. (Ed.). (2001). *Concussive Brain Trauma: Neurobehavioral Impairment and Maladaption*. London: CRC Press.

Rimel, R. W., Giordani, B., Barth, J. T., Boll, T. J., & Jane, J. A. (1981). Disability caused by minor head injury. *Neurosurgery, 9*, 221–228.

Ruff, R. M. (1999). Discipline specific approach vs. individual care. In N. R. Varney & R. J. Roberts (Eds.). *Mild Head Injury: Causes, Evaluation and Treatment*. Mahwah, NJ: Erlbaum, pp. 99–113.

Ruff, R. M. & Hibbard, K. (2003). *Ruff Neurobehavioral Inventory*. Odessa, FL: Psychological Assessment Resources.

Ruff, R. M., & Jurica, P. J. (1999). In search of a unified definition for mild traumatic brain injury. *Brain Injury, 13*, 943–952.

Ruff, R. M., Camenzuli, L. F., & Mueller, J. (1996a). Miserable minority: Emotional risk factors that influence the outcome following mild traumatic brain injury. *Brain Injury, 10*, 551–565.

Ruff, R. M., Mueller, J., & Jurica, P. J. (1996b). Estimating premorbid functioning levels after traumatic brain injury. *Neurorehabilitation, 7*, 39–53.

Sweet, J. J., Moberg, P. J., & Suchy, Y. (2000). Ten-year follow-up survey of clinical neuropsychologists. *The Clinical Neuropsychologist, 4*, 479–495.

Taylor, J. S. (1999). The legal environment pertaining to clinical neuropsychology. In J. J. Sweet (Ed.). *Forensic Neuropsychology*. Lisse, The Netherlands: Swets & Zeitlinger, pp. 419–442.

16

Mild Traumatic Brain Injury: Neuropsychological Causality Modelling

RODNEY D. VANDERPLOEG, HEATHER G. BELANGER, AND GLENN CURTISS

An individual with a mild traumatic brain injury (mTBI) will, by definition, have a Glasgow Coma Scale score (GCS) (Teasdale & Jennett, 1974) of 13–15 within 30 minutes of injury (i.e., typically by the time they are initially assessed by emergency medical personnel). Thus, within 30 minutes of injury, they obey commands and, at worst, may be disoriented and consequently have confused or inappropriate speech. Also by definition, disorientation, if present, lasts less than 1 day. Approximately 70–90% of patients who sustain TBIs have had a mild TBI (Cassidy et al., 2004). Mild TBI is believed to result when injury triggers a pathologic neurochemical cascade, but it is insufficient to produce widespread neuronal dysfunction or the axonal disruption that characterizes more severe brain injuries. The majority of these patients make excellent neurobehavioral recovery, but some have persistent and at times disabling symptoms (Carroll et al., 2004; see also Chapter 18 by Nicholson and Martelli). The formal criteria for mTBI have been defined by the American Congress of Rehabilitation Medicine (1993) (see Chapter 15 by Barth et al. for a discussion of these criteria).

In TBI cohort-based neuroimaging studies, Borg and colleagues (2004) report that 5% of individuals who have a GCS score of 15, 20% with a GCS score of 14, and 30% with GCS score of 13 have abnormal findings on clinical computed tomography (CT). However, in those with an initial GCS of 13–15 (i.e., mTBI), if clinical neuroimaging findings are present, the classification changes to "complicated mTBI," which has a 6-month outcome more similar to moderate TBI (Williams et al., 1990). In this chapter, mTBI will be used to refer only to individuals with normal initial clinical neuroimaging findings.

1. Causality in mTBI: A Traditional Medical Approach

The persistence of symptoms following mTBI in a minority of individuals has led to mTBI being a controversial diagnosis in the medical–legal arena.

Proving that mTBI is the cause of ongoing symptoms, particularly in the absence of objective findings such as neuroimaging abnormalities or clear cognitive impairments on formal neuropsychological testing, is extremely challenging. Traditionally, medical causality follows a linear model in which a specific event (infection, injury, etc.) leads to symptoms, which are verified by history, medical examination, and diagnostic tests. A diagnosis is established when findings point to one particular etiological explanation and are inconsistent with alternative etiologies.

A traditional medical model of causality in the mTBI area is dependent on several factors. First, a clear traumatic event, potentially severe enough to disrupt brain functioning, must have occurred. Second, the initial clinical presentation following that event must meet the criteria for mTBI (i.e., a physiologic disruption of brain function resulting in a relatively short period of unconsciousness or disturbed consciousness). Third, ongoing or emerging symptoms must be consistent with brain dysfunction and must not be attributable to other etiological factors. Fourth, brain injury or dysfunction must be demonstrated on one or more evaluation tests or procedures, and the specific nature of that documented impairment must be consistent with the clinical history as well as with the symptoms and problems reported.

Each of these four conditions is at times difficult to demonstrate in mTBI. First, not all traumatic injurious events are witnessed. A person may be a victim of a hit-and-run driver or a person may slip on a wet floor, fall, and have a head injury, but the fall might not have been witnessed. Second, any period of disturbed consciousness may resolve before it can be assessed and documented by medical personnel. Therefore, for both of the first two conditions necessary to establish causality, medical personnel often must rely solely on the self-report of the individual who is claiming damages. Difficulty with the third causality condition is that many if not all of the symptoms and complaints associated with mTBI overlap with normal day-to-day complaints or those of other medical or psychiatric conditions. Thus, establishing the injury-related historical emergence and course of symptoms is crucial. Again, however, such a careful historical documentation is often dependent on the individual who is claiming damages or his/her family. Finally, for the fourth condition, by definition, individuals with mTBI (at least uncomplicated mTBI) have normal findings on the medical tests most often used to demonstrate brain damage—clinical CT or magnetic resonance imaging (MRI) scans. Neuropsychological evaluation of cognitive functioning or electrophysiological studies such as electroencephalograms (EEGs) or event-related potentials can only help establish mTBI causality if a clear pattern of findings emerges that is consistent with an established medical literature of impaired performance or functional abnormalities associated with mTBI and not associated with other medical or psychiatric conditions. Unfortunately, from a causality perspective, again there is significant overlap in cognitive impairments and electrophysiological findings with multiple medical conditions such as depression, alcohol or other substance abuse, hypertension-related cerebral vascular difficulties, and multiple sclerosis, to name just a few. It is these last two causality conditions to which we turn our attention.

2.   The Medical Literature: Necessary Causality Conditions

2.1.   *Symptom Complaints: The Postconcussion Syndrome*

There is no doubt that a mTBI causes acute disruption of brain functioning. The individual who sustains a mTBI initially is at best dazed, confused, and temporarily disoriented, and often has memory gaps for the injury itself and for some period of time thereafter (seconds to hours). At worst, the individual is clearly unconscious for up to 30 minutes. Still controversial, however, are questions of how long the disruption of normal brain functioning lasts and whether symptoms and impairments continue long-term or eventually resolve.

Formal diagnostic criteria for postconcussion syndrome (PCS) vary between the *Diagnostic and Statistical Manual of Mental Disorders*, 4th ed. (DSM-IV) (American Psychiatric Association 1994) and the *International Statistical Classification of Disease and Related Health Problems*, 10th ed. (ICD-10) (World Health Organization, 1992). PCS is not an official diagnostic category in the DSM-IV. Rather, it is a set of proposed diagnostic criteria for investigation and includes not only the symptom complaints described earlier but also neuropsychological evidence of attention or memory difficulty. The ICD-10 criteria are not investigational and do not require evidence of neuropsychological dysfunction. In addition, the ICD-10 suggests that there may be hypochondriacal preoccupation, whereas the DSM-IV does not discuss this possible presentation. Despite the differences, the complex of symptom complaints is quite similar between the two classification systems. In this section, the term PCS will be used to describe the cluster of symptoms rather than specific diagnostic criteria.

2.1.1.   PCS as a Neurologically Based Disorder

Various studies have demonstrated that symptoms of PCS are found not only in brain-injured but also in normal individuals where base rates are as high as 10–20% (Mittenberg et al., 1992; Vanderploeg et al., submitted). Nonetheless, some researchers posit that persistent PCS reflects subtle neurological dysfunction allegedly beneath the detection threshold of routine diagnostic procedures such as CT, MRI, and EEG conducted shortly after injury (Hayes & Dixon, 1994; Miller, 1996; Povlishock & Coburn, 1989). Indeed, Vanderploeg and colleagues (submitted) found that compared to controls, an mTBI doubled the likelihood of a current PCS and resulted in an increased frequency of neurologic (50–250% increase) and cognitive postconcussion symptoms (75–280% increase), but minimal increase in psychological post-concussion symptoms (0–36% increase).

2.1.2.   The Role of Expectation on PCS Symptoms

Others contend, however, that PCS symptoms are the result of psychological mechanisms such as poor coping styles (Bohnen et al., 1992; Marsh & Smith, 1995), emotional reactions to an adverse event (Bryant & Harvey, 1999), or expectations of symptoms that may occur following an mTBI (Mittenberg et al., 1992). Soliciting expected symptoms using a 30-item symptom checklist for PCS, Mittenberg and colleagues (1992) demonstrated that control subjects (n = 223) asked to imagine symptoms following a head injury reported very similar symptom profiles to individuals who had experienced an mTBI (n = 100). Head-injured subjects reported an average of 13.8 symptoms (SD = 8.3), whereas the control group anticipated an average of 14.8 symptoms (SD = 7.6). Further, findings suggested that those with mTBI underestimated their premorbid problems with concentration by about 9% but reported postinjury levels of concentration problems at levels consistent with "expected post-mTBI levels" reported by control subjects. Thus, this and other studies by Mittenberg and colleagues clearly identify expectation as a psychological variable that has a significant influence on severity of PCS following mTBI.

2.1.3.   Concomitant Psychological Issues and PCS Symptoms

Other studies have demonstrated that concomitant psychiatric difficulties also are important moderators of PCS. King (1996) reported that depression, anxiety, and stress within 1 week of mild to moderate head injury were highly predictive of severity of postconcussion symptoms 3 months postinjury. Further, pre-existing psychiatric disturbance and psychosocial problems are often found in symptomatic mTBI patients (Binder et al., 1997; Fenton et al., 1993; Greiffenstein & Baker, 2001; Robertson et al., 1994) and tend to complicate recovery from mild head injury (Fann et al., 1995). Female gender, older age, social difficulties, and environmental stress are also associated with chronic symptoms (Fenton et al., 1993; Gouvier et al., 1992; Radanov et al., 1991, 1999; Santa Maria et al., 2001; Wood et al., 1984). Finally, pain (including headaches) and sleep problems are significantly associated with postconcussive symptoms (Nicholson, 2000; Perlis, Artiola, & Giles, 1997) (see Chapter 18 by Nicholson & Martelli).

Secondary gain or financial incentive (Lees-Haley & Brown, 1993; Youngjohn et al., 1995) also can play a significant role in PCS. According to a meta-analytic review that included approximately 20 different samples, the effect of financial incentive on outcome following mTBI is quite large [effect size = 0.47 (Binder & Rohling, 1996)]. That is, litigating subjects with mTBI performed on average about a half of a standard deviation more poorly than control subjects.

2.1.4.   Methodological and Patient Selection Factors and PCS Symptoms

Interpretation of findings regarding PCS are further complicated by method-ological issues. The vast majority of studies on this topic have used referred, symptomatic subjects (Gasquoine, 1997). Patients with ongoing complaints are more likely to seek treatment and compensation than those in the general population of mTBI sufferers. Identifying salient variables that exert an influence on the presence of PCS and its relationship to the natural recovery from mTBI requires the use of an epidemiologically-based or nonreferred sample. For example, Luis et al. (2003) examined the contribution of multi-ple factors in predicting persistent PCS in a nonclinical, population-based mTBI sample and found that pre-existing psychiatric difficulties, demo-graphic and social support variables, and severity of the mTBI accounted for 33% of the variance in the presence of PCS. A self-reported loss of con-sciousness (LOC) or memory gap was associated with a 57% increase in PCS symptom frequency. Altered consciousness (i.e., clear mTBI findings) had the largest adverse impact in those with less "cognitive reserve" or resilience where LOC doubled the prevalence of PCS, whereas higher levels of intelligence or cognitive reserve were protective against the long-term adverse effects of mTBI on PCS outcomes.

2.1.5.   PCS Conclusions

The evidence reviewed reveals that although the injury to the brain sustained in an mTBI, as indicated by altered consciousness, plays a role in the experi-ence of PCS, the development of PCS is, in part, dependent on self-expecta-tions regarding the likely effects of an mTBI. In addition, the presence of PCS is mediated by factors such as individual resilience (cognitive reserve), pre-existing psychological status, and psychosocial support.

2.2.   Tests of Brain Structure and Function

Evidence of mTBI from tests of brain structure and function is more fre-quently being introduced into legal proceedings. However, there are several important methodological issues to consider when evaluating the literature on neurophysiological and neuropsychological sequelae of mTBI. One is whether the study included a random selection of all individuals who sus-tained an mTBI or was limited to subsamples reporting ongoing post-mTBI symptoms. Positive findings associated with only symptomatic individuals could reflect something unique to the symptom complaints irrespective of etiology (i.e., mTBI or alternative etiological factors such as depression, anx-iety, stress, pain, or even internal thought processes such as the belief of brain damage). A second methodological concern is the postinjury evaluation time point. Positive findings within the first couple of weeks or months post-mTBI would be expected given the nature of the mild injuries and the acute disruption of brain functioning. However, whether or not this dysfunction represents a stable and chronic condition is an important medical–legal consideration. A third methodological concern is whether potential physiological, imaging, or cognitive abnormalities have any reliable external clinical correlates. If not, it is impossible to know the importance or relevance of such positive findings.

2.2.1.   Neuroimaging Findings

Neuroimaging can broadly be defined as a set of techniques that attempts to capture the structural, functional, or metabolic status of the brain. Structural imaging techniques such as clinical CT or MRI do not reflect abnormalities in patients with mild uncomplicated TBI, even in those patients with neurobehavioral deficits (Levin et al., 1987). This may be either because there is no structural brain damage or because current technology is unable to detect it. Certainly, microscopic diffuse axonal injury (DAI), if present in mTBI patients, is not detectable using traditional neuroimaging techniques (Adams et al., 1989; Mittl et al., 1994). Therefore, the discussion of positive neuroimaging findings in mild uncomplicated TBI must necessarily be limited to "experimental" techniques. Discussions of these techniques will follow.

2.2.1.1.   Structural Neuroimaging Finding

Diffusion tensor imaging (DTI) is a relatively new MRI technique that capitalizes on the diffusion of water molecules for imaging the brain. Only one study (Arfanakis et al., 2002) has been conducted with mTBI patients. Five patients with mTBI were examined within 24 hours of injury and two were retested 1 month postinjury. The mTBI patients demonstrated reduced directional axonal diffusion in white matter relative to 10 control participants. This was true for both mTBI patients within 24 hours and at 1 month postinjury. Studies have not yet been conducted to determine if chronic mTBI patients have similar abnormal DTI findings. It is also unknown whether DTI abnormalities in mTBI have clinical relevance or are predictive of outcome.

Magnetization transfer imaging (MTI) is a technique that increases the contrast between tissues. Bagley et al. (2000) scanned 28 patients of varying severity, 1–29 days postinjury. Of five patients with mTBI (GCS = 13–15), only one had abnormal magnetization transfer ratio findings. However, these authors conducted another study focusing specifically on 13 patients with mTBI (McGowan et al., 2000), 12 of whom had normal MRI scans. They found significantly lowered MTR in patients relative to controls in the splenium but not the pons. Only 2 neuropsychological measures (of the 25 given) showed a significant correlation with regional MTR values. Finally, Sinson et al. (2001) reported abnormal MTR in four patients with mTBI (GCS = 15). However, these findings were not related to outcome 3 months postinjury. In summary, MTI with mTBI patients inconsistently detects abnormalities within the first month or two following mTBI, and the meaning of these abnormalities is unclear, given the lack of association with clinical variables.

In contrast to neuroimaging techniques offering structural information about brain integrity, *magnetic resonance spectroscopy* (MRS) offers in vivo neurochemical information by detecting signals from individual solutes in body tissues. In mTBI cases (GCS = 14 or 15) with normal clinical MRI scans, Cecil et al. (1998) reported abnormal findings in the splenium of the corpus collosum in 11 of 16 patients, although it is not known if these abnormalities correlate with clinical variables. Also, given the wide range of time since injury in this study (i.e., 2 days to 8.5 years), it is impossible to know if these represent acute or long-term findings. Govindaraju and colleagues (2004) in a more recent study of more acute mTBI patients (mean of 13.3 days postinjury) found no focal abnormalities in metabolites in 15 of the 16 subjects, although group data differed significantly from control data in several regions. Specifically, decreased N-acetylaspartate/Creatine ratios in parietal white matter regions, increased Choline/Creatine ratios in occipital lobe gray matter, and decreased N-acetylaspartate/Choline ratios in occipital regions were noted in the patient group. Nonetheless, these metabolite ratios did not correlate significantly with clinical measures acutely (GCS) or at discharge (Glasgow Outcome Scale). In addition, most of these patients (10 out of 16) had abnormal CT scans, calling into question the incremental validity of the neuroimaging data.

Finally, *Magnetic source imaging* (MSI) utilizes magnetoencephalograpic (MEG) technology to acquire electrophysiological data from the brain and conventional MRI technology to acquire specific structural data. Only one study has been conducted with mTBI patients (Lewine et al., 1999) who were 2 to 38 months postinjury. Abnormalities were detected in symptomatic patients but not in asymptomatic patients. These findings suggest that there are abnormal electrophysiological findings associated with postconcussive symptoms, but not necessarily with mTBI in general.

2.2.2. Functional Neuroimaging Findings

Functional magnetic resonance imaging (fMRI) is a widely used neuroimaging technique for evaluating brain functioning through measuring cerebral blood flow. Blood flow is considered an indirect measure of brain metabolism. McAllister and colleagues (McAllister et al., 1999, 2001) used fMRI to study blood flow related to working memory in mTBI patients who were approximately 1 month postinjury. They found that patients and controls activated similar brain regions (frontal and parietal) during a working memory task but produced different brain activation patterns in response to different processing loads. This finding suggests that mTBI patients had decreased ability to allocate or modulate resources according to level of task difficulty. However, because the mTBI patients had more subjective memory complaints than controls, it is unclear if these results were a function of mTBI or self-expectations of memory difficulty. In addition, it is unknown whether these differences in brain activation persist long term.

Positron emission tomography (PET) is an imaging technique for measuring metabolic activity of cells. PET uses radioactive sugar molecules to produce images that show the metabolic activity of tissues. PET studies conducted with mTBI patients in the chronic stage are very inconsistent. Findings range from regional hypometabolism (Gross et al., 1996; Humayun et al., 1989; Ruff et al., 1994), to abnormalities in metabolism during working memory tasks (Chen et al., 2003), and to both hypometabolism and hypermetabolism in the same regions across different mTBI patients (Gross et al., 1996). PET abnormalities do seem to relate to neuropsychological performance (Gross et al., 1996), although these comparisons are sometimes made qualitatively, making interpretation difficult (Ruff et al., 1994). Furthermore, as these studies were all conducted with symptomatic patients, findings may not generalize to all persons with mTBI.

Single-photon emission–computed tomography (SPECT) has been used as a less expensive alternative to PET, with its primary application being the gross localization of regional cerebral blood flow. SPECT has been reported to be sensitive to injury in mTBI patients acutely (Audenaert et al., 2003; Hofman et al., 2001; Nedd et al., 1993), although relationships to clinical variables (e.g., neuropsychological performance) are either not demonstrated (Hofman et al., 2001), reported in a qualitative fashion (Audenaert et al., 2003), or not studied. Studies conducted with more chronic mTBI patients (i.e., 6 months or more postinjury) revealed abnormalities on SPECT (Bonne et al., 2003; Gray et al., 1992; Ichise et al., 1994; Jacobs et al., 1996; Kant et al., 1997; Umile et al., 1998, 2002; Varney & Bushnell, 1998), although all of these patients were symptomatic or recruited from clinical settings. Furthermore, these studies found no relationship or inconsistent relationships with neuropsychological testing.

2.2.3.   Neuroimaging Conclusions and Caveats

The lack of consistency with regard to study methodology makes interpretation of the mTBI neuroimaging literature difficult. For instance, the patient's mental activity during the actual scan differs across functional studies, with some studies requiring the patient to perform a task and others requiring the patient to do "nothing." Some studies include patients who require "mild sedation" during the scan, whereas others do not. Obviously, these differences may be reflected in differential rates of blood flow or metabolism. There is inconsistency with regard to controlling for sample demographic characteristics. Further, most of the studies reviewed above used relatively small samples, usually symptomatic or clinic based.

From a mTBI causality perspective, there are other problems. Hypometabolism is found in a variety of neurologic and psychiatric conditions and, therefore, is not specific to TBI. There is no unique fMRI, PET, or SPECT "profile" that has been clinically validated with regard to TBI. Depression (Dunn et al., 2002; Ketter et al., 2001; Kimura et al., 2003) and even a sad mood (Jaracz & Rybakowski, 2002) can result in frontal hypometabolism similar to that seen following mTBI. Indeed, as Deutsch (1992) demonstrated, reduction of frontal blood flow is often a result of altered mental activity rather than pathology. Further, a recent fMRI study demonstrated that a placebo administered for pain control (i.e., a placebo-based self-expectation that pain will be reduced) resulted in significant attenuation of activation in pain-related areas of the brain in response to a painful stimulus. Importantly, the magnitude of the self-reported placebo effect was correlated with the fMRI neural changes (Wager et al., 2004). Clearly, self-beliefs regarding symptoms, irrespective of any underlying brain dysfunction, can alter functional neuroimaging results. Similarly, structural MRI changes have been reported in response to learning and practicing a new complex visuospatial motor task (Draganski et al., 2004). Increased gray matter volume was found following 3 months of juggling practice, which reversed after discontinuation of juggling. One might therefore anticipate that a decrease in physical or mental activities following an mTBI might also result in at least mild structural attenuation over time.

Clearly, if changes in mood, specific self-beliefs, and increased new cognitive–motor activities can alter functional and structural neuroimaging outcomes, then interpreting neuroimaging changes as reflecting brain dysfunction in someone who suffered an mTBI is problematic. This is particularly true given that many of individuals with mTBI report mood problems, decrease their mental and physical activity levels postinjury, and have a self-belief that they are functionally and cognitively compromised as a result of their mTBI.

2.2.4. Electrophysiological Findings

2.2.4.1. EEG and QEEG

The clinical EEG measures electrical activity generated by the brain via scalp electrode recording. Although the conventional EEG is abnormal in many individuals with moderate to severe mTBIs and may provide some acute prognostic information for patients with severe TBI (Bricolo & Turella, 1973; Synek, 1990), the conventional EEG is typically normal in individuals who have sustained an mTBI (Jacome et al., 1984), even in patients with minor structural lesions on the MRI (Voller et al., 1999). Therefore, conventional EEG is not regarded as a useful tool in evaluating patients with mTBI (Gaetz & Bernstein, 2001).

With advances in computer-based signal processing technology, quantitative EEG (QEEG) analyses are possible. QEEG uses computer analyses to decompose the EEG signal into various component frequencies, and measures of coherence and phase can be computed. The utility of QEEG with mTBI is unclear. Although studies have demonstrated frequency power spectrum abnormalities in the acute phase (Fenton, 1996; Tebano et al., 1988) and in chronic, symptomatic patients (Watson et al., 1995), the utility of QEEG in chronic asymptomatic patients remains to be demonstrated.

Other authors have reported EEG coherence and/or phase abnormalities, even in chronic asymptomatic mTBI individuals (Cudmore et al., 2000; Thatcher et al., 1989), although further evidence of clinical correlates are needed. Indeed, the American Academy of Neurology and the American Clinical Neurophysiology Society deemed that QEEG should not be used in civil or criminal proceedings (Nuwer, 1997).

2.2.4.2 *Evoked Potentials (EPs) and Event-Related Potentials (ERPs)*

In mTBI, prolongation of brainstem auditory evoked potential (BAEP) wave I and III latencies have been observed soon after concussion, and prolongation of BAEP interpeak intervals (between waves I and V) have been noted on the day of injury (Noseworthy et al., 1981), but resolved by 6 weeks postinjury (Montgomery et al., 1991). Persistent PCS is not associated with significant BAEP latency delays (Gaetz & Weinberg, 2000). Also, in a group of amateur boxers ($N = 47$) with repeated concussions, no differences in BAEP results were observed when compared to other athletes with low risk of mTBI (Haglund & Persson, 1990).

In terms of cortical ERPs, acute postinjury findings have been reported. For example, Pratap-Shand et al. (1988) found increased P300 latencies and decreased amplitudes in individuals with acute mTBIs. However, these abnormalities completely resolved on retesting. Decreased P300 amplitudes have also been consistently found, even in the chronic phase up to 8 years post-mTBI in patients with active postconcussion symptoms (Bernstein, 2002), with the P300 amplitude inversely correlated with severity of postconcussion symptoms in both acute and chronic phases of mTBI (Dupuis et al., 2000; Gaetz & Weinberg, 2000; Lavoie et al., 2004; Solbakk et al., 2000). However, these P300 findings have not been investigated in the mTBI population at large.

2.2.4.3. *Electrophysiological Conclusions and Caveats*

Electrophysiological studies consistently find acute changes on QEEG variables, BAEP, and cortical ERPs (particularly P300 amplitudes). However, in prospective studies, these findings resolve and are consistent with control group performances within several weeks of injury. Where long-term abnormalities are found following mTBI, it is in patients reporting ongoing postconcussion symptoms.

2.2.5. Neuropsychological Findings

2.2.5.1. *Meta-analytic Studies*

Four meta-analytic reviews have been published on neuropsychological findings in mTBI. The first, by Binder and colleagues (1997), included only studies utilizing patients at least 3 months postinjury who had been selected because of a history of mild head trauma rather than symptom complaint. These authors calculated a total of 11 effect sizes (defined in the note to Table

16.2) from 8 different studies and found the overall effect to be quite small (d = 0.12). When effect sizes were calculated for specific neuropsychological domains, it was found that only attention had an effect size significantly greater than zero (d = 0.20). In contrast, a subsequent meta-analysis by Zakzanis et al. (1999) included 12 studies. This study differed from the Binder et al. study (1997) by including both clinic-based/referred samples and prospective studies. An overall effect size was not reported. The results of domain analysis revealed moderate to large effect sizes for all cognitive domains, with the largest for cognitive flexibility/abstraction (d = 0.72) and the smallest for manual dexterity (d = 0.44). However, it is impossible to know whether these larger effect sizes reflect the inclusion of more acute studies, as the time since injury was not specified, or whether they reflect the inclusion of clinic-based samples.

A recent meta-analysis (Schretlen & Shapiro, 2003) attempted to clarify these disparate results by examining both mTBI studies and moderate-to-severe studies and including only prospective studies. The overall effect size for mTBI was $d = 0.24$, whereas the effect size for moderate/severe mTBI was $d = 0.74$. These findings suggest that it was the inclusion of studies with clinic-based symptomatic patients that resulted in the larger effect sizes in the Zakzanis and colleagues (1999) meta-analysis. Further, these investigators found that effect sizes of mTBI were not significantly different from zero by 30–89 days postinjury. However, these investigators did not report effect sizes by different neuropsychological domains, and it is certainly possible that some domains may show residual effects not accurately reflected by the overall effect size, as was the case in Binder et al. (1997).

In an attempt to address the shortcomings of the previous meta-analytic studies, we recently conducted another meta-analysis of neuropsychological outcomes following mTBI (Belanger et al., 2005). Of primary interest was whether there were differences in effect sizes based on cognitive domain (e.g., attention, memory, etc.), time since injury, and the nature of the study participants (in litigation vs. clinic based vs. population based). Results were obtained from 39 studies with a total of 41 effect sizes.

Acute effects (less than 90 days postinjury) of mTBI were greatest for delayed memory and fluency (d = 1.03 and 0.89, respectively). However, the neuropsychological effect size associated with mTBI in population-based studies was essentially zero by 3 months postinjury, replicating the findings of Schretlen and Shapiro (2003). Findings were moderated by patient characteristics and sampling methods. Clinic-based samples (vs. population-based samples) and samples of participants in litigation were associated with greater cognitive sequelae of mTBI. Indeed, litigation was associated with stable or worsening of cognitive functioning over time. A "test validity" moderator analysis showed that the litigation effect could not be accounted for by invalid effort. Overall, the results of this meta-analysis suggest that for the mTBI population at large, there is full neuropsychological recovery by 3 months postinjury. Table 16.1 summarizes the findings.

TABLE 16.1. Moderator Analyses: Time Since Injury by Cognitive Domain by Participant Selection Context in Belanger et al. (2005)

Cognitive Domain	Litigation-Based Studies		Clinic-Based Studies		Population-Based Studies	
Time Since Injury	d (k)	Q	d (k)	Q	d (k)	Q
Averaged across domains						
< 90 Days	0.52* (2)	0.0			0.63* (23)	1649.4*
≥ 90 Days	0.78* (6)	14.1*	0.74* (11)	410.9*	0.04 (8)	49.3*
Global						
< 90 Days					0.29* (4)	66.1*
≥ 90 Days			1.32* (2)	24.5*	−0.02 (2)	0.1
Attention						
< 90 Days	0.52* (2)	0.1			0.53* (19)	1125.5*
≥ 90 Days	0.67* (5)	30.8*	0.74* (8)	84.9*	0.04 (8)	40.6*
Executive functions						
< 90 Days					0.21* (7)	47.8*
≥ 90 Days	0.59* (5)	10.9*	0.47* (6)	75.2*	−0.15 (5)	49.6*
Fluency						
< 90 Days	0.58* (1)				0.89* (6)	22.9*
≥ 90 Days	0.59* (2)	0.7	0.88* (2)	0.6	0.98* (1)	
Memory acquisition						
< 90 Days	0.53* (1)				0.35* (12)	444.3*
≥ 90 Days	0.78* (4)	20.1*	0.79* (4)	3.2	0.01 (6)	37.2*
Delayed memory						
< 90 Days	0.48* (1)				1.03* (9)	369.5*
≥ 90 Days	0.80* (5)	11.2*	0.43* (3)	15.6*	0.07 (2)	0.1
Language						
< 90 Days					0.64* (7)	46.6*
≥ 90 Days			0.20 (1)		0.21 (2)	0.1
Visuospatial skill						
< 90 Days					0.48* (6)	97.4*
≥ 90 Days	0.73* (4)	21.5*				

Note: k = number of studies; d = effect size; Q = homogeneity statistic; asterisk indicates $p < .05$

2.2.5.2. Subtle Long-Term Deficits in Complex Attention

In another recent study (Vanderploeg et al., 2005), we sought to investigate possible subtle long-term effects of mTBI on complex aspects of attention. We examined the long-term neuropsychological outcomes of mTBI an average of 8 years postinjury. These data were based on 4,462 male U.S. Army veterans and represent a nonclinic, nonreferred, population-based randomly selected sample. Individuals were categorized into one of three groups: those who (1) had not been injured in a MVA or had a head injury (HI) (Normal Control; $n = 3,214$; 73%), (2) had been injured in a MVA but did not have a HI (MVA Control; $n = 539$; 12.3%), and (3) had a HI with altered consciousness (mTBI; $n = 254$; 5.8%). Results of a multivariate analysis of variance revealed no overall differences in neuropsychological functioning across groups (Wilks' $\lambda = 0.99$, $F(30,7620) = 1.28$, $p = .14$, $\eta^2 = 0.005$).

TABLE 16.2. Means and Standard Deviations for Cognitive Test Scores Across Groups in Vanderploeg et al. (2005)

Current Performance Cognitive Test Measure	Normal Control (n = 3,057)	MVA Control (n = 521)	mTBI (n = 254)	d Normal Control	d MVA Control
General Technical Test Score (current)	109.73 (21.38)	109.72 (20.49)	107.56 (22.68)	0.10	0.10
Dominant Hand Grooved Pegs	73.38 (11.70)	73.35 (12.43)	75.19 (13.03)	0.15	0.15
PASAT Trial 1 Correct	38.58 (10.78)	38.93 (10.69)	37.64 (11.90)	0.09	0.12
WAIS-R Information Age Scale Score	9.98 (2.71)	9.80 (2.80)	9.63 (2.76)	0.13	0.06
COWA (FAS word list production)	34.63 (10.75)	34.96 (10.79)	35.20 (10.30)	−0.05	−0.02
Animal Fluency	20.49 (5.09)	20.82 (5.36)	20.70 (5.33)	−0.04	0.02
WAIS-R Block Design Age Scale Score	10.43 (2.58)	10.42 (2.68)	10.42 (2.69)	0.00	0.00
Rey-Osterrieth Copy	32.68 (3.38)	32.75 (3.02)	32.73 (3.04)	−0.02	0.01
CVLT Sum Trials 1 to 5	46.00 (8.72)	45.88 (8.47)	46.34 (9.66)	−0.04	−0.05
CVLT Long Delay Free Recall	9.84 (2.70)	9.87 (2.70)	9.83 (2.93)	0.00	0.01
CVLT Hits	13.81 (1.92)	13.89 (1.83)	13.90 (1.69)	−0.05	−0.01
Rey-Osterrieth Delayed Recall	20.09 (6.24)	20.10 (6.46)	19.78 (6.30)	0.05	0.05
WCST Number of Categories Completed	5.31 (1.38)	5.20 (1.47)	5.17 (1.54)	0.10	0.02
WCST Perseverations	14.72 (15.17)	16.09 (15.35)	14.87 (13.84)	0.01	−0.08
WCST Failures to Maintain Set	3.79 (3.46)	4.00 (3.50)	4.02 (3.47)	0.07	0.01

Note: Standard deviations are in parentheses. There were no significant univariate ANOVA differences on any measure across groups. MVA = injured in a motor vehicle accident; d = effect size (mean of control group minus mTBI group mean, divided by the pooled standard deviation of the two groups); positive d scores indicate that the mTBI group performed more poorly.

Table 16.2 shows the means and standard deviations for the 15 neuropsychological measures across the 3 groups, none of which were significant.

Subtle aspects of attention and working memory were examined by comparing the three groups on Paced Auditory Serial Addition Test (PASAT) (Gronwall, 1977) continuation rate across the four trials and on CVLT proactive interference (Trials 1 minus List B). The three groups did not differ on PASAT continuation rates across Trials 1 or 2, but did differ significantly on Trial 3 [χ^2 (2, n = 3832) = 6.55, p < .04]. The mTBI group had a significantly lower rate of PASAT continuation than did either of the two control groups. The influence of mTBI on CVLT proactive interference (Trial 1 compared to List B) was also examined. A significant proactive interference difference was observed across groups [F(2,3829) = 4.39, p < .02], and follow-up analyses revealed that the mTBI group had a larger proactive interference effect than the Normal Control group (p < .01), with the MVA Control group falling at an intermediate level. In addition, these discontinuation rates and proactive interference effects were associated with external neurologic correlates, left-sided visual imperceptions, and impaired tandem gait abnormalities, respectively. In contrast to the results of the meta-analytic studies, these results show that mTBI can have significant adverse long-term neuropsychological outcomes on subtle aspects of complex attention and working memory and that these findings are associated with distinct neurologic findings.

2.2.5.3.   Conclusions Regarding Neuropsychological Outcomes

In population-based studies of mTBI, there are acute difficulties (within the first 3 months) with virtually all aspects of neuropsychological functioning; individuals with mTBI perform about half a standard deviation (d = 0.57) more poorly than demographic-matched controls. Individuals with mTBI present with an acute profile of relatively greater problems with delayed memory recall (d = 1.03) and fluency (d = 0.89), which resolve by 3 months postinjury. However, when within-subject or repeated measures analyses are used to examine subtle aspects of complex attention and working memory, mild long-term difficulties can be found.

In contrast to this typical pattern of findings in the mTBI population at large (i.e., prospective or population-based studies), individuals with mTBI who present in the chronic phase for medical or neuropsychological evaluation or who are in litigation (i.e., groups composed of individuals reporting ongoing symptoms and problems) represent a different subsample of patients. These individuals perform more poorly on neuropsychological tests but in a manner not associated with any specific deficit pattern. In contrast to the expected recovery pattern, these individuals show stable or worsening neuropsychological abilities across time. Invalid effort (or malingering) as a possible factor accounting for the poorer performance of litigating patients was not supported by a meta-analytic moderator analysis of "symptom validity testing." Factors that might account for the chronic neuropsycho-logical problems found in litigation and clinic-based samples include self-expectations of difficulties (Mittenberg et al., 1992), emotional reactions to an adverse event (Bryant & Harvey, 1999), poor coping styles (Bohnen et al., 1992; Marsh & Smith, 1995), concomitant psychiatric difficulties (Fann et al., 1995; Trahan et al., 2001), pain (Nicholson, 2000; Perlis et al., 1997) (see also Chapter 18 by Nicholson & Martelli), or psychosocial factors (Luis et al., 2003), as well as subtle residual neurologic impairments (Vanderploeg et al., 2005).

2.2.6.   Long-Term Mental Health and Psychosocial Outcomes in mTBI

Cognitive and psychiatric difficulties may negatively impact the ability to engage in social, economic, and personal activities, resulting in increased functional morbidity and potentially enduring disability. In fact, one of the most devastating consequences of mTBI is difficulty in adequately perform-ing social roles held prior to the injury, an important contributor to subjec-tive quality of life (Brown et al., 2000). The ability to return to work or to maintain a marital relationship are two major social roles. However, postin-jury marital and employment outcomes and predictors of their success are a relatively unexplored area following mTBI.

Here, we will present some of our work in examining the long-term men-tal health and psychosocial consequences of mTBI in a large nonreferred sample. In addition, we will examine preinjury factors associated with or moderating long-term work status. In contrast to virtually all other studies to date, our study used a large, nonclinic, nonreferred, population-based ran-domly selected sample from the Vietnam Experience Study (VES) reported earlier regarding neuropsychology outcomes.

2.2.6.1   *Mental Health Outcomes*

Using this VES dataset (Vanderploeg et al., submitted), odds ratios (ORs) and 95% confidence intervals (CIs) across Normal Control, MVA/nonhead injury control, and mTBI groups for different current psychiatric conditions are presented in Table 16.3. Prevalence rates of these conditions were calcu-lated and are consistent with those reported for the general population. Alcohol and drug abuse or dependence as well as Antisocial Personality Disorder increased the likelihood for an injurious event. A significant increase in frequency of Depression was associated with mTBI. To deter-mine whether this depression group difference might be attributable to early life psychiatric problems not controlled by the covariate analyses, only par-ticipants without premilitary depression problems were examined. Again, frequency of current Depression was elevated in the mTBI group (depres-sion: adjusted OR = 1.78, CI = 1.06–3.00). Finally, no relationship was found between combat-related Posttraumatic Stress Disorder (PTSD) (which would have occurred prior to MVA or mTBI) and group membership.

TABLE 16.3. Odds Ratios and Frequency Rates for Various Psychiatric Disorders Over the Prior Year Across Groups in Vanderploeg et al. (submitted)

Disorder	Variables Controlled	Normal Control (n = 3214)	MVA Control (n = 539)	Mild Traumatic Brain Injury (n = 254)
Alcohol abuse or dependence	None	1.0 (12.5%)	1.77 (1.40–2.25)	**2.57** (1.90–3.47)
	Demographic, medical, and psychiatric	1.0	1.57 (1.21–2.03)	1.93 (1.39–2.68)
Drug abuse or dependence	None	1.0 (2.6%)	2.40 (1.59–3.63)	3.68 (2.28–5.94)
	Demographic, medical, and psychiatric	1.0	1.84 (1.19–2.84)	2.05 (1.20–3.49)
Antisocial personality disorder*	None	1.0 (8.6%)	1.73 (1.32–2.28)	**3.27** (2.39–4.47)
	Demographic, medical, and psychiatric	1.0	1.47 (1.10–1.97)	**2.27** (1.60–3.23)
Major depression	None	1.0 (5.2%)	1.54 (1.09–2.19)	**3.01** (2.05–4.43)
	Demographic, medical, and psychiatric	1.0	1.29 (0.87–1.88)	1.77 (1.13–2.78)
Generalized Anxiety Disorder	None	1.0 (8.2%)	1.41 (1.05–1.89)	**2.16** (1.51–3.09)
	Demographic, medical, and psychiatric	1.0	1.15 (0.83–1.59)	1.42 (0.95–2.13)
Combat-related PTSD	None	1.0 (6.4%)	1.41 (1.01–1.96)	1.98 (1.32–2.98)
	Demographic, medical, and psychiatric	1.0	1.16 (0.81–1.66)	1.21 (0.77–1.91)
DSM-4 PCS	None	1.0 (20.6%)	1.30 (1.05–1.61)	**2.67** (2.05–3.48)
	Demographic, medical, and psychiatric	1.0	1.04 (0.82–1.31)	**2.00** (1.49–2.69)
ICD-10 PCS	None	1.0 (19.1%)	1.40 (1.13–1.74)	**2.53** (1.93–3.31)
	Demographic, medical, and psychiatric	1.0	1.13 (0.90–1.44)	**1.80** (1.33–2.43)

Note: Odds ratios and 95% confidence intervals. The Normal Control group served as the reference group. Odds ratios are first presented without controlling any potential confounds. Next they are presented adjusting for demographic factors (age, years of education, race, and enlistment GTT score), prior or current medical conditions (history of meningitis, malaria, diabetes, hypertension, myocardial infarction heart murmur, peripheral vascular disease), and pre-injury psychiatric difficulties (anxiety, mood disorder, conduct disorder, alcohol abuse, and other drug abuse prior to military service). *For antisocial personality disorder the covariate control of childhood conduct disorder was not used, as the diagnosis of antisocial personality disorder entails a childhood diagnosis of conduct disorder. Value in brackets represent the frequency for that condition. Values in bold font indicate group is significantly different from all other groups. MVA = Motor Vehicle Accident; mTBI = mild traumatic brain injury.

PTSD related to accidents occurring subsequent to military service was also examined. Only nine participants met criteria for accident-related PTSD, none of whom were in the mTBI group. A unique relationship was found between PCS and mTBI. A history of mTBI doubled the likelihood of current PCS. In contrast, a history of injury in an MVA, but not experiencing an mTBI, did not increase the likelihood of PCS.

2.2.6.2. Psychosocial and Quality of Life Outcomes

The mTBI group also had significantly poorer psychosocial and quality of life outcomes than the two control groups (Vanderploeg et al., submitted) (see Table 16.4). Although both injury groups were more likely to be unmarried than the normal control group, individuals with a history of mTBI had a significantly higher frequency of being unmarried (adjusted OR = 2.01). A history of mTBI also increased the likelihood of employment problems (adjusted OR = 1.89), low income (adjusted OR = 1.88), and being disabled (adjusted OR = 2.90). Although the mTBI group had a less than satisfactory social support system (adjusted OR = 1.49) and a decrease in availability of social support (adjusted OR = 1.37), these findings did not reach statistical significance.

2.2.6.3. Predictors of Work Status

Also using the VES data, Vanderploeg et al., (2003) examined factors that might predict work status following mTBI. Within a head injury sample composed of both those with mTBI and those with no alteration of consciousness (minor head injury), results of a hierarchical logistic regression accounted for 23.1% of the total variance in full-time work status. Five specific variables were identified as the most important predictors of unique variance in work status: premorbid intelligence (2.6%), premorbid internalizing psychiatric difficulties (2.1%), the interactions of race by region of current residence (1.9%), education by period of altered consciousness (1.2%), and race by region of current residence by period of altered consciousness (2.4%). The geographic interaction effects will not be discussed further in this chapter (see Vanderploeg et al., 2003, for detailed discussion). Presence of disturbed consciousness (i.e., mTBI), by itself, was not predictive of work status but did interact with other factors to adversely impact work status.

Working full time was more likely in individuals of higher intelligence and without early life internalizing psychiatric difficulties (e.g., anxiety, depression, mania, psychosis). After controlling for all other main predictor variables, individuals with average cognitive abilities were two times more likely to be working full time and individuals with higher preinjury abilities were almost four times more likely to be working full time than individuals who had lower preinjury cognitive abilities. Similarly, individuals without a history of earlier life-internalizing problems were 2.3 times more likely to be working full-time than

TABLE 16.4. Odds Ratios for Psychosocial and Quality-of-Life Outcome Measures from Vanderploeg et al. (submitted)

Status	Variables Controlled	Normal Control (n = 3214)	MVA Control (n = 539)	Mild Traumatic Brain Injury (n = 254)
Not currently married	None	1.0 (23.8%)	1.37 (1.12–1.68)	**2.29** (1.76–2.98)
	Demographic, medical, and psychiatric	1.0	1.30 (1.05–1.60)	**2.01 (1.57–2.75)**
Employed less than full time	None	1.0 (11.8%)	1.23 (0.94–1.60)	**2.47** (1.82–3.34)
	Demographic, medical, and psychiatric	1.0	1.08 (0.82–1.43)	**1.89 (1.36–2.64)**
Annual income less than $10,000	None	1.0 (8.8%)	1.25 (0.92–1.68)	**2.29** (1.62–3.24)
	Demographic, medical, and psychiatric	1.0	1.10 (0.80–1.51)	**1.88 (1.29–2.74)**
Disabled	None	1.0 (2.1%)	1.74 (1.04–2.93)	**3.64** (2.12–6.23)
	Demographic, medical, and psychiatric	1.0	1.49 (0.86–2.57)	**2.90 (1.63–5.15)**
Satisfaction with social support (very or somewhat dissatisfied)	None	1.0 (6.0%)	1.22 (0.85–1.74)	**2.10** (1.39–3.15)
	Demographic, medical, and psychiatric	1.0	1.11 (0.77–1.60)	1.49 (0.96–2.33)
Availability of social support (hardly ever or never)	None	1.0 (2.6%)	1.08 (0.62–1.89)	**2.03** (1.12–3.70)
	Demographic, medical, and psychiatric	1.0	0.85 (0.48–1.51)	1.37 (0.73–2.56)

Note: Odds ratios are first presented without controlling any potential confounds. Next, they are presented controlling for demographic factors (age, years of education, race, and enlistment GTT score), prior or current medical conditions (history of meningitis, malaria, diabetes, hypertension, angina, myocardial infarction, heart murmur, peripheral vascular disease), and early life psychiatric difficulties (anxiety, depression, conduct disorder, alcohol abuse, and other drug abuse prior to military service). For the reference group, the value in parentheses represent the prevalence for that condition. Values for the other three groups represent the odds ratios and 95% confidence intervals. Values in bold indicate that the group is significantly different from all other groups. MVA = motor vehicle accident.

individuals with such a history. Finally, loss of consciousness has an indirect effect on work status postinjury, as Vanderploeg and colleagues (2003) demonstrated that level of education interacts with loss of consciousness in complex ways to affect work status.

2.2.6.4.   *Conclusions Regarding Mental Health and Psychosocial Outcomes*

These findings indicate that an mTBI can have significant long-term adverse effects on mental health and psychosocial outcomes. The rate of depression is increased two-fold following mTBI, both in relation to normal controls and MVA-injured controls. In addition, the postconcussion symptom complex is increased threefold following mTBI. Finally, work status is adversely affected by mTBI, again with about a two-fold increase in adverse outcomes. What is interesting, however, is that the direct effect of mTBI on mental health and psychosocial outcomes (as assessed by a period of altered consciousness) is modest. However, these studies show that the effects of an mTBI are mediated in part by individual resilience, as well as the extent of a supportive social environmental milieu. Intellectual capacity, educational attainment, pre-existing psychological problems, and extent of social support play significant roles in symptom experience and work status.

3.   An Alternative View of Causality in mTBI

The predictive study of employment outcome following mTBI reported earlier (Vanderploeg et al., 2003) as well as the predictive study of PCS discussed early in the chapter (Luis et al., 2003) are congruent with a multifactorial model of mTBI outcome proposed by Greiffenstein (2000). This model posits that post-mTBI outcome is the interactive product of predisposing, precipitating, and perpetuating factors. Predisposing factors represent an increased vulnerability to adverse outcome following mTBI. Precipitating factors are events such as the mTBI itself and the initial medical or social support interventions associated with it. Perpetuating factors are circumstances that perpetuate the symptoms long after the initial trigger is gone. This is a nonlinear, systemic model that posits that for the minority of individuals who experience ongoing post-mTBI problems, there are multiple predisposing factors, causative agents, and symptom mitigating and sustaining factors. Figure 16.1 illustrates such a model. Predisposing conditions are set before any injury occurs. At the moment of injury, there is a simultaneous set of causative factors interacting in complex feedback loops with predisposing factors, which can serve to intensify, perpetuate, or help alleviate symptoms. At a somewhat later point in time, additional causative factors come into play (e.g., possible medical and legal interventions). Again, these can serve to either intensity and perpetuate symptoms or to minimize and alleviate symptoms.

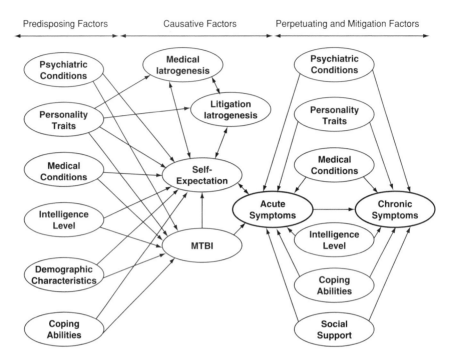

FIGURE 16.1. A systemic model of predisposing factors, causative agents, and symptom mitigating and sustaining factors, which helps explain why individuals might experience various post-mTBI problems.

3.1. Potential Causative Agents

There is no doubt that an mTBI causes acute disruption of brain functioning. In a minority of individuals, the acute disorientation and confusion is followed by the emergence of a constellation of long-term physical, emotional, and cognitive symptoms (i.e., the PCS). Whether this symptom complex is the result of ongoing neurologic brain dysfunction or other factors remains a controversial issue. However, the review detailed earlier suggests that both subtle ongoing brain dysfunction in a minority of individuals and psychological and social support factors play important roles in the emergence and persistence of PCS.

Certainly, the series of studies based on the VES dataset show that a period of altered consciousness independently predicts poorer postconcussion symptom outcomes (Luis et al., 2003) and worse mental health and psychosocial outcomes (Vanderploeg et al., submitted). In addition, a period of altered consciousness played an interactive role in association with premorbid ability (intelligence or education) in poorer postconcussion symptom and work–status outcomes. In one study, even in the chronic phase of recovery, an average of 8 years postinjury, mTBI was associated with subtle problems in complex attention and neurologic findings (Vanderploeg et al., 2005). These data strongly suggest a direct effect of mild brain dysfunction in poorer postinjury outcomes, but an effect that can be modulated through predisposing and perpetuating factors.

On the other hand, the work of Mittenberg and colleagues clearly established that expectations following mTBI play a significant role in outcomes. If there is no expectation of ongoing symptoms, as is the general case in sports-related mTBI, then there are few or no ongoing symptoms (Ferguson et al., 1999; Mittenberg et al., 1997). If there is an expectation of postinjury problems, then in at least a minority of individuals, such symptoms are more likely to occur (Mittenberg et al., 1992). In addition, because virtually everyone with an mTBI experiences acute symptoms for seconds to minutes to hours, the mere presence of these symptoms can reinforce pre-existing expectations and beliefs. Thus, both brain dysfunction and expectation play independent and interactive causative roles in PCS.

Mittenberg and colleagues have also demonstrated how the effects of expectation can be mitigated through educational and psychological interventions. Mittenberg et al. (1993) developed a treatment manual for patients in which general information about the sequelae of head trauma was presented, in addition to information about the nature, incidence, and expected recovery of symptoms. One primary post-mTBI intervention involved cognitive re-attribution of the symptoms to selective attention (i.e., paying more attention post-injury to normal daily aches, pains, and mental slips) and to expected but transient responses to stress. Cognitive behavioral interventions for anxiety and depression were also included in the treatment approach, as were instructions for gradual resumption of previous activity levels. In an effectiveness study, subjects in the treatment group reported significantly shorter average symptom duration (33 vs. 51 days) and significantly fewer symptoms (1.6 vs. 3.1) at six-month follow-up than untreated patients following mTBI (Mittenberg et al., 1996).

If such interventions can mitigate post-mTBI problems through modifying expectations or other components of the program, certainly the opposite is also likely to be true. Health care providers can iatrogenically induce or sustain post-mTBI problems by making statements such as the following: "These problems you're having clearly indicate that you had a brain injury," or "Although the CT scan of your brain was normal, I'm certain there was some brain damage that is not showing," or "Those memory lapses you are having are one indicator of ongoing brain dysfunction." Similarly, ordering a number of time-consuming and expensive diagnostic procedures following an mTBI can reinforce self-concern that "something must be wrong, otherwise why would the doctor be ordering all these tests." In an individual susceptible to worry about health problems, such statements and interventions are likely to amplify negative expectations and induce or enhance post-mTBI symptoms.

An analog to health care iatrogenesis is an attorney-based interaction that follows the same pattern. An attorney may be convinced that the client or potential client has been injured and deserves compensation for that injury. Simply taking a case, collecting the facts, and establishing a series of investigative evaluations can amplify negative expectations, particularly in a vulnerable individual.

3.2.   Predisposing and Perpetuating Factors

A number of vulnerabilities or predisposing factors to a poorer outcome following mTBI have been identified. These include pre-existing psychiatric, personality, or medical problems, lower levels of intelligence, lower levels of education, poor social support, and pre-existing poor coping resources. Other researchers have identified older age and female gender as factors related to poorer outcome. All of these predisposing factors can also become perpetuating factors in the postacute or chronic phase of recovery. Again, Figure 16.1 illustrates this multifactorial and interactive model of causation.

3.3.   Causality Conclusions

This chapter has focused on group data regarding outcomes following mTBI. However, in both the clinical and the medical–legal context, it is not the group but rather the individual who is the focus of interest. The question is no longer "What factors influence outcome following mTBI?" but rather "What is causing the symptoms or problems in this particular case?" The clinical arena can accommodate an ambiguous interactive systemic model of causality, but a legal arena is seeking to assign definitive responsibility. Also, in the individual case, it is often very difficult, if not impossible, to attribute mildly abnormal findings such as slightly more proactive memory interference than normal, mild balance difficulties, occasional visual imperceptions, headaches, dizziness, fatigue, and memory complaints to a particular etiology. Such a pattern of symptoms could represent (1) brain dysfunction, (2) a normal population variant, (3) pre-existing mental health problems (e.g., depression and anxiety), (4) pre-existing or coexisting medical problems (e.g., chronic pain syndrome, multiple sclerosis, hypertension, acquired immunodeficiency syndrome, alcohol-abuse-related complications), (5) inadequate patient effort on examination or outright malingering, or (6) a combination of these factors. Furthering the difficulty in determining etiological factors is weighing the degree to which pre-existing poor coping skills, self-beliefs/expectations, poor social support, medical iatrogenesis, or litigation-based iatrogenesis might amplify and extend residual post-mTBI problems.

A conservative but limited approach for the health care provider might lie in time-tested, clinically validated diagnostic evaluations, a careful history of preinjury and postinjury symptoms and functioning, and a reliance on the medical linear model of causality. However, an increasingly used approach relies on the examination of multiple potential predisposing factors, causative agents, and perpetuating factors that interactively influence each other. Causality determination requires (1) examination of all relevant etiological events or factors, (2) investigation of the initial clinical presentation as being more or less consistent with those potential causative agents, (3) tracking ongoing or emerging symptoms as being consistent with the medical literature regarding potential causative agents and not consistent with other potential etiological factors, and (4) examination of findings from diagnostic procedures as being consistent with the clinical history, the nature and course of symptoms, and suspected explanatory causative factors. Only if a chronologically consistent and clinically logical pattern of results emerges after an alleged causal event can findings be attributed to it.

References

Adams, J. H., Doyle, D., Ford, I., Gennarelli, T. A., Graham, D. I., & McLellan, D. R. (1989). Diffuse axonal injury in head injury: Definition, diagnosis and grading. *Histopathology, 15*, 49–59.

American Congress of Rehabilitation Medicine. (1993). Definition of mild traumatic brain injury. *Journal of Head Trauma Rehabilition, 8*, 86–87.

American Psychiatric Association. (1994). *Diagnostic and Statistical Manual of Mental Disorders: DSM-IV*. Washington, DC: American Psychiatric Association.

Arfanakis, K., Haughton, V. M., Carew, J. D., Rogers, B. P., Dempsey, R. J., & Meyerand, M. E. (2002). Diffusion tensor MR imaging in diffuse axonal injury. *American Journal of Neuroradiology, 23*, 794–802.

Audenaert, K., Jansen, H. M., Otte, A., Peremans, K., Vervaet, M., Crombez, R., de Ridder, L., van Heeringen, C., Thirot, J., Dierckx, R., & Korf, J. (2003). Imaging of mild traumatic brain injury using ^{57}Co and ^{99m}Tc HMPAO SPECT as compared to other diagnostic procedures. *Medical Science Monitor, 9*, MT112–MT117.

Bagley, L. J., McGowan, J. C., Grossman, R. I., Sinson, G., Kotapka, M., Lexa, F. J., Berlin, J. A., & McIntosh, T. K. (2000). Magnetization transfer imaging of traumatic brain injury. *Journal of Magnetic Resonance Imaging, 11*, 1–8.

Belanger, H. G., Curtiss, G., Demery, J. A., Lebowitz, B. K., & Vanderploeg, R. D. (2005). Factors moderating neuropsychological outcome following mild traumatic brain injury: A meta-analysis. *Journal of the International Neuropsychological Society, 11*, 228–236.

Bernstein, D. M. (2002). Information processing difficulty long after self-reported concussion. *Journal of the International Neuropsychological Society, 8*, 673–682.

Binder, L. M. & Rohling, M. L. (1996). Money matters: A meta-analytic review of the effects of financial incentives on recovery after closed-head injury. *American Journal of Psychiatry, 153*, 7–10.

Binder, L. M., Rohling, M. L., & Larrabee, J. (1997). A review of mild head trauma. Part I: Meta-analytic review of neuropsychological studies. *Journal of Clinical and Experimental Neuropsychology, 19*, 421–431.

Bohnen, L., Jolles, J., Twijnstra, A., Mellink, R., & Sulon, J. (1992). Coping styles, cortisol reactivity, and performance on vigilance tasks of patients with persistant postconcussive symptoms after mild head injury. *International Journal of Neuroscience, 64*, 97–105.

Bonne, O., Gilboa, A., Louzoun, Y., Kempf-Sherf, O., Katz, M., Fishman, Y., Ben-Nahum, Z., Krausz, Y., Bocher, M., Lester, H., Chisin, R., & Lerer, B. (2003). Cerebral blood flow in chronic symptomatic mild traumatic brain injury. *Psychiatry Research, 124*, 141–152.

Borg, J., Holm, L., Cassidy, J. D., Peloso, P. M., Carroll, L. J., von Holst, H., & Ericson, K. (2004). Diagnostic procedures in mild traumatic brain injury: Results of the WHO Collaborating Centre Task Force on Mild Traumatic Brain Injury. *Journal of Rehabilitation Medicine, 43S*, 61–75.

Bricolo, A. & Turella, G. (1973). Electroencephalographic patterns of acute traumatic coma: Diagnostic and prognostic value. *Journal of Neurosurgical Sciences, 17*, 278–285.

Brown, M., Gordon, W. A., & Haddad, L. (2000). Models for predicting subjective quality of life in individuals with traumatic brain injury. *Brain Injury, 14*, 5–19.

Bryant, R. A. & Harvey, A. G. (1999). Postconcussive symptoms and Posttraumatic Stress Disorder after mild traumatic brain injury. *Journal of Nervous and Mental Disease, 187*, 302–305.

Carroll, L. J., Cassidy, J. D., Peloso, P. M., Borg, J., von Holst, H., Holm, L., Paniak, C., & Pepin, M. (2004). Prognosis for mild traumatic brain injury: results of the WHO Collaborating Centre Task Force on Mild Traumatic Brain Injury. *Journal of Rehabilitation Medicine, 43 Suppl*, 84–105.

Cassidy, J. D., Carroll, L. J., Peloso, P. M., Borg, J., von Holst, H., Holm, L., Kraus, J., & Coronado, V. G. (2004). Incidence, risk factors and prevention of mild traumatic brain injury: Results of the WHO Collaborating Centre Task Force on Mild Traumatic Brain Injury. *Journal of Rehabilitation Medicine, 43 Suppl*, 28–60.

Cecil, K. M., Hills, E. C., Sandel, M. E., Smith, D. H., McIntosh, T. K., Mannon, L. J., Sinson, G. P., Bagley, L. J., Grossman, R. I., & Lenkinski, R. E. (1998). Proton magnetic resonance spectroscopy for detection of axonal injury in the splenium of the corpus callosum of brain-injured patients. *Journal of Neurosurgery, 88*, 795–801.

Chen, S. H., Kareken, D. A., Fastenau, P. S., Trexler, L. E., & Hutchins, G. D. (2003). A study of persistent post-concussion symptoms in mild head trauma using positron emission tomography. *Journal of Neurology, Neurosurgery and Psychiatry, 74*, 326–332.

Cudmore, L. J., Segalowitz, S. J., & Dywan, J. (2000). EEG coherence shows altered frontal-parietal communication in mild TBI during a dual-task. *Brain and Cognition, 44*, 86–90.

Deutsch, G. (1992). The nonspecificity of frontal dysfunction in disease and altered states: Cortical blood flow evidence. *Neuropsychiatry, Neuropsychology and Behavioral Neurology, 5*, 301–307.

Draganski, B., Gaser, C., Busch, V., Schuierer, G., Bogdahn, U., & May, A. (2004). Neuroplasticity: changes in grey matter induced by training. *Nature, 427*, 311–312.

Dunn, R. T., Kimbrell, T. A., Ketter, T. A., Frye, M. A., Willis, M. W., Luckenbaugh, D. A., & Post, R. M. (2002). Principal components of the Beck Depression Inventory and regional cerebral metabolism in unipolar and bipolar depression. *Biological Psychiatry, 51*, 387–399.

Dupuis, F., Johnston, K. M., Lavoie, M., Lepore, F., & Lassonde, M. (2000). Concussions in athletes produce brain dysfunction as revealed by event-related potentials. *Neuroreport, 11*, 4087–4092.

Fann, J. R., Katon, W. J., Uomoto, J. M., & Esselman, P. C. (1995). Psychiatric disorders and functional disability in outpatients with traumatic brain injuries. *American Journal of Psychiatry, 152*, 1493–1499.

Fenton, G., McClelland, R., Montgomery, A., MacFlynn, G., & Rutherford, W. (1993). The postconcussional syndrome: Social antecedents and psychological sequelae. *British Journal of Psychiatry, 162*, 493–497.

Fenton, G. W. (1996). The postconcussional syndrome reappraised. *Clinical Electroencephalography, 27*, 174–182.

Ferguson, R. J., Mittenberg, W., Barone, D. F., & Schneider, B. (1999). Postconcussion syndrome following sports-related head injury: Expectation as etiology. *Neuropsychology, 13*, 582–589.

Gaetz, M. & Bernstein, D. M. (2001). The current status of electrophysiologic procedures for the assessment of mild traumatic brain injury. *Journal of Head Trauma Rehabilitation, 16*, 386–405.

Gaetz, M. & Weinberg, H. (2000). Electrophysiological indices of persistent postconcussion symptoms. *Brain Injury, 14*, 815–832.

Gasquoine, P. G. (1997). Postconcussion symptoms. *Neuropsychological Review, 7*, 77–85.

Gouvier, W. D., Cubic, B., Jones, G., Brantley, P., & Cutlip, Q. (1992). Postconcussion symptoms and daily stress in normal and head injured college populations. *Archives of Clinical Neuropsychology, 7*, 193–211.

Govindaraju, V., Gauger, G. E., Manley, G. T., Ebel, A., Meeker, M., & Maudsley, A. A. (2004). Volumetric proton spectroscopic imaging of mild traumatic brain injury. *American Journal of Neuroradiology, 25*, 730–737.

Gray, B. G., Ichise, M., Chung, D. G., Kirsh, J. C., & Franks, W. (1992). Technetium-99m-HMPAO SPECT in the evaluation of patients with a remote history of traumatic brain injury: A comparison with x-ray computed tomography. *Journal of Nuclear Medicine, 33*, 52–58.

Greiffenstein, F. M. & Baker, J. W. (2001). Comparison of premorbid and postinjury MMPI-2 profiles in late postconcussion claimants. *Clinical Neuropsychologist, 15*, 162–170.

Greiffenstein, M. F. (2000). Late post-concussion syndrome as learned illness behavior: Proposal for a mulitfactorial model. *Brain Injury Source, 4*, 26–27.

Gronwall, D. A. (1977). Paced Auditory Serial Addition Task: A measure of recovery from concussion. *Perceptual and Motor Skills, 44*, 367–373.

Gross, H., Kling, A., Henry, G., Herndon, C., & Lavretsky, H. (1996). Local cerebral glucose metabolism in patients with long-term behavioral and cognitive deficits following mild traumatic brain injury. *Journal of Neuropsychiatry and Clinical Neuroscience, 8*, 324–334.

Haglund, Y. & Persson, H. E. (1990). Does Swedish amateur boxing lead to chronic brain damage? 3. A retrospective clinical neurophysiological study. *Acta Neurologica Scandinavica, 82*, 353–360.

Hayes, R. L. & Dixon, C. E. (1994). Neurochemical changes in mild head injury. *Seminars in Neurology, 14*, 25–31.

Hofman, P. A., Stapert, S. Z., van Kroonenburgh, M. J., Jolles, J., de Kruijk, J., & Wilmink, J. T. (2001). MR imaging, single-photon emission CT, and neurocognitive performance after mild traumatic brain injury. *American Journal of Neuroradiology, 22*, 441–449.

Humayun, M. S., Presty, S. K., Lafrance, N. D., Holcomb, H. H., Loats, H., Long, D. M., Wagner, H. N., & Gordon, B. (1989). Local cerebral glucose abnormalities in mild closed head injured patients with cognitive impairments. *Nuclear Medicine Communications, 10*, 335–344.

Ichise, M., Chung, D. G., Wang, P., Wortzman, G., Gray, B. G., & Franks, W. (1994). Technetium-99m-HMPAO SPECT, CT and MRI in the evaluation of patients with chronic traumatic brain injury: A correlation with neuropsychological performance. *Journal of Nuclear Medicine, 35*, 217–226.

Jacobs, A., Put, E., Ingels, M., Put, T., & Bossuyt, A. (1996). One-year follow-up of technetium-99m-HMPAO SPECT in mild head injury. *Journal of Nuclear Medicine, 37*, 1605–1609.

Jacome, D. E. & Risko, M. (1984). EEG features in post-traumatic syndrome. *Clinical Electroencephalography, 15*, 214–221.

Jaracz, J. & Rybakowski, J. (2002). [Studies of cerebral blood flow in metabolism in depression using positron emission tomography (PET)]. *Psychiatria Polska, 36*, 617–628.

Kant, R., Smith-Seemiller, L., Isaac, G., & Duffy, J. (1997). Tc-HMPAO SPECT in persistent post-concussion syndrome after mild head injury: Comparison with MRI/CT. *Brain Injury, 11*, 115–124.

Ketter, T. A., Kimbrell, T. A., George, M. S., Dunn, R. T., Speer, A. M., Benson, B. E., Willis, M. W., Danielson, A., Frye, M. A., Herscovitch, P., & Post, R. M. (2001). Effects of mood and subtype on cerebral glucose metabolism in treatment-resistant bipolar disorder. *Biological Psychiatry, 49*, 97–109.

Kimura, M., Shimoda, K., Mizumura, S., Tateno, A., Fujito, T., Mori, T., & Endo, S. (2003). Regional cerebral blood flow in vascular depression assessed by 123I-IMP SPECT. *Journal of Nippon Medical School, 70*, 321–326.

King, N. S. (1996). Emotional, neuropsychological, and organic factors: Their use in the prediction of persisting postconcussion symptoms after moderate and mild head injuries. *Journal of Neurology, Neurosurgery and Psychiatry, 61*, 75–81.

Lavoie, M. E., Dupuis, F., Johnston, K. M., Leclerc, S., & Lassonde, M. (2004). Visual p300 effects beyond symptoms in concussed college athletes. *Journal of Clinical and Experimental Neuropsychology, 26*, 55–73.

Lees-Haley, P. R. & Brown, R. S. (1993). Neuropsychological complaint base rates of 170 personal injury claimants. *Archives of Clinical Neuropsychology, 8*, 203–209.

Levin, H. S., Amparo, E., Eisenberg, H. M., Williams, D. H., High, W. J., McArdle, C. B., & Weiner, R. L. (1987). Magnetic resonance imaging and computerized tomography in relation to the neurobehavioral sequelae of mild and moderate head injuries. *Journal of Neurosurgery, 66*, 706–713.

Lewine, J. D., Davis, J. T., Sloan, J. H., Kodituwakku, P. W., & Orrison, W. W., Jr. (1999). Neuromagnetic assessment of pathophysiologic brain activity induced by minor head trauma. *American Journal of Neuroradiology, 20*, 857–866.

Luis, C. A., Vanderploeg, R. D., & Curtiss, G. (2003). Predictors of postconcussion symptom complex in community dwelling male veterans. *Journal of the International Neuropsychological Society, 9*, 1001–1015.

Marsh, H. V. & Smith, M. D. (1995). Post-concussion syndrome and the coping hypothesis. *Brain Injury, 9*, 553–562.

McAllister, T. W., Saykin, A. J., Flashman, L. A., Sparling, M. B., Johnson, S. C., Guerin, S. J., Mamourian, A. C., Weaver, J. B., & Yanofsky, N. (1999). Brain activation during working memory 1 month after mild traumatic brain injury: A functional MRI study. *Neurology, 53*, 1300–1308.

McAllister, T. W., Sparling, M. B., Flashman, L. A., Guerin, S. J., Mamourian, A. C., & Saykin, A. J. (2001). Differential working memory load effects after mild traumatic brain injury. *Neuroimage, 14*, 1004–1012.

McGowan, J. C., Yang, J. H., Plotkin, R. C., Grossman, R. I., Umile, E. M., Cecil, K. M., & Bagley, L. J. (2000). Magnetization transfer imaging in the detection of injury associated with mild head trauma. *American Journal of Neuroradiology, 21*, 875–880.

Miller, L. (1996). Neuropsychology and pathophysiology of mild head injury and the postconcussion syndrome: Clinical and forensic considerations. *The Journal of Cognitive Rehabilitation, 14*, 8–23.

Mittenberg, W., DiGiulio, D. V., Perrin, S., & Bass, A. E. (1992). Symptoms following mild head injury: Expectation as aetiology. *Journal of Neurology, Neurosurgery and Psychiatry, 55*, 200–204.

Mittenberg, W., Ferguson, R. J., & Miller, L. J. (1997). Postconcussion syndrome following sport related head injury: Expectation as etiology. *Journal of the International Neuropsychological Society, 3*, 13 (abstract).

Mittenberg, W., Tremont, G., Zeilinski, R., Fichera, S., & Rayls, K. (1996). Cognitive behavioral prevention of postconcussion syndrome. *Archives of Clinical Neuropsychology, 11*, 139–145.

Mittenberg, W., Zielinski, R. E., & Fichera, S. (1993). Recovery from mild head injury: A treatment manual for patients. *Psychotherapy in Private Practice, 12*, 37–52.

Mittl, R. L., Grossman, R. I., Hiehle, J. F., Hurst, R. W., Kauder, D. R., Gennarelli, T. A., & Alburger, G. W. (1994). Prevalence of MR evidence of diffuse axonal injury in patients with mild head injury and normal head CT findings. *American Journal of Neuroradiology, 15*, 1583–1589.

Montgomery, E. A., Fenton, G. W., McClelland, R. J., MacFlynn, G., & Rutherford, W. H. (1991). The psychobiology of minor head injury. *Psychological Medicine, 21*, 375–384.

Nedd, K., Sfakianakis, G., Ganz, W., Uricchio, B., Vernberg, D., Villanueva, P., Jabir, A. M., Bartlett, J., & Keena, J. (1993). 99mTc-HMPAO SPECT of the brain in mild to moderate traumatic brain injury patients: compared with CT—A prospective study. *Brain Injury, 7*, 469–479.

Nicholson, K. (2000). Pain, cognition and traumatic brain injury. *NeuroRehabilitation, 14*, 95–103.

Noseworthy, J. H., Miller, J., Murray, T. J., & Regan, D. (1981). Auditory brainstem responses in postconcussion syndrome. *Archives of Neurology, 38*, 275–278.

Nuwer, M. (1997). Assessment of digital EEG, quantitative EEG, and EEG brain mapping: Report of the American Academy of Neurology and the American Clinical Neurophysiology Society. *Neurology, 49*, 277–292.

Perlis, M. L., Artiola, L., & Giles, D. E. (1997). Sleep complaints in chronic postconcussion syndrome. *Perceptual and Motor Skills, 84*, 595–599.

Povlishock, J. T. & Coburn, T. H. (1989). Morphopathological change associated with mild head injury. In H. S. Levin, H. M. Eisenberg, & A. L. Benton (Eds.). *Mild Head Injury*. New York: Oxford University Press, pp. 37–53.

Pratap-Chand, R., Sinniah, M., & Salem, F. A. (1988). Cognitive evoked potential (P300): A metric for cerebral concussion. *Acta Neurologica Scandinavica, 78*, 185–189.

Radanov, B. P., Bicik, I., Dvorak, J., Antinnes, J., von Schulthess, G. K., & Buck, A. (1999). Relation between neuropsychological and neuroimaging findings in patients with late whiplash syndrome. *Journal of Neurology, Neurosurgery and Psychiatry, 66*, 485–489.

Radanov, B. P., di Stefano, G., Schnidrig, A., & Ballinari, P. (1991). Role of psychosocial stress in recovery from common whiplash [see comment]. *Lancet, 338*, 712–715.

Robertson, E., Rath, B., Fournet, G., Zelhart, P., & Estes, R. (1994). Assessment of mild brain trauma: A preliminary study of the influence of premorbid factors. *The Clinical Neuropsychologist, 8*, 69–74.

Ruff, R. M., Crouch, J. A., Troster, A. I., Marshall, L. F., Buchsbaum, M. S., Lottenberg, S., & Somers, L. M. (1994). Selected cases of poor outcome following a minor brain trauma: Comparing neuropsychological and positron emission tomography assessment. *Brain Injury, 8*, 297–308.

Santa Maria, M. P., Pinkston, J. B., Miller, S. R., & Gouvier, W. D. (2001). Stability of postconcussion symptomatology differs between high and low responders and by gender but not by mild head injury status. *Archives of Clinical Neuropsychology, 16*, 133–140.

Schretlen, D. J. & Shapiro, A. M. (2003). A quantitative review of the effects of traumatic brain injury on cognitive functioning. *International Review of Psychiatry, 15*, 341–349.

Sinson, G., Bagley, L. J., Cecil, K. M., Torchia, M., McGowan, J. C., Lenkinski, R. E., McIntosh, T. K., & Grossman, R. I. (2001). Magnetization transfer imaging and proton MR spectroscopy in the evaluation of axonal injury: Correlation with clinical outcome after traumatic brain injury. *American Journal of Neuroradiology, 22*, 143–151.

Solbakk, A. K., Reinvang, I., & Nielsen, C. S. (2000). ERP indices of resource allocation difficulties in mild head injury. *Journal of Clinical and Experimental Neuropsychology, 22*, 743–760.

Synek, V. M. (1990). Value of a revised EEG coma scale for prognosis after cerebral anoxia and diffuse head injury. *Clinical Electroencephalography, 21*, 25–30.

Teasdale, G. & Jennett, B. (1974). Assessment of coma and impaired consciousness. A practical scale. *Lancet, 2*, 81–84.

Tebano, M. T., Cameroni, M., Gallozzi, G., Loizzo, A., Palazzino, G., Pezzini, G., & Ricci, G. F. (1988). EEG spectral analysis after minor head injury in man. *Electroencephalography and Clinical Neurophysiology, 70*, 185–189.

Thatcher, R. W., Walker, R. A., Gerson, I., & Geisler, F. H. (1989). EEG discriminant analyses of mild head trauma. *Electroencephalography and Clinical Neurophysiology, 73*, 94–106.

Trahan, D. E., Ross, C. E., & Trahan, S. L. (2001). Relationships among postconcussional-type symptoms, depression, and anxiety in neurologically normal young adults and victims of mild brain injury. *Archives of Clinical Neuropsychology, 16*, 435–445.

Umile, E. M., Plotkin, R. C., & Sandel, M. E. (1998). Functional assessment of mild traumatic brain injury using SPECT and neuropsychological testing. *Brain Injury, 12*, 577–594.

Umile, E. M., Sandel, M. E., Alavi, A., Terry, C. M., & Plotkin, R. C. (2002). Dynamic imaging in mild traumatic brain injury: Support for the theory of medial temporal vulnerability. *Archives of Physical Medicine and Rehabilitation, 83*, 1506–1513.

Vanderploeg, R. D., Curtiss, G., & Belanger, H. G. (2005). Long-term neuropsychological outcomes following mild traumatic brain injury. *Journal of the International Neuropsychological Society, 11*, 228–236.

Vanderploeg, R. D., Curtiss, G., Duchnick, J. J., & Luis, C. A. (2003). Demographic, medical, and psychiatric factors in work and marital status after mild head injury. *Journal of Head Trauma Rehabilitation, 18*, 148–163.

Vanderploeg, R. D., Curtiss, G., Luis, C. A., Ordorica, P. I., & Salazar, A. M. (submitted). Long-term morbidity and quality of life following mild head injury.

Varney, N. R. & Bushnell, D. (1998). NeuroSPECT findings in patients with post-traumatic anosmia: A quantitative analysis. *Journal of Head Trauma Rehabilitation, 13*, 63–72.

Voller, B., Benke, T., Benedetto, K., Schnider, P., Auff, E., & Aichner, F. (1999). Neuropsychological, MRI and EEG findings after very mild traumatic brain injury. *Brain Injury, 13*, 821–827.

Wager, T. D., Rilling, J. K., Smith, E. E., Sokolik, A., Casey, K. L., Davidson, R. J., Kosslyn, S. M., Rose, R. M., & Cohen, J. D. (2004). Placebo-induced changes in FMRI in the anticipation and experience of pain. *Science, 303*, 1162–1167.

Watson, M. R., Fenton, G. W., McClelland, R. J., Lumsden, J., Headley, M., & Rutherford, W. H. (1995). The post-concussional state: Neurophysiological aspects. *British Journal of Psychiatry, 167*, 514–521.

Williams, D. H., Levin, H. S., & Eisenberg, H. M. (1990). Mild head injury classification. *Neurosurgery, 27*, 422–428.

Wood, F., Novak, T. A., & Long, C. J. (1984). Post-concussion symptoms: Cognitive, emotional and environmental aspects. *International Journal of Psychiatry in Medicine, 4*, 277–283.

World Health Organization. (1992). *International Classification of Diseases and Related Health Problems*. Geneva: World Health Organization.

Youngjohn, J. R., Burrows, L., & Erdal, K. (1995). Brain damage or compensation neurosis? The controversial post-concussion syndrome. *The Clinical Neuropsychologist, 9*, 112–123.

Zakzanis, K. K., Leach, L., & Kaplan, E. (1999). Mild traumatic brain injury. In *Neuropsychological Differential Diagnosis*. Exton, PA: Swets & Zeitlinger, pp. 163–171.

17

Mild Traumatic Brain Injury: Causality Considerations from a Neuroimaging and Neuropathology Perspective

ERIN D. BIGLER

"He was never quite 'himself' after that accident."

In Sinson's (2001, p. 425) commentary about new neuroimaging methods for detecting subtle effects of traumatic brain injury (TBI), he offered the above statement about a patient with mild traumatic brain injury (mTBI) and the potential long-term consequences of such an injury—that a lasting deficit may exist. There is little dispute about potential lasting effects resulting from moderate to severe TBI. Disagreement seems to center on mTBI, its existence and long-term sequelae. This chapter will review neuroimaging and neuropathology of mTBI from the perspective of causality.

1. Animal Models of mTBI

Objectivity is the hallmark of understanding a disorder and in clinical neuroscience, where present, animal models often characterize the best in objective representation of human disorders. This is true for obvious reasons of better experimental control (i.e., controlling the type and severity of injury along with age, genes, environmental effects, etc.) as well as the opportunity to directly examine neural tissue through various anatomical, physiological, histological, and biochemical measures. Given that backdrop, this chapter will start with two important animal model studies of TBI.

Zohar et al. (2003), using a rodent mTBI model, induced brain injury in mice by a "weight drop" technique impacting the head in lightly anesthetized animals, whose heads were held in place by a sponge. This model was specifically designed to mimic human concussion, and animals "concussed" in this manner were found to exhibit persistent cognitive deficits on a water maze task. What is particularly important about this study is that the mice exhibited rapid overall restoration of species-typical behavior once concussed and recovered from the light anesthesia, wherein they immediately returned to species-typical baseline activities of mouse behavior (i.e., exploration, grooming, feeding, etc.) that did not differ from their noninjured cohorts. Postmortem analyses of the brain revealed no gross abnormalities. Furthermore, no visible macroscopic lesions or abnormalities could be identified, including on high-field magnetic resonance imaging (MRI). Only in the novel learning situation of escaping from the water maze did the mice with concussion differ, exhibiting significant cognitive impairment. These findings are also consistent with other animal TBI studies (see Cernak et al., 2004; Creeley et al., 2004; Leker et al., 2002), showing the potential for mTBI to leave a lasting impairment in memory and learning, which may also be observed in humans (Ryan & Warden, 2003; Schretlen & Shapiro, 2003).

The rodent TBI model of Bramlett and Dietrich (2002) has histologically quantified the degree of structural changes in the brain related to severity of injury, in which a distinct reduction in white matter volume with concomitant increase in ventricular volume was shown. White matter damage associated with TBI can be quantitatively demonstrated in humans using MRI methods (Bigler, 2001b, 2005). A straightforward demonstration of white matter vulnerability in human mTBI can be found in the study by Goetz et al. (2004), as shown in Figure 17.1. In this case, an index of water diffusion (i.e., water

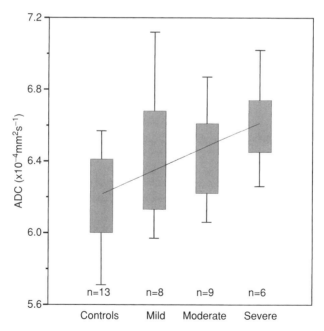

FIGURE 17.1. As a quantitative measure of white matter integrity, the "apparent diffusion coefficient" (ADC) exhibits a linear relationship to injury severity. Boxes indicate the interquartile range and whisker caps indicate the data range. Median bars and the linear regression line of the entire dataset are displayed. [From Goetz et al. (2004) with permission.]

molecules are tightly held together in normal white matter tissue, which differs from that in damaged tissue) shows increased diffusion proportional to the severity of brain injury, including mTBI. Because speed of processing is dependent on white matter integrity, it is not unexpected that diminished speed of processing is a consistent theme of neuropsychological findings in TBI, including mTBI (Mathias et al., 2004a; 2004b).

In the category of mTBI, sports concussions are some of the most well studied (Bigler & Orrison, 2004). Because athletes are motivated to return to play, some of the issues surrounding incentive to recover are maximized. Nonetheless, in sports concussion, there clearly is an initial impairment in memory and diminished speed of processing, which persists for at least a week, as shown in Figure 17.2. Also, once concussed, independent studies have demonstrated an athlete is more susceptible to subsequent concussion, clearly indicating residual effects from the original injury (Guskiewicz et al., 2003; Schulz et al., 2004). Thus, evidently even with sports concussions, at a minimum a transient brain injury occurs that disrupts neurological function, and although full "recovery" results in the vast majority, an increased vulnerability remains for subsequent concussion, suggesting subtle lingering neuropathological effects, even in those asymptotic. Furthermore, Moser et al. (2005) examined high school athletes (n=233) wherein they established baseline performance and compared a group (n=82) who sustained no concussion and had no medical and/or neuropsychological complaints to a group who had experienced one (n=56) or two or more (n=45) concussions (not in the prior six months), and those who had experienced a concussion one week before testing. They found "subtle yet significant prolonged neuropsychological effects in youth athletes with a history of two or more previous concussions (p. 300)."

In addition, the serum s-100B protein is an astroglial protein marker for cerebral tissue damage (Shirasaki et al., 2004), which, when elevated in mTBI, is associated with worse neurobehavioral outcome (Stranjalis et al., 2004). Thus, from a causation standpoint, the issues are about the persistence of sequelae, not whether mTBI exists (see also chapters 15, 16, and 19, respectively, by Barth et al., Vanderploeg et al., and Patry & Mateer, chapter 19).

2.   mTBI Nomenclature and Magnitude of the mTBI Problem

The literature is somewhat confusing with regard to mTBI nomenclature (Boake et al., 2004; Mc Cauley et al., 2005). Often concussion and mTBI are used interchangeably, and when concussive symptoms persist, it is often referred to as a persistent Postconcussive Syndrome, or PCS. Table 17.1 contains various definitional statements related to TBI that center around degree of loss of consciousness (LOC) or coma, the degree of posttraumatic amnesia (PTA), and/or presence of some indicator of injury (i.e., skull fracture). With regard to injury severity, most contemporary definitions utilize some aspect of the Glasgow

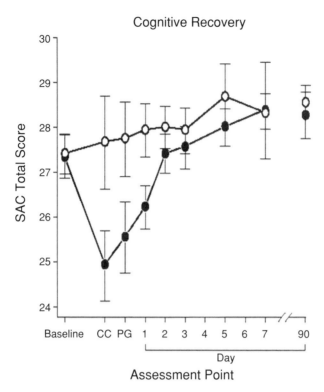

FIGURE 17.2. The immediate effects of a sports-related concussion on a simple cognitive measure—Standardized Assessment of Concussion (SAC). The beauty of this study is that baseline data on each individual subject had been obtained prior to the American collegiate football season beginning. Note the distinct drop in cognitive ability immediately after being concussed (CC), with the level of reduced SAC performance persisting at approximately the same level when assessed after the game (PG). Although remaining below their nonconcussed counterparts, cognitive scores on the SAC only become statistically indistinguishable (i.e., 95% confidence intervals overlap) from nonconcussed subjects on day 2 and remain below the nonconcussed cohort until day 7 postinjury. At 90 days, the concussed group was slightly below the control, insignificantly slow, although the reader should note the greater confidence interval in the concussed subjects. The larger range of the mean confidence interval indicates that within those concussed, there were some who still had reduced SAC scores even when assessed 90 days later. These subjects are, of course, the one of interest for lasting sequelae and the topic of this chapter. [Adapted From McCrea et al. (2003) with permission.] Note: Open circle = control; Closed circle = concussion

Coma Scale (GCS), which ranges from 3 (most severe) to 15 (least severe) (Teasdale & Jennett, 1974), with 13–15 being the traditional range for mTBI. Obviously, bone fide concussion is a brain injury and produces, however momentary or transient, some disruption in normal neurologic homeostasis.

TABLE 17.1. Definitions of mTBI and Concussion Grading Systems

Grade	Cantu[a]	Colorado[b]	Roberts[c]	American Academy of Neurology[d]	European Federation of Neurological Societies[e]
0			"Bell ringer"; no LOC; no PTA		GCS=15; no LOC, no PTA, = head injury, no TBI No risk factors[f]
1	No LOC; PTA <30 minutes	No LOC; confusion without amnesia	No LOC; PTA <30 minutes	No LOC; transient confusion; concussion symptoms or mental status abnormality resolve in <15 minutes	GCS=15; LOC <30 minutes, PTA <1 hour[f] No risk factors[f]
2	LOC <5 minutes; PTA >30 minutes and <24 hours	No LOC; confusion with amnesia	LOC <5 minutes; PTA >30 minutes and <24 hours	No LOC; transient confusion; concussion symptoms or mental status abnormality last >15 minutes	GCS=15 and risk factors[f]
3	LOC >5 minutes or PTA >24 hours	LOC	LOC >5 minutes or PTA >24 hours	Any LOC, either brief or prolonged	GCS=13–14: LOC <30 minutes, PTA <1 hour[f] with or without risk factors present[f]

Note: **LOC** = loss of consciousness; **mTBI** = mild traumatic brain injury; **PTA** = posttraumatic amnesia; **GCS** = Glasgow Coma Scale.
[a]Cantu, 1986.
[b]Kelly et al., 1991.
[c]Roberts, 1992.
[d]Quality standards subcommittee, 1997.
[e]Vos et al., 2002.[f]Risk factors are shown in Table 17.2. These are the same criteria that define complicated mTBI.
Source: Parts adapted with permission from Leclerc et al. (2001).

How quickly neurologic homeostasis returns after an injury defines the significance of any sequelae.

As inferred in Table 17.1, moderate-to-severe TBI is well defined by objective criteria that include definitive alterations in level of consciousness or frank LOC and coma (i.e., GCS scores ≤ 12) in conjunction with various objective neurological deficits and often with definitive neuroimaging findings (Silver et al., 2005). Although the level of disability is often straightforward to establish in those with moderate-to-severe TBI (Colantonio et al., 2004; Dikmen et al., 2003), that range of injury is the least frequent. In the largest study to date involving several hospitals, Udekwu et al. (2004) reports that out of 22,924 emergency room (ER) admissions for head injury, 60.2% were in the mild category (GCS ≥ 13) and 45% had a GCS of 15. The Center for Disease Control places the annual incidence of all types of TBI at about 200 per 100,000 population (see www.cdc.gov), resulting in over 1.5 million brain injuries per year in the United States (Thurman et al., 1999). Therefore, even though the majority of individuals with mTBI fully recover (Carroll et al., 2004; Dikmen et al., 2001; Rees, 2003; Schretlen & Shapiro, 2003), given that mTBI is the most frequent form of TBI, it is understandable why there are large numbers of mTBI patients seen for evaluation (Ruff, 2005; Wood, 2004).

Criteria for the presence of a brain injury can also be established by physics of impact (Bayly et al., 2005; Ommaya et al., 2002; Pittella & Gusmao, 2004; Zhang et al., 2004). Unmistakable and obvious emergency medical care is required in every case of moderate or worse TBI. In contrast, many who sustain mTBI may display only subtle or minimal symptoms acutely, which often may not be medically documented, yet the physical force dynamics present at the time of injury had been sufficient to produce a brain injury (Pellman et al., 2004). Knowing whether physical forces were sufficient to produce an mTBI may be very important in understanding a patient's symptoms following injury.

The importance of establishing injury severity is that severity is particularly important in understanding sequelae, including the presence of neuroimaging abnormalities, and is often the most important predictor of outcome (Anderson et al., 2004). The guidelines offered by Alexander (1995) and Stuss (1995) stress that TBI severity has to be defined during the acute time frame and not by severity of symptoms randomly assessed after trauma. However, one does have to consider the potential for delayed neuropathological effects related to trauma-induced neuroinflammatory reactions that might not be immediately expressed (Grossman et al., 2004; Holmin & Hojeberg, 2004). For example, the relationship between GCS and mortality is linear, and although few die from mTBI, it does occur (Corbo & Tripathi, 2004; Denton & Mileusnic, 2003; Udekwu et al., 2004). In Stuss's guidelines, in evaluating mTBI, he stressed the importance of determining whether symptoms/problems are proportional to severity, with one "underlying golden rule: everything must make sense" (Stuss, 1995, p. 1251). Understanding this principle and that a majority of mTBI patients are classified as "recovered" (Hooper et al., 2004) are *key* to understanding the neuropsychology, including neuroimaging, of mTBI.

3. Trauma, Degenerative Changes, Cerebral Atrophy, and TBI, Including mTBI

As introduced earlier, cerebral atrophy (reduced brain volume, increased ventricular volume, and greater prominence of cortical sulci) is a well-established, objective, and identifiable consequence of TBI. As shown in Figures 17.3 and 17.4, TBI-related cerebral atrophy is proportional to the severity of brain injury (Bigler, 2005). The fewest atrophic changes occur in mTBI but occur nonetheless (MacKenzie et al., 2002; Zhang et al., 2004). Likewise, Govindaraju et al. (2004, p. 730) examined volumetric proton spectroscopic imaging of the whole brain in mTBI patients 1 month postinjury and found "widespread metabolic changes following mTBI in regions that appear normal ..." on conventional MRI. This supports the notion that nonspecific damaging effects can occur in mTBI at a subtle, microscopic level of injury (see also Hurley et al., 2004).

4. Pathophysiology of mTBI

At the immediate point of acute injury, basic pathophysiological processes in TBI may be mechanical, where physical forces stretch, tear, or completely shear axons and/or underlying vasculature, or biochemical, where neuronal metabolic cycles are disrupted or produce neurotoxic cascades that disrupt or damage cellular integrity (Povlishock & Katz, 2005). Secondary TBI effects that damage the brain occur in the form of edema and a variety of neuroinflammatory responses (Graham et al., 2002; Povlishock & Katz, 2005).

There is ongoing debate about what constitutes the mildest form of mTBI and how neurobehavioral function may be altered (Gaetz, 2004; Mickeviciene et al., 2004; Rees, 2003). As already stated, most who sustain mTBI "recover," indicating the potential transient nature of mTBI. A most appropriate example of an individual with such transient effects followed by "recovery" is Picabo Street, the Olympic downhill competitive racer, who, in 1998, lost control and slammed into the retaining barrier, losing consciousness for 45 seconds, an event clearly captured on television. Within a few days, she was medically cleared to race again and won the Super Giant Slalom (super-g) gold medal in the Nagano, 1998 Winter Olympics.

As outlined in Table 17.1, the minimal effects to produce mTBI distinctly alter normal neurological homeostasis. How quickly neurological normalcy returns in part defines the mildest form of mTBI (Guskiewicz et al., 2003; McCrea et al., 2003). Transient disruption of neural function in mTBI has been characterized as something akin to a brief seizure (McCrory & Berkovic, 2000; Shaw, 2002). This is an appropriate analogy because in a more significant mTBI, a brief trauma-induced seizure may occur immediately after the impact (McCrory & Berkovic, 2000). In the mildest form of mTBI, this disruption in the delicate biochemical balance that underlies

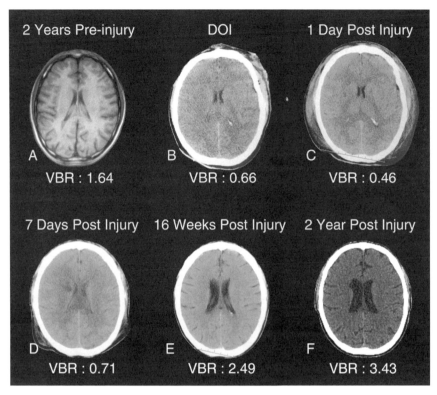

FIGURE 17.3. This case nicely demonstrates the type of nonspecific ventricular dilation that accompanies moderate-to-severe TBI and might also be seen in mTBI. In this case, the patient had an MRI performed 2 years prior to injury, because of headaches. No abnormalities were found (see top left). Quantitative analysis included the calculation of the ventricle-to-brain ratio (VBR), which represents total ventricular volume divided by total brain volume times 100. The normal VBR for individuals under 40 years of age is approximately 1.5, with a standard deviation of 0.5 (Blatter et al., 1995). As such, the preinjury VBR is well within normal limits. The day-of-injury CT demonstrates generalized cerebral edema evidenced by loss of white–gray matter boundaries, effacement of the ventricular system, and lack of definition for cortical sulci. VBR based on imaging approximately 2 hours after admission demonstrates markedly reduced VBR, indicative of the trauma-induced generalized brain swelling, that persists more than a week. When scanned 16 weeks postinjury, significant ventricular dilation was present that eventually plateaued at more than 3 standard deviations above the normal mean. Note the ventricular prominence along with the width and depth of the cortical sulci.

neural transmission returns quickly to its baseline state and may not be associated with any permanent structural or neurochemical changes that are deleterious to neurological function (McCrea et al., 2003). Keeping within the seizure analogy in those with epilepsy, once a seizure runs its

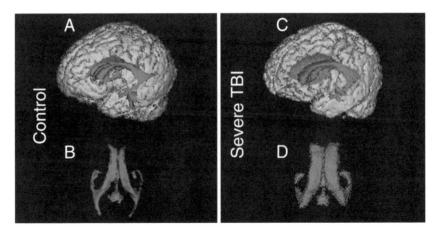

FIGURE 17.4. Three-dimensional (3D) reconstruction of the ventricular system of the patient from Figure 17.3 is shown (C) compared to an age-matched control (A). Note the generalized enlargement of the ventricular system. The ventricular enlargement is even more readily recognized when the 3D ventricle is isolated and shown in dorsal view in the TBI patient (D) compared to the control (B). Again, note the diffuse nature of ventricular dilation indicative of global brain volume loss associated with TBI.

course, rapid cognitive and neurobehavioral function may be restored, wherein the patient returns to baseline function (Aldenkamp & Arends, 2004).

As injury moves along the continuum toward complicated mTBI (see Table 17.2), a better defined structural as well as pathophysiological process occurs with improved prediction of neurobehavioral sequelae (Silver et al., 2005). For example, there is ample evidence that the frontal and temporal regions of the brain are most vulnerable in TBI, including mTBI (Bigler, 2005). Basal forebrain structures, the ventral striatum, and limbic structures, including mesial temporal lobe structures like the hippocampus and amygdala, are especially vulnerable to brain injury (Salmond et al., 2005; Wilde et al., 2005). Because these frontotemporolimbic regions are the most susceptible to injury where macroscopic damage can be identified, there is little reason not to assume that these same regions are also the most susceptible in mTBI as well. Furthermore, damage to these regions may be explanatory of the neurobehavioral sequelae of mTBI (Bigler, 2004).

The scan taken over 1 year postinjury in Figure 17.5 demonstrates these points. This patient sustained an mTBI in a motor vehicle accident (MVA); her GCS at the scene was rated 14, but was 15 by the time she was evaluated in the ER. The scan clearly shows numerous hemosiderin deposits, indicators of prior hemorrhagic lesions, scattered throughout the frontal lobes. Hemosiderin deposits are often located right on the margin of gray/white matter and it is this

TABLE 17.2. Factors Associated with Complicated mTBI Based on the Recommendations for the Selection of Patients for CT Imaging of the Head Based on Meta-Analysis of 83,636 Patients Admitted with mTBI

Patients with any one of the following signs or symptoms should have CT scanning of the head immediately requested:

1. GCS < 13 at any point since the injury
2. GCS < 15 at 2 h after the injury
3. Suspected open or depressed skull fracture
4. Any sign of basal skull fracture
5. Posttraumatic seizure
6. Focal neurological deficit
7. More than one episode of vomiting
8. Amnesia for more than 30 minutes

CT should also be immediately requested in the following patients provided they have experience some LOC or PTA since injury

1. Age > 65 years
2. Coagulopathy
3. Dangerous mechanism of injury: pedestrian struck by motor vehicle; occupant ejected from car; fall greater than 3 ft

Note: mTBI = mild traumatic brain injury; CT = computerized tomography; GCS = Glasgow Coma Scale; LOC = loss of consciousness; PTA = posttraumatic amnesia.
Source: Adapted from Dunning et al. (2004) with permission.

finding that often is interpreted as a neuroimaging indicator of diffuse axonal injury (DAI) (Besenski, 2002). In a young patient with no prior history of head injury and no other risk factor for intracranial hemorrhage, the presence of hemosiderin become *sine qua non* indicators of shear injury, because that is the mechanism that leads to tearing of the microvasculature and bleeding into brain parenchyma. Accordingly, part of the vulnerability of brain injury is not just injury to brain tissue but also the vasculature that supports it, resulting in neurotransmitter and metabolic changes (Buczek et al., 2002; Lovell et al., 2004). Thus, shearing of blood vessels, reflected by the presence of hemosiderin secondary to trauma, is in the same class as axonal injury from trauma (Graham et al., 2002). Furthermore, scattered small deposits of hemosiderin have been shown to be present at postmortem, below the detection of neuroimaging in mTBI (Bigler, 2004). This means that in cases of TBI, what is detected at the macroscopic end of structural neuroimaging may only represent part of the actual underlying pathophysiology (see Kushi et al., 2003). Because much of the pathology may be at the microscopic level, functional neuroimaging may be more suitable for the detection of subtle deficits associated with mTBI, where a consistent theme of functional neuroimaging studies is slowed processing speed, likely a result of disrupted white matter integrity (Bigler & Orrison, 2004; McAllister et al., 1999). Matching these findings with those showing cognitive differences in terms of speed of processing in mTBI (Felmingham et al., 2004;

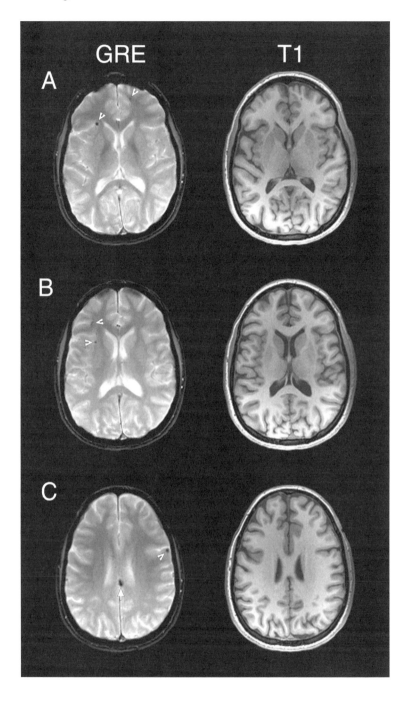

Mathias et al., 2004a; 2004b) makes for a compelling argument for some form of white matter perturbation as the basis for many mTBI sequelae when they persist (see Huisman et al., 2004).

5.   Other Variables in mTBI

5.1.   Complicated Versus Uncomplicated mTBI: mTBI Severity and Outcome

The mildest forms of experimental concussion typically show rapid return to baseline (see Shaw, 2002), as is the case in human mTBI. However, when symptoms, particularly PTA, persists after a concussion, thereby reaching criteria for Grade 3 or any factors listed in Table 17.2 representing "complicated" mTBI (see Borgaro et al., 2003), as a group such individuals are at increased likelihood for residual deficits (Ibanez et al., 2004) and to have positive imaging findings (Bigler, 2005).

5.2.   Age, Time of Injury, and Long-Term Outcome

It is now well known that dynamic changes in brain development occur over one's life span (Salat et al., 2004; Sowell et al., 2004). Accordingly, TBI that occurs during strategic periods of brain development or aging might have particularly disruptive effects on outcome (Wilde et al., 2005). In two prospective studies examining neurobehavioral sequelae up to 25 years post-mTBI in childhood, McKinlay et al. (2002, 2004) have shown that children with complicated mTBIs had a much higher likelihood of being diagnosed with a neuropsychiatric disorder. Hawley et al. (2004), in a parental survey conducted up to 6 years after children with complicated mTBIs (all were hospitalized), found significantly increased parental endorsement for such things as personality change (20%), mood swings (18.2%), headaches (15.6%), problems with attention (14.1%), temper outbursts (13%), and tiredness (11.5%). In the matched non-mTBI control sample whose parents completed the same questionnaires, Hawley et al. (2004) found headaches were ranked at a

---

FIGURE 17.5. Illustration of residual lesions associated with mTBI defined by hemosiderin deposits, best identified in the gradient recalled echo (GRE) sequence (left column), where small hemorrhagic lesions show up as dark spots (see arrows). There is also a large lesion in the posterior corpus callosum (see arrowhead), a common place for shearing. Note the preponderance of frontal locations of the hemosiderin deposits. The T1 imaging (right column) nicely depicts anatomy, which shows no distinct abnormalities, yet some prominence of the right Sylvian fissure (viewer's left) is evident. The patient's neuropsychological and neurobehavioral changes were consistent with the MRI findings.

frequency of 4.4%, with all of the other behaviors rated no higher than 2.2% and most at 0.0% (see also Hooper et al., 2004). Likewise, at the other end of the age spectrum, some speculate that mTBI has more of an effect in older individuals and that this relates to diminished brain reserve and resiliency effects associated with aging (Bigler, 2006).

6.   Subjective Symptomology in mTBI

The fact that most of the symptomology associated with mTBI is subjective in nature and nonspecific is a core feature of the controversy associated with persistent mTBI sequelae (Alexander, 1995; Evans, 1994, 2004a, 2004b; Vos et al., 2002). If one refers to the American Psychiatric Association *Diagnostic and Statistical Manual*, 4th ed. (DSM-IV), *all* of the neurobehavioral features of PCS (i.e., persistent mTBI) have subjective elements that overlap with numerous neurologic and neuropsychiatric disorders. This lack of specificity often makes it difficult to know what symptoms are attributable to the injury and what may be the result of correlated, preinjury, or unrelated conditions (Luis et al., 2003; Vanderploeg et al., 2003). Therefore, the time line of symptom onset postinjury and recognition and reliance on good base rate research on postconcussive symptoms is critical.

   Appropriately done, base-rate research comes from well-designed, prospective, population-based studies in which researchers have no vested interest in the outcome of the study, merely reporting the base-rate symptomology. For example, in a study from the Netherlands, Stulemeijer et al. (2004) recently examined the prevalence rate of subjective PCS symptoms in a cohort of 450 consecutive mTBI patients (83% had a GCS of 15, 10% had 14, and 7% had 13) who were followed and reassessed 6 months postinjury. Sixty-eight percent reported one or more persistent symptoms at 6 months post-injury; the most frequent symptoms were fatigue (69%), forgetfulness (60%), and increased irritability (59%). In the matched patient control group consisting of those with traumatic ankle or wrist orthopedic injury but no head injury, only 20% endorsed any PCS symptomology at 6 months postinjury, with the top three being fatigue (73%), sleep problems (60%) and increased irritability (53%). These base-rate issues are also dealt with in Chapter 16 by Vanderploeg et al.

   Given the list of subjective symptoms commonly endorsed by mTBI patients, often those patients who continue to endorse somatic symptoms in the absence of "objective" findings supporting their symptom endorsement have been considered to have some form of a somatization disorder (Binder & Campbell, 2004; Larrabee, 2005). Indeed, somatization may occur with a higher frequency in mTBI. However, difficult to explain symptoms may represent a much more complicated circumstance than represented by labeling the condition as being under the umbrella of somatoform disorder or medically unexplained (Richardson & Engel, 2004). For example, pituitary–hypothalamic regions may be particularly vulnerable to TBI (Agha et al., 2004a, 2004b; Bondanelli et al.,

2004; Elovic, 2003), including mTBI. As exemplified by demyelinating disorders, white matter damage is associated with fatiguability (Attarian et al., 2004; Lobentanz et al., 2004; Tartaglia et al., 2004) and a common theme of almost any neurological disorder is some disruption in stamina, both physical and mental, where complaints of fatigue and motivation are commonplace (Alves et al., 2004; Habib, 2004; Staub & Bogousslavsky, 2001; van der Werf et al., 2001).

As already mentioned, a variety of immune responses are acutely and subacutely initiated by TBI, which, at this time, are poorly understood (Raghupathi, 2004). Also, limbic, striatal, and frontotemporal regions are particularly vulnerable in TBI, and residing within these brain regions are centers for drive, motivation, and emotional regulation. Sleep disturbance is a common mTBI sequelae and sleep deprivation impairs working memory and differentially activates the dorsolateral prefrontal cortex (Chee & Choo, 2004). Mild TBI patients often complain of not being able to tolerate stress as they had done preinjury and, interestingly, increased stress may adversely influence protein kinase C (PKC) signaling in prefrontal cortical areas, and elevated PKC levels are associated with impaired working memory (Birnbaum et al., 2004). Similar prefrontal regions are altered by pain as well (Apkarian et al., 2004; Newberg et al., 2005). Posttraumatic Stress Disorder could be a factor in mTBI (Glaesser et al., 2004; Harvey et al., 2003) and may coexist with mTBI, and in certain individuals, the brain injury itself may play a predisposing role in the elicitation of PTSD.

Finally, having been in a traumatic event such as an accident and the event now being the reference point for symptom onset, various attributional factors may also be at play in how the patient perceives symptoms and their cause (Gunstad & Suhr, 2004).

To conclude, there may be a variety of neuropsychiatric features that corelate to "subjective" postconcussive symptomology. Accordingly, it can be argued that the so-called subjective symptoms associated with mTBI may, indeed, have a neurobiological basis, notwithstanding the play of factors such as attribution of cause to the event, and other cognitive sets and expectations. Along these lines, it should be noted that "subjective" symptoms have been shown in other disorders (i.e., progressive neurological disorders) to truly be the *first* symptoms of the disorder (Jorm et al., 2004; van der Flier et al., 2004).

6.1. Objective Neurocognitive Findings in mTBI

Often "objective" findings of neurocognitive deficits specific to mTBI are difficult to clearly delineate and demonstrate (Binder et al., 1997; Frencham et al., 2004; Schretlen & Shapiro, 2003). The typical patient who has sustained an injury does not have a preinjury neuropsychological battery of tests for comparison. Thus, inferences about premorbid abilities have to be made (Skeel et al., 2004) to interpret the postinjury test. But the same applies to postinjury patterns; there is no unique data marker of definitive long-term neuropsychological sequelae on neuropsychological battery performance, and inferences have to be made. Returning to Stuss's (1995) recommendations, mTBI deficits, if demonstrated at all on neuropsychological tests, should be in proportion to the injury and, therefore, should generally be "mild" or "subtle" as well, typically expressed as impairments in sustained attention/concentration, short-term memory, and executive function along with changes in mood regulation and affect. Nevertheless, the confluence of such impairments may lead to quite evident functional impairments, depending on the individual involved and his or her context at work, home, in school, and so on.

7. Heterogeneity of TBI and Outcome

Outcome from brain injury is very heterogenous. Patients with what appear to be very similar lesions will often have very different outcomes (Bigler, 2001a). In fact, studies examining the degree of lesion burden in any type of brain injury, not just TBI, where "lesion burden" is usually defined as the total volume of identifiable lesions, find at best that overall lesion burden accounts for only part of the variance (Anderson et al., 2004; Levin et al., 2004; Rovaris et al., 2003). Undoubtedly, there are complex factors at play in trying to predict outcome, most of which are poorly specified at this time but generally fall into two broad but not mutually exclusive categories: (1) vulnerability or susceptibility factors and (2) degree of cognitive reserve or resilience. Such factors as prior head injury, pre-existing neurological disorder (e.g., epilepsy), presence of learning disability at the time of injury, pre-existing neuropsychiatric disorder, and level of educational attainment prior to injury (Bigler, 2006) all impact the likelihood of persistent mTBI sequelae. Accordingly, at the time of injury there are significant individual differences based on constitutional, genetic, and environmental factors that all have the potential to impact expression of mTBI symptomology, recovery, and outcome.

7.1. Remote, Long-Term Consequences of mTBI

The simple answer to the question about the persistent effects of mTBI is that its lasting effects are not known at this time. Studies to date indicate that TBI alters the risk ratios for neuropsychiatric disorders, including disorders of depression, suicide, and dementia (see Silver et al., 2005). The interaction of genetic predisposition and head injury may also be a factor (Koponen et al., 2004; Mayeux, 2004; Mayeux et al., 1995). How chronic mTBI-related problems are manifested in cognition, behavior, and neuroimaging findings over one's life span and how these problems can be separated from pre-existing or comorbid problems is the challenge in establishing the causality effects of mTBI. In this context, much of the psychiatric morbidity associated with mTBI may need to be viewed in the context of life-span vulnerability factors, not at just a single point of assessment. Thus, two individuals who sustain identical mTBIs may have dissimilar outcomes depending on their genetic and neuropsychiatric constitution and constellation of vulnerability factors at the time of injury. In such cases, individuals with prior neuropsychiatric history (i.e., depression) may be more vulnerable to the effects of mTBI over one's life span. Similarly, Guskiewicz et al. (2003) and Schulz et al. (2004) have independently documented the greater susceptibility of sustaining a sports-related concussion in those with previous concussion. If concussion were truly benign, having sustained a prior concussion should not alter the likelihood of a subsequent concussion.

8.   Diagnostic Issues

8.1.   Can Neuropsychological Tests Alone Diagnose mTBI?

There is not sufficient specificity in neuropsychological test findings to "diagnose" mTBI, independent of other critical clinical information. Neuropsychological testing is well designed to demonstrate potential problems within various cognitive domains, such as memory and executive function, provided sufficient patient compliance and effort during assessment. However, without the history and time line of symptom onset, severity, and duration, neuropsychological test findings alone cannot be used to "diagnose" mTBI.

8.2.   The Importance of History: The Time Line of Symptom Onset

Several empirical studies have assessed the importance of history and the time line of symptom onset in making correct diagnoses (Hampton et al., 1975; Peterson et al., 1992; Sandler, 1980). Interestingly, these studies generally report high diagnostic accuracy rates based solely on history-taking, underscoring the importance of history and time line of symptom onset in establishing the correct diagnosis. In mTBI, obviously there is a known event. Applying the guidelines outlined by Stuss (1995), assessing the patient's preinjury status compared to postinjury, with the aid of neuropsychological test and neuroimaging findings, typically an accurate assessment of the patient's problems and their long-term relevance can be made. In other words, when the clinical time line and clinical picture make sense, in the context of an appropriate comprehensive assement, the probability of obtaining a valid assessment is optimized.

8.3.   Comorbidity and mTBI

Cormorbidity has already been alluded to, but, in conclusion, it needs emphasis again. A variety of disorders have similar symptoms to mTBI or may coexist with it, including disorders of mood, chronic pain, and PTSD (Harvey et al., 2003). Problems with mood may impact neurocognitive performance (Thompson et al., 2005). Persistent headache is a common sequelae of concussion (Evans, 2004b), and headache alone has its associated neuropsychological sequelae (Collins et al., 2003). Likewise, because the patient has been involved in physical trauma to the body, often physical injuries associated with chronic pain syndromes may accompany mTBI (Nicholson & Martelli, 2004). Finally, being involved in medicolegal proceedings is associated with its own degree of stress, which may also negatively impact a patient's emotional state and ability to perform neuropsychological tests (Feinstein et al., 2001). Some of these issues are addressed in Chapter 18 by Nicholson and Martelli.

9.   How Is Causality Handled in the Adversarial Legal Process? Polarization and Bias in Forensic Neuropsychological Evaluations of mTBI: Effort, Malingering, and Validity of Performance

In neuropsychological assessment, conclusions must be based on an examination of a valid clinical presentation by the patient that includes test performance and history given. In the context of valid performance, considerable research has examined the problems associated with effort, malingering, and related factors as they pertain to neuropsychological assessment in cases of mTBI (Moore & Donders, 2004; Vanderploeg & Curtiss, 2001). For the most part, the appropriately trained and ethically-guided clinician is well equipped to handle these problems when they arise and provide reasonable explanations for their clinical significance, including the diagnosis of malingering (disingenuous or poor effort intentionally done to exaggerate a deficit) when it is present.

Obviously, in litigation, where the degree of compensation has the potential to affect the level of "impairment" exhibited by a patient (Binder, 2002; Feinstein et al., 2001; Freeman & Rossignol, 2000), understanding the factors around explicit incentives (conscious or not) that might influence a mTBI patient's behavior are important (Feinstein et al., 2001). As described by Larrabee (2005), the potential for frank malingering is present in any forensic case and needs to be clearly and straightforwardly addressed in assessment.

Because subjective symptoms characterize mTBI and most individuals "recover" following injury, there is clearly the potential for overdiagnosis of impairments associated with mTBI (i.e., false positives). Oppositely, to ignore genuine symptomology, which fits with the known sequelae of mTBI, would constitute a misdiagnosis (i.e., false negatives). The key to accurate diagnosis is to keep both of these types of error to a minimum, best implemented within a conservative scientific approach to assessment and knowledge of the current scientific literature of known mTBI sequelae, including neuropsychological findings, combined with Stuss's (1995) guidelines. Genuine residual deficits can and do result from mTBI, but as outlined in this volume, there should be both external and internal consistency between the patient's history of injury and his or her premorbid and postmorbid status.

Unfortunately, the guidelines offered above are sometimes ignored by either side when litigation is involved. For example, overdiagnosis of mTBI sequelae occurs when the clinician over relies on poor neuropsychological test performance alone without carefully examining the patient's history or level of effort during testing. Oppositely, the retained defense expert who views his or her role as generating as many points as possible to discredit genuine mTBI symptoms will produce an evaluation that has little bearing on the patient's actual condition. For example, such an expert often will go to extraordinary lengths questioning neuropsychological test validity, the veracity of the patient's claimed deficits, and/or the patient's performance on neuropsychological tests, or the test selection used by the expert. This approach attempts to either show that methods of neuropsychological assessment are useless in detecting what they purport, that the deficits pre-existed, or are not genuine (i.e., the patient is malingering) or are at least not at the level endorsed and portrayed by the patient (i.e., poor effort, disingenuous). In such cases there is no real interest in understanding legitimate TBI symptoms, but only to provide "alternative" explanations that avoid acknowledgment of the effects of any acquired brain injury.

An example of this is given in Figure 17.6: a case of severe TBI. Indisputably, this patient's MRI displays massive structural damage in the

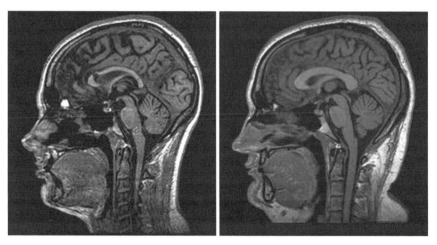

TBI   Normal

FIGURE 17.6. The patient on the left had sustained a severe TBI (see text for description), clearly evident in the chronic-phase MRI done several years postinjury. Note the frontal atrophy (dark areas of cerebrospinal) fluid in these sagittal images of the TBI patient contrasted to a control at a similar plane. Also, note the generalized atrophy of the corpus callosum, reduction in size of the fornix, and a complete shear lesion of the anterior aspect of the corpus callosum. The defense psychologist who evaluated this patient made the diagnosis of anxiety disorder.

view shown, particularly in the frontal region. The psychologist retained by the defense concluded, in DSM-IV parlance, that this patient did have a "cognitive disorder, not otherwise specified" but that it was in "partial remission" and that her greater problem was "anxiety disorder, with depressive and anxious components" with, of course, no mention that such symptoms are commonplace with severe brain injury (see Jorge et al., 2004). This psychologist, who in deposition admitted to only doing defense work, also further qualified the "cognitive disorder" as being influenced by "psychogenic" factors of depression and anxiety and that "inconsistent" effort may have "undermined" her performance on neuropsychological tests. So, ignoring the history of severe brain injury—the amount of structural damage as objectively shown in Figure 17.6—the defense psychologist issued a report that bore little resemblance to the actual problems of this patient, a true disservice to the field of forensic psychology. It was also enlightening to note the exorbitant fees received by this defense psychologist, for a single neuropsychological "forensic" consultation. If such statements are made about a straightforward severe TBI case, it takes little imagination to know what the "defense expert" would say about neuropsychological and neuroimaging findings in mTBI.

10.   Guidelines and Conclusions

The objectivity of neuroimaging, both functional and structural, adds to the objectivity of findings associated with mTBI and provides, in part, the basis for understanding causality. Future structural as well as functional neuroimaging methods will likely resolve some controversies associated with outcome following both uncomplicated and complicated mTBI. From the standpoint of establishing causality, the neuropathological basis for persistent symptomology associated with complicated mTBI is more straightforward, as reviewed earlier. The neuroimaging and neuropathological studies, to date, point toward a subtle disruption in the integrity of frontotemporal and limbic systems that regulate working memory and executive and emotional function. Speed of processing also appears to be affected, most likely via impairment in white matter integrity. The guidelines offered by Stuss (1995) are reasonable ones to assist the expert in evaluating the effects of mTBI consistency within each of the patients' history of injury, their premorbid status, and their postmorbid status, as well as between the severity of their injury and their postmorbid status. Neuropsychological assessment methods are best suited as functional measures of the patient's current status, rather than aiding in establishing the diagnosis of "brain damage" in mTBI. Part of the reason for the lack of diagnostic specificity of neuropsychological testing in mTBI is that the neuropsychological battery is not only assessing the sum total of trauma effects, including any related to pain, but also changes in psychosocial status, and stress-mediated problems as well as premorbid factors. History of symptom expression should guide the clinician, in conjunction with neuropsychological patterns of strengths and weaknesses, where consideration is given to preinjury or related possible confounding factors, to determine the relevant forensic implications of mTBI. Finally, experts should simply be good scientists and practitioners and do what they have been trained to do—validly assess the symptoms of the patient and, in the framework of causality as outlined in this chapter, assess whether there is a relationship between symptoms and injury.

References

Agha, A., Rogers, B., Sherlock, M., O'Kelly, P., Tormey, W., Phillips, J., &Thompson, C.J. (2004a). Anterior pituitary dysfunction in survivors of traumatic brain injury. *Journal of Clinical Endocrinology and Metabolism, 89(10)*, 4929–4936.

Agha, A., Thornton, E., O'Kelly, P., Tormey, W., Phillips, J., & Thompson, C. J. (2004b). Posterior pituitary dysfunction after traumatic brain injury. *Journal of Clinical Endocrinology and Metabolism, 89(12)*, 5987–5992.

Aldenkamp, A. P. & Arends, J. (2004). Effects of epileptiform EEG discharges on cognitive function: is the concept of "transient cognitive impairment" still valid? *Epilepsy and Behavior, 57 (Suppl. 1)*, S25–S34.

Alexander, M. P. (1995). Mild traumatic brain injury: Pathophysiology, natural history, and clinical management. *Neurology, 45*, 1253–1260.

Alves, G., Wentzel-Larsen, T., & Larsen, J. P. (2004). Is fatigue an independent and persistent symptom in patients with Parkinson disease? *Neurology, 63(10)*, 1908–1911.

Anderson, V. A., Morse, S. A., Catroppa, C., Haritou, F., & Rosenfeld, J. V. (2004). Thirty month outcome from early childhood head injury: A prospective analysis of neurobehavioural recovery. *Brain, 127(Pt. 12)*, 2608–2620.

Apkarian, A. V., Sosa, Y., Sonty, S., Levy, R. M., Harden, R. N., Parrish, T. B., Gitelman, D.R. (2004). Chronic back pain is associated with decreased prefrontal and thalamic gray matter density. *Journal of Neuroscience, 24(46)*, 10,410–10,415.

Attarian, H. P., Brown, K. M., Duntley, S. P., Carter, J. D., & Cross, A. H. (2004). The relationship of sleep disturbances and fatigue in multiple sclerosis. *Archives of Neurology, 61(4)*, 525–528.

Bayly, P.V., Cohen, E.P., Leister, D. Ajo, Leuthardt, E.C., & Genin, G.M. (2005). Deformation of the human brain induced by mild acceleration. *Journal of Neurotrauma, 22*(8), 2005, 845–856.

Besenski, N. (2002). Traumatic injuries: Imaging of head injuries. *European Radiology, 12(6)*, 1237–1252.

Bigler, E. D. (2001a). Neuropsychological testing defines the neurobehavioral significance of neuroimaging-identified abnormalities. *Archives of Clinical Neuropsychology, 16(3)*, 227–236.

Bigler, E. D. (2001b). Quantitative magnetic resonance imaging in traumatic brain injury. *Journal of Head Trauma Rehabilitation, 16(2)*, 1–21.

Bigler, E. D. (2004). Neuropsychological results and neuropathological findings at autopsy in a case of mild traumatic brain injury. *Journal of the International Neuropsychology Society, 10(5)*, 794–806.

Bigler, E. D. (2005). Structural Imaging. In J. M. Silver, T. W. McAllister, T. W., & S. C. Yudofsky (Eds.). *Textbook of Traumatic Brain Injury*, 2nd ed., Washington DC: American Psychiatric Publishing.

Bigler, E. D. (2006). Neuroimaging correlates of functional outcome. In N. D. Zasler, D. I. Katz, & R. D. Zafonte (Eds.). *Brain Injury Medicine: Principles and Practice*. New York: Demos Medical Publishing.

Bigler, E. D. (2006). Traumatic brain injury and cognitive reserve. In Y. Stern (Ed.). *Cognitive Reserve*. New York: Psychology Press (in press).

Bigler, E. D. & Orrison, W. W., Jr. (2004). Neuroimaging in sports-related brain injury. In M. R. Lovell, R. J. Echemendia, J. T. Barth, & M. W. Collins (Eds.). *Traumatic Brain Injury in Sports*. Lisse, The Netherlands: Swets and Zeitlinger, pp. 71–93.

Binder, L. M. & Campbell, K. A. (2004). Medically unexplained symptoms and neuropsychological assessment. *Journal of Clinical* and *Experimental Neuropsychology, 26(3)*, 369–392.

Binder, L. M., Rohling, M. L., & Larrabee, J. (1997). A review of mild head trauma. Part I: Meta-analytic review of neuropsychological studies. *Journal of Clinical and Experimental Neuropsychology, 19(3)*, 421–431.

Binder, R. L. (2002). Liability for the psychiatrist expert witness. *American Journal of Psychiatry, 159(11)*, 1819–1825.

Birnbaum, S. G., Yuan, P. X., Wang, M., Vijayraghavan, S., Bloom, A. K., Davis, D. J., Gobeske, K. T., Sweatt, J. D., Manji, H. K., & Arnsten, A. F. (2004). Gobeske, K. (2004). Protein kinase C overactivity impairs prefrontal cortical regulation of working memory. *Science, 306(5697)*, 882–884.

Blatter, D. D., Bigler, E. D., Gale, S. D., Johnson, S. C., Anderson, C. V., Burnett, B. M., Parker, N., Kurth, S., & Horn, S. D. (1995). Quantitative volumetric analysis of brain MR: Normative database spanning 5 decades of life. *American Journal of Neuroradiology, 16(2)*, 241–251.

Boake, C., McCauley, S. R., Levin, H. S., Contant, C. F., Song, J. X., Brown, S. A., Goodman, H. S., Brundage, S. I., Diaz-Marchan, P. J., & Merritt, S. G. (2004). Limited agreement between criteria-based diagnoses of postconcussional syndrome. *Journal of Neuropsychiatry and Clinical Neuroscience, 16(4)*, 493–499.

Bondanelli, M., De Marinis, L., Ambrosio, M. R., Monesi, M., Valle, D., Zatelli, M. C., Fusco, A., Bianchi, A., Farneti, M., & degli Uberti, E. C. (2004). Occurrence of pituitary dysfunction following traumatic brain injury. *Journal of Neurotrauma, 21(6)*, 685–696.

Borgaro, S. R., Prigatano, G. P., Kwasnica, C., & Rexer, J. L. (2003). Cognitive and affective sequelae in complicated and uncomplicated mild traumatic brain injury. *Brain Injury, 17(3)*, 189–198.

Bramlett, H. M. & Dietrich, W. D. (2002). Quantitative structural changes in white and gray matter 1 year following traumatic brain injury in rats. *Acta Neuropathology (Berlin), 103(6)*, 607–614.

Brown, A. W., Leibson, C. L., Malec, J. F., Perkins, P. K., Diehl, N. N., & Larson, D. R. (2004). Long-term survival after traumatic brain injury: A population-based analysis. *NeuroRehabilitation, 19(1)*, 37–43.

Buczek, M., Alvarez, J., Azhar, J., Zhou, Y., Lust, W. D., Selman, W. R., & Ratcheson, R. A. (2002). Delayed changes in regional brain energy metabolism following cerebral concussion in rats. *Metabolism and Brain Disease, 17(3)*, 153–167.

Cantu, R. C. (1986). Guidelines for return to contact sports after cerebral concussion. *Physician and Sports Medicine, 14*, 75–83.

Carroll, L. J., Cassidy, J. D., Peloso, P. M., Borg, J., von Holst, H., Holm, L., Paniak, C., & Pepin, M. (2004). Prognosis for mild traumatic brain injury: Results of the WHO Collaborating Centre Task Force on Mild Traumatic Brain Injury. *Journal of Rehabilitative Medicine, (43 Suppl.)*, 84–105.

Cernak, I., Vink, R., Zapple, D. N., Cruz, M. I., Ahmed, F., Chang, T., Fricke, S.T., & Faden, A.I. (2004). The pathobiology of moderate diffuse traumatic brain injury as identified using a new experimental model of injury in rats. *Neurobiologic Disorders, 17(1)*, 29–43.

Chee, M. W. & Choo, W. C. (2004). Functional imaging of working memory after 24 hr of total sleep deprivation. *Journal of Neuroscience, 24(19)*, 4560–4567.

Colantonio, A., Ratcliff, G., Chase, S., Kelsey, S., Escobar, M., & Vernich, L. (2004). Long-term outcomes after moderate to severe traumatic brain injury. *Disability and Rehabilitation, 26(5)*, 253–261.

Collins, M. W., Field, M., Lovell, M. R., Iverson, G., Johnston, K. M., Maroon, J., Fu, F. H. (2003). Relationship between postconcussion headache and neuropsychological test performance in high school athletes. *American Journal of Sports Medicine, 31(2)*, 168–173.

Corbo, J. & Tripathi, P. (2004). Delayed presentation of diffuse axonal injury: A case report. *Annals of Emergency Medicine, 44(1)*, 57–60.

Creeley, C. E., Wozniak, D. F., Bayly, P. V., Olney, J. W., & Lewis, L. M. (2004). Multiple episodes of mild traumatic brain injury result in impaired cognitive performance in mice. *Academy of Emergency Medicine, 11(8)*, 809–819.

Denton, S. & Mileusnic, D. (2003). Delayed sudden death in an infant following an accidental fall: A case report with review of the literature. *American Journal of Forensic Medicine and Pathology, 24(4)*, 371–376.

Dikmen, S., Machamer, J., & Temkin, N. (2001). Mild head injury: Facts and artifacts. *Journal of Clinical and Experimental Neuropsychology, 23(6)*, 729–738.

Dikmen, S. S., Machamer, J. E., Powell, J. M., & Temkin, N. R. (2003). Outcome 3 to 5 years after moderate to severe traumatic brain injury. *Archives of Physical and Medical Rehabilitation, 84(10)*, 1449–1457.

Dunning, J., Stratford-Smith, P., Lecky, F., Batchelor, J., Hogg, K., Browne, J., Sharpin, C., & Mackway-Jones, K. (2004). A meta-analysis of clinical correlates that predict significant intracranial injury in adults with minor head trauma. *Journal of Neurotrauma, 21(7)*, 877–885.

Elovic, E. P. (2003). Anterior pituitary dysfunction after traumatic brain injury, Part I. *Journal of Head Trauma Rehabilitation, 18(6)*, 541–543.

Evans, R. W. (1994). The postconcussion syndrome: 130 years of controversy. *Seminars in Neurology, 14(1)*, 32–39.

Evans, R. W. (2004a). The postconcussion syndrome and whiplash injuries: A question-and-answer review for primary care physicians. *Primary Care, 31(1)*, 1–17.

Evans, R. W. (2004b). Post-traumatic headaches. *Neurology Clinics, 22(1)*, 237–249.

Feinstein, A., Ouchterlony, D., Somerville, J., & Jardine, A. (2001). The effects of litigation on symptom expression: A prospective study following mild traumatic brain injury. *Medicine Science Law, 41(2)*, 116–121.

Felmingham, K. L., Baguley, I. J., & Green, A. M. (2004). Effects of diffuse axonal injury on speed of information processing following severe traumatic brain injury. *Neuropsychology, 18(3)*, 564–571.

Freeman, M. D. & Rossignol, A. M. (2000). Effect of eliminating compensation for pain and suffering on the outcome of insurance claims. *New England Journal of Medicine, 343(15)*, 1118–1119.

Frencham, K. A., Fox, A. M., & Maybery, M. T. (2004). Meta-analytic review of neuropsychological research in mild traumatic brain injury since 1995. *Brain Impairment, 5(Suppl.)*, 79–80.

Gaetz, M. (2004). The neurophysiology of brain injury. *Clinical Neurophysiology, 115(1)*, 4–18.

Glaesser, J., Neuner, F., Lutgehetmann, R., Schmidt, R., & Elbert, T. (2004). Posttraumatic Stress Disorder in patients with traumatic brain injury. *BMC Psychiatry, 4(1)*, 5.

Goetz, P., Blamire, A., Rajagopalan, B., Cadoux-Hudson, T., Young, D., & Styles, P. (2004). Increase in apparent diffusion coefficient in normal appearing white matter following human traumatic brain injury correlates with injury severity. *Journal of Neurotrauma, 21(6)*, 645–654.

Govindaraju, V., Gauger, G. E., Manley, G. T., Ebel, A., Meeker, M., & Maudsley, A. A. (2004). Volumetric proton spectroscopic imaging of mild traumatic brain injury. *American Journal of Neuroradiology, 25(5)*, 730–737.

Graham, D. I., Gennarelli, T. A., & McIntosh, T. K. (2002). Trauma. In D. I. Graham & P. L. Lantos (Eds.). *Greenfield's Neuropathology*, 7th ed. New York: Arnold, pp. 823–898.

Grossman, K. J., Goss, C. W., & Stein, D. G. (2004). Effects of progesterone on the inflammatory response to brain injury in the rat. *Brain Research, 1008(1)*, 29–39.

Gunstad, J. & Suhr, J. A. (2004). Cognitive factors in Postconcussion Syndrome symptom report. *Archives of Clinical Neuropsychology, 19(3)*, 391–405.

Guskiewicz, K. M., McCrea, M., Marshall, S. W., Cantu, R. C., Randolph, C., Barr, W., Onate, J. A., & Kelly, J. P. (2003). Cumulative effects associated with recurrent concussion in collegiate football players: The NCAA Concussion Study. *Journal of the American Medical Association, 290(19)*, 2549–2555.

Habib, M. (2004). Athymhormia and disorders of motivation in Basal Ganglia disease. *Journal of Neuropsychiatry and Clinical Neuroscience, 16(4)*, 509–524.

Hampton, J. R., Harrison, M. J., Mitchell, J. R., Prichard, J. S., & Seymour, C. (1975). Relative contributions of history-taking, physical examination, and laboratory investigation to diagnosis and management of medical outpatients. *British Medical Journal, 2(5969)*, 486–489.

Harvey, A. G., Brewin, C. R., Jones, C., & Kopelman, M. D. (2003). Coexistence of Posttraumatic Stress Disorder and traumatic brain injury: Towards a resolution of the paradox. *Journal of the International Neuropsychology Society, 9(4)*, 663–676.

Hawley, C. A., Ward, A. B., Magnay, A. R., & Long, J. (2004). Outcomes following childhood head injury: A population study. *Journal of Neurology, Neurosurgery, and Psychiatry, 75(5)*, 737–742.

Holmin, S. & Hojeberg, B. (2004). In situ detection of intracerebral cytokine expression after human brain contusion. *Neuroscience Letters, 369(2)*, 108–114.

Hooper, S. R., Alexander, J., Moore, D., Sasser, H. C., Laurent, S., King, J., Bartel, S., & Callahan, B. (2004). Caregiver reports of common symptoms in children following a traumatic brain injury. *NeuroRehabilitation, 19(3)*, 175–189.

Huisman, T. A., Schwamm, L. H., Schaefer, P. W., Koroshetz, W. J., Shetty-Alva, N., Ozsunar, Y., et al. (2004). Diffusion tensor imaging as potential biomarker of white matter injury in diffuse axonal injury. *American Journal of Neuroradiology, 25(3)*, 370–376.

Hurley, R. A., McGowan, J. C., Arfanakis, K., & Taber, K. H. (2004). Traumatic axonal injury: Novel insights into evolution and identification. *Journal of Neuropsychiatry and Clinical Neurosciences, 16(1)*, 1–7.

Ibanez, J., Arikan, F., Pedraza, S., Sanchez, E., Poca, M. A., Rodriguez, D., & Rubioa, E. (2004). Reliability of clinical guidelines in the detection of patients at risk following mild head injury: Results of a prospective study. *Journal of Neurosurgery, 100(5)*, 825–834.

Jorge, R. E., Robinson, R. G., Moser, D., Tateno, A., Crespo-Facorro, B., & Arndt, S. (2004). Major depression following traumatic brain injury. *Archives of General Psychiatry, 61(1)*, 42–50.

Jorm, A. F., Masaki, K. H., Davis, D. G., Hardman, J., Nelson, J., Markesbery, W. R., Petrovich, H., Ross, G. W., & White, L. R. (2004). Memory complaints in nondemented men predict future pathologic diagnosis of Alzheimer disease. *Neurology, 63(10)*, 1960–1961.

Kelly, J. P., Nichols, J. S., Filley, C. M., Lillehei, K. O., Rubinstein, D., & Kleinschmidt-DeMasters, B. K. (1991). Concussion in sports. Guidelines for the prevention of catastrophic outcome. *Journal of the American Medical Association, 266(20)*, 2867–2869.

Koponen, S., Taiminen, T., Kairisto, V., Portin, R., Isoniemi, H., Hinkka, S., & Tenovuo, O. (2004). APOE-epsilon4 predicts dementia but not other psychiatric disorders after traumatic brain injury. *Neurology, 63(4)*, 749–750.

Kushi, H., Saito, T., Makino, K., & Hayashi, N. (2003). Neuronal damage in pericontusional edema zone. *Acta Neurochirurgica, 86, (Suppl.)*, 339–342.

Larrabee, G. J. (Ed.). (2005). *Fornesic Neuropsychology: A Scientific Approach*. New York: Oxford University Press.

Leclerc, S., Lassonde, M., Delaney, J. S., Lacroix, V. J., & Johnston, K. M. (2001). Recommendations for grading of concussion in athletes. *Sports Medicine, 31(8)*, 629–636.

Leker, R. R., Shohami, E., & Constantini, S. (2002). Experimental models of head trauma. *Acta Neurochir 83(Suppl.)*, 49–54.

Levin, H. S., Zhang, L., Dennis, M., Ewing-Cobbs, L., Schachar, R., Max, J., et al. (2004). Psychosocial outcome of TBI in children with unilateral frontal lesions. *Journal of the International Neuropsychology Society, 10(3)*, 305–316.

Lobentanz, I. S., Asenbaum, S., Vass, K., Sauter, C., Klosch, G., Kollegger, H., et al. (2004). Factors influencing quality of life in multiple sclerosis patients: Disability, depressive mood, fatigue and sleep quality. *Acta Neurology Scandavia, 110(1)*, 6–13.

Lovell, M. R., Echemendia, R. J., Barth, J. T., & Collins, M. W. (2004). *Traumatic Brain Injury in Sports*. Lisse, The Netherlands: Swets and Zeitlinger.

Luis, C. A., Vanderploeg, R. D., & Curtiss, G. (2003). Predictors of postconcussion symptom complex in community dwelling male veterans. *Journal of the International Neuropsychology Society, 9(7)*, 1001–1015.

MacKenzie, J. D., Siddiqi, F., Babb, J. S., Bagley, L. J., Mannon, L. J., Sinson, G. P., & Grossman, R. I. (2002). Brain atrophy in mild or moderate traumatic brain injury: A longitudinal quantitative analysis. *American Journal of Neuroradiology, 23(9)*, 1509–1515.

Mathias, J. L., Beall, J. A., & Bigler, E. D. (2004a). Neuropsychological and information processing deficits following mild traumatic brain injury. *Journal of the International Neuropsychology Society, 10(2)*, 286–297.

Mathias, J. L., Bigler, E. D., Jones, N. R., Bowden, S. C., Barrett-Woodbridge, M., Brown, G. C., & Taylor, J. D. (2004b). Neuropsychological and information processing performance and its relationship to white matter changes following moderate and severe traumatic brain injury. *Applied Neuropsychology, 11*.

Mayeux, R. (2004). Dissecting the relative influences of genes and the environment in Alzheimer's disease. *Annals of Neurology, 55(2)*, 156–158.

Mayeux, R., Ottman, R., Maestre, G., Ngai, C., Tang, M. X., Ginsberg, H., et al. (1995). Synergistic effects of traumatic head injury and apolipoprotein-epsilon 4 in patients with Alzheimer's disease. *Neurology, 45(3 Pt. 1)*, 555–557.

McAllister, T. W., Saykin, A. J., Flashman, L. A., Sparling, M. B., Johnson, S. C., Guerin, S. J., et al. (1999). Brain activation during working memory 1 month after mild traumatic brain injury: A functional MRI study. *Neurology, 53(6)*, 1300–1308.

McCauley, S.R., Boake, C., Pedroza, C., Brown, S.A., Levin, H.S., Goodman, H.S., & Merritt, S.G. (2005). Postconcussional disorder: Are the DSM-IV criteria an improvement over the ICD-10? *Journal of Nervous and Mental Disease 193*, 540–550.

McCrea, M., Guskiewicz, K. M., Marshall, S. W., Barr, W., Randolph, C., Cantu, R. C., et al. (2003). Acute effects and recovery time following concussion in collegiate football players: The NCAA Concussion Study. *Journal of the American Medical Association, 290(19)*, 2556–2563.

McCrory, P. R. & Berkovic, S. F. (2000). Video analysis of acute motor and convulsive manifestations in sport-related concussion. *Neurology, 54(7)*, 1488–1491.

McKinlay, A., Dalrymple-Alford, J. C., Horwood, L. J., & Fergusson, D. M. (2002). Long term psychosocial outcomes after mild head injury in early childhood. *Journal of Neurology, Neurosurgery, and Psychiatry, 73(3)*, 281–288.

McKinlay, A., Dalrymple-Alford, J. C., Horwood, L. J., & Fergusson, D. M. (2004). Adverse outcomes associated with childhood mild head injury continue into adulthood: A 25 year follow-up of a birth cohort. *Brain Impairment, 5*, 81.

Mickeviciene, D., Schrader, H., Obelieniene, D., Surkiene, D., Kunickas, R., Stovner, L. J., & Sand, T. (2004). A controlled prospective inception cohort study on the post-concussion syndrome outside the medicolegal context. *European Journal of Neurology, 11(6)*, 411–419.

Moser, R.S., Schatz, P., & Jordan, B.D. (2005). Prolonged effects of concussion in high school athletes. *Neurosurgery, 57*(2), 300–306.

Moore, B. A. & Donders, J. (2004). Predictors of invalid neuropsychological test performance after traumatic brain injury. *Brain Injury, 18*, 975–984.

Newberg, A. B., Lariccia, P. J., Lee, B. Y., Farrar, J. T., Lee, L., & Alavi, A. (2005). Cerebral blood flow effects of pain and acupuncture: a preliminary single-photon emission computed tomography imaging study. *Journal of Neuroimaging, 15(1)*, 43–49.

Nicholson, K. & Martelli, M. F. (2004). The problem of pain. *Journal of Head Trauma Rehabilitation, 19(1)*, 2–9.

Ommaya, A. K., Goldsmith, W., & Thibault, L. (2002). Biomechanics and neuropathology of adult and paediatric head injury. *British Journal of Neurosurgery, 16(3)*, 220–242.

Pellman, E. J., Powell, J. W., Viano, D. C., Casson, I. R., Tucker, A. M., Feuer, H., et al. (2004). Concussion in professional football: Epidemiological features of game injuries and review of the literature—Part 3. *Neurosurgery, 54(1)*, 81–96.

Peterson, M. C., Holbrook, J. H., Von Hales, D., Smith, N. L., & Staker, L. V. (1992). Contributions of the history, physical examination, and laboratory investigation in making medical diagnoses. *Western Journal of Medicine, 156(2)*, 163–165.

Pittella, J. E. & Gusmao, S. N. (2004). The conformation of the brain plays an important role in the distribution of diffuse axonal injury in fatal road traffic accident. *Arquivos de Neuropsiquiatria, 62(2B)*, 406–412.

Povlishock, J. T. & Katz, D. I. (2005). Update of neuropathology and neurological recovery after traumatic brain injury. *Journal of Head Trauma Rehabilitation, 20(1)*, 76–94.

Quality Standards Subcommittee. (1997). Practice parameter: The management of concussion in sports [summary statement]. *Neurology, 48*, 581–585.

Raghupathi, R. (2004). Cell death mechanisms following traumatic brain injury. *Brain Pathology, 14(2)*, 215–222.

Rees, P. M. (2003). Contemporary issues in mild traumatic brain injury. *Archives of Physical Medicine Rehabilitation, 84(12)*, 1885–1894.

Richardson, R. D. & Engel, C. C., Jr. (2004). Evaluation and management of medically unexplained physical symptoms. *The Neurologist, 10(1)*, 18–30.

Roberts, W. (1992). Who plays? Who sits? Managing concussions in sports. *Physician Sports Medicine, 20*, 66–72.

Rovaris, M., Agosta, F., Sormani, M. P., Inglese, M., Martinelli, V., Comi, G., & Filippi, M. (2003). Conventional and magnetization transfer MRI predictors of clinical multiple sclerosis evolution: A medium-term follow-up study. *Brain, 126(Pt. 10)*, 2323–2332.

Ruff, R. (2005). Two decades of advances in understanding of mild traumatic brain injury. *Journal of Head Trauma Rehabilitation, 20(1)*, 5–18.

Ryan, L. M. & Warden, D. L. (2003). Post concussion syndrome. *International Reviews in Psychiatry, 15(4)*, 310–316.

Salat, D. H., Buckner, R. L., Snyder, A. Z., Greve, D. N., Desikan, R. S., Busa, E., Morris, J. C., Dale, A. M., & Fischl, B. (2004). Thinning of the cerebral cortex in aging. *Cerebral Cortex, 14(7)*, 721–730.

Salmond, C. H., Chatfield, D. A., Menon, D. K., Pickard, J. D., & Sahakian, B. J. (2005). Cognitive sequelae of head injury: Involvement of basal forebrain and associated structures. *Brain, 128(Pt. 1)*, 189–200.

Sandler, G. (1980). The importance of the history in the medical clinic and the cost of unnecessary tests. *American Heart Journal, 100(6 Pt. 1)*, 928–931.

Schretlen, D. J. & Shapiro, A. M. (2003). A quantitative review of the effects of traumatic brain injury on cognitive functioning. *International Reviews in Psychiatry, 15(4)*, 341–349.

Schulz, M. R., Marshall, S. W., Mueller, F. O., Yang, J., Weaver, N. L., Kalsbeek, W. D.,& Bowling, J. M. (2004). Incidence and risk factors for concussion in high school athletes, North Carolina, 1996–1999. *American Journal of Epidemiology, 160(10)*, 937–944.

Shaw, N. A. (2002). The neurophysiology of concussion. *Progress in Neurobiology, 67(4)*, 281–344.

Shirasaki, Y., Edo, N., & Sato, T. (2004). Serum S-100b protein as a biomarker for the assessment of neuroprotectants. *Brain Research, 1021(2)*, 159–166.

Silver, J. M., McAllister, T. W., & Yudofsky, S. C. (Eds.). (2005). *Textbook of Traumatic Brain Injury*, 2nd ed. Washington DC: American Psychiatric Publishing.

Sinson, G. (2001). "He was never quite 'himself' after that accident": Exploring the long-term consequences of mild traumatic brain injury. *American Journal of Neuroradiology, 22(3)*, 425–426.

Skeel, R. L., Sitzer, D., Fogal, T., Wells, J., & Johnstone, B. (2004). Comparison of predicted-difference, simple-difference, and premorbid-estimation methodologies for evaluating IQ and memory score discrepancies. *Archives of Clinical Neuropsychology, 19(3)*, 363–374.

Sowell, E. R., Thompson, P. M., & Toga, A. W. (2004). Mapping changes in the human cortex throughout the span of life. *The Neuroscientist, 10(4)*, 372–392.

Staub, F. & Bogousslavsky, J. (2001). Fatigue after stroke: A major but neglected issue. *Cerebrovascular Disease 12(2)*, 75–81.

Stranjalis, G., Korfias, S., Papapetrou, C., Kouyialis, A., Boviatsis, E., Psachoulia, C., & Sakas, D. E. (2004). Elevated serum S-100B protein as a predictor of failure to short-term return to work or activities after mild head injury. *Journal of Neurotrauma, 21(8)*, 1070–1075.

Stulemeijer, M., Brauer, J., Bleijenberg, G., & Vos, P. E. (2004). Post-concussion symptoms 6 months after mild traumatic brain injury: A controlled study. *Neurology, 62(Suppl. 5)*, A372.

Stuss, D. T. (1995). A sensible approach to mild traumatic brain injury. *Neurology, 45(7)*, 1251–1252.

Tartaglia, M. C., Narayanan, S., Francis, S. J., Santos, A. C., De Stefano, N., Lapierre, Y., & Arnold, D. L. (2004). The relationship between diffuse axonal damage and fatigue in multiple sclerosis. *Archives of Neurology, 61(2)*, 201–207.

Teasdale, G. & Jennett, B. (1974). Assessment of coma and impaired consciousness: A practical scale. *Lancet, 2*, 81–84.

Thompson, J. M., Gallagher, P., Hughes, J. H., Watson, S., Gray, J. M., Ferrier, I. N., & Young, A. H. (2005). Neurocognitive impairment in euthymic patients with bipolar affective disorder. *British Journal of Psychiatry, 186*, 32–40.

Thurman, D. J., Alverson, C., Dunn, K. A., Guerrero, J., & Sniezek, J. E. (1999). Traumatic brain injury in the United States: A public health perspective. *Journal of Head Trauma Rehabilitation, 14(6)*, 602–615.

Udekwu, P., Kromhout-Schiro, S., Vaslef, S., Baker, C., & Oller, D. (2004). Glasgow Coma Scale score, mortality, and functional outcome in head-injured patients. *Journal of Trauma, 56(5)*, 1084–1089.

van der Flier, W. M., van Buchem, M. A., Weverling-Rijnsburger, A. W., Mutsaers, E. R., Bollen, E. L., Admiraal-Behloul, F., Westendorp, R. G., & Middelkoop, H. A. (2004). Memory complaints in patients with normal cognition are associated with smaller hippocampal volumes. *Journal of Neurology, 251(6)*, 671–675.

van der Werf, S. P., van den Broek, H. L., Anten, H. W., & Bleijenberg, G. (2001). Experience of severe fatigue long after stroke and its relation to depressive symptoms and disease characteristics. *European Neurology, 45(1)*, 28–33.

Vanderploeg, R. D. & Curtiss, G. (2001). Malingering assessment: Evaluation of validity of performance. *NeuroRehabilitation, 16(4)*, 245–251.

Vanderploeg, R. D., Curtiss, G., Duchnick, J. J., & Luis, C. A. (2003). Demographic, medical, and psychiatric factors in work and marital status after mild head injury. *Journal of Head Trauma Rehabilitation, 18(2)*, 148–163.

Vos, P. E., Battistin, L., Birbamer, G., Gerstenbrand, F., Potapov, A., Prevec, T., Stepan Ch, A., Traubner, P., Twijnstra, A., Vecsei, L., & von Wild, K. (2002). EFNS guideline on mild traumatic brain injury: Report of an EFNS task force. *European Journal of Neurology, 9(3)*, 207–219.

Wilde, E. A., Hunter, J. V., Newsome, M. R., Scheibel, R. S., Bigler, E. D., Johnson, J. L., Fearing, M. A., Cleavinger, H. B., Li, X., Swank, P. R., Pedroza, C., Roberson, G. S., Bachevalier, J., & Levin, H. S. (2005). Frontal and temporal morphometric findings on MRI in children after moderate to severe traumatic brain injury. *Journal of Neurotrauma, 22(3)*, 333–334.

Wood, R. L. (2004). Understanding the 'miserable minority': A diathesis-stress paradigm for post-concussional syndrome. *Brain Injury, 18(11)*, 1135–1153.

Zhang, L., Yang, K. H., & King, A. I. (2004). A proposed injury threshold for mild traumatic brain injury. *Journal of Biomechanical Engineering, 126(2)*, 226–236.

Zohar, O., Schreiber, S., Getslev, V., Schwartz, J. P., Mullins, P. G., & Pick, C. G. (2003). Closed-head minimal traumatic brain injury produces long-term cognitive deficits in mice. *Neuroscience, 118(4)*, 949–955.

18

Confounding Effects of Pain, Psychoemotional Problems or Psychiatric Disorder, Premorbid Ability Structure, and Motivational or Other Factors on Neuropsychological Test Performance

Keith Nicholson and Michael F. Martelli

1. Introduction

As is true of any psychological test or measure, neuropsychological assessment techniques provide samples of behavior. A multitude of measures have been developed to assess memory, attention, verbal or nonverbal abilities, sensory and motor function, executive control functions, emotion, and social behavior, to name just some of the major neuropsychological categories of interest. Within each of these domains, a myriad of more specific behaviors can be assessed, e.g., different components of mnemonic function such as learning of structured versus unstructured material or rate of forgetting. In a neuropsychological assessment, there is typically some interest in how such samples of behavior may be related to the operation or functioning of the brain, that is, what the brain–behavior relationships involved may be. There is also very often an interest in how such samples of behavior may reflect abnormal brain function or what the clinical–pathological correlation may be (i.e., the relationship between a clinical entity and lesions or damage to the brain). A very large literature continues to accumulate documenting what the clinical–pathological correlations are in such conditions as traumatic brain injury (TBI), Alzheimer's disease, stroke, and numerous other clinical entities. Many clinical entities have been shown to have quite specific neuropsychological profiles or patterns of test results. However, in many cases, there is a problem of how specific the neuropsychological test results are. There are many reasons why a person may do poorly on any given neuropsychological test. This chapter will explore some of the confounding factors affecting the interpretation of results obtained on neuropsychological assessment, with particular focus on those confounding factors that may be most pertinent for the differential diagnosis of the neuropsychological sequelae of TBI.

2.   Pain

As may be apparent to those who have experienced significant pain, this has the potential to interfere with aspects of cognition or other function. Pain-related impairment of function may be most important in cases of postconcussive syndrome (PCS). Most surveys that have been conducted of this syndrome identify headache as the primary problem (Alves et al., 1993; Brown et al., 1994; Edna & Cappelen, 1987; Evans, 2004; Jacobsen et al., 1987; Middleboe et al., 1992; Rutherford, 1979). Keidel and Diener (1997) suggested that the incidence of posttraumatic headache is 90% soon after trauma. Evans (2004) reviewed studies indicating that the incidence of posttraumatic headache is poorly understood, with estimates ranging from approximately 30% to 90% at 3 months post-head trauma, with 8–35% at 1 year post-trauma and with some 24% having persistent headaches at 4 years post-trauma. In contrast, some prospective studies have not found that there is any increased incidence of headache subsequent to head trauma (Mickeviciene et al., 2004).

Evans (2004) noted that the etiology of posttraumatic headache is also poorly understood. However, contrary to expectation on the basis of brain injury, posttraumatic headache is more common in those having minor head injury or mild traumatic brain injury as compared to those with more severe traumatic brain injury (Couch & Bearss, 2001; Uomoto & Esselman, 1993), possibly because sensitization effects may be more prominent, with trauma being more fully experienced in those who have little or no loss of consciousness (Miller, 2000; Nicholson, 1998). Uomoto and Esselman (1993) found that only 5% of a sample of mild head or TBI patients were without pain, whereas a large proportion (78%) of the moderate–severe head-injured patients reported no pain problems. However, Lahz and Bryant (1996) found that pain was also reported in many, i.e., 52% of moderate–severe traumatic brain injury patients. Headache was, again, the most common complaint or problem. In addition to headache, there are often other pain problems such as neck and back pain following injury.

Numerous studies involving an acute experimental pain challenge in normal controls, i.e., when a painful stimulus is delivered to healthy subjects, document that this may result in performance or cognitive deficits (see Hart et al., 2000; Nicholson, 2000a; Nicholson et al., 2001 for recent reviews). In some paradigms, the performance decrement is very large. Numerous studies of persons with nonexperimental acute or chronic pain problems also document that such clinical pain can interfere with aspects of performance (see Hart et al., 2000; Nicholson, 2000a; Nicholson et al., 2001 for recent reviews).

Many of these studies involve chronic pain patents with no history of brain injury. Again, performance deficits may be very large. Several more recent studies continue to document an association between pain or even the anticipation of pain and cognitive or related problems (e.g., Apkarian et al., 2004a; Collins et al., 2003; Dick et al., 2003; Houlihan et al., 2003; Van Damme et al., 2004). The acute pain challenge and acute or chronic clinical pain studies indicate that attention, concentration, memory, and speed of processing are most affected, those functions that may also be most affected with TBI (see chapter 19 by Patry and Mateer, in this volume).

Importantly, there is marked variability in whether or not pain may be associated with cognitive deficits, as there are some persons with chronic pain who have no such complaints or problems. In addition to pain itself, there are often associated difficulties such as sleep disturbance, psychoemotional distress or specific psychiatric disorder, marital or other interpersonal difficulties, medication side effects, or other problems. Sleep disturbance is a prominent problem associated with chronic pain (Menefee et al., 2000) as well as TBI (Mahmood et al., 2004). Pilcher and Huffcutt (1996), in a meta-analysis of the effects of sleep disturbance, found that sleep deprivation can markedly impair human performance. The mean effect size of sleep disturbance on cognitive tasks was −1.36, but acute sleep deprivation resulted in a much larger performance decrement (effect size of −3.01), indicating that some adaptation occurred in the more chronic conditions.

Several other factors have been found to be associated with cognitive or other performance deficits in chronic pain patients. In one study, Eccleston et al. (1997) found that somatic preoccupation accounted for attentional deficits. Several studies have found that depression or other psychoemotional problems were associated with cognitive deficits in chronic pain patients (Grace et al., 1999; McCracken & Iverson, 2001; Schnurr & MacDonald, 1995), including studies involving persistent PCS (Fann et al., 1995; King, 1996; Trahan et al., 2001). Wade and Hart (2002) studied the relationship of different components of pain with performance on a simple measure of verbal attention. Utilizing a four-stage model of pain processing that differentiates between pain intensity (suggested to be assessing the sensory–discriminative component of pain), unpleasantness, suffering, and pain behavior, it was found that only suffering and pain behavior were related to attentional problems. Hart et al. (2003) subsequently reviewed research concerning the role of emotional distress and other aspects of suffering in the cognitive impairment of pain patients. It was concluded that pain-related negative emotions and stress potentially impact cognitive functioning independent of the effects of pain intensity. Research suggested that specific central nervous system structures and processes, e.g., the anterior cingulate cortex or the hypothalamic–pituitary–adrenal cortical axis, can mediate effects.

Eccleston and Crombez (1999), on reviewing the literature, suggested that pain interrupts attention, which then interferes with memory, speed of processing, or other functions. Such an interference effect is a common interpretation of the cognitive or performance deficits that may be seen in chronic pain. However, it may also be that pain has more specific effects on actual brain function. Functional imaging or other studies of the effect of acute pain challenge or chronic pain have well documented that most all of the brain may be adversely affected, although more discreet abnormalities are usually noted, especially with acute pain challenge paradigms (Coghill et al., 2003; Nicholson, 2000b; Wager et al., 2004). It should also be noted that merely anticipating the experience of pain will result in similar or identical changes in brain function as application of an actual painful stimulus (Wager et al., 2004).

There may also be significant structural brain changes associated with chronic pain. Apkarian et al. (2004b) found that chronic low back pain was associated with reduction of neocortical gray matter equivalent to the gray matter lost in 10–20 years of normal aging. This was most evident in the bilateral dorsolateral prefrontal and right thalamic cortex and was associated with such pain characteristics as pain duration or whether pain was neuropathic. Various other psychologic or psychiatric conditions such as depression, anxiety disorders, or schizophrenia are also well known to have structural and/or functional imaging abnormalities (Kanner, 2004). These studies underscore the artificiality of mind–body dualism and reinforce the truism that all psychological processes have some underlying neurobiological substrate. Whereas changes in brain structure or function may have an effect on and alter aspects of behavior, either temporarily or on a more permanent basis, it should also be realized that experience or psychosocial factors may have an effect on brain function, either temporarily or on a more permanent basis (Mayer & Saper, 2000).

We suspect that posttraumatic headache, in addition to other pain and related problems, have seriously confounded interpretation of neuropsychological test results in studies of mild TBI or persistent PCS. Whereas prospective studies of mild traumatic brain or head injury indicate that there is limited and discrete neuropsychological sequelae in the immediate postinjury period with resolution within days to weeks and few, if any, long-term sequelae (Binder et al., 1997; Carroll et al., 2004; Dikmen et al., 1995, 2001; Vanderploeg et al., Chapter 16), some portion of persons experiencing head trauma go on to develop persistent PCS. Importantly, a head injury does not mean a brain injury. Whereas trauma to the head may cause persistent problems with headaches, this may be unrelated to the effects of TBI. In addition, it has been demonstrated that symptoms of persistent PCS, e.g., headache, irritability, dizziness, fatigue, anxiety, plus concentration and memory problems or complaints, are common in the general population or following injury that does not involve the head or brain (Lees-Haley et al., 2001; Mittenberg et al., 1992; Putnam et al., 1999; Vanderploeg et al., submitted). Smith-Seemiller et al. (2003) found that chronic pain patients endorsed symptoms similar to or consistent with those with a mild TBI, concluding that symptoms of PCS were not unique to mild TBI and could be seen in other conditions such as chronic pain.

Pain and related problems may also have confounded the interpretation of studies with moderate–severe TBI patients. Taylor et al. (1996) compared the performance of nonimpact whiplash patients, chronic pain patients with documented moderate-to-severe brain injury who continued to complain of chronic pain, and patients with chronic pain but no evidence of head injury. There were no significant differences among groups on several neuropsychological tests. Dikmen et al. (1995) noted that there was substantial variability in outcome in a large-scale study of TBI and called for an examination of factors that may mitigate or exacerbate the effects of brain injury. Similarly, Lannoo et al. (2001) found that almost half of moderate–severe TBI patients showed no impairment of neuropsychological function in comparison with trauma patients with injuries to parts of the body other than the head.

3.   Psychoemotional Problems and Psychiatric Disorder

Psychoemotional problems or psychiatric disorders can markedly interfere with aspects of neuropsychological function. Estimates of the prevalence of psychiatric disorder in the general population indicate that these are common. Narrow et al. (2002) noted that the major large-scale epidemiological surveys in the United States had yielded estimates for 1-year mental and addictive disorder prevalence rates approaching 30% and lifetime rates approaching 50%. However, when attempts were made to include only those cases with clinically significant symptomatology, the estimate of the 1-year prevalence rate for any mental or substance use disorder was reduced to 18.5%. According to this estimate, over the course of a year, close to one in five individuals might present with a clinically significant disorder. In certain populations, such as TBI, the prevalence rates may be much higher given that such individuals may be more vulnerable to becoming involved in accidents or injuries resulting in a brain injury (Tate, 2003).

Depression is common in the general population (Shenal et al., 2003) and there is increased likelihood of depression when there is some other comorbid condition such as pain (Davis et al., 2000; Fishbain et al., 1997), traumatic brain injury (Williams & Evans, 2003), or Posttraumatic Stress Disorder (PTSD) (O'Donnell et al., 2004). The DSM-IV (American Psychiatric Association, 1994) criteria for depression include interference effects on aspects of cognition, i.e., attention or memory. Numerous studies have concluded that there are cognitive or neuropsychological deficits associated with depression, especially with such functions as effortful processing, attention, memory, processing speed, and executive functioning, although this may be most evident in particular subsets of depressed individuals (Burt et al., 1995; Christensen et al., 1997; Cohen et al., 2001; Elderkin-Thompson et al., 2004; Fleming et al., 2004; Fossati et al., 2004; Hammar et al., 2003;

Koetsier et al., 2002; Ottowitz et al., 2002; Post et al., 2000; Ravnkilde et al., 2000). It should also be noted that depressed persons may report more cognitive or other problems than are apparent on objective investigation, likely the result of negative thinking or catastrophizing (Farrin et al., 2003). Again, depression is known to be associated with a number of abnormalities of brain function (Shenal et al., 2003).

There are also often neuropsychological deficits associated with stress, anxiety, or anxiety disorders (Birnbaum et al., 2004; Kuelz et al., 2004; Nitschke et al., 2000; Toren et al., 2000). PTSD is one especially important anxiety disorder having a high comorbidity with traumatic brain injury, especially mild traumatic brain injury (Bryant et al., 1999; Miller, 2000; Sharp & Harvey, 2001; Williams & Evans, 2003). Several studies have found cognitive deficits or impairments on neuropsychological test performance in persons with PTSD (Horner & Hamner, 2003), although this is somewhat controversial (Crowell et al., 2002; Danckwerts & Leathem, 2003). There is also strong evidence that there are some specific abnormalities of brain functioning in PTSD or other psychological trauma (Weber & Reynolds, 2004).

Numerous other psychiatric disorders may have a pronounced effect on the results of neuropsychological assessment (e.g., schizophrenia) (Chan et al., 2004). In addition, a host of poorly understood and medically unexplained syndromes are associated with significant neuropsychological deficits (Binder & Campbell, 2004). There may also be significant interference effects on aspects of cognition or behavior with many or most prescription or nonprescription (i.e., street) drugs or alcohol, although effects vary depending on whether there is acute intoxication, multiple drug abuse, duration of use, or other factors (Barker et al., 2003; Stein & Strickland, 1998; Verdejo-Garcia et al., 2004).

4.   Premorbid Ability Structure and Other Premorbid Factors

The interpretation of neuropsychological test results, as any scientific data, is dependent on some frame of reference. The most common frame of reference in neuropsychological assessments is a relevant control group; that is, an examinee's scores are compared to the scores of a sample of other individuals who have also been administered the tests to be interpreted. If the examinee performs poorly in comparison with others, it can be concluded that there is a deficit possibly associated with the effects of traumatic brain injury or other pathological process affecting the integrity of brain function. It is common to conclude that there is an impairment if scores fall 2 or more standard deviations below the control group mean (i.e., below the 2nd percentile). However, it may have been that the person would have performed poorly on the test in question prior to the brain injury because they were always weak in that area. Conversely, if the examinee did much better than most of the control group (e.g., score falling at the 90th percentile), it might be concluded that there were no adverse neuropsychological sequelae attributable to the effects of TBI. However, it may have been that the examinee had previously or premorbidly been functioning at a superior level of ability (e.g., at the 99th percentile) and that the brain injury had actually resulted in a significant loss. In some situations, a decline from the 99th to the 90th percentile would be devastating.

An especially important measure in neuropsychological assessments is that of an individual's general level of intellectual ability. Intelligence is known to be strongly related to performance on neuropsychological tests (Diaz-Asper et al., 2004); that is, those who are more intelligent tend to do better on many measures and vice versa. Whereas there are methods that have been developed to estimate the premorbid level of intellectual ability from current test performance, past educational achievement, or other demographic factors, this has met with limited success (Powell et al., 2003). Furthermore, although intelligence is useful as a general indicator of how a person may perform on neuropsychological tests, there is marked normal intraindividual variability in neuropsychological test performance (Schretlen et al., 2003). In other words, most people do much better or much worse on some measures than others, reflecting strengths or weaknesses in their ability structure; that is, they have relatively good or poor memory, visuospatial or verbal abilities, and so forth. It is generally much more difficult to provide an accurate estimate of the premorbid status of most neuropsychological functions. Furthermore, Posthuma et al. (2002) noted that more than 50% of the normal population will obtain five or more impaired scores on an expanded Halstead Reitan Battery (Heaton et al., 1991). As such, what might be interpreted as an injury-related deficit may actually represent premorbid ability structure. The ideal situation would be to have results of neuropsychological testing conducted prior to a TBI in order to compare with performance subsequent to such injury, but this is seldom available. As such, it is often unclear how current test performance may compare with what would have been expected on the basis of the premorbid level of ability.

In addition to premorbid variability in functions that tend to be the focus of neuropsychological assessments, i.e., cognitive functions such as attention, memory, etc., the premorbid personality organization and psychiatric or psychosocial history of persons presenting with possible sequelae secondary to TBI may also be important. It has long been suspected that physiological factors, i.e., effects associated with brain injury, may early on play a part in cases of PCS, but that psychological factors may subsequently become more important (Lishman, 1973, 1988).

Several studies have found that premorbid psychosocial factors may have a pronounced effect on response to injury. Fenton et al. (1993) found that those presenting with persistent problems following a mild head injury reported twice as many adverse life events or social difficulties occurring in the year preceeding the injury in comparison with those whose symptoms had resolved as would normally be expected. Greiffenstein and Baker (2001) found that premorbid personality profiles, in a small sample of TBI patients, were all abnormal and, unexpectedly, that postinjury profiles showed a decrease in global psychopathology. MacMillan et al. (2002) found that premorbid coping liabilities, e.g., a history of prior psychiatric problems and substance abuse, predicted subsequent employment and independent living status in a sample of TBI patients. Luis et al. (2003) found that the most salient predictors of persistent PCS were early life psychiatric difficulties such as anxiety or depression, limited social support, lower intelligence, and interactions among these variables. Martelli et al. (2002) have recently reviewed the role of preinjury factors affecting disability following TBI. There have also been some excellent discussions about the importance of premorbid psychosocial factors and postinjury adaptation, often within the context of diathesis (vulnerability)–stress models (e.g., Kay, 1999).

5.   Effort and Malingering

In the past several years, there has been increasing attention paid to the issue of whether examinees may be malingering, i.e., purposefully trying to do poorly for the purpose of secondary gain or compensation, or not putting forth good effort during testing and thus producing a profile of results that may not accurately reflect (i.e., underestimating) actual ability or functional status. Binder and Rohling (1996), in a review of the effects of mild TBI, reported a moderate effect size (0.47) for the effect of financial compensation seeking across numerous studies assessing a variety of dependent variables. It was noted that, in some instances, mild TBI patients seeking compensation showed significantly poorer functioning than did those with a moderate or severe TBI. However, it was also noted that there may not be an improvement in function following financial settlement, suggesting that factors other than compensation may be pertinent. Whereas some of those seeking compensation may have been malingering or purposely putting forth poor effort, it may also be that some were presenting with a host of other problems (e.g., pain, sleep disturbance, depression, etc., as described earlier), which could have resulted in increased level of disability/impairment leading to litigation or compensation seeking.

Binder et al. (2003), citing numerous studies of mild head injury with chronic symptoms in a medicolegal context that employed specific measures to assess invalid responding and motivation during neuropsychological assessment, suggested that the base rates for probable malingering or invalid responding were as high as 32–60% in this population. It was thought that the base rates were likely much lower in other nonmedicolegal settings or with moderate–severe TBI subjects. Slick et al. (1999) had earlier suggested that a distinction be made among definite, probable, and possible malingering of neurocognitive dysfunction. According to this formulation, the criteria for definite malingering involves (1) presence of a substantial external incentive, (2) definite negative response bias (i.e., below chance performance on one or more forced choice measures of cognitive function), and (3) behaviors meeting the second criterion were not fully accounted for by psychiatric, neurological, or developmental factors. Below-chance level of performance on forced choice techniques (e.g., Hiscock & Hiscock, 1989) provides strong evidence of conscious dissimulation or malingering, given that this suggests that the examinee must have known the correct response in order to provide a wrong response more often than could be expected if they were responding just "by chance." However, with the usual probability level (i.e., .05), approximately 1 in 20 who are actually responding only at chance may be incorrectly classified as malingering. In some forced-choice paradigms, which involve more effortful processing, persons with severe headache, affective distress or psychiatric disorder, sleep disturbance, and so forth may actually be performing at chance.

The Slick et al. (1999) criteria for probable malingering are (1) the presence of substantial external incentive, (2) two or more types of evidence from neuropsychological testing (excluding definite negative response bias) or one type of evidence from neuropsychological testing and one or more types of evidence from self-report, and (3) behaviors meeting the second criterion were not fully accounted for by psychiatric, neurological, or developmental factors. There are a number of problems associated with assessment of the several possible types of evidence for the second criterion. We will focus on just one of these—probable response bias—given the prominent role that such evidence has assumed in medicolegal assessments. Probable response bias is defined as "performance on one or more well-validated psychometric tests or indices designed to measure exaggeration or fabrication of cognitive deficits is consistent with feigning" (Slick et al., 1999, p. 553). In our opinion, most of these techniques suffer from the important limitation that it is unknown to what extent various possible confounding factors such as pain (especially perhaps headache), psychoemotional distress or psychiatric disorder, sleep disturbance, and/or other factors may impact performance.

Few studies have attempted to determine what effect confounding factors may have on symptom validity testing techniques, but some suggest this may be significant. Davidson et al. (1991) found that chronic pain patients performed relatively poorly on the 15 Item Test. Binder and Willis (1991) found that a mixed psychiatric group of patients did relatively poorly on the Portland Digit Recognition Test. Bierly et al. (2001) found that endorsement of somatic symptoms on the Hamilton Anxiety and Depression Scale was associated with the at-chance or below-chance level of performance on the Sternberg Recognition Memory Test in a small subset of TBI patients. Grillo et al. (1994) examined the relationship between personality disorders on the MCMI-II and response bias on MMPI-2 validity indicators and found that the presence of personality disorder, rather than malingering, contributed to exaggerated results in a personal injury population. Moore and Donders (2004) investigated failed validity criteria in a 3-year series of TBI rehabilitation referrals and found that both psychiatric history and financial compensation seeking were associated with an almost fourfold increase in likelihood of invalid responding.

Several studies with many different populations (i.e, TBI, depression, pain, toxic encephalopathy, etc.) have found very high rates of below "cutoff" responding interpreted as poor effort or possibly malingering and, therefore, invalidating other results (e.g., Rohling et al. 2002; van Hout et al., 2003). Such cutoffs are typically determined as the level of performance or score that well discriminates the performance of healthy normal controls and selected patient groups versus those instructed to simulate malingering or those seeking compensation. However, we suspect that some combination of confounding factors as discussed above may well result in a below-cutoff level of responding and, thus, that some of those being labeled as malingering or putting forth suboptimal effort may be false positives.

6.   Conclusion

Whereas neuropsychological techniques may provide sensitive and standardized measures of multiple cognitive or other functions, interpretation may be confounded by the effects of pain, psychoemotional distress or psychiatric disorder, sleep disturbance, premorbid ability structure, motivational lapses or conscious dissimulation, or other factors. Such confounding factors are common in many patient populations such as persistent PCS. Most studies have focused on one or another of these factors, although it is likely that a combination is operative in most cases. It is expected that there will be continued progress addressing these issues with further clarification of the sensitivity and specificity of neuropsychological techniques.

References

Alves, W., Macciocchi, S. N., & Barth, J. T. (1993). Postconcussive symptoms after uncomplicated mild head injury, *Journal of Head Trauma Rehabilitation, 8*, 48–59.

American Psychiatric Association (1994). *Diagnostic and Statistical Manual of Mental Disorders*, 4th ed. Washington DC: American Psychiatric Association.

Apkarian A. V., Sosa Y., Krauss B. R., Thomas P. S., Fredrickson B. E., Levy R. E. Harden R., & Chialvo D. R. (2004*a*). Chronic pain patients are impaired on an emotional decision-making task. *Pain, 108*, 129–136.

Apkarian, A. V., Sosa, Y., Sonty, S., Levy, R. M., Harden, R. N., Parrish, T. B., & Gitelman, D. R. (2004b). Chronic back pain is associated with decreased prefrontal and thalamic gray matter density. *Journal of Neuroscience, 24*, 10410–10415.

Barker, M. J., Greenwood, K. M., Jackson, M., & Crowe, S. F. (2003). Persistence of cognitive effects after withdrawal from long-term benzodiazepine use: A meta-analysis. *Archives of Clinical Neuropsychology, 19*, 437–454.

Bierly, R. A., Drake, A. I., Date, E. S., Rosner, M., Warden, D., & Salazar, A. M. (2001). Biased responding: A case series demonstrating a relationship between somatic symptoms and impaired recognition memory performance for traumatic brain injured individuals. *Brain Injury, 15*, 697–714.

Binder, L. M. & Campbell, K. A. (2004). Medically unexplained symptoms and neuropsychological assessment. *Journal of Clinical and Experimental Neuropsychology, 26*, 369–392.

Binder, L. M., Kelly, M. P., Villaneuva, M. R. & Winslow, M. M. (2003). Motivation and neuropsychological test performance following mild head injury. *Journal of Clinical and Experimental Neuropsychology, 25*, 420–430.

Binder, L. M. & Rohling, M. L. (1996). Money matters: A meta-analytic review of the effects of financial incentives on recovery after closed-head injury. *American Journal of Psychiatry, 153*, 7–10.

Binder, L. M., Rohling, M. L. & Larrabee, J. (1997). A review of mild head trauma. Part I: Meta-analytic review of neuropsychological studies. *Journal of Clinical and Experimental Neuropsychology, 19*, 421–431.

Binder, L. M. & Willis, S. C. (1991). Assessment of motivation after financially compensable minor head trauma. *Psychological Assessment, 3*, 175–181.

Birnbaum, S. G., Yuan, P. X., Wang, M., Vijayraghavan, S., Bloom, A. K., Davis, D. J., Gobeske, K. T., Sweatt, J. D., Manji, H. K., & Arnsten, A. F. T. (2004). Protein kinase C overactivity impairs prefrontal cortical regulation of working memory. *Science, 306*, 882–884.

Brown, S. J., Fann, J. R., & Grant, I. (1994). Postconcussional disorder: Time to acknowledge a common source of neurobehavioral morbidity. *Journal of Neuropsychiatry and Clinical Neurosciences, 6*, 15–22.

Bryant, R. A., Marosszeky J. E., Crooks J., Baguley I. J., & Gurka, J. A. (1999). Interaction of Posttraumatic Stress Disorder and chronic pain following traumatic brain injury. *Journal of Head Trauma Rehabilitation, 14*, 588–594.

Burt, D. B., Zembar, M. J., & Niederehe, G. (1995). Depression and memory impairment: A meta-analysis of the association, its pattern, and specificity. *Psychological Bulletin, 117*, 285–305.

Carroll, L. J., Cassidy, J. D., Peloso, P. M., Borg, J., von Holst, H., Holm, L., Paniak, C., & Pepin, M. (2004). Prognosis for mild traumatic brain injury: results of the WHO Collaborating Centre Task Force on Mild Traumatic Brain Injury. *Journal of Rehabilitation Medicine, 43* (Suppl) 84–105.

Chan, M. W. C., Yip, J. T. H., & Lee, T. M. C. (2004). Differential impairment on measures of attention in patients with paranoid and nonparanoid schizophrenia. *Journal of Psychiatric Research, 38*, 145–152.

Christensen, H., Griffiths, K., MacKinnon, A., & Jacomb, P. (1997). A quantitative review of cognitive deficits in depression and Alzheimer-type dementia. *Journal of the International Neuropsychological Society, 3*, 631–651.

Coghill, R. C., McHaffie, J. G., & Yen, Y. (2003). Neural correlates of interindividual differences in the subjective experience of pain. *PNAS, 100*, 8538–8542.

Cohen, R., Lohr, I., Paul, R., & Boland, R. (2001). Impairments of attention and effort among patients with major affective disorders. *Journal of Neuropsychiatry and Clinical Neurosciences, 13*, 385–395.

Collins, M. W., Field, M., Lowell, M. R., Iverson, G., Johnston K. M., Maroon J., & Fu, F. H. (2003). Relationship between postconcussion headache and neuropsychological test performance in high school athletes. *American Journal of Sports Medicine, 31*, 168–174.

Couch, J. R. & Bearss, C. (2001). Chronic daily headache in the post-traumatic syndrome: Relation to extent of head injury. *Headache: The Journal of Face and Head Pain, 41*, 559–564.

Crowell, T. A., Kieffer, K. M., Siders, C. A., & Vanderploeg, R. D. (2002). Neuropsychological findings in combat-related Posttraumatic Stress Disorder. *The Clinical Neuropsychologist, 16*, 310–321.

Danckwerts, A. & Leathem, J. (2003). Questioning the link between PTSD and cognitive dysfunction. *Neuropsychology Review, 13*, 221–235.

Davidson, H., Suffield, B., Orenczuk, S., Nantau, K., & Mandel, A. (1991). Screening for malingering using the Memory for Fifteen Items Test (MFIT). Presented at the 1991 International Neuropsychological Society Annual Meeting.

Davis, P. J., Reeves, J. L., Hastie, B. A., Graff-Radford, S. B., & Naliboff, B. D. (2000). Depression determines illness conviction and pain impact: A sructural equation modelling analysis. *Pain Medicine, 1*, 238–246.

Diaz-Asper, C. M., Schretlen, D. J., & Pearlson, G. D. (2004). How well does IQ predict neuropsychological test performance in normal adults. *Journal of the International Neuropsychological Society, 10*, 82–90.

Dick, B. D., Connolly, J. F., McGrath, P. J., Finley, G. A., Stroink, G., Houlihan, M. E., & Clark, J. (2003). The disruptive effect of chronic pain on mismatch negativity. *Clinical Neurophysiology, 114*, 1497–1506.

Dikmen, S. S., Machamer, J. E., & Temkin, N. R. (2001). Mild head injury: Facts and artifacts. *Journal of Clinical and Experimental Neuropsychology, 23*, 729–738.

Dikmen, S. S., Machamer, J. E., Winn, H. R., & Temkin, N. R. (1995). Neuropsychological outcome at 1-year post head injury. *Neuropsychology, 9*, 80–90.

Eccleston, C. & Crombez, G. (1999). Pain demands attention: A cognitive–affective model of the interruptive function of pain. *Psychological Bulletin, 125*, 356–366.

Eccleston, C., Crombez, G., Aldrich, S., & Stannard, C. (1997). Attention and somatic awareness of chronic pain. *Pain, 72*, 209–215.

Edna, T. H. & Cappelen, J. (1987). Late postconcussional symptoms in traumatic head injury. An analysis of frequency and risk factors, *Acta Neurochir (Wien), 86*, 12–17.

Elderkin-Thompson, V., Kumar, A., Mintz, J., Boone, K., Bahng, E., & Lavretsky, H. (2004). Executive dysfunction and visuospatial ability among depressed elders in a community setting. *Archives of Clinical Neuropsychology, 19*, 597–611.

Evans, R. W. (2004). Post-traumatic headaches. *Neurologic Clinics, 22(1)*, 237–249. Philadelphia: Saunders.

Fann, J. R., Katon, W. J., Uomoto, J. M., & Esselman, P. C. (1995). Psychiatric disorders and functional disability in outpatients with traumatic brain injuries. *American Journal of Psychiatry, 152*, 1493–1499.

Farrin, L., Hull, L., Unwin, C., Wyles, T., & David, A. (2003). Effects of depressed mood on objective and subjective measures of attention. *Journal of Neuropsychiatry and Clinical Neurosciences, 15*, 98–104.

Fenton, G., McClelland, R., Montgomery, A., MacFlynn, G., & Rutherford, W. (1993). The postconcussional syndrome: Social antecedents and psychological sequelae. *British Journal of Psychiatry, 162*, 493–497.

Fishbain, D. A., Cutler, R., Rosomoff, H. L., & Rosomoff, R. S. (1997). Chronic pain-associated depression: Antecedent or consequence of chronic pain? *Clinical Journal of Pain, 13*, 116–37.

Fleming, S. K., Blasey, C., & Schatzburg, A. F. (2004). Neuropsychological correlates of psychotic features in major depressive disorders: A review and meta-analysis. *Journal of Psychiatric Research, 38*, 27–35.

Fossati. P, Harvey, P., Le Bastard, G., Ergis, A., Jouvent, R., & Allilaire, J. (2004). Verbal memory performance of patients with a first depressive episode and patients with unipolar and bipolar recurrent depression. *Journal of Psychiatric Research, 38*, 137–144.

Grace, G. M., Nielson, W. R., Hopkins, M., & Berg, M. A. (1999). Concentration and memory deficits in patients with fibromyalgia syndrome. *Journal of Clinical and Experimental Neuropsychology, 21*, 477–487.

Greiffenstein, F. M. & Baker, J. W. (2001). Comparison of premorbid and postinjury MMPI-2 profiles in late postconcussion claimants. *Clinical Neuropsychology, 15*, 162–170.

Grillo, J., Brown R. S., Hilsabeck R., Price, J. R., & Lees-Haley, P. R. (1994). Raising doubts about claims of malingering: Implications of relationships between MCMI-II and MMPI-2 performances. *Journal of Clinical Psychology, 50*, 651–655.

Hammar, A., Lund, A., & Hugdahl, K. (2003). Selective impairment in effortful infor-mation processing in major depression. *Journal of the International Neuropsychological Society, 9*, 954–959.

Hart, R. P., Martelli, M. F., & Zasler, N. D. (2000). Chronic pain and neuropsycho-logical functioning. *Neuropsychology Review, 10(3)*, 131–149.

Hart R. P., Wade, J. B., & Martelli, M. F. (2003). Cognitive impairment in patients with chronic pain: The significance of stress. *Current Pain and Headache Reports, 7*, 1–12.

Heaton, R. K., Grant, I., & Matthews, C. G. (1991). *Comprehensive Norms for an Extended Halstead–Reitan Neuropsychological Test Battery.* Odessa, FL, Psychological Assessment Resources.

Hiscock, M. & Hiscock, C. K. (1989). Refining the forced choice method for the detection of malingering. *Journal of Clinical and Experimental Neuropsychology, 11*, 967–974.

Horner M. D. & Hamner, M. B. (2003). Neurocognitive functioning in Posttraumatic Stress Disorder. *Neuropsychology Review, 12*, 15–30.

Houlihan, M. E., McGrath, P. J., Connolly, J. F., Stroink, G., Finley, G. A., Dick, B., & Phi, T.-T. (2003). Assessing the effect of pain on demands for attentional resources using ERPs. *International Journal of Psychophysiology, 51*, 181–187.

Jacobsen, J., Baadsgaard, S. E., & Thompson, S. (1987). Prediction of post-concus-sional sequelae by reaction time test. *Acta Neurologica Scandinavia, 75*, 341–345.

Kanner, A. M. (2004). Is major depression a neurologic disorder with psychiatric symptoms. *Epilepsy and Behavior, 5*, 636–644.

Kay, T. (1999). Interpreting apparent neuropsychological deficits: What is really wrong? In J. J. Sweet (Ed.). *Forensic Neuropsychology: Fundamentals and Practice.* Lisse, The Netherlands: Swets & Zeitlinger, pp. 145–184.

Keidel M., & Diener H. C. (1997). Post-traumatic headache. *Nervenarzt, 68*, 769–777.

King, N. S. (1996). Emotional, neuropsychological, and organic factors: Their use in the prediction of persisting postconcussion symptoms after moderate and mild head injuries. *Journal of Neurology, Neurosurgery and Psychiatry, 61*, 75–81.

Koetsier, G. C., Volkers, A. Tulen, J. H. M., Passchier, J., van den Broek, W. W., & Bruijn, J. A. (2002). CPT performance in major depressive disorder before and after treatment with imipramine or fluvoxamine. *Journal of Psychiatric Research, 36*, 391–397.

Kuelz, A. K., Hohagen, F., & Voderholzer, U. (2004). Neuropsychological performance in obsessive–compulsive disorder: A critical review. *Biological Psychology,*
65, 185–236.

Lahz, S. & Bryant, R. A. (1996). Incidence of chronic pain following traumatic brain
injury. *Archives of Physical Medicine and Rehabilitation, 77,* 889–891.

Lannoo, E., Colardyn, F., Jannes, C., & de Soete, G. (2001). Course of neuropsychological recovery from moderate-to-severe head injury: A 2-year follow-up. *Brain*
Injury, 15, 1–13.

Lees-Haley, P. R., Fox, D. D., & Courtney J. C. (2001). A comparison of complaints
by mild brain injury claimants and other claimants describing subjective experiences immediately following their injury. *Archives of Clinical Neuropsychology, 16,*
689–695.

Lishman, W. A. (1973). The psychiatric sequelae of head injury: A review.
Psychological Medicine, 3, 304–318.

Lishman, W. A. (1988). Physiogenesis and psychogenesis in the 'post-concussional
syndrome.' *British Journal of Psychiatry, 153,* 460–469.

Luis C., Vanderploeg R. D., & Curtiss, G. (2003). Predictors of postconcussion symptom complex in community dwelling male veterans. *Journal of the International*
Neuropsychological Society, 9, 1001–1015.

MacMillan, P. J., Hart, R. P., Martelli, M. M., & Zasler, N. D. (2002). Pre-injury status and adaptation following traumatic brain injury. *Brain Injury, 16,* 41–49.

Mahmood, O., Rapport, L. J., Hanks, R. A., & Fitchtenberg, N. L. (2004).
Neuropsychological performance and sleep disturbance following traumatic brain
injury. *Journal of Head Trauma Rehabilitation, 19,* 378–390.

Martelli, M. F., Bender, M. C., Nicholson, K., & Zasler, N. D. (2002). Masquerades
of brain injury. Part V. Preinjury factors affecting disability following traumatic
brain injury. *Journal of Controversial Medical Claims, 9,* 1–7.

Mayer, E. A. & Saper, C. B. (Eds.). (2000). *The Biological Basis for Mind Body*
Interactions. Progress in Brain Research, Vol. 122, Amsterdam: Elsevier.

McCracken, L. M. & Iverson, G. L. (2001). Predicting complaints of impaired cognitive
functioning in patients with chronic pain. *Journal of Pain and Symptom Management,*
21, 392–397.

Menefee, L. A., Cohen, M. J. M., Anderson, W. R., Doghramji, K., Frank, E. D., &
Lee, H. (2000). Sleep disturbance and nonmalignant chronic pain: A comprehensive review of the literature. *Pain Medicine, 1,* 156–172.

Mickeviciene, D, Schrader, H., Obelieniene D., Surkiene, D., Kunickas, R., Stovner,
L. J., & Sand, T. (2004). A controlled prospective inception cohort study on the
post-concussion syndrome outside the medicolegal context. *European Journal of*
Neurology, 11, 411–419.

Middleboe, T., Birket-Smith, M., Andersen, H. S., & Friis, M. L. (1992). Personality
traits in patients with postconcussional sequelae, *Journal of Personality Disorders, 6,*
246–255.

Miller, L. (2000). Neurosensitization: A model for persistent disability in chronic pain,
depression, and Posttraumatic Stress Disorder following injury. *Neurorehabilitation,*
14, 25–32.

Mittenberg, W., DiGiulio, D. V., Perrin, S., & Bass, A. E. (1992). Symptoms following
mild head injury; expectation as aetiology. *Journal of Neurology, Neurosurgery and*
Psychiatry, 55, 200–204.

Moore, B. A. & Donders, J. (2004). Predictors of invalid neuropsychological test performance after traumatic brain injury. *Brain Injury, 18*, 975–984.

Narrow, W. E., Rae, D. S., Robbins, L. N., & Regier, D. A. (2002). Revised prevalence estimates of mental disorders in the United States. *Archives of General Psychiatry, 59*, 115–123.

Nicholson, K. (1998). The neuropsychology of pain. Special presentation. National Academy of Neuropsychology Annual Conference.

Nicholson, K. (2000a). Pain, cognition and traumatic brain injury. *NeuroRehabilitation, 14*, 95–103.

Nicholson, K. (2000b). At the crossroads: Pain in the 21st century. *NeuroRehabilitation, 14*, 57–67.

Nicholson, K., Martelli, M. F., & Zasler, N. D. (2001). Does pain confound interpretation of neuropsychological test results. *NeuroRehabilitation, 16*, 225–230.

Nitschke, J. B., Heller, W., & Miller, G. A. (2000). Anxiety, stress, and cortical brain function. In J. C. Borod (Ed.). *The Neuropsychology of Emotion*. Series in Affective Science. New York: Oxford University Press, pp. 298–319.

O'Donnell, M. L., Creamer, M., & Pattison, P. (2004). Posttraumatic Stress Disorder and depression following trauma: Understanding comorbidity. *American Journal of Psychiatry, 161*, 1390–1397.

Ottowitz, W. E., Dougherty, D. D., & Savage, C. R. (2002). The neural network basis for abnormalities of attention and executive function in major depressive disorder: Implications for application of the medical disease model to psychiatric disorders. *Harvard Review of Psychiatry, 10*, 86–99.

Pilcher, J. J. & Huffcutt, A. I. (1996). Effects of sleep deprivation on performance: A meta-analysis. *Sleep, 19*, 318–326.

Post, R. M., Denicoff, K. D., Leverich, G. S., Huggins, T., Post, S. W., & Luckenbaugh, D. (2000). Neuropsychological deficits of primary affective illness: Implications for therapy, *Psychiatric Annals, 30*, 485–494.

Posthuma, A. Podrouzek, W., & Crisp, D. (2002). The implications of Daubert on neuropsychological evidence in the assessment of remote mild traumatic brain injury. *American Journal of Forensic Psychology, 20(4)*, 21–23.

Powell, B. D., Brossart, D. F., & Reynolds, C. R. (2003). Evaluation of the accuracy of two regression-based methods for estimating premorbid IQ. *Archives of Clinical Neuropsychology, 18*, 277–292.

Putnam, S. H., Ricker, J. H., Ross, S. R., & Kurtz, J. E. (1999). Considering premorbid functioning: Beyond cognition to a conceptualization of personality in post-injury functioning. In J. J. Sweet (Ed.). *Forensic Neuropsychology*. Lisse, The Netherlands: Swets & Zetlinger, pp. 39–81.

Ravnkilde, B., Videbech1, P., Clemmensen, K., Egander, A., Rasmussen, N. A., & Rosenberg, R. (2002). Cognitive deficits in major depression. *Scandinavian Journal of Psychology, 43*, 239–251.

Rohling, M. L., Green, P., Allen, L. M., & Iverson, G. L. (2002). Depressive symptoms and neurocognitive test scores in patients passing symptom validity tests. *Archives of Clinical Neuropsychology, 17*, 205–222.

Rutherford, W. H. (1979). Postconcussion symptoms: Relationship to acute neurological indices, individual differences, and circumstances of injury. In H. S. Levin, H. M. Eisenberg, & A. L. Benton (Eds.). *Mild Head Injury*. New York: Oxford University Press, pp. 217–228.

Schnurr, R. F. & MacDonald, M. R. (1995). Memory complaints in chronic pain. *Clinical Journal of Pain, 11*, 103–111.

Schretlen, D. J., Munro, C. A., Anthony, J. C., & Pearlson, G. D. (2003). Examining the range of normal intraindividual variability in neuropsychological test performance. *Journal of the International Neuropsychological Society, 9*, 864–870.

Sharp, T. J. & Harvey, A. G. (2001). Chronic pain and Posttraumatic Stress Disorder: Mutual maintenance? *Clinical Psychology Review, 21*, 857–877.

Shenal, B. V., Harrison, D. W., & Demaree, H. A. (2003). The neuropsychology of depression: A literature review and preliminary model. *Neuropsychology Review, 13*, 33–42.

Slick, D. L., Sherman, E. M. S., & Iverson, G. L. (1999). Diagnostic criteria for malingered neurocognitive dysfunction: Proposed standards for clinical practice and research. *The Clinical Neuropsychologist, 13*, 545–561.

Smith-Seemiller, L., Fow, N. R., Kant, R., and Franzen, M. D. (2003). Presence of post-concussion syndrome symptoms in patients with chronic pain versus mild traumatic brain injury. *Brain Injury, 17*, 199–206.

Stein, R. A. & Strickland, T. L. (1998). A review of the neuropsychological effects of commonly used prescription medications. *Archives of Clinical Neuropsychology, 13*, 259–284.

Tate, R. L. (2003). Impact of pre-injury factors on outcome after severe traumatic brain injury: Does post-traumatic personality change represent an exacerbation of premorbid traits. *Neuropsychological Rehabilitation, 13*, 43–64.

Taylor, A., Cox, C., & Mailis, A. (1996). Persistent neuropsychological deficits following whiplash: Evidence for chronic mild traumatic brain injury? *Archives of Physical Medicine and Rehabilitation, 77*, 529–535.

Toren, P., Sadeh, M., Wolmer, L., Eldar, S., Koren, S., Weizman, R., & Laor, N. (2000). Neurocognitive correlates of anxiety disorders in children: A preliminary report. *Journal of Anxiety Disorders, 14*, 239–247.

Trahan, D. E., Ross, C. E., & Trahan, S. L. (2001). Relationships among postconcussional-type symptoms, depression, and anxiety in neurologically normal young adults and victims of mild brain injury. *Archives of Clinical Neuropsychology, 16*, 435–445.

Uomoto, J. M. & Esselman, P. C. (1993). Traumatic brain injury and chronic pain: Differential types and rates by head injury severity. *Archives of Physical Medicine and Rehabilitation, 74*, 61–64.

Van Damme, S. V., Crombez, G., & Eccleston, C. (2004). The anticipation of pain modulates spatial attention: Evidence for pain-specificity in high-pain catastrophizers. *Pain, 111*, 392–399.

van Hout, M. S. E., Schmand, B., Wekking, E. M., Hageman, G., & Deelman, B. G. (2003). Suboptimal performance on neuropsychological tests in patients with suspected chronic toxic encephalopathy. *NeuroToxicology, 24*, 547–551.

Vanderploeg, R. D., Curtiss, G., Luis, C. A., Ordorica, P. I., & Salazar, A. M. (submitted). Long-term morbidity and quality of life following mild head injury.

Verdejo-Garcia, A., Lopez-Torrecillas, F., Gimenez, C. O., & Perez-Garcia, M. (2004). Clinical implications and methodological challenges in the study of the neuropsychological correlates of cannabis, stimulant, and opioid abuse. *Neuropsychology Review, 14*, 1–41.

Wade, J. B., & Hart, R. P. (2002). Attention and the stages of pain processing. *Pain Medicine, 3*, 30–38.

recover at different rates. Attention, memory, and executive functions typically remain the most pervasively impaired (Dikmen et al., 1995; Goldstein & Levin, 1995; Kersel et al., 2001; Kinsella, 1998; van Zomeren & Brouwer, 1994).

A recent meta-analysis suggested greater and more persistent impairment of overall cognitive functioning following moderate or severe TBI compared to mild TBI (Schretlen & Shapiro, 2003). Nevertheless, there exists significant interindividual variability in the performance of adults with severe brain injury (Dikmen et al., 1995). Several injury-related variables have been linked to prognosis. These include coma depth (Levin et al., 1990) and length (Dikmen et al., 1990), pupillary abnormalities (Levin et al., 1990), duration of PTA (Ellenberg et al., 1996), diffuse injury (Wilson et al., 1995), and evidence of mass lesions (Williams et al., 1990). However, no injury-related variable has been shown to be consistently correlated with outcome and none predicted the extent of recovery 2 years post-TBI in a prospective study (Lannoo et al., 2001).

2.   The Comprehensive Neuropsychological Assessment

The range and nature of cognitive deficits following a moderate or severe TBI can vary considerably depending on both injury- and recovery-related factors (Sohlberg & Mateer, 2001) as well as on other patient-related variables. The frequent coexistence of both diffuse and focal damage also precludes the inference of deficits in particular cognitive domains based on neuroimaging findings. A comprehensive assessment helps ensure that relevant areas of deficits are not overlooked.

2.1.   Clinical Interview and Collateral Information

A clinical interview provides information about the brain-injured individual's experience of his or her own cognitive abilities, the consistency between self-reports and other sources of data, premorbid characteristics such as emotional difficulties, and various other factors (e.g., sleep disturbances) that may impact symptoms and cognition.

Interviews with people who knew the patient well before and after the event that led to a TBI can provide information regarding changes in functional and cognitive abilities as well as alterations in personality, behavior, or emotional functioning. Collateral interviews are especially important if the patient is a poor informant because of impaired self-awareness.

Academic, vocational, military, and medical records can assist in estimating premorbid functioning. They can also aid in determining the extent to which premorbid deficits, medical conditions, including psychiatric difficulties, and medications may be contributing to current test performance. Psychotropic medications may be given to clients with TBI to alleviate physiological, behavioral, or emotional symptoms. Several of these substances, as well as nonpsychotropic drugs, can impact cognitive functions (see Stein & Strickland, 1998, for a review). Neuroimaging and neurosurgical reports as well as emergency room notes, admission information, and discharge summaries are useful to support or disconfirm hypotheses based on other data. These records can also provide information on presence and severity of brain damage at the time of injury or admission, potential medical complications, and course of recovery.

The review of raw test data from previous neuropsychological assessments, if available, allows the comparison of past and current test scores. The neuropsychologist can also verify the accuracy of the scoring and interpretations derived from prior scores in light of recent scientific findings.

2.2.   Neuropsychological Testing

For the proper neuropsychological assessment of moderate to severe TBI, the individual should have emerged from PTA and be able both to focus attention and actively participate in the assessment (Kinsella, 1998). In a recent survey, 33 neuropsychologists with extensive experience in the area of TBI recommended initial assessments at 3 and 6 months postinjury and follow-ups at 1 and 2 years for individuals with moderate or severe brain injury. Assessment at resolution of PTA was also recommended (Sherer & Novack, in press).

3.   Neuropsychological Assessment Domains and Relevant Groups Findings in Moderate to Severe TBI

Patients who have sustained a moderate to severe TBI usually undergo a neuropsychological evaluation during later stages of rehabilitation or in the chronic stage of recovery. Therefore, most of the research reviewed in this section is based on patients who were in these stages of recovery. Also, most findings pertain exclusively to serve TBI because relatively few studies have included a subgroup of patients with a moderate TBI.

Moderate and severe TBI are usually characterized by diffuse damage because of diffuse axonal injury and secondary pathological processes. Given the mechanics of injury, the ventral and lateral surfaces of the frontal and temporal lobes are particularly vulnerable. As a result, the most common sequelae of TBI involves disturbances in functions mediated largely by these areas or susceptible to diffuse injury, namely attention and processing speed, learning and memory, and executive functions.

3.1.   Attention

3.1.1.   Assessing the Construct of Attention

Attention remains an elusive construct with no agreed-upon definition. This is most likely attributable to its multidimensional nature (Ponsford, 2000), with attention encompassing several mental operations (e.g., Bate et al., 2001). These include speed of processing, immediate span of attention, sustained attention or vigilance, selective or focused attention, divided attention, and working memory.

There is no single test of attention; rather, different tests were designed to measure different components of attention. Tests differ both in their parameters (e.g., stimulus presentation rate, self-paced or externally paced responding, emphasis on automatic or controlled processing demands, amount of structure provided) (Spikman et al., 1999). Attention tests are also differentially sensitive to impairment. The more sensitive measures emphasize speed and require simultaneous attention to several pieces of information (Cicerone, 1997).

The assessment of everyday attention poses a challenge for neuropsychologists. One issue concerns the inability of commonly used measures of attention to elicit the kind and extent of attentional impairments experienced by individuals with TBI in their everyday life. Additionally, attentional deficits that may be occurring in real-world settings may not be apparent during testing because testing occurs within a limited period of one-to-one interaction in a quiet and highly structured environment (Kerns & Mateer, 1996).

3.1.2.   Research Findings Pertaining to Attention in Moderate to Severe TBI

People with moderate or severe TBI can present with a range of attentional difficulties, given the severity of injury and the multiple pathologies that can potentially underlie attention deficits (Kinsella, 1998). Residual attentional impairments also typically last longer than in those with milder injuries and may persist for at least 1 year (van Zomeren & Brouwer, 1994). However, the neuropsychological literature is replete with controversy over the nature of the deficits, and neuropsychologists' views are divided as to whether the deficits represent true attentional difficulties or reduced speed of processing (see Cossa & Fabiani, 1999, for a review).

3.1.2.1.   Speed of Processing

Slowed speed of processing is the most consistently reported finding in the area of attention and TBI. Indeed, several studies failed to find deficits in specific aspects of attention but reported that measures requiring speed of processing are particularly sensitive to severe TBI, even 2–5 years postinjury (Spikman et al., 2000). Measures that have yielded group differences include simple and choice reaction time (RT) tasks as well as the Symbol Digit Modalities Test (SDMT), Stroop, Digit Symbol, and Paced Auditory Serial Addition Test (PASAT) (Bate et al., 2001; Ponsford & Kinsella, 1992; Spikman et al., 1996, 1999; Stuss et al., 1989). Speed of performance on problem-solving and motor tasks has been highly associated with estimates of injury severity (Dikmen et al., 1995).

Reaction time measures are thought to measure mainly speed of processing because minimal conscious control is required for adequate performance

(Spikman et al., 1999). With severe TBI, reaction time seems to be disproportionately affected by increases in task complexity (e.g., Ponsford & Kinsella, 1992; see also van Zomeren & Brouwer, 1994, for a review).

Ponsford and Kinsella (1992) suggested that individuals with severe TBI may tend to sacrifice speed to maintain accuracy, as they observed group differences in accuracy solely when tasks were not self-paced. A similar pattern of performance was noted by others (e.g., Stuss et al., 1985). Despite the evidence for reduced speed of processing following severe TBI, brain-injured individuals have occasionally been reported to perform similarly to persons without injury on particular speed of processing measures, such as the Color-Word subtest of the Stroop (Spikman et al., 2000).

3.1.2.2.   Immediate Span of Attention

Although Digit Span may be impaired in the acute stages following TBI, scores improve more rapidly than for Digit Symbol within the first 6 months postinjury (Kersel et al., 2001). After an average of 8 months post-TBI, performance was comparable to that of persons without a brain injury (Bate et al., 2001; Leclercq et al., 2000).

3.1.2.3.   Sustained Attention/Vigilance

Of the relatively few studies that have focused on sustained attention in moderate to severe TBI, many found either a reduction (e.g., Bate et al., 2001; Loken et al., 1995; van Zomeren & Brouwer, 1987) or fluctuation (e.g., Ringholz & Boake, 1987) of the level of arousal. Nevertheless, such problems have not been universally reported (e.g., Levin et al., 1988; Ponsford & Kinsella, 1992).

The Conners Continuous Performance Test (CPT), commonly used in clinical practice to measure sustained attention, has shown sensitivity to both focal and diffuse injury, with greater deficits being associated with diffuse damage (Riccio et al., 2002). In a study by Loken et al. (1995), individuals with severe TBI who were tested with the CPT an average of 2 months postinjury showed impairment in overall vigilance and sustained allocation of attention over time. In contrast, other studies did not find deterioration of vigilance (Levin et al., 1988; Ponsford & Kinsella, 1992) or reduced accuracy (Ponsford & Kinsella, 1992) in persons with severe TBI.

The Test of Everyday Attention (TEA) comprises two subtests designed to measure vigilance, namely the Lottery Task and Telephone Search while Counting. Both subtests were performed more poorly by a group of people with severe TBI than by a control group in a study by Robertson et al. (1996). Another study reported recovery in sustained attention beyond 1 year post-TBI based on the Lottery subtest (Bate et al., 2001).

3.1.2.4.   Selective (or Focused) Attention

The performance of individuals with severe TBI on several measures utilized in clinical practice did not reveal deficits in focused attention in a study by

Ponsford and Kinsella (1992). Similarly, in a review of the effects of head injury on attention, van Zomeren and Brouwer (1994) concluded that little empirical data support common complaints of heightened distractibility However, they pointed out that a small body of evidence exists for increased sensitivity to interference several months after a TBI.

More recent studies have reported the presence of deficits in selective attention, often based on cancellation and visual search tasks. Visual selective attention was impaired on the Map Search, Telephone Search, and Visual Elevator subtests of the TEA within 1 year of a severe TBI and at more than 2 years postinjury in a study of individuals with severe TBI (Bate et al., 2001). Scores on the first two measures were also impaired in another study (Robertson et al., 1996). Map Search was able to better differentiate between patients and controls compared to other attentional measures (with the exception of the Color-Word subtest of the Stroop) (Bate et al., 2001). Individuals with TBI also showed deficits on the total accuracy score of the Ruff 2 & 7 Selective Attention Test (Bate et al., 2001). An experimental task used by Schmitter-Edgecombe and Kibby (1998) revealed problems with the suppression of attention to visual distractors except when attention was cued to the target location. In contrast to the above findings of selective attention deficits, no impairment was noted by Bate et al. (2001) on Elevator Counting, an auditory selective attention subtest of the TEA.

3.1.2.5. Divided Attention

It has not been unequivocally established that divided attention is impaired following severe TBI (Park et al., 1999; van Zomeren & Brouwer, 1994; Veltman et al., 1996). Weak performance on divided attention tasks has sometimes been attributed to slowed speed of processing (Ponsford & Kinsella, 1992; van Zomeren & Brouwer, 1994). Van Zomeren and Brouwer (1994) reviewed evidence for divided attention impairments and concluded that a nonspecific slowing of both perceptual–motor and cognitive processes increases with task complexity and seems to account for group differences. More recent studies have criticized several earlier investigations of divided attention. Park et al. (1999) indicated that most of the dual tasks used involved motor and perceptual components such as manual tracking rather than working memory. Furthermore, Schmitter-Edgecombe (1996) pointed out that studies did not appropriately address the ability to divide attention concurrently over multiple effortful tasks, with paradigms usually involving the presentation of distractors during a reaction time task.

One view holds that a deficit of control mechanisms underlies the poor performance of persons with severe TBI on divided attention tasks by persons with severe TBI (e.g., McDowell et al., 1997; Vilkki et al., 1996). Weak scores were observed under dual-task conditions even when statistically controlling for slower performance (Azouvi et al., 1996). The severity of the deficit may depend on the type of cognitive operation performed. Greater impairment was noted when dual tasks required more controlled processing of stored information or working memory rather than straightforward storage and retrieval of information, as in digit span measures (Park et al., 1999). Consistent with this hypothesis, Leclercq et al. (2000) reported a greater decrement of reaction time in persons with very severe diffuse injury compared to those without a TBI when a simple reaction time task was performed concurrently with a self-paced random number generation task. Nevertheless, a group of patients who were in various stages of recovery following a severe TBI showed greater decrements than healthy individuals on a simple visual reaction time task when simultaneously performing an articulation or digit span task (McDowell et al., 1997). A different type of study found that severity of divided attention impairments may be contingent on both the type of cognitive operation performed and on the dependencies among tasks. Specifically, Brouwer et al. (2001) reported that individuals with chronic severe TBI performed adequately on independent dual tasks but were impaired when performance on one task depended on the information presented in the other task. By contrast, the performance of the control group was similar across conditions.

The PASAT is measure of divided attention often used in clinical practice. It has been deemed one of the more sensitive attention measures following mild TBI (Cicerone, 1997). In studies of individuals with moderate to severe TBI, the PASAT is usually impaired, although it is uncertain whether there is a disproportionate deterioration in performance with faster presentation rates (Bate et al., 2001; Ponsford & Kinsella, 1992).

3.2.   Learning and Memory

3.2.1.   Assessing the Construct of Memory

A three-stage model of memory functioning underlies most of the research on memory dysfunction in TBI (Bauer et al., 1993). The three stages, namely encoding or registration, storage/rehearsal, and retrieval of new information, can be selectively impaired and have been identified through factor analysis (e.g., Vakil & Blachstein; 1993). Memory is closely related to attention, with attentional difficulties precluding adequate registration of the to-be-remembered information.

A comprehensive assessment requires the evaluation of at least three aspects of memory. Encoding ability is inferred from the acquisition of new material, retention of information from performance on delayed recall measures, and recognition from the ability to discriminate previously presented items from new stimuli.

Memory is typically evaluated in both the auditory and visual modalities through the use of both verbal and nonverbal material because of potential modality or material-specific deficits, particularly following focal brain damage. Immediate and delayed free recall can also be selectively impaired. Cued recall assesses the ability to benefit from cues and can help distinguish retrieval from storage deficits. The use of a recognition format also serves this purpose and is particularly useful when individuals are unable to copy, draw, or respond verbally. The quality of encoding and retrieval can be inferred from the use of active learning strategies.

3.2.2.   Research Findings Pertaining to Memory in Moderate to Severe TBI

Impairment of new learning and memory is deemed to be characteristic of moderate to severe TBI and is often enduring (Levin, 1989). However, the specific nature of the memory deficits remains unclear (i.e., encoding, consolidation, retrieval). Furthermore, the relationship between injury-related variables and memory performance is not straightforward. A link has been found between such variables and the level (Wiegner & Donders, 1999), but not the pattern (Curtiss et al., 2001), of memory performance.

The various aspects of verbal learning and memory are commonly evaluated by asking an individual to learn a list of words such as the California Verbal Learning Test (CVLT). Of the various scores derived from the CVLT, the General Verbal Learning factor (Total Trials 1–5) was found to best discriminate persons with moderate to severe TBI from non-brain-injured individuals with an 84–88% accuracy rate (Gardner & Vrbancic, 1998). However, individuals with a TBI may be more likely to be classified as impaired when the CVLT is used as opposed to the Rey Auditory Verbal Learning Test (RAVLT) (Stallings et al., 1995). According to the authors, this may be partly because of differences in normative samples in the two studies and also because of reduced semantic clustering by patients with TBI on the CVLT.

On the Wechsler Memory Scale-III (WMS-III), the Visual Memory Index was found to be more sensitive than the Auditory Memory Index to bilateral or diffuse brain injury (Hawkins, 1998). Additionally, it showed a relatively high level of sensitivity (71.4%) to TBI, being the second most sensitive of the Wechsler indices to such injury (Taylor & Heaton, 2001).

3.2.2.1.   *Evidence for an Encoding Deficit*

A reduced rate of verbal and visual learning, typically attributed to an encoding deficit, has been reported by several investigators (Blachstein et al., 1993; Crosson et al., 1988; DeLuca et al., 2000; Shum et al., 2000). Conversely, others have found learning to be intact (Vanderploeg & Eichler, 1990; Vanderploeg et al., 2001). In a study by Kersel et al. (2001), the ability to learn a list of words on the RAVLT improved between 6 months and 1 year postinjury but remained impaired in more than half of the patients with severe TBI. Poor recall following the initial presentation of to-be-learned material is also frequently observed and may be related more (or equally) to attentional difficulties (Sohlberg & Mateer, 2001).

3.2.2.2.   Evidence for a Consolidation Deficit

A consolidation deficit involves difficulties with the maintenance, elaboration, and storage of novel information in long-term memory. In a study by Vanderploeg et al. (2001), individuals with severe TBI showed a more rapid rate of forgetting than those without a brain injury. This was indicated by a disproportionate impairment on delayed recall compared to immediate recall measures. Because the investigators controlled for acquisition differences and for ceiling effects on recall and recognition measures, they attributed their findings to a consolidation deficit. A more rapid rate of forgetting has also been reported in other studies (Stuss et al., 1985, Zec et al., 2001), regardless of whether they controlled for acquisition differences between groups. Nevertheless, similar rates of forgetting by patient and control groups were found by DeLuca et al. (2000) when groups were equated for initial levels of learning. Shum et al. (2000) also found retention to be intact.

Previously learned information interferes with new learning in non-brain-injured individuals. This proactive interference effect may be reduced in people who sustained a severe TBI (Vanderploeg et al., 2001), potentially because they possess more limited old information secondary to a consolidation deficit. However, findings in this area have been inconsistent (e.g., Crosson et al., 1988; Goldstein et al., 1989; Numan et al., 2000).

3.2.2.3.   Evidence for a Retrieval Deficit

Some authors have argued for the presence of a retrieval deficit based on poorer performance on delayed free recall compared to cued recall and recognition measures (Crosson et al., 1988; Curtiss et al., 2001). Others (e.g., DeLuca et al., 2000) did not report this pattern of performance. The failure of several studies to control for ceiling effects makes it difficult to infer the status of retrieval abilities.

3.2.2.4.   Variability in Patterns of Memory Impairment

The patterns of memory impairment manifested by individuals with severe TBI are highly variable. Two studies have identified active, passive, disorganized, and deficient learning and memory styles (Deshpande et al., 1996; Millis & Ricker, 1994). Deshpande et al. (1996) also observed a combination of disorganized and deficient learning styles also observed in one of the studies (Deshpande et al., 1996).

Different aspects of memory may also be affected to various degrees across patients with TBI. Curtiss et al. (2001) differentiated subgroups with deficits in consolidation, retrieval, and retention based on CVLT performance after an average of 1 year postinjury. The authors also identified subgroups of patients with intact memory performance who used either an active or a passive encoding strategy. In a prospective study, patients who were assessed both 6 months and 1 year after a severe TBI and who showed poor delayed recall on the RAVLT had different underlying difficulties (Kersel et al., 2001). About 60% had retrieval problems, with intact performance on a recognition test, and the remainder experienced difficulties with retention. In the study by Curtiss et al. (2001), individuals with a retrieval deficit performed more poorly on other neuropsychological measures, including other memory tests.

3.2.2.5. Application of Active Strategies

Patients with severe TBI may have difficulty applying active strategies during learning and memory tasks. They have shown less spontaneous clustering of words compared to persons without a brain injury, indicating a passive approach to learning (Blachstein et al., 1993; Crosson et al., 1988; Levin & Goldstein, 1986). Although some authors have postulated an encoding deficit (Crosson et al., 1988; Levin & Goldstein, 1986; Stallings et al., 1995), others have argued that it could also, or alternatively, be related to inefficient retrieval strategies because recall is often inconsistent across trials (Blachstein et al., 1993; Paniak et al., 1989; Vanderploeg et al., 2001). According to Levin and Goldstein (1986), the reduced use of semantic clustering strategies does not seem to be the result of an inability to process semantic knowledge (Levin & Goldstein, 1986).

3.2.2.6. Intrusion Errors

A tendency to retrieve items that were not presented or to answer "yes" to items not previously encountered has been observed on verbal (Crosson et al., 1988; Zec et al., 2001) and visual (e.g., Levin & Goldstein, 1986; Shum et al., 2000) recall and recognition tasks.

3.2.2.7. Long-Term Effects of TBI on Memory

Goldstein and Levin (1995) reported the presence of long-term nonspecific memory impairment affecting both encoding and retrieval of verbal and visual information. However, the rate of memory recovery over a 2-year period varies considerably across people with severe TBI (Levin, 1989). In one study conducted an average of 3.25 years postinjury, patients with PTA greater than 3 weeks were impaired on the Logical Memory subtest of the WMS and on the delayed recall trial of the Rey Complex Figure Test compared to orthopedic controls (Bennett-Levy, 1984). Another study reported that a group that had sustained a severe TBI an average of 10 years earlier performed more poorly than a spinal cord injury group on several verbal and visual memory tests (Zec et al., 2001). Measures included the Buschke Selective Reminding Test, RAVLT, and WMS-R. Individuals with TBI recalled fewer words across trials and showed greater forgetting after a delay, indicating problems with learning and retention. They also committed more false-positive errors on delayed recognition. A study by Sbordone et al. (1995) suggested that memory may continue to improve until at least 10 years postinjury.

3.3. Executive Functions

3.3.1.   Assessing the Construct of Executive Functions

Executive functions refer to a variety of capabilities necessary to organize and carry out goal-directed behaviors, such as the ability to initiate, plan, sequence, organize, and self-regulate one's actions to reach functional goals. Executive functions also encompass self-awareness. They are thought to be associated predominantly with frontal lobe structures and function.

Several of the constructs subsumed under the term "executive functions" are difficult to quantify using traditional neuropsychological instruments (Damasio & Anderson, 1993). This is partly because dysfunction is most apparent in novel situations or during the performance of novel problem-solving tasks, which is incompatible with the standardized and structured nature of the tests and testing environment. Consequently, the sensitivity of executive function tests to existing deficits may be limited (Rankin & Adams, 1999). In addition, current measures assess only one or a few of the cognitive processes subsumed under the term "executive functions" and thus may fail to capture the complexity of cognitive and behavioral alterations (Cripe, 1996). Another problem concerns the timed nature of several tests, which confounds the effects of slowed processing speed with executive function deficits (Spikman et al., 2000).

3.3.2.   Research Findings Pertaining to Executive Functions in Moderate to Severe TBI

Executive functions are often compromised in individuals with moderate or severe TBI because the frontal lobes are commonly injured. Focal cortical contusions to the frontal lobes, hemorrhages involving frontal–subcortical circuitry, diffuse injury, or secondary damage and delayed complications may all disrupt executive functions. The specific effects of TBI on frontal functions largely depend on the type, severity, and location of injury, as well as on the depth and laterality of focal lesions.

Motivational problems such as denial, irritability, apathy, and unawareness (Chervinsky et al., 1998) are often linked to reduced responsiveness to reward or to a difficulty producing goal-directed behaviors. Self-awareness has been correlated with severity of injury based on the GCS upon admission (Prigatano et al., 1998). Severe TBI is typically associated with a limited or lack of awareness of behavioral and cognitive alterations, particularly within the first year postinjury (Prigatano, 1999). Comparison of self-ratings with ratings made by relatives indicates that persons with a severe TBI underestimate the severity of their behavioral, emotional, and social difficulties (Prigatano, 1996). Additionally, they frequently underestimate the extent of the memory deficits uncovered using objective measures (e.g., Baddeley et al., 1987). The validity of memory self-reports by patients with a severe TBI appears to be influenced by both neurogenic and psychogenic factors (Boake et al., 1995). Anosognosia refers to impaired awareness resulting directly from the injury. It is associated with executive dysfunction and may be chronic with more severe TBI.

Verbal fluency, as measured by the Controlled Oral Word Association Test (COWAT), is one of the executive skills most consistently reported to be impaired following a severe TBI (Cockburn, 1995; Leclercq et al., 2000). One year postinjury, 42% of patients continued to still perform in the severe range on the COWAT, with most patients failing to implement any strategy to facilitate word recall (Kersel et al., 2001). This finding is consistent with Ruff et al.'s (1986) hypothesis that impairment of verbal fluency in TBI is related to cognitive inflexibility.

Differences have also been observed between patients and controls on the Wisconsin Card Sorting Test (WCST) (Cockburn, 1995; Hartman et al., 1992). Another commonly administered measure, the Trail Making Test (TMT), has revealed more variable impairment. Although Veltman et al. (1996) reported cognitive flexibility to be comparable to that of controls, based on the TMT another study found group differences on Part B of the test when an assessment was conducted 2–5 years postinjury (Spikman et al., 2000).

Scores on the Stroop interference index do not suggest a reduced ability to inhibit a prepotent response following a severe TBI (Bate et al., 2001; Ponsford & Kinsella, 1992; Trexler & Zappala, 1988). On the other hand, the revised Strategy Application Test has shown sensitivity to TBI as well as to injury severity (Levine et al., 2000). This task requires inhibition or reversal of the response pattern previously reinforced.

Performance on the Tower of London (TOL) is typically spared in individuals with a severe TBI (Cockburn, 1995; Levin et al., 1991; Ponsford & Kinsella, 1992; Spikman et al., 2000). They are able to solve as many problems as healthy controls. However, this test assesses planning ability within a structured setting. An individual could thus perform adequately but have difficulty formulating plans in daily unstructured situations. Persons with a severe TBI have been reported to take longer to perform the TOL (Ponsford & Kinsella, 1992), but this finding is not universal (Spikman et al., 2000; Veltman et al., 1996). The Ecological Planning Task and the Tinkertoy Test are two measures of planning ability that also failed to reveal group differences in accuracy 2–5 years postinjury (Spikman et al., 2000). Conversely, a measure that is relatively unstructured and requires a self-generated strategy without externally provided cues (Executive Route Finding task) was performed more poorly by persons with TBI, particularly those with focal frontal injuries (Spikman et al., 2000).

3.4.   Intellectual Functioning

The Wechsler Adult Intelligence Scale (WAIS) is the most commonly used measure of intellectual functioning. On the revised version (WAIS-R), the likelihood that an individual is correctly classified as having sustained a TBI (of any degree of severity) or not based on either the Full Scale IQ (FSIQ) or on a combination of the Verbal IQ (VIQ) and Performance IQ (PIQ) is about 71% (Crawford et al., 1997). However, there is lack of consensus regarding the association between severe TBI and a significant VIQ–PIQ discrepancy. One study reported a lower PIQ than VIQ (Sherrill-Pattison et al., 2000). By contrast, Hawkins et al. (2002) suggested that such a discrepancy is unlikely in the subacute phase of recovery and that its absence does not imply a lack of sequelae from TBI. At 1 year post-TBI, the FSIQ may remain lower than its premorbid level, but intellectual functioning appears to be among the cognitive domains least affected by a severe TBI (Kersel et al., 2001).

Compared to the WAIS-R, the WAIS-III has the advantage of yielding four factor scores. Of these, Processing Speed (PS) has shown greater sensitivity to TBI than Perceptual Organization (PO) (73% vs. 56%) at a cutoff of one standard deviation. However, both factors correctly identifying 84% of healthy individuals as not having sustained a TBI (Taylor & Heaton, 2001). Hawkins (1998) found the PS factor to be most sensitive to various forms of brain dysfunction, particularly to two disorders including TBI. Because the PS factor can help differentiate between mild and moderate to severe TBI, Martin et al. (2000) emphasized the importance of administering both subtests comprising the PS factor, namely Digit Symbol and Symbol Search. However, the PS factor may not be useful in cases of focal injury and may be negatively impacted by depression (Hawkins, 1998). It is therefore necessary to rely on additional cognitive measures to determine the presence of brain injury. No discrepancy between the other factors derived from the WAIS-III has been reported in a TBI sample (Hawkins, 1998).

Although factor scores can yield important information, subtests comprising a factor should also be examined because subtests can be differentially sensitive to brain dysfunction. For example, within the Working Memory Index, Letter-Number Sequencing has shown greater sensitivity to TBI than Digit Span or Arithmetic (Donders et al., 2001). In the same study, the Matrix Reasoning subtest did not distinguish individuals with moderate to severe TBI from healthy controls.

3.5.   Language and Communication

Following a TBI, the nature of any language or communication disorder is largely dependent on the nature, localization, and severity of the TBI injury. Aphasia is relatively rare in individuals who have sustained a TBI. By contrast, communication dysfunction is more common and is usually secondary to pragmatic versus phonological, syntactic, or semantic impairments (Martin & McDonald, 2003; McDonald, 2000).

Various types of communication difficulty have been observed in subsets of individuals with TBI within the comprehension, expression, or affective aspects of communication. Comprehension may be impaired because of an inability to ignore the literal meaning of utterances and thus to grasp the meaning of more subtle and abstract language (e.g., sarcasm, humor). Such difficulties also impact language production. Furthermore, speech may be disorganized and/or tangential, inefficiently convey information, and contain socially inappropriate comments. Dysprosodia (i.e., the loss of expressive intonation or rhythm when speaking) and difficulty recognizing emotions based on facial expressions interfere with effective communication (Martin & McDonald, 2003). The communication problems experienced by some individuals with TBI are most typically viewed as stemming from an interaction between language and other cognitive abilities, such as executive functions (McDonald, 2000).

In a sample of individuals with severe TBI assessed 2 years postinjury, the types of pragmatic errors observed in conversation included inefficient provision of information, provision of redundant information being given, and failure to structure discourse. However, total utterances and conversation duration were comparable to those of a group of non-brain-injured people with orthopedic injuries (Snow et al., 1998).

3.6.   Visuospatial Skills

Difficulties in this area may be secondary to various disrupted processes in visual perception, including visual acuity, recognition, organization, and scanning (Lovell & Franzen, 1994). A qualitative approach is particularly useful when assessing visuospatial skills. Observation of the strategies used and of the kinds of difficulties encountered on tests with a visuospatial component can yield information about the localization of injury (Kaplan et al., 1991). Studies on visual–perceptual functioning in cases of severe TBI have produced mixed results. On the Block Design subtest of the WAIS-R or WAIS-III, half of a sample of patients with a severe TBI remained impaired, mostly to a severe degree, 6 months postinjury (Kersel et al., 2001).

3.7.   Motor Skills

Fine and gross motor skills can be selectively impaired after a TBI with either focal or diffuse injury and may impact test scores in various cognitive domains. Studies assessing speed of finger tapping in TBI have found it to be related to injury severity (Dikmen et al., 1995; Prigatano & Borgaro, 2003) and recovery (Haaland et al., 1994). Diffuse injury may account for the bilateral impairment in finger tapping speed associated with severe TBI (Prigatano & Borgaro, 2003).

3.8.   Anosmia

The prevalence of anosmia in cases of moderate to severe TBI is estimated to be approximately 20% (Costanzo & Zasler, 1992). A study by Callaban and Hinkebein (2002) reported that more severe TBI is associated with greater risk of severe anosmia (61% of their sample) and unawareness of this problem

(48% of their sample). In this population, it is therefore prudent to assess for potential anosmia. Callaban and Hinkebein (2002) recommended the administration of the full Smell Identification Test because the screening test failed to detect 20% of people who showed anosmia on the full version. The presence of anosmia does not necessarily imply a brain injury. It may be related more strongly to damaged olfactory bulbs (Yousem et al., 1999).

4. Issues to Consider When Interpreting Neuropsychological Findings in the Context of a TBI

Measurement issues such as reliability, validity, predictive power, and normative frames of reference must be taken into consideration when interpreting the results of a neuropsychological evaluation. Confounding issues must also be taken into account and are discussed in other chapters of this volume.

4.1. Reliability

Reliability refers to the extent to which a person's score on a test is free from errors of measurement. Test–retest reliability is particularly important when assessing individuals with a TBI who are involved in litigation because they often will have undergone several assessments. When test–retest reliability is high, clinicians can have more confidence that the obtained scores reflect the individual's true level of functioning. However, some tests lack reliability data or their reliability coefficients fall below an acceptable level of 0.8 (Williams, 2001). This makes it difficult to determine the extent to which variations in performance across time are the result of natural recovery from a TBI, practice effects, temporary variables (e.g., fatigue or fluctuations in attention), or a combination of these. Practice effects are particularly problematic when tests involve novelty and they might mask the effects of a TBI. However, the impact of practice effects is usually reduced over repeated assessments and with a greater test–retest interval. Test reliability, as well as validity, is also sensitive to changes within a testing session, such as fluctuations in levels of fatigue or motivation. Therefore, it is necessary to monitor the level of alertness and engagement of the patient. The use of several measures tapping the same construct can help somewhat to address the issue of low reliability.

4.2. Validity

Test scores are only useful if they are measuring the ability of interest (Tulsky & Haaland, 2001), i.e., if they have adequate construct validity. Dysfunction within one or more cognitive processes related to the ability a test was designed to measure may also impact test scores (Rankin & Adams, 1999) and contribute to variable performance across tests given to assess a single construct.

An area of critical importance in TBI is criterion validity, which refers to how well scores on a particular test are associated with a variable assumed to directly measure a behavior or characteristic of interest. In the TBI population, the link between scores and neuroanatomical findings is often inconsistent (e.g., Levin et al., 1991).

Most tests were designed and validated to detect and attempt to localize brain injury rather than to predict everyday functioning. However, the forensic neuropsychologist is often asked to also determine whether such an injury will negatively impact the person's ability to live independently, manage finances, drive, return to work or school, or maintain competitive employment. Therefore, an important psychometric test property is ecological validity. Tests may have good diagnostic potential but, nevertheless, be weakly associated with everyday abilities (Sbordone & Guilmette, 1999).

There are limited and conflicting empirical findings on the relationship between test scores and functional skills. The overall correlation is low to moderate (0.2 to 0.5), with particularly poor prediction when test performance falls in the borderline to average range (Williams, 1996). A review by Sbordone and Guilmette (1999) concluded that no single test can accurately predict everyday functioning in a patient with a brain injury. An individual's functioning will depend on the interaction between their strengths/deficits and the demands of the environment (Sbordone & Guilmette, 1999). Although individual scores are not highly related to everyday functioning, a general consistency between multiple neuropsychological measures and reports of functional abilities within a person's environment suggests a greater degree of ecological validity (Sbordone & Purisch, 1996).

Characteristics of the testing environment and modification of test administration are designed to optimize performance, but in so doing, they may mask or underestimate the severity of behavioral and cognitive deficits. This, in turn, reduces the ability to generalize the results to a person's everyday functioning, particularly in noisy, complex, and disorganized environments. It can also lead to the erroneous conclusion that the person with a TBI is able to function effectively in real-world settings despite an inability to do so (Sbordone & Guilmette, 1999).

4.3. Positive and Negative Predictive Power

Positive predictive power in the context of TBI refers to the likelihood that a person has a TBI based on a score falling in the "impaired" range (i.e., a relatively poor score). Negative predictive power refers to the likelihood that the person does not have a TBI given their score in the "normal" range (i.e., a relatively good score). Predictive power is especially important when test scores reveal impairment in the absence of neuroradiological and neurological findings (Bauer, 1997).

When interpreting test scores, a false-negative error occurs when a person truly is impaired but the score falls in the unimpaired range. Potential causes of false-negative errors include a high level of premorbid functioning, use of compensatory strategies, lack of sensitivity of current measures to frontal lobe dysfunction, and other causes (Rankin & Adams, 1999). A false-positive error occurs if the score indicates impairment when in reality no such deficit exists.

4.4. Base Rates

The current prevalence of a disorder, symptom, or pattern of test scores within a specified population is termed "base rate". Consideration of base rates can be helpful, as they influence the diagnostic significance of symptoms and test scores (Gouvier et al., 1998). For example, several symptoms associated with TBI, such as requiring a long time to think, being forgetful, and having poor concentration, are also relatively common in the general population (Gouvier et al., 1998). Without consideration of base rates, the likelihood that a person has a severe TBI based on a score in the "impaired" range could be overestimated (Faust & Nurcombe, 1989). When considering factor scores from the WAIS-III as well as the Auditory and Visual Memory factor scores from the WMS-III, 46% of a nonclinical sample was classified as "impaired" (one standard deviation below the mean) on at least one factor score and 14% were "impaired" on at least two factor scores (Taylor & Heaton, 2001). Similarly, the median percentage of scores falling in the "impaired" range based on the same criterion was 10% based on a comprehensive test battery (Heaton et al., 1991). Intraindividual intertest variability is also similar in those with and without a TBI (Crawford et al., 1997), and variability on the WAIS-R is the rule rather than the exception in the general population (Kaufman, 1990).

The base rate of a diagnosis of severe TBI in a given population determines the likelihood that a particular person has or does not have a severe TBI and is accurately diagnosed (Labarge et al., 2003). With a lower base rate, the likelihood that someone has a severe TBI based on test results (positive predictive power) is reduced (Retzlaff & Gibertini, 1994). The importance of base rates has been demonstrated in the interpretation of the WAIS-III FSIQ–WMS-III GMI discrepancy as a reflection of memory decline (Hawkins & Tulsky, 2001). Specifically a small discrepancy in favor of FSIQ may signify memory decline in those with a low IQ, with an increasing risk of false positive as the IQ level rises. This issue is particularly important in TBI because a disproportionate number of patients have lower than average IQ (Putnam & Adams, 1992).

4.5.   Normative Frames of Reference

Test scores obtained by an individual with a TBI are interpreted not only in the context of the person's premorbid abilities and are also compared to test scores achieved by non-brain-injured people with similar demographic characteristics. The scores are interpreted based on the number of standard deviations above or below the mean of the normative sample (Anastasi & Urbina, 1997). Use of a large normative sample stratified across a wide range of demographic characteristics helps to determine whether or not a low score is the result of injury or whether or not it can be attributed to factors such as normal variability or demographic characteristics (Tulsky & Haaland, 2001). The norms are especially useful when a person may be showing subtle deficits. Appropriate norms based on sex, age, education, and ethnicity are often essential for valid test interpretation (Axelrod & Goldman, 1996) and accuracy of diagnosis (Dick et al., 2002) because there can be significant variability in the classification of raw scores depending on the normative frame of reference (Kalechstein et al., 1998). Current norms are typically based on white middle- to upper-class segments of society and various problems exist in terms of their applicability to individuals from ethnic minority groups.

4.6.   Approaches to Data Interpretation

The interpretation of test scores as indicative of impairment and reflective of a brain injury requires several levels of analysis, in addition to those pertaining to psychometric issues and confounding factors. As discussed earlier, evaluation of the level of performance is achieved by comparing a person's score to results obtained by similar individuals (e.g., those with similar demographic backgrounds). However, according to Kay (1999), the first step when examining test data is to determine whether there are any absolute, relative, or questionable deficits independent of etiology. Absolute deficits refer to scores that reflect clear impairment for anyone. Relative deficits are scores that may represent impairment for a particular person based on that person's premorbid functioning. Questionable deficits refer to scores that may constitute relative deficits. Interpretation of test results cannot be solely based on level of performance or the risk of making either a false-positive or false-negative error increases (Rankin & Adams, 1999).

An important consideration when interpreting test results is whether or not a person's pattern of test scores makes sense from a neuroanatomical perspective and whether or not the pattern corresponds to known profiles of deficits given the nature of the brain injury (Kay, 1999; Rankin & Adams, 1999). Exploring the match between the severity of injury and the test results is also important. This approach to test interpretation can potentially help to localize brain lesions (Rankin & Adams, 1999).

Right–left differences refer to the comparison of sensory and motor functioning for each side of the body. Results can be compared to those obtained during a neurological examination. Lateralized impairment is often interpreted as indicative of brain injury to a particular hemisphere but may also be attributable to peripheral conditions or premorbid variability (Rankin & Adams, 1999).

Various signs are pathognomonic of brain injury, but they are relatively rare in clinical practice. Examples of such signs include aphasia, alexia, agraphia, acalculia, apraxia, visual neglect, visual field cuts, and agnosia (Rankin & Adams, 1999). Dissociations of subcomponents of language (e.g., graphomotor vs. verbal output; reading vs. auditory comprehension) do not occur without a localized lesion.

5. Conclusion

Group studies have revealed persisting neuropsychological impairments, particularly within the domains of attention, memory, and executive functions, in many, although not all, individuals who have sustained a moderate to severe TBI. Such deficits can have a profound impact on psychosocial and vocational functioning. Nevertheless, the presence, type, and pattern of deficits vary across individuals and no single neuropsychological tool has been shown to capture the full range and extent of deficits, highlighting the importance of a comprehensive neuropsychological assessment. A thorough evaluation of the data gathered from the assessment with consideration of psychometric issues and confounding variables is crucial to properly interpret any neuropsychological deficits as attributable to a TBI.

References

Anastasi, A., & Urbina, S. (1997). *Psychological Testing*, 7th ed. Upper Saddle River, NJ: Prentice-Hall.

Axelrod, B. N. & Goldman, R. S. (1996). Use of demographic corrections in neuropsychological interpretation: How standard are standard scores? *The Clinical Neuropsychologist, 10(2)*, 159–162.

Azouvi, P., Jokic, C., Van der Linden, M., Marlier, N., & Bussel, B. (1996). Working memory and supervisory control after severe closed head injury. A study of dual task performance and random generation. *Journal of Clinical and Experimental Neuropsychology, 18(3)*, 317–337.

Baddeley, A., Harris, J., Sunderland, A., Watts, K. P., & Wilson, B. (1987). Closed head injury and memory. In H. S. Levin, J. Grafman, & H. M. Eisenberg (Eds.). *Neurobehavioral Recovery from Head Injury*. New York: Oxford University Press, pp. 295–317.

Bate, A. J., Mathias, J. L., & Crawford, J. R. (2001). Performance on the Test of Everyday Attention and standard tests of attention following severe traumatic brain injury. *The Clinical Neuropsychologist, 15(3)*, 405–422.

Bauer, R. M. (1997). Brain damage caused by collision with forensic neuropsychologist. Paper presented at the meeting of the International Neuropsychological Society.

Bauer, R. M., Tobias, B., & Valenstein, E. (1993). Amnestic disorders. In K. M. Heilman & E. Valenstein (Eds.). *Clinical Neuropsychology*, 3rd ed. New York: Oxford University Press, pp. 523–602.

Bennett-Levy, J. M. (1984). Long-term effects of severe closed head injury on memory: Evidence from a consecutive series of young adults. *Acta Neurologica Scandinavica, 70*, 285–298.

Blachstein, H., Vakil, E., & Hoofien, D. (1993). Impaired learning in patients with closed-head injuries: An analysis of components of the acquisition process. *Neuropsychology, 7(4)*, 530–535.

Boake, C., Freelands, J. C., Ringholz, G. M., & Nance, M. L. (1995). Awareness of memory loss after severe closed-head injury. *Brain Injury, 9(3)*, 273–283.

Brouwer, W., Verzendaal, M., van der Naalt, J., Smit, J., & van Zomeren, E. (2001). Divided attention years after severe closed head injury: The effect of dependencies between the subtasks. *Brain and Cognition, 46(1–2)*, 54–56.

Callaban, C. D. & Hinkebein, J. H. (2002). Assessment of anosmia after traumatic brain injury: Performance characteristics of the University of Pennsylvania Smell Identification Test. *Journal of Head Trauma Rehabilitation, 17(3)*, 251–256.

Chervinsky, A. B., Ommaya, A. K., & deJonge, M. (1998). Motivation for traumatic brain injury rehabilitation questionnaire (MOT-Q): Reliability, factor analysis, and relationship to MMPI-2 variables. *Archives of Clinical Neuropsychology, 13(5)*, 433–446.

Cicerone, K. D. (1997). Clinical sensitivity of four measures of attention to mild traumatic brain injury. *The Clinical Neuropsychologist, 11(3)*, 266–272.

Cockburn, J. (1995). Performance on the Tower of London test after severe head injury. *Journal of the International Neuropsychological Society, 1(6)*, 537–544.

Cossa, E. M. & Fabiani, M. (1999). Attention in closed head injury: A critical review. *International Journal of Neurological Sciences, 20*, 145–153.

Costanzo, R. M. & Zasler, N. D. (1992). Epidemiology and pathophysiology of olfactory and gustatory dysfunction in head trauma. *Journal of Head Trauma Rehabilitation, 7(1)*, 15–24.

Crawford, J. R., Johnson, D. A., Mychalkiw, B., & Moore, J. W. (1997). WAIS-R performance following closed-head injury: A comparison of the clinical utility of summary IQs, factor scores, and subtest scatter indices. *The Clinical Neuropsychologist, 11(4)*, 345–355.

Cripe, L. I. (1996). The ecological validity of executive function testing. In R. J. Sbordone & C. J. Long (Eds.). *Ecological Validity of Neuropsychological Testing*. New York: St. Lucie Press, pp. 171–202.

Crosson, B., Novack, T. A., & Trennery, M. R. (1988). California Verbal Learning Test (CVLT) performance in severely head-injured and neurologically normal adult males. *Journal of Clinical and Experimental Neuropsychology, 10(6)*, 754–768.

Curtiss, G., Vanderploeg, R. D., Spencer, J., & Salazar, A. M. (2001). Patterns of verbal learning and memory in traumatic brain injury. *Journal of the International Neuropsychological Society, 7(5)*, 574–585.

Damasio, A. R. & Anderson, S. W. (1993). The frontal lobes. In K. M. Heilman & E. Valenstein (Eds.). *Clinical Neuropsychology*, (3rd ed.). New York: Oxford University Press, pp. 409–460.

DeLuca, J., Schultheis, M. T., Madigan, N. K., Christodoulou, C., & Averill, A. (2000). Acquisition vs. retrieval deficits in traumatic brain injury: Implications for memory rehabilitation. *Archives of Physical Medicine and Rehabilitation, 81*, 1327–1333.

Deshpande, S. A., Millis, S. R., Reeder, K. P., Fuerst, D., & Ricker, J. H. (1996). Verbal learning subtypes in traumatic brain injury: A replication. *Journal of Clinical and Experimental Neuropsychology, 18(6)*, 836–842.

Dick, M. B., Teng, E. L., Kempler, D., Davis, D. S., & Taussig, I. M. (2002). The Cross-Cultural Neuropsychological Test Battery (CCNB): Effects of age, education, ethnicity, and cognitive status on performance. In F. R. Ferraro (Ed.). *Minority and Cross-Cultural Aspects of Neuropsychological Assessment: Studies on Neuropsychology, Development, and Cognition.* Bristol, PA: Swets & Zeitlinger, pp. 17–44.

Dikmen, S., Machamer, J., & Temkin, M. (1990). Neuropsychological recovery in patients with moderate to severe head injury: 2 year follow-up. *Journal of Clinical and Experimental Neuropsychology, 12(4)*, 507–519.

Dikmen, S. S., Machamer, J. E., Winn, H. R., & Temkin, N. R. (1995). Neuropsychological outcome at 1-year post head injury. *Neuropsychology, 9(1)*, 80–90.

Donders, J., Tulsky, D. S., & Zhu, J. (2001). Criterion validity of new WAIS-III subtest scores after traumatic brain injury. *Journal of the International Neuropsychological Society, 7(7)*, 892–898.

Ellenberg, J. H., Levin, H. S., & Saydjari, C. (1996). Posttraumatic amnesia as a predictor of outcome after severe closed head injury. *Archives of Neurology, 53*, 782–791.

Faust, D. & Nurcombe, B. (1989). Improving the accuracy of clinical judgment. *Psychiatry, 52*, 197–208.

Gardner, S. D. & Vrbancic, M. I. (1998). Which California Verbal Learning Test factors discriminate moderate and severe head injury from normals? *Brain and Cognition, 37(1)*, 10–13.

Goldstein, F. C. & Levin, H. S. (1995). Post-traumatic and anterograde amnesia following closed head injury. In A. D. Baddeley, B. A. Wilson, & F. N. Watts (Eds.). *Handbook of Memory Disorders.* New York: Wiley, pp. 187–209.

Goldstein, F. C., Levin, H. S., & Boake, C. (1989). Conceptual encoding following severe closed head injury. *Cortex, 25*, 541–554.

Gouvier, W. M. D., Hayes, J. S., & Smiroldo, B. B. (1998). The significance of base rates, test sensitivity, test specificity, and subjects' knowledge of symptoms in assessing TBI sequelae and malingering. In C. R. Reynolds (Ed.). *Detection of Malingering During Head Injury Litigation.* New York: Plenum Press, pp. 55–79.

Haaland, K. Y., Temkin, N., Randahl, G., & Dikmen, S. (1994). Recovery of simple motor skills after head injury. *Journal of Clinical and Experimental Neuropsychology, 16*, 448–456.

Hartman, A., Pickering, R. M., & Wilson, B. A. (1992). Is there a central executive deficit after severe head injury? *Clinical Rehabilitation, 6*, 133–140.

Hawkins, K. A. (1998). Indicators of brain dysfunction derived from graphic representations of the WAIS-III/WMS-III technical manual clinical samples data: A preliminary approach to clinical utility. *The Clinical Neuropsychologist, 12(4)*, 535–551.

Hawkins, K. A. & Tulsky, D. S. (2001). The influence of IQ stratification on WAIS-III/WMS-III FSIQ–General Memory Index discrepancy base-rates in the standardization sample. *Journal of the International Neuropsychological Society, 7(7)*, 875–880.

Hawkins, K. A., Plehn, K., & Borgaro, S. (2002). Verbal IQ–performance IQ differentials in traumatic brain injury samples. *Archives of Clinical Neuropsychology, 17(1)*, 49–56.

Heaton, R. K., Grant, I., & Matthews, C. G. (1991). *Comprehensive Norms for an Expanded Halstead–Reitan Battery: Demographic Corrections, Research Findings, and Clinical Applications*. Odessa, FL: Psychological Assessment Resources.

Kalechstein, A. D., van Gorp, W. G., & Rapport, L. J. (1998). Variability in clinical classification of raw test scores across normative data sets. *The Clinical Neuropsychologist, 12(3)*, 339–347.

Kaplan, E., Fein, D., Morris, R., & Delis, D. (1991). *WAIS-R as a Neuropsychological Instrument*. San Antonio, TX: The Psychological Corporation.

Kaufman, A. S. (1990). *Assessing Adolescent and Adult Intelligence*. Boston: Allyn & Bacon.

Kay, T. (1999). Interpreting apparent neuropsychological deficits: What is really wrong? In J. J. Sweet (Ed.). *Forensic Neuropsychology: Fundamentals and Practice*. Lisse, The Netherlands: Swets & Zeitlinger, pp. 145–183.

Kerns, K. A. & Mateer, C. A. (1996). Walking and chewing gum: The impact of attentional capacity on everyday activities. In R. J. Sbordone & C. J. Long (Eds.). *Ecological Validity of Neuropsychological Testing*. New York: St. Lucie Press, pp. 147–169.

Kersel, D. A., Marsh, N. V., Havill, J. H., & Sleigh, J. W. (2001). Neuropsychological functioning during the year following severe traumatic brain injury. *Brain Injury, 15(4)*, 283–296.

Kinsella, G. J. (1998). Assessment of attention following traumatic brain injury: A review. *Neuropsychological Rehabilitation, 8(3)*, 351–375.

Labarge, A. S., McCaffrey, R. J., & Brown, T. A. (2003). Neuropsychologists' abilities to determine the predictive value of diagnostic tests. *Archives of Clinical Neuropsychology, 18(2)*, 165–175.

Lannoo, E., Colardyn, F., Jannes, C., & de Soete, G. (2001). Course of neuropsychological recovery from moderate-to-severe traumatic brain injury: A 2-year follow-up. *Brain Injury, 15(1)*, 1–13.

Leclercq, M., Couillet, J., Azouvi, P., Marlier, N., Martin, Y., Strypstein, E., & Rousseaux, M. (2000). Dual task performance after severe diffuse traumatic brain injury or vascular prefrontal damage. *Journal of Clinical and Experimental Neuropsychology, 22(3)*, 339–350.

Levin, H. S. (1989). Memory deficit after closed-head injury. *Journal of Clinical and Experimental Neuropsychology, 12(1)*, 129–153.

Levin, H. S. & Goldstein, F. C. (1986). Organization of verbal memory after severe closed head injury. *Journal of Clinical and Experimental Neuropsychology, 8(6)*, 643–656.

Levin, H. S., Eisenberg, H. M., Gary, H. E., Marmarou, A., Foulkes, M. A., Jane, J. A., Marshall, L. F., & Portman, S. M. (1991). Intracranial hypertension in relation to memory functioning during the first year after severe head injury. *Neurosurgery, 28*, 196–200.

Levin, H. S., Gary, H. E., Eisenberg, H. M., Ruff, R. M., Barth, J. T., Kreutzer, J., High, W. M., Portman, S., Foulkes, M. A., Jane, J. A., Marmarou, A., & Marshall, L. F. (1990). Neurobehavioral outcome one year after severe head injury: Experience of the Traumatic Coma Data Bank. *Journal of Neurosurgery, 73*, 699–709.

Levin, H. S., Goldstein, F. C., High, W. M., & Eisenberg, H. M. (1988). Disproportionately severe memory deficit in relation to normal intellectual functioning after closed head injury. *Journal of Neurology, Neurosurgery, and Psychiatry, 51(10)*, 14–20.

Levine, B., Dawson, D., Boutet, I., Schwartz, M. I., & Stuss, D. T. (2000). Assessment of strategic self-regulation in traumatic brain injury: Its relationship to injury severity and psychosocial outcome. *Neuropsychology, 14(4)*, 491–500.

Loken, W. J., Thornton, A. E., Otto, R. L., & Long, C. J. (1995). Sustained attention after severe closed head injury. *Neuropsychology, 9(4)*, 592–598.

Lovell, M. R. & Franzen, M. D. (1994). Neuropsychological assessment. In J. M. Silver, S. C. Yadofsky, & R. E. Hales (Eds.). *Neuropsychiatry of Traumatic Brain Injury*. Washington, DC: American Psychiatric Press, pp. 133–160.

Martin, E. & McDonald, S. (2003). Weak coherence, no theory of mind, or executive dysfunction? Solving the puzzle of pragmatic language disorders. *Brain and Language, 85*, 451–466.

Martin, T. A., Donders, J., & Thompson, E. (2000). Potential of and problems with new measures of psychometric intelligence after traumatic brain injury. *Rehabilitation Psychology, 45*, 402–408.

McDonald, S. (2000). Putting communication disorders in context after traumatic brain injury. *Aphasiology, 14(4)*, 339–347.

McDowell, S., Whyte, J., & D'Esposito, M. (1997). Working memory impairments in traumatic brain injury: Evidence from a dual-task paradigm. *Neuropsychologia, 35(10)*, 1341–1353.

Millis, S. R. & Ricker, J. H. (1994). Verbal learning patterns in moderate and severe traumatic brain injury. *Journal of Clinical and Experimental Neuropsychology, 16(4)*, 498–507.

Numan, B., Sweet, J. J., & Ranganath, C. (2000). Use of the California Verbal Learning Test to detect proactive interference in the traumatically brain injured. *Journal of Clinical Psychology, 56(4)*, 553–562.

Paniak, C. E., Shore, D. L., & Rourke, B. P. (1989). Recovery of memory after severe closed head injury: Dissociations in recovery of memory parameters and predictors of outcome. *Journal of Clinical and Experimental Neuropsychology, 11(5)*, 631–644.

Park, N. W., Moscovitch, M., & Robertson, I. H. (1999). Divided attention impairments after traumatic brain injury. *Neuropsychologia, 37(10)*, 1119–1133.

Ponsford, J. L. (2000). Attention. In G. Groth-Marnat (Ed.). *Neuropsychological Assessment in Clinical Practice: A Guide to Test Interpretation and Integration*. New York: Wiley, pp. 355–400.

Ponsford, J. L. & Kinsella, G. (1992). Attentional deficits following closed-head injury. *Journal of Clinical and Experimental Neuropsychology, 14(5)*, 822–838.

Prigatano, G. P. (1996). TBI patients tend to underestimate: A replication and extension to patients with lateralized cerebral dysfunction. *The Clinical Neuropsychologist, 10(2)*, 191–201.

Prigatano, G. P. (1999). *Principles of Neuropsychological Rehabilitation*. NewYork: Oxford University Press.

Prigatano, G. P. & Borgaro, S. R. (2003). Qualitative features of finger movement during the Halstead finger oscillation test following traumatic brain injury. *Journal of the International Neuropsychological Society, 9*, 128–133.

Prigatano, G. P., Bruna, O., & Mataro, M. (1998). Initial disturbances of consciousness and resultant impaired awareness in Spanish patients with traumatic brain injury. *Journal of Head Trauma Rehabilitation, 13(5)*, 29–38.

Putnam, S. H. & Adams, K. M. (1992). Regression-based prediction of long-term outcome following multidisciplinary rehabilitation for traumatic brain injury. *The Clinical Neuropsychologist, 6(4)*, 383–405.

Rankin, E. J. & Adams, R. L. (1999). The neuropsychological evaluation: Clinical and scientific foundations. In J. J. Sweet (Ed.). *Forensic Neuropsychology: Fundamentals and Practice*. Lisse, The Netherlands: Swets & Zeitlinger, pp. 85–119.

Retzlaff, P. D. & Gibertini, M. (1994). Neuropsychometric issues and problems. In R. D. Vanderploeg (Ed.). *Clinician's Guide to Neuropsychological Assessment*. Hillsdale, NJ: Erlbaum, pp. 185–209.

Riccio, C. A., Reynolds, C. R., Lowe, P., & Moore, J. J. (2002). The continuous performance test: A window on the neural substrates for attention? *Archives of Clinical Neuropsychology, 17(3)*, 235–272.

Ringholz, G. M. & Boake, C. (1987). *Inconsistent Attention in Survivors of Chronic Closed-Head Injury*. Paper presented at the 15th annual meeting of the International Neuropsychological Society.

Robertson, I. H., Ward, T., Ridgeway, V., & Nimmo-Smith, I (1996). The structure of normal human attention: The test of everyday attention. *Journal of the International Neuropsychological Society, 2(6)*, 525–534.

Ruff, R. M., Evans, R. W., & Light, R. H. (1986). Automatic detection vs. controlled search: A paper and pencil approach. *Perceptual and Motor Skills, 62*, 407–416.

Sbordone, R. J. & Guilmette, T. J. (1999). Ecological validity: Prediction of everyday and vocational functioning from neuropsychological test data. In J. J. Sweet (Ed.). *Forensic Neuropsychology: Fundamentals and Practice*. Lisse, The Netherlands: Swets & Zeitlinger, pp. 227–254.

Sbordone, R. J. & Purisch, A. D. (1996). Hazards of blind analysis of neuropsychological test data in assessing cognitive disability: The role of psychological pain and other confounding factors. *NeuroRehabilitation, 7*, 15–26.

Sbordone, R. J., Liter, J. C., & Pettler-Jennings, P. (1995). Recovery of function following severe traumatic brain injury: A retrospective 10-year follow-up. *Brain Injury, 9(3)*, 285–299.

Schmitter-Edgecombe, M. (1996). Effects of traumatic brain injury on cognitive performance: An attentional resource hypothesis in search of data. *Journal of Head Trauma Rehabilitation, 11(2)*, 17–30.

Schmitter-Edgecombe, M. & Kibby, M. K. (1998). Visual selective attention after severe closed head injury. *Journal of the International Neuropsychological Society, 4(2)*, 144–159.

Schretlen, D. J. & Shapiro, A. M. (2003). A quantitative review of the effects of traumatic brain injury on cognitive functioning. *International Review of Psychiatry, 15*, 341–349.

Sherer, M. & Novack, T. A. (in press). Neuropsychological assessment after traumatic brain injury in adults. In G. Prigatano, C. M. Cullum, & N. Pliskin (Eds.). *Demonstrating Utility and Cost-Effectiveness in Clinical Neuropsychology*. Philadelphia: Psychology Press.

Sherrill-Pattison, S., Donders, J., & Thompson, E. (2000). Influence of demographic variables on neuropsychological test performance after traumatic brain injury. *The Clinical Neuropsychologist, 14(4)*, 496–503.

Shum, D. H. K., Harris, D., & O'Gorman, J. G. (2000). Effects of severe traumatic brain injury on visual memory. *Journal of Clinical and Experimental Neuropsychology, 22(1)*, 25–39.

Snow, P., Douglas, J., & Ponsford, J. (1998). Conversational discourse abilities follow-ing severe traumatic brain injury: A follow-up study. *Brain Injury, 12(11)*, 911–935.

Sohlberg, M. M. & Mateer, C. A. (2001). *Cognitive Rehabilitation: An Integrative Neuropsychological Approach*. New York: Guilford Press.

Spikman, J. M, Deelman, B. G., & van Zomeren, A. H. (2000). Executive functioning, attention and frontal lesions in patients with chronic CHI. *Journal of Clinical and Experimental Neuropsychology, 22(3)*, 325–338.

Spikman, J. M., Timmerman, M. E., van Zomeren, A. H., & Deelman, B. G. (1999). Recovery versus retest effects in attention after closed head injury. *Journal of Clinical and Experimental Neuropsychology, 21(5)*, 585–605.

Spikman, J. M., van Zomeren, A. H., & Deelman, B. G. (1996). Deficits of attention after closed-head injury: Slowness only? *Journal of Clinical and Experimental Neuropsychology, 18(5)*, 755–767.

Stallings, G., Boake, C., & Sherer, M. (1995). Comparison of the California Verbal Learning Test and the Rey Auditory Verbal Learning Test in head-injured patients. *Journal of Clinical and Experimental Neuropsychology, 17(5)*, 706–712.

Stein, R. A. & Strickland, T. L. (1998). A review of the neuropsychological effects of commonly used prescription medications. *Archives of Clinical Neuropsychology, 13(3)*, 259–284.

Stuss, D. T., Ely, P., Hugenholtz, H., Richard, M. T., Larochelle, S., Poirier, C. A., & Bell, I. (1985). Subtle neuropsychological deficits in patients with good recovery after closed head injury. *Neurosurgery, 17*, 41–46.

Stuss, D. T., Stethem, L. L., Hugenholtz, H., Picton, T., Pivik, J., & Richard, M. T. (1989). Reaction time after head injury: Fatigue, divided and focused attention, and consistency of performance. *Journal of Neurology, Neurosurgery, and Psychiatry, 52(6)*, 742–748.

Taylor, M. J. & Heaton, R. K. (2001). Sensitivity and specificity of WAIS-III/WMS-III demographically-corrected factor scores in neuropsychological assessment. *Journal of the International Neuropsychological Society, 7(7)*, 867–874.

Teasdale, G. & Jennett, B. (1974). Assessment of coma and impaired consciousness: A practical scale. *Lancet, 2*, 81–84.

Trexler, L. E. & Zappala, G. (1988). Neuropathological determinants of acquired attention disorders in traumatic brain injury. *Brain and Cognition, 8(3)*, 291–302.

Tulsky, D. S. & Haaland, K. Y. (2001). Exploring the clinical utility of WAIS-III and WMS-III. *Journal of the International Neuropsychological Society, 7(7)*, 860–862.

Vakil, E. & Blachstein, H. (1993). Rey Auditory-Verbal Learning Test: Structure analysis. *Journal of Clinical Psychology, 49(6)*, 883–890.

Vanderploeg, R. D. & Eichler, S. R. (1990). *Performance of the Severely Traumatic Brain Injured on the CVLT*. Paper presented at the annual meeting of the American Psychological Association.

Vanderploeg, R. D., Crowell, T. A., & Curtiss, G. (2001). Verbal learning and mem-ory deficits in traumatic brain injury: Encoding, consolidation, and retrieval. *Journal of Clinical and Experimental Neuropsychology, 23(2)*, 185–195.

van Zomeren, A. H. & Brouwer, W. H. (1987). Head injury and concepts of attention. In H. S. Levin, J. Grafman, & H. M. Eisenberg (Eds.). *Neurobehavioral Recovery from Head Injury*. New York: Oxford University Press, pp. 398–415.

van Zomeren, A. H. & Brouwer, W. H. (1994). *Clinical Neuropsychology of Attention*. New York: Oxford University Press.

Veltman, J. C., Brouwer, W. H., van Zomeren, A. H., & Van Wolffehaar, P. C. (1996). Central executive aspects of attention in subacute severe and very severe closed head injury patients: Planning, inhibition, flexibility, and divided attention. *Neuropsychology, 10(3)*, 357–367.

Vilkki, J., Virtanen, S., Surma-Aho, O., & Servo, A. (1996). Dual task performance after focal cerebral lesions and closed head injuries. *Neuropsychologia, 34(11)*, 1051–1056.

Wiegner, S. & Donders, J. (1999). Performance on the California Verbal Learning Test after traumatic brain injury. *Journal of Clinical and Experimental Neuropsychology, 21(2)*, 159–170.

Williams, A. D. (2001). Psychometric concerns in neuropsychological testing. *NeuroRehabilitation, 16(4)*, 221–224.

Williams, D. H., Levin, H. S., & Eisenberg, H. M. (1990). Mild head injury classification. *Neurosurgery, 27*, 422–428.

Williams, J. M. (1996). A practical model of everyday memory assessment. In R. J. Sbordone & C. J. Long (Eds.). *Ecological Validity of Neuropsychological Testing*. New York: St. Lucie Press, pp. 129–145.

Wilson, J. T. L., Hadley, D. M., Wiedmann, K. D., & Teasdale, G. M. (1995). Neuropsychological consequences of two patterns of brain damage shown by MRI in survivors of severe head injury. *Journal of Neurology, Neurosurgery, and Psychiatry, 59(3)*, 328–331.

Yousem, D. M., Geckle, R. J., Bilker, W. B., Kroger, H., & Doty, R. L. (1999). Posttraumatic smell loss: Relationship of psychophysical tests and volumes of the olfactory bulbs and tracts and the temporal lobes. *Academic Radiology, 6*, 264–272.

Zec, R. F., Zellers, D., Belman, J., Miller, J., Matthews, J., Ferneau-Belman, D., & Robbs, R. (2001). Long-term consequences of severe closed head injury on episodic memory. *Journal of Clinical and Experimental Neuropsychology, 23(5)*, 671–691.

Section 6

Conclusions

20

Conclusions on Psychological Knowledge in Court: PTSD, Pain, and TBI

GERALD YOUNG, KEITH NICHOLSON, AND ANDREW W. KANE

This volume has elucidated various concepts and issues in psychology and law related to psychological injury and has established a knowledge base and framework to help practitioners in both professions, and related professions, to more effectively understand and deal with issues related to their work. The area of psychological injury concerns damage or dysfunction in one's thought processes, emotions, and/ or behavior causally related to an event at claim for damages (Schultz & Brady, 2003). Koch (2005) noted that in psychological injury cases, *Diagnostic and Statistical Manual of Mental Disorders*, 4th ed. (DSM-IV) diagnoses such as Posttraumatic Stress Disorder (PTSD) are often made (American Psychiatric Association, 1994, 2000), but also that there might be emotional reactions or states that do not meet DSM criteria or are not within the scope of this classification system, yet still substantially compromise functional activity.

Schultz and Brady (2003) described three types of psychological injury or psychological sequela following personal injury: (1) mental or "physical–mental" ones, such as PTSD or depression, as may happen because of injury involving loss of part of the body, (2) neuropsychological ones, and (3) pain-related ones. Although phrased somewhat differently, the three types of psychological injury identified by Schultz and Brady correspond to the three major sections of this book, on the psychological concepts of PTSD/distress, chronic pain, and TBI. Many cases involving these types of psychological injury lead survivors to consult with an attorney and can lead to lawsuits alleging tortious action wherein psychological expertise may be needed to establish the nature and legitimacy of litigants' claims.

Schultz (2003) called the area of psychological injury a confused minefield and quagmire. To meet *Daubert* and similar challenges (see Kane, Chapter 2), psychologists must be knowledgeable of their field and apply their knowledge judiciously in comprehensive assessments of individuals. The chapters in this volume demonstrate that the knowledge base upon which psychological assessors must rely is expanding and that practitioners need to keep abreast of these developments in psychology as well as relevant developments in law.

We have assembled foremost researchers and practitioners who are familiar with both the psychological literature and its legal implications. Together, they have presented knowledge about the three areas, how to properly evaluate individuals who might be experiencing these psychological difficulties, which assessment instruments meet acceptable reliability and validity requirements, and how to detect threats to validity and other confounding factors.

In the following, we comment on the particular sections comprising the book.

1.   Section Commentaries

After an introductory first chapter by the editors, Kane, in Chapter 2, described the nature and purpose of expert testimony and the rules and regulations governing evidence law. The *Daubert* trilogy specifies that for evidence to be admissible in court, judges, in their gatekeeping function, must consider such factors as reliability of the evidence (or its validity in psychological terms), its relevance or soundness, replicability, falsifiability, publication in peer-reviewed journals and error rates, in addition to other criteria of good science. Kane concluded that psychologists need to be aware of the population-level scientific research (the nomothetic level) relating to their cases at hand, thereby increasing the acceptability of evidence concerning any one individual (the idiographic level).

These rules and regulations, as enunciated in the *Daubert* trilogy and the Federal Rules of Evidence in the United States and equivalent laws and case law in Canada, demand that the highest standards of science in psychological research be brought to court in testimony about individuals offered to triers of fact. However, research in any field of psychology is affected by ongoing developments and changes in basic definitions and concepts that are continually subject to critical refinement. The law requests a clear degree of certainty in the conclusions offered in evidence for court, and some may interpret changing definitions and concepts in our field as a sign of uncertainty on our part.

At the same time, psychologists reason that the law formulates definitions and concepts that may be hard to translate into psychological terms, such as specifying a "disability" as "permanent." For example, disability concerns functional impairments, and the court is interested in whether there have been and will continue to be economic losses because of these; however, psychologists are not trained in economic considerations. Moreover, psychologists may have a difficult time assessing the prognosis of any psychological disability because it is an expression of multiple factors, which for any one case may be difficult to project into the future. However, statements may be made to a reasonable degree of psychological certainty.

To conclude, psychologists arrive at conclusions consistent with their professional competencies, as part of the evidence that they offer in court. Their conclusions are supported by the data that they have gathered on an individual and their knowledge of the pertinent scientific literature. However, our definitions and concepts are aimed at understanding human behavior and psychological processes, not legal terms, thresholds, or requirements. There may be an overlap, generalization, or transfer possible across the two disciplines, but the differences between them may negate clear application from psychology to law. The two professions need to continue to coordinate their work on these issues.

This volume will help the practicing professional, whether in psychology, law, or related disciplines, appreciate the recent scientific developments and research in the field of psychological injury and bridge the differing approaches in the fields while finding commonalities. Just as psychology is evolving, with gradual improvements in its understanding and application, so is the law's understanding of our profession. It should be noted that the *Daubert* criteria on the nature of the scientific process and what renders research both reliable and valid are issues of contention in their own right.

2.   Comment on the PTSD/Distress Section

The chapters in this section addressed a wide range of issues concerning Posttraumatic Stress Disorder (PTSD). PTSD is diagnosed in a minority of individuals exposed to a traumatic event. Many individuals exposed to traumatic events do not develop PTSD or other psychological disorders. They manifest resiliency, in part because of strong social support. Young and Yehuda emphasized that in those who do develop PTSD, it is a product of multiple causes characterized by individual differences. For example, those who develop PTSD may have been rendered vulnerable by risk factors, such as preincident traumatic experiences and psychopathology. However, peritraumatic factors are also important to consider. Weiss and Ozer (Chapter 5) reviewed the multiple factors predictive of PTSD status. For example, their research and the research of others indicate that the experience of trauma may be marked by dissociation, panic, and related peritraumatic factors that are strongly predictive of the development of PTSD. Moreover, the interpretation of the nature of the traumatic incident appears to be an important variable in determining who will develop PTSD. Also, individuals respond differently to some degree to type of trauma. According to Polusny and Arbisi, a traumatic event may elicit different psychological reactions depending on the type of traumatic event involved, such as sexual assault versus other types. They emphasized the need for comprehensive assessments. O'Donnell and colleagues discussed the methodological limitations evident in the research to date on PTSD after serious injury and the comorbidity of PTSD and depression. Ultimately, the onset and development of PTSD after trauma reflects a confluence of multiple factors.

The chapters in this section indicate that although we know a great deal about PTSD, we also have a great deal to learn. Psychologists, in their evaluations of individuals, must cautiously draw conclusions based on the best scientific research available and the best scientific methods of analyzing the data gathered.

3.   Comment on the Chronic Pain Section

The chapters in this section highlight several important themes. Chronic pain is a prevalent and prominent condition. Many chronic pain problems result from trauma or other injury that may be the subject of medicolegal proceedings. Pain is currently viewed as multidimensional, with both experiential (e.g., sensory, affective–motivational, and cognitive–evaluative) as well as behavioral components. The widely accepted and predominant biopsychosocial model of pain stipulates that both biomedical and psychosocial factors are important in understanding or treating chronic pain. Melzack and Katz, (Chapter 7), noted the effect that mind–body dualism has had on thinking about pain. As has also been true of numerous other medical and nonmedical phenomena, there has been a strong tendency to think about pain in terms of *either* biomedical (i.e., body) *or* psychological (i.e., mind) factors.

Gatchel and Kishino, (Chapter 8), noted that biomedical reductionism had a stifling effect on the exploration or understanding of how psychosocial factors might be involved in various medical problems, including pain. The gate control theory of Melzack and Wall (1965), which emphasized the close interaction between psychosocial and physiological processes affecting pain, was a landmark shift in thinking about chronic pain. Melzack and Katz noted that psychological factors, which had been dismissed as "reactions to pain" prior to the advent of the gate control theory, were subsequently seen to be an integral part of pain processing. They presented further discussion about the neuromatrix theory of pain, which has shifted focus to how the brain is involved in processing and actively organizing the experience of pain. They also noted that many pain problems that had been suggested to reflect some psychopathological process have been found to have a neurobiological basis. They question whether Pain Disorder should be included in a manual of mental disorders, because of problems with the criteria, its artificial division of psychological and biomedical factors, and its pejorative connotation.

Gatchel and Kishino, suggested that concepts such as "psychogenic pain" and "pain prone personality" are outdated. These concepts had historically been interpreted in terms of mind–body dualism (e.g., psychogenic, as meaning that there is no organic basis for the pain problem or that pain is "all in the mind"). However, all mental processes have a neurobiological substrate and there are many shades of meaning to the term "psychogenic", which, essentially, just means that psychological processes may be related to the behavior or phenomenon at hand (Nicholson, 2000). Similarly, it is now widely accepted that most behavior or psychological processes are some function of a Person × Situation interaction, in which "person" could involve aspects of personality (Mischel, 2004). Gatchel and Kishino eventually suggested that "the proper question to pose is not whether personality characteristics cause pain, but what are their relative contributions to the pain perception process" (Chapter 8, pg 155).

Pincus, in her chapter, made the important distinction between risk and vulnerability factors, in chronic pain. She noted that there is not a necessary causal relationship between risk factors and subsequent chronic pain and that there is still poor evidence for the role of vulnerability factors, defined as relatively stable characteristics (typically genetic or acquired early in life) that are causally linked to chronic pain or other pathological process, although there are promising suggestions for the latter. Pincus noted that researchers have universally adopted the central theoretical proposition of the gate control theory that psychological states, including emotion and cognition, are part and parcel of pain processing. She discussed in detail many cognitive and emotional factors that have been investigated in chronic pain patients, noting methodological problems, and concluded with a discussion of a promising model in which the normally independent schemata of self, pain, and illness become enmeshed.

Sherman and Ohrbach, (Chapter 11), noted that the subjective "experience of pain can never fully be confirmed or disconfirmed with absolute certainty by an external observer" (pg 193). Many so-called "objective" signs, such as various imaging techniques, are noted to have poor reliability or validity. In contrast, assessment of "higher-order" functioning or psychological processes is considered necessary to understand an individual's report of pain, and this might be successfully accomplished using a variety of techniques and instruments.

Young and Chapman, (Chapter 10), noted that there is a reliable co-occurrence of negative affective states (e.g., depression, anger, anxiety) and pain, but the exact nature of causal relationships remains unclear. They considered pain as an emergent constructed conscious experience and described a nonlinear dynamical systems approach to chronic pain. Such models make it clear that simple linear causal relationships often do not reflect the nature of phenomena such as chronic pain. Young and Chapman developed five-step stage models of both the development of chronic pain from an acute to a chronic state and response to therapy, illustrating that pain is not a static process. They proposed that assessors of patients presenting with chronic pain need to specify complications identified in their presentation.

4.   Comment on the PTSD/Comorbid Pain Section

The study of the mutual maintenance of pain and PTSD is in its infancy, both in terms of the theoretical models that have been proposed and the empirical research that has been undertaken. The work of Blanchard and Hickling (1997), as described in Chapter 12 with Freidenberg and Malta, has spurred research in the area. Otis, Pincus, and Keane presented a Triple Vulnerability Model of the comorbidity of chronic pain and PTSD, which described a common biological vulnerability, a common early psychological vulnerability that included feeling a lack of control, and a more specific psychological vulnerability in which one learned to focus anxiety on specific situations. Among other factors, Asmundson and Taylor demonstrated that anxiety sensitivity is a primary risk factor in developing comorbid chronic pain and PTSD.

In Chapter 10 in the pain section, Young and Chapman proposed that a nonlinear dynamic systems conceptualization may help explain chronic pain and its relationship to PTSD. Finally, the concept of a system that helps cohere pain and PTSD into one complex that is quite difficult to treat can be expanded to include the effects of traumatic brain injury.

Asmundson and Taylor argued that until we better understand the exact nature of the PTSD–pain linkage and know better how to treat clients having the conditions comorbidly, it will be difficult for assessors to determine causality in any one individual case. The mutual maintenance and exacerbation that can take place when chronic pain and PTSD co-occur can complicate, delay, or even undermine recovery.

5. Comment on the Traumatic Brain Injury Section

The five chapters in the traumatic brain injury (TBI) section of the book illustrate the complexity of issues in the field of psychological injury and TBI. In Chapter 15, Barth, Ruff, and Espe-Pfeifer noted that mild TBI occurs frequently following motor vehicle accidents, falls, or other injuries that may become subject to medicolegal proceedings. Although there are several somewhat different definitions of mild TBI, there is full resolution in most cases. However, some 10–20% of individuals may go on to present with persistent difficulty, which is sometimes referred to as the persistent Postconcussive Syndrome (PPCS).

Bigler, (Chapter 17), discussed at greater length the possible neuropathological substrate of mild TBI, making the important distinction of grades of mild TBI. Bigler contended that in cases of mild TBI, there is one golden rule: everything must make sense. He noted that the results of neuropsychological assessments are not diagnostic of mild TBI, but may provide information on the level of functioning that can be associated with mild TBI. It is noted by Bigler that there are complex factors at play in trying to predict outcome, most of which are poorly specified at this time.

Vanderploeg, Belanger, and Curtiss in Chapter 16 discussed the meaning and definitions of mild TBI and PPCS. They reviewed criteria for the traditional medical model of causality of mild TBI and presented a multifactorial model of PPCS. The model may help explain the long-term psychological effects found in a minority of mild TBI victims. They presented their well-controlled research in support of the model. They added that although the nomothetic database in the area is improving and will continue to improve, the application to the individual idiographic case remains problematic, requiring careful consideration.

Nicholson and Martelli, (Chapter 18), reviewed some of the important possible confounding factors that may need to be considered in the interpretation of neuropsychological test data following TBI. Pain, especially headaches, sleep disturbance, psychoemotional disturbance and psychiatric disorder, and effort or dissimulation are highlighted as being of particular relevance for appropriate differential diagnosis of mild TBI or more significant TBI.

The case of moderate to severe TBI also presents challenges to the forensic neuropsychological assessor. Patry and Mateer indicated that group outcome studies find that there are often deficits in attention, memory, and executive functions, in particular, although there is much interindividual variability. Patry and Mateer offered a comprehensive review of the research in fundamental neuropsychological functions, noting many methodological problems or limitations in the knowledge base. Ultimately, approaches such as theirs represent the best that psychology has to offer the court. Research that meets the most stringent scientific standards needs to continue to be undertaken and made available to professionals offering evidence to court.

6. Conclusions

First, we offer conclusions pertaining to psychological issues relevant to knowledge in court, and then we address some implications for testimony in court.

Psychology
1. The chapters in this book offer theoretical and empirical support for a biopsychosocial or similar multifactorial point of view. We also consider these to be the most useful and representative of what is actually occurring in most cases and wish to emphasize that most symptom presentations will be the result of an interaction of biomedical and psychosocial factors. Progress is being made in understanding the dynamics, individual pathways, and multiple mechanisms involved in the development and course of PTSD, chronic pain, and TBI.
2. Theory needs to be tested by sound empirical investigation, which, in turn, leads to better theory. For example, in the fields of PTSD, chronic pain, and TBI, more prospective longitudinal research is needed to investigate better the course of the conditions and all of the influences that contribute to their determination. More research is needed on measures of outcome that are relevant to court.

3. In the three fields of PTSD, chronic pain, and TBI, the best models are ones that are comprehensive and that acknowledge multicausality. They should consider pretrauma, peritrauma, posttrauma, and other relevant factors. They should involve biopsychosocial and related models, including Person × Environment, Diatheses × Thesis, and Vulnerability/risk × Coping/resilience models.
4. These multifactorial theoretical models apply not only to the group data in population-level studies but also to individual assessment; that is, individual assessments should be comprehensive and examine the multiplicity of possible causal influences.
5. In the evidence provided to court, psychologists should avoid using pejorative terms that lack scientific precision. As scientists, psychologists should emphasize their data and the direct conclusions that can be reasonably drawn from that data in the context of current theoretical models.

Court. This volume started with a discussion by Kane on evidence law. We return to his presentation regarding the scientific attitude needed by practicing psychologists. In evaluating an individual reporting psychological injury, the psychologist must first have state-of-the-art knowledge of the scientific literature of concern, whether on PTSD, chronic pain, traumatic brain injury, or other problems. The psychologist must be able to evaluate the quality of the research, in terms of its reliability, or replicability, and in terms of its validity, or soundness (keeping in mind that "validity" in psychological terms is labeled "reliability" in *Daubert*). Second, the psychologist must use the most appropriate techniques, including selection of the most appropriate psychological instruments as part of the comprehensive assessment undertaken of the individual, and, again, the scientific literature must be consulted with a critical perspective. Third, the psychologist must proceed in a scientific fashion when analyzing the data gathered in an individual case. In all phases of her or his work, the psychologist functions from a scientific perspective. Ultimately, this is the optimal way of meeting any *Daubert* challenge about the value of evidence offered in court (Kane explores some of these issues at length in Young, Kane, and Nicholson (2006), the companion volume to this volume).

Also, when psychologists and plaintiffs enter the legal arena, they are subject to pressures that they would not encounter otherwise. The possibility of financial damages in tort claims may place pressure on individuals to either consciously or unconsciously exaggerate their symptoms. Similarly, psychologists are subject to their own biases. Psychologists need to screen for the individual's level of effort in the cases that they assess and to check their own biases at the same time, so that the best possible evidence is offered to the court. (For development of some of these themes, see the section by Nicholson in Young et al., 2006).

This book presents a range of issues covering the law and the three areas of psychology reviewed, on PTSD/distress, chronic pain, and traumatic brain injury. The scientific underpinnings and state of the art continually improve in psychology. Researchers in the field need to consider (1) definitional and diagnostic issues, including base rates, course, and outcome, (2) improving the psychological instruments available while respecting the traditions established in the field, and (3) improving our understanding of the nature of psychological injury, PTSD, chronic pain, and TBI and their causes. (For development of some of these themes, see the section by Young in Young et al., 2006).

Together, the current volume and the companion volume by Young et al. (2006) help explicate evidence law and psychological knowledge in the major fields of psychological injury. Moreover, they explain pertinent concepts related to causality and causation, examining them from the perspective of the law, psychology, and medicine, in particular. We maintain that as our research knowledge grows, we will be better able to undertake comprehensive and defensible psychological assessments that address questions relevant for court purposes. The co-editors hope that these volumes will assist both professionals and students in the field of psychological injury practice.

References

American Psychiatric Association. (1994). *Diagnostic and Statistical Manual of Mental disorders*, 4th ed. Washington, DC: American Psychiatric Association.

American Psychiatric Association. (2000). *Diagnostic and Statistical Manual of Mental Disorders: Text Revision*, 4th ed. Washington, DC: American Psychiatric Association.

Blanchard, E. B. & Hickling, E. J. (1997). *After the Crash: Assessment and Treatment of Motor Vehicle Accident Survivors*. Washington, DC: American Psychological Association.

Koch, W. J. (2005). The implications of "psychological injuries" for clinical psychology training programs. *Canadian Psychology, 46*, 41–45.

Melzack, R., & Wall, P. D. (1965). Pain mechanisms: A new theory. *Science, 150*, 971–979.

Mischel, W. (2004). Toward an integrative science of the person. *Annual Review of Psychology, 55*, 1–22.

Nicholson, K. (2000). At the crossroads: Pain in the 21st century. *NeuroRehabilitation, 14*, 57–67.

Schultz, I. Z. (2003). The relationship between psychological impairment and occupational disability. In I. Z. Schultz & D. O. Brady (Eds.), *Psychological Injuries at Trial.* Chicago, IL: American Bar Association, pp. 65–101.

Schultz, I. Z. & Brady, D. O. (2003). Preface: Definition and introduction to psychological injuries. In I. Z. Schultz & D. O. Brady (Eds.). *Psychological Injuries at Trial*. Chicago, IL: American Bar Association, pp. 13–17.

Young, G., Kane, A.W., & Nicholson, K. (Eds.). (2006). *Causality: Psychological Evidence in Court*. New York: Springer-Verlag.

Index